A Survey of Agricultural Economics Literature
VOLUME 1

The three volumes in *A Survey of Agricultural Economics Literature* have been prepared by and published for the American Agricultural Economics Association. The general editor of the survey volumes is Lee R. Martin.

Volume 1, *Traditional Fields of Agricultural Economics, 1940s to 1970s.* Lee R. Martin, editor.

Volume 2, *Quantitative Methods in Agricultural Economics, 1940s to 1970s.* George G. Judge, Richard H. Day, S. R. Johnson, Gordon C. Rausser, and Lee R. Martin, editors.

> **On Estimating the Parameters of Economic Relations** by George G. Judge. **Discussion** by Richard J. Foote.
>
> **Economic Optimization.** "On Economic Optimization: A Nontechnical Survey" by Richard H. Day. "Optimization Models in Agricultural and Resource Economics" by Richard H. Day and Edward Sparling. "Agricultural Production Function Studies" by Roger C. Woodworth.
>
> **Systems Analysis and Simulation: A Survey of Applications in Agricultural Economics** by S. R. Johnson and Gordon C. Rausser.
>
> **Developments in Agricultural Economics Data** by M. L. Upchurch.

Volume 3, *Economics of Welfare, Development, and Natural Resources in Agriculture, 1940s to 1970s.* Lee R. Martin, editor.

> **Economics of Rural Poverty** by D. Lee Bawden and W. Keith Bryant.
>
> **Rural People, Communities, and Regions.** George S. Tolley, coordinator. "Economic Bases for Growth" by Clark Edwards. "Rural Development: Problems and Prospects" by Dean Jansma, Hays Gamble, Patrick Madden, and Rex Warland. "Population Distribution: Migration and Settlement Patterns" by Marion Clawson.
>
> **Agriculture in Economic Development.** "Africa" by Carl Eicher. "Asia" by John W. Mellor. "Latin America" by G. Edward Schuh.
>
> **Natural Resources** by Emery N. Castle, Maurice M. Kelso, Herbert H. Stoevener, and Joe B. Stevens.
>
> **Philosophic Foundations of Agricultural Economics Thought** by Glenn L. Johnson.
>
> **Organization and Performance of Agricultural Markets** by Peter Helmberger, Gerald R. Campbell, and William D. Dobson.

A
SURVEY OF
AGRICULTURAL
ECONOMICS
LITERATURE
VOLUME 1

Traditional Fields
of Agricultural Economics,
1940s to 1970s

LEE R. MARTIN,

editor

Published by the University of Minnesota Press, Minneapolis,
for the American Agricultural Economics Association

Library of Congress Catalog Number 76-27968

ISBN 0-8166-0801-6

Contents

PART II. The Analysis of Productive Efficiency in Agricultural
Marketing: Models, Methods, and Progress
Ben C. French

PART IV. Postwar Policies Relating
to Trade in Agricultural Products
D. Gale Johnson

PART V. Agricultural Price Analysis and Outlook
William G. Tomek and Kenneth L. Robinson

PART VII. Technical Change in Agriculture
Willis Peterson and Yujiro Hayami

Foreword

In March 1968 C. E. Bishop, president of the American Agricultural Economics Association, appointed a committee to investigate the need for a major survey of the agricultural economics literature published from the 1940s to the 1970s. The committee found that an extensive assessment of this body of literature would indeed be of value to research workers, teachers, and extension workers and graduate students in agricultural economics; teachers, research workers, and graduate students in economics and economic statistics, sociology, geography, political science, and anthropology; and teachers, research workers, and graduate students in technical agriculture. In the end the committee was assigned the responsibility for planning the project and commissioning authors to prepare the papers.

The members of the committee were Glenn L. Johnson (Michigan State University), M. M. Kelso (University of Arizona), James E. Martin (Virginia Polytechnic Institute), M. L. Upchurch (Economic Research Service of the United States Department of Agriculture), and Lee R. Martin, chairman (University of Minnesota). Early in 1969 James E. Martin resigned from the committee, and several new members — John P. Doll (University of Missouri), Peter G. Helmberger (University of Wisconsin), J. Patrick Madden (Pennsylvania State University), and Edward W. Tyrchniewicz (University of Manitoba) — were appointed.

As its first step, the committee tentatively identified the fields to be covered and commissioned highly regarded members of the profession to draw up outlines of the coverage to be undertaken in the different fields. These outlines were used in the selection of economists to prepare the surveys and in negotiating agreements with prospective authors. Once the surveys were prepared, the committee again obtained assistance from highly competent members of the profession to make critical, constructive evaluations of each survey draft. In the case of the preparation of outlines and the review of papers, the committee sought to strike a representative balance among differing viewpoints in each field. For the preparation of the papers themselves, the committee obtained the services of outstanding agricultural economists with special competence in the respective fields.

In connection with the papers published in this volume, substantial assistance was provided by the following individuals:

PART I. Farm Management and Production Economics, 1946-70. *Preparation of outlines:* John P. Doll, Albert R. Hagan, Charles E. Harshbarger, and Joseph C. Headley. *Review of paper:* John P. Doll, Earl O. Heady, Glenn L. Johnson, and Max R. Langham.

PART II. The Analysis of Productive Efficiency in Agricultural Marketing: Models, Methods, and Progress. *Preparation of outlines:* Peter G. Helmberger and Frank J. Smith. *Review of paper:* Emerson M. Babb, Peter G. Helmberger, Harold M. Riley, and James D. Shaffer.

PART III. Policy for Commercial Agriculture, 1945-71. *Preparation of outlines:* James T. Bonnen, John A. Schnittker, Vernon L. Sorenson, and Arley D. Waldo. *Review of paper:* Willard W. Cochrane, David MacFarlane, Lauren K. Soth, and Luther G. Tweeten.

PART IV. Postwar Policies Relating to Trade in Agricultural Products. *Preparation of outlines:* Martin E. Abel and James P. Houck. *Review of paper:* T. K. Warley, Larry J. Wipf, and Lawrence W. Witt.

PART V. Agricultural Price Analysis and Outlook. *Preparation of outlines:* James P. Houck, Lester V. Manderscheid, and Edward W. Tyrchniewicz. *Review of paper:* James P. Houck, Richard A. King, and Edward W. Tyrchniewicz.

PART VI. Agricultural Finance and Capital Markets. *Preparation of outlines:* Chester B. Baker, William H. Heneberry, John A. Hopkin, and George D. Irwin. *Review of paper:* Peter J. Barry, Fred Garlock, George D. Irwin, Lawrence A. Jones, Warren F. Lee, and John B. Penson.

PART VII. Technical Change in Agriculture. *Preparation of outlines:* Vernon W. Ruttan. *Review of paper:* Zvi Griliches and Vernon W. Ruttan.

This list includes only the official reviewers who acted on behalf of the association and the committee. Many other individuals who assisted the authors of the papers in various ways are cited in the notes preceding each paper. The authors were urged to incorporate into their papers the comments and suggestions provided by the respective reviewers, but final decisions about the content of the papers were left to the discretion of the authors.

The Committee on Publication of Postwar Literature Review arranged for publication of the three-volume set of literature reviews. The members of this committee are Emerson M. Babb (chairman), J. P. Madden, and John C. Redman. Neil Harl provided valuable assistance in the publication phase to both committees.

On behalf of the members of the association and the Literature Review Committee I wish to express sincere gratitude to the authors of the papers in this volume and to the advisors, reviewers, and others who participated in the planning and implementation of the project as a whole.

Finally, I would like to direct readers' attention to current literature reviews of some closely related fields of agricultural economics — reviews that both complement and supplement the reviews in this volume and the two companion volumes. The following reviews have been published in an Australian journal, *Review of Marketing and Agricultural Economics*:

> G. Weinschenck, W. Henrichsmeyer, and F. Aldinger (1969). "The Theory of Spatial Equilibrium and Optimal Location in Agriculture: A Survey." 37:3-70.
>
> Ulf Renborg (1970). "Growth of the Agricultural Firm: Problems and Theories." 38:51-101.
>
> John L. Dillon (1971). "An Expository Review of Bernoullian Decision Theory in Agriculture: Is Utility Futility?" 39:3-80.
>
> Roger W. Gray and David J. S. Rutledge (1971). "The Economics of Commodity Futures Markets: A Survey." 39:57-113.
>
> Harold F. Breimyer (1973). "The Economics of Agricultural Marketing: A Survey." 41:115-165.
>
> Jock R. Anderson (1974). "Simulation: Methodology and Application in Agricultural Economics." 42:3-55.

An additional article commissioned by the *Review of Marketing and Agricultural Economics* but not yet published is "Public Utility Pricing" by David Gallagher.

Another important set of literature reviews in agricultural economics is being published in the British *Journal of Agricultural Economics*. To date the following review articles have been published:

G. H. Peters (1973). "Land Use Studies in Britain: A Review of the Literature with Special Reference to Applications of Cost-Benefit Analysis." 21:171-214.

T. E. Josling (1974). "Agricultural Policies in Developed Countries: A Review." 25:229-264.

C. S. Barnard (1975). "Data in Agriculture. A Review with Special Reference to Farm Management Research, Policy and Advice in Britain." 26:289-333.

D. I. Bateman (1976). "Agricultural Marketing: A Review of the Literature of Marketing Theory and Selected Applications." 27:171-225.

Also worthy of note is Marguerite C. Burk's "Survey of Interpretations of Consumer Behavior by Social Scientists in the Postwar Period," *Journal of Farm Economics* 49:1-31.

Lee R. Martin
Survey Editor

October 1976

Part I. Farm Management and Production Economics, 1946-70

Earl O. Heady, more than anyone else, influenced the course of farm management and production economics after World War II. It is fitting therefore that the guiding concept for this chapter be based on a quotation from one of his articles: "The thesis behind [the article] is that the advancement in a scientific field grows not out of unqualified acceptance of the status quo but by frequent appraisal of the road ahead" [109].

No logical base may exist for inferring the future from the evidence of the past. However, I know of no way to appraise the road ahead for farm management and production economics except to use past developments and evolving concerns in farm management and production economics as cues for the future. I write in terms of the image I have of developments and concerns in this subject matter area. I hope that what I relate may remind us that as students of social science our central task is to work not only to increase the power and capacity of our science — its methodology, analytical tools, and techniques — but also to apply this capacity in solving problems of growing social concern. This review covers primarily the period from 1946 through 1970. Earlier and later literature is sometimes referenced to provide either background or continuity to the developments within this period. The references are by no means exhaustive, but I believe they are a fair and ample representation of the literature on farm management and production economics.

H. R. J.

Farm Management and Production Economics, 1946-70

Harald R. Jensen
Professor of Agricultural and Applied Economics
University of Minnesota

The Need for Research and Education in Farm Management

Since World War II farm management specialists and production economists have increasingly emphasized that the changes bearing on the farm-household decision-making unit and the imperfect knowledge about these changes have created the need for additional research and education in farm management. Farm operators or managers, they have reasoned, must organize and operate their farms in a highly dynamic setting.

Prices, weather, technology, institutions, and people – their needs, moods, attitudes, goals, and values – change to influence profits and losses in farming. In this dynamic setting wrong decisions can easily result, wrong not only in terms of the needs of the decision-making units but also in terms of social needs. Private and public costs of wrong decisions can be very high. Thus, it was argued that research and education are needed in farm management to reduce errors and the costs of errors in allocating and using farm resources.

To reduce errors and their costs or to increase resource efficiency, research and education in farm management and production economics focused on (1) assisting farm decision makers in the best use of their resources in ways compatible with the changing needs, values, and goals of society, (2) assisting public policy makers and administrators in determining private and public consequences of alternative policy programs on farm resource use, (3) testing traditional and developing theory or postulates of the firm as a basis for un-

3

derstanding the behavior of the farm firm and for improving firm management, (4) studying the economic effects of technological and institutional changes on agricultural production and resource use, and (5) studying individual farm, area, and regional adjustments in resource use.

The dynamic setting in which our farmers operated following World War II included the heavy demand of war-torn nations for food products, fibers, and livestock feeds, a high rate of growth in our own economy which required increasing supplies of labor and capital resources to meet the demands of the industrial and service sectors, and a technological explosion in agriculture which assured adequate food and fiber supplies from our agricultural industry with employment of decreasing quantities of labor. This outburst of technology was made possible by the availability of large supplies of low-priced fossil energy relative to the supplies and prices of human energy.

In this dynamic setting farm management specialists and production economists saw a need for research and education to improve overall resource efficiency. Seen as underlying such improvement was the adoption by farmers of the most profitable technology, expanding farm size to exhaust economies to size, transferring labor out of agriculture for employment in secondary and tertiary industries where its marginal value productivity was assumed to be higher.

But the need based on resource efficiency has not gone unquestioned. Glenn Johnson [152] pointed out that some of the really tough problems in agriculture involve something other than the economists' pet efficiency norm. Other norms, said Johnson, were security, equity, progress, freedom, mercy, and justice. If equilibrium in terms of profit maximization is the pet efficiency norm that Johnson had in mind, then it is quite clear that attainment of this norm does not necessarily guarantee attainment of other possible norms, that there then are possible trade-offs among norms and that emphasis on one may be costly in terms of failure to realize others. Perhaps the need for research and education in farm management and production economies was visualized and consummated with too narrow a view of efficiency. Moreover, perhaps we have arrived at a situation where the remaining resources in agriculture can be utilized more efficiently there than elsewhere in terms of their marginal value products, and hence the need for research and education in farm management and production economics no longer rests in any large measure on moving resources out of agriculture. Perhaps the need now is for technological assessment in terms of a wider set of norms that may change as problem solving progresses.

It has been argued that the need for research and education in farm management and production economics grows out of some unique characteristics of the farming industry. The argument was that the farming industry is com-

prised of relatively small single-proprietorship firms — primarily family operations. Given its relatively small size, the typical farm firm has not been able
to invest its own resources in research and development for its own benefit.
But since World War II our nation's farms have grown considerably. The
industrial developers and producers of feed, fertilizer, seed, and pest and
weed control are heavily involved in research and education as a basis for
maintaining or expanding the farm market. In some areas of agriculture, such
as the egg, broiler, and turkey subsectors, production has been vertically integrated with other processes or functions. Moreover, in some sections of the
country corporate farming, as supplementary to off-farm business activity,
has replaced small single-proprietorship farm firms. In short, the post-World
War II era has seen some rather far-reaching changes in the farming structure.
The question has been raised, therefore, whether public expenditure for research and extension education can continue to be justified and, if so, on
what grounds.

But the problems before us should be grounds enough for continuing public expenditure for research and education in farm management and production economics. However, the grounds change as the problems change in kind,
scope, and urgency. As we look ahead, the need for public support for research and education in farm management and production economics springs
not only from a growing emphasis on efficient food production in a competitive world but also from a growing emphasis on conservation of energy, on a
cleaner physical environment, and on a more humane and equitable social environment.

Our Heritage — Accounts and Surveys,
Economic Theory, Statistics

Viewing our heritage with the close of World War II as the vantage point, we
move the clock back to the beginning of this century and trace the developments in subject matter and method forward in time. My purpose here is not
to provide any detailed or lengthy account of these developments but to supply an overview that describes the setting for post-World War II review. A
number of excellent references are available for those wishing more detail on
the pre-World War II period [32, 166, 198, 218, 226, 237, 259, 260, 271,
272, 277].

Farm management evolved along two conceptual streams, which Johnson
[155] described as the "endowed" and the "unendowed." Johnson described
the "unendowed" as a group of production men who were not in a position
to inherit economic thought from the classicists and the neoclassicists. Farm
management courses were developed and taught by men who considered

themselves "farm managers," not economists, and they approached their subject matter as empiricists. Among these early pioneers were I. P. Roberts, an agronomist at Cornell University, who taught cost accounts; T. F. Hunt, an agronomist at Ohio State and later Cornell, who lectured on public problems, the history of agriculture, and farm management; G. F. Warren, a horticulturalist at Cornell, who initiated cost route studies; W. J. Spillman, an agronomist in the Office of Farm Management, USDA, who used statistical techniques in the economic analysis of agricultural experimental data. Through the ideas of these men concepts with economic content in a farming context evolved — concepts such as enterprise costs and returns, enterprise combination, labor income, and factors affecting farm earnings and net farm returns. This interest in the business side of farming led to the development of farm management as a field of study.

Thus, farm management as a field of study in the United States evolved from this earlier conceptual stream based on analysis of data obtained from farmers through sample surveys and cost account routes. These data were descriptive of the operation of the several enterprises on a given farm and of the entire farm, either currently or for the preceding year. The analyses converged on costs and returns for major products, sources of inputs, earnings, and expenditures for the farm as a whole and on factors affecting costs and earnings. Methodologically, the orientation of the "unendowed" was positivistic in the sense of describing what farmers were doing. However, when what the most successful farmers were doing was suggested as something for the less successful to emulate, the orientation became prescriptive. The approach was empirical because the knowledge gained came directly from the experience of farmers. It was at the same time inductive, particularly in its application to the factors affecting farm profits, which involved studies of relationships. Studies of relationships, S. Warren [272] maintained, must be repeated frequently in time and place because when the same relationships appear in different places at different times we approach a point where it is safe to generalize.

In his account of the "endowed" Johnson [155] reminded us that "as marginal analysis reached a climax with Alfred Marshall, agricultural economics was just beginning to emerge as a discipline in the land-grant colleges." The members of this new profession were the fortunate heirs of the theoretical thought that the classicists and neoclassicists had developed. Trained in economics, H. C. Taylor [257] pioneered in emphasizing the application of economic principles to problems in agriculture. Sherman Johnson and Kenneth Bachman [166] described the 1920s as a period wherein great strides were made in developing the scope and method of production economics. They highlighted the period by relating that this was the time when budgeting was developed as a research tool grounded in the economic principles of production.

Production economics as an integrated field (building from firm to area to region to the whole economy) began to develop at this time. The works of W. J. Spillman and E. Lang [243, 244] were particularly noteworthy in spearheading a development relating to the quantification of production functions in forms for use in economic analysis. The 1920s was the period wherein H. R. Tolley, J. D. Black, and M. Ezekiel pioneered in the use of statistical analysis of input-output relationships derived from farm sample survey data. J. D. Black [26] integrated the numerous developments of the period into the framework of classical and neoclassical theory of firm and producing area. His *Introduction to Production Economics* was the first full and formal synthesis of the field of production economics.

In the 1930s we were witness to an extensive application of farm budgeting, the research tool developed in the 1920s. The tool was widely used in research and extension to analyze the impact of the numerous federal farm programs that were implemented to help combat drought and depression. In the 1930s the Bankhead-Jones Act was passed to encourage experimental work designed to provide estimates of production relationships. Experimental work initiated in the 1930s led to the publication in the 1940s of what has become some of the most extensively used production function data on milk, pork, beef, and eggs [6, 98, 148, 204]. The 1930s also produced some significant advances in the theory of the firm, which along with advances in statistical theory [55, 136, 236] set the stage for post-World War II developments in farm management and production economics. However, even before then, the notion that the farm was a business firm that could be analyzed and understood with use of neoclassical economic theory and modern statistical theory was gaining momentum.

Farm Management and Production Economics since World War II

The topics in this section represent some of the major changes and concerns in farm management and production economics in this period.

Changes in the Underlying Methodology

Shortly after World War II Heady [109] published an article that foreshadowed the nature of developments that dominated farm management and production economics teaching, research, and extension in the postwar era. He wrote of the strengths of farm management and production economics with a methodological foundation in neoclassical theory and modern statistics.

He wrote of the weaknesses of traditional farm management methods, methodologically rooted in descriptive positivism, empiricism, and inductive procedures. He outlined the analytical setting for farm production economics research as the portion of economic theory dealing with the economics of the firm or the principles of production. He pointed out that the principles of production provide the models in farm management economics that serve as the fundamental hypotheses for research; these principles, he added, also provide the framework for construction of the appropriate empirical analysis — the nature of the data needed to specify the problem, the sample or experimental design, and the appropriate statistical analysis — for solving specific problems. Heady saw farm management research as relating to the study of efficiency and productivity of farm resources. He delineated its specific objectives "(1) to guide individual farmers in the best use of their resources and in a manner compatible with the welfare of society and (2) to provide fundamental analysis of the efficiency of farm resource combinations which can serve as a basis for bettering the public administration of resources where agricultural policy or institutions which condition production efficiency are concerned" [109]. This statement of objectives reflects Heady's concern over the need to link micro and macro aspects of production efficiency to a greater degree than had been done in the past; because of micro-macro relations he saw little academic justification for differentiating between farm management and production economics. Some years later Johnson [149] argued strongly for differentiation because he saw farm management on the way to being dominated by production economics, which he viewed as detrimental to both farm management and production economics.

In discussing problem concepts Heady visualized scientific research as a problem solving activity with these basic steps: (1) formulation of models and criteria establishing the ideal or practical optimum (the conditions that must hold here are to be made explicit for the attainment of a given end; hence, the model provides the theoretical solution and serves as the a priori hypothesis for establishing quantitative relationships from data that can be identified and measured); (2) determination of the extent to which the existing situation deviates from the optimum and why; and (3) establishment of the appropriate means and quantitative data that provide the basis for action to close or narrow the gap between the existing situation and the optimum.

Heady outlined the basic types of problems to be solved in production, such as level of production, method of production, enterprise combination, scale of operations, timing of production, and adjustment to change and uncertainty. He outlined the data needed for solving these problems, namely, physical input-output ratios and price ratios. At the same time he deplored the search for new profit-maximizing principles when the need was for basic technical and price data for use with existing principles. He ended the article with a critique of traditional research procedures (factors affecting farm profits studies) in farm production economics and some comments on sample design and statistical estimation; he closed by emphasizing the need to explain the gap between existing resource use and the optimal, suggesting that variables other than economic ones helped to explain the gap. In the pages of this article, then, we have the blueprint of the methodology that was to guide most of the research and education in farm management and production economics in the postwar period.

Two decades earlier Black [26] had also emphasized the application of economic principles to the solution of problems in production. In the years that followed other writings transmitted a similar emphasis, such as Benedict's articles [19, 20] on the use of opportunity costs in farm management budgeting and Johnson's article [165] on the theory of enterprise combination. Black and associates' text [27] on farm management, which appeared in 1947, gave particular emphasis to the broad principles of comparative advantage and interregional competition and to those involved in adjusting to markets and prices.

Proponents of the methodology articulated by Heady and others before him were soon confronted by individuals who had been schooled in the traditional and historic methodological approach to farm management research and education — the descriptive, empirical, and inductive approach through farm surveys and accounts. In the summer of 1949, under the sponsorship of the Farm Foundation working through the North Central Farm Management Research Committee, a farm management workshop on research methodology was held at Black Duck, Minnesota. Glenn Johnson has aptly described the conflicting methodological positions that were brought into sharp focus at that workshop: "The empiricists regarded themselves as closer to reality and hence more practical and realistic than the users of theory. The other group in turn considered its members as trained deductively as well as inductively. The empiricists sometimes regarded theory as a source of dangerous preconceptions. Those using theory regarded empiricism, without systematic use of theory, as a source of spurious unmeaningful conclusions" [155]. Johnson was of the opinion that the Black Duck workshop brought the conflict to a head and laid the groundwork for union of the two groups. As Johnson now agrees, however, it is doubtful that a union ever occurred. My opinion is that those who since the 1920s had been arguing for use of economic principles and statistics in farm management and production economics plus those who through the 1940s had been trained in neoclassical economic theory and modern statistics, already at the time of the Black Duck workshop had assured through work, study, and training that neoclassical economic theory would provide the methodological foundation for much of the work in farm management and production economics in the post-World War II era.

Adding form and content to the methodology already sketched out in his "Elementary Models in Farm Production Economics Research," Heady [110] emphasized the role of theory and equilibrium analysis in research and outlined basic steps for empirical research. Briefly these steps included (1) formulating the problem either in terms of doubt, confusion, or felt difficulty or in terms of departure from ideal or optimum conditions (for the latter or the normative the equilibrium conditions of economics, he said, serve directly to identify the problems — i.e., equilibrium explains the conditions under which a given end is maximized), (2) formulating the hypothesis, (3) designing empirical procedures, (4) assembling and processing data, and (5) interpreting findings. In the process of empirical research Heady emphasized the importance of explaining the means of moving from the existing state to the theoretical (or empirical) optimum. He defined agricultural economics as economics applied to agriculture with the former drawing on the latter for its basic laws and analytical models.

A further rounding out of the methodology came with the distinctions Heady developed [105, 116] between short-run transformation curves and long-run planning curves (with their implications for understanding firm behavior) and with the economic logic he originated for farm enterprise diversification and its empirical applications. These conceptual developments pointed to a new synthesis that was about to appear. Drawing on advances in neoclassical theory of the firm by Hicks [136], Carlson [55], Schultz [236], and others and on the developments in statistics and mathematical economics of the 1940s, Heady [107] brought forth his landmark work, *Economics of Agricultural Production and Resource Use*, which became the central source for guiding farm management and production economics research and education in the post-World War II period. The book, organized into four parts, begins with the scope and nature of production economics. The second part, devoted to planning under perfect knowledge, is the theoretical core (static economic production theory) of the book. The third part, dealing with planning under imperfect knowledge, is mostly an exposition of precautions and formal and informal insurance schemes that can be used as adjustments to risk and uncertainty. The final part deals with aggregative aspects of production.

Some Results Reflecting the New Methodology

Various textbooks and extension programs may remind us that the new methodology had a far-reaching impact on resident and extension education in farm management and production economics. In *Farm Management* (1947) Black and associates [27] exposed many advanced farm management students to the broad principles of comparative advantage, interregional competition, cost analysis, and production adjustments to markets and prices. In graduate teaching in production economics Heady's *Economics of Agricultural Production and Resource Use*, along with the numerous references in that book, became standard reading and seminar materials. Bradford and Johnson's *Farm Management Analysis* [35], published in 1953, found use at both undergraduate and graduate levels. This book attempted to integrate the old ("unendowed" approach) with the new ("endowed" approach), but it did not really succeed. In 1954 Heady and Jensen's *Farm Management Economics* [122] was published. It was conceived for use in undergraduate teaching; although it has a separate chapter on economic principles or theory, the application of that theory is developed throughout the book. The following year Beneke's *Managing the Farm Business* [21] was published for use particularly by vocational agriculture students in high schools. In 1958 Bishop and Toussaint's *Introduction to Agricultural Economics Analysis* [24] made its appearance, and it has found use in both graduate and undergraduate teaching. In 1968 Doll and associates came forth with *Economics of Agricultural Production, Markets, and Policy* [74], which provides a succinct treatment of production economics theory for advanced undergraduates and graduates.

Interests in increasing total output per farm continued high at the end of World War II and extension farm management specialists put forth considerable effort toward injecting more economic analysis into the evaluation of technical data. In the early 1950s additional work was devoted to the economic evaluation of cropping systems and the economics of fertilizer use. More generally, extension farm management specialists were pointing out how economics could be used to solve farmers' problems. Bottum [33] noted that most farmers had no interest in economic data and principles per se and that extension specialists were trying to raise the economic literacy of the general public by teaching economic principles and economic reasoning with problems. In addressing himself to the use of economic theory in extension programs Lanpher [181] in 1961 stated that as a general rule farm management specialists were making constant and practical application of economic theory. He noted that only a negligible amount of extension farm management work failed to use such principles or concepts as diminishing returns and marginal analysis, opportunity costs, and fixed and variable costs. He observed the stepped-up interest and activity in teaching economic principles to farmers, noting that some regional farm management extension committees had actually published bulletins to serve as guides in teaching principles to farmers. Thus he saw economic theory as an analytical tool to be taught to farmers, at least in its elementary forms, and to county or field extension staffs. In the early 1960s the farm management school approach became one of the primary methods used by extension farm management across the country. The approach continues to be used extensively for teaching the application of economics to the management of farm-households.

After World War II Heady [109] pointed out that the real limitations to our efforts in farm management were the lack of technological and price data to use with existing principles. He appeared to be saying that a well-developed body of theory was in place but was far from fully exploited in its applications. To make it work for us and to make our efforts pay off, we should utilize this theory for model building. The models in turn would serve to guide the development of the much needed technical data which did not exist in a form for effective use in decision making. The particular body of theory that stood ready to be exploited was that which Heady [107] had put together in Part II of his book. It became an important source of models for guiding the development of technical data.

The development of technical data for use in farm management and production economics began with the inventorying of existing data, published and unpublished, in the crop and animal science departments of land-grant colleges and universities. The North Central Farm Management Research Committee organized itself into subcommittees to explore these sources, but very little data were found that provided information on production relationships. At the same time individual and group efforts turned toward conceptualization and model construction as frameworks for developing the necessary data for farm and production economics analyses. At the annual meeting of the American Agricultural Economics Association in Montreat in 1950 the farm management program emphasized discussion of the common analytical tools of economic theory available for problem analysis together with the developments needed in this theory.[1] Applications of firm theory to factor-product, factor-factor, product-product, and scale relationships and the developments needed in static theory were noted. Problems specifically identified were those involving (1) production functions subject to physiological limitations such as concentrate limit in animal feeding, (2) the estimation of value productivity functions where the lumping of inputs into categories influences the marginal value productivities of inputs, and (3) alternative production techniques and enterprise combinations.

During the 1950s many journal articles, notes, and papers were produced and numerous conferences and workshops were held — all concerned with model construction and having implications for the development of technical data and the use of these data in decisions on resource use. Antedating the 1950s was Heady's article [108] on the economics of rotations, in which he laid out the economic logic for choice of cropping system and suggested an experimental design to generate the technical data for this model. Drawing on data from the USDA Technical Bulletin 815 a short time later, Heady [112] developed a model on the economics of feeding dairy cows for milk production. He pointed out that it is the quantitative physical and value relationships for several categories of resources and products that determine their optimum use and combination. He considered the article to have both methodological and practical application, but he wrote it primarily to inspire other social and physical scientists to work on the problems of the methodological procedures employed. Heady suggested that staff people from animal husbandry, agronomy, and production economics should work cooperatively in generating this kind of information. Redman [222] added to the conceptualizations on the milk production function. He described the characteristics and economic implications of the milk production function suggested by dairy feeding standards and noted the inconsistencies between the production function implied by feeding standards and by the economists. Interests in the nature of feed-milk production relationships grew in intensity with the Mighell-Heady-Olson [127, 191, 193] exchange. Most of the controversy here seemingly grew out of the use that Heady and Olson had made of Bulletin 815 data for estimating milk isoproduct contours. Since it was pointed out from the very beginning and argued to the end that the experiments underlying these data really were not designed for estimating isoproduct contours, the exchange served little to clarify issues. Mighell argued in the final rebuttal that for farmers the factor-product relationship is more important than the factor-factor relationship. Mighell may be right, but neither he nor anyone else, including the farmer, is likely to gain much from pursuing this argument. When forage is free-fed, it is the value of the added milk plus the value of the forage saved minus the value of the grain added that must be accounted for as grain feeding is increased. In other words, both factor-product and factor-factor relationships are involved and must be considered in the analysis.

In 1952 one section of the annual meeting of the American Agricultural Economics Association was devoted to "Sources and Use of Data in Farm Management Analysis." McPherson [189] noted that the discipline of economics is bordered on one side by the disciplines of individual and social behavior and on the other by the technical studies of production. He added that regardless of the accuracy of farm management formulas farm management research cannot be accurate unless data from the technical and social disciplines are accurate and complete. He concluded that in the development of knowledge the division of labor had gone too far for optimum efficiency in research. At the same sectional meeting Allen [2] saw the ideal in technical data as a complete inventory of input-output ratios, but Haver [99] cautioned against stressing the need for data without thought of how farmers would use such data.

In 1953 Baum and Walkup [18] gleaned what was known about intratemporal and intertemporal input-output (feed and meat) relationships in fryer production and developed the economic implications of these relationships. Additional model building and technical data development in poultry production emerged from Iowa State College in 1956 with emphasis on least-cost rations and optimum marketing weight [118, 126].

Early concept and model formation on fertilizer-crop production relations focused on the evaluation of various functional forms and on the need for cooperative efforts between agronomists and economists in developing input-output data. Johnson [160], in combining experimental data and various estimating equations, found that the optimal rate of fertilizer application varied considerably with the functional form of the estimating equations used. With the objective of facilitating development of information for the farmer's decision making Redman and Allen [223] elucidated agronomic and economic concepts to improve understanding between agronomists and economists and to spur them to work together to develop information on basic production relationships. Ibach [144] also emphasized the need to establish a working partnership with the natural scientists and pointed out that the discovery of important input-output relationships and the use of them to develop better management on farms are still a long way off. At the same time he illustrated the various kinds of answers that can be obtained through use of production functions as applied to problems of fertilizer economics. The Tennessee Valley Authority was also involved in the early post-World War II work on integrating the conceptual understanding of agronomists, production economists, and statisticians for the design of experiments and development of fertilizer use data [143].

To lay the groundwork for technical data development a number of conferences were held to increase conceptual understanding not only within our own discipline but also between farm management and production economists and crop and livestock production specialists. Participants at one conference addressed problems involved in estimating resource productivity and returns to scale and suggested some estimating procedures [123]. Those at another conference discussed agronomic-economic relationships in fertilizer and crop production data development and use, focusing on general methodological considerations and experimental design and prediction problems, on fitting functions to data, and on applying or using the data [17]. A symposium sponsored by the Michigan Agricultural Experiment Station brought together a group of agronomists, economists, nutritionists, and statisticians to exchange ideas and to explore the possibilities for cooperative research and education on nutritional and economic aspects of feeding dairy cows [140].

In 1957 Heady [111] outlined conditions necessary for cooperative research between economists and physical scientists and put forth some special considerations in selecting algebraic forms of functions. Other considerations in technical data development and data use in this period were statistical problems in joint research, problems of inference from experimental data to farm situations, use of production function analysis with capital constraints, variance estimates for marginal physical products, and substitution rates and the inclusion of time in choice of factor inputs [39, 40, 72, 73, 150, 185, 252, 263]. In regard to time Brown and Arscott [39] noted that in traditional production theory optimal factor combinations are usually estimated in a timeless setting, placing limits on its application to problems in which time is an important variable. In these situations, therefore, rather than providing answers to questions of what is the least-cost factor combination for producing a given output and what is the optimal level of output — questions which ignore time — we should be providing answers to questions such as this: Given some fixed time period for the production process in a subperiod of production, what is the most profitable factor combination and what is the optimal length of time for the subperiods of production, considering the longer overall production period? They visualized this specification of time in the model as particularly applicable to problems in livestock and poultry feeding, where various lots or batches can be produced, over the time span of, say, a year.

After presenting the production economics logic for allocating scarce resources among competing enterprises, Doll [72] applied this logic to some empirical data to determine the optimal allocation of a limited amount of fertilizer between corn and barley.

Much of the conceptualization and model construction for technical data development along with data developments during the first decade following World War II were synthesized in Heady and Dillon's *Agricultural Production Functions* [121]. This book is an excellent summary of concepts and research procedures relating to physical and firm production functions and traces the development of production function analysis — functional forms, problems of specification, collection, and analyses of data for functional estimates, and economic applications. It ends with a description of the recent research based on production function analysis.

The conceptualizations, the model building, the informal communications, and the conferences, workshops, and the like that took place among agricultural economists, physical scientists, and statisticians led to a number of multidisciplinary experimental efforts. These experiments were designed and put into operation to produce technical data that quantitatively specified some of the basic input-output relationships in crop and livestock production considered essential to economic analysis. The major efforts reported here have been widely publicized in the literature. Multidisciplinary endeavors have also been undertaken elsewhere, such as the fertilizer and crop production experimentation at Purdue University, the University of Kentucky, and North Carolina State University.

In 1953 an article in the *Journal of Farm Economics* reported on the effectiveness of cooperative research between animal scientists and economists [134]. The article included a plea to other schools to extend and improve upon the data which had been developed through this research. In this article Heady and his co-workers presented data from an experiment designed to develop production surfaces and isoproduct contours relating corn and soybean meal inputs to pork output.[2] Least-cost rations were computed and a simplifying technique (a pork costulator) was developed to make it easy for farmers to use these data in hog ration decisions. In the following year Heady and Pesek [128] published certainly the most comprehensive study of its kind that had yet appeared; in it agronomists and economists had jointly designed an experiment which produced estimates of corn production surfaces from varying combinations of N and P_2O_5. Analysis of the data specified the economic optima for fertilizer use. A number of studies since then have sought to determine the crop yield effects of fertilizer and other variables such as rainfall, soil moisture at seeding or planting time, irrigation waters, and multiharvest periods [80, 86, 138, 175, 196, 209].

In 1966 Hoffnar and Johnson [139] reported on nine years of cooperative agronomic-economic research in Michigan. The major goal in this research was to design experiments that would produce reliable estimates of economically optimum rates of fertilizer. Particular attention was given to problems of within treatment variance and of making inferences from plots to actual farm situations.

Paralleling the kind of work done earlier on production relationships in pork and corn production, Heady and associates [129] in 1956 reported on the first experiment ever designed to permit estimation and prediction of milk production surfaces and the quantities of milk, grain, and hay associated with this structure. The data generated through this experiment were used to show how to arrive at optimal rations and levels of milk production. The study was described as methodological, and the authors suggested that it could serve as a foundation for further study at Iowa State College and elsewhere. A second report on a milk production function study at Iowa State followed some years later [124]. Variables other than hay and grain — namely, cow characteristics such as body weight and age and environmental variables such as temperature — were included in the latter study. On the basis of the study the authors concluded that future experiments could lead to improved estimates of milk production functions if cow characteristics were considered along with feed variables in the design.

In 1967 Hoover and associates [141] at Kansas State University reported on a multidisciplinary study where economists, nutritionists, and statisticians had worked together on a milk production function study designed to complement the study done at Iowa State University. The results from this study were reported to be highly supportive of the findings from the Iowa experiments. In other words, the Kansas study provided additional evidence of slight nonlinearity in the milk production function and decreasing marginal rates of substitution of grain for hay. The nature of the milk production surfaces and the shape and position of the isoquants from the Kansas and Iowa studies were highly similar. The Kansas study also suggested that in addition to feed auxiliary variables such as cow characteristics and environmental variables should be designed into the experiment.

To round out the review of literature on milk production function studies, two additional reports should be noted. Using data from the Iowa experiment in dairy feeding, Coffey and Toussaint [62] made some comparisons between optimum feeding and most profitable stomach capacity feeding. They concluded that optimum rations lie near the stomach capacity limit for most prices of hay, grain, and milk. Moreover, feeding hay free choice to cows yields higher returns than does limited feeding when body weight changes and additional feeding expenses were considered (i.e., for most feed-milk price ratios). The results also showed that the milk isoquants are almost straight, if not linear. Paris and associates [211] added further to our knowledge of milk production functions in a report of a feeding experiment from which they developed isoquants for whole milk, fat, 4 percent fat-corrected milk, and skim milk. The fat isoquants were convex to the origin while the whole and skim milk isoquants were concave. The offsetting differences, i.e., the relative efficiency attained in transforming feed into fat versus the relative inefficiency of transforming feed into the nonfat components of milk, resulted in 4 percent fat-corrected milk isoquants with almost straight line segments, a finding substantially in agreement with the Iowa findings.

Much of the model building and technical data development in farm management and production economics have centered on fertilizer and feeds as key variables, but intensive efforts have been made to generate other kinds of data for production planning. The development of information on the labor input comes to mind here. In 1949 Vaughan and Hardin's [269] *Farm Work Simplification* appeared. This publication was a landmark study on farm labor, a synthesis of much of the research that had been done during the war years. The acute manpower shortages during the war and early postwar years resulted in the need to increase worker productivity. One response to this situation was to find ways to simplify farm work. The American Farm Economic Association established a Work Simplification Committee, and in 1942 the National Farm Work Simplification Project was established and funded. At Purdue University the Purdue Motion and Time Study Laboratory, under the direction of E. C. Young, was organized and set up as an integral part of the national project. Farm management research workers from Florida, Kentucky, Minnesota, New Jersey, New York, South Carolina, and Vermont also became involved in this effort, and the additional names of M. E. Brunk [42], G. B. Byers and E. R. Young [47], R. M. Carter [57], S. A. Engene [82], H. Woodworth [282], and E. C. Young and I. R. Bierly [284] became associated with farm work simplification studies. The underlying purpose of these studies was to save time by eliminating unnecessary work or motions and to develop easier, faster, and more economical ways of doing farm jobs.

Most of the other postwar studies on the labor input had a different focus but had some similarities with the earlier time and motion studies. The large amounts of budgeting or programming in the postwar period called for vast quantities of labor data. But the emphasis was not primarily that of finding ways to save labor. The focus was rather on estimating the amount of labor actually used on farms in producing crops and livestock under different methods and at different scales. The estimated amounts of labor used or the labor coefficients could then be employed in budgeting or programming studies. But the later labor studies resembled the earlier time and motion studies in the sense that both looked at labor in relation to tasks and various ways of performing these tasks. This approach is particularly useful in budgeting or programming farms with widely different resource situations. First, the labor coefficients are developed for specific production methods and hence should be more accurate than coefficients developed from an average of various production methods. Moreover, labor coefficients developed by tasks (e.g., grain feeding, silage feeding, milking, manure handling) and by different ways of performing these tasks can be organized to reflect the amount of labor required by different systems, such as alternative dairy chore systems. Labor information in this form enhances the value of budgeting and programming for farm planning by allowing the choice of system to fit particular resource situations.

Aune and Day [7] and Fuller and Jensen [88] used a task function approach and regression analysis in developing relationships between dairy herd size and dairy chore labor requirements given various methods for performing the various tasks. Their studies showed that increases in herd size are related to some labor economies. Langvatn [180] also showed decreasing time per cow as the size of the dairy herd increased. Seagraves [238] compared synthesized and labor record estimates of labor requirements in broiler production. He noted that a number of alternative procedures are available for estimating labor requirements, and he emphasized the importance of specifying beforehand the purpose for wanting to know labor requirements because that may influence the procedure used.

Changing technology, often having far-reaching effects on whole systems of production, calls for a sustained effort in developing technical data as a basis for production planning. Drawing on his research experience with swine production systems, Kadlec [168] emphasized the growing importance of information on alternative production processes and encouraged researchers to seek complete knowledge of the various production systems with an awareness of alternative technologies. He urged greater use of experiments and a multidisciplinary approach in developing data.

Reviewing the effort at conceptualization and model construction for the development of technical data for use in farm management and production economics studies, my judgment is that outside of the Purdue experiments generating technical data for alternative swine production systems, the Michigan fertilizer and crop production experiments, and the Kansas feed and milk production experiments, the comprehensive multidisciplinary approaches to the development of these data have been mostly at Iowa State University. Given the need for technical data for farm production analysis and planning, it is something of a puzzle why comprehensive multidisciplinary efforts have not been more widespread and numerous. One possible explanation is that multidisciplinary efforts require the building of bridges — the establishing of communications and working relations among disciplines — which is not always easy to accomplish. Another possible explanation is that because of constantly changing technology physical production relationships are continually changing, and for this reason data can soon become obsolete, generating a certain feeling of frustration and resulting in reluctance on the part of researchers to get involved in comprehensive efforts that may absorb much time and many other resources. A third possibility is that such studies may not have a high economic payoff; given the variations that do exist in climate and soils, it may make little difference whether a farmer applies 150 or 200 pounds of fertilizer. A fourth possible explanation is that production economists may have turned most of their time and interests toward model building and testing which can be based on assumptions of various data sets and forms. Again, with the introduction of linear programming shortly after World War II so much of the effort of farm management and production economists has been involved with developing this technique that there is an increased willingness to accept discrete data in the form of the best estimates provided by the physical scientists. But, whatever the explanation, if the kinds or classes of problems that have been addressed over the last decade in station bulletins, circulars, and reports are an accurate reflection of the data needs of the period, then the overwhelming needs focus on data for analyzing enterprise combination and method of production problems.

In the preceding pages we have reviewed the postwar research devoted to the development of technical data for use in economic analysis of farm production problems. Let us now examine the farm management research that was published in the bulletins, circulars, and reports produced by a sample of twenty-nine land-grant colleges and universities through the 1960s. Much of this farmer-oriented research of course drew on the technical data developed and referenced above, but it also drew on other data sources such as farmers and physical scientists.

Farm management and production economics specialists devoted the great bulk of their farm-oriented research effort toward developing information and guides for farmers to use in choosing enterprises and methods of production. The largest single group of studies dealt with enterprise costs and returns, with enterprise combinations, or with enterprise adjustments to changing technology or prices. Numerous studies dealt with the economics of a single enterprise (beef, dairy, cotton, or fruit) and many, through budgeting or programming, determined optimal enterprise combinations within varying resource situations and constraints. Methods of production studies were devoted to providing cost information on alternative ways of producing crops and livestock involving alternative irrigation systems, fertilizer combinations, fertilizer and seed, labor-machinery-equipment combinations, alternative rations, and dryland versus irrigation farming. Given our economy, rich in alternative farm technologies and highly dynamic in developing new technologies, it is not surprising that a great deal of effort was devoted to providing guidance in choice of production methods. Nor is it surprising that the choice of enterprise was regarded as a most important decision problem, because comparative advantage shifts as technologies, prices, and institutions change.

Next in order of frequency but ranking considerably below enterprise and production method studies were studies which yielded information (1) on how to improve decisions on farm size, farm finance, and purchases of inputs, (2) on what institutional arrangements — such as agricultural policies and credit and leasing terms — exist, and (3) on how to improve data collection and handling.

Since large numbers of farmers are involved with choices on farm size, many farm management and production economists responded with studies on economies to size and on management problems associated with increased size. Since increasing farm size often required financing, numerous studies sought answers to questions on financing expansion, capital needs, cash flows, and the use of credit, debt load capacity, financing through father-son partnership, and corporate arrangements.

Farmers often have the opportunity of either buying inputs outright or hiring or renting the use of them. To provide information for these choices, a fair number of studies were made on the costs of owning versus renting land and on the costs of owning versus renting power, machinery, and equipment. Other cost studies developed information for constructing and operating complete systems such as those for irrigation of crops, for forage handling, and for swine feeding. Other cost studies simply sought to improve market information by gathering data on prices paid for land or hired labor, for the rental services of land and machinery, and for used machinery.

Most of the studies on institutions were set up to provide information for the farmer's use in evaluating the effects of various agricultural policies and institutional arrangements, such as the effects of wheat, corn, or cotton policy, grazing fees and permits, and minimum wages, and the effects of various taxes such as real estate, sales, income, and social security taxes. Extension farm management specialists particularly have provided much needed information on social security and income taxes. Other studies on institutions have dealt with matters such as the effects of pollution controls on farm costs and returns and the effects of varying farm bargaining power arrangements on farm incomes and consumer costs. Others have developed information on various contracts, such as those used in egg and broiler production.

Studies to improve data collection and handling treated subjects such as mail-in farm accounts, coding farm records, collecting and organizing input-output data in farm management handbooks, programmed budgeting techniques, and computer programming. A number of studies yielded information on the productivity of various resources, and others treated problems growing out of risk and uncertainty, such as yield and income variability.

Not all information used by farm managers was developed from studies by farm management or production economists. Commercial farm managers suggest that information from physical and biological scientists also has value in farm management. A sampling of the articles in the *Journal of the American Society of Farm Managers and Rural Appraisers* over the postwar period suggested that professional farm managers find use for purely technical data. About one-fourth of the articles were devoted to technical information on such matters as pasture practices, bloat, performance testing, fertility and nutritional balance, rations, grain fumigation, European corn borer, weed killers, and machinery design. A somewhat smaller proportion was devoted to appraisal and leasing of land and to land booms and taxes. About three-fifths of the sample articles provided economic information and were contributed primarily by farm management and production economists within the land-grant system. These articles furnished information on subjects such as costs of production, credit, land valuation, risk and insurance, decision shortcuts, capitalization, least-cost machinery, linear programming, computerized accounting and other management technologies, economics of beef production, competitive position of hogs, demand-supply and prices, and financing of agriculture.

In retrospect then, research for the farmer's use has ranged over a wide variety of topics and problems, suggesting that the management of farms is a complex business. At the same time the great bulk of the research has focused on methods of production and farm enterprise studies. Perhaps the postwar price-cost squeeze in agriculture and the resulting narrow profit margins partially explain this emphasis. Information from the studies could help guide farmers in reducing production costs through the recombination of factors and in increasing gross income through recombinations of enterprises, in this manner widening profit margins or preventing them from getting narrower. In addition, the existence of numerous alternative technologies and of technological, institutional, and market changes provides the opportunities and the continuous need for evaluating the choices of production methods and of the crops and/or livestock to produce.

Analytical Techniques

The previous section focused on some results associated with the shift to the neoclassical static firm theory as the new methodological base. In this section we examine the most important analytical techniques that have been used, together with this theory, as the essential tools for analysis in the post-World War II period. The discussion is limited primarily to micro applications — mathematical programming, simulation, regression, gaming, and flow-of-funds.

Frederick Waugh set the stage for the far-reaching developments in mathematical programming that took place in farm management and production economics following World War II. In 1951 he wrote, "The main purpose of this paper is to test a method of determining the least expensive combination of feeds which meets or surpasses each of several stated requirements. The 'linear programming' techniques recently developed by Koopmans, Dantzig, and others are used to provide a definitive solution to this problem" [274]. The first decade following the war can be considered a development period for mathematical programming. By the beginning of the second decade it had become a standard technique that was used in nearly all departments of agricultural economics, particularly in farm management and production economics.

In 1953 Waugh [273] reminded us that agricultural economists had long used an informal type of programming, referred to as the budget method, which he described as not very systematic in that it relied very strongly on judgment and intuition. He mentioned at that time that linear programming had had few practical applications to real economic problems, but he did refer to some promising studies that were under way. Among these were studies by Richard King and his associates at North Carolina State University and by Walter Fisher and Leonard Schruben of Kansas State. Waugh saw linear programming as a technique that would have wide application, one that might prove as important as multiple regression. The extensive application in succeeding years attests to the accuracy of his prediction.

Accuracy in forecasting also should be attributed to Fisher and Schruben [85], who predicted that by the 1960s linear programming would be explored and its limitations would be understood. They contributed to the development of this technique by extending Waugh's one-product example to two or more products and to alternative price situations. They also commented on the relationship between linear programming and the isoproduct contour or function.

King [174] drew our attention to the possibilities of the new analytical tool in solving some practical problems in agriculture. For a manager with given resources who must decide on input and enterprise combinations, he outlined four techniques for finding a solution: budgeting analysis; production function, cost function, and revenue function analysis; isoproduct contour analysis; and activity analysis. After demonstrating activity analysis he outlined some implications of the new technique: (1) it provides a mathematical test to indicate whether the most profitable production plan has been suggested; (2) it offers a way of using information now available in the crops and animal sciences departments which may be unsuitable for estimating production functions but which can be used to compare a limited number of specific techniques of production; (3) it serves to emphasize the specification of the resources available to farmers; (4) it supplies a method for showing the profitability of new combinations of resources or larger quantities of resources; (5) it is a tool for analyzing the impact of public programs on a farming area; and (6) it points to the need for the addition of matrix algebra to the economist's mathematical kit. Twenty years later most of us would probably say that these indeed were the implications and then some.

Emphasizing the power and versatility of the new technique, Swanson and Fox [255] applied activity analysis to the problem of livestock enterprise selection in 1954, a time when its use was still limited because of excessive computational work. Commenting on its "apparent complexity," Heady [115] laid some groundwork from which expansion in use of the tool could take place by a simplified presentation of the underlying logic and computational procedures.

Further developments in linear programming as an analytical technique appeared in the mid-1950s. Boles [30] systematically unfolded its application to farm management problems in a step-by-step procedure (a sterling piece of pedagogy) and pointed to its principal advantages over budgeting. Swanson [254] illustrated the solving of a linear programming problem through the use of an electronic computer. Babbar, Tintner, and Heady [8] presented an exploratory analysis for an Iowa farm situation with variations in input-output coefficients which in turn influenced probable outcomes in production plans. Smith [240] illustrated how linear programming can deal with situations in which the opportunity cost of using an input, produced or available on the farm, is different from the price of that input — a two-price problem for inputs. Peterson [214] showed how linear programming can be used for the simultaneous selection of optimal crop and livestock enterprises.

At the annual meeting of the American Farm Economic Association in 1955 McCorkle [188] discussed linear programming as a tool in farm management analysis. Because of frequently appearing problems involving choice from numerous alternatives and because of the adaptability of linear programming to various kinds of problems, he regarded it as a very important tool. He warned, however, that it is no panacea for farm management analysis and suggested that fieldwork, experimental evidence, and careful formulation of the problem are still keys to successful farm management analysis.

In a joint meeting of the American Farm Economic Association and other associations, Bishop, Katzman, and Swanson [23, 170, 251] reported on various applications of mathematical programming. Bishop demonstrated the use of linear programming in evaluating part-time farming. Swanson pointed out how linear programming was especially applicable to corn belt farms that support a wide range in choice of enterprises, including complex interrelationships between crops and livestock. Both Bishop and Swanson indicated the usefulness of linear programming in determining the sensitivity of solutions to price changes, particularly where the optimal solution relates to a relatively long production period. Swanson suggested than an important use of linear programming is as a check on the general nature of recommendations made to farmers. Katzman, following Waugh's pioneering effort on a similar problem, illustrated the use of linear programming in providing an exact and unique solution to the problem of determining a least-cost broiler diet meeting certain nutritive requirements.

Candler [48] reported on a procedure whereby linear programming solutions can be provided easily for a large number of capital situations — solutions based on capital as a continuous variable. This procedure can provide results that fit a number of farms with similar "other" resources but with varying capital availabilities.

In view of the fact that linear programming was still being done extensively on desk calculators in 1956, Boles [31] presented a method for condensing a problem so as to reduce the number of iterations that need be performed. Although linear programming had been regarded exclusively as a tool for private decision making on resource use, Heady [106] visualized how it could be used to provide a framework for selecting important problems for research. Using ranch management to illustrate his point, he suggested that if linear programming solutions indicate that forage supplies in August limit the scale of operations, then research should be devoted to increasing forage supplies in August, not to increasing them in June.

In 1957 Candler [49] illustrated variable price programming. He viewed it as an efficient technique for evaluating the effects of price changes compatible with a given farm production plan, for evaluating the effects of changing support prices on farm income and optimum production plans, and for estimating normative supply functions for a farm or region. To emphasize the practical application of linear programming solutions, Puterbaugh and associates [219] presented a farm situation, production possibilities, a solution tableau, and an analysis of this tableau and its stability. Noting the orientation that the linear programming effort appeared to be assuming until the late 1950s, McAlexander and Hutton [186] pointed out that most of it had been of a maximizing type. They then proceeded to discuss several methods for setting up minimization type problems and related the minimization form to the maximization form so that those who had worked only with the latter would be able to benefit from the presentation.

Heady and Candler's *Linear Programming Methods* [119], a handy reference book for teaching and research, was published in 1958. The information on preparing and coding data for computers, on shortcuts and checks, and on mapping can be valuable in the research time it may save. Moreover, the detailed description of the step-by-step procedures of numerical analysis is helpful to both teacher and student.

Coutu [64] viewed linear programming as an excellent teaching device in working with low-income farmers. In going through the processes of identifying resource restrictions, classifying resources relative to productivity levels, and so on, Coutu reasoned that the farm management worker gets involved with the farmers in evaluating alternatives and in evaluating goals and objectives with the result that he acts more as a teacher than an adviser. Knudtson and Cochrane [176] used linear programming to derive a supply function for flax at the firm level.

Articles on dynamic programming began to appear in the late 1950s. Loftsgard and Heady [183] argued that farm and home plans could be made more realistic by including time and more farm-household interdependence. Then with a dynamic programming model (dynamic in the Hicksian sense in that inputs and outputs are dated) they solved the optimum for any one year. This optimum was a function of the optima in previous years, of the availability of capital and the returns on capital in previous years, and of the need for household consumption at different points in time. The procedure specified the plans for the transitional years before the optimal plan is reached; heretofore, programming or budgeting typically had provided a plan for some future time with no information covering the period between that plan and the existing one. Candler [51], reflecting on this study, pointed out that there was no real difference formally between normal linear programming and Hicksian dynamic programming. He added that if the only difference between years is the supply of capital, as was suggested by the description of the "case farm situation," then we have a problem in which parametric programming would reduce the computing burden.

The linearity assumption underlying the standard programming model has been of concern to farm management and production economists. Giaever and Seagraves [90] in 1960 were concerned about the large number of enterprises that often were included in the optimal solutions of linear programs, possibly because they did not allow for economies to size. They attempted to extend or improve programming techniques by examining several procedures for solving programming problems when economies to size exist. Candler and Manning [53] described a modified simplex procedure for linear programming problems with one or two input coefficients displaying decreasing average costs. They drew on parametric programming as a means of examining all points on the relevant section of the production surface to find the plan yielding the highest income.

The continuity assumption of orthodox linear programming which permits a variable to take on any value (integer or noninteger) in the optimal solution may pose something of a problem in situations involving indivisibilities. In the early 1960s Musgrave [201] showed how integer and mixed integer programming could be used to overcome that problem as well as the problem of increasing returns. (See also [184].)

Parametric programming was developed to measure how sensitive a solution is to variation in the technical and/or price coefficients. The parameter most often varied was product price, although some interesting studies using variable factor pricing have also been made. Among these was a study that Weeks [275] designed to estimate the conditions under which wheat would be fed to livestock. The model was developed to select simultaneously the animals to be fed and their rations; the solutions were obtained by parametrically varying the price of wheat. Varying the price changed the marginal opportunity cost of alternative livestock enterprises so as to suggest that the choice of feeding ration and feeding activity should be made simultaneously.

With time, programming models have become more and more intricate, usually as a consequence of trying to construct them so that they more accurately mirror the planning reality wherein at least some of the variation is of a stochastic nature. Merrill [190] made a comparative analysis of a multiperiod stochastic linear programming model and a "linear team" programming model to determine their application to a farm planning problem. Each of the models considered both time and uncertainty. From the comparison he concluded that the optimal solutions differed little. Apparently the differences in the profitability of the activities was so large relative to the variances of the profits that accounting for variability in profits made essentially no difference in the optimal solutions.

Recently Candler and associates [52] have described their experiences in designing computer programs for farm management extension use. They argued that we have given too little attention to the gap between the software requirements for research and those for extension use. They reasoned that the needs in extension were more demanding than in research and that this at least partly explained the gap. They contended that in extension there was a strong need for clarity, speed, and reliability. Too there was a philosophical difference between extension and research in that a research worker often wants to change the structure of the problem while the extension worker takes the structure as a given and wants to know how the optimal farm plan changes when yields, factor, and product prices are changed.

But despite the possible lag in the development of computer software for extension uses, extension workers have made far-reaching applications of linear programming and electronic data processing (EDP). Soon after the advent of linear programming in agricultural economics, extension farm management specialists began to explore its use in developing farm plans for individual farmers. Over the past fifteen years many farms have been the focus of pilot projects to test the feasibility of linear programming in farm planning and to explore it as a tool for economic education. A few of these pilot projects are Purdue's Top Farmer program, Nebraska's least-cost feed project, Penn State's educational service project, Oklahoma's Feedmix program, Missouri's cattle feeder ration program, and Ohio State's whole farm program. Much concern and criticism have evolved over the high costs of programming individual farms. Various efforts have been made to reduce these costs by mechanizing the data-gathering process and by reducing the overhead costs per farm. One approach is to linear program typical or representative farms, but this method has not met with great success because of the difficulties of adapting the results to the uniqueness of individual farms. Also, most individual farmers are not likely to work from a bulletin in adapting linear programming results from a typical farm to their own. In the past few years efforts have been under way in many states to build a standardized matrix, to be held in computer memory, for which individual coefficients can be changed to meet the desires of individual farmers. The procedure reduces the amount of time used in working with the individual farmer and reduces the amount of new input data needed for each linear programming run. The Automatic Corn Budget developed at Purdue illustrates the procedure [52].

In conjunction with or separate from the linear programming effort over the past ten years extension farm management has been involved with a number of computerized farm record projects. Examples are the Michigan State Today's Electronic Farm Records for Management (TELFARM) and the Wisconsin electronic records program. In some instances extension personnel have worked directly with farmers on these projects, but in other instances they have worked through commercial firms, helping them develop and implement computerized farm record projects as services to farmers. Computer programs developed by extension often have been used by commercial firms as the basis for their own programs.

The extension-operated computer farm record projects have most often relied on the mail-in method for obtaining the data from farm records. The record projects have served as a mechanism for conducting many other traditional extension farm management programs and for budgeting, programming, and counseling on management problems. Throughout the development and operation of the record projects there has been a sustained interest in tying the record to forward planning. Plaunt [215], in discussing the application of EDP to problems of farm record keeping and farm business analysis, saw the development of a comprehensive EDP farm record system as a way of getting detailed physical and financial information on inputs and outputs for each major production process within the farm business. In his view, once that information was on hand, a wide assortment of other research and extension goals would be attainable.

To date, however, there has not been much success in formally tying record keeping to a forward planning process. One project in the northeastern United States does have a component whereby the farmer can feed a forward plan for the coming year into the computer. The computer then runs comparisons of this plan with his record as it evolves through the year. Illinois also has a project wherein farm records by EDP are tied to forward planning via linear programming.

Testing of remote terminals for use in farm management extension programs has been widespread in the last few years. An estimated fifty to sixty separate computer applications for use through remote terminals have been prepared in various states. Approximately fifteen states have tested the use of remote terminals and about ten of these have terminals in field offices. At the same time considerable effort is being expended in building data banks for storage and retrieval of information. Generally, many view the use of remote terminals as a successful effort, and many believe there is tremendous potential for further use of them in extension farm management in the near future, particularly as the inventory of computer software in the form of decision aids develops.

At the beginning of the 1960s a survey report revealed that almost all departments of agricultural economics used linear programming in research (mostly in farm management and production economics), that the majority of the departments taught it, and that 30 percent used it or planned to use it in extension [83]. The same report noted that most of the modifications at that time in the standard programming model were transportation, variable pricing, and dynamic programming. Through the 1960s other modifications were made — modifications to handle discontinuities, scale variants, time, and uncertainty. The post-World War II period saw linear programming develop as an educational and research tool, numerous refinements in the standard model to make it applicable to a variety of situations, and the adoption of it throughout the country in farm management and production economics, research, and education. On the basis of the station bulletins and circulars from a sample of land-grant colleges and universities, mathematical programming now ranks along with budgeting as the most widely used analytical techniques in farm management and production economics.

Even though the main reliance has been placed on budgeting and programming, other analytical tools or techniques have also been explored and used at the micro level. Burt and Allison [44] used dynamic programming (as defined by Bellman) for deciding when to leave land fallow rather than planting wheat under dryland conditions. This Markovian model involved a multistage decision process in which the task was to find a sequence of decisions that maximized or minimized the objective function. Soil moisture at wheat planting time was the variable on which the decision was based.

Simulation is one of the new techniques and is certainly in the exploratory and developmental stages. Suttor and Crom [250] have argued that computers have made large complex models feasible in terms of time and costs and that the numerical solutions of simulation models make them particularly useful for examining policy issues of firms and of other decision-making units. Halter and Dean [97] reported on the possibilities of using computer simulation in evaluating management policies under uncertainty of prices and weather. They warned against the use of simulation at the firm level when answers can be developed with simpler techniques. At the same time they did suggest that there are a goodly number of questions at the firm level for which adequate answers cannot be provided by other techniques. Zusman and Amiad [285] reported on the results of applying simulation techniques to solve the decision problems on a farm in the Negev region (Israel), which has low and variable rainfall. One of their objectives was to appraise the usefulness of this technique for solving farm management problems. In its use for farm management they alluded to its high cost in terms of man and computer time, but on the positive side they added that once a model has been developed for one farm it can be adapted to other farms with minor modifications and that a farm manager equipped with a program simulating his farm can keep it up to date at very low cost. They viewed it as a promising tool for use mainly by extension workers and operators of large farms with access to computers in farm planning and management under uncertain weather conditions. Patrick and Eisgruber's study [213] showed that simulation models can be used to approximate the farmer's decision-making process with reasonable accuracy. Anderson [4] described a simulation program designed to determine the optimal crop pattern on irrigated farms. The optimal pattern was based on making the most efficient use (that is, the use that would produce the highest net income) of the predicted water supply throughout the season. An interesting feature of this program is its several decision points: an irrigation organization allocates water to farms and irrigators, and farm managers decide on the crops to irrigate and on the order in which to irrigate them. Ikerd and Schupp [145] developed a decision model for continuous sequence production processes of variable length. Their computer simulation program compared continuous sequences of fixed lengths with the variable length model. When there is continuous sequence production, the problem becomes one of maximizing profits per unit of time rather than for any single production process.

Most who have firsthand experience with the use of simulation for firm-level problems suggest that we consider simpler techniques for answering questions before deciding on simulation. The costs of developing the programs are high, and given that fact simulation appears at this time to be more appropriate as a tool for macro problems.

Regression, of course, is a tool used widely in aggregate production function analysis, which is reviewed elsewhere. It is also a tool much used in partial production function analysis of certain biological processes within the firm, such as specifying fertilizer and crop yield relations and feed and milk relations, which have already been discussed. It has been used but little for estimating enterprise production functions. Using Illinois enterprise cost accounting data from twenty-seven dairy-hog farms, Beringer [22] fitted four functions (three enterprise functions and one aggregate function) for the whole farm. His comparison of the enterprise functions with the aggregate function suggested that the former provided more meaningful estimates for management than the latter. However, the errors of the regression coefficients were very large, and the intercorrelations among the independent variables were high. The high intercorrelations, along with the other problems usually associated with this type of analysis, suggests that more study is needed if the procedure is to be useful to firm managers. Beringer's effort would appear to be a step in that direction, because certainly whole farm production function analysis has a role only as a general guide to macro policy decisions.

Game theory has been used sparingly as an analytical technique in farm management analysis. It is a technique used for decision making under uncertainty. Dillon [70] reported on an application of game theory to choice of cattle feeding program, using various decision criteria. He drew no strong conclusions, but he did put the theory to an empirical test. At present game theory can be described as an orderly way of viewing decision making and therefore it may serve as a source of hypotheses for testing. Whether the knowledge and application of game theory by farm operators will improve decision making is an open question.

An analytical technique that has added an important new dimension to farm management analysis is the flow-of-funds analysis. Mueller [199] has described this technique as embodying no production plans of its own other than matching sources and uses of funds in a given period. He saw it as complementary to budgeting or linear programming in evaluating the potential effects of proposed production plans on the financial position of the firm. It might also be added that the expected financial position of the firm in the planning process may also affect a farmer's choice of production plans. Flow-of-funds analysis provides a way of integrating financial management with farm and household planning or management.

The Development of Regional Activities[3]

In the spring of 1946 a small group of agricultural economists met in St. Paul, Minnesota, to identify issues that needed to be faced in farm management research.[4] This meeting was the source of extensive developments in farm management and production economics. A meeting in the fall of 1946 in Madison, Wisconsin, was essentially an extension of the St. Paul meeting. The participants in the Madison meeting recommended that the experiment station directors of the north central region be asked to name members to a regional farm management research committee and suggested that the Farm Foundation act as a catalytic agent to bring interested individuals together to discuss lines of work, ideas, or problems and to take suitable action. They felt that not many farm management problems lent themselves to regional study, but they did believe that a regional farm management research committee could make its most important contributions in research methodology. The directors approved the recommendations of the Madison group, and in April 1947 a committee of agricultural economists active in farm management became known as the North Central Farm Management Research Committee.

THE NORTH CENTRAL FARM MANAGEMENT
RESEARCH COMMITTEE (NCFMRC)

From its very beginning the NCFMRC recognized the importance of acting as a forum for discussion of research problems and methods, but it also engaged in actual research. A proposed study of the economics of soil conservation became the first to be approved and funded as a regional project. The early 1950s saw the fruits of the work on this project in the form of theses, articles, and bulletins on the economics of cropping systems, on fertilizer use, on harvesting and storing forage crops, on livestock feeding, on obstacles to soil conservation, and on budgeting techniques. Since adjustments to soil conservation farming in many instances meant increased forage production on farms, the NCFMRC soon became involved in grain-forage substitution relationships in livestock production. This involvement took the form of searching the existing data from livestock feeding experiments, organizing meetings and conferences with livestock nutritionists, and planning and conducting livestock feeding experiments in cooperation with livestock nutritionists. The purpose of this was to obtain data in a form applicable to an economic analysis of grain-forage substitution and level of feeding in livestock production. Similar arrangements were made between NCFMRC members and crop and soil specialists to get at the economics of fertilizer use.

The NCFMRC members recognized both micro and macro aspects of the soil conservation problem. It was observed that study of the economics of soil conservation must recognize both the individual farm and social aspects, differentiating between those practices that were profitable for the individual farmer and those that were not but were vital to the general welfare. However, the NCFMRC never dealt in a substantive way with the externalities of the soil conservation problem and consequently missed a great opportunity for developing socially comprehensive guides to resource use. It was recognized that time considerations for the individual farmer were likely to differ from those for society and that because of this difference some practices would be of economic interest to the individual farmer and some would not but could be of interest to society. Not recognized, or at least not brought into the analysis, was the consideration of farming practices profitable to the individual farmer but so costly to society that farmers who engaged in such practices might be expected to reimburse the public for the social cost.

The need for management grows out of risk and uncertainty, and in the early 1950s some NCFMRC members became interested in the study of manaagerial processes. What later became known as the Interstate Managerial Study had its beginning at this time. In the early to middle 1950s the committee members also began to focus on what later became widely known as the price-cost squeeze in commercial agriculture. Linear programming was also introduced at this time and discussed within the committee as a new research technique, and the committee held a conference on the problem of farm size and resource productivity [123].

In the last half of the 1950s the committee set to work to improve the information and data available for farm and home planning. This period also saw the earlier planning for the Interstate Managerial Study grow into a large study of managerial processes in farming. The study was not a formal NCFMRC effort, but the personnel who planned and conducted it were also members of the NCFMRC. During the same period the NCFMRC organized work conferences on agricultural adjustments in a growing economy, on supply responses, and on dairy feeding. It was involved in cooperative studies between animal nutritionists and farm management specialists or production economists on livestock feeding experiments — primarily involving dairy and other ruminant livestock. Largely as a result of the activities of the agricultural adjustment subcommittee of the NCFMRC, the end of the decade saw a blossoming forth of aggregate supply response study proposals and study programs. The NCFMRC's regional project proposal on supply response for hogs and beef cattle was given formal approval by the directors. Another regional aggregate supply response study under way at this time was the Lake States Milk Supply Response Study, again not a formal effort by the NCFMRC but involving members of it. These supply response studies turned out to be of little help to policy makers except to suggest to them what production could be given certain price and resource constraints. However, for use in predicting supply response, the models providing the framework for these studies had little value. The models were inadequately constrained, largely owing to failure in identifying and specifying realistic behavioral equations in the models. At the end of the decade a study of the human factor in farm management was funded.

In the 1960s seminars on expectations and basic managerial research suggested that the subject of management continued to command attention. Conferences or symposia on the farm firm — growth, financing, basic structural modifications as related to structural changes in the economy as a whole —

showed sustained interest in how the farm firm grows, how growth and change are financed, and the implications for the farm firm of vertical integration and other structural changes in the economy. A seminar on supply function work indicated that study continued in that area. Another seminar revealed a renewed interest in the use of farm records, largely in records as an information system (mail-in or other) that could possibly be utilized with greater effectiveness in farm decision making through the use of electronic equipment. Other discussions focused on the role of farm management research and of United States research analysts in developing countries. In the 1960s the NCFMRC showed interest not only in structuring alternative farm management information systems but also in the storage and retrieval of this information, and it arranged to cooperate with the USDA in creating a data bank for farm planning.

The regional effort in farm management and production economics, stretching over more than two decades (1947-70) was highly instrumental in making farm management an integral part of applied agricultural economics. Throughout its history the NCFMRC never lost sight of its initial goal, namely, to serve as a forum for the discussion of problems and research methods. Through the earlier period of its history the single most important contribution of the NCFMRC, particularly as a result of the efforts of Earl Heady and Glenn Johnson, was improvement in research methods at the micro level and a wide diffusion in the use of these methods. In fact, throughout its history the use of theoretical models (with foundations in economics) for analyzing problems has been important in the basic approach of the NCFMRC.

Further evaluation of the regional effort in farm management can perhaps best be accomplished by noting what appear to be the central concerns of the parties that contributed to this regional effort. The experiment station directors who facilitated the regional effort by approving meetings, allocating funds, and advising on administrative matters were ordinarily concerned over whether research proposals, activities, and results had a regional orientation. Directors would tend to regard with favor project proposals that addressed themselves to problems regional in scope, to integrated research efforts by the participating states, and to research results that permitted strong inferences to be made to populations extending at least beyond the boundaries of one state. Possibly only three north central regional research projects, two of them informal (i.e., without regional funds) and one formal (regionally approved and funded) met this test. The first two of these were the Interstate Managerial Study and the Lake States Milk Supply Response Study, and the third was the Supply Response and Adjustments for Hogs and Beef Cattle Study. In all three instances state participants agreed on a common model or analytical framework to assure a fully integrated approach.

The Farm Foundation, which provided meeting facilities and funds for travel, conferences, publications, and secretarial and other services, was (as intended) an effective catalytic agent in bringing individuals together to discuss lines of work, policies, ideas, and problems. The enthusiastic and intensive efforts of Joseph A. Ackerman, the foundation's director for many years, did much to stimulate others who were involved in regional study. Particularly over the first decade of regional work the foundation emphasized that regional committees produce what will be useful to farm people.

The USDA, which always had representation on the NCFMRC, has had a long history of helping to coordinate and strengthen the joint efforts among states and between states and the agency. The USDA was anxious to fulfill this role in its relation with the NCFMRC, and these responsibilities were ably carried out by C. W. Crickman and others. In addition, the USDA often supplemented state and regional funds to support the work of the NCFMRC.

Earlier we noted that the primary concern of NCFMRC members was to utilize the regional mechanism to improve research methodology. This in no way implies that they were not interested in engaging in regional research aimed at finding solutions to farm problems. It has already been mentioned that in its first decade of work the NCFMRC regarded as its biggest contribution the improvement of research methods at the micro level. The improved methods were in turn applied at both state and regional levels to problems of farm resource use, such as choice of cropping system, level of fertilizer application, fertilizer and feed combinations, and level of soil conservation. Then in the wake of World War II the nation's farmers were caught up in a price-cost squeeze and the concomitant problems of aggregate farm product supply responses, farm size, and resource productivity. The result was that NCFMRC concern shifted considerably to macro level problems. This writer recalls Earl Heady saying in the early 1950s that it would be a mistake for the NCFMRC to go over the same ground again. In the general problem of agricultural adjustments NCFMRC members felt that the area of aggregate supply responses in relation to changing product prices, changing technology and factor prices, and changing farm size and farm numbers was the one in which little information was available to help guide policy makers and farmers in resource use. Moreover, the methodology for handling these problems was not very well developed. Thus, although the NCFMRC did not entirely neglect micro level problems (in most models for aggregate analysis, aggregate adjustments to varying prices and so on were built up from typical farm adjustments to the included variables), much of its work through most of the 1950s and the early 1960s was devoted to macro level problems. In 1960, however, there were those in the NCFMRC who voiced uneasiness about what appeared to them to be a macro orientation in the work of the NCFMRC specifically and among farm management workers generally. Some felt that the NCFMRC and farm management had shifted too far away from the objective of providing farmers with information that would help them to make better decisions. Moreover, they thought a continuation of this emphasis would lead others to move in and to work on farm operator problems. In addition to their concern over the increased emphasis on macro problems, some NCFMRC members felt that time and effort devoted to training foreign students was diverting attention from critical problems in the domestic micro area. Through the 1960s some NCFMRC members continued to be troubled by what they regarded as the committee's failure to stimulate research of immediate value to individual farm operators. Although this did not deter the committee from establishing a subcommittee on foreign farm management, it did result in considerable micro reorientation through the 1960s, reflected in the establishment of a new farm records subcommittee and subcommittees on livestock, crops, and soil management. Thus, the regional effort in farm management appears to have completed a cycle which began with emphasis on the micro, shifting to the macro, and then back to the micro. At the time of this writing the regional endeavor in agricultural economics has been reorganized. All existing regional research committees in agricultural economics have been closed out, and three regional committees have been set up. What emphasis farm management and production economics will have in this new organization is not clear, but farm management is likely to be viewed and studied in a closer relation to marketing and processing — to agribusiness generally — and to reflect more realistically the structural changes taking place in agriculture. But whatever the future of regional efforts in farm management or production economics, it is clear at this point that the NCFMRC has been an important forum for discussing and delineating problem areas in farm management and production economics and for improving and diffusing research methods.

THE SOUTHERN FARM MANAGEMENT RESEARCH COMMITTEE (SFMRC)

The SFMRC was also created in the late 1940s under the sponsorship of the Farm Foundation. Early sessions of the committee and its subcommittees were devoted to the review and discussion of research methods and empirical procedures applicable to problems in farm management and production economics. These considerations covered a broad range of subject matter including budgeting techniques, production functions, and sampling procedures. As the field of farm management and production economics developed in terms of alternative empirical techniques, the committee continued to serve as a vehicle for updating the skills of committee members, and, through them, of professionals in the south. For example, in the late 1950s a workshop on linear programming was conducted in Raleigh, North Carolina [241]. A similar session in Stillwater, Oklahoma, in 1970 was devoted to simulation.

The SFMRC has served as a clearinghouse for emerging ideas and as a source of information relating to planned and existing work in the region. Each year a subcommittee has issued a list of publications released by the various participating states. Clearly this activity has improved communications between institutions in the region.

Early in its history the SFMRC initiated an extensive review of farm management and production economics problems. This consideration culminated in the selection of a project dealing with the estimation of supply functions for major southern commodities based on aggregated typical firm supply functions. The project was initiated in 1958 after an intensive workshop session in which alternative research methods and procedures were considered. The supply response study was terminated in 1968 when a livestock project was initiated. During the late 1960s and early 1970s the committee focused its attention on the potential role of production economists in rural development research.

In retrospect, it is clear that the SFMRC had a major impact on the quality and quantity of farm management research produced in the south. Further, the committee greatly enhanced the capacity of professionals within the region to carry out future research projects through its continuing emphasis on the professional development of individuals and groups.

THE NORTHEAST FARM MANAGEMENT RESEARCH COMMITTEE (NEFMRC)

Over the past two decades the NEFMRC was an influential force in research, teaching, and extension programs in the northeast. This committee too was organized under the sponsorship of the Farm Foundation and was composed of appointed agricultural economists from the land-grant colleges in the region.

The purposes of the committee are described well in a quotation from the trust agreement of the foundation: "To stimulate and conduct research and experimental work for the study of any economic, social, educational, or scientific problem of importance to any substantial portion of the rural population of the country, including problems of production, marketing, and purchasing, and the sound coordination of the agricultural with the industrial, financial, and mercantile life of the country."

The committee initiated its work in 1951 with its mission clearly focused on problem identification and solution within a regional framework. Its early efforts were aimed at the development of a regional project in which most representatives might cooperate. Such emphasis led to a formal regional project on the economics of forage production and utilization. This action reflected the heavy emphasis on dairying in the region and the continuing necessity to improve production efficiency.

The development of a formal regional project gave impetus to the role the NEFMRC played in the ensuing years. Specific problems were identified and their main aspects were discussed. If sufficient interest in a problem was generated in two or more states, a subcommittee composed of agricultural technicians and specialists not necessarily of the parent committee was appointed. Such subcommittees developed regional projects to find solutions to problems and reported on progress to the regional research committee. Over some twenty years such problems as labor management, equipment efficiency, farm size and production cost relationships, irrigation, milk supply responses, and the relation of farming to the urban fringe were studied, and nearly two hundred reports based on the results were published.

An educational program for its own members was another facet of NEFMRC operations. A standing subcommittee on research methods used some time at each semiannual meeting to discuss developments in research methods and empirical procedures applicable to problems in production economics. This activity had substantial benefits to the cooperating members. More uniformity in procedures and a continuing advance in techniques led to the application of more sophisticated theory and analytical tools. The quality of research results of the subcommittee improved greatly with beneficial results to the users. One major development in this area was the publication of *Budgeting — Tool of Research and Extension in Agricultural Economics*. This bulletin became a standard guide for budgeting in the United States and in foreign countries. Throughout the period the research committee was in constant touch with a panel committee in extension farm management, giving rise to a two-directional flow of information. Problems of field importance were referred to the research group and results of research projects were used by extension workers.

Few developments in agricultural economics in the northeast have had as much influence on the scope and method of farm management and production economics research as the regional committees sponsored by the Farm Foundation. Benefits to problem identification and solution and improvements in research methods resulted, and, more importantly, the capacity of current and future research and extension workers in farm management and production economics was enhanced.

THE WESTERN FARM MANAGEMENT RESEARCH COMMITTEE (WFMRC)

The WFMRC was organized in 1955 by the Western Agricultural Economics Research Council with the promise of financial support by the Farm

Foundation. Eleven adjoining western states and the USDA each appointed one representative to the first annual meeting, which was held in July 1955 at Fort Collins, Colorado. Representatives from Texas and Hawaii were included later in the regional committee. At the initial meeting areas of research considered important to western agriculture were discussed. These included problems of scale of operation, management alternatives in plant husbandry, management alternatives in animal husbandry, enterprise combinations, the impact of technology, research methodology, the effect of institutional arrangements, and financial management.

The functions of the WFMRC were initially defined very broadly, giving the committee ample scope in which to define its objectives and operating procedures. "The functions developed by the Committee and agreed upon by the Council included: (1) Annually review, identify, and evaluate emerging regional economic problems in the farm maangement areas; describe and evaluate ongoing research; determine additional research needed; and develop methods and tools for attacking new and important problems for western agriculture. (2) Develop and propose regional research projects as needed. (3) Improve the quality and effectiveness of regional research by providing a forum to facilitate an exchange of ideas and information concerning researchable problems of relevance in western agriculture. (4) Provide an annual report to the WAERC which summarizes the activities of the Committee."[5]

To fulfill the first two functions the WFMRC developed and implemented research on forage harvesting, machinery use, appraisal of opportunities for adjusting farming to prospective markets, capital-labor substitution and demand for agricultural labor in the western region, and economic growth of the agricultural firm. To fulfill the third objective it was emphasized that workers in closely related research areas must be kept informed; whenever possible resource specialists from outside the region were called upon to participate in the exchange of ideas and information.

Like other regional committees the WFMRC held a number of conferences, symposia, and workshops. Reports emerging from these meetings have helped to develop subject matter in various areas, particularly in management and firm growth.

Agricultural Adjustments and Aggregative Analysis

Accumulated personal savings, pent-up domestic demands, resource needs to convert the domestic economy from war to peacetime activities and to rebuild the war-torn economies of Western Europe all contributed to high levels of industrial activity and employment and a high level of growth in the overall economy following World War II. But it was not long before it was apparent that United States agriculture was not sharing in that growth. War demands had left us with an expanded agricultural producing plant. The agricultural production capacity of Western Europe recovered rather quickly, and the adoption of new technology on United States farms added further to domestic production capacity. Farm product prices declined, surpluses accumulated, and the costs of inputs climbed as the industrial and agricultural sectors bid for the materials going into those inputs. Discussions began to focus on the price-cost squeeze in agriculture and on agricultural adjustment problems. Laborers were moving out of agriculture in search of better jobs and more income, the total number of farms was beginning to decrease, and the acre-size of farms was beginning to increase at rapid rates.

Farm management and production economists soon became heavily involved in finding solutions to the United States price-cost squeeze farm problem and in developing educational programs to describe the problem and suggest action leading to solution. Some aspects of this involvement have already been noted in the preceding section. In this section we will first discuss the general agricultural adjustment literature and then turn our attention to the literature with a more specific focus, such as supply response and farm size adjustments (including projections of sizes and numbers), interregional analysis, and work in the international area. The first portion of this section represents a micro-to-macro shift of emphasis in farm management and production economics — from a micro orientation until about the mid-1950s to a macro orientation from then into the 1960s. Later in this section we review some of the literature in aggregate productivity analysis. Farm management production economists have long been concerned with resource productivities as a basis for factor shares and resource adjustments for increased efficiency, but, as we will note, aggregate productivity estimation continues to have problems.

The book *Agricultural Adjustment Problems in a Growing Economy*, published in 1956, marks the first large concerted effort by agricultural economists to assess the problem, what was known about it, and how they might go about solving it [120]. The book contains papers presented at a conference organized and sponsored by the North Central Farm Management Research Committee and the Farm Foundation.

Using aggregate production function analysis and assuming that the pre-World War II period of 1936-39 reflected a reasonably good degree of adjustment, Swanson [253] sought to determine whether the 1950-53 period represented a departure from the 1936-39 period in degree of adjustment. His analysis showed that the years intervening between the two periods had disturbed the adjustments in land and labor in such a way that more land and less labor should have been used in the postwar period.

In 1957 Heady [113] noted that progress in product demand expansion and in production control had been and would continue to be small in its contribution to adjusting the economic structure of agriculture. He argued that our efforts need to be concentrated on the supply side or what he termed the orthodox solution of reducing the labor force in agriculture and moving the surplus population from farms to other industries where its marginal value productivity was higher. This he viewed as the long-run solution, emphasizing the need for education as a means of attaining it. He urged that increases in extension education budgets were needed to develop education programs that would provide farm people with an understanding of the long-run economic situation. Intensive efforts in economic education, he argued, were more likely to solve the adjustment problem than all the efforts used in deriving interdependence coefficients, inverse matrices, and structural equations and in gathering and refining empirical data.[6]

Tompkin [262] set out to determine the nature and extent of production adjustments to price changes farmers had made and should make in the future. He did this by observing the changes actually made by a sample of farmers over a two-year period and by programming the farms for optimal changes within a given asset structure. This is an interesting approach for determining how farmers actually do respond to price changes in the short run, but information on what changes motivate farmers to alter asset structures is also needed.

While national farm policy sought production adjustments through land retirement, most farm management and production economists emphasized moving farm labor into other sectors as the long-run solution. Some, however, saw the solution to the overproduction problem in the movement of land, labor, and capital resources simultaneously [177].

SUPPLY RESPONSE

Much of the work by farm management and production economists in regard to agricultural adjustments was focused more narrowly on supply response studies. The approach used in many of these studies was to build aggregate responses from firm levels. Discussions began to evolve around positive versus normative supply response estimates, representative farms, and aggregation biases.

Richard Day [66] took a look at the aggregation problem inherent in the representative (typical or benchmark) firm approach combined with linear programming models of the firm to arrive at regional or national aggregates of production. The question Day set out to answer was, To what extent must a group of firms be alike in order for a single model to represent the aggregate of the individual decisions without causing distortions? He showed that firms in the aggregate can exhibit wide variations in scale and expected net returns as long as these are proportional.

Sheehy and McAlexander [239] studied the effect of the selection of benchmark farms on aggregation bias. They discussed possible biases associated with a conventional method of selection and presented an alternative which did not overcome problems associated with profit maximization and static assumptions that eliminate nonmonetary motives and dynamic elements. Frick and Andrews [87] studied aggregation bias by comparing four methods of summing farm supply functions. The method of grouping farms on the basis of the most limiting resource, considering the order in which each resource became restrictive, showed the smallest amount of bias. But this method also has limitations in that it ignores farm size, does not easily make possible weight adjustments for farm numbers in various "restriction" classes, and is difficult to apply to more than one product.

The so-called normative supply response studies were based mostly on linear programming techniques, while some of the positive supply response studies were based on the producer panel technique in which actual responses from a sample of farms are studied over time. Conneman [63] described and evaluated the Cornell producer panel which was initiated in 1959, when one was also begun in Minnesota. He listed several advantages of this technique: It is a procedure for estimating actual supply response, adjusted for entry and exit of firms and other dynamic aspects; it provides a basis for testing various hypotheses in regard to supply response; it is a good source of descriptive data and generates data of the kind needed for Markov process projections. Several disadvantages could also be listed, such as the difficulty of maintaining a representative sample over time and the relatively long period involved in generating supply response data. Furthermore, although past responses can be described, they are not so easily explained and may not serve very effectively in predicting future response.

Day [65] and Barker and Stanton [16] reviewed research on estimating supply response based on linear programming models and representative farms. Day called our attention to estimating errors associated with construction of representative farms and aggregation bias. Barker and Stanton discussed the interrelationships among various approaches, such as linear programming, recursive programming, and producer panels. They concluded that over the preceding five years progress had been made in the study of supply but that economists were still a long way from developing usable estimates of regional and national supply from individual farm data. They raised the question, Is it realistic to hope to use individual farm data in estimating agricultural supply? Their reply was that in the mid-1960s the problems were clearer than the solutions. The logic of building from the bottom up, they maintained, still had appeal despite the problems of aggregation, data collection, and programming. It is probably correct to say that theirs is a fair appraisal of where we stand today. However, since Day and Barker and Stanton made their reviews, other approaches to supply response have been introduced. Wipf and Bawden [280] tested the reliability of supply functions derived from empirically estimated production functions and found them to be generally unreliable (overestimating considerably) when compared with actual output and with supply elasticities estimated by regression analysis of time series. Schechter and Heady [232] presented a methodological study using simulation to derive response surfaces in the feed grain program. Changes in loan rates in the system were made, and the consequences of these changes in feed grain stock accumulations, treasury costs, incomes of participating farmers, and net farm income were observed.

FARM SIZE ADJUSTMENTS

Farm management and production economists were generally of the opinion that to improve resource efficiency and farm family incomes labor needed to move out of agriculture into better income-producing off-farm occupations and that as labor moved out and farm numbers decreased family incomes on the remaining farms would increase with the absorption of the freed land resources. An underlying assumption in this logic was that in the adjustment process there were some significant economies to size to be exploited in farming. In discussing alternative opportunities for cost reductions in farming, Bachman and Barton [10] in 1954 urged a stepping up of the trend toward larger farms, emphasizing that such an adjustment would be among the most fruitful ones for the decade ahead. They argued that this adjustment would improve efficiency and income per worker. From about 1955 to 1965 a fair number of studies were made to determine the nature of cost economies or diseconomies to size in farming.

Using regression analysis, Ottoson and Epp [210] found no cost advantages for farms above 160 acres, but a number of other studies showed important economies to size in farm production. Hopkin [142] analyzed a cross section of the cattle feeding industry and concluded that cattle feeding as predominantly practiced in California was a decreasing cost industry. Miller and Back [195] studied size and efficiency of farms in the Great Plains area and concluded that farmers there lagged in adjustments in size and efficiency in relation to the potential adjustments made possible by technology. Using alternative approaches (budgeting, mathematical programming, and regression) Carter and Dean [56] studied cost-size relationships for cash crop farms in California. Their study showed substantial economies up to $150,000 of output. They also concluded that a wide range of farms will continue to exist because unit costs are approximately constant over a wide range.

Farm size adjustment studies typically gave no attention to the social and community impact of fewer farms. Raup [221] aluded to this void in past studies and to what he considered to be other shortcomings of existing studies when he stated that they do not consider after-tax position, they are static (i.e., do not show growth patterns), they fail to show the capacity of different sizes to adjust to rising land values, they do not provide for growth in management, and they fail to discuss changes in size in relation to social and community effects.

Most economies to size studies have shown that important economies to size exist but that most of these are exhausted within the scope of a family farm operation. Krause and Kyle [178] took issue with this conclusion when pointing to the shortcomings of past research of size. They suggested that past studies had primarily emphasized internal technical and engineering economies with a focus on family-sized units and single product analysis. Ignored were economies of buying and selling and common ownership of related farm and nonfarm activities. Identified as incentives for establishing large-scale units were higher net product prices as a result of eliminating some marketing steps, decreasing costs because of volume discounts, opportunities for organizing off-season supplementary business activities that may lower labor and machinery costs, better business management, and federal income tax incentives.

In studying farm size some farm management and production economists have used cohort and Markov process analysis to project the expected future number and size distirbution of farms. Kanel [169], using cohort analysis, measured the differences in the way in which various age groups participated in agricultural adjustments. His study showed that for the 1950s the limited number of young people entering farming had been a major factor in the decrease in farm numbers since older farmers in the 1950s left farming at about the same rate as in several previous decades. Stanton and Kettunen [246] used Markov process analysis to project numbers and sizes of dairy farms in New York. The use of different assumptions about the number of entrants, they discovered, had important implications for the future structure of the industry. Hallberg [93] pointed to situations in which it would be inappropriate to use the first-order Markov chain model for projecting future size distribution of firms. Since the model is based on the assumption that the transition probabilities remain constant over time, it would be inappropriate to use it, Hallberg said, where structural characteristics of the industry are changing. In these situations he suggested use of a method based on multiple regression techniques whereby the constant transition probabilities are replaced by probabilities as a function of various factors, including structural characteristics of the industry.

AGGREGATE PRODUCTIVITY ANALYSIS

Since the development of the Cobb-Douglas production function, agricultural economists and particularly farm production economists have engaged in aggregate productivity analysis, in productivity comparisons among farms in different geographic locations, and in productivity estimates for farms in a given location. In these efforts the objective has been to locate resource adjustment problems and to specify needed shifts in resource use.

Aggregate productivity analysis has always been fraught with problems, and much of the literature in the post-World War II period is devoted to estimation problems and suggestions for overcoming those problems. Trant [264] suggested procedures for adjusting C-D value products for price changes so as to eliminate annual surveys. Griliches [91] discussed the effects of specification bias. Halter, Carter, and Hocking [96] pointed to the advantages of the flexible transcendental predicting function. Chandler [60] suggested using factor income for gross product in measuring changes in productivity. Amick and Purcell [3] presented a procedure for overcoming high intercorrelations among independent variables. Mundlak [200] discussed the problem of product aggregation and suggested ways of overcoming that problem. Yotopoulos [283] addressed the problem of using capital stock as a proxy for the annual flow of services from capital stock. Vandenborre and McCarthy [266] wrote on the matter of comparing marginal value productivities with individual factor prices, and Ulveling and Fletcher [265] discussed the use of constant elasticities of production for describing input-output relationships.

In other studies productivity estimation was the main objective. Using Cobb-Douglas, Heady and Shaw [130] estimated the marginal value productivity of resource categories in different farming regions in the United States. They analyzed the effects of different quantities of resources on the value of marginal products and made not only interarea comparisons but also comparisons between strata of farms within an area and between marginal value productivities and factor prices. Heady and Strand [132], using average productivity measurements and citing production efficiency as a major goal of economic organization at the level of the firm-household and at the level of the national economy, provided some insights into the relative efficiency of United States agricultural producing regions. Heady and Auer [117] used a time series production function in estimating resource productivities for individual crops by states to provide some insights into the sources of production increases in recent years for various crops. Focusing on a particular farm input surrounded by controversy because of possible side effects, Headley [100] used Cobb-Douglas to estimate the marginal value productivity of pesticides. The results showed pesticides to be a highly productive input, but Headley pointed to the need for better data on crop and livestock response to pest control and on side effects.

Given the problems of specification bias, intercorrelations among input categories, and problems growing out of aggregating inputs and outputs, it is questionable whether aggregate production function analysis should play any role beyond that of a diagnostic technique in the preliminary stages of analysis (i.e., for suggesting possible resource malallocations). Plaxico [216] demonstrated clearly how product and input aggregation procedures influence values and hence the reliability of the productivity estimates, and he questioned the usefulness of Cobb-Douglas analysis for intrafarm and interarea adjustments. Schultz [235] has questioned the whole process of accounting and measuring of costs and returns in production function analysis and argued that it would be a mistake to attribute all of the difference between estimates of agricultural output and input to technical improvements. He suggested that it was high time that rigorous production economics be used to assess carefully the costs and returns of technical improvements. Hildebrand [137] used data from farm management association records in 1950-52, in some experiments with the C-D function. Over this period and for various stratifications he observed extreme variability and irregularity in the estimates of elasticities and marginal value productivities. His results suggested that productivity was being picked up in a haphazard fashion without any observable pattern of bias.

INTERREGIONAL COMPETITION

The post-World War II studies on interregional competition are rooted in the conceptual developments in comparative advantage, budgeting, types of farming, supply estimation, and interregional competition that antedate that war. As early as 1903 Spillman [242] discussed systems of farming. In the 1920s Black [26] addressed himself to an analysis of comparative advantage among producing areas of a country and between countries. Elliott [81] mapped United States agriculture into 514 type-of-farming areas based on the 1930 census. The plan was that facts on agricultural production areas were to be gathered in the form of both aggregative trends and representative farms. Through budget analyses, then, needed adjustments to changes in demand, prices, and technology could be anticipated. In the 1930s Mighell and Black [194] budgeted samples of dairy farms in New England and the Lake States, synthesized short-run supply curves from these budgets, and ended with an empirical analysis ranging over firms, type-of-farming areas to interregions. In anticipation of war production needs S. E. Johnson and others in the Bureau of Agricultural Economics in 1940 began what came to be known as wartime food production capacity studies. Potentials for expansion of crops and livestock were built up from areas and states to regions and the nation, and the relative production advantages were appraised as a basis for establishing county and state production goals. The price-cost squeeze of postwar agriculture was the focus for numerous studies undertaken to guide micro and macro adjustments in agriculture, among these the interregional competition studies. It was the developments in mathematical programming, however, that really made it possible to enhance greatly the size of interregional competition models and to study interregional competition in a systematic and manageable way. All through the 1960s and into the 1970s Heady, Egbert, and others at Iowa State University and in the USDA were involved in a vast undertaking with the major objective of formulating and testing mathematical models that were increasingly more realistic in explaining the regional and commodity interdependencies within United States agriculture [38, 76, 77, 78, 125, 131, 133, 276]. Initial models included wheat and feed grains, later soybeans and cotton, and finally forage, hog, beef, and dairy production. Another comprehensive interregional study constructed to study adjustments was the "national model" of the Economic Research Service. During the postwar period a considerable number of other studies were done on interregional competition, including Day's work [68] on recursive programming that contributed significantly to model building, Dennis and Sammet's [69] on interregional competition in frozen strawberries, Schrader and King's [234] on location of cattle feeding, Buchholz and Judge's [43] on interregional analysis of the feed-livestock economy, and various regional farm management research committees' supply response studies.

Participation in the International Area

During the post-World War II period an increasing number of farm management and production economics specialists became involved in development work in Africa, Asia, Latin America, and other developing areas. Most of the research effort was of an aggregative type with either project or sector orientation. Examples in point are Ohio State University's capital formation project in Brazil, Michigan State University's agricultural sector analyses in Nigeria and South Korea, and Iowa State University's sector study in Thailand.

It can be argued that sector studies were a logical approach to problems in developing countries with scarce resources and central planning, particularly when central planners were brought into the study process. The argument in support of this approach stems from the much greater opportunity for influencing decision making on resource use, but planning at the farm level cannot be neglected. In a recent book review Glenn Johnson argued that planning individual farms and extension activities to assist individual farmers are very important in developing countries but that central planning agencies have usually neglected this area of assistance.[7] At the same time the involvement of United States farm management and production economics specialists in farm-level extension activities in these countries has not been overwhelming either. However, United States farm management and production economics specialists have been involved in a far-reaching effort to train students and staff from these countries. The training has taken several forms, such as formal degree instruction for graduate students, cooperative research, seminars, and workshops.

The Changing Structure of Agriculture

Since World War II the nation's farming structure has changed in at least two major ways. One change, particularly in some subsectors of the industry, has blurred the boundary line between what is a farm firm and what is not a farm firm. Vertical integration has obscured the boundary lines between farm operators and such input suppliers as feed and fertilizer dealers, processors, canners, and hatchery operators. The other major change is the rapid horizontal growth of the farm firm. The nature of this growth has given rise to much study and discussion of the rapidly increasing capital requirements in farming and has stimulated much thought on the financial management which appears to be becoming an integral part of farm management. Both vertical and horizontal integration have implications for farm management and production economics.

In 1960, the annual meeting of the American Farm Economic Association included a section on the farm of the future. Stewart [248] focused his main attention on changes in number, size, organization, capital, and managerial requirements of selected types of farms by 1975. He saw the small marginal units as being least able to adjust but the typical family farm as becoming larger and more specialized, buying more of its services, and adopting labor-saving and output-increasing technology. He envisioned that vertical integration would dominate the poultry industry and that large-scale factory-type feeding operations would become increasingly important in the west and southwest.

At about the same time van Vleet [268], in a penetrating article, analyzed the increasing capital requirements in relation to the problem of getting started in farming. He traced the increased capital requirements to increases in capital values (especially in land), the substitution of capital and land for labor, and the drive for social progress. He stated that the main burden for sustaining increased farm income requirements had fallen to capital expansion of the farming unit. He then traced the concomitant implications of the large increase in farm capital — commensurate managerial capacity, larger savings margins, and larger buffers against risk — and identified the large capital investments required for increased mechanization, expansion in buildings and facilities, and broad expansion in production inputs. He alluded to the interdependence of the various capital elements, suggesting that access to real estate is no longer adequate as an entrance to a farming career. He then indicated how the general change in the basis of access to farming had opened the way for a growing urban-based investment in farming — hobby farming, suburban dabbling, suitcase farmers leaning on other income, and the cream-skimming operations of those seeking an investment return, capital gains, tax benefits, and other advantages of land ownership plus the integrated business operations. He maintained that these changes moved land values out of the manageable range for ordinary commercial farmers; to meet this situation he recommended high technical and managerial competence, farming training, and access to credit.

The extent of the literature on vertical integration suggests that farm management and production economists have shown much less concern over this type of change in the farming structure than over change in structure through horizontal integration. Some have sought to explain vertical integration and what it means for farm maangement, but many more have addressed themselves to the question of increasing farm size through horizontal expansion and the associated capital and financial maangement needs. With the limited information available in 1957 Mighell [192] reviewed vertical integration in the context of farm management. He commented on its present status, on what it purportedly does to reduce risk and increase scale and efficiency, on some problems associated with it, and on some suggestions for research and extension education. In response to the high degree of interest in vertical integration in 1958 Castle [59] outlined some of the implications of this structural change for farm management research. He saw the clientele shifting from the farm manager to the personnel within the integrated firm. He suggested that research interests might shift to the basic production relationships in the integrated business, to decisions on choice of contract, to new constraints, and to resource supplies. Roy [228] in 1965 used budgeting techniques to evaluate alternative broiler contracts. Butz [46] addressed the question of the effects of off-farm management inputs on the management factor in agriculture. Although his discussion does not pertain exclusively to vertical integration, it does definitely have reference to the broadening of the management function for a business unit beyond the farm operator. Butz concluded that the effect of off-farm management inputs had been substantial, and he expected them to play an even more important role in speeding up adoption of new technology, in improving managerial capabilities, and in helping producers to reduce unit costs of production and to increase income.

One wonders why farm management and production economists have devoted so little effort to studying and analyzing vertical integration in relation to the management of farms. It is a fact that the real thrust of vertical integration has been in poultry and egg production. It is also generally true that farm management has never showed much interest in poultry. Hence, when vertical integration swept through the poultry industry, farm maangement and production economists may have felt no significant change in their operating base, or they may have felt that off-farm firms were providing the necessary research and education inputs, and therefore efforts could be put to better use elsewhere.

The new realignment of regional research committees appears to encourage research and study on the vertical dimensions of the structure of commercial agriculture. The regional committee on commercial agriculture is concerned with the management of all agricultural firms; it recognizes a field of management that has general relevance to various decision-making units, but it also recognizes that a farm firm is not always easily distinguished from other agricultural firms. This committee is concerned with understanding growth of all types of agricultural firms and with systems analysis of agricultural subsectors, encompassing processes and interrelationships from production to consumption. Some small amount of research has been done in agriculture using a subsector systems approach, such as the hog-pork subsector project centered at Purdue University and the citrus project in Florida. If more of this type of analysis is to get under way, it will require closer working relations between farm management and marketing than we have had to date.

Changes in the structure of farming through the increase in farm size and the decrease in farm numbers have produced considerable activity among farm management and production economists. The literature deals with a number of different topics, such as the need for more information on emerging financial problems — how to obtain additional capital and credit, how to improve financial management and control, and how to attain farm firm growth.

Wirth [281] outlined the major financial stages as establishment, expansion, and consolidation and pleaded for basic financial information, especially net worth statements, operating statements, and statements of the outlays for family living and for nonfarm investments. He suggested aggregating data from farm account projects in various states to improve information on financial flows and analysis. Baker and Holcomb [13] discussed the emerging financial problems of farmers and lenders in a changing agriculture. They identified the farmer's need for the development of managerial skills in finance, specifically the management of reserves, seasonal financing, insurance, capital gains, and land transfers and the lender's need to predict managerial success beyond the range of the operator's experience, to identify in advance how desirable loans may turn into trouble loans because of a series of poor marketing years, and to know how to overcome the lending limits of banks which are inadequately capitalized. Brake [36], in examining the capital and credit requirements of farmers in relation to likely future structural changes in American agriculture, expected that these needs would increase further and that structural changes would accompany such an increase, partly because of the way credit institutions adapt to meet capital needs. He saw research as being able to make important contributions in the areas of firm growth, acquisition and control of capital, capital flows in and out of agriculture, and disinvestment from farming. In future farm financing Nelson [203] saw equity capital making up a smaller percentage of the total with more of the equity capital coming from gifts and inheritance and with credit used to a greater extent. In the vertical integration of the poultry industry feed dealers, hatcherymen, and processors have been important sources of production credit, but Rogers [225] pointed out that the question of capital for fixed investments was still unanswered. Neuman [206] addressed the problem of capital requirements and financing practices for restructuring southern agriculture and showed the structure of farm organization that would be necessary to raise the minimum level of farm operator earnings to a level approximating the wage rates for factory workers. He suggested that financial management and financial control problems were likely to increase relative to production and farm organization problems. He indicated that to gain perspective on the future credit needs in agriculture continuing study is needed at both firm and industry levels. Baker and Hopkin [14] suggested that if the traditional owner-operator pattern is to continue to dominate agriculture growth and economic viability must replace the debt-free balance sheet. They estimated that had output been constrained to a market clearing level, then 306,000 cost-minimizing farms in the north central region could have done the job in 1959, when it actually took 1.2 million farms to produce an output that was only slightly above the market clearing level.

As the structure of farming has changed through increases in farm size and rising capital requirements of individual farms, farm management extension specialists sharply stepped up their programs in financial management. In the early 1960s the four regional farm management extension committees worked with the agricultural committee of the American Bankers Association to develop a banker's handbook for each region. This handbook has served bankers as a useful reference in working with farmers throughout the country. As the interest in financial management has increased, the availability of extension training for personnel of lending institutions has also increased. In the past few years extension farm management has developed a number of different cash flow budgeting techniques, some of which make use of remote terminals and computers.

Most farm management and production economists have viewed increases in farm size (farm firm growth) as desirable. I make this statement on the basis that the central concern in firm growth literature appears to be to identify and assess the significance of those factors that limit growth. Lacking are studies devoted to the social and community costs that may follow in the wake of such growth. In order to explain growth, however, it is of course necessary to identify the variables important to the process. Using a capital accumulation model in which the proportion of retained net earnings and borrowed funds is the policy variable of interest to the firm's entrepreneur, Halter [94] found that the rate of capital accumulation with respect to the retention ratio is dependent on the specific growth equation, a conclusion at variance with that of a study which allowed the firm to issue stock. Hence, he concluded that the problem of specifying growth models for farm firms of the type (he used a linear and homogeneous production function, increasing expansion costs, and constant prices and technology) he discussed was an empirical problem, not an analytic problem. Johnson and associates [164] studied the relative influence of initial asset position, investment policy, and crop yield variability on farm growth. Patrick and Eisgruber [213] concluded that managerial ability and long-term loan limits were the major factors limiting farm firm growth. Boehlje and White [29] demonstrated that the growth process and the terminal size differ with the objective function. Vandeputte and Baker [267] argued that proper specification of tax liabilities and consumption behavior is an important problem in designing models for the study of firm growth.

Firm growth indeed has opened up a broad spectrum for research, and mathematical programming and simulation techniques have been very helpful in probing into growth problems which involve time, dynamics, and imperfect knowledge. Walker and Martin [270] identified conditions in agriculture which they saw as leading to growth pressures. They then specified what they thought should go into a firm growth research package. This package, they said, should do a better job of dealing with finance, managerial capacity, imperfect knowledge, and the time and life cycle of the firm. They then touched on dynamic linear programming and simulation as analytical techniques, the latter allowing some ex ante experimentation before committing resources to growth. Irwin [146], in discussing the Walker-Martin paper, outlined some accounting relationships as a way of isolating growth sources which in turn suggested research opportunities. These accounting relationships were described

as follows: "Basically, growth can be thought of as the accumulation of resources resulting from reinvestment of net savings by the farm operator. Net
savings for a year is equal to the tax adjusted difference between per unit
gross income and variable costs, multiplied by volume, from which we sub-
tract fixed costs and consumption expenditures and to which we add off-farm
income. Gross, in turn, is the result of marketing efficiency in purchasing inputs, technical efficiency in using them, and initial resources available for production" [146].

The papers, articles, and reports that have been written on firm growth,
along with those yet to be done, will perhaps some day be synthesized into a
theory of growth. Whether it makes sense to talk about such a theory in
terms of equilibrium conditions is not clear. Perhaps growth means continuous disequilibria, at least until some desired size of operation is reached. Possibly growth means a movement toward various equilibria at different points
in time and ultimately to a near equilibrium. In any event Baker [11] has argued that the equilibrium conditions traditionally used by economists are inadequate when it comes to building models involving financial components.
He suggested that one important modification was related to liquidity. Credit
or borrowing capacity constitutes an important source of liquidity, and consequently borrowing gives rise to a cost in the form of loss of liquidity as well
as a cost in terms of interest on the loan. He therefore argued that optimizing
criteria must consider liquidity losses related to borrowing. At another point
he [12] reasoned that in reference to equilibrium, optima are determined not
only by product price ratios but also by farmer expectations of lender behavior in regard to alternative enterprises. He added that financial components
will become increasingly important, in addition to price ratios, in models constructed for prescriptive and behavioral research.

The Development of a Dichotomy

In 1957 Glenn Johnson [149] saw farm management being dominated by
agricultural economics and well on its way to being dominated by production
economics. He also saw groups resisting this domination, groups that viewed
farm management as something more than economics. The resistance groups
identified by Johnson appear to be farm firm oriented. If we view this loose
federation of resisters as one group and the farm management and production
economists with a strong economics orientation as another, we have something of a dichotomy. A few years later Johnson wrote, "Farm management
research with a 'production-economics' orientation has become increasingly:
(a) less focused on the practical problem of managing farms, and (b) more
focused on methodological and theoretical issues of less and less relevance to
the solution of practical farm management problems" [157]. At about the

same time Kelso [172] detected a tendency among production economists to select problems on which they can test their skills in using new analytical tools, not necessarily the problems of the greatest economic significance. In 1969 Williams [279] described what he viewed as a breakdown in communication between people in the basic discipline of production economics on the one hand and extension personnel on the other. He added that for some there is intellectual satisfaction in building models and in successively relaxing constraints in the hope of analyzing through this process relationships and interactions that will uncover understanding of the real world. He felt that production economics had turned more and more to research methodolgy and policy implications while farm management extension had remained as empirical as ever but with computers doing the arithmetic.

Enough has been written to suggest to us in farm management and production economics that perhaps a dichotomy of those who are primarily farm firm or micro oriented versus those who are primarily professionally oriented (toward our peers within agricultural economics or economics) has indeed developed and that we should spend some time analyzing the implications of this development. The methodological orientation of farm management and production economics after World War II has already been discussed in the present chapter. One of the results of this orientation was the search for technical data that expressed the various production relations (factor-product, factor-factor, and so on). This search diverted considerable effort in farm management and production economics away from work with agriculturalists directly on farm management problems to work directly with agriculturalists on methodological issues and experimentation. The postwar period also saw the adoption of linear programming and a strong movement to develop its potential, to test its power, and to modify it, and as a result much energy has been devoted to model building and testing. Moreover, not many years had passed after the war before agriculture as a whole suffered a malaise (the price-cost squeeze) and attention was diverted from micro to macro problems. Within the same period extension farm management had retained its micro orientation with some shift in emphasis from economic education for its farmer clientele to computerized farm record systems and decision aids (computer programs) for use with remote terminals as services to farmers.

If this dichotomous development aptly describes what has evolved, then we need to consider what implications it has for the future. Although the efforts of the professionally oriented branch of this dichotomy probably reflect a period of consolidation of postwar developments in economic theory and statistics and their applications, it is difficult to see how this branch can remain alive unless it seeks out a clientele and sets to work on socioeconomic problems of significance to that clientele. To the extent that extension farm management devotes its energies to providing management services rather than education, it may be entering a field in which it has no comparative advantage and in which, except for engaging in the development of such services, it may be a questionable allocation of public resources.

Limitations of Static Economic Firm Theory and Profit Maximization

Since World War II the foundation for most of the work in farm management and production economics was static economic theory with profit maximization as the goal or norm. Shortly after the war Heady [110] wrote that when a research problem is defined in terms of departure from ideal or optimum conditions (a normative approach) the equilibrium conditions of economics serve directly to identify and outline the problem. The equilibrium conditions, he said, explained the circumstances under which a given end is maximized. He did mention that a problem also could be defined in terms of doubt, confusion, or felt difficulty. My own impression after surveying the postwar literature is that research problems have been defined largely in terms of departures from the ideal. Moreover, the ideal has been, in most instances, profit maximization, which under competitive conditions has been considered synonymous with resource efficiency.

Stedry [247] drew some interesting comparisons between market and behavioral theories of the firm. He described behavioralists as those who wish to learn how organizations really behave and why. In market theory interest in the firm per se is limited to assumptions about behavior, and the implications of these assumptions are directed to predicting the behavior of an aggregation of firms. He went on to say that economic market theory and the profit maximizing principle have gone hand in hand and that market theory has had little to say about the internal structure or management of the firm. He added that given the fundamental assumption of profit maximization, the internal conditions (i.e., the necessary and sufficient conditions) for equilibrium can be deduced. For most economists, Stedry stated, the model is considered adequate provided that the macro economic predictions derived from it fit the corresponding economic data fairly well. Perhaps it is fitting to say then that the methodological underpinning of farm management and production economics following World War II was framed in this mold of macro predictive theory and consisted of micro normative theory with profit maximization as the norm. The narrow focus placed a great deal of strain on the methodological framework from the very beginning of the postwar period. Given the multiple values and objectives of farm-household decision-making units, problem definition in terms of profit disequilibria may simply have been cast too narrowly, particularly in view of the dynamic environment in which farm-households operated.

Shortcomings of the static equilibrium theory were recognized throughout the postwar period. At the American Farm Economic Association's annual meeting in 1950 the limitations of farm management analysis based on static economic theory were discussed and the need to incorporate risk and uncertainty into the analysis was emphasized [9, 84, 103, 147, 153, 205]. Risk and uncertainty considerations such as dynamics, instability, planning horizons, and expectations were mentioned, and needed developments in risk trend and dynamic theories were sketched out.

In 1949 Heady [110] had written that the study of risk and uncertainty and the dynamics of the firm is one of the most neglected areas in farm management. The management problems associated with handling risk and uncertainty have often been singled out as part of the explanation for the gap between a farm operator's existing situation and the optimal or equilibrium situation. Hence, a fair amount of the literature has been addressed to various ways of adjusting to risk and uncertainty, such as increasing accuracy in expectation formulations [5, 28, 41, 197, 278], increasing resource or plant flexibility [9, 233], and reducing yield and income variability [1, 15, 50, 105, 135, 167, 245, 249], to narrow the gap. Adjustments such as these were, in a manner of speaking, adjuncts to static economic theory with some modifications in profit maximization as the decision criterion. In the 1960s, however, with the developments in dynamic programming, quadratic programming, stochastic linear programming, game theory, simulation, and Bayesian decision theory, the approach to farm planning was enriched through the incorporation of a variety of decision criteria into the objective functions. The literature speaks of LaPlace equaprobability, Savage regret, the Hurwicz pessimism-optimism criterion, Wald maximum, variants of the Bayes criterion, and risk preference; it discusses how to find a sequence of decisions that will maximize or minimize the appropriate objective function. It also addresses the concepts of utility or expected utility with consideration for skewness, variance, and expected yields and discusses growth models with different objective functions such as maximum subjective expected returns, mean standard deviation of returns, and maximum expected returns with minimum income side conditions [29, 44, 45, 54, 67, 71, 97, 161, 163, 187, 208, 256]. Whether these approaches will find their way into the actual planning of farms is difficult to know, but the existence of techniques for farm planning with probability distributions, strategies, and alternative decision criteria may serve to enhance the relevancy of farm planning to more farm families or other decision units.

Another development pointing to limitations of the framework of static economic theory and profit equilibrium was the farm and home planning of the 1950s which viewed the farm firm and the household as an integrated decision-making unit. The recognition in farm and home development of multiple goals and of farm-household interdependence was a shift away from the profit-maximizing firm under static theory. Incorporating time, along with farm-household interdependencies, in a dynamic linear programming model emphasized the shortcomings of the static economic and profit-maximizing framework a bit more [104, 183]. Moreover, incorporating time into such a model provides plans for getting from the existing situation to a specified goal at some future point in contrast to timeless planning, which provides no information between the existing and the optimal. Having the skills and tools to fill this gap with planning information should enhance the value of farm and home planning.

A fair amount of the postwar literature is devoted to studies of managerial behavior which set out to develop hypotheses about this behavior and to test the hypotheses. The methodological orientation of the studies was positivistic and behavioral. The immediate objective was to identify and describe farm firm managerial processes — the functional behavior related to the organization and operation of the farm firm. The ultimate objective was to improve the managerial processes. Once it was known what the processes were and how they were performed, presumably further studies would indicate how they might be improved. In terms of the ultimate objective the studies took on a normative cast. In the sense that in these studies researchers sought to learn how farm firms behave and what causes them to behave the way they do, their methodological framework was the behavioral theory of the firm — and certainly something of a challenge to the methodological framework of static economic theory and the profit-maximizing norm. The conceptualizations and empirical studies of managerial or decision processes have without question significantly modified our approaches to the teaching of farm management in both residence and extension.

Much of the literature on managerial or decision processes under review here had its roots in the Interstate Managerial Study and the Management Resource in Farming study. Both studies lent support to the view that farm management as a study stretches across numerous disciplines.

In 1952 Glenn Johnson [151] published an article that was a forerunner to the Interstate Managerial Study, which he spearheaded. Johnson related our typical methods of thinking to our concepts of management. He suggested that the empiricist working without theory failed to develop worthwhile managerial concepts, that the conomic theorist's approach (static theory) or the rationalist's approach was equally unproductive, but that the experimentalist's approach based on realistic assumptions and using inductive and deductive logic was productive. This meant, he said, that our approach will be both theoretical and empirical, both deductive and inductive, and that answers will be sought to theoretical and factual problems of risk, uncertainty, and management. He reviewed the progress that had been made on managerial concepts and on risk and uncertainty problems with special reference to the works of Knight, Hart, Hicks, Schackle, Katona, Wald, von Neumann, and Morgenstern. He mentioned that Schultz's "Theory of the Firm and Farm Management Research" [236] in 1939 marked a turning point in farm management thinking, and he noted the empirical studies on risk, uncertainty, and management contributed by Brownlee, Gainer, Reiss, Williams, and Schickele and his own empirical study based on thirty-one Kentucky farms. Johnson identified sources and uses of information for handling managerial problems growing out of risk and uncertainty. He noted that data useful in solving these probelms are largely subjective, dealing with value patterns and with the processes the managers use. Understanding the value patterns, the processes, and the different problems, Johnson argued, would help us in farm and home planning, in understanding farm people, and in identifying subjects of interest to farmers and in these ways would make our research and education efforts more productive.

At the annual meeting of the American Farm Economic Association in 1955 a section of the program was devoted to progress and problems in decision-making studies with specific reference to the Interstate Managerial Study.[8] The nature of this study was outlined and the universe of farms studied was described along with the Friedman-Savage utility hypothesis, which was being tested. Some problems of method were discussed, as were the implications of the study for farm management teaching and research and for farm and home development.

A year later Ciriacy-Wantrup [61] pointed out that farm management research since World War II had been of the normative type and that it sought to determine economic optima and (in its extension phase) to assist farmers in attaining them. Only recently, he said, referring to the Interstate Managerial Study, had studies been initiated that focused on understanding the processes and motive of farm management decisions in reality. He reasoned that normative farm management research was significant in making adjustments after a policy had been put into effect but that research dealing with how farmers do respond has greater significance for establishing policy. He felt that greater emphasis on the positive response of farmers was needed in the years ahead.

In 1957 Glenn Johnson [149] described the array of disciplines important to the managerial process. He viewed economics as a necessary but not a sufficient framework for management. He saw organization theory growing out of political science and public affairs, decision theory growing out of mathematics and statistics, human behavior theory growing out of sociology and psychology, and managerial theory in economics evolving from risk and uncertainty theory and theory of games. He pointed out how students of the managerial process who had examined the assumptions underlying static production economics theory had found it wanting.

In the same year Plaxico and Wiegmann [217] suggested that until we know much more about how farmers actually make decisions, what information they use, how risk and uncertainty considerations enter into their decision making, and until we have a better idea of what they seek to maximize, we cannot be sure of the real usefulness of research based on static profit-maximizing, cost-minimizing models. Using information from the Interstate Managerial Study Boyne and Johnson [34] described the relevance of static theory in its applications to farm organization and operation, to the managerial process, and to aggregate supply and price analysis. They concluded that static theory played a minor role in organization but that it played an important role in farm operation with important consequences for supply and price analysis. In farm operation farmers tended to respond more readily to input price decreases and product price increases than to price countermovements — a phenomenon which Boyne and Johnson attributed largely to the role of fixed asset theory. They pointed out that budgeting, linear programming, and marginal analysis, dependent as these are on fixed assets, appeared useful but inadequate in explaining price response because asset fixities were not determined endogenously. They contended that the usual forms of marginal analysis would be considerably more effective in explaining aggregate response to price change if they were adjusted for consideration of fixed asset theory and theory of managerial behavior assuming imperfect knowledge.[9]

Again drawing on information from the Interstate Managerial Study, Johnson [154] discussed types and sources of information that farmers used in decision making, the importance they attached to different kinds of information, and the difficulties they encountered in obtaining different kinds of information.

Halter and Beringer [95] constructed utility estimates relative to certain farm managerial characteristics using data from the Interstate Managerial Study and the von Neumann-Morgenstern index for measuring cardinal utility. Their analysis suggested that farmers with relatively high marginal utility for monetary gains and low marginal disutility for monetary losses were in high-risk types of farming.

Drawing on a sample of Alabama farmers, Lee and Chastain [182] sought to attain information on the extent of problem identification and to learn whether farm managers recognized opportunities for adjustment associated with these problems. They emphasized the importance of problem recognition in managerial adjustments to change. Study of the managerial function of problem identification was not a part of the Interstate Managerial Study and is considered by those involved in the study to be a serious omission.

In 1961 Johnson and associates [158] summarized many of the individual studies completed under the Interstate Managerial Study; some of the individual studies have been reviewed here. In addition to describing the setting for the study, the book discusses types and sources of information used by farmers, knowledge situations, analytical processes, expectation formulation, decision making, utility of gains and losses, and decisions to take action and responsibility as well as some implications of the study for the farmer's response to price changes. The study was important as a venture into an area about which little was known. One of its weaknesses was that it was a broad, general study and therefore the results cannot be regarded as very conclusive. The results of the study also have limited application because of the kind of manager hypothesized in the study — a rational economic man who observes, gathers information, analyzes it, decides, acts, and accepts responsibilities for action taken. In fairness to the study, however, it should be said that responses were solicited from farmers with both profit maximization and total family satisfaction as goals. Perhaps the most important contribution of the study has been its impact on farm management teaching. As a result of the study farm management has acquired a new role in which it goes beyond the analytical function and attempts to define problems, to identify and assemble relevant information, to specify alternative possible solutions, to decide on and take action, and to evaluate the performance of all of these functions.

Drawing on his experience in teaching decision making, Brannen [37] outlined the elements in the decision process and discussed how training can help managers improve their decision making. He described the elements in the decision-making process as defining the problem, delineating the goal, recognizing alternatives, recognizing and collecting needed information, selecting and evaluating alternatives, and making a decision in terms of a plan of action. As a discussant of the Brannen paper, Baker [37] pointed out that teaching managers how to improve decision making presumed knowledge of how farmers learn. Baker noted that many farmers were willing to pay a substantial price for the privilege of being nonrigorous in decision making. From this premise he argued for the importance of using case materials to demonstrate the consequences of slipshod decision making, to point out that not all problems are equally important, and to demonstrate the importance of evaluating the payoffs in relation to specific farm family needs.

Hagan [92] conceived of managerial resources as being direct and indirect. He regarded those originating on the farm through the operator, his family, and his employees as direct and those originating off the farm, such as professional management, integration services, contractual services, and institutional resources (government programs, financial institutions, and cooperatives) as indirect. He then classified farms as adequate, inadequate, part-time, and semiretirement and noted the management needs of each type. Thus, Hagan suggested that there are different kinds of managerial needs and different kinds of managerial resources, and for best results we need to match these up. Others have addressed themselves to the question of how the managerial resource is affected by some of the broad changes in agriculture. Paul Johnson [162] addressed the question of the effect of off-farm migration on managerial resources in agriculture, and Butz [46] discussed the effects of off-farm management inputs on the managerial resource in commercial agriculture. Butz concluded that off-farm management inputs would play an even greater role in speeding up the adoption of new technology, improving managerial capabilities, and helping producers reduce unit production costs and increase income.

Partenheimer [212] examined the question of executive skills and executive capacity in farm management, noting that this topic has received short shrift in farm management textbooks. Execution or action, he said, is an attempt to implement a decision and executive skills include at least physical, technical, and supervisory skills. He arqued that the exercise of these skills becomes part of the management process, and he noted that this stance brought him into conflict with Glenn Johnson, who had stated that management is not an input. Partenheimer reasoned that management is an input that includes executive skills. Admitting that the theory on the executive function is far from complete, he formulated hypotheses and proposed that the testing of them would provide additional information in this connection.

Routhe [227] contended that considerable support existed for the thesis that decision-making processes should be the core of a farm management education program. He outlined steps in the decision-making process and suggested how to apply these to youth and prospective farmers, to young commercial farmers, and to established commercial farmers. He challenged extension economists in farm management to cast educational materials into a decision-making framework and suggested that extension workers apply the decision-making processes in their own efforts. Routhe hypothesized that if extension economists were to do this, then service training for leaders in agriculture, management workshops for young commercial farmers, and career explorations for youth and prospective farmers would receive high priority.

Tedford [261] discussed the analytics of decision making. He pointed out that according to Luce and Raiffa the bulk of our formal theory falls into the certainty class whereas most decisions fall into the risk and uncertainty class.

He discussed decision making under certainty and deferred decision making under uncertainty and noted that models for analyzing problems under uncertainty are game theoretic or probabilistic.

Langham [179] offered another dichotomy, namely, decision problems of a recurring nature versus those of a nonrecurring nature. The nonrecurring problems, he noted, are the ones that give us the most trouble. He said that in trying to quantify and solve decision problems we are in fact trying to minimize the experience and the abilities required for good decision making. We are trying simultaneously to help the decision maker and to replace him. Langham suggested that such attempts indicate our impatience with apprenticeship and the individual case study approach. In an age in which time is scarce, he continued, we look upon observational learning experiences as wasteful; furthermore, we may be substituting training for education of decision makers. He concluded by saying that our efforts to aid in decision making could result in poorer decisions and less of the human satisfaction which people normally gain from personal decision making.

In a sectional program of the American Farm Economic Association in 1965 entitled "The Management Factor in Commercial Agriculture" Kelsey [171] suggested that to improve managerial ability we need a managerial process model in order to know what we are trying to improve. Kelsey believed that in extension teaching and research we had contributed most to improving the management process through specifying and analyzing alternatives. Headley [101] proposed that management be defined through a "workable definition." To arrive at such a definition he suggested obtaining empirical observations from the manager based on his biography, skills and ability tests, and daily behavior. This set of observations would serve as predictors. A second set of observations, "criterion variables," would be based on financial and efficiency measures from the manager's farm records and subjective ratings from county agents, bankers, and others. The primary interest is to determine whether the "predictor variables" can predict the "criterion variables." If there is a strong relationship between the sets of variables, that relationship would then define management. In addressing the question of how the management factor in commercial agriculture could be improved, Nelson [202] emphasized the need to equate the managerial input with other resources used in farming by identifying and measuring the characteristics associated with managerial ability. Rieck [224] suggested that in the teaching of management we focus on three principles — namely, learning takes place in small increments, the recognition of similarities between past experience and present problems leads to the discovery of a concept of decision making, and the individual must take an active part in the learning process if learning is to take place. On the topic of new tools for the manager Kennedy [173] first laid out the scope of management under three problem headings — production and organization problems, administrative problems, and marketing problems. For the first problem he suggested the tools of improved budgets, systematic programming, linear programming, dynamic programming, operations research, supply forecasting, and planning guides. For the second problem he suggested the tools of reliable input-output data, interdisciplinary research, electronic accounting and data processing, operational timing studies, meteorological forecasting, management consulting firms, and commercial servicing. For the third problem he suggested the tools of market and demand forecasting, futures trading, research and extension publications, improved credit, and contractual farming.

Rushton and Shaudys [229] used a social systems model in an attempt to clarify the criterion problem in research on farm managerial ability. They viewed the farm firm as a subsystem of the farm family which has certain values, goals, and resources. Thus, we see a continuing concern about identifying, measuring, and improving management. Our failure to come up with answers that will allay or eliminate these concerns no doubt contributes to the fuzziness of the boundaries surrounding farm management as a discipline.

A development in statistical decision theory that may have important implications for improving decision making is the Bayesian approach in which optimal action is determined on the basis of prior probabilities and then the optimal action is revised in the light of additional information. Eidman and associates [79] empirically applied the Bayesian approach to management decisions under uncertainty. The choice in the study was between contract and independent production of turkeys, and the major random variables were product prices and mortality rates. Optimal action was first determined where only prior probabilities of states of nature were available. Optimal strategies were then determined where information from a price forecasting model was available and posterior probabilities of the states of nature were determined. They concluded that the value of the additional information from the forecasting model was considerable.

A concept which points to limitations of static firm theory is that of a fixed asset developed by Glenn Johnson and associates. In traditional firm theory the acquisition cost of an asset equals its salvage value, and in equilibrium these two values are equal to the marginal value product of the asset or resources. Johnson argued that these conditions may hold for some assets, such as seed and tractor fuel, but for many assets acquisition costs and salvage values differ considerably; an asset is fixed if its marginal value product falls between its acquisition cost and its salvage value. This concept has been applied to problems in forage evaluation and has been used in linear programming models that emphasize estimation of supply functions [75, 120, 159].

Another recent development that emphasizes the shortcomings of the methodological framework built on static economic theory and profit maximization involves the firm growth models which incorporate time, imperfect knowledge, household consumption, financial flows, and other variables in tracing out growth patterns and providing planning information between the current and some future time period [29, 213]. Firm growth models that particularly provide freedom from maximizing profits are those that utilize simulation techniques. Simulation frees one from optimizing a decision rule, but it is very demanding in other respects, such as requiring specification of rates of change in variables.

Another post-World War II development that appears to be placing some stress or strain on the methodological framework of static economic theory and profit maximization is the farm management identity crisis. In a book published in 1953 J. D. Black [25] wrote that "when the economics of agricultural production is reduced to terms of the individual farm, it becomes what is ordinarily known as farm management. Any textbook in real farm management is a treatise on the economics of production of the individual farm" [25].[10] In 1956 Ciriacy-Wantrup [61] saw production economics as dealing primarily wtih the combination and allocation of productive factors. He noted that these problems were important to farm management but that they did not circumscribe the whole field. In other respects Ciriacy-Wantrup viewed production economics as broader than farm management, stating that factor combination and allocation could not be understood adequately if the analysis were confined to farm management. Perhaps Plaxico and Wiegmann [217] said the same when they suggested that farm management and production economics were not synonymous terms but overlapping terms, each including areas not encompassed by the other. In 1957 Glenn Johnson [149] wrote that farm management now tends to be considered as a subfield of production economics and production economics in turn is a subfield of agricultural economics and economics. In the same year he wrote, "Farm management is far broader than economics. It extends from deep in the physical sciences on the one hand to deep in philosophic value theory and ethics on the other" [156]. He commented further in 1963: "Though the new orientation [referring to the postwar orientation of isolating problems that could be solved by finding the equilibria defined in static production economic theory] concentrated on problems and, in this sense, differed significantly from the immediately preceding fact-finding research in the field of farm management, it contained a serious flaw . . . The flaw involved the narrowness of the problems considered which tended to be defined in terms of the disequilibria of static production economic theory. This concentration made farm management a narrow problem-solving subfield of production economics which, in turn, was a subfield of general economics" [157]. In 1967 Ruttan [230] wrote that the field of farm management had never satisfactorily resolved the question of whether it should confine itself to the economics of farm management (production economics) or whether production economics is simply one of the applied behavioral, social, biological, and physical science disciplines upon which the field of farm management is based. Williams [279] expressly viewed production economics as only one of the basic disciplines of farm management.

In short, farm management faces an identity crisis. There is no clear notion of what farm management is. Glenn Johnson [149] has even suggested that maybe farm management is an impossible academic discipline because management is pervasive and shows up in many disciplines and that perhaps farm management is, just a point of view. If we do not know what farm management is, then most assuredly it is difficult to determine what its methodological orientation or foundation is.

Outlook for the Future

This paper began with a quotation from Heady to the effect that advancement in a scientific field grows not out of unqualified acceptance of the status quo but out of frequent appraisal of the road ahead. Through the years since World War II the literature has been enriched by a number of excellent reviews and appraisals, some of which focused broadly on agricultural economics while others specifically addressed production economics and, farm management [58, 102, 114, 155, 157, 230, 231, 279]. As we noted earlier our central task is to increase the power and capacity of our science — its methodology and its analytical tools and techniques so as to become more effective in solving current social problems — and also to apply this capacity to solving problems of growing social concern. Looking at the production function work and the developments in mathematical programming, simulation, and other analytical techniques that have extended theory to include time, imperfect knowledge, and various decision criteria, I have the impression that considerable progress has been made in increasing the power of our applied science to handle the growing complexity of our problems. To be demonstrated yet, it seems to me, is whether this development will be effective in solving problems of increasing social concern. Williams [279] has pointed out that "the growing emphasis on uncertainty and on inter-disciplinary approaches to input-output analysis on the biological side, and to decision making and behavioral studies on the social science side, has been well-meaning enough. But these new efforts have not yet paid off in terms of their influences upon practitioners of either extension or farm management."

As applied scientists we are going to be judged in the end by our dedication and skill in solving problems of social concern. As a basis for increasing our effectiveness in these areas it may be helpful to focus on the farm management identity crisis and on some orientation questions.

The Farm Management Identity Crisis[11]

As we noted in the previous section, Ruttan's question — whether farm management as an academic field should confine itself to the economics (or production economics) of farm management or whether production economics is simply one of the applied behavioral, social, biological, and physical science disciplines on which the field of farm management is based — remains unanswered. On the other hand, we noted Glenn Johnson's conclusion that farm management had become a narrow problem-solving subfield of production economics, which in turn is a subfield of economics.

From its very beginning farm management was a multidisciplinary study. Originally what was known in farm management as a study came directly from the farms. Farms produced crops and livestock and used land, seed, buildings, labor, tools, machinery, and management for the production of these crops and livestock. Originally the study of farm management involved the gathering of data on the outputs and the inputs. Over time specialized bodies of knowledge and information, often called disciplines, developed. The disciplines reflected in the data gathered in the early days of farm management were mostly technical ones dealing with crops, livestock, farm power, and machinery.

Before the study of farm management was very old, it began to employ principles, theory, and information from economics and later from agricultural economics. From the beginning farm management study involved subject matter from statistics, at least of a descriptive sort. However, some time elapsed before farm management actually began to integrate the theory and tools — sampling theory, regression, frequency distributions — from modern statistics into its study and analysis. Later, farm management drew on concepts and techniques (Bayesian analysis, game theory, mathematical programming) from various areas such as statistics, mathematics, social psychology, and econometrics for handling risk and uncertainty considerations and for maximizing or minimizing specified objectives in decision making. With the advent of computer technology farm management began to utilize concepts from applied mathematics in the form of simulation techniques for handling problems of risk and uncertainty for the farming system and for measuring the consequences of introducing changes into the system. In addition, farm management study has applied concepts from operations research in handling management problems related to inventory, resource allocation, sequencing, replacement, information search, and competition.

The Interstate Managerial Study, which was conceived as a means of obtaining knowledge of managerial processes, provided firsthand empirical support to the widely held view of farm management as a broad interdisciplinary problem-solving study. The farm operator's performance of the functions of (1) observing and gathering information on prices, production, institutions, and people, (2) analyzing the information, (3) making decisions, and (4) acting and accepting consequences for action taken revealed the interdisciplinary nature of this study.

The north central regional project on the human factor in management (later known as Management Resource in Farming) was planned for the purpose of measuring the managerial ability of farmers. This attempt to measure managerial ability indirectly through factors such as age, experience, education, and other variables of a socioeconomic and psychological nature also lent support to the view of farm management as a study stretching across numerous disciplines. Hence, given the nature of the unit on which the study of farm management focuses, and given the functions that a manager of such a unit must perform to solve the problems he encounters, farm management as a study must necessarily continue in a multidisciplinary vein.

According to Ruttan, "If farm management is defined as a field which is concerned with the application of the full range of behavioral, social, biological, and physical sciences (or even of the social and behavioral sicences) to the management of the farm firm, the implications for the organization of agricultural economics, as an academic field, become extremely difficult" [230]. Not only will it be difficult for agricultural economics as an academic field, it will be difficult for farm management unless some integrating force exists. Questions that need to be resolved for farm management are: What is management? What is to be managed? Who does the management? What is the unit of analysis? Who are the clientele? What are the decision criteria? What are the allocative principles? For if farm management is multidisciplinary and encompasses behavioral, social, biological, and physical sciences (Ruttan) or encompasses statistics, logic, sociology, home economics, psychology, philosophic value theory, physical and biological sciences, and economics (Johnson, [149]), then an important additional question exists: Do these many disciplines exist as parallel fields, each with its own methodology, key variables and fundamental relationships, allocative principles, and decision criteria as these pertain to management in each discipline, or are there linkages among the variables from each discipline that tie the disciplines together into a general theory serving as a foundation for a managerial science? Or is there one of these many disciplines that is an integrating discipline? Or is the manager at one time a psychologist, at another time an agronomist, and at another time an economist?

Ruttan [230] suggested that agricultural economics departments might seek to achieve a broad staffing pattern like that used in business schools with a management science approach, which would at least bring in staff members trained in the several social and behavioral sciences. Such a pattern would serve to bring several disciplines concerned with management under one administrative unit, but it is questionable whether it would serve as an integrating force among the various disciplines; if Ruttan has in mind primarily the business management component of business schools, then the approach to management may be no more integrated than the approach in farm management and production economics. Newman and associates [207] noted that in business *several* approaches to management — approaches involving several disciplines — are used. One approach is productivity with emphasis on scientific management, personnel management, internal financial management, and technological aids to productivity. A second approach is behavioral and focuses on human relations, communication, and how people behave under varying conditions. A third approach is based on the rationalistic model, which centers on micro economic theory, profit maximizing, game theory, systems analysis, and operations research techniques. A fourth approach is institutional and places the emphasis on understanding the practices, customs, and laws under which a manager operates.

Another response, according to Ruttan [230], is to follow the pattern evolving in many agribusiness programs of establishing a close program integration with the business schools. The effect of this response, as Ruttan sees it, would be to restructure agricultural economics specializations (a) with the firm-oriented farm management and agricultural business management curriculum and research programs more closely integrated with similar programs in the schools of business and (b) with the policy-oriented areas in agricultural economics continuing their close association with departments of economics. There certainly are structural changes in agriculture, such as vertical integration and rapid growth of the capital base of farm firms which necessitates increased attention to financial flows and management, and there is common understanding and usage of many of the same analytical techniques — all of which provides a logical base for a closer association with schools of business. However, as a means of integrating multidisciplines into an approach to management, this pattern appears to face the same problems as Ruttan's first suggestion.

If farm management is defined less broadly, i.e., as the economics of farm production or as the production economics of the farm firm, Ruttan sees no conflict with the trend in the evolution of the two fields of farm management and production economics during the last several decades. The academic field of farm management would focus on the production economics and the economic organization of the farm firm, leaving the commercial farm manager, or his advisers, to integrate the findings from agricultural economics and other disciplines into decisions at the firm level. This has been the subject matter approach of farm management economics where economics with its various decision criteria and allocative principles is the integrating discpline for the manager or his advisers in making decisions. This approach is a pragmatic approach to the farm management identity problem. It does not solve completely the "problem versus departments and disciplines" dilemma of the applied sciences. Farm management requires an overriding commitment to problem solving, and problem solving requires the ability to perceive and use concepts and factual relations from many disciplines. But all applied sciences have a problem focus, and to the extent that problems are multifaceted (as most of them in the real world are) satisfactory solutions require information and knowledge from more than one discipline — at least given the structure of colleges, universities, and the development of knowledge. Disciplines or branches of learning or fields of study can be defined broadly or narrowly. Whether we can develop them broadly for satisfactory application to and solution of problems is quite a different matter. The modern dilemma is that if we are to know a field in depth we are forced either to define disciplines more narrowly or to divide them into subdisciplines at the very time when problems have become increasingly complex, requiring information from a broadening spectrum for satisfactory solution. The implications of these developments for farm management are that it must continue to draw on various disciplines in its problem-solving activity and that the mix on which it must draw will differ as problems differ or change.

Glenn Johnson [157] saw the problem orientation of farm mangement following World War II as differing markedly from the preceding fact-finding orientation. But he also saw a serious flaw in this new orientation which he described as the narrowness of the problems considered. These, he said, tended to be defined in terms of the disequilibria of static production economics theory. He reasoned that this concentration had made farm management a narrow problem-solving subfield of production economics. He added that problems definable in terms of disequilibria are solvable through recommendations for establishing equilibria and that as long as the marginality conditions are met for an equilibrium existing problems are not directly discernible or solvable solely within the theory and hence can easily be overlooked. Here he suggested that the focus of economic theory on disequilibria can distract attention from the really relevant problem — the inadequate resources of some of the units making up the initial asset ownership pattern.

At least part of the solution to the problem is to build models that are less constricting. One approach here is for professionals with interests in farm management economics and production economics to expand the theory and models by relaxing the basic assumptions underlying static production economics theory. The basic assumptions taken as given are perfect knowledge, the state of the art, tastes and preferences, timelessness, institutions, and motivations. If we have the skills, interests, and energy to work toward incorporating these "givens" into the theoretical systems and models, production economics theory will become broader in scope and will more nearly meet the needs of solving important problems in managing farms and other units. Progress has been made in incorporating some of the "givens" into our models as variables and in expanding the objective function beyond profit maximization. Just what the payoff from this progress will be is difficult to predict, but most assuredly specialized training and skills are required to formulate complex models, to develop computer software, and to operate the equipment that will generate solutions. Large commercial firms and governmental units may be able to afford these investment and operational outlays, but small firms and small governmental units may need to purchase the services. Also, there is a question of how sophisticated decision-making units really should become. As Baker [37] pointed out, many farmers may be willing to pay a relatively high price for the privilege of being nonrigorous in decision making; and as Langham [179] suggested, in our attempts to help the decision maker we may be replacing him with adverse effects to him and to the quality of the human decision.

Orientations for the Future

For the foreseeable future, research and resident and extension teaching as related to the farm firm and household should be conceived as farm management economics. The focus should be on problems of concern to the specified clientele. The methodological base should combine the standard model of profit maximization under certainty with behavioral theories or constructs that have something to say about how individuals and organizations respond to imperfect knowledge, risk, uncertainty, and multiple goals. With this orientation the discipline of farm management economics will have a home in agricultural or applied economics, complementarities will exist between farm management economics and production economics, and the available theory, tools, and techniques can be put to work in solving crucial economic and social problems.

At the same time efforts should be directed toward the possibility of tying the various disciplines or parts of disciplines together into an integrated managerial theory and science that can be applied to both private and public decision making by individuals or groups. In the context of the farm as a whole or the farm firm-household, farm management historically has had to draw on information from various disciplines to solve its problems. Thus, farm management is basically an integrating study and the advances in multidisciplinary orientations in agricultural colleges are in no small way attributable to the efforts of farm management and production economists. These advances are the building blocks for future problem solving.

As mentioned earlier, my review of the literature indicates that considerable progress has been made in increasing the power of our applied science in handling increasingly complex problems. Nevertheless, it is not yet clear what payoff this development will have in solving problems. With an eye to the future, however, we should bear in mind that as farm and agribusiness firms become more commercialized the managers of these firms stand more in need of, and hence are more likely to use, the sophisticated economic information and the results from the analytical techniques that have been developed. Moreover, an increasing number of individuals, the future managers of these firms, are being trained in farm management classes in which students solve problems and make decisions in simulated farming situations using electronic equipment. The strong student interest in this approach suggests opportunities for further development.

A clearer, more specific orientation to our clientele is needed. To be effectively engaged in problem-solving activities we must know who our clientele are. We must also know what their problems, goals, and values are — and possibly we should be prepared to help them to articulate these. We must identify clearly our units of analysis — a farm firm, a farm firm-household, a set of farm feed processing firms, an area, a region, a nation. If we wish to improve decision making, we must get involved with the decision makers or the policy makers of these units.

If our clientele is both private and public, then our analysis must single out those alternative acts that complement or compete with each other in private and public areas and show the private and social costs of attaining or not attaining compatibility where interests and objectives deviate. The same kind of analysis is needed within the private sector when various parties with diverse interests and objectives enter into a decision-making process such as that obtaining in tenant-landlord, father-son, farm firm-household, partnership, and corporation relationships. If the clientele is public, then the interests, the goals, and the problems of the various groups of people within the area must be identified and the analysis must show how policy interventions affect the needs and objectives of these different groups.

Farm management and production economics, it has been said, has become oriented toward research techniques, research methods, and theory rather than problems [157, 230, 279]. Perhaps this might also be described as professional orientation versus problem orientation. Certainly a profession must devote a portion of its energies and efforts to the tools of its trade, but hiding behind computers, techniques, and models is not going to solve our social and economic problems. I do think our university system encourages the diversion of staff energies toward the publication of material in professional journals. To the extent that this is an avenue to salary increases and promotion, there is probably enough pragmatism in all of us to cause us to traverse it. But this course is a hazardous one to the extent that it diverts us from becoming personally involved in finding solutions to problems of growing economic, social, and political concern.

Farm management and production economics has been accused of being identified too much with positivism, that it must become more normative [157]. Glenn Johnson has suggested that specialization and a tendency toward positivism have been responsible for lack of productivity in terms of problem solving. Certainly if such a tendency leads us away from problem solving, then again we are treading dangerous ground. It is difficult to assess what the right amount of positivism and normativism is in an applied science, but it seems to me that Ciriacy-Wantrup [61] has wisely urged us to use some of both. He suggested that normative farm management research is significant in making adjustments after a policy has been put into effect. For establishing policy, Ciriacy-Wantrup reasoned that research on how farmers respond is of greater significance than normative research in developing a policy and in deciding on its implementation. In this sense it appears to me that farm management and production economics needs some orientation in both directions, even at the firm level, in developing policy and adjusting to it.

It has been suggested that research in farm management and production economics has primarily sought information for private rather than public decision making [217, 230]. Plaxico and Wiegmann, drawing on information from their review in the late 1950s of past and current research in farm management and production economics, found that estimates of interfarm and interindustry relationships have been considered to have little value relative to intrafarm relationships. My review of journal articles and technical and station bulletins indicates that this lack of emphasis has changed little, if any, since then. But perhaps if one looks at the use of production economics in the areas of resource and regional economics the conclusion would be different. Ruttan argued, particularly in reference to developing countries, that it is a misuse of professional talent to treat farm operators, and even extension workers, as the primary clientele for microeconomic research. He emphasized the importance of producing information on the consequences of alternative public decisions to administrators and policy makers. Actually information is needed at both levels.

During the 1930s and 1940s we saw a great deal of interest and effort devoted to evaluating the expected consequences of alternative agricultural policies on farm resource use. Interest in agricultural price and income policy has dwindled, but there are many other state and national policies (or nonpolicies) that influence resource use. As various agricultural and nonagricultural groups bid for resources — land, water, fuel, labor — there are both private and social costs that need to be weighed against returns in alternative uses. The handling of waste and effluent involves similar kinds of analyses. As actions of farm firms or other decision-making units are circumscribed by environmental controls, studies are much needed to evaluate the conomic impact of the controls. The analytical tools and techniques of farm management and production economics are well suited for evaluating farm firm benefits and the costs associated with alternative possible solutions and for assessing the costs society may need to bear if it wants results.

As agribusiness firms and industries move in to provide more and more managerial services to farmers, consideration should be given to the possibility of shifting professional resources to the study of interfarm and interindustry problems and relations and to a study of the micro effects of alternative policies with policy makers and administrators as the primary clientele.

Through a review of literature of a professional group it is possible to learn something about the objectives underlying the professional efforts or work of that group. Glenn Johnson appraised the pronouncements of leading agricultural economists on the state of their field and in 1954 distilled a list of beliefs and values that appeared to be held by a substantial portion of the profession [152]. Three of the beliefs dealt with objectives underlying the work of the profession:

> Agricultural economics research exists to serve farmers, and if it fails to do so it will cease to exist. It is also widely held that research exists to serve nonfarm groups handling and consuming farm products. A very substantial number of our profession hold that it also exists to serve society in general. These beliefs and convictions fairly well define the problems on which agricultural economists are expected to work.

> Service research, teaching, and extension work are crowding out fundamental research work to the long-run detriment of the profession.

> The traditional efficiency norm of economics is a necessary but insufficient basis for judgment in doing research on the problems addressed to agricultural economists.

At about the same time Ratchford [220] outlined the objectives of extension economics work and in referring to the Smith-Lever Act stated that under it we could work to improve the welfare of individual farm families, the welfare of agriculture, or — most important of all in Ratchford's view — the economic welfare of society in general.

In 1948 Heady wrote, "Farm management research relates to the study of the economic efficiency and productivity of farm resources. Its specific objectives are (1) to guide individual farmers in the best use of their resources and in a manner compatible with the welfare of society and (2) to provide fundamental analyses of the efficiency of farm resource combinations which can serve as a basis for bettering the public administration of resources where agricultural policy or institutions which condition production efficiency are concerned" [109]. In the same article he stated, "The individual farm and broader industry or social objectives are sometimes looked upon as incongruous. They are not however. Both channel to the same end in respect to resource efficiency. . . . Agriculture as a competitive industry provides an environment in which the best use of resources by the individual firm can result in the most efficient use of resources from the standpoint of society with the exceptions noted."[12]

Hence, even though the objectives as outlined above from Johnson and Ratchford might imply incompatibility between those who set out to serve the interests of farmers and those who keep society's interests to the fore, I think most farm management specialists and production economists in the post-World War II period have proceeded in the belief that in most instances efforts to serve either actually served both in terms of resource efficiency. Moreover, I think fairly strong evidence exists to support the argument that the farm management and production economics recommendations for agricultural adjustment in the postwar period were compatible with national policy. The recommendations in terms of profit maximization for individual farms and overall resource efficiency favored bigger and fewer farms, substitution of capital for labor, and movement of labor out of agriculture into off-farm employment where its value product or wage was assumed to be higher. These recommendations do not appear to be at odds with a national policy that has encouraged unionization of labor and minimum wages, has subsidized research and education in agriculture, and has subsidized credit in agriculture which in turn has lowered capital costs and demands for labor as labor-saving technology has been substituted for labor.

But I think we have entered a period marked by a reorientation in objectives. In 1969 Williams [279] hoped that in retrospect the 1960s would be seen as the period when the influence of humanism in the sciences, including economics, matured. In 1970 Castle [58] referred to a recurrent theme running through discussion in land-grant education circles to the effect that if universitites could but reorder their priorities and organize to tackle "real" social problems rather than simply the problem of the increasing agricultural output the result would be a rebirth of the land-grant philosophy. At the same time he characterized the 1960s as a period in agricultural economics when small conceptions of social problems were discarded and subspecializations such as farm management, marketing, and resource or land economics tended to yield to broader categories, as did agricultural economics itself. In 1972 Heady wrote, "Over the long run, institutions are likely to be better financed and gain broader public support if they concern themselves more with the people and problems of greatest social urgency" [102]. In the same year Danial Fusfeld [89] wrote, "The problems of the present indicate the path of the future. A reconstruction of economics — a new synthesis and a new paradigm — will have to move toward greater concern for humane values, toward a humane economy on a world wide scale. A humane economy requires more than prosperity and economic growth, more than efficient allocation of resources. It demands changes in the framework of economic institutions to achieve greater equality and freedom.[13] It requires dispersal of the economic power and governmental authority that support the present disposition of income, wealth and power. It requires a social environment that brings a sense of community and fellowship into human relationships. It demands compatibility among man, his technology, and the natural environment. And all of these things must be done on a world wide scale. These are the goals of the future, to which economists and everyone else will have to devote their energies." I close with a plea for farm management and production economics to move ahead in this spirit, to move ahead with the times. Problems of human development in the rural-urban complex, of our use or misuse of our natural environment and fossil energy, should identify the future clientele and the future directions for farm management and production economics.

Notes

1. See *J. Farm Econ.* 32:1100-1181, November 1950

2. This experiment also included information on feed conversion rates with and without aureomycin, which did have a significant effect. A later study shows that temperatures (both low and high) also influence feed conversion rates in swine. See R. Amick and J. Purcell, "Influence of Temperature on Feed Conversion by Swine," *J. Farm Econ.* 46:1227-1231, December 1964.

3. I am particularly indebted to Irving Fellows of the University of Connecticut, James Plaxico of Oklahoma State University, George Dawson of New Mexico State University, and Gerald Dean of the University of California in Davis for help in developing this section. I have described the activities of the North Central Farm Management Research Committee, of which I was long a member, in some detail. Since the basic purposes underlying the activities of similar committees elsewhere were the same, regardless of geography, much of the information about NCFMRC applies also to the other regional committees.

4. Members of this group were Andrew Boss, University of Minnesota, chairman; Sherman Johnson, USDA; H. C. M. Case, University of Illinois; George Pond, University of Minnesota; O. B. Jesness, University of Minnesota; Walter Wilcox, University of Wisconsin; Joe Ackermann and Frank Peck, Farm Foundation. They met on the St. Paul campus of the University of Minnesota on April 8-9, 1946.

5. From "Farm Management Committee of WAERC — History" in *Forces Restructuring Production and Marketing in Commercial Agriculture*, Western Agricultural Economics Research Council, Committee on the Economics of Range Use and Development, Report No. 10 (jointly with the Marketing Research Committee and the Farm Management Research Committee), Conference Proceedings, Tucson, Arizona, November 19-21, 1968, p. 248.

6. An interesting ex post observation can be made here. Heady at this time estimated that a decrease in the number of commercial farms to 2.5 million (a decrease of nearly a million from 1955) would make possible reasonable scale economies and favorable returns to farm labor. In 1970 we had 2.9 million commercial farms. Heady suggested that the farm labor force could be decreased by 50 percent from the 1950 level (from 9.3 to 4.6 million). In 1971 farm employment stood at 4.2 million.

7. See *International Development Review* 15:24, 1973/3 for G. L. Johnson's review of M. P. Collinson's *Farm Management in Peasant Agriculture: A Handbook for Rural Development Planning in Africa*, Praeger Special Studies, 1972.

8. See "Progress and Problems in Decision Making Studies," *J. Farm Econ.* 37:1097-1125, December 1955, for several reports on the Interstate Managerial Study.

9. In the concept of fixed asset used here an asset is fixed if its marginal value product falls between its acquisition price or cost and its salvage value. Differences between acquisition cost and salvage value are not considered in traditional marginal analysis. Reference is made to this concept at a later point.

10. In a footnote to this quotation Black writes, "It must be confessed that some have been written that have left out a good deal of this economics."

11. Identity problems are really not peculiar to farm management. Given the various names that are now being used for units previously identified as agricultural economics, it is quite clear that agricultural economics too has an identity problem. Even colleges and institutes of agriculture have identity problems.

12. The exceptions were the divergencies that grow out of uncertainty and other imperfections in the market, leasing arrangements and other institutional factors, and segments in agriculture that are not competitive.

13. In a seminar Ruttan argued that in recent years much had been done in measuring the contributions of the natural sciences and technology to growth in agricultural and industrial output but that similar progress had not been made in conceptualizing the contribution of new knowledge to the process of institutional change. He reasoned that the value of new knowledge in the social sciences comes primarily from its contribution to the process of institutional change. Hence, the primary rationale for public investment is the development of the capacity in the social sciences to produce institutional innovations that are more efficient than current institutions.

References

[1] Afzal, M., J. McCoy, and F. Orazem. "Development of Inventory Models to Determine Feed Reserves for Beef Cattle Production under Climatic Conditions." *J. Farm Econ.* 47:948-962, November 1965.

[2] Allen, C. W. "Discussion." *J. Farm Econ.* 34:817-819, December 1952.

[3] Amick, R., and J. Purcell. "An Application of Residual Analysis for Determining Relationships between Selected Variables and Unit Cost." *J. Farm Econ.* 44:1423-1427, December 1962.

[4] Anderson, R. "A Simulation Program to Establish Optimum Crop Patterns on Irrigated Farms Based on Preseason Estimates of Water Supply." *Am. J. Agr. Econ.* 50: 1586-1590, December 1968.

[5] Athearn, J. "Price Expectations, Plans, and Decision Making among Ohio Commercial Cattle Feeders." *J. Farm Econ.* 38:126-143, February 1956.

[6] Atkinson, L. J., and J. W. Klein. *Feed Consumption and Marketing Weight of Hogs.* USDA Tech. Bul. 894, 1945.

[7] Aune, H., and L. Day. "Determining the Effect of Size of Herd and Equipment on Dairy Chore Labor." *J. Farm Econ.* 41:569-583, August 1959.

[8] Babbar, M., G. Tintner, and E. O. Heady. "Programming with Consideration of Variations in Input Coefficients." *J. Farm Econ.* 37:333-341, May 1955.

[9] Bachman, K. L. "Relation of Economic Theory to the Analysis of Empirical Data in Farm Management Research." *J. Farm Econ.* 32:1159-1168, November 1950.

[10] Bachman, K. L., and G. Barton. "Farm Cost Structure and Opportunities for Cost Reduction." *J. Farm Econ.* 36:991-999, December 1954.

[11] Baker, C. "Credit in the Production Organization of the Firm." *Am. J. Agr. Econ.* 50:507-520, August 1968.

[12] ———. "Financial Organization and Production Choices." *Am. J. Agr. Econ.* 50: 1566-1577, December 1968.

[13] Baker, C., and J. Holcomb. "The Emerging Financial Problems in a Changing Agriculture." *J. Farm Econ.* 46:1200-1206, December 1964.

[14] Baker, C., and J. Hopkin. "Concepts of Finance Capital for a Capital-Using Agriculture." *Am. J. Agr. Econ.* 51:1055-1064, December 1969.

[15] Barber, E., and P. Thair. "Institutional Methods of Meeting Weather Uncertainty in the Great Plains." *J. Farm Econ.* 32:391-410, August 1950.

[16] Barker, R., and B. Stanton. "Estimation and Aggregation of Firm Supply Functions." *J. Farm Econ.* 47:701-712, August 1965.

[17] Baum, E. L., E. O. Heady, and J. Blackmore, eds. *Methodological Procedures in the Economic Analysis of Fertilizer Use Data.* Ames: Iowa State College Press, 1956.

[18] Baum, E. L., and H. G. Walkup. "Some Economic Implications of Input-Output Relationships in Fryer Production." *J. Farm Econ.* 35:223-235, May 1953.

[19] Benedict, M. R. "The Opportunity Cost Basis of the Substitution Method in Farm Management." *J. Farm Econ.* 14:384-405, July 1932.

[20] ———. "The Opportunity Cost Basis of the Substitution Method in Farm Management." *J. Farm Econ.* 14:541-557, October 1932.

[21] Beneke, R. R. *Managing the Farm Business.* New York: Wiley, 1955.

[22] Beringer, C. "Estimating Enterprise Production Functions from Input-Output Data on Multiple Enterprise Farms." *J. Farm Econ.* 38:923-930, November 1956.

[23] Bishop, C. "Programming Farm-Nonfarm Allocation of Farm Family Resources." *J. Farm Econ.* 38:396-407, May 1956.

[24] Bishop, C., and W. D. Toussaint. *Introduction to Agricultural Economics Analysis.* New York: Wiley, 1958.

[25] Black, J. D. *Introduction to Economics for Agriculture.* New York: Macmillan, 1953, p. 120.

[26] ———. *Introduction to Production Economics.* New York: Henry Holt, 1926.

[27] Black, J. D., M. Clawson, C. R. Sayre, and W. W. Wilcox. *Farm Management*. New York: Macmillan, 1947.

[28] Boan, J. "A Study of Farmers' Reactions to Uncertain Price Expectations." *J. Farm Econ.* 37:90-95, February 1955.

[29] Boehlje, M., and T. White. "A Production-Investment Decision Model of Farm Firm Growth." *Am. J. Agr. Econ.* 51:546-563, August 1969.

[30] Boles, J. "Linear Programming and Farm Management Analysis." *J. Farm Econ.* 37:1-24, February 1955.

[31] ———. "Short Cuts in Programming Computations." *J. Farm Econ.* 38:981-990, November 1956.

[32] Boss, A. "Forty Years of Cash Accounts." *J. Farm Econ.* 27:1-17, February 1945.

[33] Bottum, J. C. "Methods of Presenting Economic Data to Farmers." *J. Farm Econ.* 34:837-841, December 1952.

[34] Boyne, D., and G. L. Johnson. "A Partial Evaluation of Static Theory from Results of the Interstate Managerial Survey." *J. Farm Econ.* 40:458-469, May 1958.

[35] Bradford, L. A., and G. L. Johnson. *Farm Management Analysis*. New York: Wiley, 1953.

[36] Brake, J. "Impact of Structural Changes in Capital and Credit Needs." *J. Farm Econ.* 48:1536-1545, December 1966.

[37] Brannen, S. "Teaching Managers How to Improve Their Decision-Making Processes." Discussion by C. Baker. *J. Farm Econ.* 43:1278-1286, December 1961.

[38] Brokken, R. F., and E. O. Heady. *Interregional Adjustments in Crop and Livestock Production — A Linear Programming Analysis*. USDA Tech. Bul. 1396, July 1968.

[39] Brown, W. G., and G. H. Arscott. "A Method for Dealing with Time in Determining Optimum Factor Input." *J. Farm Econ.* 40:666-673, August 1958.

[40] Brown, W. G., and A. M. M. Oveson. "Production Functions from Data over a Series of Years." *J. Farm Econ.* 40:451-457, May 1958.

[41] Brownlee, O., and W. Gainer. "Farmers' Price Anticipation and the Role of Uncertainty in Farm Planning." *J. Farm Econ.* 32:266-275, May 1949.

[42] Brunk, M. E. *Celery Harvesting Methods in Florida*. Florida Agr. Exp. Sta. Res. Bul. 404, 1944.

[43] Buchholz, H. E., and G. G. Judge. *An Interregional Analysis of the Feed-Livestock Economy*. Dept. Agr. Econ. AERR 75, University of Illinois, 1965.

[44] Burt, O., and J. Allison. "Farm Management Decisions with Dynamic Programming." *J. Farm Econ.* 45:121-136, February 1963.

[45] Burt, O., and R. Johnson. "Strategies for Wheat Production in the Great Plains." *J. Farm Econ.* 49:881-899, November 1967.

[46] Butz, D. "The Effect of Off-Farm Management Inputs." *J. Farm Econ.* 47:1443-1445, December 1965.

[47] Byers, G. B., and E. R. Young. *How to Save Time in Pulling Tobacco Plants*. Kentucky Agr. Coll. Leaflet 90, 1945.

[48] Candler, W. "A Modified Simplex Solution for Linear Programming with Variable Capital Restrictions." *J. Farm Econ.* 38:940-955, November 1956.

[49] ———. "A Modified Simplex Solution for Linear Programming with Variable Prices." *J. Farm Econ.* 39:409-428, May 1957.

[50] ———. "The Optimum Fodder Reserve — An Inventory Problem." *J. Farm Econ.* 41:257-262, May 1959.

[51] ———. "Reflections on Dynamic Programming Models." *J. Farm Econ.* 42: 920-926, November 1960.

[52] Candler, W., M. Boehlje, and R. Saathof. "Computer Software for Farm Management Extension." *Am. J. Agr. Econ.* 52:71-80, February 1970.

[53] Candler, W., and R. Manning. "A Modified Simplex Procedure for Problems with Decreasing Average Cost." *J. Farm Econ.* 43:859-875, November 1961.

[54] Carlson, G. "A Decision Theoretic Approach of Crop Disease Prediction and Control." *Am. J. Agr. Econ.* 52:216-223, May 1970.

[55] Carlson, S. *A Study of the Pure Theory of Production.* London: King, 1939.

[56] Carter, H., and G. Dean. "Cost-Size Relationships for Cash-Crop Farms in a Highly Commercialized Agriculture." *J. Farm Econ.* 43:264-277, May 1961.

[57] Carter, R. M. *Saving Labor through Farm Job Analysis: I. Dairy Barn Chores.* Vermont Agr. Exp. Sta. Bul. 503, 1943.

[58] Castle, E. "Priorities in Agricultural Economics for the 1970s." *Am. J. Agr. Econ.* 52:831-840, December 1970.

[59] ———. "Vertical Integration and Farm Management Research." *J. Farm Econ.* 40:434-439, May 1958.

[60] Chandler, C. "The Relative Contribution of Capital Intensity and Productivity to Changes in Output and Income in the U.S. Economy, Farm and Non-Farm Sectors, 1946-58." *J. Farm Econ.* 44:335-348, May 1962.

[61] Ciriacy-Wantrup, S. "Policy Considerations in Farm Management Research in the Decade Ahead." *J. Farm Econ.* 38:1301-1311, December 1956.

[62] Coffey, J., and W. Toussaint. "Some Economic Aspects of Free Choice Feeding of Dairy Cows." *J. Farm Econ.* 45:1213-1218, December 1963.

[63] Conneman, G. "Farm Panels as a Source of Farm Management Data: The Cornell Producer Panel." *Am. J. Agr. Econ.* 51:1206-1210, December 1969.

[64] Coutu, A. "Planning of Total Resource Use on Low-Income and Part-Time Farms." *J. Farm Econ.* 39:1350-1359, December 1957.

[65] Day, L. "Use of Representative Farms in Studies of Interregional Competition and Production Response." *J. Farm Econ.* 45:1438-1445, December 1963.

[66] Day, R. "On Aggregating Linear Programming Models of Production." *J. Farm Econ.* 45:797-813, November 1963.

[67] ———. "Probability Distributions of Field Crop Yields." *J. Farm Econ.* 47: 713-741, August 1965.

[68] ———. *Recursive Programming and Production Response.* Amsterdam: North Holland Pub. Co., 1963.

[69] Dennis, C. C., and L. L. Sammet. "Interregional Competition in the Frozen Strawberry Industry." *Hilgardia* 31:499-611, 1961.

[70] Dillon, J. "Theoretical and Empirical Approaches to Program Selection within the Feeder Cattle Enterprise." *J. Farm Econ.* 40:1921-1931, December 1958.

[71] Dillon, J., and E. O. Heady. "Free Competition, Uncertainty, and Farmer Decision." *J. Farm Econ.* 43:643-651, August 1961.

[72] Doll, J. P. "The Allocation of Limited Quantities of Variable Resources among Competing Enterprises." *J. Farm Econ.* 41:781-789, November 1959.

[73] Doll, J. P., E. H. Jebe, and R. O. Munson. "Computation of Variance Estimates for Marginal Physical Products and Marginal Rates of Substitution." *J. Farm Econ.* 42:596-607, August 1960.

[74] Doll, J. P., V. J. Rhodes, and J. G. West. *Economics of Agricultural Production, Markets, and Policy.* Homewood, Ill.: Richard D. Irwin, 1968.

[75] Edwards, C. "Resource Fixity and Farm Organization." *J. Farm Econ.* 41: 747-759, November 1959.

[76] Egbert, A. C., and E. O. Heady. *Regional Adjustment in Grain Production — A Linear Programming Analysis.* USDA Tech. Bul. 1241, June 1961.

[77] ———. *Regional Analysis of Production Adjustments in the Major Field Crops: Historical and Prospective — An Application of Spatial Linear Programming.* USDA Tech. Bul. 1294, 1963.

[78] Egbert, A. C., E. O. Heady, and R. F. Brokken. *Regional Changes in Grain Production — An Application of Spatial Linear Programming.* Iowa Agr. Exp. Sta. Res. Bul. 521, 1964.

[79] Eidman, V., G. Dean, and H. Carter. "An Application of Statistical Decision Theory to Commercial Turkey Production." *J. Farm Econ.* 49:852-868, November 1967.

[80] Eidman, V., J. C. Lingle, and H. Carter. "Optimum Fertilization Rates for Crops with Multi-Harvest Periods." *J. Farm Econ.* 45:823-830, November 1963.

[81] Elliott, F. F. *Types of Farming in the United States.* U.S. Department of Commerce, Census Bureau, Washington, D.C., 1933.

[82] Engene, S. A. "Review of Papers on Farm Work Simplification." *J. Farm Econ.* 28:337-340, February 1946.

[83] Eisgruber, L., and E. Reisch. "A Note on the Application of Linear Programming by Agricultural Economics Departments of Land Grant Colleges." *J. Farm Econ.* 43:303-307, May 1961.

[84] Fellows, I. F. "The Application of Static Economic Theory to Farm Management Problems." *J. Farm Econ.* 32:1100-1112, November 1950.

[85] Fisher, W., and L. Schruben. "Linear Programming Applied to Feed-Mixing under Different Price Conditions." *J. Farm Econ.* 35:471-483, November 1953.

[86] French, B. "Functional Relationships for Irrigated Corn Response to Nitrogen." *J. Farm Econ.* 38:736-747, August 1956.

[87] Frick, G., and R. Andrews. "Aggregation Bias and Four Methods of Summing Farm Supply Functions." *J. Farm Econ.* 47:696-700, August 1965.

[88] Fuller, E. I., and H. R. Jensen. *Herd Size Effects on Labor for Loose Housing Chore Tasks.* Minnesota Agr. Exp. Sta. Bul. 462, 1962.

[89] Fusfeld, D. R. "Post-Post-Keynes: The Shattered Synthesis." *Saturday Review*, January 22, 1972, pp. 36-39.

[90] Giaever, H., and J. Seagraves. "Linear Programming and Economies of Size." *J. Farm Econ.* 42:103-117, February 1960.

[91] Griliches, Z. "Specifications Bias in Estimating Production Functions." *J. Farm Econ.* 39:8-20, February 1957.

[92] Hagan, A. "Alternative Sources of Managerial Resources on Farms." *J. Farm Econ.* 44:1450-1460, December 1962.

[93] Hallberg, M. "Projecting the Size Distribution of Agricultural Firms — An Application of a Markov Process with Non-Stationary Transition Probabilities." *Am. J. Agr. Econ.* 51:289-302, May 1969.

[94] Halter, A. "Models of Firm Growth." *J. Farm Econ.* 48:1503-1509, December 1966.

[95] Halter, A., and C. Beringer. "Cardinal Utility Functions and Managerial Behavior." *J. Farm Econ.* 42:118-132, February 1960.

[96] Halter, A., H. Carter, and J. Hocking. "A Note on the Transcendental Production Function." *J. Farm Econ.* 39:966-974, November 1957.

[97] Halter, A., and G. Dean. "Use of Simulation in Evaluating Management Poli-

cies Under Uncertainty: Application to a Large-Scale Ranch." *J. Farm Econ.* 47:557-573, August 1965.

[98] Hanson, P. L. "Input-Output Relationships in Egg Production." *J. Farm Econ.* 31:687-696, November 1949.

[99] Haver, C. B. "Discussion." *J. Farm Econ.* 34:819-821, December 1952.

[100] Headley, J. "Estimating the Productivity of Agricultural Pesticides." *Am. J. Agr. Econ.* 50:13-23, February 1968.

[101] ———. "How Can It Be Recognized?" *J. Farm Econ.* 47:1437-1439, December 1965.

[102] Heady, E. O. "Allocations of Colleges and Economists." *Am. J. Agr. Econ.* 54:934-944, December 1972.

[103] ———. "Application of Recent Economic Theory in Agricultural Production Economics." *J. Farm Econ.* 32:1125-1139, November 1950.

[104] ———. "Basic Logic in Farm and Home Planning in Extension Education." *J. Farm Econ.* 38:80-92, February 1956.

[105] ———. "Diversification in Resource Allocation and Minimization of Income Variability." *J. Farm Econ.* 34:482-496, November 1952.

[106] ———. "Economic Concepts in Directing and Designing Research for Programming Use of Range Resources." *J. Farm Econ.* 38:1604-1616, December 1956.

[107] ———. *Economics of Agricultural Production and Resource Use.* New York: Prentice-Hall, 1952.

[108] ———. "Economics of Rotations." *J. Farm Econ.* 30:645-664, November 1948.

[109] ———. "Elementary Models in Farm Production Economics Research." *J. Farm Econ.* 30:201-225, May 1948.

[110] ———. "Implications of Particular Economics in Agricultural Economics Methodology." *J. Farm Econ.* 31:837-850, November 1949.

[111] ———. "Organization Activities and Criteria in Obtaining and Fitting Technical Production Functions." *J. Farm Econ.* 39:360-369, May 1957.

[112] ———. "A Production Function and Marginal Rates of Substitution in the Utilization of Feed Resources by Dairy Cows." *J. Farm Econ.* 33:485-498, November 1951.

[113] ———. "Progress in Adjusting Agriculture to Economic Change." *J. Farm Econ.* 39:1336-1347, December 1957.

[114] ———. "Public Purpose in Agricultural Research and Education." *J. Farm Econ.* 43:566-581, August 1961.

[115] ———. "Simplified Presentation and Logical Aspects of the Linear Programming Technique." *J. Farm Econ.* 36:1035-1048, December 1954.

[116] ———. "Uncertainty in Market Relationships and Resource Allocation in the Short Run." *J. Farm Econ.* 32:240-257, May 1950.

[117] Heady, E. O., and L. Auer. "Imputation of Production to Technologies." *J. Farm Econ.* 48:309-322, May 1966.

[118] Heady, E. O., S. Balloun, and G. Dean. *Least Cost Rations and Optimum Marketing Weights for Turkeys.* Iowa Agr. Exp. Sta. Res. Bul. 443, 1956.

[119] Heady, E. O., and W. Candler. *Linear Programming Methods.* Ames: Iowa State College Press, 1958.

[120] Heady, E. O., H. Diesslin, H. R. Jensen, and G. L. Johnson, eds. *Agricultural Adjustment Problems in a Growing Economy.* Ames: Iowa State College Press, 1956.

[121] Heady, E. O., and J. Dillon. *Agricultural Production Functions*. Ames: Iowa State University Press, 1961.

[122] Heady, E. O., and H. R. Jensen, *Farm Management Economics*. New York: Prentice-Hall, 1954.

[123] Heady, E. O., G. L. Johnson, and L. S. Hardin, eds. *Resource Productivity, Returns to Scale, and Farm Size*. Ames: Iowa State College Press, 1956.

[124] Heady, E. O., J. Madden, N. Jacobson, and A. Freeman. "Milk Production Functions Incorporating Variables for Cow Characteristics and Environment." *J. Farm Econ.* 46:1-19, February 1964.

[125] Heady, E. O., H. C. Madsen, K. J. Nicol, and S. H. Hargrove. "National and Interregional Models of Water Demand, Land Use, and Agricultural Policies." *Water Resources Research* 9:777-791, August 1973.

[126] Heady, E. O., and R. W. McAlexander. *Least Cost Rations and Optimum Marketing Weight for Broilers*. Iowa Agr. Exp. Sta. Res. Bul. 442, 1956.

[127] Heady, E. O., and R. O. Olson. "Mighell on Methodology." *J. Farm Econ.* 35:269-276, May 1953.

[128] Heady, E. O., and J. Pesek. "A Fertilizer Production Surface." *J. Farm Econ.* 36:466-482, August 1954.

[129] Heady, E. O., J. Schnittker, S. Bloom, and N. Jacobson. "Isoquants, Isoclines, and Economic Predictions in Dairy Production." *J. Farm Econ.* 38:763-779, August 1956.

[130] Heady, E. O., and R. Shaw. "Resource Returns and Productivity Coefficients." *J. Farm Econ.* 36:243-257, May 1954.

[131] Heady, E. O., and M. Skold. *Projections of United States Agricultural Capacity and Interregional Adjustments in Production and Land Use with Spatial Programming Models*. Iowa Agr. Exp. Sta. Res. Bul. 539, 1965.

[132] Heady, E. O., and E. Strand. "Efficiency within American Agriculture." *J. Farm Econ.* 37:524-537, August 1955.

[133] Heady, E. O., and N. K. Whittlesey. *A Programming Analysis of Interregional Competition and Surplus Capacity of American Agriculture*. Iowa Agr. Exp. Sta. Res. Bul. 538, 1965.

[134] Heady, E. O., R. Woodworth, D. Catron, and G. Ashton. "Productivity and Substitution Coefficients in Pork Output." *J. Farm Econ.* 35:341-354, August 1953.

[135] Helfenstine, R. "Estimating Variations in Production and Income Over Time in Farm Plans for the Great Plains." *J. Farm Econ.* 41:262-267, May 1959.

[136] Hicks, J. R. *Value and Capital*. London: Clarendon Press, 1939.

[137] Hildebrand, J. "Some Difficulties with Empirical Results from Whole-Farm Cobb-Douglas-Type Production Functions." *J. Farm Econ.* 42:897-904, November 1960.

[138] Hildreth, R. J. "Influence of Rainfall on Fertilizer Profits." *J. Farm Econ.* 39:522-524, May 1957.

[139] Hoffnar, B. R., and G. L. Johnson. *Cooperative Agronomic-Economic Experiments at Michigan State University*. Michigan Agr. Exp. Sta. Res. Bul. 11, 1966.

[140] Hoglund, C. R., G. L. Johnson, C. A. Lassiter, and L. D. McGilliard, eds. *Nutritional and Economic Aspects of Feed Utilization by Dairy Cows*. Ames: Iowa State College Press, 1958.

[141] Hoover, L., P. Kelley, G. Ward, A. Feyerherm, and R. Chodda. "Economic Relationships of Hay and Concentrate Consumption to Milk Production." *Am. J. Agr. Econ.* 49:64-78, February 1967.

[142] Hopkin, J. "Economies of Size in the Cattle Feeding Industry of California." *J. Farm Econ.* 40:417-429, May 1958.

[143] Hutton, R. F. *An Appraisal of Research on Economics of Fertilizer Use.* TVA, Division of Agricultural Relations, Agricultural Economics Branch, Rep. No. T55-1, 1955.

[144] Ibach, D. "Use of Production Functions in Farm Management Research." *J. Farm Econ.* 35:938-956, December 1953.

[145] Ikerd, J., and A. Schupp. "A Decision Model for Continuous Sequence Production Processes of Variable Length: An Application to Hog Marketing." *Am. J. Agr. Econ.* 51:1159-1163, December 1969.

[146] Irwin, G. "Discussion: Firm Growth Research Opportunities and Techniques." *J. Farm Econ.* 48:1532-1535, December 1966.

[147] James, H. B. "Limitations of Static Economic Theory in Farm Management Analysis." Discussions by S. A. Engene, L. C. Cunningham, and R. E. L. Greene. *J. Farm Econ.* 32:1113-1124, November 1950.

[148] Jensen, E., J. W. Klein, E. Rauchenstein, T. E. Woodward, and R. H. Smith. *Input-Output Relationships in Milk Production.* USDA Tech. Bul. 815, 1942.

[149] Johnson, G. L. "Agricultural Economics, Production Economics, and the Field of Farm Management." *J. Farm Econ.* 39:441-450, May 1957.

[150] ———. "Discussion: Economic Implications of Agricultural Experiments." *J. Farm Econ.* 39:390-397, May 1957.

[151] ———. "Handling Problems of Risk and Uncertainty in Farm Management Analysis." *J. Farm Econ.* 34:807-817, December 1952.

[152] ———. "Major Opportunities for Improving Agricultural Economics Research in the Decade Ahead." *J. Farm Econ.* 36:829-840, December 1954.

[153] ———. "Needed Developments in Economic Theory as Applied to Farm Management." Discussion by C. B. Haver. *J. Farm Econ.* 32:1140-1158, November 1950.

[154] ———. "New Knowledge of Decision-Making Processes." *J. Farm Econ.* 40: 1393-1404, December 1958.

[155] ———. "Results from Production Economics Analysis." *J. Farm Econ.* 37: 206-222, May 1955.

[156] ———. "The Role of Management in Planning Farms for Optimum Fertilizer Use." In *Economic and Technical Analysis of Fertilizer Innovations and Resource Use,* E. Baum, E. O. Heady, J. Pesek, C. Hildreth, eds. Ames: Iowa State College Press, 1957.

[157] ———. "Stress on Production Economics." *Australian J. Agr. Econ.* 7:12-26, 1963.

[158] Johnson, G. L., A. Halter, H. R. Jensen, and D. Thomas, eds. *A Study of Managerial Processes of Midwestern Farmers.* Ames: Iowa State University Press, 1961.

[159] Johnson, G. L., and L. S. Hardin. *Economics of Forage Valuation.* Agr. Ext. Serv., Sta. Bul. 623, Purdue University, 1955.

[160] Johnson, P. R. "Alternative Functions for Analyzing a Fertilizer-Yield Relationship." *J. Farm Econ.* 35:519-529, November 1953.

[161] ———. "Do Farmers Hold a Preference for Risk?" *J. Farm Econ.* 44:200-207, February 1962.

[162] ———. "Effects of Off-Farm Migration of Managers on Managerial Resources in Agriculture." *J. Farm Econ.* 44:1462-1471, December 1962.

[163] Johnson, S. "A Re-examination of the Farm Diversification Problem." *J. Farm Econ.* 49:610-612, August 1967.

[164] Johnson, S., K. Tefertiller, and D. Moore. "Stochastic Linear Programming and Feasibility Problems in Farm Growth Analysis." *J. Farm Econ.* 49:908-919, November 1967.

[165] Johnson, S. E. "The Theory of Combination of Enterprises on Individual Farms." *J. Farm Econ.* 15:656-667, October 1933.

[166] Johnson, S. E., and K. L. Bachman. "Introduction: Development of Production Economics in Agriculture." In *Economics for Agriculture: Selected Writings of John D. Black*, J. P. Cavin, ed. Cambridge, Mass.: Harvard University Press, 1959.

[167] Jones, L. "Stabilizing Farming by Shifting Wheat Land to Grass in the Northern Great Plains." *J. Farm Econ.* 32:375-390, August 1950.

[168] Kadlec, J. "Production Management Research for Farm Decision Making — the Livestock Enterprises." *J. Farm Econ.* 46:1172-1178, December 1964.

[169] Kanel, D. "Farm Adjustments by Age Groups, North Central States 1950-1959." *J. Farm Econ.* 45:47-60, February 1963.

[170] Katzman, I. "Solving Feed Problems Through Linear Programming." *J. Farm Econ.* 38:420-429, May 1956.

[171] Kelsey, M. "Is It an Art or Science?" *J. Farm Econ.* 47:1433-1436, December 1965.

[172] Kelso, M. "A Critical Appraisal of Agricultural Economics in the Mid-Sixties." *J. Farm Econ.* 47:1-16, February 1965.

[173] Kennedy, R. "New Tools for the Manager." *J. Farm Econ.* 47:1452-1456, December 1965.

[174] King, R. A. "Some Applications of Activity Analysis in Agricultural Economics." *J. Farm Econ.* 35:823-833, December 1953.

[175] Knetsch, J. L. "Moisture Uncertainties and Fertility Response Studies." *J. Farm Econ.* 41:70-76, February 1959.

[176] Knudtson, A., and W. Cochrane. "A Supply Function for Flax at the Firm Level." *J. Farm Econ.* 40:117-123, February 1958.

[177] Kottke, M. "Withdrawal of Resources out of Agriculture in an Expanding Urban Industrial Economy." *J. Farm Econ.* 42:1508-1509, December 1960.

[178] Krause, K., and L. Kyle. "Economic Factors Underlying the Incidence of Large Farming Units: The Current Situation." *Am. J. Agr. Econ.* 52:748-761, December 1970.

[179] Langham, M. "Discussion: Analytics of Decision Making." *J. Farm Econ.* 46:1362-1364, December 1964.

[180] Langvatn, H. N. "An Approach to the Effect of Size and Combination of Enterprises on Farm Labor Consumption." *J. Farm Econ.* 42:79-89, February 1960.

[181] Lanpher, B. "Use of Economic Theory in Farm Management." *J. Farm Econ.* 43:1490-1496, December 1961.

[182] Lee, J., and E. Chastain. "The Role of Problem Recognition in Managerial Adjustments." *J. Farm Econ.* 42:650-659, August 1960.

[183] Loftsgard, L., and E. O. Heady. "Application of Dynamic Programming Models for Optimum Farm and Home Plans." *J. Farm Econ.* 41:51-62, February 1959.

[184] Maruyama, Y., and E. I. Fuller. "Alternative Solution Procedures for Mixed Integer Programming Problems." *J. Farm Econ.* 46:1213-1218, December 1964.

[185] Mason, D. D. "Statistical Problems in Joint Research." *J. Farm Econ.* 39:370-381, May 1957.

[186] McAlexander, R., and R. F. Hutton. "Determining Least-Cost Combinations." *J. Farm Econ.* 39:936-941, November 1957.

[187] McConnen, R. "Decision Theory, Climatic Variability, and 'Best' Short-Run Management Strategies." *J. Farm Econ.* 43:1340-1341, December 1961.

[188] McCorkle, C., Jr. "Linear Programming as a Tool in Farm Management Analysis." *J. Farm Econ.* 37:1222-1235, December 1955.

[189] McPherson, W. W. "Sources and Use of Technical Data in Farm Management Analysis." *J. Farm Econ.* 34:799-806, December 1952.

[190] Merrill, W. "Alternative Programming Models Involving Uncertainty." *J. Farm Econ.* 47:595-610, August 1965.

[191] Mighell, R. L. "A Further Note on the Equal Product Function." *J. Farm Econ.* 35:29-43, February 1953.

[192] ———. "Vertical Integration and Farm Management." *J. Farm Econ.* 39:1666-1669, December 1957.

[193] ———. "What is the Place of the Equal-Product Function?" *J. Farm Econ.* 35:29-43, February 1953.

[194] Mighell, R. L., and J. D. Black. *Interregional Competition in Agriculture.* Cambridge: Harvard University Press, 1951.

[195] Miller, L., and W. Back. "Effect of Scientific Progress on Size and Efficiency of Farms in the Plains." *J. Farm Econ.* 40:1250-1262, December 1958.

[196] Moore, C. V. "A General Framework for Estimating the Production Function for Crops Using Irrigation Water." *J. Farm Econ.* 43:876-888, November 1961.

[197] Morrison, T., and G. G. Judge. "Impact of Price Expectations and Uncertainties on Decision Making by Poultry Farms." *J. Farm Econ.* 37:652-663, November 1955.

[198] Mosher, M. L. "Thirty Years of Farm Financial and Production Records in Illinois." *J. Farm Econ.* 27:24-37, February 1945.

[199] Mueller, A. "Flow-of-Funds Analysis in Farm Financial Management." *J. Farm Econ.* 48:661-667, August 1966.

[200] Mundlak, Y. "Specification and Estimation of Agricultural Production Functions." *J. Farm Econ.* 45:433-443, May 1963.

[201] Musgrave, W. "A Note on Integer Programming and the Problem of Increasing Returns." *J. Farm Econ.* 44:1068-1076, November 1962.

[202] Nelson, A. G. "The Management Factor in Commercial Agriculture: How Can It Be Improved?" *J. Farm Econ.* 47:1446-1448, December 1965.

[203] ———. "Financing Representative Farms in 1975." *J. Farm Econ.* 42:1380-1390, December 1960.

[204] ———. *Relation of Feed Consumed to Food Products Produced in Fattening Cattle.* USDA Tech. Bul. 900, 1945.

[205] Nesius, E. J. "Some Problems of Joint Use of Theory and Empirical Data in Farm Management Research." *J. Farm Econ.* 32:1169-1181, November 1950.

[206] Neuman, D. "Capital Requirements and Financing Practices for Restructuring Southern Agriculture." *J. Farm Econ.* 48:1550-1560, December 1966.

[207] Newman, W. H., C. E. Summer, and E. K. Warren. *The Process of Management.* Englewood Cliffs, N.J.: Prentice-Hall, 1967. (See chapter 2.)

[208] Officer, R., and A. Halter. "Utility Analysis in a Practical Setting." *Am. J. Agr. Econ.* 50:257-277, May 1968.

[209] Orazem, F., and R. B. Herring. "Economic Aspects of the Effects of Fertilizer, Soil Moisture, and Rainfall on the Yields of Grain Sorghum in the 'Sandy Lands' of Southwest Kansas." *J. Farm Econ.* 40:697-708, August 1958.

[210] Ottoson, H., and A. Epp. "Size of Farm and Farming Efficiency in Northeastern Nebraska." *J. Farm Econ.* 38:803-812, August 1956.

[211] Paris, Q., F. Malossini, A. Pilla, and A. Romita. "A Note on Milk Production Functions." *Am. J. Agr. Econ.* 52:594-598, November 1970.

[212] Partenheimer, E. "Executive Skills and Executive Capacity in Farm Management." *J. Farm Econ.* 44:1475-1482, December 1962.

[213] Patrick, G., and L. Eisgruber. "The Impact of Managerial Ability and Capital Structure on Growth of the Farm Firm." *Am. J. Agr. Econ.* 50:491-506, August 1968.

[214] Peterson, G. "Selection of Maximum Profit Combinations of Livestock Enterprises and Crop Rotations." *J. Farm Econ.* 37:546-554, August 1955.

[215] Plaunt, D. "Use of High-Speed Computers for Farm Record Keeping and Data Collection in Farm Business Analysis." *J. Farm Econ.* 45:1192-1199, December 1963.

[216] Plaxico, J. "Problems of Factor-Product Aggregation in Cobb-Douglas Value Productivity Analysis." *J. Farm Econ.* 37:664-675, November 1955.

[217] Plaxico, J., and F. Wiegmann. "Allocation of Resources in Farm Management and Production Economics Research." *J. Farm Econ.* 39:86-93, February 1957.

[218] Pond, G. A., S. A. Engene, T. R. Nodland, S. O. Berg, and C. W. Crickman. *The First Sixty Years of Farm Management Research in Minnesota, 1902-1962.* Dept. Agr. Econ., Agr. Econ. Rep. 283, University of Minnesota, 1965.

[219] Puterbaugh, H., E. Kehrberg, and J. Dunbar. "Analyzing the Solution Tableau of a Simplex Linear Programming Problem in Farm Organization." *J. Farm Econ.* 39:478-489, 1957.

[220] Ratchford, C. B. "Selecting Economic Data to Present to Farmers." *J. Farm Econ.* 34:828-836, December 1952.

[221] Raup, P. "Economies and Diseconomies of Large-Scale Agriculture." *Am. J. Agr. Econ.* 51:1274-1283, December 1969.

[222] Redman, J. C. "Economic Aspects of Feeding for Milk Production." *J. Farm Econ.* 34:333-345, August 1952.

[223] Redman, J. C., and S. Q. Allen. "Some Interrelationships of Economic and Agronomic Concepts." *J. Farm Econ.* 36:453-465, August 1954.

[224] Rieck, R. "How Can It Be Taught?" *J. Farm Econ.* 47:1449-1451, December 1965.

[225] Rogers, G. "Credit in the Poultry Industry." *J. Farm Econ.* 45:409-415, May 1963.

[226] Roth, W. J., and H. R. Tolley. "Recent Trends in Farm Management Research." In *Research in Farm Management: Scope and Method.* Social Science Research Council Bul. 13, 1932.

[227] Routhe, H. "The Application of Decision-Making Processes in Extension Work in Farm Management." *J. Farm Econ.* 44:1497-1508, December 1962.

[228] Roy, E. "A Method of Comparing Contract Proposals for Broiler-Chicken Production." *J. Farm Econ.* 47:973-978, November 1965.

[229] Rushton, W., and E. Shaudys. "A Systematic Conceptualization of Farm Management." *J. Farm Econ.* 49:53-63, February 1967.

[230] Ruttan, V. "Issues in the Evolution of Production Economics." *J. Farm Econ.* 49:1490-1499, December 1967.

[231] ———. "Production Economics for Agricultural Development." *Indian J. Agr. Econ.* 23:1-14, April-June 1968.

[232] Schechter, M., and E. O. Heady. "Response Surface Analysis and Simulation Models in Policy Choices." *Am. J. Agr. Econ.* 52:41-50, February 1970.

[233] Schickel, R. "Farmers Adaptations to Income Uncertainty." *J. Farm Econ.* 32:356-374, August 1950.

[234] Schrader, L. F., and G. A. King. "Regional Location of Beef Cattle Feeding." *J. Farm Econ.* 44:64-81, February 1962.

[235] Schultz, T. W. "Output-Input Relationships Revisited." *J. Farm Econ.* 40:924-932, November 1958.

[236] ———. "Theory of the Firm and Farm Management Research." *J. Farm Econ.* 21:570-586, August 1939.

[237] ———. "Theory of the Firm and Farm Management Research." *J. Farm Econ.* 21:583-584, August 1939.

[238] Seagraves, J. "Estimating Labor Requirements — A Broiler Production Example." *J. Farm Econ.* 42:1516-1517, December 1960.

[239] Sheehy, S., and R. McAlexander. "Selection of Representative Benchmark Farms for Supply Estimation." *J. Farm Econ.* 47:681-695, August 1965.

[240] Smith, V. "Perfect vs. Discontinuous Input Markets: A Linear Programming Analysis." *J. Farm Econ.* 37:538-545, August 1955.

[241] Southern Agricultural Experiment Stations and the Farm Foundation with the cooperation of FERD, ARS, and USDA. *Farm Size and Output Research: A Study in Research Methods.* Southern Cooperative Series Bul. 56, 1958.

[242] Spillman, W. J. "Systems of Farm Management in the United States" in *Yearbook of the United States Department of Agriculture 1902.* Washington, D.C.: Government Printing Office, 1903.

[243] ———. *Use of the Exponential Yield Curve in Fertilizer Experiments.* USDA Tech. Bul. 348, 1933.

[244] Spillman, W. J., and E. Lang. *The Law of Diminishing Returns.* New York: World Book Co., 1924.

[245] Staniforth, S. "Combating Uncertainty in Agricultural Production." *J. Farm Econ.* 36:87-97, February 1954.

[246] Stanton, B., and L. Kettunen. "Potential Entrants and Projections in Markov Process Analysis." *J. Farm Econ.* 49:633-642, August 1967.

[247] Stedry, A. C. "Market versus Behavioral Theories of the Firm and Basic Managerial Research" in *Production Economics in Agricultural Research.* Conference Proceedings AE-4108, University of Illinois, March 1966.

[248] Stewart, H. L. "The Organization and Structure of Some Representative Farms in 1975." *J. Farm Econ.* 42:1367-1379, December 1960.

[249] Stovall, J. "Income Variation and Selection of Enterprises." *J. Farm Econ.* 48:1575-1579, December 1966.

[250] Suttor, R., and R. Crom. "Computer Models and Simulation." *J. Farm Econ.* 46:1341-1350, December 1964.

[251] Swanson, E. "Application of Programming Analysis to Cornbelt Farms," *J. Farm Econ.* 38:408-419, May 1956.

[252] ———. "Problems of Applying Experimental Results to Commercial Practice." *J. Farm Econ.* 39:382-389, May 1957.

[253] ———. "Resource Adjustments on 146 Commercial Cornbelt Farms, 1936-1953." *J. Farm Econ.* 39:502-505, May 1957.

[254] ———. "Solving Minimum-Cost Feed Mix Problems." *J. Farm Econ.* 37:135-139, February 1955.

[255] Swanson, E., and K. Fox. "The Selection of Livestock Enterprises by Activity Analysis." *J. Farm Econ.* 36:78-86, February 1954.

[256] Tadros, M., and G. Casler. "A Game Theoretic Model for Farm Planning Under Uncertainty." *Am. J. Agr. Econ.* 51:1164-1167, December 1969.

[257] Taylor, H. C. *Introduction to the Study of Agricultural Economics.* New York: Macmillan, 1905.

[258] ———. *Outlines of Agricultural Economics.* New York: Macmillan, 1925.

[259] ———. "Research in Agricultural Economics." *J. Farm Econ.* 10:33-41, January 1928.

[260] Taylor, H. C., and A. D. Taylor. *The Story of Agricultural Economics.* Ames: Iowa State College Press, 1952.

[261] Tedford, J. "Analytics of Decision Making." *J. Farm Econ.* 46:1353-1362, December 1964.

[262] Tompkin, J. R. "Response of Farm Production Unit as a Whole to Prices." *J. Farm Econ.* 40:1115-1128, December 1958.

[263] Tramel, T. E. "Alternative Methods of Using Production Functions for Making Recommendations." *J. Farm Econ.* 39:790-793, August 1957.

[264] Trant, G. "Adjusting for Changes in Price Levels in Value Productivity Studies." *J. Farm Econ.* 37:563-566, August 1955.

[265] Ulveling, E., and L. Fletcher. "A Cobb-Douglas Production Function with Variable Returns to Scale." *Am. J. Agr. Econ.* 52:322-326, May 1970.

[266] Vandenborre, R., and W. McCarthy. "Determination of Optimal Input Levels in Cobb-Douglas Analysis." *J. Farm Econ.* 49:940-942, November 1967.

[267] Vandeputte, J., and C. Baker. "Income, Taxes, Consumption, Savings." *Am. J. Agr. Econ.* 52:521-527, November 1970.

[268] van Vleet, H. "Increased Capital Requirements and the Problem of Getting Started in Farming." *J. Farm Econ.* 40:1613-1622, December 1958.

[269] Vaughan, L. M., and L. S. Hardin. *Farm Work Simplification.* New York: Wiley, 1949.

[270] Walker, O., and J. Martin. "Firm Growth Research Opportunities and Techniques." *J. Farm Econ.* 14:2-9, January 1932.

[271] Warren, G. F. "The Origin and Development of Farm Economics in the United States." *J. Farm Econ.* 14:2-9, January 1932.

[272] Warren, S. W. "Forty Years of Farm Management Surveys." *J. Farm Econ.* 27: 18-23, February 1945.

[273] Waugh, F. V. "Applicability of Recent Developments in Methodology to Agricultural Economics." *J. Farm Econ.* 35:692-706, December 1953.

[274] ———. "The Minimum Cost Dairy Feed." *J. Farm Econ.* 33:299-310, August 1951.

[275] Weeks, E. "Maximum Profit Livestock Rations That Include Wheat." *J. Farm Econ.* 47:669-680, August 1965.

[276] Whittlesey, N. K., and E. O. Heady. *Aggregate Economic Effects of Alternative Land Retirement Programs: A Linear Programming Analysis.* USDA Tech. Bul. 1351, 1966.

[277] Wilcox, W. W., S. E. Johnson, and S. W. Warren. *Farm Management Research, 1940-1941: A Report by the Subcommittee on Farm Management.* Social Science Research Council Bul. 52, 1943.

[278] Williams, D. B. "Price Expectations and Reactions to Uncertainty by Farmers in Illinois." *J. Farm Econ.* 33:20-39, February 1951.

[279] ———. "Production Economics, Farm Management, and Extension." *Am. J. Agr. Econ.* 51:57-70, February 1969.

[280] Wipf, L., and D. Bawden. "Reliability of Supply Equations Derived from Production Functions." *Am. J. Agr. Econ.* 51:170-178, February 1969.

[281] Wirth, M. "Lifetime Changes in Financial Problems of Farmers." *J. Farm Econ.* 46:1191-1197, December 1964.

[282] Woodworth, H. "Farm Management Research Needs in New England." *J. Farm Econ.* 26:503-513, August 1944.

[283] Yotopoulos, P. "From Stock to Flow Capital Inputs for Agricultural Production Functions: A Microanalytic Approach." *J. Farm Econ.* 49:476-479, May 1967.

[284] Young, E. C., and I. R. Bierly. "The Future of Farm Work Simplification Research." *J. Farm Econ.* 28:331-337, February 1946.

[285] Zusman, P., and A. Amiad. "Simulation: A Tool for Farm Planning under Conditions of Weather Uncertainty." *J. Farm Econ.* 47:574-594, August 1965.

Part II. The Analysis of Productive Efficiency
in Agricultural Marketing:
Models, Methods, and Progress

I am indebted to Emerson Babb, Harold F. Breimyer, Hoy F. Carman, Carleton C. Dennis, Peter G. Helmberger, Gordon A. King, Richard A. King, Samuel H. Logan, Lee R. Martin, Loy L. Sammet, and James D. Shaffer for very helpful comments on earlier drafts of this paper. Carlos Benito and Steven Buccola provided valuable assistance in assembling the large number of research reports. Special thanks go to Alice Munoz for typing the manuscript(s) and the long list of references.

B. C. F.

The Analysis of Productive Efficiency in Agricultural Marketing: Models, Methods, and Progress

Ben C. French
Professor of Agricultural Economics
University of California, Davis

Although the efficiency of the marketing system has been a matter of public interest for many years, attempts to improve it through economic research were quite limited until the passage of the Agricultural Marketing Act of 1946. This act provided an expression of official concern with efficiency, a set of broad goals, and, most importantly, money to support research. It stated, among other things, that "a sound, efficient, and privately operated system for distributing and marketing agricultural products is essential to a prosperous agriculture and is indispensable to the maintenance of full employment and to the welfare, prosperity, and health of the Nation." To aid in achieving such a system, it further declared, "it is the intent of Congress to provide for . . . continuous research to improve the marketing, handling, storage, processing, transportation and distribution of agricultural products" [3] .

Measured in terms of dollars spent and reports issued, it would appear that the congressional intent has indeed been carried out. In the period since World War II the United States Department of Agriculture and the state experiment stations (with federal help) have allocated between $4 million and $8 million per year to projects dealing with efficiency in various parts of the marketing system for agricultural products.[1] The results of these expenditures are described in some seven hundred research reports and journal articles concerned with productive efficiency and a substantial number of similar publications dealing with related studies of interregional competition and pricing efficiency.[2]

93

In this paper I describe and evaluate the contributions of the many studies of productive efficiency to the field of agricultural market analysis and to the improvement of marketing operations. More specifically, I attempt to set forth and tie together the emerging elements of theory which seem especially relevant to the study of marketing efficiency, to review and evaluate the empirical methodology that has been developed, to summarize (within broad limits) some of the major results and findings of the empirical studies, and finally to offer some suggestions about future directions and development in this type of research.

The subject matter in this review is restricted primarily to the area of productive efficiency in the expectation that efficiency of the pricing and exchange system in the competitive or structural sense will be covered in other reviews.[3] Limitation of the scope in this manner seemed necessary because of the large amount of research activity and the extensive body of literature pertaining to the subject. Since pricing and productive efficiency may sometimes be interrelated, the boundaries imposed should be regarded as matters of convenience, not as clear delineations.

On the Meaning of Efficiency

Economists, in writing about efficiency, have been quick to point out that it is a deceptively complex concept. Waugh [95], for example, made this observation: "An unsophisticated student might make two false assumptions: first, that it is easy to define (and to measure) the efficiency of agricultural marketing; and second, that almost everyone is in favor of efficiency. Actually, the concept of efficiency is very difficult when applied to a complex problem such as the marketing of farm products. And actually the public may prefer to keep some known inefficiencies, rather than to adopt new methods — especially if the prospective improvements in efficiency might reduce employment, decrease price competition, or lead to greater concentration of economic power." The definition and dimensions of efficiency vary at different levels within the market economy and become increasingly complex as we move from the firm to an industry or group and finally to the total system.

The individual marketing firm (or any other firm) is said to be *technically efficient* if its production function yields the greatest output for any set of inputs, given its particular location and environment. If some other production function is used, the ratio of output obtained with this function to output obtained with the best function, given the input combinations, is a measure of the degree of technical efficiency (see Farrell [210] and Timmer [246]). Neoclassical economic theory has traditionally assumed that firms operate with technically efficient production functions; since this is not always true in the real world, the determination of technical efficiency is quite important for applied economists. Leibenstein [49] refers to actual productive performance relative to the production frontier as "X-efficiency." As reasons for deviations from the frontier he includes incomplete knowledge of available techniques, motivation, learning, and psychological factors. Cyert and March [21] have developed the concept of "organizational slack" as another factor accounting for such deviations.

Firms that are technically efficient still may be inefficient in a pricing sense if they fail to combine inputs so that marginal revenue products are equal to factor prices (or marginal factor costs). Firm *pricing efficiency*, or preferably *allocative efficiency*, is measured relative to the efficient production function as the ratio of cost with optimal input proportions to cost with the input proportions actually used (Bressler and King [14], Farrell [210], and Timmer [246]). The product of the index of technical efficiency and the index of allocative efficiency is a measure of *economic efficiency* of the firm. A firm that is efficient both technically and allocatively has an economic efficiency index of 1.0. Note that a plant may be both technically and economically efficient for its scale but inefficient with respect to its optimum scale. Optimum scale may also vary with relative factor prices (see Seitz [236]).

The total marketing system or an industry subsystem may be said to be efficient if (a) all firms are economically efficient as noted above, (b) the industry is organized to utilize capacity and to take full advantage of scale and location economies, and (c) the industry operates under exchange mechanisms that generate prices which conform to a competitive standard such as the perfect market. The degree to which (a) and (b) are achieved together is commonly referred to as *productive efficiency*, and the degree to which (c) is achieved is referred to as *pricing efficiency* (Bressler and King [14]).[4] Helmberger [36] has coined the term "O-efficiency" to describe the efficiency of alternative organizational configurations under (b) above and overlapping (c) as well. He includes the mix of conscious planning and unconscious market coordination as factors affecting O-efficiency. The prospects for accurate measurement of departures from O-efficiency, however, are described as "downright dismal."

The rigorous definitions of technical, allocative, and pricing efficiency derived from static neoclassical theory are strictly valid only in a timeless framework. Since real economic systems are characterized by uncertainty and continual changes in technology and environmental factors, measurement of efficiency at a single point in time may be illusory or misleading. What we need to know is the optimal utilization of resources and organization of industries over periods of time, given the facts of uncertainty and change. Efficiency thus should be measured as a function of time paths of system behavior relative to some optimal path. Progress on formulating such a dynamic framework appears to have been very limited to date.

Research supported by public funds must also consider the broader social implications of the results such as the external costs of new systems and production techniques and the way in which research benefits are distributed. Defining and measuring efficiency in this general context is very difficult. Members of a work group at the 1955 National Workshop on Agricultural Marketing, after struggling with the problem at length, decided that at all levels efficiency may be defined simply as the ratio of ends to resources. "What makes the strategic difference between the individual and the group is the differing content each might give to ends and resources" [87]. The ends relevant to the examination of efficiency of the economy may differ from those of total agriculture, or the agricultural marketing system, or an industry, or a firm. Further, as we move from the firm to more aggregative levels in the system, there is less and less agreement on which ends are relevant. Therefore, there is less and less agreement on what is truly efficient.

This uncomfortable state of affairs led Kohls [47] to call for workers in policy and workers in marketing to join forces. He further suggested that methods must be found by which the talents of other social scientists can be utilized. Although progress with respect to the last point appears to have been somewhat limited, the emergence of the "systems approach" seems likely to shift research approaches substantially in the direction desired by Kohls. The systems approach has been described by Churchman [18] as "a continuing debate between various attitudes of mind with respect to society." It focuses on the performance of total systems, with clear recognition that the optimization process may require some trade-off in efficiency among subsystems. This is consistent with Waugh's statement that some known inefficiencies may actually be preferred.

Economic research relating to productive efficiency may lead to improved marketing performance (1) by determining the relative efficiency of existing alternative production methods, scale of operations, and business practices, thereby aiding individual marketing firms to move to the most efficient production function for their environment (Leibenstein's X-efficiency), or to an improved position on a given production function, and (2) by formulating models of efficient organization within market areas or industries. The latter may serve as planning guides for industry groups and as aids to policy formulation for public agencies and legislative bodies.[5]

Efficiency may also be improved by developing new production techniques which lead to higher-level production functions. This is primarily an engineering or biological problem. Economists may be concerned, however, in at least three ways: in the allocation of resources to technological research and development; in cost-benefit studies of new production techniques under varying factor costs and environmental conditions; and in evaluating the effects of new techniques on the economic organization and structure of the industry and the broader benefits to society. The study of the welfare effects of the tomato harvester by Schmitz and Seckler [71] provides an excellent example of an approach to the latter type of concern.

Formulation of a Theoretical Framework

It has been argued effectively that there need be no special economic theory of marketing (Mehren [56]). This would seem particularly true in the production of marketing services; the essential guides for empirical analyses relating to efficiency in agricultural marketing are or should be provided by the general body of microeconomic theory of the firm.

While accepting this view (see, for example, Boger [9]), marketing economists of the 1940s and 1950s discovered that the neoclassical theory, as formulated in the textbooks of that period, left much to be desired for their purposes.[6] There were two major sources of difficulty. First, much of the conventional firm theory was aimed at developing a base for explaining resource allocation, market price, total output, and factor shares with rather less concern for the development of a base for empirical analysis.[7] Second, and perhaps more importantly, the theory was expressed in a single dimension — *rates* of output and *rates* of input. Marketing operations, on the other hand, involved the added dimensions of time (length of operation), space, and form that, until recently, were accorded little attention in micro-theory texts.

Elaborations of the neoclassical theory during the past two decades have provided a more suitable framework for empirical studies of marketing efficiency. Many of these elaborations have been formulated without any particular reference to agricultural marketing (see Dano [22] , Ferguson [29] , Naylor and Vernon [63] , and Shepard [76]) and may be considered a part of the current general core of microeconomic theory. No attempt will be made here to review such developments. There are, however, several types of modifications and extensions, growing substantially out of the work of agricultural economists, which are particularly relevant to marketing firm management and the study of marketing efficiency. They have involved (1) more precise and detailed specifications of production organization and methods of combining inputs, (2) incorporation of the length of operation as an added dimension of plant cost functions, (3) further elaboration of the nature of multiple service operations, (4) explicit development of the spatial dimensions of firm efficiency, and (5) formulation of models pertaining to total systems.

Production Systems in Marketing Firms

Agricultural systems transform raw materials such as seeds or feed and inputs of chemicals, water, and energy into products such as bales of cotton, tons of apples, or numbers of slaughter-weight steers. *Marketing* systems transform the products of agricultural production systems and inputs such as chemicals, water, and energy into intermediate products such as mixed feeds and into consumer products distributed geographically and temporally. Although resting on the same basic concepts of productive activity, the two systems differ in the conceptualization of the product, the time flow of inputs and outputs, and to some degree the interdependence of the separate plant processes.

In contrast to the more easily recognized and defined products of farm firms, the product of marketing firms is the *service* involved in transforming or transferring the basic farm products. The quantity of a service such as packaging fresh apples and arranging for their sale and shipment may be closely correlated with the physical volume of product handled. In many cases, however, the service is a complex bundle involving time, space, and form dimensions which may be difficult to measure. The output of a supermarket, for example, consists of the service associated with assembling six thousand or so items in a convenient location where they are readily available to consumers. The measurement of this product is considerably more difficult than is suggested by the usual presentation of neoclassical production theory. This still substantially unresolved problem in the analysis of sales-oriented firms will be discussed further in a later section.

Farm firm inputs are applied to fixed land or livestock units and outputs are obtained at intermittent intervals. Usually it is possible to vary the amount of farm inputs continuously since input and output rates are measured seasonally. Inputs of many marketing firms, on the other hand, are applied to time flows of raw farm products from which outputs emerge in continuous streams. An important result of this difference, at least for purposes of empirical analysis, is that labor cost functions which often would be continuous in farm firms may be discontinuous step functions in marketing firms. The discontinuities arise from the commonly used pricing system for labor which requires that workers be paid for time on the job rather than time actually worked. Although some farm labor is fixed per season, the inputs of hourly paid labor typically can be varied so that time on the job and time worked coincide. In marketing firms labor inputs must be purchased in whole units even though the rate of material flow might require fractional man-hours per unit of time – thus the step-type function. Continuous cost functions in empirical models of marketing firms, therefore, must be regarded generally as approximations adopted for ease of manipulation, not as precise measures of cost-output relationships.

The more careful scrutiny of production systems required for effective studies of marketing efficiency made postwar agricultural economists increasingly aware of a fact engineers presumably took for granted — that most plant operations consist of many processes. Following Jantzen [45] and Kutish [48], French, Sammet, and Bressler [401] referred to these processes as *stages*. Most stages are organized sequentially about the flow of materials through the plant. A fruit-packing operation, for example, might be divided into stages such as receiving raw produce, dumping produce on conveyers, grading, packing, lidding, loading, receiving container materials, and assembling container materials. A meat-packing operation might involve processes such as receiving, slaughtering, dressing, cooling, and delivery. Nonsequential stages include overall management, record keeping, cleaning, maintenance, and storage operations. Activities within the latter stages may often occur at times that do not coincide exactly with the operations of flow-oriented stages and may relate to total output within some time period, such as a day, rather than to rates of flow.

Compatibility of product and material flow among sequential stages is maintained by adjusting input levels at each stage to the flow of output from the previous stage and by providing temporary storage between stages to smooth out irregularities in rates of outputs among processes. Such storage increases with the degree of irregularity of flow and, of course, adds to the cost of operation.

Processes often are organized in parallel fashion. This may occur in two ways — as a series of identical machines within a process or as a series of usually identical production lines across processes. A fruit-packing plant, for example, may have many identical packing stations within the grading stage. It may also have several production lines, each of which includes a nearly complete sequence of stages. Joel Dean [23] referred to this as "unit segmentation."

Plants with parallel organizations typically vary rates of output by varying the number of identical production units in use. In the common case where equipment units and labor are combined in fixed proportions, this produces a discontinuous stair-step type cost function that is linear in overall shape. Where it is possible to vary labor input per machine or production line by crowding workers or increasing the machine speed, the steps in the function will be less regular, and diminishing returns may occur with respect to the utilization of each machine. Optimum utilization requires that as output rates are increased each *identical* machine or production line is operated at the same rate (see French, Sammet, and Bressler [401, pp. 551-553] and Dano [22, pp. 111-114]).[8] The total function associated with varying the number of machines will be linear-homogenous in general shape.

If stages and production lines are appropriately defined to be independent except for the flow of materials between them, each may be thought of as having its own production function.[9] Thus, we have many "plants" within a plant, and the single production function of neoclassical theory is actually an aggregation of many component production functions. While this does not invalidate the concepts and conclusions of the neoclassical formulations, it suggests some possible modifications with regard to determining optimum input combinations and approaches to efficient organization of marketing systems.

An obvious point is that factors are combined stage by stage or process by process. The stage then is the appropriate initial focal point for managerial input decisions and for the empirical measurement of cost functions.

In many cases factor proportions are fixed by the technology used, and the problem of determining optimum factor combinations becomes trivial in the short run and not directly meaningful in the long run. Consider a given plant in the short run with a specified production system producing a particular set of marketing services. Examination of the activities within and between stages will reveal in most instances that the opportunities for factor substitution are highly restricted. For example, chemicals and packaging materials are not substitutes for labor, and ordinarly labor energy cannot be substituted for electrical or mechanical energy used to operate machinery. Often the inputs become embodied in the product in such a way that changing the inputs defines a new product. Some substitution may be possible within classes of inputs — for example, among chemicals or, in rare cases, among types of labor — but such opportunities would appear to be rather limited.

The main factor substitution possibilities are between labor and machinery, which may require changes in the production technology.[10] Under these circumstances we are not concerned with factor substitution as such but with the selection of the best production function. If we are suitably vague in defining inputs, including an amorphous view of capital, we can, of course, define a long-run production function which embodies the best parts of all possible short-run production functions. This is the neoclassical approach (see [29, p. 154] and [249]). Optimum input combinations are then determined by the usual mathematical manipulations of calculus. Such a functional concept may be useful in formulating models to explain the price system and broad categories of resource allocation, but it is of limited value to the empirical analyst or a plant manager. What is required is stage-by-stage examination of alternative production techniques and selection of the sets of techniques which minimize costs of producing any volume of marketing services,

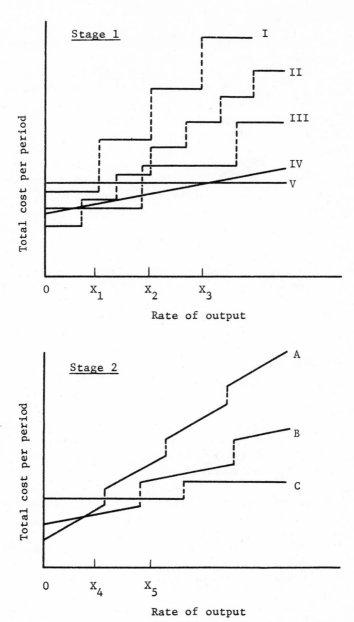

Figure 1. Cost functions for alternative technologies at two plant stages, with operating time per demand or sale period held at a specific figure. Source: French, Sammet, and Bressler [401].

given the environment within which the firm must operate. Aggregation over stages then defines the optimum combination of factors.

The nature of the selection procedure is illustrated in figure 1. The hypothetical stage cost functions shown represent several alternative production techniques for two of the independent plant stages, defined in terms of specific combinations of equipment and variable inputs. If input substitution were possible, least-cost combinations of inputs would be implied. Each curve shows the total stage cost per seasonal period — including operating costs and returns above variable costs required to maintain and replace the durable factors — expressed in relation to the rate of output. The time of operation per seasonal period is held constant. The curve representing each production technique may be viewed as an "envelope" to the cost curves of plants of different size and employing different quantities of the same type of inputs (all using the same basic production technique). The intercept values represent the minimum inputs if production is to occur at all.

Another envelope may be drawn to the curve representing the different production techniques to obtain the long-run cost functions for each stage. In the example technique II in stage 1 is least costly if hourly volume is less than OX_1. Technique III is least costly if output is between OX_1 and OX_2; technique IV is least costly for rates of output between OX_2 and OX_3; and beyond OX_3 technique V is least costly. Note that technique I fails to be the most economical for any output and so is eliminated in determining the envelope.

A similar envelope is obtained for stage 2 and for each of the other plant stages. These functions may then be aggregated (including costs of a general nature) to determine the long-run cost or planning curve. If hours of operation per seasonal period are held at a different level, a different set of stage functions is obtained and, thus, a different long-run cost curve. In fact, there will be a whole family of planning functions, one for each length of operating period, which means that time of operation is itself a variable in the cost function. This point will be developed more fully in the next section.

As the number of alternative production techniques available at each stage increases, the magnitude of the possible discontinuities in the long-run cost function tends to decrease, although their total number may increase. There is a further relative decrease in the magnitude of the discontinuities (and again a further increase in the number) as the stage cost functions are aggregated into an overall cost curve. The long-run cost curve with variable techniques thus approaches a continuous function, and in a purely theoretical extreme it would be continuous, although this is quite unlikely for most types of plants.

Plant Costs and the Length of Operation

It is convenient to think of marketing firms as faced with two types of demand. One is the demand of consumers or other firms for the final physical product and the other is the demand of agricultural producers and shippers for marketing services such as packing, processing, and storage. Although consumer demands often remain fairly stable, the demand for marketing services may fluctuate substantially throughout the year, mainly because of seasonal changes in farm production and harvest rates. Marketing firms commonly adjust to these changing demands by varying both the length of operation within a particular time period and the rate of output. This adds a dimension to output that until recently has received little attention in economic models of the firm.[11] Although the range of variability in the length of operation may be restricted by the perishability of the product and the flow pattern of the harvest, there are enough degrees of freedom to make this an important decision variable for many firms.

There are two types of length-of-operation decisions. Within short periods such as a day or a week, the firm must determine the combination of hours of operation and rate of output in the existing plant that will minimize the costs of producing any given total volume of marketing services. In formulating long-range plans, the firm must determine the optimum combination of plant size and seasonal length of operation for any expected seasonal volume of marketing service to be produced. The first type of decision has important implications for the shape of short-run cost functions and the second adds to the complexity of determining optimum plant scale. Both are important to the empirical analyst as well as firm managers.

Consider a firm producing a single marketing service within a production or marketing period of arbitrary length T. During this period the plant is to be operated at some constant rate of output Q for a length of operation t, ($t \leq T$). The total quantity of service produced is thus

(1) $S_T = Qt$.

Input requirements for each rate of output flow are prescribed as in the previous section or, more generally, are combined in optimum proportions as specified by neoclassical theory. For simplicity at the outset, the variable operating cost function in the rate dimension will be represented as a continuous approximation to the more realistic discontinuous function:

(2) $C = f(Q)$,

where C is the rate of total variable cost per unit of time and Q is the rate of output per unit of time.

Case I. No storage costs. Let us assume for the moment that (2) is independent of the length of operation — i.e., that fatigue is not a factor and that pay rates do not change — and that added storage costs are not incurred as output rates per unit of time exceed demand per unit of time. The cost per hour for any given rate of output then remains constant as the hours of operation are expanded up to t = T. The total variable cost incurred during the period T is

(3) $\text{TVC}_T = Ct = f(Q)t.$

A general form of this relationship is illustrated in figure 2. Note that although cost increases nonlinearly in the rate dimension in this illustration, it increases linearly in the time dimension.

To determine the rate of output and the length of operation which minimize cost for any S_T, form the Lagrangian function

(4) $L = f(Q)t + \lambda(S_T - Qt)$

and set the partial derivatives with respect to Q, t and λ equal to zero:

(5) $\dfrac{\partial L}{\partial Q} = t\dfrac{\partial f}{\partial Q} - \lambda t = 0$

(6) $\dfrac{\partial L}{\partial t} = f(Q) - \lambda Q = 0$

(7) $\dfrac{\partial L}{\partial \lambda} = S_T - Qt = 0$

Solving (5), (6), and (7) gives the minimum cost rate of output, Q^* and length of operation t^*, provided S_T is such that $S_T \le Q^*T$ (i.e., $t^* \le T$) and subject to the usual second-order conditions. From (5) and (6) we obtain

(8) $\lambda = \dfrac{\partial C}{\partial Q} = \dfrac{C}{Q},$

which indicates that the optimum output rate Q^* will be such that marginal cost in the rate dimension is equal to average variable cost. This, of course, is the rate at which average variable cost is a minimum.

As S_T is increased, a point is reached where $t^* = T$ and further increases in S_T can be accomplished only by expanding in the rate dimension. The length of operation becomes a constant in (3) and we return to the usual neoclassical model.

The equilibrium value of S_T is determined by the conditions of demand facing the firm. Very often the demand for a marketing service during a specified production and marketing period is predetermined by weather, cultur-

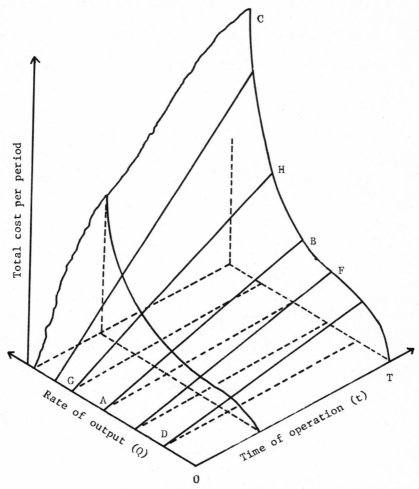

Figure 2. A cost surface for producing a single product by varying both rate and time of operation. Storage costs are assumed to be zero. Source: French, Sammet, and Bressler [401].

al, and biological factors. The price of the service may also be predetermined by conditions of supply and demand established over longer periods and by industry-wide competition. In such cases the firm simply adjusts its short-period output of service (S_T) to equal the predetermined quantity demanded, provided the price of the service exceeds marginal cost. A rational manager would not, of course, permit production to go beyond the point where marginal cost is equated with price.

In the conceptually more general but probably less common case, the demand for a marketing service during T may vary with its price. Letting the quantity produced equal the quantity demanded and imposing (5), (6), and (7), the optimizing model for S_T may be expressed as

$$(9) \quad NR_T = P_S S_T - f(Q)t = R(S_T) - \lambda^* S_T, \text{ if } S_T \leq Q^*T$$

$$(10) \quad NR_T = P_S S_T - f(Q)T = R(S_T) - f(\frac{S_T}{T})T, \text{ if } S_T > Q^*T$$

where NR_T is net revenue, P_S is the price of the service, $R(S_T)$ is the total revenue function, and λ^* is the marginal cost when $Q = Q^*$ (or equivalently, the minimum value of average variable cost) and the remaining terms are as defined above. If the initial solution of (9) yields $S_T > Q^*T$, the optimum value is determined by (10), which is the neoclassical model.

Under the conditions specified above, it is clear that an efficient manager would, to the extent possible, adjust to changing demands for marketing services by varying the length of operation, with the output rates set to minimize the cost per unit of service per unit of time. An important consequence for theorists is that realized cost functions associated with changes in the length of operation tend to be linear over most of the range of actual output variation, even though the plant cost function conceivably may be nonlinear in the rate dimension. This will also hold for the more realistic case of discontinuous cost functions, both linear and nonlinear. Another consequence is that the often observed practice of equating price with average cost may also equate marginal cost and price, thus suggesting a closer correspondence between business practice and economic theory.

If fatigue were a significant factor, output rates might decline slightly as the length of operation increased, and cost would be a nonlinear function of time. In practice this seems very unlikely since worker inputs are usually set to keep up with machines and adequate rest periods are normally built into the input structure. Institutional restrictions such as minimum pay periods or overtime rates imposed by union contracts may limit the range of variation in length of operation and add discontinuities to the cost function in this dimension.[12] These factors may become less restrictive, however, as the defined length of production period T increases.

Case II. Inventory considerations. If the length of operation is such that $t \leq T$, it is likely that the rate of output will, during some periods, exceed the rate at which the transformed products flow to the next level in the marketing system. Thus, inventories will accumulate for a time before being reduced during the interval from t to T when the output flow is stopped. So far it has been assumed that the variable storage costs associated with such inventory accumulation are negligible. This seems to be a reasonably accurate assumption for many marketing firm operations. In some cases, however, added cooling or handling costs may be incurred, so the previous analysis needs to be extended to encompass this possibility.

Production period storage costs — costs incurred within the time interval T, as distinct from costs of providing longer periods of storage services — are a function of the rate of output, the length of operation, and the rate of shipment or movement of product. The latter may be irregular, or may be continuous at a rate no greater than the rate of production, or may follow some other definite pattern.[13] Each type of product movement generates a different pattern of inventory accumulation and, therefore, a different storage cost function. Generally, the function will be nonlinear.[14]

The optimum combination of rate of output and length of operation is determined as specified previously in equations (4) to (7) with the storage cost function simply added to the production cost function. The net result is that the optimum rate of output is reduced slightly, compared with the case having no storage costs, and the length of operation is slightly increased (provided, of course, $t^* < T$). This is evident since, for given S_T, storage costs increase with increases in the rate of output and decrease with the length of operation. In the commonly encountered situation of linear and discontinuous cost functions and uniquely engineered plant capacities, the optimum output rate may occur at a "corner position" and thus remain unchanged with the addition of production period storage costs.

Case III. Dynamic extensions. Very often changes in the state of the production and marketing system from one production period to the next affect the firm's cost function and restrict the possible range of output variation. For example, breakdowns may occur, labor supplies or other inputs may be limited, product inventories (other than normal storage operations) may be carried over, and biological or weather factors may affect worker performance. The values of these events (referred to as "state variables") in the current period often are influenced by the state of the system and decisions made in previous periods. Thus, the optimization process must be developed with regard to a sequence of decisions, rather than independently for each period as in the previous analysis.

The simple static model developed above may be transformed into a dynamic framework by combining the production cost equation (3) with the production period storage cost equation and isolating the variables (previously treated as constants) which define the state of the system during each production period. Total variable cost in period i of length T becomes

(11) $\text{TVC}_{Ti} = f(Q_i, t_i, z_{1i}, z_{2i}, \ldots, z_{ni})$,

where Z_{1i}, Z_{2i}, . . . , Z_{ni} represent variables which define the state of the system in each period and the other terms are as defined previously. Note that since $S_{Ti} = t_i Q_i$, t_i may be replaced by $\dfrac{S_{Ti}}{Q_i}$.

The criterion function of the firm is the discounted sum of net returns over K production periods of length T. The problem is to maximize this function subject to the difference equations which express the state variables in period i as functions of values in previous periods. The problem might be specified as

$$(12) \quad \text{Max} \sum_{i=1}^{K} \; [P_s S_{Ti} - f(Q_i, S_{Ti}, Z_{1i}, \ldots, Z_{ni})] \; B^{i-1},$$

subject to

$$Z_{1i} = h_1(Z_{1i-1}, \ldots Z_{ni-1}, Q_{i-1}, S_{Ti-1}, u_{1i})$$

.

.

.

$$Z_{ni} = h_n(Z_{1i-1}, \ldots Z_{ni-1}, Q_{i-1}, S_{Ti-1}, u_{ni})$$

$$S_{Ti} = r(i, v_i)$$

$$Z_{10} = b_{10}, Z_{20} = b_{20}, \ldots Z_{n0} = b_{n0}.$$

The term B is a discount factor; u and v reflect uncontrollable factors; $b_{10} \ldots b_{n0}$ are initial values of the state variables, $Z_1 \ldots Z_n$, Q_i is the decision variable; and S_{Ti} is treated here as a state variable, although the model could easily be specified to include it as another decision variable.

The type of model illustrated by (12) is readily recognized as a *control problem* which involves choosing time paths for certain variables (in this case, Q_i), called *control variables*, from a given class of time paths called the *control set* (see, for example, [43, 16, 81]).[15] The solution procedures required for dynamic control problems are beyond the scope of this paper.[16] The formulation is suggestive, however, of the type of model extensions which ultimately may be required to deal more realistically and effectively with the production decisions of marketing firm managers.

The long-run cost curve is an envelope concept which, in neoclassical theory, specifies the minimum cost per unit of time in relation to rate of plant output per unit of time. However, for many agricultural marketing firms which do not operate throughout the year, the minimum cost associated with a particular rate of output differs, depending on whether the seasonal length of operation (the sum of various production period hours of operation over the total operating season) is long or short. Moreover, production techniques that are labor intensive may be most efficient for plants with short seasons, while capital intensive techniques with higher fixed costs and lower unit variable costs may be selected by plants with longer seasons. Long-run cost functions thus involve considerations of both rate of output and seasonal length of operation.

For long-run planning purposes we need to know the scale of plant (measured in terms of expected rate of output) which gives the least cost for any seasonal volume of marketing service to be produced. The computational procedures involved vary with the degree of control over the seasonal length of operation. In the extreme case where the length is rigidly prescribed by harvest conditions or other factors, the planning curve is determined in accordance with the neoclassical model. Each seasonal volume of service is associated with a particular output rate or design capacity, and the cost function measured in terms of rates of output is directly convertible to a function of seasonal volume. However, there is a different planning curve for each possible length of season.

Frequently seasonal marketing firms are able to influence the length of seasonal operation by control of planting dates or by incurring added transportation or storage costs. The problem then is to find the minimum cost combination of both plant scale and length of seasonal operation for all possible seasonal volumes of service to be produced.

To illustrate the computational process, consider a simple long-run cost model of the general form

(13) $TC_K = g(Q, t_K)$,

where TC_K is the total seasonal cost, Q is rate of output, and t_K is length of seasonal operation.[17] The total cost involves two components — an envelope function wherein each point represents the cost for a specific plant operating at its designed capacity rate, or slightly to the left if the short-run average cost functions are truly U-shaped; and transportation, storage, or other costs which may increase directly with increases in the seasonal length of operation. The long-run planning function is determined by first forming the Lagrangian function

(14) $V = g(Q, t_K) + \mu(S_K - Qt_K)$

and setting the partial derivatives with respect to Q, t_K and μ equal to zero:

(15) $\dfrac{\partial V}{\partial Q} = \dfrac{\partial g}{\partial Q} - \mu t_K = 0$

(16) $\dfrac{\partial V}{\partial t_K} = \dfrac{\partial g}{\partial t_K} - \mu Q = 0$

(17) $\dfrac{\partial V}{\partial \mu} = S_K - Qt_K = 0$

Solving (15), (16), and (17) for Q and t_K as functions of S_K and substituting in (13) gives

(18) $TC_K = G(S_K)$,

which is the long-run planning or economies of scale curve, assuming the appropriate second-order conditions which guarantee minimum cost values.

Since economies of scale involve an envelope concept representing least-cost operations, each plant depicted on the curve is assumed always to produce at a uniform rate. This is clearly the most efficient way. But many marketing firms faced with uncontrollable seasonal variations in demand for services cannot produce the same quantity of service during each time period. Given the need to adjust readily and efficiently, the firms might choose plant production techniques different from those they would choose if the same season volume of services could be produced at uniform rates. A planning curve such as (18), based on uniform operation, thus might be inappropriate for such firms.

To derive planning curves for plants faced with such variable demands it is necessary to specify the pattern of seasonal variation expected to prevail. Envelope functions with final forms similar to (18) then can be derived for all patterns of interest, although the added intraseasonal dimensions may produce a formidable computational task. For firms able to adjust to changes in intraseasonal demand by varying the short period length of operation (see previous discussion), the marginal cost remains constant over a wide range of output (values of S_T), and the planning curves for plants with variable outputs may differ little from plants with uniform outputs. Scale curves based on the latter thus may be practical substitutes. Where institutional factors restrict this type of adjustment process, the more involved development may be required (see, for example, Logan [52], Fitzpatrick and French [315], and Daellenbach and Fletcher [517]).

Uncontrollable variation in volume among seasons presents a similar problem in applying economies of scale analyses. The most efficient plant for a given uniform season volume may not be the most efficient for the same average but variable season volume. Again a family of scale curves can be developed in relation to mean season volume for each pattern of interseasonal variation of interest. In many cases the choice of plant scale and production technique may be essentially the same for uniform and flexible interseason operations, for the reasons suggested above. The main factor is the degree to which firms are free to adjust to changing demands by varying the length of seasonal operation (in total hours) rather than the rates of output.

Multiple-Service Plant Operations

Many firms engaged in agricultural processing or marketing operations produce more than one product or marketing service. Even if we think of the firm as producing a single type of service, such as packing fresh fruit for shipment to market, the service may differ qualitatively with the forms of packages used or the distribution of grades. Thus, multiple outputs are effectively the rule rather than the exception.

Neoclassical theory provides us with a mathematically elegant model of multiple-product production which is useful for conceptualizing the resource allocation and product mix decisions (see, for example, Henderson and Quandt [37, pp. 95-98], Ferguson [29, pp. 201-211], and Naylor and Vernon [63, pp. 123-128]) but which is quite inadequate as a framework for measuring production and cost functions in marketing firms. There are two major shortcomings in addition to the limitations of the single-product neoclassical model noted previously. First, because of the model's generality and the many variables involved, it is virtually impossible to estimate its parameters with the types of statistical data ordinarily available. Second, as a base for economic-engineering synthesis of production and cost functions, it offers few clues to the nature of the functions involved or the parameters to be determined. It assumes away or leaves unspecified a substantial part of the problem of interest to the empirical analyst and the firm manager.

Instead of one general multiple-product model, what is required is a set of models which will enable the researcher to infer from the type of multiple production some expected characteristics of the firm's production and cost functions. Bressler and King [14] classify multiple-product operations into five general cases: case 1, joint (marketing) services in fixed proportions; case 2, outputs with varying composition; case 3, independent services from a single plant; case 4, single services that may be applied to several physical commodities; and case 5, joint services with variable proportions. Since inferences with respect to these classifications may differ for short-run and long-run production, we shall first examine each case for a given plant and production technology and then see how the conclusions may be modified in long-run situations.

Bressler and King [14] argue that all of the multiple-production situations can be broken down into variants of the single-product model (also see Dano [22, p. 166]). Cases 1 and 2 are analytically equivalent to the single-product case. The joint products are simply redefined to be single products. In the second case — typical of many biological growth situations — the composition of the product varies as the rates of input change but in a uniquely determined manner, so that production decisions are made in a single-product framework.

Case 3 includes situations in which one commodity may be processed during one part of the year and another at a different time or two or more products may be processed (or services may be produced) simultaneously but on separate production lines. In either situation, although there is some sharing of fixed factors such as the building and perhaps common costs such as sorting the basic raw product, the variable cost functions are independent. Thus, output decisions may be made separately for each product or service.

Case 4 (which appears to overlap somewhat with case 3) involves the application of a particular marketing service such as packing, transportation, or storage to different commodities or subgroups of commodities. Although the marketing firm may appear to be producing many different products, the production process involves only a single basic service. When a common capacity factor is fully utilized, the commodities to which the service may be applied become alternatives. Dano [22] refers to this type of situation appropriately as multiple products with *alternative processes*. The optimum commodity mix may be determined by programming methods. If the commodity mix of applications is given, the optimization problem is to schedule the output flow to minimize costs of transferring from one commodity to another, subject to the time sequence of demands.[18] Although integer programming or other operations research techniques may be applicable in such cases (see Wagner [94] and Muth and Thompson [59]), the solution often may be fairly simple or even obvious. In any event the component cost functions involved are all single-product relationships.

Case 5 is distinguished from the others by the requirement that a change in the rate of output of one service affects the marginal costs of producing the other services. It is not possible to relate cost to the rate of output of each product independently of the rate of production of other commodities. Although this is often represented as the realistic or general case, Bressler and King [14] argue that on closer examination all such situations will be found to fall into one of the first four categories. They note that "proportions are not varied through a continuous function but by discrete changes in technology, changes in cultural practices, in breeds and varieties of crops and livestock in crop rotation, and so on. We have been unable to find a single case where, with a given set of technology and inputs, anything but a unique set of outputs would result."

In what at first glance might appear to be a contrary example, Reed and Sammet [479] point out that as the allocation of a given flow of raw material among grades or package forms is changed, the marginal costs of producing the different product forms may be affected because of changes in flow rates in branch lines. This, however, violates the proposition that output rates of some products may be held constant while those of others are varied. It is actually a case of *alternative processes* wherein the component stage activities may be analyzed in terms of single-product equations.

Even if examples can be found of short-run production that is truly "joint with variable proportions," it seems clear that this occurs infrequently. The reduction of most multiple-product situations to single-product variants with respect to cost determination is obviously important to the empirical analyst for it enables him to deal with separable components in the measurement process. It does not eliminate the need for joint determination of the optimum output mix, particularly in the case of alternative products, but it allows the problem to be placed in a programming framework that is more readily solved with modern computer algorithms.

The long-run cost function for a multiple-product firm (which is not treated very extensively in the economic literature) is a multidimensional envelope to cost functions for plants designed to operate at all different output levels and combinations of levels for a given set of products (see Bressler [12]). Within this framework the single-product plant is a special case in which the design outputs of all commodities considered except one are set at zero.

Referring to the Bressler and King classifications of multiple-product situations, but now in a long-run context, it is clear that cases 1 and 2 may still be regarded analytically as variants of the single product model. Case 4 also appears to be amenable to formulation as essentially a single-product model (or a combination of single-product models). In case 3, however, the joint costs such as shared buildings and equipment, which remain constant for a given plant, become variable costs in a planning function. The selection of the best production technique and the level of the jointly shared cost thus may depend on the output rates for all the commodities involved. At least a portion of the productive activities in case 3, therefore, may shift to case 5 for purposes of long-run planning, although case 5 was rejected by Bressler and King as nonexistent in the short run.

Even the most simple of the truly interdependent multiple-product models is quite complex. Incorporating further considerations of uncertainty and the possible need for short-run flexibility and adaptability in the long-run planning model creates what is indeed a formidable problem for the empirical analyst. Two approaches have been tried. The first is to attempt to reduce multiple-product situations to single-product dimensions through some index of output (see Dean [23, pp. 296-313] ; National Commission on Food Marketing [229, pp. 139-152]). In view of the uncertainties involved in long-run planning, this may often be a practical and useful way of measuring of scale economies. However, it provides limited information regarding costs of alternative product mixes. The second approach is a stage-by-stage analysis, which permits a separation of activities into those which may be considered in a single-product framework and those which require truly joint consideration. The stage and component functions then may be recombined to model the total process of multiple production (for example, see Reed and Sammet [479]). These approaches are discussed in greater depth in the methodological sections of this paper.

Spatial Components of Marketing Cost

Supplies of raw agricultural products handled by a single plant typically are acquired from widely dispersed points. The assembled and transformed products, in turn, may be sent to widely scattered markets or customers. The theory of the marketing firm thus needs to include a framework for analyzing the efficiency of collection and delivery systems and the relation between plant volume and total assembly and distribution costs.[19]

THE COLLECTION OR DELIVERY COST FUNCTION

Let us consider first the costs associated with operating a single vehicle on a single route of given design. Following the general approach of Bressler [11], Judge and Baker [361], and Clarke [538], the total variable cost may be subdivided into components which can be analyzed separately with respect to the individual variable involved. The basic identity takes the form

$$(19) \quad C_T = W_1(T_1 + T_2 + T_3 + T_4) + W_2 D + W_3$$

where

C_T = total variable cost per trip,
W_1 = hourly cost of the driver,
T_1 = travel time,
T_2 = time spent loading at farm collection points or unloading at customer delivery points,
T_3 = time at plant,
T_4 = miscellaneous and personal time,
W_2 = operating cost of vehicle per mile,
D = total distance traveled, and
W_3 = cost of plant loading and unloading per trip.

An analysis of the component costs suggests the following set of relationships:

(20) $T_1 = \dfrac{D}{S}$

(21) $S = f_1(N, V, X)$

(22) $T_2 = \displaystyle\sum_{i=1}^{N} f_2(V_{si})$

(23) $T_3 = f_3(V)$

(24) $T_4 = k$

(25) $W_2 = f_4(S, V, X, N)$

(26) $W_3 = f_5(V)$

where

S   =   average speed,
N   =   number of stops,
V   =   total volume per trip,
X   =   a composite of effects of road conditions, terrain,
          type of vehicle, and legal restrictions,
V_{si} =   volume per stop for stop i, and
k   =   a constant.

Substituting (20) to (26) in (19) gives an equation which, even after consolidating terms, is awkward to handle. However, it becomes much more manageable with a few simplifying assumptions. First, we might let the average speed, S, be constant and independent of V and N. Second, we might replace individual volumes per stop in (22) with the average volume, giving $T_2 = Nf_2(\overline{V}_s)$. Third, the average hourly operating cost of the vehicle might be regarded as unaffected by V and N within a given average environment. These assumptions, which seem likely to have relatively small effects in most cases, permit us to express the collection or delivery function as

(27) $C_T = b_0 + B_1 D + b_2 Nf_2(\overline{V}_s) + h(V)$

where

$b_0 = W_1 k$

$b_1 = \dfrac{W_1}{S} + W_2$

$b_2 = W_1$

$$h(V) = W_1 f_3(V) + f_5(V).$$

Equation (27) is, of course, restricted to the range such that

$$(28) \ T_1 + T_2 + T_3 + T_4 = T \le H$$

where H = daily hour limit or, alternatively, $\frac{D}{S} + Nf_2(\overline{V}_s) + f_3(V) + k \le H$. The total variable cost *per season* is the sum of costs per trip, to which may be added a value to cover costs associated with investment or ownership (such as taxes, license, time depreciation, interest, insurance, and garaging). In addition to its analytical uses this type of function may provide some guidance in establishing service charges for delivering commodities such as fluid milk, particularly with respect to the influence of volume per stop on cost [537, 538, 542, 554]. However, the allocation of indirect costs such as travel time and fixed investment costs is arbitrary. Such costs might, for example, be allocated on a customer basis by dividing by the total number of stops or on a volume per customer basis by dividing by season volume. The charge for the customer service component $(W_1 T_2)$ would be the same in either case, but the allocation of other costs would differ.

The discussion so far has ignored the problem of efficient route organization. To achieve minimum cost, travel patterns must be specified to minimize the total route mileage. This may be particularly challenging when the plant volume requires the operation of several routes. There is no general theory of optimum route organization. However, the operations research literature dealing with the "traveling salesman problem" provides several solution algorithms (see Bellmore and Neuhauser [7], Schruben and Clifton [276], and Hallberg and Kriebel [266]). Because of still unsolved difficulties in handling the more complex routing problems, solutions in practice have typically been of a trial-and-error nature (see Boutwell and Simmons [535]).

The achievement of optimum route efficiency is further complicated by the need to select the most efficient equipment for each set of distance and volume requirements. In simple cases equations such as (27) and (28) may be formed for each type of vehicle and the least-cost method readily determined for all conditions. More generally, however, the choice of equipment may interact with the route organization, with many combinations of equipment possible. Formal models for this type of problem are not well developed. For a related approach applicable to single-point pickup, see Henry and Burbee [565].

ASSEMBLY AND DISTRIBUTION COST FUNCTIONS

Assembly or distribution cost functions show how the total acquisition or distribution costs vary with the level of plant output.[20] The functions are unique to each plant location, the specific character depending on the distribution of supply sources (or customers) available to the plant and the density of production at each source. Some generalization about the likely overall form is possible, however, by introducing some simplifying abstractions. The model, which follows approaches used by Olson [718], Henry and Seagraves [567], Williamson [733], and French [265], will be in terms of assembly, but it can be reversed to apply to distribution activities as well.

Consider a plant located at the center of a circular supply plane with production spread nearly continuously throughout the area and the density of supply roughly constant throughout the plane. Assume for the moment a single stop for each load. Imposing these conditions on (27) and expressing on a cost per season basis gives

$$(29) \quad C_S = Q(a_0 + a_1 \bar{D})$$

where

C_S = total variable assembly cost per season,
Q = total volume per season, and
$\bar{D}$ = average one-way travel distance.

If the plant is visualized as located at the origin of a set of polar coordinates, then (see [265])

$$(30) \quad \bar{D} = \frac{2}{3} wr$$

where

r = radius of circular supply area, and
w = a factor for converting from air distance to road distance.

Since the volume assembled (Q) is equal to average density multiplied by the area of the supply plane, the radius can be expressed as

$$(31) \quad r = \sqrt{\frac{Q}{\pi P}}$$

where

P = density of supply per unit of area.

Substituting in (29) gives

$$(32) \quad C_S = Q(a_0 + \frac{2}{3} a_1 w \, \frac{Q^{1/2}}{\pi^{1/2} \, p^{1/2}}).$$

Dividing (32) by Q gives an average unit assembly cost function which increases at a decreasing rate as the volume assembled increases.

Cost functions with similar shapes are obtained for rectangular supply areas with roads running along section lines [265] and for models based on route assembly where each load is picked up at several stops [535].[21]

Since (32) includes only variable costs, it is applicable only to short-run cost models. Whether an assembly cost function can be regarded as fully meaningful in this context is perhaps open to question since the area of the plant supply plane is likely to be fixed in the short run. Changes in short-run output are more likely to be associated with changes in average density of supply.

A restricted long-run assembly cost function (for a particular vehicle type) is obtained by adding the cost of ownership or rental of transport equipment to (32). This imposes discontinuities at points where additional vehicles must be added, but it leaves the general shape of the function unchanged. A more general long-run assembly cost function would, of course, involve changes in transport method for greater distances. The rate of increase in assembly cost thus would be slightly less than suggested by (32) for larger volumes assembled. Similar considerations apply to the distribution of final products, particularly for commodities such as milk sold in local markets.

Although actual assembly or distribution cost functions will be modified by geographic configurations and real market factors, the general result regarding shape is quite significant. For the theorist, it suggests a factor which may be important in limiting plant size, even in cases where internal plant diseconomies of scale are absent. For the empirical analyst, it indicates the need to include assembly and distribution costs in the long-run planning curve. And for management, it is clearly an important factor influencing the location of the plant, the source of supplies, and the prices to be paid for raw products.

Total Systems Analysis

The economic theory or set of theories needed for guidance in studies of marketing systems for industries or areas may be separated into two parts — theory relating to systems design and theories of competitive equilibrium and behavior, both extended into spatial and vertical dimensions. The first component of theory focuses on the strict goals of minimum cost organization. The second provides a basis for considering the interaction between system organization and competitive behavior. The latter is essential in evaluating the desirability of alternative organizational structures and in formulating plans for implementing research findings.

DESIGN THEORY

An engineer-economist setting out to design an efficient marketing system might view the system as a single plant on a grand scale. The stage and flow concepts discussed earlier can be extended readily to this larger system. Fresh fruit, for example, may pass through marketing stages such as transportation to a packing plant, packing, storage, shipment to central warehouses, transportation to retail stores, and final sales to consumers. Just as plant organizations are defined in terms of both methods and scale of production lines, the organization of a marketing system can be defined in terms of plant production methods and scale of plant. The design of a total system is somewhat more complex, however, because of the dispersion of raw product sources and markets and the consequent need to specify the *location* of each plant at each stage in the system.

The design problem facing the engineer-economist is to select the shipping patterns, plant techniques, plant scales, location, and number of plants at each stage to minimize some function of total cost. The cost of concern here is for the total system, but it could be the costs of processing firms, raw material owners, transport facility owners, consumers, or some other component [717]. The models constructed to solve this type of problem differ with respect to the assumptions about the continuity or discontinuity of space.[22] For the continuous case, we draw on the classical location models as presented by Losch [53] and Beckman [6] and extended first to agricultural marketing systems by Bressler and colleagues [11] at Connecticut and later by Williamson [733] and Olson [718]. The discontinuous case is formulated in a programming framework as applied particularly by Stollsteimer [726], King and Logan [707, 711], and others. It is difficult to separate the theory and its application in these cases, and so further discussion will be reserved for the methodological sections elsewhere in this paper.

Since the output at one level of a marketing system becomes an input at the next level, the system designer must also be concerned with the vertical coordination of activities. For a given system, the problem is to determine the best flow patterns of materials and sequences of activities. For the longer run, the problem is to select combinations of plant capacities among levels that will be "harmonious"[23] and to develop vertical arrangements that are optimum with respect to both their cost and risk.

The theory of vertical integration of processes within plants as developed by Dano [22, pp. 149-162] would appear as applicable to a given marketing system, as to a plant. However, Dano's model is static and deterministic whereas many coordination problems arise because of uncontrollable weather and biological factors and the wide range of individual producing units. Theoretical frameworks which would encompass these added dimensions of uncertainty and dynamics are not well defined. Several types of operations research models appear promising in empirical application. Niles [64] has developed a simulation model for producer-processor coordination in the sugar beet industry, and Belden and Schrader [626] have formulated a linear programming model of an integrated turkey production and marketing system.

Queuing theory, scheduling theory, and dynamic programming may also prove useful in this type of analysis.

Conceptual frameworks for analyzing the long-run economies of vertical arrangements have been formulated by Mighell and Jones [57], Baligh and Richartz [4], and Logan [51]. The Mighell-Jones study is a landmark work. It was perhaps the first thorough and rigorous development of both the economic and institutional base for vertical coordination in agricultural production and marketing activities.[24] The work by Baligh and Richartz deals more generally and in greater theoretical depth with economic factors determining the vertical organization of marketing systems. Logan extends the analytical framework in a firm growth context, with emphasis on firm utility functions and risk factors.

COMPETITIVE BEHAVIOR

Whether the efficient system designed by an engineer-economist is achievable, or even desirable, depends on the decision-making framework and the competitive environment within which it will operate. Although a least-cost system design may appear consistent with the norms of perfect competition (and its extension to the perfect market concept [77]), the centralized decision structure required for achievement and the spatial monopolies associated with exclusive territories may in fact lead to pricing systems that are far less than perfect (Bressler and King [14, pp. 153-155]). Our theoretical framework for the analysis of regional or industry market organization, therefore, must include competitive as well as pure cost considerations.

Consideration of competitive behavior brings us into the realm of Helmberger's O-efficiency [36] (see the earlier discussion of efficiency concepts). The problem is to select from among the various possible organizational configurations of an economy the particular configuration which maximizes some welfare criteria. Since these configurations involve space, time, form, and vertical dimensions as well as competitive interactions, the problem is exceedingly complex. Although there have been some efforts to incorporate imperfect competition into quantitative spatial models (Williamson [733], Bobst and Waananen [687], Kloth and Blakley [708], and DeHaven [696]), most relevant theory provides only broad concepts rather than models that may be applied directly to empirical analysis of marketing systems.[25] Helmberger [36] describes the general theory available as "informal and very weak." Additional theoretical modeling seems clearly needed in this area.[26]

Estimation of Plant Cost Relationships

The discussion so far has been aimed at developing theoretical concepts which have been accorded limited space in standard neoclassical works and which seem essential to the study of efficiency in agricultural marketing. We turn now to a consideration of the empirical methodology and the scope of research concerned with cost and efficiency in the individual firm. Subsequent sections will deal with studies of efficient organization for industries, markets, and market areas.

Approaches to estimating plant cost and efficiency relationships may be grouped into three broad categories: (1) descriptive analysis of accounting data, which mainly involves combining point estimates of average costs into various classes for comparative purposes, (2) statistical analysis of accounting data, which attempts to estimate functional relationships by econometric methods, and (3) the economic-engineering approach, which "synthesizes" production and cost relationships from engineering data or other estimates of the components of the production function. Classifying all studies into these single categories, as will be done for convenience in the discussion that follows, often may be somewhat arbitrary since two or more approaches are frequently combined. A study which relies mainly on descriptive analysis may, for example, include some statistical analysis — and *vice versa*. There is also considerable variation in the degree of sophistication in statistical studies and, consequently, in their degree of departure from descriptive analysis. Economic-engineering studies may also rely on statistical estimation based on accounting data for some components. Moreover, many descriptive comparisons of costs rely mainly on data generated by quasi-engineering types of measurements.

Studies using any of these approaches share the common objective of providing guides to management that will in some way aid in improving efficiency. There are, however, some separable objectives which are achievable only through the use of particular approaches. These objectives, and the approach or approaches for each, are as follows:

1. Describe average cost experience to provide standards of comparison among firms; approach (1).
2. Describe and compare costs in firms following different business practices or operating in different ways; approaches (1) and (2).
3. Measure short-run cost functions to provide managerial tools for decision making; approaches (2) and (3).
4. Compare the efficiency of alternative production methods or techniques under different operating circumstances; approach (3).
5. Develop improved production techniques; approach (3).
6. Evaluate the effects of plant scale on cost; approaches (1), (2), and (3).
7. Test theoretical hypotheses; approaches (2) and (3).
8. Measure and compare relative total efficiency among firms and at different times; approaches (2) and (3).

9. Provide basic estimates of relationships for use in area or industry studies; approaches (2) and (3).

The fact that more than one approach is listed as consistent with a particular objective does not mean that the approaches are equally effective in achieving the objective. Differences in effectiveness will be discussed in subsequent sections.

Descriptive Analysis of Accounting Data

The computational procedures involved in this approach are straightforward and simple. Typically, average accounting cost records for a particular time period are obtained from a sample of plants. The degree of breakdown in these costs is variable, ranging from broad categories such as labor, materials, insurance, and taxes to more detailed records by department or plant stage. The cost data supplied by the plants sometimes may be supplemented by direct observations or interviews. Occasionally the investigator may attempt some standardization of the methods of reporting and allocating costs within and among plants.

The sample plants usually are classified according to factors such as size, location, type of containers used, degree of mechanization, or some other operating practice. Averages of the average costs are computed for each grouping and for each cost component. Frequently, the range in cost is given also and sometimes the data are presented for each plant in the sample. An effort is made to explain variations in cost among plants in accordance with the variations in class averages (such as by volume) and by other factors thought to affect costs based largely on the general observations and experience of the researcher.

The descriptive approach was the first method used to study marketing firm efficiency. It was virtually the only approach used in the few marketing firm cost studies made before 1940 (for examples, see [5, 27, 78, 80, and 83]). It is still widely used today.

The reference section of this article lists about a hundred research reports, published since 1949, which have followed essentially this approach, although perhaps not all would agree on their placement in this category. Very likely there are others that have escaped the attention of the author. Table 1 shows how these studies have been distributed in time and among major types of agricultural marketing activities. The nearly even split before and after 1960 suggests that the approach has remained popular. Moreover, measures of this type are frequently included in studies of a more analytical nature that are discussed elsewhere in this paper.

There appear to be four main reasons for the popularity of this approach.

Table 1. Descriptive Studies of Plant Cost Records: Distribution by Time,
Commodity, and Function, 1949-71

Commodity Group and Function	Published before 1960[a]	Published 1960 and later[a]
Fresh fruit and vegetable packing	[97, 99, 119, 127, 150, 152, 170, 180, 186, 187, 191, 193]	[124, 190]
Dairy production processing	[98, 104, 110, 132, 144, 155, 183]	[103, 125, 138, 148, 161, 176]
Milk collection and delivery	[105, 147, 157, 158, 159]	[149]
Poultry and egg packing and processing	[101, 120, 122, 128, 162]	[142, 171, 172, 175, 184, 194]
Egg collection	[146]	[123, 139]
Elevator and milling operations	[106, 143, 160, 174, 185]	[109, 108, 129, 133, 154, 164, 169, 189]
Cotton ginning	[131, 136, 168, 178, 179, 192]	[115, 116, 117, 118, 151]
Livestock auctions	[135, 153, 156, 188]	[102, 134]
Other[b]	[92, 100, 107, 121, 130, 140, 173, 177]	[96, 111, 112, 113, 114, 126, 137, 141, 145, 163, 165, 166, 167, 181, 182, 195]

[a]Numbers in brackets refer to publications listed in the reference section.

[b]Fruit and vegetable processing, sugar processing, crawfish peeling, cattle feeding, grocery manufacturing, retail food store operations, slaughter plants, wholesale operations.

First, it is relatively cheap compared to economic-engineering analysis or to statistical studies. Second, it is easily understood by plant managers. Third, since the costs are "real," they provide a means for managers to relate their own cost experience to the experience of others. Thus, they suggest potential gains from improvement and may point to the direction of search for means of achieving such improvement. Finally, they may provide a record of cost experience useful to agencies and groups interested in broader questions pertaining to levels of marketing costs and margins — for example, the National Commission on Food Marketing in 1966.

There are, however, significant limitations to the approach. First, unless the record-keeping system is highly standardized among plants, the costs compared may vary widely — especially among component costs — simply because of differences in accounting classification or allocation systems and the time of purchase of durable inputs.[27] Second, in addition to differences in accounting systems, plant costs are affected by so many factors — managerial efficiency, scale, production methods, input prices, degree of plant utilization, environmental conditions, and random variations in plant performance — that the types of cross classification or groupings typically possible usually do not permit clear separations of the influence of individual factors. Finally, this type of study gives us only snapshots of past experience. It provides no quantitative measures of parameters and few general clues regarding the types of functional relationships suggested by our micro-theory framework.

Statistical Analysis of Accounting Data

Statistical analysis uses much the same data as descriptive analysis. It is distinguished from the latter by its attempts to develop quantitative estimates of production and cost functions or to test theoretical hypotheses about them.

The primary focus here will be on cost functions. Although production function studies have encompassed many types of economic activity including agriculture (see Walters [249]), there have been few applications to agricultural marketing firms (exceptions are found in Kelley et al. [220, 221]). In view of this and the extensive body of literature dealing with econometric estimation of production functions (see Walters [249], Brown [15], and Nadiri [60]), it seems best to limit the discussion to aspects of methodology most directly relevant to the evaluation of agricultural marketing firm studies. It should be noted, however, that many of the points to be made pertaining to cost functions also apply to the measurement of production functions.[28]

The first applications of statistical approaches to cost measurement appeared in the late 1930s and 1940s in studies of nonagricultural firms by Dean [205, 206, 207], Dean and James [208], Yntema [254], Wylie and Ezekiel [253], and others. The methodology developed in these studies was extended and applied to a wide variety of production activities during the 1950s and 1960s. Many of the studies are reviewed or referenced in Walters [249] and Johnston [219]. Few applications to agricultural marketing firms are mentioned by these authors — in part because many were published later, but probably also owing to unfamiliarity with the work in this area. In any case, the statistical approach has been used in studies of agricultural marketing or related activities such as livestock auctions [200, 204, 225, 227, 228, 251, 252], grain elevator and milling operations [199, 220, 221, 232, 239, 245, 255, 256], cattle feedlots [209, 216, 218], retail food store operations [212, 229], dairy products processing [215, 222, 223, 224, 233], meat packing [214, 231, 235], and farm supply stores [217].

Nearly all of the studies cited in the preceding paragraph have been concerned with estimates of long-run cost functions from cross-section data. Only three [215, 217, 235] have involved the analysis of time series data, and even these have used cross-section data also. However, this very likely understates the actual and potential importance of time series analysis because it is commonly used to estimate some components of cost variation in economic-engineering studies to be discussed later in this paper and is widely used (often combined with cross-section data) in studies of other types of production activity.

If we can judge from the relatively small number of reports published, the statistical approach has been considerably less popular in studies of marketing firm efficiency than straight descriptive analysis of the economic-engineering approach. Offhand, this may seem surprising since research costs of statistical analysis are not especially high and the state of statistical science is generally well advanced. The explanation appears to be in the difficult specific methodological issues encountered, the limited uses of purely statistical analysis, and the availability of an alternative approach (economic-engineering) which, although more costly, may be more satisfactory for many purposes.

The analyst who sets out to measure plant cost functions by statistical techniques typically has available a set of observations on total cost and output from a sample of plants for a single accounting period such as a year. Less commonly, he may have data for several years, or he may have costs and outputs for each plant for time series of shorter accounting periods such as a week or a month. Attempts to derive theoretical cost curves from such data are jeopardized by possible distortions or biases owing to the character and treatment of the data or inappropriate specification and measurement in relation to the true model of cost behavior.[29]

DATA PROBLEMS

Statistical studies using accounting records face all of the data limitations of descriptive studies. The data defects may be of greater importance, however, because of the potential for biasing quantitative functional estimates. The five problems most commonly encountered are identified in the following list. (For further discussion, see Dean [23, pp. 303-324], Malmgren [226], Johnston [219, pp. 26-30], and Sammet [69, pp. 113-119].)

1. Measures of durable input costs, in the form of depreciation figures, may vary among plants owing to differences in accounting systems, the acquisition dates of the factors, and depreciation rules that do not accurately reflect the real input cost. Where data can be obtained from plants using uniform accounting systems, the degree of distortion may be reduced but clearly not eliminated.

2. Accounting values are averages for a period of time and may conceal variations in rates of output and plant utilization within accounting periods. Data on plant hours and rate variations for each period may be required for a more meaningful analysis. Using data for shorter accounting periods may also be desirable, although that can lead to another difficulty — the matching of outputs with the periods for which the associated costs are reported. In general, detailed records which permit analysis by plant components may be preferred, although in some cross-section studies disaggregated comparisons have proved unreliable because of variations among plants in the way costs are allocated to components or departments (see Thuroczy and Schlegel [245]).

3. Factor prices, including variable factors, may vary among plants owing to locational and institutional rigidities and over time owing to price level changes. Efforts to correct for price differences by using standardized values or adjusting by some price index have been criticized since the procedure takes no account of factor substitution as prices vary. There is not complete agreement, however, on the nature of the potential bias that may result from such adjustments (Johnston [219, pp. 170-176]). Walters argues that the degree of bias is likely to be small compared to the original price distortion [249, p. 42].

4. Time series of long duration may reflect variations in the physical plant structure and production technique. This may not be bad for some types of comparative purposes, but clearly the researcher must have some measure of the nature of any change of this kind.

5. Cost values for multiple-product plants may involve arbitrary and variable systems of allocating costs among products. Because of the difficulties in measuring output in multiple-service firms, plant scale is sometimes represented by an input such as number of workers or physical assets (for example, see [229]). Stigler argues that "there is no defense except convenience for measuring output by one input" [79].[30] More commonly, total sales is used as an output measure. If the output mix and component prices remain fairly stable over time and among plants, this may be a satisfactory approximation. Otherwise, it may be a rather misleading index. Where the number of products or services is small, output may be measured in multiple dimensions, but this generates identification problems which often cannot be resolved satisfactorily with the types and sizes of sample data available. The problem of measuring scale for integrated operations still seems open (for further discussion, see Smith [242]).

SPECIFICATION AND MEASUREMENT PROBLEMS

Most of the marketing firm cost studies cited earlier have failed in some way to account fully for the underlying process which generates the historical records of cost and output. Consequently, what is estimated often turns out to be some descriptive function rather than the basic cost functions suggested by the theoretical framework appropriate to the production of marketing services.

Cost functions from time series data. In studies using time series data to estimate short-run cost functions, the major specification problem relates to the separation of rate of output and length of operation dimensions. If output varies from one accounting period to another by variations in the length of operation, the cost-volume relationship will be linear (see the earlier discussion of the theoretical framework). On the other hand, if length of operation remains constant and rates of output vary, the function may be nonlinear, although as we noted earlier there may often be reasons to expect approximate (discontinuous) linearity in the rate dimension as well. In any case, simply relating total cost to total volume per accounting period confuses the effects of the two dimensions and typically imparts a linear bias to the cost estimates. Much of the historical controversy over the shape of marginal and average cost curves appears traceable to this kind of confusion. The solution to the problem, other than to use an engineering approach, is to obtain accounting data in sufficient detail to separate cost components and outputs associated with changes in rates, length of operation, or discrete time periods such as a day or a week and so to formulate the statistical model in a manner consistent with the theoretical considerations discussed earlier.

Average regressions from cross-section data. In cases where cross-section data have been available it has been (and apparently still is) common practice to compute average seasonal costs for each plant, to plot this against volume per season, and to fit an average regression line which is represented to be a measure of some type of long-run cost function (for example, see [200, 204, 212, 223, 228, 233, and 251]). The shortcomings of this procedure have been recognized for so long that its persistence is surprising. The authors of the well-known study on cost behavior published by the National Bureau of Economic Research in 1943 [19] noted: "Not only may each plant be producing at some other level on its short-run average cost curve than the tangency point with the envelope, but with changes in price in any period it is certain to be out of long-run equilibrium. The fact that many establishments have grown piecemeal, and hence may have larger costs for a particular scale than a firm planned for that scale, will also distort the statistical relationship out of all resemblance to its analytical counterpart." In 1944 Erdman [28] made a similar point with regard to some of the early cost studies of agricultural marketing firms, and Bressler [13] in 1945 noted that such average regression lines "combine and confuse cost changes that result from more complete utilization of a plant of a given scale with the cost changes that accompany changes in scale."

A related type of criticism, commonly referred to as the "regression fallacy," was later developed by Stigler [79] and Friedman [32]. Stigler gives an example of three firms which *on the average* produce the same output per year but with random fluctuations around the average. Because of large fixed costs, in a particular year the plants with lower than average volume show higher average accounting costs while those with larger than average volume show lower average costs. "This fall in average cost with output would seem to show that there are definite economies of large-scale production, and yet actually the result is due only to the facts that all costs are not variable in the short-run and that output is subject to chance fluctuations." (Also see Johnston [219, pp. 188-192].)

In yet another criticism Friedman [32] has argued that in a competitive industry all firms would have the same average costs if specialized differences were properly capitalized. Variations in outputs from one firm to another would be due either to mistakes or the existence of specialized resources controlled by the firm. Cross-section data would thus reveal nothing about economies of scale. Walters [249] and Johnston [219] have noted that this objection would not apply in an imperfectly competitive world. Johnston particularly stresses the influence of the size of the market (local demand). The local demand and the assembly and distribution costs appear to be the main factors which permit the existence of agricultural marketing firms of widely differing scale. Since there has been substantial controversy among economists regarding the extent and nature of economies of scale, it would seem that imperfect information could also account for some real cross-section variation in plant size.

Although average regressions of the type described are highly suspect and clearly cannot be regarded as estimates of theoretical economies of scale curves, we still must ask whether they have any other value. Two points have been advanced which tend to support the notion that some meaningful interpretations may be possible. First, Johnston considers an example in which plant sizes vary, but the output of each plant is subject to "transient" variations around some normal level. The degree of distortion in the average regressions turns out to be small in this case, and Johnston concludes that "the statistical results confirm the hypothesis of economies of scale, although the *extent* of the economies may have sometimes been exaggerated." This is not too comforting, however, since an average regression which is able to confirm the existence of economies of scale may still miss badly on the level and the shape of the long-run cost function.

A more substantial point is developed by Walters [248] for the case where product demand, and therefore output, is variable. He formulates the concept of an expected cost curve based on costs of operating at a range of output rates and then argues that "the results of empirical studies should normally be interpreted as estimates of an expected cost function."[31] Just how they should be interpreted in cases where differences in management efficiency, historical growth factors, or data distortions are also important is not clear.

Attempts to avoid the regression fallacy have taken several forms. Most commonly a measure of capacity has been incorporated as a variable in the statistical analysis (for examples, see [225, 229, and 232]). A family of short-run cost functions may be obtained from the cross-section function by holding the capacity variable constant at various levels. Another approach is to classify plants by size, fit cross-section cost-volume relationships for each group (perhaps including a capacity variable within groups if the range is large), and then to draw an envelope function to obtain the scale curve [216, 256]. Two other approaches have been used in cases where both time series and cross-section data are available. One is to combine the two series into a single analysis of covariance model, allowing separately for individual plant and time effects (for example, see [217]). The other alternative is to develop short-run cost functions from time series for each plant and then to construct an envelope function (perhaps graphically) to the short-run cost curves [251].

Note that each of the methods of adjusting for the regression fallacy still produces an average regression but the things averaged may differ. The first two cases average differences due to management efficiency, environmental factors, and accounting variations. The analysis of covariance approach corrects for management and other differences in level of cost among plants and averages slopes of cost functions among firms. This may produce a peculiar hybrid type of function that is difficult to interpret (see Johnson [217, p. 184]).[32] The last method develops short-run time series cost functions for each firm, with the envelope to these functions coming the closest of the four to approximating the theoretical concept of a long-run cost curve.

Frontier functions. For the case where only cross-section data are available, Bressler [13] has suggested that instead of fitting average functions the long-run cost function might be estimated as an envelope function to the bottom of the cost-volume scatter diagram. He noted that "such a curve would be more defensible as an approach to economies of scale than the average regression, for at least it may approach the true curve." Although application of the envelope approach to the analysis of cross-section cost data has been very limited, it has received considerable attention with respect to production functions.[33] First brought into prominence by Farrell [210] and Farrell and Fieldhouse [211] as a basis for measuring productive efficiency, the frontier production function concept has been elaborated and extended by Bressler [203], Boles [201, 202], Seitz [236, 237, 238], Sitorus [241], Aigner and Chu [196], and Timmer [246, 247].

The basic approach to obtaining a frontier function is to constrain errors to one sign, fitting either least lines or least squares with linear or quadratic programming techniques. Timmer [246] identifies three variants of the approach: (1) The Farrell and Fieldhouse approach, with further programming elaborations by Boles, transforms all observations on plant outputs and inputs to a unit activity basis (inputs per unit of output) and derives an efficient unit isoquant in input-output space. A measure of scale is required if the plants are of different size. The iterative procedure used to estimate the efficient unit isoquant does not require the specification of a functional form. (2) Aigner and Chu specify a particular form of production function (in this case Cobb-Douglas) and fit this function with the error term constrained to be negative. (3) Timmer [247] formulates a "chance constrained" model which may build on either the Farrell or the Aigner and Chu approaches. In this case the frontier is estimated in a probabilistic fashion by constraining some percentage of the observations (say, 3 percent) to fall ouside the frontier surface. The objective is to eliminate extreme observations which might be the result of data errors. This may require considerable judgment on the part of the researcher, particularly if the sample of observations is small.

Only one application of the frontier approach to agricultural marketing firms was uncovered. In this study O'Connor and Hammonds [230] used the Farrell approach to measure efficiency in meat-handling systems.[34] They concluded that it was inferior to an alternative UOP (unit output price) profit model developed by Lau and Yotopoulos. However, in view of the progress suggested in other applications, the general approach appears to merit further exploration. But it is still subject to many of the data and specification problems of the more conventional methods.

Form of the cost function. Another perplexing problem facing the cost and efficiency analyst — one which may apply to production functions as well as to cost functions and to both frontier and average functions — is the specification of the form of the function to be fitted to the data. That it is indeed a problem has been amply demonstrated by Stollsteimer, Bressler, and Boles [244]. Taking the cross-section data used by Phillips [232] to estimate cost functions for mixed feed mills, they showed that it was possible to develop a wide variety of cost relationships, most based on seemingly quite plausible assumptions about cost behavior and each yielding highly respectable measures of correlation and reliability. A measure of capacity was used in all cases so that the regression fallacy was not an issue.

Stollsteimer, Bressler, and Boles [244] note how such different results could be obtained from one set of basic data and still yield correlation coefficients and t-ratios which suggest high degrees of reliability:

In part, this situation can be explained by the fact that changes in equation form were accompanied by compensating changes in the regression coefficients of the independent variables. . . . The changes in estimated slopes of the regression surface which accompanied changes in equation form apparently take place in such a way that each of the alternative models fit the observed cost-volume points quite well. However, when these alternative slopes are projected to the long-run situation, the alternative models yield quite different results.

Their conclusions are devastating:

Our general conclusion must be that the analysis of such cross-section data may result in high correlations and apparently significant regression coefficients, without providing the basis for confidence in the results as even rough approximations of the basic cost relations involved. . . . To be specific with respect to this study of feed mills costs, we are at a loss when faced with the problem of selecting among the several alternative formulations — although we would reject some and limit the range of applicability of others on logical grounds as noted earlier. We do not know whether long-run average cost levels are relatively high or low or if they are characterized by minor declines as scale is increased or by pronounced economies of scale extending over wide ranges in capacity. In a similar way, we find it impossible to forecast the effects of volume on costs for a plant of particular capacity. We would find it difficult or impossible to advise plant owners and managers as to the probable cost consequences of building larger or smaller plants or of combining the volumes for two or three plants in a single operation. Faced with this great diversity of empirical findings, we may well wonder if cost functions derived from cross-section data are fact or fantasy.

Although these dismal findings apply directly only to the cross-section models described above, the general conclusions and criticisms appear applicable to much of the cross-section analysis published to date. Some of the objections may be reduced through more careful data selection and by obtaining more detailed information about each plant, but this may require direct observation which soon moves us away from pure statistical cross-section analysis to the economic-engineering approach.

THE SURVIVOR TECHNIQUE

To complete our discussion of statistical approaches we need to consider briefly an alternative method of measuring scale economies called the "survivor technique."[35] Originated in its modern form by Stigler [243], it has been applied to many manufacturing industries by Saving [234], Weiss [250], Shepherd [240], and the staff of the Federal Trade Commission [213]. Some forty food industries have been included in varying degree (see especially [213]).

The survivor technique is conceptually appealing and mechanically simple. It is based on the hypothesis that plant sizes which are efficient will survive and plant sizes which are inefficient will decline. The distribution of value added by plant size class (usually measured in terms of numbers of employees) is computed for two or more census years and the changes in relative shares are compared. Data other than census figures could be used, of course, if available. Plants in size classes which show increases in shares are presumed to be "optimal." The smallest group which shows an increase in its relative share is classed as the "minimum efficient size."

The survivor technique avoids many of the problems encountered with cross-section analysis while retaining the advantage of being based on actual market results. Although no functional relationships are derived, the estimates of minimum efficient size, and the optimum size range if reliable and meaningful, could serve managers and policy makers about as well as functional estimates for some purposes. Unfortunately, the technique has many shortcomings.

A major problem is the fact that plants may survive for many reasons other than their internal efficiency (see Bain [198]). Furthermore, efficient scale may be influenced by environmental conditions pertaining to the extent of the market, sources of raw materials, and length of operation which usually are not revealed by the data used. The use of employment as a measure of size introduces the possibility of further bias caused by innovations that substitute capital for labor. Other problems relate to the method of measuring survival (by relative shares of sales, absolute growth, or number of plants) and to the data itself, particularly the changes in classifications between census years.

These limitations cast considerable doubt on the validity of the estimates obtained and the usefulness of this technique as a tool for agricultural marketing analysts. It may have some value when used with other approaches and when screened against other evidence, such as static size distribution and an analysis of the influences at work on plant sizes (Shepherd [240]). But Shepherd concludes that "the results fall short of the early promise of the survivor technique: the failures are many, the proven successes few."

The Economic-Engineering Approach

The alternative to descriptive and statistical analysis of plant accounting data is to synthesize cost functions from engineering, biological, or other detailed specifications of input-output relationships. This approach has come to be referred to most commonly as economic-engineering analysis. It has also been called the building block approach, the engineering approach, or the synthetic approach.

The technique, as applied to agricultural marketing firms, was originated in the early 1940s by R. G. Bressler, Jr., and his associates at the University of Connecticut. The excellent series of research bulletins produced by this group, under the overall title *Efficiency in Milk Marketing in Connecticut,*[36] provided a foundation which was eagerly embraced by many agricultural economists newly involved in efficiency studies following the enactment of the Agricultural Marketing Act of 1946.

The synthetic method of model building was further refined and elaborated in the early 1950s, with the work at the University of California (to which Bressler had transferred his services) in particular serving as a prototype for many studies to follow. The California approach is described in detail in French, Sammet, and Bressler [401], Clarke [537], Boles [311], and Sammet [69]. Other early contributors to the development of the economic-engineering research methodology included Brewster [485], C. French [318], and Homme [267]. In a somewhat parallel development Chenery [258, 259] and Ferguson [262] pioneered the use of engineering data to estimate production and cost functions in nonagricultural firms. Subsequent applications in industry appear to have been less extensive than in agricultural marketing operations. For examples, see the trucking study by Smith [277] and the mathematical programming models of Isard [268] and Manne [270].

SCOPE OF RESEARCH

The economic-engineering approach, as defined here, encompasses studies ranging from simple descriptive comparisons of labor time requirements, through industrial engineering-oriented studies of methods improvement, to detailed estimates of short-run and long-run cost functions. All of these studies share the common feature of concern with micro-components of plant production functions. Some idea of the extent of this type of research may be obtained from table 2. The bracketed numbers in the table refer to 345 plant efficiency studies published since 1950. They are grouped by time period, by commodity or function, and according to the character or objectives of the study. The table excludes studies pertaining to farm supply operations such as bulk fertilizer handling and blending.

The 107 economies of scale studies listed in the table have been separated into two groups based on differences in approach. The studies classed as "economies of scale only" are developed from model plants in which costs of alternative production techniques receive only implicit consideration. The

Table 2. Economic-Engineering Analysis of Plant Efficiency in Agricultural Marketing: A Classification of Studies, 1950-75

Primary Focus of Studies[a]

Commodity and Function	Economies of Scale Only		Economies of Scale and Methods of Efficiency		Methods of Efficiency		Descriptive Cost Models	
	Before 1960	1960 and Later	Before 1960	1960 and Later	Before 1960	1960 and Later	Before 1960	1960 and Later
Cattle feeding		[284, 285, 286, 287, 288, 289, 290, 294]		[282, 283, 293]				[281, 291, 292]
Cotton assembly and ginning		[295, 298, 299, 300, 301, 302, 303, 304]				[297]	[296]	[305]
Dairy products processing	[306, 308, 311, 314, 316, 317, 325, 330, 350]	[329, 333, 335, 336, 343, 351]		[307, 331, 345]	[312, 318, 319, 320, 321, 322, 323, 324, 339, 342, 346]	[315, 328, 340, 341, 344]	[313, 334, 337, 349]	[309, 310, 326, 327, 332, 338, 347, 348]
Egg packing assembly, and distribution		[353, 356, 360, 363, 364, 365]		[352, 355, 359]	[362, 367]	[357, 369]	[354, 361]	[358, 366, 368]
Fresh fruit and vegetable packing and assembly	[461]		[372, 398, 400, 401, 457]	[373, 389, 392, 409, 424, 431]	50 studies[b]	[371, 375, 380, 414, 422, 423, 427, 429, 430, 444, 459, 463]	[402, 403, 404, 406, 408, 411, 425, 434, 436, 440, 441, 455]	[376, 383, 412, 433, 437, 438, 439, 440, 453]
Fruit and vegetable processing	[480]	[473, 476]	[467, 478]	[465, 468, 469, 472, 474, 475, 479]	[470]	[466, 477]		[471]
Elevator and milling operations	[488, 494, 502]	[481, 483, 489, 490, 495, 501, 505, 506, 512]	[485, 486, 497]		[482, 487, 491]	[484, 492, 493, 499, 503, 507, 510]	[496]	[498, 500, 504, 508, 509, 511, 513]

Table 2. Economic-Engineering Analysis of Plant Efficiency in Agricultural Marketing: A Classification of Studies, 1950-75 (Cont.)

| | Primary Focus of Studies[a] | | | | | | | |
| Commodity and Function | Economies of Scale Only | | Economies of Scale and Methods of Efficiency | | Methods of Efficiency | | Descriptive Cost Models | |
	Before 1960	1960 and Later	Before 1960	1960 and Later	Before 1960	1960 and Later	Before 1960	1960 and Later
Meat packing and assembly		[516, 518, 527]		[522, 524]		[514, 515, 519, 520, 521, 528, 529]		[517, 523, 525, 526]
Milk collection and delivery					[531, 532, 541, 546, 547, 549]	[534, 536, 543, 545]	[530, 533, 537, 538, 539]	[535, 540, 542, 544, 548, 550, 551, 552, 553, 554]
Poultry processing and assembly	[555, 557, 561, 562, 570, 573]	[558, 565, 574, 575]	[556]		[560]	[564, 576]	[563, 569]	[559, 566, 567, 568, 571, 572]
Wholesale and retail food store operations	[599]				[577, 580, 581, 583, 585, 586, 587, 589, 591, 592, 594, 597, 598, 600, 603, 604, 605, 606, 608]	[578, 579, 582, 588, 590, 595, 596, 601, 602, 607]		[584, 593]
Miscellaneous	[612, 616, 620]		[619, 621]		[611, 613, 618, 623, 625]	[610, 622]		[609, 614, 615, 617, 624]

[a]Numbers in brackets refer to publications listed in the reference section.

[b]Fruit and vegetable methods efficiency studies before 1960: [370, 374, 377, 378, 379, 381, 382, 384, 385, 386, 387, 388, 390, 391, 393, 394, 395, 396, 397, 399, 405, 407, 410, 413, 415, 416, 417, 418, 419, 420, 421, 426, 428, 432, 435, 442, 443, 445, 446, 447, 448, 449, 450, 451, 452, 454, 458, 460, 462, 464].

second group of studies synthesize total long-run cost functions from efficient component functions with best production techniques determined as outlined earlier in the theory section. These studies will be considered more fully later in the discussion.

The 152 studies classed under "methods efficiency" typically deal with single components of marketing firm activities such as a stage or a group of activities within a plant. The major focus is on developing improved production techniques or comparing the efficiency of alternative existing techniques. Although the effects of scale on choice of technique may be considered in some cases, the reports are not listed as economies of scale studies since they do not pertain to total plant operations.

The 86 reports classed as "descriptive cost models" include mostly comparative analyses based on time or work sampling studies or measures of cost functions for a single plant. Many of these studies are similar to descriptive analysis of accounting data, except that some of the data have been obtained by quasi-engineering measurements of labor time requirements rather than from accounting records.

The studies are separated into two publication time periods to see if there has been any significant change in research output or emphasis. Assuming that table 2 includes high and equal proportions of studies published before and after 1960, three things are revealed. First, the total number of studies published during the 1960s and early 1970s is almost the same as that during the 1950s, but the commodity distribution has shifted considerably. Operations such as meat packing, cattle feeding, and cotton ginning, which received little attention from synthesizers in the 1950s were brought more fully into the fold in the 1960s. Finally, there has been a shift toward greater emphasis on complete plant studies, rather than individual plant processes, as indicated by the increase in studies dealing with economies of scale and the decrease in studies concerned only with methods improvement.

THE ECONOMIC-ENGINEERING TECHNIQUE

If the reader were to select at random one of the studies listed in table 2 with the expectation that a review of the contents would provide a good guide to economic-engineering methodology, the chances are good that he would be sadly disappointed or, worse yet, would be misled and misinformed. Although the list includes many excellent studies, the reports have varied widely in the depth, rigor, and skill with which they have been developed and in the character and objectives of the analysis. The economic-enginneering technique thus is better described in terms of what seems to have evolved as standard good practice, given particular study objectives, than in terms of methods that have actually been followed. Our focus is on studies combining process or stage analyses into functional estimates which may reveal the nature of short-run cost functions, the comparative costs of alternative production methods under a range of conditions, and economies of scale.

The nature of economic-engineering analysis perhaps can be described most clearly in terms of a series of procedural steps.[37]

1. *System description.* The economic-engineering method requires much greater familiarity with technical aspects of production than does the typical analysis of accounting data. The researcher thus must become familiar, through plant visits and consultations, with the production systems and organization of activities within and among the firms of concern. To begin his analysis he must be able to delineate the various plant stages and to specify fully the nature and sequence of operations to be performed within the plant or the system being studied. Typically, process flow charts and detailed job descriptions are developed to aid in visualizing the system structure.

2. *Specification of alternative production techniques.* Unless the research is concerned only with the development of a short-run cost function for a single plant, the researcher must consider the variations in production technique that might be employed at each stage of the plant operation. For example, a fruit-packing plant might have a choice of three different types of equipment to use in the grading stage, two alternatives for box filling, and so on. In addition, there are alternative choices in building construction, layout, and in-plant transportation which may not relate to any particular "in-line" stage. For collection or delivery systems there are alternative choices of vehicle and methods of loading and unloading. Information on these alternatives is obtained by consultation with managers, engineers, and manufacturers and by visits to a cross section of plants using various production techniques. The sample of plants selected for economic-engineering analysis thus is purposive rather than random.

3. *Estimation of the production function.* The total plant production function is obtained by combining the production functions for the various operating stages or components. The "building blocks" for the stage production functions are the building and equipment capacities and the associated input-output relationships for labor, chemicals, energy, and materials.

Equipment capacities may be determined by measurements in plants selected for detailed study or from manufacturers' and/or engineers' specifications. Building space requirements are determined by space requirements for equipment, work space, storage, and traffic movement. Typically, these requirements are determined by observations in sample plants. Alternative building designs and constructions are developed by consultation with building contractors or construction engineers.

The specification of equipment, layout (or route organization and distance for collection and delivery systems), and building space generally prescribes the types of jobs to be performed, although some variation in crew organization and work procedures may be possible. Labor performance standards for various tasks may be developed from any of several sources. Most commonly they are derived from work measurement data obtained by time, production, or work sampling studies in a sample of plants which utilize the various production techniques to be considered. More rarely, standard work tables may be used.[38] A source requiring somewhat less time and expense is the technique of crew survey based on informal observation of crew organization and interviews with plant personnel [69]. If detailed payroll records are available, they may sometimes be used as a means of estimating labor requirements, but normally they are better used as a means of checking the engineering estimates (see [69, 401]).

Input-output relationships for chemicals and energy may be determined by engineering formulas and studies of various machine and process requirements (see Chenery [258] and Smith [278]). For agricultural marketing firms, they are frequently estimated by simple specifications of requirements per hour of machine operation or directly in cost terms from plant record data [69].

Given the basic input-output standards plus appropriate allowances for rest periods, delays, breakdowns, and the like, the production function for each stage is obtained by a simple tabular arrangement. Average output rates are specified and the corresponding input rates determined from the performance standards and technical specifications. Note that most "in-line" stages (with grading an important exception) involve only a single output or "through-put" variable. At one end of the plant this may consist of units of raw material or animals to be processed. In other parts of the plant the stage outputs consist of various partially processed or finally processed products.

Production functions must also be specified for "off-line" activities such as record keeping, receiving raw materials, supervision, custodial inputs, plant preparation, off-season activities, and the like. Some of these inputs are related to the hours or days of operation for a particular plant, not to specific outputs. Others tend to be fixed per season if the plant operates at all, but are zero otherwise. Added together, these component production functions form a multidimensional total plant production function, and ultimately a total cost function, that would be impossible to estimate by ordinary statistical analysis of total aggregated accounting data. Plant record data may, however, serve a very important and often neglected purpose — that of establishing the credibility and character of the estimated component production functions. The synthesized functions may reflect standardized conditions not found in any particular plant, and comparison with actual input-output observations can provide a type of "ball park" check plus an indication of the level of performance being modeled.

4. *Synthesis of cost functions.* Once the production functions have been specified, the cost functions are determined by applying factor prices. Short-run cost functions are obtained by specification of a set of production techniques and their capacities (thus defining a particular plant) and computing variable operating costs for a range of output rates up to or in excess of the design capacity limits. Time and partial product dimensions can be eliminated or varied by specifying operating conditions such as length of season and ratios of each stage product to the final product or products.

To develop long-run cost functions, consideration must be given to all alternative stage production techniques and to the measurement of prices of durable inputs. The usual procedure for the latter is to specify an expected life of the equipment, divide this into the installed cost, and add an amount to cover the cost of borrowed capital, taxes, insurance, and, in some cases, a portion of average maintenance costs.

The long-run cost function may be derived by either of two approaches. The most common practice has been to construct several model plants of varying capacities, perhaps for alternative lengths of season, and then to fit envelope functions either explicitly or implicitly (see references in table 2 under "scale only"). With plants designed to have specific engineered capacities, this involves fitting the function to the lower measure of cost associated with design capacity. The model plant approach is most appropriate in cases where production techniques are fairly standardized or where the researcher is confident of being able to select *a priori* the best methods for each of his model plants. Otherwise there is some risk of obtaining biased estimates of the true scale curve because of overlooked technical possibilities.

In cases in which several alternative production techniques are available at several stages, the possible number of model plants may be very large. Consequently, the most efficient procedure may be to estimate long-run cost functions by stages (or to determine by stages the best technique for each output range and length of season) and then to combine these cost functions into a total long-run cost function. Variants of this procedure are used in the studies classed under "economies of scale and methods efficiency" in table 2. Very often a smoothed function is fitted to the synthesized cost-volume and length of run observations so that the cost function may be represented in more convenient equation form.

CRITIQUE OF THE ECONOMIC-ENGINEERING APPROACH

Table 2 shows that studies using the economic-engineering approach have outnumbered studies based exclusively on accounting records almost three to one.[39] This suggests some important comparative advantages. The economic-engineering approach avoids many of the problems encountered in strictly statistical studies. Moreover, it can be applied in cases wherein accounting record data are not available, and it can more readily handle cost functions with multiple products and the added dimensions of length of operation. And it is usually the only approach possible when the objective is to compare methods or develop improved methods of operation.

A major limitation of the economic-engineering approach is its high research cost. The amount of technical detail required to synthesize cost functions can be very expensive compared with the analysis of accounting data. Moreover, as the size and complexity of the operation increases, so does the possibility that the model builder will omit some aspect of cost (Black [257]). In principle, however, large and complex operations can be synthesized as well as smaller ones if the researcher is willing and able to devote the time and care necessary to obtain and organize the massive technical data. Although the economic-engineering approach has not been applied to the study of super plants such as in automobile manufacturing, it has been used successfully in some fairly large food processing operations (see [473, 479, and 524]). But in view of the expense involved, the objectives and expected benefits should be weighed very carefully against the research cost in each individual study.

One means of reducing the costs of synthesizing cost functions is by systematic tabulation of accumulated information on physical input-output relationships. Such data can be used in other studies involving similar operations. Although often cited as an advantage of the synthetic approach, recent publications by a southern marketing committee (Project SM-30) represent the first coordinated efforts along these lines (see [431, 474, and 475]). More recently, Sammet [272] has suggested a basis for evaluating the transferability of such microeconomic data over time.

Another still undeveloped possibility for reducing research costs is the use of a more aggregative approach combining economic-engineering, accounting, and statistics. Input standards and cost components might be analyzed in terms of broad aggregates while still avoiding many of the problems associated with accounting data only.

The economic-engineering approach has been criticized for the general lack of findings pertaining to diseconomies of scale. This has been attributed to the use of constant input coefficients (especially for labor) and the inability to measure or account for coordination problems as plant scale increases. Furthermore, although the engineering approach may handle technical aspects of production processes with considerable accuracy, estimates pertaining to management, sales, and service activities are apt to be very crude [213, p. 95]. Walters has suggested that in some cases the separate plant processes may intersect with one another and so may not be additively separable [249]. These points are difficult to dispute as generalizations. In practice, however, the magnitude of distortion may be fairly small, particularly in view of the many other problems encountered with the statistical approach.

A related point made by Black [257] and others is that "the estimates derived from synthesis are cut adrift from the standard measures of reliability." Although perhaps attributing a bit too much to measures of reliability in standard statistical analyses, given the nature of the data problems outlined earlier, this is a valid criticism of many synthetic studies. Synthetic estimates clearly need to be checked against alternative sources of information, particularly actual plant performance data.

On balance the economic-engineering approach appears to offer more in terms of analytical power (at a higher cost) than either the descriptive approach or the statistical approach. However, the optimal choice of method depends on the objectives of the study and the funds and data available. An amalgamation of all three approaches may be appropriate in some cases.

The Evidence on Economies of Scale

Of all the factors that may affect marketing efficiency, the relation of cost to scale has received by far the most attention. In view of the empirical and theoretical interest, an attempt has been made to tabulate the results of these studies in a way that reveals something about the relative magnitudes and extent of economies of scale. This proved to be a difficult task since many different commodities and units of measurement are involved. Moreover, even studies dealing with the same commodities and the same units of measurement may differ significantly in the time units used (per hour, per day, per week, per season) and the associated specifications of conditions. In some cases the conditions are not clearly stated at all.

In order to make sense out of all this for summary and comparative purposes, all cost-scale findings were expressed in relative terms. The largest plant considered in each study was given a scale value of 100 and the reported average unit cost for that scale was also given a value of 100. Costs were tabulated for plants ranging in scale from 10 to 80 percent of the scale of the largest plant. These costs were then expressed as a percentage of the cost in the largest plant.

The results of these tabulations for both the economic-engineering studies and the statistical analyses of cross-section data are given in table 3. Not all of the scale studies listed in table 2 are included. Omitted are several that proved especially difficult to interpret or which dealt with only a single plant process or component rather than the total plant operation. Most of the studies included presented cost-scale relationships for a variety of situations. The values given in table 3 pertain to what appear to be the conditions most commonly

Table 3. Economies of Scale in Agricultural Marketing Plants: A Summary of Findings in Selected Studies, 1950-74

Source	Commodity and Function	Output Units	Volume Range	Relative Average Total Unit Cost* Plant Scale Values+					
				10%	20%	40%	60%	80%	100%
Economic-Engineering Studies									
1. [285] King, 1962	Feed beef (commercial)	1,000 head	10-70 per year	--	128	111	104	102	100
2. [294] Williams and McDowell, 1965	Feed beef (drylot)	1 million lbs. gained	.25-12.75 per 120 day period	116	111	104	103	101	100
3. [287] Malone and Rogers, 1965	Feed beef ("warm-up")	1 head	300-2,400 per year	--	107	104	101	101	100
4. [289] McCoy and Wakefield, 1966	Feed beef (farm)	1 head	50-1,150 per year	139	115	100	100	100	100
5. [283] Hunter and Madden, 1966	Feed beef (commercial)	1 head	135-15,300 per year	113	107	103	101	101	100
6. [288] McCoy and Hausman, 1967	Feed beef (commercial)	1,000 head	4-64 per year	114	109	102	101	100	100
7. [284] Irrer and Jones, 1971	Feed beef	1 head	200-2,000 per year	132	127	111	103	101	100
8. [298] Covey and Hudson, 1963	Gin cotton	1 bale	6,000-22,000 per season	--	--	124	113	107	100
	Assemble and gin[a]								
	High density			--	--	116	109	104	100
	Medium density			--	--	115	108	104	100
	Low density			--	--	107	103	101	100
9. [299] Lafferty, 1964	Gin cotton	1 bale	16,000-65,000 per season	128 (25%)	121 (33%)	115 (50%)	109 (67%)	103 (75%)	100
10. [302] Thompson and Ward, 1964	Gin cotton	1 bale	8-12 per hour				106 (66%)	102 (83%)	100
11. [301] Metcalf, 1965	Gin cotton	1 bale	2.4-9.6 per hour	156 (25%)	138 (33%)	126 (50%)	113 (67%)	107 (75%)	100
	Assemble, store, and gin[b]								
	High density			146 (25%)	131 (33%)	122 (50%)	110 (67%)	106 (75%)	100
	Medium density			145 (25%)	131 (33%)	121 (50%)	111 (67%)	106 (75%)	100

142

	Low density			138 (25%)	125 (33%)	118 (50%)	109 (67%)	104 (75%)	100
12. [295] Anderson, 1966	Gin cotton	1 bale	4,436-13,440 per season	--	--	136	121	107	100
	Assemble and gin[c]								
	High density			--	--	123	113	106	100
	Medium density			--	--	121	113	105	100
	Low density			--	--	114	109	104	100
13. [304] Wilmot, Stedronsky, Looney, and Moore, 1967	Gin cotton	1 bale	4,620-18,480 per season	--	--	123	114	105	100
14. [300] Looney and Wilmot, 1971	Gin cotton	1 bale	4,620-27,720 per season	147 (16%)	134 (22%)	115 (44%)	109 (66%)	102 (83%)	100
15. [325] Henry, Bressler, and Frick, 1948	Process whole milk	1 qt.	228-4,560 per day	177	149	130	120	109	100
16. [350] Walker, Preston, and Nelson, 1953	Manufacture butter and nonfat dry milk	1,000 lbs. (input)	45-255 per day		151	120	113	107	100
17. [316] Frazer, Nielsen, and Ladd, 1956	Manufacture butter	1 million lbs.	.2-2.2 per season	422	206	144	125	111	100
18. [330] Kolmer, Homme, and Ladd, 1957	Spray-dry nonfat dry milk in butter-powder plants	1 million lbs. powder	1-3.175 per season	--	--	136	114	107	100
19. [314] Conner, Webster, and Owens, 1957	Bottle milk	1 packaged unit	1,000-19,500 per day	183	130	115	109	104	100
20. [311] Boles, 1958	Evaporate milk	1,000 696-lb. cases	300-1,150 per season	--	--	139	117	107	100
21. [343] Strain and Christensen, 1960	Process fluid milk	1 qt.	1,684,100-26,945,600 per year	161	137	116	109	102	100
22. [333] Miller and Graf, 1970	Manufacture cottage cheese	1 lb.	75,000-2,000,000 per season	247	210	161	127	111	100
23. [329] Knudtson and Koller, 1960	Manufacture butter	1 million lbs.	21.9-109.5 per season	--	181	133	114	105	100
24. [222] Knudtson, 1958	Manufacture butter	1 million lbs.	9-77 per year	--	185	140	120	110	100
25. [307] Babb and Taylor, 1962	Manufacture ice cream	1,000 gals.	100-350 per year	--	--	176	128	108	100
26. [351] Webster et al., 1963	Process fluid milk	1 qt.	6,000-10,000 per day	197 (6%)	135	110 (50%)			100

Table 3. Economies of Scale in Agricultural Marketing Plants: A Summary of Findings in Selected Studies, 1950-74 (Cont.)

Source	Commodity and Function	Output Units	Volume Range	Relative Average Total Unit Cost* Plant Scale Values+					
				10%	20%	40%	60%	80%	100%
27. [329] O'Connell and Snyder, 1964	Process fluid milk products	1 unit^d	1,929,911-30,878,576 per year	162	135	113	105	103	100
28. [345] Taylor, Bartlett, and C. French, 1964	Manufacture ice cream	1,000 gals.	100-500 per year	- -	251	152	122	113	100
29. [695] Cobia and Babb, 1964	Package fluid milk only	1 qt.	5,000-130,000 per day	129	119	110	106	103	100
[685] Babb, 1967	Package and distribute			124	115	108	104	102	100
	Package, distribute, and assemble			122	114	107	103	101	100
30. [331] Lilwall and Hammond, 1970	Manufacture cheddar cheese	1,000 lbs.	50-1373.4 per day	162	127	109	105	101	100
31. [356] Gallimore and Sternberger, 1962	Hatch chicks	1 million chicks	1.022112-17.52192 per year	148	136	117	109	104	100
32. [364] Pedersen, 1965	Hatch turkeys	1 salable poult	319.738-6,394.752 per year	139	128	114	106	103	100
33. [363] Pedersen, 1967	Hatch chicks	1 million salable pullets	.379-3.79 per year	123	112	107	103	101	100
34. [352] Bird, 1960	Pack eggs	1 30-doz. case	6-96 per hour	133	118	108	105	103	100
35. [365] Peeler and King, 1963	Pack eggs	1 30-doz. case	649-10,384 per week	117	109	103	101	100	100
36. [359] Jones, 1964	Pack eggs	1 30-doz. case	14,560-249,600 per year	121	114	106	103	101	100
37. [353] Byers and Callahan, 1965	Pack eggs	1 30-doz. case	100-4,000 per week	146	120	108	103	101	100
	Assemble pack^e			132	110	99	97	97	100

38. [372] Bird, 1958	Pack fresh potatoes	10-lb. sack	500-5,000 per hour	--	134	112	105	100	100
39. [401] French, Sammet, and Bressler, 1956	Pack fresh pears	1,000 lbs.	2,000-20,000 per season	159	126	110	106	103	100
40. [461] Thor, 1959	Pack fresh citrus[f]	1 3/5-bu. box	120,000-850,000 per season	--	111	104	101	101	100
41. [457] Stallings and Sammet, 1959	Pack fresh plums	100 28-lb. crates	.5-12.0 per hour	157	124	111	104	101	100
42. [398] French and Gillette, 1959	Pack fresh apples	1 bu.	25-1,000 per hour	122	113	105	101	100	100
	Assemble and pack[g]								
	High density			118	110	103	100	99	100
	Medium density			111	104	99	97	98	100
	Low density			109	103	97	96	97	100
43. [424] Mathia and King, 1963	Pack fresh sweet potatoes	1 bu.	20,000-80,000 storable capacity	--	--	102	101	100	100
44. [373] Bohall, Farrish, and Podany, 1964	Pack green-ripe tomatoes	40-lb. carton	300-925 per hour			113 (32%)	103 (59%)		100
45. [389] Carman, 1967	Pack fresh apples	1 bu.	100-500 per hour	--	122	106	103	101	100
46. [422] Mathia, 1967	Store apples	1 carton	10,000-80,000 per season	110 (12.5%)		105 (25%)		100 (50%)	100
47. [423] Mathia, 1969	Pack fresh blueberries	12-pt. flat	9,375-75,000 per season	138	120	108	103	100	100 100
48. [480] Scott, 1959	Can passion fruit	1 lb. (input)	20,000-80,000 per day		111 (25%)		104 (50%)		
49. [467] Dennis, 1958	Grade and freeze strawberries	1,000 lbs.	5-25 per hour	--	130	111	105	102	100
50. [478] Reed, 1959	Assemble and process lima beans for freezing[h]	1,000 lbs.	5-30 per hour	--	113	105	102	101	100
51. [465] Davis and Hutchings, 1960	Process peas for freezing	1 lb.	5,000-30,000	--	108	103	103	102	100
52. [479] Reed and Sammet, 1963	Freeze spinach, other vegetables	1,000 lbs.	5-30 per hour	--	113	106	101	100	100
53. [469] Goble, 1964	Grade and freeze strawberries	1 lb.	400,000-2,000,000 per season	--	--	111	105	102	100
54. [467] Reed, 1967	Can sweet corn	1 case[i]	20-40 tons per hour			108 (50%)		103 (75%)	100

Table 3. Economies of Scale in Agricultural Marketing Plants: A Summary of Findings in Selected Studies, 1950-74 (Cont.)

Source	Commodity and Function	Output Units	Volume Range	Relative Average Total Unit Cost* Plant Scale Values+					
				10%	20%	40%	60%	80%	100%
55. [472] Law and Beeson, 1967	Flake sweet potatoes	1 lb. (input)	6,000-24,000 per hour	- -	- -	105	102	101	100
56. [473] Mathia, Pearson, and Ela, 1970	Can lima beans	1 case[i]	100-1,500 per hour	121 (7%)		113 (27%)	105 (53%)	102	100
	Can leafy greens		100-1,500 per hour	134 (7%)		118 (27%)	107 (53%)	103	100
57. [476] Pearson, Mathia, and Ela, 1970	Can okra	1 case[i]	100-800 per hour	194 (12%)		108 (50%)		102	100
	Can dry beans		100-1,500 per hour	131 (7%)	115 (27%)	106 (53%)		102	100
58. [485] Brewster, 1954	Process cottonseed oil	1 ton seed	10,600-105,600 per season	- -	129	105	102	101	100
59. [494] Hall, 1955	Handle grain	1 bu.	250,000-1,500,000 per season	193 (17%)	172 (27%)	145	130	130	100
	Store grain			223 (2%)	142 (16%)	119 (33%)		110 (50%)	100
60. [512] Yager, 1963	Handle grain	1 bu.	235,000-1,053,000 per season	201 (22%)	181 (28%)	119 (54%)	126 (59%)	103 (93%)	100
	Store grain		65,000-247,000 per season	154 (26%)	112	117 (50%)	126 (65%)	101 (85%)	100
61. [489] Burbee, Bardwell, and Brown, 1965	Mix broiler feed	1 ton	5,434-90,577 per season	185	156	125	113	106	100
	Mix and distribute[j]								
	High density			145	125	112	104	101	100
	Medium density			124	110	99	97	99	100
	Low density			107	97	91	93	97	100
62. [483] Austin and Nelson, 1966	Mix commercial feed	1,000 tons	6-52 per year (approx.)	- -	181	135	116	108	100

No. [Ref]	Author, year	Activity	Unit	Size range						
63. [506]	Vosloh, 1968	Mix commercial feed	1 ton	80-300 per day	--	--	133	117	108	100
64. [505]	Van Ausdle and Oldenstadt, 1969	Handle grain	1,000 bu.	70-375 per season	--	257	164	123	109	100
		Store grain		50-260 per season	--	160	117	106	103	100
65. [481]	Anderson and Helgeson, 1974	Mix commercial feeds	1,000 bu.	100-2,000 per year	375	--	150	--	--	100
		Assemble and mix commercial feeds	1,000 cwt.		246	--	120	--	--	100
66. [495]	Holder, Morrison, and Traylor, 1974	Mill rice		500-7,000 per year	171	131	114	109	104	100
67. [524]	Logan and King, 1962	Slaughter beef	1,000 head	15-250 per year	129	122	113	107	104	100
68. [522]	Logan, 1966	Slaughter beef	1 head	20-120 per hour	--	133	116	108	101	100
69. [518]	Franzmann and Kuntz, 1966	Slaughter beef	1,000 head	37-265 per year	--	104	100	98	99	100
70. [516]	Cassell and West, 1967	Slaughter hogs	1,000 head	.7-10.5 per week	150	139	124	114	107	100
		Assemble and slaughter[k]								
		High density			136	120	107	104	102	100
		Medium density			128	114	114	110	105	100
		Low density			111	106	104	103	101	100
71. [527]	Schnake, Franzmann, and Hammons, 1968	Process meat[l]	1 lb.	50,000-250,000 per week	--	126	120	--	--	100
72. [612]	Bird, 1964	Freeze-dry chicken	1 million lbs. water removed	2-16 per season	--	171	135	115	101	100
73. [616]	Gibb and Riley, 1961	Livestock auction	1 head sold	10,000-110,000 per season	253 (9%)	167 (18%)	137 (32%)	123 (50%)	110 (73%)	100
74. [620]	Kuehn, 1971	Livestock auction	1 LMU[m]	8,000-130,000 per season	176	141	114	106	103	100
75. [557]	Baum, Faris, and Walkup, 1952	Process fryers	1,000 fryers	200-9,000 per day	123	112	107	103	101	100
76. [555]	Abbott, 1954	Process turkeys	1 turkey	60-1,200 per hour	140 (5%)	117 (25%)		102 (50%)		100
77. [561]	Donald and Bishop, 1957	Process broilers	1,000 lbs.	25-400 per week	132	118	108	103	101	100
78. [570]	Rogers and Bardwell, 1959	Process broilers	1 broiler	150-10,000 per hour	138	124	110	105	102	100
79. [573]	Rogers, et al., 1958	Process broilers and other fowl[n]	1 bird	150-5,000 per hour	145	128	116	107	103	100

Table 3. Economies of Scale in Agricultural Marketing Plants: A Summary of Findings in Selected Studies, 1950-74 (Cont.)

Source	Commodity and Function	Output Units	Volume Range	Relative Average Total Unit Cost* Plant Scale Values+					
				10%	20%	40%	60%	80%	100%
80. [562] Farrish and Seaver, 1959	Process broilers	1 broiler	15,000-75,000 per hour	--	140	109	103	101	100
81. [566] Henry, Chappell, and Seagraves, 1960	Service, assemble, and process broilers	1 bird	1,800-9,600 per hour						
	High density			--	97	96	96	98	100
	Medium density			--	106	100	99	99	100
	Low density			--	115	106	103	101	100
82. [574] Rogers and Rinear, 1963	Process tom turkeys	1 million lbs.	4-76 per year (approx.)	140	120	107	104	102	100
83. [558] Burbee and Bardwell, 1964	Hatch chicks and process broilers	1 million broilers	1.19-19.76 per year	139	124	115	109	104	100
	Hatch, assemble, process, and distributeo								
	High density			130	115	106	103	102	100
	Medium density			123	112	104	102	101	100
	Low density			--	113	105	100	99	100
84. [575] Rogers and Smith, 1966	Further processing of poultry: Cooked chicken parts	1 million lbs.	1-15 per year	114	106	103	101	100	
	Statistical Studies								
85. [233] Purcell and Penny, 1955	Process and package milk in paper cartons	1 qt.	1,000-34,000 per day	139	127	117	111	103	100
86. [222] Knudtson, 1958	Manufacture butter	1 million lbs.	9-77 per year	--	240	164	136	116	100
87. [215] Hanlon and Koller, 1969	Process butter and nonfat dry milk	1 million lbs.	140-470 per year (approx.)	--	--	106	101	100	100
88. [231] Parsons and Guise, 1971	Export Abattoirp	1 cattle equiv.q	18,000-155,000 per year	--	283	167	133	113	100
89. [561] Donald and Bishop, 1957	Process broilers	1 broiler	150-4,000 per hour	102	89	88	91	95	100

			head capacity						
91. [209] Dietrich, 1969	Feed cattle	1,000 head							
92. [232] Phillips, 1956	Mix feeds	1,000 tons (input)	20-150 per year	164	141	121	110	102	100
93. [245] Thuroczy and Schlegel, 1959	Mill rice	1 cwt. (input)	100,000-1,500,000 per year	128	116	109	103	102	100
94. [225] Lindberg and Judge, 1958	Livestock auction	1 animal unit^r	4,000-75,000 per year	192	144	115	108	104	100
95. [252] Wootan and McNeely, 1966	Livestock auction	1 animal unit^s	50,000-350,000 per year	121	109	104	102	101	100
96. [204] Broadbent and Perkinson, 1971	Country hog market	1 hog-unit equivalent^t	10,000-140,000 per year (approx.)	239	191	152	136	121	100
97. [251] Wilson and Kuehn, 1971	Livestock auction	1 LMU	1,500-27,000 per year	132	115	106	103	101	100
98. [212] Farstad and Brensike, 1952	Retail meat	1,000 lbs. (input)	.4-10 per month	277	169	123	116	108	100

*Expressed as a percentage of the largest plant cost.

+Expressed as a percentage of the scale of the largest plant. It was not possible to tabulate values for exactly 10, 20, 40, 60 and 80 percent in all cases. The actual percentages for which values were tabulated are given in parentheses in the body of the table.

a300, 200, and 50 bales per square mile, respectively, available for ginning.

b100, 75, and 25 bales per square mile, respectively, available for ginning.

c300, 200, and 50 bales per square mile, respectively, available for ginning.

d1 unit equals 1 quart for all fluids except cream; 1 unit equals 1/4 quart of cream.

eAssembly costs reported for only one production density.

fIncludes picking, hauling, packing, and selling.

g30,000, 1,500, and 75 field crates (bushels) per square mile, respectively, available for packing.

hAssembly here refers only to linear field-to-plant transportation costs.

i1 case contains 24 No. 303 cans or equivalent.

j32.73, 6.55, and 1.31 tons of feed distributed per square mile, respectively.

k100, 50, and 12 hogs per square mile, respectively, available for slaughtering.

lRefers to sausages and other cured and smoked meats.

m1 LMU (livestock marketing unit) = 1 beef animal, 3 calves, 4 hogs, or 5 sheep.

nThis refers to processing exclusive of evisceration. All other processing studies reviewed included evisceration.

o25,000, 5,000, and 1,000 birds per square mile, respectively, available for processing.

PAbattoir for export meats from Australia only.

q1 cattle equivalent = 1 beef animal, 8.3 sheep, 8 pigs, or 3 calves.

r1 animal unit = 1 beef animal, 1 hog, or 6 sheep.

s1 animal unit = 1 beef animal, 1 hog, or 6 sheep.

t1 hog-unit equivalent = 1 beef animal, 4 hogs, 5 sheep, or 8 feeder pigs.

encountered. The relationships for other variants usually do not differ much in relative terms.

This type of relative comparison is very imperfect since the size of the largest plant which serves as the base measure varies considerably among studies, even for studies dealing with the same commodity. Therefore, we need to be very careful in interpreting these findings. Nevertheless, it seems possible to reach some tentative conclusions.

First, although substantial variability is observed, there appears to be some consistency in findings among studies dealing with particular types of commodities. For example, dairy processing plants and elevator and milling operations, which involve larger inputs of capital items relative to labor, show greater scale economies than plants for egg or fruit and vegetable packing.

Second, plants that are, for example, only 20 percent of the size of the largest plant considered have costs from 10 to 40 percent higher than the largest plants for high labor operations and from 30 to more than 100 percent higher for the capital intensive operations such as dairy processing. For high-labor operations, most of the in-plant scale economies have been achieved at a scale equal to 60 percent of the largest plant. The more capital-intensive operations still show significant gains at 80 percent of the largest plant scale.

If we restrict consideration to in-plant operations, only two of the studies listed (based on either economic-engineering or statistical analysis) show any diseconomies of scale within the size ranges considered. And even these cases (Franzmann and Kuntz [518] and Donald and Bishop [561]) seem open to question. However, if we include assembly or distribution costs, the picture changes a bit. The studies by French and Gillette [398], Henry et al. [566], Burbee and Bardwell [558], Byers and Callahan [353], Burbee et al. [489], and Cobia and Babb [695] all show the optimum scale shifting back to the range of 40 to 80 percent of the largest plant, depending on the level of supply density or the transportation system. Several other studies (Covey and Hudson [298], Metcalf [301], and Anderson [295]), all dealing with cotton, do not show the optimum scale shifting with the addition of assembly cost, but the magnitude of scale economies is reduced.

Because of differences in volume range and commodity coverage, it is difficult to make meaningful general comparisons between the results of statistical studies (last section of table 3) and the economic-engineering models. The two direct comparisons included in table 3 produced rather divergent results. The study by Knudtson [222] (table 3, items 24 and 86) concluded that the statistical analysis overstates the economies of scale. Whether this can be generalized seems doubtful since the type of data and sample could affect the statistical results. A study by Donald and Bishop (table 3, items 77 and 89) developed a synthetic function with continually decreasing costs and a statistical cost function with decreasing and then increasing costs (item 89). However, the authors indicated little confidence in their statistical function because of nonstandardized procedures with respect to hours of operation, uniforms for workers, and packaging operations.

The widespread existence of economies of scale, with the largest plant almost always showing the least cost, is clearly an important force in shaping the future development of the marketing system. In dealing with the specific implications of these findings, however, it is important to recognize that scale is only one of several factors affecting the level of plant cost. The model scale curves are standardized for operating conditions and abstract from the real-world concern with uncertainty and change. Moreover, they all pertain only to plants, not firms, and thus reveal little about possible advantages or disadvantages for multiplant firms. Considering the significance of increasing assembly costs and the flatness of many scale curves in the medium to large range, it is easy to see how a scale disadvantage may often be offset by other cost and market factors. The evaluation of the potential impact of these scale findings thus requires consideration of specific location and growth patterns and the relation of existing plant size and cost distributions to the estimated scale curves. Most of the plant studies referred to in table 3 did not explore the broad economic implications of their findings in depth, if at all. In the next section we shall consider some studies that have.

Applications and Extensions of Plant Efficiency Research

As the methodology of plant efficiency research advanced beyond the formative stages and as empirical applications became more widespread, the plant studies began to provide essential inputs into several other types of studies. These include (1) firm optimizing studies, (2) feasibility studies, (3) studies of efficient organization of market regions or industries, and (4) studies of wholesale market organization.[40]

Firm Optimizing Studies

Whereas cost and efficiency research provides management with information to aid in the decision process, firm optimizing research focuses on improving the skills of management in making decisions. There are two aspects involved — one concerned with the organizational and behavioral structure of management and the other with developing quantitative tools by which optimizing solutions may be obtained.

Except for occasional conceptual articles (Kohls [634] and C. French [630]), agricultural marketing firm analysis relating to the first aspect has consisted mainly of educational activities and reports published by the Farmer Cooperative Service and the various state agricultural extension services. Although Leibenstein [49], in his article on X-efficiency, has suggested that motivational factors and improved managerial skills may be very important in shifting firms from an interior position to the frontier of their production possibilities, agricultural marketing firm research pertaining to this apsect has been very limited. Agricultural economists have tended to view the area as belonging to the general field of firm management (rather than as a specialized area for marketing firm analysis) or as a teaching related activity.[41] It might be noted, however, that the measurement of managerial performance is still one of the weakest elements of firm efficiency analysis, particularly in economic-engineering studies.

Research on the second aspect has consisted mainly of case study illustrations of how operations research tools (especially linear programming) may be used to solve short-run decision problems. This type of study has been developed most extensively by James Snyder and Charles French and their colleagues at Purdue. Examples of their research and several similar types of studies by others are listed in the reference section (items [626] to [644]). The problem of determining optimum product mix has received the most attention. The procedures applied are based on generally standard operations research models.

Feasibility Studies

A time-honored approach to the development of rural areas has been to encourage the establishment of processing or marketing facilities in regions where they have not existed in the past or to expand facilities in existing areas. Successful developments of this sort may increase marketing and production opportunities for farm resources and provide more jobs and investment for the area. Feasibility studies have, as one objective, the evaluation of the likely degree of success of such ventures (Woodard [682]). Feasibility analysis may also be required when existing firms are contemplating changes in their operations such as mergers or consolidations, expansions of present facilities, adoption of new technologies, relocation, addition of new services or product lines, and expansion of market area (Schermerhorn [673] and Hammond [658]).

Dalrymple, in a comment appended to the paper by Woodard [682], argued that "there is no clearly defined area of feasibility as such. Rather, it is a hybrid made up of a number of areas of work within agricultural economics alone." Although this is undoubtedly correct, it is possible to identify four components or phases that are common to most studies which deal with questions relating to feasibility: (1) analysis of final product demand, (2) analysis of processing, assembly, and distribution costs, (3) analysis of raw product acquisition costs and (where appropriate) farm costs and returns, and (4) a final budgeting model which evaluates expected benefits (or losses) from the venture considered. Let us look at a highly simplified description of the analytical processes required.[42]

The demand phase brings together all available information on consumption and utilization trends, competition and production in other areas, commodity price levels and price elasticities, income elasticities, and institutional requirements for product marketing. This must be translated into a set of anticipated prices, f.o.b. plant, for the range of possible product volumes considered.

The second phase requires estimates of processing and assembly costs (ideally, estimates of long-run cost functions). In some cases the assembly cost component may be regarded as part of the grower cost. The processing or handling cost function is expanded to include several alternative rates of return on investment. Often consideration is given to several possible plant locations and several lengths of operating season. The estimated costs plus return on investment for various volumes and situations are then subtracted from the schedule of expected prices to obtain a "raw product fund" (see Dahle, Jones, and Nichols [651]). This determines the maximum amount the processor can pay per unit of raw product for the various situations considered.

The third phase estimates the probable acquisition cost to the processing plant. If the commodity is already produced in the area but not processed, existing prices and opportunity costs for alternative crops may establish the minimum level of prices that must be paid. However, an assessment must be made of supplies available at these prices. If the commodity has not been produced in large quantities, production costs must be synthesized. This requires consultation with production specialists. The syntheses may involve simple budgeting studies or more complex linear programming analysis for model farms such as those by Hammond et al. [660] and Stollsteimer, Coutu, and Dahle [678]. The most difficult part is to estimate the total regional production available at various prices and return rates.

The last phase combines the first three to estimate expected returns to processing and production for the several situations and volume levels considered. A complete study might also include an evaluation of expected environmental and community effects.

Although long a matter of concern to extension specialists in agricultural marketing and to the technical assistance staff of the USDA Farmer Cooperative Service, feasibility analysis apparently did not attract much research attention until the 1960s. This probably was owing to the fact that these studies usually build on previous cost analyses and it was not until the late 1950s that there was an accumulation of research findings and familiarity with the economic-engineering approach which is at the heart of most such studies. A look at the reference section shows that at least thirty-eight reports on feasibility (items [645] to [682]) have been published since the early 1960s. Very likely there are others that have been overlooked.[43] Twelve reports deal with vegetable processing, nine with livestock related operations, and the rest with a variety of products. Much of the leadership for this type of research has been provided by the economics group at North Carolina State University (see [658, 659, 660, 666, 676, and 678]).

Efficient Organization within Market Areas

Research dealing with with efficiency of marketing areas or marketing sub-industry organization has focused mainly on the determination of the optimum number, size, and location of marketing facilities. Two classes of models have emerged. One group treats space as continuous for purposes of defining optimal marketing areas for individual firms, and the other specifies finite numbers of markets, locations, and raw material sources.

THE CONTINUOUS SPACE APPROACH

Consider a region with approximately uniform average density of raw product supplies and/or spatial density of demand. Take a long-run average cost function, estimated as described earlier, and add to it average assembly and/or distribution cost functions, also estimated as described. Take the first derivative with respect to plant volume, set it equal to zero, and solve for the volume that minimizes the combined average plant, assembly, and distribution cost. Divide this volume into the total regional supply (or demand for distribution cost functions). The result is a crude approximation of the optimum number of plants for the region and the assembly or distribution area for each plant. Arbitrarily locate one plant. This then determines the locations of all other plants.

Note that in this case assembly or distribution cost functions based on circular supply areas would not be appropriate since the areas would have to overlap to blanket the entire region. With direct road patterns, hexagonal areas would be most efficient. For a hexagon circumscribed by a circle of radius r, the area is $2.598\ r^2$ and the average one-way air travel distance is .6685 r (see Beckmann [6, p. 471]). These values may be substituted in equations having the form of (30), (31), and (32) to obtain an assembly cost function based on hexagonal supply areas. Where roads form a square grid system, a square supply area is most efficient (see French [265] for the development of assembly cost functions in such a case). The difference in efficiency among these forms is very small, however.

This approach to optimum size and numbers of agricultural marketing plants was first used by Olson [718] in a study of milk assembly. Williamson [733] later elaborated the model into a more general spatial equilibrium framework for plant location, including both competitive and monopsonistic cases. He also showed how, under some fairly heroic assumptions, the model can be applied to cross-section data to obtain statistical estimates of the relation of optimum plant size to supply density. Variants of the Olson and Williamson models have been applied to grain elevator size and location by Von Oppen and Hill [729] and Araji and Walsh [684], to livestock markets by Miller and Henning [715], to optimum milk plant size by Cobia and Babb [694] and Babb [685], to cotton ginning and warehousing by Wilmot and Cable [734], and to petroleum distribution to farms by Haskell and Manuel [697]. The several other studies which have combined processing and assembly or distribution costs (see table 3) have dealt somewhat implicitly with optimum numbers (if not location) as well as size.

The major difficulty with the continuous space approach is, of course, that supply density typically is not uniform and supply areas are not regular and continuous in shape.[44] Moreover, there often are limited numbers of realistic choices of efficient locations, and the plant cost functions may not be independent of these locations. Under these circumstances the continuous model may give very poor approximations to realistically efficient size and location solutions.

THE DISCRETE SPACE APPROACH

The alternative to the continuous approach is to group supply sources and market territories into finite numbers of point locations and to consider some predetermined set of feasible potential plant locations. As in the continuous case, we still need to know the transportation cost functions (or all point-to-point rates) and the long-run processing or handling cost function. One of the first models for solving this type of problem was developed by Stollsteimer [726] as a basis for determining the optimum number, size, and location of pear-packing plants in a fairly homogenous pear-producing region (also see Hoch [699], Mathia [713], Stollsteimer [725], and Stollsteimer, Courtney, and Sammet [723]). The problem may be stated algebraically. Minimize

$$(33) \quad TC_{(J, J_k)} = \sum_{j=1}^{J} P_j X_j | J_k + \sum_{i=1}^{I} \sum_{j=1}^{J} C_{ij} X_{ij} | J_k$$

with respect to plant numbers ($J \leq L$) and locations J_k [$k = 1 \ldots , (\frac{L}{J})$], subject to

$$\sum_{j=1}^{J} X_{ij} = X_i,$$

$$\sum_{i=1}^{I} X_{ij} = X_j,$$

$$\sum_{i=1}^{I} \sum_{j=1}^{J} X_{ij} = X,$$

where X_{ij}, $X_j \geq 0$ and $C_{ij} > 0$,

TC = total processing and assembly cost,

P_j = unit processing costs in plant j (j = 1 ... J < L), located at L_j,

X_{ij} = quantity of raw material shipped from origin i to plant j located at L_j,

X_i = quantity of raw material available at origin i per production period,

X_j = quantity of material processed at plant j per production period,

X = total quantity of raw material produced and processed,

C_{ij} = unit cost of shipping material from origin i to plant j located with respect to L_j,

J_k = one locational pattern for J plants among the possible combinations of locations for J plants given L possible locations, and

L_j = a specific location for an individual plant (j = 1 ... J).

The ease or difficulty of solving this problem is affected by the presence or absence of economies of scale, the form of the processing cost function, the effects of location on plant cost, and the number of sources and potential plant locations to be considered. In his original application of the model Stollsteimer introduced the strategic assumption (supported by empirical analysis) that the long-run total cost function for pear packing could be approximated by a linear equation with a positive intercept. The solution then was obtained in three stages.

First, the minimum assembly cost was computed for each possible number of plants. This was accomplished by considering all possible combinations of locations for each number of plants and selecting the particular pattern giving the least assembly cost. If processing or handling costs varied by location, they were simply added to the transportation costs in the first stage minimization. Second, the total processing plant cost was expressed as a linear function of plant numbers. With constant long-run marginal cost, the slope component of processing cost is affected only by total volume and not by plant numbers, but the intercept component increases directly with plant numbers. The third step was to add the minimized assembly cost (a decreasing function of plant numbers) to the increasing processing cost function and to determine the number of plants which minimize combined total cost. The exact locations and plant volumes were obtained by reference to the first stage minimization process.

The basic Stollsteimer model has been extended to encompass multiple-product plants by Polopolus [722] and to handle discontinuous plant cost functions by Chern and Polopolus [692]. The latter permits some relaxation of the restrictive assumption regarding the form of the long-run plant cost function. Other modifications and extensions have included a procedure for testing the sensitivity of the model to changes in parameters (Ladd and Halvorson [709]) and a method of approximate optimization which may greatly reduce the very large amount of computer time required for cases in which the number of potential plant locations is large (Warrack and Fletcher [731]).

Applications of the Stollsteimer model are discussed by Mathia and King [714] (sweet potato processing, 1962), Peeler and King [719] (egg packing, 1964), Polopolus [722] (vegetable processing, 1965), Sanders and Fletcher [724] (egg packing, 1966), Warrack and Fletcher [730] (feed manufacturing, 1970), Hicks and Badenhop [698] (livestock auction markets, 1971), Stollsteimer, Courtney, and Sammet [723] (pear packing, 1975), and Jesse, Schultz, and Bomben [705] (decentralized tomato processing, 1975).

Although the Stollsteimer model may be used to determine optimum plant location, size, and numbers with respect to either assembly or distribution systems, it is not applicable to situations where both must be considered. One approach to this problem has been to use a transshipment model which is a modification of the basic linear programming transportation model (King [706]). The transshipment model, by classifying each production or consumption area as a possible shipment or transshipment point, gains considerable computational advantage. The first application to agricultural marketing was in a study of livestock slaughter plant location by King and Logan [707]. A "heuristic" technique was used to handle the problem of economies of scale. This involved first specifying a set of (low) costs for all locations, solving, then examining the result for consistency with the economies of scale curve, revising costs, solving again, and so on until no further significant cost reductions were achieved.

The transshipment model was further developed by Hurt and Tramel [704] to handle more than one level of processing, more than one plant at each level, and more than one final product. Leath and Martin [710] extended the model to include inequality restraints, and Toft, Cassidy, and McCarthy [728] developed a procedure for testing the sensitivity of the model to change in cost elements of the model. Applications to the analysis of market area efficiency have included, in addition to the King-Logan study, a study of fluid milk plant location in Washington by Bobst and Waananen [687], milk manufacturing plant location in Louisiana and Mississippi by Alexander and Ashley [683], slaughter plant location in Queensland, Australia, by Cassidy, McCarthy, and Toft [691], meat freezing plant location in New Zealand by Brodie and McCarthy [688], a study of cotton processing facilities by Hudson and Jesse [703], and plant location for a honey packer by Holroyd and Lessley [701].

Other variants of linear and nonlinear programming procedures have also been used. The basic transportation model was used by Pherson and Firch [720] to determine optimum warehouse location for a multi-plant meatpacking firm, by Lytle and Hill [712] in a study of country elevators, and by Clay and Martin [693] in a study of retail farm machinery dealerships in Virginia. Carley [690] and Hopkin et al. [702] apparently also used the transportation model in studies of fluid milk plants in Georgia and feed-mixing plants in New England, although the procedures are not clearly specified in either report. Miller and King [716] further extended and compared several classes of programming models and computational procedures. These models were applied to the determination of minimum cost locations for peanut-grading plants [717].

Several techniques have been developed to accommodate the computational difficulties that arise with nonlinear long-run total processing cost functions. The Chern-Popopolus extension of the Stollsteimer model to handle discrete functions and the King-Logan heuristic procedure have been mentioned. Kloth and Blakley [708] used separable programming in a study of optimum dairy plant location in the United States. This procedure, which was further elaborated by Baritelle and Holland [686], approximates all nonlinear functions by piecewise-linear functions. Candler, Snyder, and Faught used concave programming to formulate a model to determine optimum rice mill location. The results are reported in Holder, Shaw, and Snyder [700]. Experience with these techniques to date suggests that the best choice of method may vary with the characteristics of the individual problem.

As we have moved from consideration of plant size and location in local assembly areas to the inclusion of wider distribution systems and then to larger geographic areas, the analytical models have overlapped increasingly with the more general models of interregional competition and spatial allocation. Eventually they merge. Any further consideration of location models thus takes us beyond the scope of this paper. Readers interested in a review of spatial equilibrium and location models should see Weinschenck, Henrichsmeyer, and Aldinger [732] and Takayama and Judge [727].

AREA EFFICIENCY IN GENERAL

The studies just described focused almost exclusively on the design aspects of efficient area organization. From them we may learn, for example, that two plants located at points x and y would in the long run be more efficient than the present twelve for some projected levels of supply and/or demand. Although such information may be of general value in formulating both public and private goals, the results are apt to be rather sterile in the absence of some central planning authority. The models tell us what could be achieved if we could start from the beginning, but they typically provide few clues to how to get there from where we are, if indeed it would be desirable to do so.

We need models which would serve as guides in the establishment of public policies and incentive systems aimed at encouraging an orderly shift toward the optimum structure. The analytical problem is formidable. Consideration must be given to ownership and vertical coordination aspects, the forces of imperfect competition and local monopoly, uncertainty, and technological and environmental changes.[45] The models would need to be extended into a dynamic framework which would encompass the adjustment process over time.[46] This would provide a basis for comparing and evaluating alternative policies and programs aimed at achieving the efficiency goal. With the possible exception of a few milk marketing and interregional competition studies, the studies concerned with production efficiency on the one hand and pricing efficiency and market structure on the other have traveled largely separate paths. If research on area efficiency is to have any real applied value, we will need to merge these concepts into a single dynamic systems approach.

Central Market Studies

The evolutionary process by which city wholesale markets have developed has been far from perfect.[47] The situation in the late 1930s was described by W. C. Crow [743] : "Antiquated, improperly designed and equipped markets, too many markets within a city, inadequate facilities for handling truck receipts, markets without rail connections, unregulated hours, lack of information on supplies, and unethical practices are among the most important problems in the wholesale fruit and vegetable markets of the large cities of the country. The solution of these problems offers one of the most fertile fields for reducing marketing costs with consequent benefits to growers, consumers, and produce dealers."

After World War II the United States Department of Agriculture, with limited experiment station cooperation, initiated a series of studies of whole-sale food distribution facilities that eventually covered nearly every major city in the United States. A number of examples of such studies are listed in the reference section (items [735] to [763]). The list is by no means exhaustive.

Studies of these markets have been of two types. One group has focused on descriptive aspects of market organization — the number and size of different types of firms, activities and services, costs and margins, and changes in the market structure. They provide background information. The more numerous group aims directly at improving the efficiency of the market. The approach has been described as "facility planning." Although it is difficult to identify a set of principles of facility planning, some fairly standardized research procedures have emerged.

The basic orientation is that of the economic-engineering approach. A typical study begins with a systematic description of the current facilities, market organization, and costs. Inadequacies are identified, and plans are made for improving the system. This may involve simply altering existing facilities or, more commonly, developing plans for new facilities at alternative sites. Usually this includes rather detailed specifications and layouts. Costs and returns are estimated for the new system and methods of financing are considered. Finally, the potential benefits of the new system are evaluated.

Although the systems developed are not necessarily optimal, they ordinarily represent realistically achievable improvements and include within them the plans for getting there. In this sense they go a desirable step beyond most studies of area efficiency dealing with optimum size, numbers, and locations. A possible shortcoming, however, is the failure to include all costs in the analysis, particularly the procurement costs of retailers.

Evaluation of Progress and Achievement

The analytical system concerned with marketing efficiency has evolved through several phases. The end of World War II found us with an inadequate theoretical framework and an undeveloped empirical methodology; most empirical work was directed toward internal plant operations. Then followed a period of concern with developing approaches and concepts appropriate to more sophisticated analysis. Studies at that time continued to focus mainly on plants and production processes. In the late 1950s and early 1960s these studies were extended to encompass assembly and distribution activities. Then came the feasilibity studies and area efficiency studies which have been the central focus of much recent work.

We now have available a very good *static* theoretical framework for measuring costs and analyzing the efficiency of individual firms. It builds on realistic specifications of the way plants operate and incorporates the important dimensions of length of operation and space. It also suggests a means of dealing more effectively with multiple-product operations, although this aspect needs some further testing and elaboration, particularly with regard to economies of scale. Relatively little attention has been given to the operations of firms with several plants, but the problem of so extending static plant theory does not appear formidable. Our theory still does not provide a good framework for incorporating uncertainty, growth, technical change, and variability into cost models. In dealing with integrated operations and total market systems, we find a good framework for the *design* of efficient systems but a far less satisfactory framework for handling the related competitive structures.

Methodological approaches to cost measurement have become well established, with economic-engineering emerging as clearly the most powerful, most effective, and most widely used method. It is also the most costly method. Inexpensive descriptive analysis of accounting data may be suitable if the objective is only to describe practices and reported cost experience. Problems may arise, however, when an attempt is made to generalize from descriptive data with regard to the effects of scale and other factors affecting costs. The authors of many of the hundred or so descriptive studies reviewed were unable to resist the temptation to do so, and the effectiveness of their work suffered accordingly.[48]

Although statistical approaches to cost measurement have evolved well beyond the early naive models which fitted regressions to scatter diagrams of average annual cost and volume data, they are still subject to severe data and specification problems. So far, the results of pure statistical models have been unimpressive and generally uncertain. Statistical analysis may, however, be important for some components of economic-engineering models.

Methods of solving programming problems required to determine optimum numbers, sizes, and locations of facilities within marketing areas have developed rapidly in recent years. Although our capability in this area is now well advanced, we are likely to see further developments in the use of computers to deal with increasingly complex structures.

It is clear that we now have substantial capability for effective study of alternative production techniques, economies of scale, and organizational structures in agricultural marketing. How we are likely to apply this capability in the future is discussed in the remaining pages.

The several hundred studies included in this review vary widely in the depth of the analysis and in the skill and rigor with which the findings have been developed and reported. Many are excellent, but others leave much to be desired. The shortcomings most often observed (and this includes many studies using the economic-engineering approach) have been (a) failure to exploit the available data to the fullest, (b) a tendency to confuse and combine the various dimensions and components of cost, and (3) inadequate or nonexistent measures or indications of reliability. The first and second deficiencies arise when studies are developed without a carefully formulated theoretical base. This means that the empirical analysis cannot bring out all of the cost interrelationships involved and those measured may be of uncertain character.

Regarding reliability, it could perhaps be argued that many studies are written for business managers who are concerned mainly with results and are not interested in technical details. But even a lay reader might like to see some evidence of the precision and representativeness of the estimates. Economic-engineering studies do not automatically generate measures of reliability, but it is possible to compare the final cost predictions against actual observations (with due consideration for capacity utilization and technology) and to evaluate the reasons for their differences. This is rarely done.

Another problem that became evident in the course of constructing the summary of economies of scale findings is the frequent failure to provide adequate explanation and detail. Often the reader has no way of being sure of the specifications of the model, the exact conditions to which it applies, or even what it really means. If professional economists have this problem, one cannot help but wonder about the value of such reports to the average marketing firm manager.

To evaluate the public benefits accruing from the analytical system described in this paper we need to consider the general contributions to economic knowledge, the direct effects on marketing costs and prices, and the side effects on employment, income distribution, economic growth, and related factors. Unfortunately, there are few quantitative measures of these effects. About the best that we can do is to compile a list of favorable and unfavorable indicators and then attempt to form some conclusion on the benefit-cost ratio.

On the favorable side, the sheer volume of published reports on marketing efficiency is impressive. These studies have undoubtedly contributed to our general understanding of the marketing system and marketing processes in ways that are difficult to measure in monetary terms. The importance of cost and efficiency studies in providing materials for the National Commission on Food Marketing studies in 1966 is one example (see [61, 62, 163, 164, 165, and 229]).

The theoretical and conceptual developments have contributed to many course offerings in agricultural economics and also have much broader significance. Unfortunately, the available evidence seems to suggest that this work is not well known to general economists.

Studies pertaining to plant location, consolidation, feasibility, and operating methods have become major activities of the agricultural extension services and the USDA Farmer Cooperative Service. Efficiency models have contributed significantly to these programs. However, reports of such technical assistance often are not widely distributed, and so the extent of the contribution is difficult to document.

Many instances can be cited of research that has had a direct impact on the marketing system — for example, reduced labor costs from studies of handling apples in the northwest, milk delivery studies and their relation to volume pricing in California, scale and feasibility studies which have led to consolidations, and wholesale market studies which have brought about improvements in city markets. Most such improvements appear to have been of eventual benefit to consumers by leading to lower prices. In addition to such specific gains, Trelogan and Townshend-Zellner [82] have shown that productivity has increased in the total marketing system relative to the increased volume of services demanded of it. However, there is no way of determining how much of this was a result of economic research.

On the less favorable side, we still do not know the extent to which the research results have actually been used. We do know that not all of the research has been good research and that not all of it has been well presented. But even economic research that is good in a technical sense (which might describe the bulk of studies) may often be overlooked or ignored by private firms. The plain fact is that, except for a few isolated cases, we do not have much evidence one way or another. At this point we can only hope that the findings have had and will have positive benefits in excess of their cost.

It might be noted that the annual expenditures on marketing efficiency research have been very small relative to the total agricultural marketing bill (probably less than 2/100 of 1 percent of the total). Thus only relatively small improvements in marketing efficiency are required to cover the taxpayers' cost. My subjective judgment, based on the performance measures I have examined, is that the returns to the public have been at least positive. Whether the benefits have matched the legislators' optimistic perception of what originally seemed possible is another matter. Although we may agree with Leibenstein [49] that "improvement in X-efficiency is a significant source of increased output," the record suggests that economic efficiency research alone can provide only modest gains, particularly compared with the gains made possible by technological developments, and by its nature the impact is extremely difficult to evaluate.

The future of marketing efficiency analysis will be shaped to a large extent by our reactions to three issues or points of concern: (1) the potential impact of efficiency research on the structure of the economy, (2) needs and attitudes toward research for public decision making versus private decision making, and (3) possible applications to previously neglected and new areas of research.[49]

It has been suggested that possibly the main thrust of developments in marketing efficiency analysis may be to challenge the idea that the market is a better coordinator and planner than a centralized system would be. The models and information generated could lead to a restructuring of the economy with more centralization, more concentration, and more government controls.

Reactions to this suggestion may vary with viewpoints on the trade-off between efficiency and control and the plausibility of the suggestion itself. If one accepts the proposition and is concerned about the undesirable effects of more centralized control, the answer is to curtail expenditures on this type of research. An alternative is to construct models that show the way to improved efficiency while retaining substantial individuality among decision units.

As originally conceived and developed, productive efficiency research was aimed almost entirely at the private decision-making sector. It was expected that competitive forces would reflect cost savings forward to consumers in the form of lower prices and/or back to producers in higher returns. While this still seems likely, rapidly advancing technology, industrialization of marketing and farming, and growth of firm size have made firm efficiency a less important issue in many minds than concentration, integration, quality of the environment, and "people" problems. With these changes in attitude there appears to be increasing reluctance to utilize public funds to support research pertaining to private sector efficiency.

Efficiency research for public decision-making purposes involves the development of larger systems models which may be used to evaluate market structure and performance, marketing control devices, and administered pricing programs. This will require closer ties between models of productive efficiency and models of pricing efficiency. We need to extend industry and area efficiency models to include vertical coordination, imperfect competition and local monopoly, uncertainty, and technological and environmental changes.[50] In developing optimum system designs we must recognize what exists and include in the models plans for formulating realistic programs or policies to guide the shift toward the optimum structure. To compare and evaluate alternative policies and programs in a dynamic framework, we may need to incorporate concepts and procedures from control theory (which is concerned with optimal time paths for decision variables), and probably we will want to draw heavily on concepts in modern decision theory. Simulation may have an increasing role also.

More aggregative types of plant studies, as opposed to detailed economic-engineering studies, may suffice as inputs into the broader models. However, access to the essential cost and price data is a point of concern. Although marketing firm cooperation has been generally good (French [263]), large complex organizations may be understandably reluctant to participate in this type of study. Should this prove to be a serious obstacle, the public interest might require some type of legislative authorization to provide the needed access.

Although extension of marketing firm efficiency analysis to encompass public policy objectives may be desirable, the wisdom of completely abandoning methods improvement studies might be questioned, particularly if supported more by private interests. If Leibenstein [49] is correct in his assessment of the great potential for improving X-efficiency through motivation, better knowledge of technical opportunities, and learning activities, possibly we should be doing more, not less, in this area. Bloom [8], in a recent study of the food industry, states that there is urgent need for increased research effort with respect to the possibilities of improving productivity through implementation of system economies in food distribution. He suggests that some of the necessary research should be undertaken by trade associations, individual companies, and other private groups but that other projects are so complex and have so many interrelationships with other industries that they are beyond the scope of privately financed research efforts. "Quasi-governmental agencies" are suggested as the appropriate place for such projects.

Much of the work proposed by Bloom and Leibenstein seems to require private initiative and an extension or technical assistance more than a research approach. Thus we are still left with some uncertainty about the role of the publicly supported research economist. Dobson and Matthes [24] argue that benefits may accrue from firm-specific work by (1) providing experience that contributes to the improvement of teaching and other research programs, (2) contributing to regional development studies, (3) helping to maintain competitive environments by focusing on smaller firm efficiency, and (4) developing joint studies with several firms cooperating.

Future studies must build on past developments and there are still some neglected areas. For example, we now know a great deal about technical economies of scale, but very little has been done on multiplant operations and pecuniary economies in purchasing inputs. There have been few studies of retail service operations such as farm machinery dealerships, farm supply operations, and grocery stores. And we still have not gone very far in presenting scale economies in a framework that involves variability of output and includes dynamic considerations such as firm growth and expenditures for research and development.

The methods, models, and expertise associated with marketing efficiency analysis would appear to have much to contribute to other types of research. Rural development seems a particularly promising area. In addition to feasibility studies research on the efficiency of providing rural services such as health care is needed (for an example, see Doherty [25]). Methods of solid waste disposal also lend themselves to this type of analysis. Finally, Abbot [1], Currie [20], King [46], Folz [30], and others have noted the need for and potential benefits of studies aimed at improving the efficiency of marketing systems in developing countries.

In conclusion, it appears to me that this review may coincide with the end of an era. The analytical systems for research and our perceptions of problems have evolved in such a way that we increasingly focus on issues that cross traditional production, marketing, and pricing lines. The emergence of Commercial Agriculture Committees to replace separate Farm Management and Agricultural Marketing Committees and the recent reorganization of the USDA Economic Research Service along commodity and analytical lines are indicators of this change. Although we shall certainly continue to be concerned with efficiency in agricultural marketing, future reviewers are likely to have difficulty in identifying it as a distinct area of study.

Notes

1. It is impossible to determine exactly the amount of federal and state funds actually utilized for cost and efficiency research or to separate clearly the expenditures on productive efficiency from pricing efficiency, interregional competition, and related studies. The figures cited have been developed from data obtained from M. L. Upchurch when he was administrator of the USDA Economic Research Service and have been supplemented by rough estimates (see [31, p. 426]).

2. The definitions and distinctions among these types of efficiency are made clear elsewhere in this review.

3. See especially "Organization and Performance of Agricultural Markets" by Peter Helmberger, Gerald R. Campbell, and William D. Dobson in *A Survey of Agricultural Economics Literature: Volume 3, Development, Welfare, and Natural Resources in Agriculture* (University of Minnesota Press, 1977).

4. Note that pricing efficiency as used in this context is not the same as pricing efficiency for the individual firm. To avoid confusion, it seems preferable to refer to firm pricing efficiency as *allocative efficiency* (Timmer, [246]), although allocation decisions are involved in both cases.

5. For additional discussion of these points, see [84, 85, 86, 87, 89, 90, 91, 260, and 264].

6. Reference is made to model formulations in books such as Hicks [38], Carlson [17], Samuelson [70], Schneider [72], and Henderson and Quandt [37].

7. For discussion relating to this point, see Machlup [54].

8. This may be strictly true only where each machine cost function is continuous. With discontinuous functions there may be small ranges in which output rates on one

machine could be slightly increased and another correspondingly decreased without affecting total costs.

9. A stage is independent of another stage if the activities included within the stage are "separable" from other stages. The choice of the amount and type of input at stage i can then be made independently of the choice at stage j. For further discussion, see French, Sammet, and Bressler [401, p. 574] and Sammet [69, p. 50]. The basic mathematical concepts of separability were first developed by Leontief [50].

10. If machine speeds can be varied, some minor short-run substitution of labor and machinery may be possible. For example, operating a forklift truck at higher speeds would increase the rate of machine input relative to labor input, provided that the labor time saved need not be paid for or can be put to other uses. The practical range of such substitution would appear, however, to be highly restricted.

11. The importance of the time dimension in short-run production theory was recognized in the early 1950s by Kutish [48] and French, Sammet, and Bressler [401]. It was discovered and elaborated somewhat later by several general economists (Alchian [2]), Hirschleifer [39], Dano [22], and Georgescu-Roegen [33, 34]), who apparently were unaware of the earlier literary development by Kutish or the more quantitative models developed by French, Sammet, and Bressler. In fact, Hirschleifer noted that his "rather extensive survey of the literature in both economic theory and business economics . . . failed to turn up any significant attention devoted to this topic." Apparently he did not examine the literature of agricultural economics.

12. For a discussion of managerial choice under institutional restrictions such as overtime pay rates, see Doll, Rhodes, and West [26].

13. For a graphic illustration, see French, Sammet, and Bressler [401, p. 566].

14. To illustrate, if shipment rates are constant and the total quantity produced during T is shipped or moved out during T (no inventory carry-over), the production period storage cost function will have the form

$$TSC = \frac{wtT(Q - R)}{2},$$

where w is the storage cost per unit of product per unit of time, R is the rate of product movement, and the other terms are as defined previously (see Horowitz [41, pp. 245, 246]). Since $S_T = tQ$, substituting for t gives a nonlinear function of Q. Since quantity produced (S_T) equals quantity shipped (RT), the cost function may be expressed with R eliminated as

$$TSC = \frac{wtT}{2} Q(1 - \frac{t}{T}) = \frac{wQ}{2}(tT - t^2).$$

15. If the production period, T, is made smaller and smaller, S_{Ti} merges with Q_i (or disappears) and (12) approaches a continuous time model which is called a functional. For a theoretical formulation of factory processes in terms of funtionals (including recognition of the rate and length of operation dimensions), see Georgescu-Roegen [33, 34]. His discussion does not, however, deal explicitly with the optimization aspect of the control problem described.

16. For examples of solution approaches and additional references on control theory see [16, 43, 63 (chapter 11), 74 (chapter 3), 81]. Also see "Systems Analysis and Simulation: A Survey of Applications in Agricultural Economics" by S. R. Johnson and Gordon C. Rausser in *A Survey of Agricultural Economics Literature: Volume 2, Quantitative Methods in Agricultural Economics, 1940s to 1970s* (University of Minnesota Press, 1977).

17. Approaches to the derivation of such functions will be discussed in the methodology sections. For empirical examples, see French, Sammet, and Bressler [401 (pp. 633-700) and 478].

18. Pfouts [67] treats this cost as a continuous function of quantities of fixed factor transferred from the production of one commodity to another. In practice, such costs seem likely to vary discretely. For example, the entire plant may be adjusted to handle one commodity for another period. The switching cost then is fixed and independent of volume produced so the model still decomposes into a set of essentially single-product components with respect to cost variation.

19. The spatial dimension of productive activity is largely neglected in the standard works on neoclassical theory — perhaps reflecting the view that the basic concepts are readily applied to all types of economic activity. The extensive literature on transportation economics, which deals mainly with policy or institutional factors, includes some theoretical models for transport firms — see, for example, [65 and 66]. However, the theoretical concepts most applicable to agricultural marketing firms, as contrasted to specialized transportation firms, have been developed mainly by agricultural economists as part of their empirical studies.

20. Increased volumes of raw products may be acquired by extending the geographic supply area or by raising prices (or lowering service charges) to induce more production in nearby areas. Similarly, depending on location, increased volumes may be shipped to more distant markets at higher cost or sold in nearby markets at lower prices. The present discussion focuses on the geographic aspects. For consideration of the problem of increasing nearby production density versus expanding supply areas, see Henry and Seagraves [567].

21. Boutwell and Simmons [535] show that with route assembly the marginal and average costs of assembly may remain constant over a moderate distance from the plant. Increased volume is handled by adding routes of approximately equal distance instead of extending the length of haul of individual vehicles. Eventually, however, a radius is reached beyond which further extensions require some increase in travel per unit of product assembled.

22. For a general discussion of the differences in approach, see Weinschenck, Henrichsmeyer, and Aldinger [732, pp. 39-48].

23. The concept of harmonious combinations of capacities among stages was first developed by Jantzen [45] and later elaborated by Brems [10]. See also French, Sammet, and Bressler [401, p. 555]. It involves searching for a common denominator of all of the durable factors that may be employed at the various stages — a common denominator reppresenting the output rates that minimize the average total unit cost of production.

24. This comment is not intended as a slight to the contributions of earlier writers on this subject such as Mueller and Collins [58] and Seaver [73]. However, the Mighell-Jones study went considerably beyond these in formulating theoretical structures.

25. For examples of general works on location theory, see [6, 35, 40, 44, and 53]. Beckman suggests that the powerful tools of linear programming have a "tendency to reduce location problems to a format where the geometry of space completely disappears and is replaced by an abstract framework of matrices." He deplores "the exclusive or even predominant use of this approach."

26. These concepts are treated more fully in "Organization and Performance of Agricultural Markets" by Peter Helmberger, Gerald R. Campbell, and William D. Dobson in *A Survey of Agricultural Economics Literature: Volume 3, Development, Welfare, and Natural Resources in Agriculture* (University of Minnesota Press, 1977).

27. The shortcomings of accounting data are explored more fully in the section on statistical analysis.

28. Statistical estimation in general is treated in "On Estimating the Parameters of Economic Relations: A Review" by George G. Judge in *A Survey of Agricultural Economics Literature: Volume 2, Quantitative Methods in Agricultural Economics, 1940s to 1970s* (University of Minnesota Press, 1977).

29. The conceptual issues and major criticisms of statistical approaches to measuring cost and production functions have been reviewed at some length by Walters [249] and Johnston [219]. Readers interested in a full treatment are referred to these articles. The discussion here summarizes only the major points as they relate particularly to studies of marketing firms.

30. It is appropriate, however, to use a physical measure such as floor space, provided short-run cost functions are computed for each size (in relation to a measure of output); the long-run cost function then is derived as an envelope to the short-run curves. See Henderson and Quandt [37, p. 75] for a discussion of the theoretical basis for this approach.

31. Economies of scale with variable outputs were discussed in the earlier theoretical section on long-run cost functions.

32. Analysis of covariance has been used more extensively to attempt to estimate production functions, particularly for agricultural operations. The assumptions and interpretations involved in covariance analysis of production functions may differ somewhat from the application to cost functions.

33. Only two examples of cross-section cost envelopes could be found — one by Stollsteimer, Bressler, and Boles [244] and the other by Donald and Bishop [561]. Both were fitted graphically.

34. Mathia and Hammond [55] used a modification of the Farrell approach to measure economic efficiency in a sample of apple-packing plants. However, their frontier function was developed from engineering data, not statistically from the observations.

35. Some might argue that while the survivor technique is clearly an empirical technique, it is not a statistical approach in the sense used above. Two other approaches can be identified in this general category: One approach is to obtain managers' opinions about optimum size [197]. The other approach has been called the "lowest labor cost method" [213]. The ratio of wage payment to value of shipments is computed from census data in a particular industry for plants grouped by employment size. The plants with the lowest labor cost as a percentage of sales are presumed to be the most efficient. Because of the seemingly obvious limitations of these approaches, they will not be elaborated further.

36. These reports are listed and partially summarized by Bressler [11].

37. For further discussion, see [69, 261, 267, 271, 273, 279, 280, 401].

38. For a description of work measurement methods and the use and application of standard data, see Sammet [69 (pp. 141-223), 269, 274, 275].

39. This may slightly overstate the relative importance of economic-engineering studies since some of the reports listed in table 2 are descriptive comparisons based on engineering measurements, such as time study, and thus are only a step removed from descriptive analyses of accounting data. Furthermore, tables 1 and 2 undoubtedly overlook some publications. Even so, the ratio is great.

40. Plant efficiency research has also provided an important input in many studies of interregional competition which are not considered in this paper. See "On Economic Optimization: A Nontechnical Survey" by Richard H. Day in *A Survey of Agricultural Eco-*

nomics Literature: Volume 2, Quantitative Methods in Agricultural Economics, 1940s to 1970s (University of Minnesota Press, 1977).

41. See Vincent [644] for a bibliography on managerial economics.

42. See Schermerhorn [673], Woodard [682], and Polopolus [721] for additional details.

43. See Dalrymple [652] for a list of related studies. Much of the feasibility work of the Farmer Cooperative Service has been reported only in documents prepared for internal use by the FCS and its clients.

44. Density can, of course, be specified as a continuous function of space. Measuring such a function is likely to be quite difficult.

45. The Bobst-Waananen study [687] makes a stride in this direction by introducing possible institutional or legal restrictions on market concentration. However, the means of achieving even the restricted optimum are not specified.

46. The study by Lytle and Hill [712] gives some consideration to the adjustment process by evaluating the short-run effects of alternative capital structures on the optimal number and type of country elevators.

47. The term "wholesale market" is used here to include groups of businesses which comprise the food distribution center for some city or area. It also includes some assembly markets such as the farmers' market at Benton Harbor, Michigan.

48. This is not to suggest that a descriptive study cannot be analytical and rigorous. It can, but considerable care must be exercised in drawing quantitative inferences from the data of such studies.

49. For further discussion pertaining to the directions of needed future marketing research, including marketing efficiency and firm management research, see Shaffer [75] and the proceedings of the 1968 Nebraska seminar on better economic research [91].

50. For discussions and examples of environmental issues in agricultural marketing, see Rogers and Vertrees [68], Vertrees [93], and Hudson, Cole, and Smith [42].

References

General References

[1] Abbot, J. C. "Marketing Issues in Agricultural Development Planning." In *Markets and Marketing in Developing Economies*, R. Moyer and S. C. Hollander, eds. Homewood, Ill.: Irwin, 1968.

[2] Alchian, A. "Costs and Output." In *The Allocation of Economic Resources: Essays in Honor of B. F. Haley* by M. Abramovitz and others. Stanford University Press, 1959.

[3] Agricultural Marketing Service. *Compilation of Statutes Relating to Marketing Activities.* USDA Agr. Handbook 130, 1958.

[4] Baligh, H. H., and L. E. Richartz. *Vertical Market Structures.* Boston: Allyn and Bacon, 1967.

[5] Bartlett, R. W. *Increasing the Efficiency of Milk Distribution.* University of Illinois, Dept. Agr. Econ., AE-693, 1937.

[6] Beckmann, M. *Location Theory.* New York: Random House, 1968.

[7] Bellmore, M., and G. L. Neuhauser. "The Traveling Salesman Problem: A Survey." *Oper. Res.* 16:538-558, May-June 1968.

[8] Bloom, G. F. *Productivity in the Food Industry.* Cambridge: MIT Press, 1972.

[9] Boger, L. L. "Application of Principles of Production Economics to Achieve

Efficiency in Marketing." In *Marketing Efficiency in a Changing Economy*. Report of the National Workshop on Agricultural Marketing, 1955. USDA, AMS, AMS-20, 1955.

[10] Brems, H. "A Discontinuous Cost Function." *Am. Econ. Rev.* 42:577-586, September 1952.

[11] Bressler, R. G., Jr. *City Milk Distribution*. Cambridge: Harvard University Press, 1952.

[12] ———. *Efficiency in the Production of Marketing Services*. Social Science Research Council Project in Agricultural Economics. Economic Efficiency Series, Paper 7. University of Chicago, 1950.

[13] ———. "Research Determination of Economies of Scale." *J. Farm Econ.* 27: 526-539, August 1945.

[14] Bressler, R. G., Jr., and R. A. King. *Markets, Prices, and Interregional Trade*. New York: Wiley, 1970.

[15] Brown, M., ed. *The Theory and Empirical Measurement of Production*. National Bureau of Economic Research. New York: Columbia University Press, 1967.

[16] Burt, O. R. "Control Theory for Agricultural Policy: Methods and Problems in Operational Models." *Am. J. Agr. Econ.* 51:394-404, May 1969.

[17] Carlson, Sune. *A Study of the Pure Theory of Production*. London: P. S. King and Sons, 1939.

[18] Churchman, C. W. *The Systems Approach*. New York: Dell, 1968.

[19] Committee on Price Determination. *Cost Behavior and Price Policy*. Conference on Price Research. New York: National Bureau of Economic Research, 1943.

[20] Curie, L. "Marketing Organization for Underdeveloped Countries." In *Markets and Marketing in Developing Countries*, P. Moyer and S. C. Hollander, eds. Homewood, Ill.: Irwin, 1968.

[21] Cyert, R. M., and J. B. March. *A Behavioral Theory of the Firm*. Englewood Cliffs, N.J.: Prentice-Hall, 1963.

[22] Dano, S. *Industrial Production Models*. New York: Springer-Verlag, 1966.

[23] Dean, J. *Managerial Economics*. Englewood Cliffs, N.J.: Prentice-Hall, 1951.

[24] Dobson, W. D., and R. C. Matthes. "University-Agribusiness Cooperation: Current Problems and Prognosis." *Am. J. Agr. Econ.* 53:557-564, November 1971.

[25] Doherty, N. J. G. *Efficiency in the Distribution and Utilization of Hospital Services*. USDA, ERS, ERS-492, 1971.

[26] Doll, J. P., V. J. Rhodes, and J. G. West. *Economics of Agricultural Production, Markets, and Policy*. Homewood, Ill.: Irwin, 1968.

[27] Dow, G. F. "Reducing Cost of Distributing Milk in Maine." *J. Farm Econ.* 21:309-314, February 1939.

[28] Erdman, H. E. "Interpretation of Variations in Cost Data for a Group of Individual Firms." *J. Farm Econ.* 26:388-391, May 1944.

[29] Ferguson, C. E. *The Neoclassical Theory of Production and Distribution*. Cambridge: At the University Press, 1969.

[30] Folz, W. E. "The Relevance of Marketing Research to Economic Development." *Proceedings, Western Farm Economics Association Annual Meeting*, 1964.

[31] French, B. C. "The Food Marketing Commission and Marketing Efficiency." *J. Farm Econ.* 49:425-435, May 1967.

[32] Friedman, M. Comment in *Business Concentration and Price Policy*. Universities-National Bureau of Economic Research, Conference Series, No. 5. Princeton: Princeton University Press, 1955.

[33] Georgescu-Roegen, N. "The Economics of Production." *Am. Econ. Rev.* 60: 1-9, May 1970.

[34] ———. "Process Analysis and the Neoclassical Theory of the Firm." *Am. J. Agr. Econ.* 54:279-294, May 1972.

[35] Greenhut, M. L. *Microeconomics and the Space Economy.* Chicago: Scott, Foresman, 1963.

[36] Helmberger, P. "O-Efficiency and the Economic Organization of Agriculture." In *Agricultural Organization in the Modern Industrial Economy.* North Central Regional Research Committee on Agricultural Marketing, NCR 20. Ohio State University, 1968.

[37] Henderson, J. M., and R. E. Quandt. *Microeconomic Theory.* 2d ed. New York: McGraw-Hill, 1971.

[38] Hicks, J. R. *Value and Capital.* 2d ed. Oxford: Clarendon Press, 1946.

[39] Hirschleifer, J. "The Firm's Cost Function: A Successful Reconstruction?" *J. Bus.* July 1962.

[40] Hoover, E. M. *The Location of Economic Activity.* New York: McGraw-Hill, 1948.

[41] Horowitz, I. *An Introduction to Quantitative Business Analysis.* 2d ed. New York: McGraw-Hill, 1972.

[42] Hudson, B. L., G. L. Cole, and R. C. Smith. *An Economic Analysis of Poultry Processing Wastewater in Delaware.* Delaware Agr. Exp. Sta. Bul. 383, 1970.

[43] Intriligator, M. D. *Mathematical Optimization and Economic Theory.* Englewood Cliffs, N.J.: Prentice-Hall, 1971.

[44] Isard, W. *Location and Space-Economy.* New York: Wiley, 1956.

[45] Jantzen, I., ed. "Voxende Udbytte i Industrien." *Nationalökonomisk Tidsskrift* 62:1-62, 1924. Translated in *Basic Principles of Business Economics and National Calculation.* Copenhagen, 1939.

[46] King, R. A. "Product Markets and Economic Development." In *Economic Development of Tropical Agriculture,* W. W. McPherson, ed. Gainesville: University of Florida Press, 1968.

[47] Kohls, R. L. "Toward a More Meaningful Concept of Marketing Efficiency." *J. Farm Econ.* 38:68-73, February 1956.

[48] Kutish, J. L. "A Theory of Production in the Short Run." *J. Pol. Econ.* 61: 25-42, February 1953.

[49] Leibenstein, H. "Allocative Efficiency vs. 'X-Efficiency.' " *Am. Econ. Rev.* 56:392-415, June 1966.

[50] Leontief, W. "Introduction to a Theory of the Internal Structure of Functional Relationships." *Econometrica* 15:361-373, April 1947.

[51] Logan, S. H. "A Conceptual Framework for Analyzing Economies of Vertical Integration." *Am. J. Agr. Econ.* 51:834-847, November 1969.

[52] ———. "The Effects of Short-Run Variations in Supplies of Cattle and Costs of Slaughtering in California." *J. Farm Econ.* 45:625-630, August 1963.

[53] Losch, A. *The Economics of Location.* New Haven: Yale University Press, 1954.

[54] Machlup, F. "Theories of the Firm — Marginalist, Behavioral, Managerial." *Am. Econ. Rev.* 57:1-33, March 1967.

[55] Mathia, G. A., and L. H. Hammond. "Measuring Economic Efficiency: An Application to Apple Marketing Facilities." *Proceedings, Marketing Section, Association of Southern Agricultural Workers,* 1967.

[56] Mehren, G. L. "The Theory of the Firm and Marketing." In *Theory in Marketing*, R. Cox and W. Alderson, eds. Chicago: Irwin, 1950.

[57] Mighell, R. L., and L. A. Jones. *Vertical Coordination in Agriculture*. USDA, ERS, Agr. Econ. Rep. 19, 1963.

[58] Mueller, W. F., and N. R. Collins. "Grower-Processor Integration in Fruit and Vegetable Marketing." *J. Farm Econ.* 39:1471-1483, December 1957.

[59] Muth, J. F., and G. L. Thompson. *Industrial Scheduling*. Englewood Cliffs, N.J.: Prentice-Hall, 1963.

[60] Nadiri, N. I. "Some Approaches to the Theory and Measurement of Total Factor Productivity: A Survey." *J. Econ. Lit.* 8:1137-1177, December 1970.

[61] National Commission on Food Marketing. *Organization and Competition in the Dairy Industry*. NCFM Tech. Study 3, 1966.

[62] ———. *Organization and Competition in the Poultry and Egg Industries*. NCFM Tech. Study 2, 1966.

[63] Naylor, T. H., and J. M. Vernon. *Microeconomics and Decision Models of the Firm*. New York: Harcourt, Brace, and World, 1969.

[64] Niles, J. A. "Coordination of Agricultural Production and Processing Operations — with Special Reference to the Problem of Scheduling." Unpub. Ph.D. dissertation, Department of Agricultural Economics, University of California, Davis, 1972.

[65] Norton, H. S. *Modern Transportation Economics*. Columbus, Ohio: Merrill, 1963.

[66] Oi, W. Y., and A. P. Hunter, Jr. *Economics of Private Truck Transportation*. Dubuque, Iowa: William C. Brown, 1965.

[67] Pfouts, R. W. "The Theory of Cost and Production in the Multi-Product Firm." *Econometrica* 29:650-658, October 1961.

[68] Rogers, G. B., and J. C. Vertrees. "Agriculture, Marketing and the Environment — Problems and Research Needs." USDA, ERS, MTS-182, 1971.

[69] Sammet, L. L. "Economic and Engineering Factors in Agricultural Processing Plant Design." Unpublished Ph.D. dissertation, University of California, Berkeley, 1958.

[70] Samuelson, P. A. *Foundations of Economic Analysis*. Cambridge: Harvard University Press, 1947.

[71] Schmitz, A., and D. Seckler. "Mechanized Agriculture and Social Welfare: The Case of the Tomato Harvester." *Am. J. Agr. Econ.* 52:569-577, November 1970.

[72] Schneider, E. *Pricing and Equilibrium*. New York: Macmillan, 1951.

[73] Seaver, S. "An Appraisal of Vertical Integration in the Broiler Industry." *J. Farm Econ.* 39:1487-1497, December 1957.

[74] Sengupta, J. K., and K. A. Fox. *Optimization Techniques in Quantitative Economic Models*. Amsterdam: North Holland Publishing, 1969.

[75] Shaffer, J. D. *A Working Paper Concerning Publicly Supported Economic Research in Agricultural Marketing*. USDA Econ. Res. Ser., 1968.

[76] Shepard, R. W. *Theory of Cost and Production Functions*. Princeton: Princeton University Press, 1970.

[77] Shepherd, G. S., and G. A. Futrell. *Marketing Farm Products*. 5th ed. Ames: Iowa State University Press, 1969.

[78] Spencer, L. "Research in Costs of Distributing Milk." *J. Farm Econ.* May 1936.

[79] Stigler, G. J. *The Theory of Price*. Rev. ed. New York: Macmillan, 1952.

[80] Tinley, J. M. "Problems of Creamery Operating Efficiency in California." *J. Farm Econ.* 17:732-735, November 1935.

[81] Tintner, G. "What Does Control Theory Have to Offer?" *Am. J. Agr. Econ.* 51:383-393, May 1969.

[82] Trelogan, H. C., and N. Townshend-Zellner. "On Benefits of Agricultural Marketing Research." *J. Farm Econ.* 47:36-50, February 1965.

[83] Tucker, C. K. *The Costs of Handling Fluid Milk and Cream in Country Plants.* Cornell Agr. Exp. Sta. Bul. 473, 1929.

[84] USDA. *Agricultural Marketing Research: Its Use, Appraisal, and Prospect.* Report of the National Workshop on Agricultural Marketing, 1956. AMS-60, 1956.

[85] ———. *How State Marketing Service Agencies Can Assist in Reducing Marketing Costs.* Report of the National Marketing Service Workshop, 1956. AMS-195, July 1957.

[86] ———. *Market Organization and Facilities.* Report of the National Workshop on Agricultural Marketing, 1953. ARS, 1953.

[87] ———. *Marketing Efficiency in a Changing Economy.* Report of the National Workshop on Agricultural Marketing, 1955. AMS-20, 1955.

[88] ———. *Marketing Margins and Efficiency.* Report of the National Workshop on Agricultural Marketing, 1950. ARA, 1950.

[89] ———. *Marketing Research Notes from National Workshop,* 1949. ARA, 1949.

[90] ———. *Marketing, the Yearbook of Agriculture.* Washington, D.C., 1954.

[91] ———. *Proceedings: A Seminar on Better Economic Research on the U.S. Food and Fiber Industry.* USDA Econ. Res. Ser., 1969.

[92] ———. *Special Studies of Marketing Costs and Practices.* AMS Marketing Res. Rep. 240, 1958.

[93] Vertrees, J. G. *The Poultry Processing Industry; A Study of the Impact of Water Pollution Control Costs.* USDA, ERS, Marketing Res. Rep. 965, June 1972.

[94] Wagner, H. M. *Principles of Operations Research.* Englewood Cliffs, N.J.: Prentice-Hall, 1969.

[95] Waugh, F. V., ed. *Readings on Agricultural Marketing.* See section 4, "Efficiency." Ames: Iowa State University Press, 1954.

Descriptive Analysis of Accounting Data

[96] Agnew, D. B. *Labor Costs of Killing Hogs From Packers' Accounting Records.* Paper presented at meeting of Southern Division, National Independent Meat Packers Association. Washington, D.C., 1962.

[97] Aronow, W. A., and J. E. Bryan. *Prepackaging Tomatoes.* USDA, PMA, Marketing Res. Rep. 20, 1952.

[98] Bartlett, R. W., and F. T. Gothard. *Measuring Efficiency of Milk Plant Operation.* Illinois Agr. Exp. Sta. Bul. 560, 1952.

[99] Bere, R. L., and M. E. Cravens. *Labor and Material Costs and Machinery Investment in Apple Grading and Packing: Thirty Ohio Apple Growers, 1954-1955.* Ohio State University Agr. Exp. Sta., A. E. 256, 1955.

[100] Bitting, H. W. *Factors Affecting Costs of Wholesale Distribution of Frozen Foods.* USDA, AMS, Marketing Res. Rep. 327, 1959.

[101] Blair, P. T., and J. B. Barlow. *An Economic Study of the Broiler Processing and Distribution System in Mississippi.* Mississippi Agr. Exp. Sta. M.R. 19, 1957.

[102] Bobst, B. W. *Area Comparisons of Auction Market Selling Costs and Returns for Cattle and Calves in the South.* Southern Cooperative Ser. Bul. 154, 1971.

[103] Bowring, J. R. *Planning for Cost Reduction in Milk Processing and Distribution.* New Hampshire Agr. Exp. Sta. Res. Mimeo 24, 1960.

[104] Bowring, J. R., H. C. Moore, and A. W. Chadbourne, Jr. *Reducing Costs of Processing Milk by Consolidating Operations.* New Hampshire Agr. Exp. Sta. Res. Mimeo 25, 1959.

[105] Bowring, J. R., and K. A. Taylor. *Transition to the Bulk Assembly of Milk in Northern New England.* Hampshire, Agr. Exp. Sta. Bul. 453, 1958.

[106] Brensike, J., and W. R. Askew. *Costs of Operating Selected Feed Mills, As Influenced by Volume, Services, and Other Factors.* USDA, AMS, Marketing Res. Rep. 79, 1955.

[107] Bright, I. *The Wage Factor in Retailing Meat in Four Cities.* USDA, AMS, Marketing Res. Rep. 202, 1957.

[108] Briscoe, N. A., A. J. Baker, and E. M. Corley. *Cost Characteristics and Management Decisions of Oklahoma Cooperative Grain Elevators.* Oklahoma Agr. Exp. Sta. Bul. P-545, 1966.

[109] Briscoe, N. A., K. B. Boggs, A. C. Geis, and H. Ponder. *A Business Study of Single-Unit Cooperative Grain Elevators.* Oklahoma Agr. Exp. Sta. Bul. B-562, 1960.

[110] Butz, D. E., and E. F. Koller. *Costs of Drying Milk in Minnesota Plants.* Minnesota Agr. Exp. Sta. Bul. 413, 1952.

[111] Cain, J. L. *Management Guide to Cost Control: Average Cost to Pack Sweet Corn.* Maryland Agr. Ext. Ser., 1971.

[112] Cain, J. L., and J. L. Runyan. *Economies of Size in Selected Affiliated Wholesale Food Marketing Firms — 1963.* Maryland Agr. Exp. Sta. Misc. Pub. 644, 1968.

[113] Camps, T. H. *Costs and Practices of Selected Cooperatives in Operating Bulk-Feed Trucks.* USDA, FCS, General Rep. 132, 1965.

[114] Campbell, J. R. *Returns, Costs and Profits for Raw Sugar Mills in Louisiana for 1969 Grinding Season.* Louisiana State University, Dept. Agr. Econ., DAE Res. Rep. 427, 1969. (Also see earlier similar reports going back to 1958.)

[115] Campbell, J. D. *Costs of Ginning Cotton by Cooperatives at Single-Gin and Two-Gin Plants, California and Texas, 1962.* USDA, FCS, Marketing Res. Rep. 640, 1964.

[116] ———. *Potential for Reducing Cooperative Cotton Ginning Costs in Arkansas.* USDA, FCS Res. Rep. 17, 1971.

[117] ———. *Reducing Cooperative Cotton Ginning Costs in Oklahoma: Three Suggested Ways.* USDA, FCS Res. Rep. 9, 1970.

[118] Campbell, J. D., and R. C. Soxman. *Baling Cotton at Gins: Practices and Costs.* USDA, FCS, Marketing Res. Rep. 386, 1960.

[119] Capel, G. L., R. E. L. Greene, and L. J. Kushman. *Packing Costs and Grading Efficiency in Florida and Alabama Potato Packing Houses.* Florida Agr. Exp. Sta., Agr. Econ. Mimeo Rep. 59-7, 1958.

[120] Clayton, P. C., and R. E. Cray. *Labor Efficiency in Egg Assembling and Grading Plants.* Ohio Agr. Exp. Sta. Res. Bul. 773, 1956.

[121] Collins, E. C., and J. K. Savage, Jr. *Costs of Canning Sweet Corn in Selected Plants.* USDA, FCS, Marketing Res. Rep. 184, 1957.

[122] Conlogue, R. M. *Candling and Cartoning Eggs at Country Plants.* USDA, AMS, Marketing Res. Rep. 366, 1959.

[123] ———. *Costs of Procurement and Assembly of Eggs in Three Midwestern States.* USDA, ERS, ERS-92, 1962.

[124] Cravens, M. E., and R. L. Bere. *Grading, Packaging, and Selling of Apples under Ohio Conditions.* Ohio Agr. Exp. Sta. Res. Bul. 881, 1961.

[125] Cross, R. H., and R. D. Aplin. *Milk Container Box Costs and Trippage.* Cornell Agr. Exp. Sta., Agr. Econ. Res. 253, July 1968.

[126] Crowder, R. T., and M. E. Juillerat. *Variation in Labor Efficiency and Selected Costs among Virginia Meat Packing Firms.* Virginia Agr. Exp. Sta. Bul. 542, 1962.

[127] Davis, G. B., and L. C. Martin. *Packaging Late Crop Potatoes at Shipping Point and at Terminal Market.* Oregon Agr. Exp. Sta. Bul. 527, 1952.

[128] Eastwood, R. A., and J. J. Scanlan. *Operating Cost of 15 Cooperative Poultry Dressing Plants.* USDA, FCA Bul. 70, 1952.

[129] Eiland, J. C., and L. O. Sorenson. *Economics of Grain Drying at Kansas Local Elevators.* USDA, FCS and AMS, Marketing Res. Rep. 449, 1961.

[130] Farstad, E., C. B. Cox, R. C. Kramer, and C. D. Phillips. *Retailing Meat in the North Central States.* Purdue Agr. Exp. Sta. Bul. 622, 1955.

[131] Fortenberry, W. H., and Z. M. Looney. *Cotton Ginning Efficiency and Costs in the Rio Grande and Pecos Valleys, Season of 1949-50 and 1950-51.* USDA, PMA, 1952.

[132] Frazer, J. R., V. H. Nielsen, and J. D. Nord. *The Costs of Manufacturing Butter.* Iowa State University Agr. Exp. Sta. Res. Bul. 389, 1952.

[133] Ghetti, J. L., A. S. Schienbein, and R. C. Kite. *Costs of Storing and Handling Grain in Commercial Elevators, 1967-68 and Projections for 1969-70.* USDA, ERS, ERS-401, 1969.

[134] Grinnell, G. E., G. B. Byers, and Z. C. Saufley. *Factors Influencing the Efficiency of Livestock Auction Markets in Kentucky.* Kentucky Agr. Econ. Ext. Inf. Ser. 3, 1969.

[135] Henning, G. F., and M. B. Evans. *Livestock Auction Markets in Ohio.* Ohio Agr. Exp. Sta. Res. Bul. 743, 1954.

[136] Holder, S. H., and O. L. McCaskill. *Cost of Electric Power and Fuel for Driers in Cotton Gins, Arkansas and Missouri.* USDA, ERS-138, 1963.

[137] Hudson, J. F., and W. J. Fontenot. *Profitability of Crawfish Peeling Plants in Louisiana.* Louisiana State University, Dept. Agr. Econ., DAE Res. Rep. 400, 1970.

[138] Hurt, V. G. *Cost of Processing and Distributing Grade "A" Milk in Mississippi.* Mississippi Agr. Exp. Sta. Bul. 748, 1967.

[139] Jack, R. L., and A. A. Kader. *Cost of Collecting Eggs from Farms by Firms Located in West Virginia.* West Virginia Agr. Exp. Sta. Bul. 571, 1969.

[140] Johnson, S. *Load Size and Delivery Labor Cost in Milk Distribution.* Connecticut (Storrs) Agr. Exp. Sta. Bul. 264, 1950.

[141] Jones, D. L., and F. H. Wiegmann. *Production Practices, Costs and Returns in the Cattle Feeding Industry, North Louisiana, 1967.* Louisiana State University, Dept. Agr. Econ., DAE Res. Rep. 387, 1968.

[142] Jones, H. B., and J. C. Thompson. *Marketing Costs and Labor Productivity in Commercial Egg Packing Plants.* Georgia Agr. Exp. Sta. Bul. N.S. P-3, 1962.

[143] Jorgens, J. R. S., and D. Snodgrass. *Handling-Storing Costs of County Grain Warehouses in Washington.* Washington Agr. Exp. Sta. Bul. 536, 1952.

[144] Juers, L. E., and E. F. Koller. *Costs of Drying Milk in Specialized Drying Plants.* Minnesota Agr. Exp. Sta. Bul. 435, 1956.

[145] Koenig, D., and E. H. Brown. "Analysis of Store Deliveries." In *Operating Results of Food Chains.* New York State College of Agriculture, Cornell University, 1963-64.

[146] Korzan, G. E., A. B. David, and D. D. MacPherson. *Costs of Distributing Milk in the Portland Market.* Oregon Agr. Exp. Sta. Bul. 442, 1952.

[147] Koudele, J. W. *Egg and Other Produce Procurement Costs.* Kansas State College Agr. Exp. Sta. Circ. 304, 1954.

[148] Lacasse, A., and L. Spencer. *Costs and Efficiency in the Operation of Milk Manufacturing Plants in the New York-New Jersey Milkshed.* Cornell University, Dept. Agr. Econ., AE Res. 26, 1960.

[149] Lasley, F. A., and S. F. Whitted. *Cost Factors in Milk Assembly (Bulk or Can Handling).* Missouri Agr. Exp. Sta. Res. Bul. 884, 1965.

[150] Libeau, C. P., and K. M. Bird. *An Analysis of Potato Packing Costs in Idaho, 1950-1951 Seasons.* Idaho Agr. Exp. Sta. Bul. 208, 1954.

[151] Looney, Z. M., and D. L. Shaw. *Cotton Gin Operating Costs in the Midsouth, 1968-69 and 1969-70.* USDA, ERS, Marketing Res. Rep. 942, 1971.

[152] Lyman, R. D., and A. J. Heinicke. *Grading and Packing Apples out of Storage.* Cornell University Agr. Exp. Sta., 1949.

[153] Malphrus, L. D. *Livestock Auction Operations in South Carolina.* South Carolina Agr. Exp. Sta. Bul. 467, 1958.

[154] Manuel, M., and R. L. Epard. *An Economic Analysis and Recommendations for Improving the Management of Kansas Grain Cooperatives.* Kansas Agr. Exp. Sta. Bul. 497, 1967.

[155] McKay, A. W., and F. R. Manson. *Labor Efficiency and Equipment Utilization in Maryland Milk Receiving Plants.* Maryland Agr. Exp. Sta., Dept. Agr. Econ., Misc. Pub. 270, 1956.

[156] McNeely, J. G., and G. E. Turner. *Texas Livestock Auction Markets — Operating Costs and Returns.* Texas Agr. Exp. Sta. Misc. Pub. 118, 1954.

[157] Metzger, H. B. *Costs of Obtaining Pasteurized Milk — A Comparison for Subdealers and Small Processor-Distributors.* Maine Agr. Exp. Sta. Bul. 515, 1953.

[158] Metzger, H. B., and C. W. Pierce. *Milk Marketing by Producer-Distributors.* Pennsylvania State College Agr. Exp. Sta. Bul. 544, 1951.

[159] Miller, A. H. *Bulk Handling of Wisconsin Milk — Farm to Plant.* Wisconsin Agr. Exp. Sta. Res. Bul. 192, 1956.

[160] Mitchell, J. A., D. Jackson, and C. B. Gilliland. *Labor and Power Utilization at Cottonseed Oil Mills.* USDA, AMS, Marketing Res. Rep. 218, 1958.

[161] Monroe, W. *Multiquart Containers — Their Effect on Milk Packaging and Handling Costs in Selected Cooperatives.* USDA, FCS, General Rep. 90, 1961.

[162] Mortenson, W. P. *A Study of Egg Handling in Wisconsin.* University of Wisconsin, Dept. Agr. Econ., 1959.

[163] National Commission on Food Marketing. *Organization and Competition in the Fruit and Vegetable Industry.* NCFM Tech. Study 4, 1966.

[164] ———. *Organization and Competition in Milling and Baking Industries.* NCFM Tech. Study 5, 1966.

[165] ———. *Studies of Organization and Competition in Grocery Manufacturing.* NCFM Tech. Study 6, 1966.

[166] Nyberg, A. J., and R. B. How. *Regional Differences in Costs of Canning Snap Beans.* Cornell University, Dept. Agr. Econ., AE Res. 150, 1964.

[167] Ott, L. *Frozen Foods: Margins, Costs, and Returns in Relation to Display Space.* USDA, ERS, ERS-235, 1965.

[168] Paulson, W. E. *Income and Cost Analysis, Cooperative Cotton Gins and Coop-*

178   BEN C. FRENCH

erative Supply Associations of Texas, Season 1949-50. Texas Agr. Exp. Sta. Bul. 803, 1955.

[169] Phillips, R. Costs of Procuring, Manufacturing, and Distributing Mixed Feeds in the Midwest. USDA, AMS, Marketing Res. Rep. 388, 1960.

[170] Podany, J. C. Costs of Marketing Florida Potatoes. USDA, AMS, Marketing Res. Rep. 233, 1958.

[171] Raskopf, B. D., and J. F. Miles. Labor Efficiency in Broiler Processing Plants in the South. Southern Cooperative Series Bul. 112, 1966.

[172] Ratcliffe, H. E. Why Egg Handling Costs Vary in Selected Cooperatives. USDA, FCS, Marketing Res. Rep. 552, 1962.

[173] Reid, R. J., V. J. Rhodes, and E. R. Kiehl. Economic Survey of Small Slaughtering Plants in Missouri. Missouri Agr. Exp. Sta. Res. Bul. 636, 1957.

[174] Richey, P. S., and T. D. Johnson. Factors to Be Considered in Locating, Planning, and Operating Country Elevators. USDA, PMA, Marketing Res. Rep. 23, 1952.

[175] Rogers, G. B., and E. H. Rinear. Costs and Efficiency in Turkey Processing Plants. USDA, MED, ERS-26, 1961.

[176] Roof, J. B. Milk Receiving Costs during Shift from Can to Bulk. USDA, FCS, General Rep. 77, 1960.

[177] Ruttan, V. W., and W. Fishel. Cost and Efficiency in Indiana Tomato Canning Plants. Purdue University Agr. Exp. Sta. Res. Mimeo ID-25, 1958.

[178] St. Clair, J. S., and A. L. Roberts. Quality and Cost of Ginning American-Egyptian Cotton — Seasons 1952-53 and 1953-54. USDA, AMS, Marketing Res. Rep. 199, 1957.

[179] St. Clair, J. S., and A. L. Roberts. Quality and Cost of Ginning Upland Cotton in Arizona. Arizona Agr. Exp. Sta. Bul. 277, 1956.

[180] Samuels, J. K., and G. L. Capel. Citrus Packinghouse Costs in California. USDA, FCA, Circ. C-138, 1951.

[181] Sanders, A., T. L. Frazier, and J. H. Padgett. An Appraisal of Economic Efficiencies within Livestock Slaughter Plants. Georgia Agr. Exp. Sta. Bul. N.S. 122, 1964.

[182] Schruben, L., and R. E. Clifton. Truck Delivery Costs of Manufactured Feed. Kansas Agr. Exp. Sta. Circ. 393, 1965.

[183] Scott, R. A. Labor Utilization in Small-Volume Milk Pasteurizing and Bottling Plants. Cornell University Agr. Exp. Sta. Bul. AE 850, 1953.

[184] Shafer, C. E. Marketing Practices and Costs of Texas Egg Producer-Wholesalers. Texas Agr. Exp. Sta. Bul. 1011, 1964.

[185] Sharp, J. W., and C. P. Baumel. A Financial Analysis of Ohio Elevator Operations. Ohio Agr. Exp. Sta. Res. Bul. 813, 1958.

[186] Smith, R. J., and J. M. Tinley. Economic Factors in Packing and Marketing Lemons in Cartons versus Standard Wooden Boxes. California Agr. Exp. Sta., Giannini Foundation Mimeo Rep. 159, 1953.

[187] Stallings, D. G. Marketing Domestic Dates — Packinghouse Practices and Costs. USDA, AMS, Marketing Res. Rep. 373, 1959.

[188] Stevens, I. M. R., and R. L. Fox. Improving Livestock Marketing Efficiency — A Study of Nine Cooperative Livestock Markets in Ohio, Indiana, and Michigan. USDA, Farmer Cooperative Service, 1958.

[189] Storey, D. A., and R. A. Gillifillan. Illinois Country Grain Elevator Financial Organization and Operation, a 1961-62 Study. Illinois Agr. Exp. Sta. Bul. 702, 1964.

[190] Thompson, J. C., Jr. Apple Storage Costs in New York State. Cornell University Agr. Exp. Sta. Res. 87, 1962.

[191] Tinley, J. M., and G. W. Parks. *Consolidation of Citrus Packing Houses in the Ontario-Cucamonga Area.* California Agr. Exp. Sta., Giannini Foundation Mimeo Rep. 154, 1953.

[192] Tussey, G. W., and R. A. King. *Costs of Ginning Cotton In North Carolina, 1957.* North Carolina State AE Inf. Ser. 72, 1959.

[193] Voegeli, L. J., E. F. White, B. Masters, and P. L. Breakiron. *Packing and Shipping Lettuce in Fiberboard Cartons and Wooden Crates — A Comparison.* USDA, AMS, Marketing Res. Rep. 86, 1955.

[194] White, M. *Relationships of Marketing Methods to Costs of Assembling, Grading, and Packaging Table Eggs.* Auburn University Agr. Exp. Sta. Bul. 348, 1963.

[195] Wissman, D. J. *Comparative Costs of Slaughtering Cattle in Michigan Packing Plants.* Michigan State University Agr. Econ. Rep. 10, 1965.

Statistical Analysis of Accounting Data

[196] Aigner, D., and S. Chu. "On Estimating the Industry Production Function." *Am. Econ. Rev.* 58:826-39, September 1968.

[197] Bain, J. *Barriers to New Competition.* Cambridge: Harvard University Press, 1956.

[198] Bain, J. S. "Survival-Ability As a Test of Efficiency." *Am. Econ. Rev.* 59: 99-104, May 1969.

[199] Baumel, P. C., and W. A. Fuller. "Estimates of the Productivity of Management Practices in Local Agribusiness Firms." *J. Farm Econ.* 46:857-865, November 1964.

[200] Beaton, N. J., and J. H. McCoy. *Economic Characteristics of Kansas Livestock Auctions.* Kansas State University Agr. Exp. Sta. Bul. 537, 1970.

[201] Boles, J. N. "Efficiency Squared — Efficient Computation of Efficiency Indexes." *Proceedings, Western Farm Economics Association Annual Meeting,* 1966.

[202] ———. *The 1130 Farrell Efficiency System — Multiple Products, Multiple Factors.* Giannini Foundation of Agricultural Economics, University of California, Berkeley, 1971.

[203] Bressler, R. G. "The Measurement of Productive Efficiency." *Proceedings, Western Farm Economics Association Annual Meeting,* 1966.

[204] Broadbent, E. E., and S. R. Perkinson. *Operational Efficiency of Illinois Country Hog Markets.* University of Illinois, Dept. Agr. Econ., AERR 110, 1971.

[205] Dean, J. "Department Store Cost Functions." In *Studies in Mathematical Economics and Econometrics,* Oskar Lange, ed. London: Cambridge University Press, 1942.

[206] ———. *The Relation of Cost to Output for a Leather Belt Shop.* National Bureau of Economic Research, Tech. Paper 2, 1941.

[207] ———. *Statistical Cost Functions of a Hosiery Mill.* Chicago: University of Chicago Press, 1941.

[208] Dean, J., and W. R. James. *The Long-Run Behavior of Costs in a Chain of Shoe Stores.* Chicago: University of Chicago Press, 1942.

[209] Dietrich, R. A. *Costs and Economies of Size in Texas-Oklahoma Cattle Feedlot Operations.* Texas Agr. Exp. Sta. Bul. 1083, 1969.

[210] Farrell, M. J. "The Measurement of Productive Efficiency." *J. Royal Stat. Soc.* 120:253-281 (Series A, Part 3), 1957.

[211] Farrell, M. J., and M. Fieldhouse. "Estimating Efficient Production Functions under Increasing Returns to Scale." *J. Royal Stat. Soc.* 125:252-267 (Series A, Part 2), 1962.

180   BEN C. FRENCH

[212] Farstad, E., and J. V. Brensike. *Costs of Retailing Meats in Relation to Volume.* USDA, BAE Marketing Res. Rep. 24, 1952.

[213] Federal Trade Commission. *The Structure of Food Manufacturing,* NCFM Tech. Study 8, 1966.

[214] Gum, R. L., and S. H. Logan. "Labor Productivity in Beef Slaughter Plants," *J. Farm Econ.* 47:1457-1461, 1965.

[215] Hanlon, J. W., and E. F. Koller. *Processing Costs in Butter-Nonfat Dry Milk Plants.* Minnesota Agr. Exp. Sta. Bul. 491, 1969.

[216] Hopkin, John A. "Economies of Size in the Cattle-Feeding Industry of California." *J. Farm Econ.* 40:417-429, 1958.

[217] Johnson, P. R. "Some Aspects of Estimating Statistical Cost Functions." *J. Farm Econ.* 46:179-187, 1964.

[218] Johnson, R. D., and A. R. Eckert. *Cattle Feeding Costs in Nebraska by System of Feeding and Size of Operation.* Nebraska Agr. Exp. Sta. and USDA, SB 496, 1968.

[219] Johnston, J. *Statistical Cost Analysis.* New York: McGraw-Hill, 1960.

[220] Kelley, P., J. H. McCoy, H. Tucker, and V. T. Altau. *Resource Returns and Productivity Coefficients in Central and Western Kansas Country Elevators of Modern Construction.* Kansas State College Agr. Exp. Sta. Tech. Bul. 88, 1957.

[221] Kelley, P. L., H. Tucker, and M. L. Manuel. *Resource Returns and Productivity Coefficients in the Kansas Cooperative Grain Elevator Industry.* Kansas State College Agr. Exp. Sta. Tech. Bul. 84, 1956.

[222] Knudtson, A. C. "Estimating Economies of Scale." *J. Farm Econ.* 40:750-756, August 1958.

[223] Knudtson, A. C., and E. F. Koller. *Manufacturing Costs in Minnesota Creameries.* Minnesota Agr. Exp. Sta. Bul. 442, 1957.

[224] Knutson, R. D., and E. F. Koller. *Costs and Margins in Minnesota Fluid Milk Plants.* Minnesota Agr. Exp. Sta. Bul. 483, 1967.

[225] Lindberg, R. C., and G. G. Judge. *Estimated Cost Functions for Oklahoma Livestock Auctions.* Oklahoma Agr. Exp. Sta. Bul. B-502, 1958.

[226] Malmgren, H. B. "What Conclusions Are to Be Drawn from Empirical Cost Data?" *J. Indus. Econ.* 7:136-144, March 1959.

[227] McDowell, J. I., D. L. Wold, and E. E. Anderson. *Cost-Volume Relationships at North Dakota Livestock Auctions.* North Dakota Agr. Exp. Sta. Bul. 452, 1965.

[228] Murra, G. E., and T. G. Mire. *The Organization, Operation, and Costs of Livestock Auctions in Louisiana.* Louisiana State University, Dept. Agr. Econ., DAE Res. Rep. 361, 1967.

[229] National Commission on Food Marketing. *Organization and Competition in Food Retailing.* (See chapter 7, "Economies of Scale in Food Retailing," and Appendix D.) NCFM Tech. Study 7, 1966.

[230] O'Connor, W. O., and T. M. Hammonds. "Measurement of Economic Efficiency of Central Fabrication versus Carcass-Meat-Handling Systems." *Am. J. Agr. Econ.* 57:665-675, November 1975.

[231] Parsons, S. A., and J. W. B. Guise. "An Analysis of the Costs of Operation of Export Abattoirs in Australia." *Quart. Rev. Agr. Econ.* 24:45-56, January 1971.

[232] Phillips, R. "Empirical Estimates of Cost Functions for Mixed Feed Mills in the Midwest." *Agr. Econ. Res.* 8:1-8, January 1956.

[233] Purcell, J. C., and N. M. Penny. *Cost of Processing and Distributing Milk in the South.* Georgia Agr. Exp. Sta. Bul. 45, 1955.

[234] Saving, T. R. "Estimation of Optimum Size of Plant by the Survivor Technique." *Quart. J. Econ.* 75:569-607, November 1961.

[235] Schneidau, R. E., and J. Havlicek, Jr. *Labor Productivity in Selected Indiana Meat Packing Plants.* Purdue University Agr. Exp. Sta. Res. Bul. 769, 1963.

[236] Seitz, W. D. "The Measurement of Efficiency Relative to a Frontier Production Function." *Am. J. Agr. Econ.* 52:505-511, November 1970.

[237] ———. "The Measurement of Productive Efficiency." Unpublished Ph.D. dissertation, University of California, Berkeley, 1968.

[238] ———. "Productive Efficiency in the Steam Generating Industry." *J. Pol. Econ.* 79:878-886, July/August 1971.

[239] Sharp, J. W., and P. W. Lytle. *An Intrafirm Analysis of Financial Statements of Country Elevators.* Ohio Agr. Res. Dev. Center, Wooster Res. Bul. 1043, 1970.

[240] Shepherd, W. G. "What Does the Survivor Technique Show about Economies of Scale?" *Southern Econ. J.* 34:113-122, July 1967.

[241] Sitorus, B. L. "Productive Efficiency and Redundant Factors of Production in Traditional Agriculture of Underdeveloped Countries." *Proceedings, Western Farm Economics Association Annual Meeting,* 1966.

[242] Smith, C. "Survey of the Empirical Evidence on Economies of Scale." In *Business Concentration and Price Policy.* Universities-National Bureau of Economic Research Conference Series, No. 5. Princeton: Princeton University Press, 1955.

[243] Stigler, G. J. "The Economies of Scale." *J. Law Econ.* 1:54-71, October 1958.

[244] Stollsteimer, J. F., R. G. Bressler, and J. N. Boles. "Cost Functions from Cross-Section Data — Fact or Fantasy?" *Agr. Econ. Res.* 13:79-88, July 1961.

[245] Thuroczy, N. M., and W. A. Schlegel. *Costs of Operating Southern Rice Mills.* USDA, AMS, Marketing Res. Rep. 330, 1959.

[246] Timmer, C. P. "On Measuring Technical Efficiency." *Food Research Institute Studies,* vol. 9, no. 2. Stanford University, 1970.

[247] ———. "Using a Probabilistic Frontier Production Function to Measure Technical Efficiency." *J. Pol. Econ.* 79:776-794, July/August 1971.

[248] Walters, A. A. "Expectations and the Regression Fallacy in Estimating Cost Functions." *Rev. Econ. Stat.* 42:210-215, May 1960.

[249] ———. "Production and Cost Functions: An Econometric Survey." *Econometrica* 31:1-66, January/April 1963.

[250] Weiss, L. "The Survival Technique and the Extent of Suboptimal Capacity." *J. Pol. Econ.* 72:246-261, June 1964.

[251] Wilson, E. M., and J. P. Kuehn. *A Cost Analysis of the Livestock Auction Markets in West Virginia.* West Virginia Agr. Exp. Sta. Bul. 600T, 1971.

[252] Wootan, C. V., and J. G. McNeely, *Factors Affecting Auction Market Operating Costs.* Texas A & M University Exp. Sta. Bul. 1056, 1966.

[253] Wylie, K. H., and M. Ezekiel. "The Cost Curve for Steel Production." *J. Pol. Econ.* 48:777-821, December 1940.

[254] Yntema, T. O. "Steel Prices, Volume and Costs." In *Temporary National Economic Committee Papers,* vol. 1. U.S. Steel Corporation, 1940.

[255] Zasada, D. "The Cost of Handling and Storing Grain in Manitoba Country Elevators." *Canadian J. Agr. Econ.* 18:45-59, February 1970.

[256] Zasada, D., and O. P. Tangri. *An Analysis of Factors Affecting the Cost of Handling and Storing Grain in Manitoba Country Elevators.* University of Manitoba Faculty of Agricultural and Home Economics, Res. Rep. 13, 1967.

Economic-Engineering Analysis

GENERAL ARTICLES

[257] Black, G. "Synthetic Method of Cost Analysis in Agricultural Marketing Firms." *J. Farm Econ.* 37:270-279, May 1955.

[258] Chenery, H. B. "Engineering Production Functions." *Quart. J. Econ.* 43:507-537, November 1949.

[259] ———. "Process and Production Functions from Engineering Data." In *Studies in the Structure of the American Economy* by W. Lwonteif et al. New York: Oxford University Press, 1953.

[260] Elliott, W. H. "Possibilities for Reducing Handling Costs." Report of the National Marketing Service Workshop, 1954. USDA, AMS, AMS-9.

[261] Farris, D. E. "Determining Internal Economies to Scale in Fruit and Vegetable Processing Plants." *Proceedings, Marketing Section, Association of Southern Agricultural Workers*, 1963.

[262] Ferguson, A. R. "Empirical Determination of a Multi-dimensional Cost Function." *Econometrica* 18:217-235, July 1950.

[263] French, B. C. "Industry Cooperation in Studies of Fruit and Vegetable Packing House Efficiency." *J. Farm Econ.* 37:1209-1214, December 1955.

[264] ———. "New Techniques in Plant Efficiency Research." *Proceedings, Western Farm Economics Association Annual Meeting*, 1951.

[265] ———. "Some Considerations in Estimating Assembly Cost Functions for Agricultural Processing Operations." *J. Farm Econ.* 42:767-778, November 1960. Reprinted in *Readings in the Economics of Agriculture*, K. A. Fox and H. G. Johnson, eds. Homewood, Ill.: Irwin, 1969.

[266] Hallberg, M. C., and W. R. Kriebel. *Designing Efficient Pickup and Delivery Route Systems by Computer.* Pennsylvania State University Agr. Exp. Sta. Bul. 782, 1972.

[267] Homme, H. A. "Estimation and Use of Cost Functions in Iowa Creameries." *J. Farm Econ.* 35:931-937, December 1953.

[268] Isard, W., E. W. Schoaler, and T. Victorisz. *Industrial Complex Analysis and Regional Development: A Case Study of Refinery-Petrochemical-Synthetic-Fiber Complexes in Puerto Rico.* New York: Wiley, 1959.

[269] Malcolm, D. G., and L. L. Sammet. "Work Sampling Applications." *J. Indus. Eng.* 5:4-6, 23, May 1954.

[270] Manne, A. S., and H. M. Markovitz, eds. *Studies in Process Analysis.* New York: Wiley, 1961.

[271] Sammet, L. L. "Systems Engineering in Agriculture." *Agr. Eng.* 40:663, 685-687, March 1959.

[272] ———. "Transferability of Microeconomic Data over Time: An Illustration." *Am. J. Agr. Econ.* 56:614-621, August 1974.

[273] Sammet, L. L., and B. C. French. "Economic-Engineering Methods in Marketing Research." *J. Farm Econ.* 35:924-930, December 1953.

[274] Sammet, L. L., and J. B. Hassler. "Use of the Ratio-Delay Method in Processing Plant Operations." *Agr. Econ. Res.* 3:124-134, October 1951.

[275] Sammet, L. L., and D. G. Malcolm. "Work Sampling Studies; Guides to Analysis and Accuracy Criteria." *J. Indus. Eng.* 5:9-13, July 1954.

[276] Schruben, L. W., and R. E. Clifton. "The Lockset Method of Sequential Programming Applied to Routing, Delivery and Pickup Trucks." *Am. J. Agr. Econ.* 50:854-867, March 1968.

[277] Smith, V. L. "Engineering Data and Statistical Techniques in the Analysis of Production and Technological Change: Fuel Requirements in the Trucking Industry." *Econometrica* 25:281-301, April 1957.

[278] ———. *Investment and Production.* Cambridge: Harvard University Press, 1961.

[279] Thor, E., J. W. Devault, and A. H. Spurlock. *A Method of Allocating Citrus Packinghouse Costs.* Florida Agr. Exp. Sta., Agr. Econ. Mimeo Rep. 58-1, 1957.

[280] Thor, E., M. Revzan, and J. B. Siebert. *A Guide for Measuring Relative Profitableness of Alternative Work Methods in Agricultural Packing and Processing Operations.* California Agr. Ext. Serv., Giannini Foundation Inf. Ser. 65-4, December 1965.

CATTLE FEEDING

[281] Carter, H. O., G. W. Dean, and P. H. Maxwell. *Economies of Cattle Feeding on Imperial Valley Field Crop Farms.* California Agr. Exp. Sta. Bul. 813, 1965.

[282] Gilliam, H. C., L. A. Ihnen, and W. D. Toussaint. *An Economic Analysis of Selected Systems for Feeding Beef Cattle in North Carolina.* North Carolina State University A. E. Inf. Ser. 112, 1964.

[283] Hunter, E. C., and J. P. Madden. *Economies of Size for Specialized Beef Feedlots in Colorado.* USDA, Agr. Econ. Rep. 91, 1966.

[284] Irrer, T. M., and B. F. Jones. *Economies of Size in Indiana Beef Cattle Feedlots.* Purdue University Agr. Exp. Sta. Bul. 881, 1971.

[285] King, G. A. *Economies of Scale in Large Commercial Feedlots.* California Agr. Exp. Sta., Giannini Foundation Res. Rep. 251, 1962.

[286] Logan, S. H. *Economies of Scale in Cattle Feeding.* Supplement 3 to NCFM Tech. Study 1, *Organization and Competition in the Livestock and Meat Industry.* National Commission on Food Marketing, 1966.

[287] Malone, J. W., and L. F. Rogers. *Economies of Size of Warm-Up Cattle Feedlot Operations in Nevada.* University of Nevada, Coll. Agr. Bul. 6, 1965.

[288] McCoy, J. H., and C. Hausman. *Economies of Scale in Commercial Cattle Feedlots of Kansas — An Analysis of Nonfeed Costs.* Kansas State Univesity Agr. Exp. Sta. Tech. Bul. 151, 1967.

[289] McCoy, J. H., and H. D. Wakefield. *Economies of Scale in Farm Cattle Feedlots of Kansas — An Analysis of Nonfeed Costs.* Kansas State University Agr. Exp. Sta. Tech. Bul. 145, 1966.

[290] Morris, W. H. M. *Economies to Scale in Cattle Feeding in the U.S.* Purdue University, Dept. Agr. Econ, 1970.

[291] Petit, J. A., Jr., and G. W. Dean. *Economies of Farm Feedlots in the Rice Area of the Sacremento Valley.* Califronia Agr. Exp. Sta. Bul. 800, 1964.

[292] Richards, J. A., and G. E. Korzan. *Beef Cattle Feedlots in Oregon — A Feasibility Study.* Oregon State University, Special Rep. 170, 1964.

[293] Webb, T. F. *Improved Methods and Facilities for Commercial Cattle Feedlots.* USDA, AMS, Marketing Res. Rep. 517, 1962.

[294] Williams, W. F., and J. I. McDowell. *Costs and Efficiency in Commercial Dry-Lot Cattle Feeding.* Oklahoma State University Agr. Exp. Sta., P-509, 1965.

COTTON ASSEMBLY AND GINNING

[295] Anderson, R. F. *Costs of Assembling and Ginning Cotton in Georgia Related to Size of Gin.* Georgia Agr. Exp. Sta. Bul. N.S. 153, 1966.

[296] Cable, C. C., Jr., and Z. M. Looney. *Effects and Costs of Cleaning Lint in Arkansas Cotton Gins.* Arkansas Agr. Exp. Sta. Bul. 595, 1957.

184   BEN C. FRENCH

[297] Cable, C. C., Jr., Z. M. Looney, and C. A. Wilmot. *Utilization and Cost of Labor for Ginning Cotton.* USDA, Agr. Econ. Rep. 70, 1965.

[298] Covey, C. D., and J. F. Hudson. *Cotton Gin Efficiency As Related to Size, Location, and Cotton Production Density in Louisiana.* Louisiana State University Agr. Exp. Sta. Bul. 577, 1963.

[299] Lafferty, D. G. *Cost Relationships in High-Capacity Cotton Gins.* Southern Cooperative Ser. Bul. 88, 1964.

[300] Looney, Z. M., and C. A. Wilmot. *Economic Models for Cotton Ginning.* USDA, ERS, Agr. Econ. Rep. 214, 1971.

[301] Metcalf, A. V. *Assembling, Storing, and Ginning Cotton in the Mississippi Delta.* Missouri Agr. Exp. Sta. Res. Bul. 878, 1965.

[302] Thompson, R. G., and J. M. Ward. *An Economic Analysis of Cotton Gin Plants — High Plains, Rolling Plains, and Lower Rio Grande Valley of Texas.* Texas Agr. Exp. Sta. Bul. 1020, 1964.

[303] Thompson, R. G., J. M. Ward, and J. W. Graves. *Cotton Ginning Costs from Model Gin Plant Analysis.* Texas Agr. Exp. Sta., Dept. Econ. Soc. Inf. Rep. 64-3, 1964.

[304] Wilmot, C. A., V. L. Stedronsky, Z. M. Looney, and V. P. Moore. *Engineering and Economic Aspects of Cotton Gin Operations — Midsouth, West Texas, Far West.* USDA, ERS, Agr. Econ. Rep. 116, 1967.

[305] Wilmot, C. A., and H. Watson. *Power Requirements and Costs of High-Capacity Cotton Gins.* USDA, ERS, Marketing Res. Rep. 763, 1966.

DAIRY PRODUCTS PROCESSING

[306] Aplin, R. D. *Country Reload Plants for Bulk Milk: Specifications and Costs.* Cornell University Agr. Exp. Sta., AE-1, 1959.

[307] Babb, E. M., and J. C. Taylor. *Use of Economic-Engineering Techniques in Planning Ice Cream Operations.* Purdue University Ext. Ser. Mimeo EC-240, 1962.

[308] Baum, E. L., R. D. Riley, and E. E. Weeks. *Economies of Scale in the Operation of Can and Tank Milk Receiving Rooms, with Special Reference to Western Washington.* Washington Agr. Exp. Sta. Tech. Bul. 12, 1954.

[309] Beal, G. M., and Y. K. Rao. *Economics of Milk Manufacturing Labor and Plant Utilization.* Maryland Agr. Exp. Sta. Misc. Pub. 536, 1965.

[310] Blanchard, W. H., G. McBride, and A. L. Rippen. *A Cost Analysis of Fluid Milk Packaging Operations.* Michigan State University Agr. Exp. Sta. Tech. Bul. 285, 1962.

[311] Boles, J. N. "Economies of Scale for Evaporated Milk Plants in California." *Hilgardia* 27:621-722. California Agr. Exp. Sta., Giannini Foundation Monograph 7, 1958.

[312] Carter, R. M., K. P. Brundage, and A. Bradfield. *Labor and Equipment Use in Milk-Receiving Plants.* Vermont Agr. Exp. Sta. Bul. 563, 1951.

[313] Conner, M. C., L. Spencer, and C. W. Pierce. *Specifications and Cost for a Milk Pasteurizing and Bottling Plant.* Virginia Polytechnic Institute Agr. Exp. Sta. Bul. 463; Northeast Regional Publication 16, 1953.

[314] Conner, M. C., F. C. Webster, and T. R. Owens. *An Economic Analysis of Model Plants for Pasteurizing and Bottling Milk.* Virginia Polytechnic Institute Agr. Exp. Sta. Bul. 484, 1957.

[315] Fitzpatrick, J. M., and C. E. French. *Impact of Seasonality of Milk Supplies on Labor Costs and Efficiency in Dairy Manufacturing Plants.* Purdue University Agr. Exp. Sta. Res. Bul. 774, 1964.

[316] Frazer, J. R., V. H. Nielsen, and C. W. Ladd. *Manufacturing Costs: Whole Milk Creameries.* Iowa State College Agr. Exp. Sta. Spec. Rep. 17, 1956.

[317] Frazer, J. R., V. H. Nielsen, and J. D. Nord. *The Cost of Manufacturing Butter.* Iowa Agr. Exp. Sta. Res. Bul. 389, 1952.

[318] French, C. E. *Research Procedure in Evaluating Milk Receiving Labor in Indiana.* Purdue University Agr. Exp. Sta. Bul. 575, 1952.

[319] French, C. E., and H. R. Varney, Jr. *Labor Utilization in Cold Storage and Empty Bottle Rooms.* Purdue University Agr. Exp. Sta. Res. Bul. 677, 1959.

[320] French, C. E., G. B. Wood, and V. C. Manhart. *Labor Utilization in Receiving Rooms of Indiana Milk Plants.* Purdue University Agr. Exp. Sta. Bul. 576, 1952.

[321] Hall, C. W. "Can Washer Selection for the Dairy Plant." Michigan Agr. Exp. Sta., *Quart. Bul.* 35:461-466, May 1953.

[322] ———. "Efficient Milk Can Conveyor Design for Dairy Plants." Michigan Agr. Exp. Sta., *Quart. Bul.* 35:198-202, November 1952.

[323] ———. "Operational Costs in a Dairy Plant — 1952." Michigan Agr. Exp. Sta., *Quart. Bul.* 36:107-129, August 1953.

[324] ———. "Weigh Can Selection for the Dairy Plant." Michigan Agr. Exp. Sta., *Quart. Bul.* 35:310-316, February 1953.

[325] Henry, W. F., R. G. Bressler, Jr., and G. E. Frick. *Efficiency of Milk Marketing in Connecticut. No. 11, Economies of Scale in Specialized Pastuerizing and Bottling Plants.* Connecticut (Storrs) Agr. Exp. Sta. Bul. 259, 1948.

[326] Hines, F. K., and L. V. Blakley, *Costs of Manufacturing Cheese in Oklahoma.* Oklahoma Agr. Exp. Sta., Dept. Agr. Econ., P-531, 1966.

[327] Johnson, A., D. O. Forker, and D. A. Clarke. *Operations and Costs of Manufacturing Dairy Products in California.* California Agr. Exp. Sta., Giannini Foundation Res. Rep. 272, 1964.

[328] Kerchner, O. G. *Economic Aspects of Flexible Dairy Manufacturing Plants.* Minnesota Agr. Exp. Sta. Bul. 487, 1968.

[329] Knudtson, A. C., and E. F. Koller. *Processing Costs of Whole Milk Creameries.* Minnesota Agr. Exp. Sta. Tech. Bul. 236, 1960.

[330] Kolmer, L., H. A. Homme, and G. W. Ladd. *Spray Drying Costs in Low-Volume Milk Plants.* Iowa State College Agr. Exp. Sta., Spec. Rep. 19, 1957.

[331] Lilwall, N. B., and J. W. Hammond. *Cheddar Cheese Manufacturing Costs.* Minnesota Agr. Exp. Sta. Bul. 501, 1970.

[332] Mengel, J., G. Devino, and A. Bradfield. *Specifications and Costs for a 100,000 Quarts per Day Fluid Milk Processing Plant.* Rutgers Exp. Sta. Bul. 825, 1969.

[333] Miller, R. H., and T. F. Graf. *An Economic Analysis of Cottage Cheese Marketing.* Wisconsin College of Agriculture Res. Bul. 278, 1970.

[334] Monroe, W. J., and S. A. Walker. *An Economic Study of Small Fluid Milk Plant Problems in Northern Idaho.* Idaho Agr. Exp. Sta. Bul. 255, 1956.

[335] Nolte, G. M., and E. F. Koller. *Milk Assembly and Processing Costs in the Butter-Dry Milk Industry.* Minnesota Agr. Exp. Sta. Bul. 507, 1972.

[336] O'Connell, P., and W. E. Snyder. *Cost Analysis of Fluid Milk Processing and Distribution in Colorado.* Colorado State University Agr. Exp. Sta. Tech. Bul. 86, 1964.

[337] Owens, T. R., and W. T. Butz. *Specifications and Costs for Processing Operations in Small Market Milk Plants.* Pennsylvania State University Agr. Exp. Sta. Bul. 625, 1957.

[338] Owens, T. R., and D. A. Clarke, Jr. *Class III Milk in the New York Milkshed.*

III. Costs of Manufacturing Dairy Products. USDA, AMS, Marketing Res. Rep. 400, 1960.

[339] Page, C. M., and S. A. Walker. *Building Designs for Dairy Processing Plants.* Idaho Agr. Exp. Sta. Bul. 297, 1953.

[340] Roof, J. B. *Milk Receiving Costs during Shift from Can to Bulk.* USDA, FCS, General Rep. 77, 1960.

[341] Simmons, R. L. *Case Handling Costs in Fluid Milk Plants.* North Carolina State College, Agr. Inf. Ser. 81, 1960.

[342] Stein, F., A. G. Mathis, and L. F. Herrman. *Costs of Butterfat Sampling and Testing Programs.* USDA, AMS-212, 1957.

[343] Strain, J. R., and S. K. Christensen. *Relationship between Plant Size and Cost of Processing Fluid Milk in Oregon.* Oregon State College Agr. Exp. Sta. Tech. Bul. 55, 1960.

[344] Taylor, J. C. *Ice Cream Manufacturing Plants in the Midwest — Methods, Equipment and Layout.* USDA, AMS, Marketing Res. Rep. 477, 1961.

[345] Taylor, J. C., T. E. Bartlett, and C. E. French. *Effects of Volume on Costs of Ice Cream Manufacturing.* Purdue University Agr. Exp. Sta. Res. Bul. 779, 1964.

[346] Taylor, J. C., and R. W. Brown. *Fluid Milk Plants in the Southeast — Methods, Equipment, and Layout.* USDA, AMS, Marketing Res. Rep. 232, 1958.

[347] Townsend, T. W., P. L. Kelley, and A. Feyerherm. *Labor Coefficients for a Surplus Milk Plant As Determined by Work Sampling.* Kansas State University Agr. Exp. Sta. Tech. Bul. 122, 1962.

[348] Tracy, P. H. *Layouts and Operating Criteria for Automation of Dairy Plants Manufacturing Ice Cream and Ice Cream Novelties.* USDA, ARS, Marketing Res. Rep. 750, 1966.

[349] Utter, K. L., W. S. Rosenberger, H. Homme, and G. Shepherd. *Methods and Costs of Processing and Delivering Fresh Concentrated Milk in Rural Areas.* Iowa State Agr. Exp. Sta. Spec. Rep. 14, 1953.

[350] Walker, S. H., H. J. Preston, and G. T. Nelson. *An Economic Analysis of Butter — Nonfat Dry Milk Plants.* Idaho Agr. Exp. Sta. Res. Bul. 20, 1953.

[351] Webster, F., A. Bradfield, J. R. Bowring, H. C. Moore, and K. A. Taylor. *Economies of Size in Fluid Milk-Processing Plants.* Vermont Agr. Exp. Sta. Bul. 636, 1963.

EGG PACKING, ASSEMBLY, AND DISTRIBUTION

[352] Bird, K. *An Analysis of Egg Handling Costs and Efficiency.* Oklahoma State University Exp. Sta. Bul. B-568, 1960.

[353] Byers, G. B., and S. A. Callahan. *Estimating Costs, Potential Efficiencies, and Profit Margins in Assembling, Processing, and Distributing Eggs.* Kentucky Agr. Exp. Sta. Bul. 701, 1965.

[354] Earle, W. *Time and Travel Requirements in Country Egg Receiving Stations.* Cornell University Agr. Exp. Sta. Bul. AE 741, 1950.

[355] Gallimore, W. W., and A. P. Stemberger. *Costs of Egg Marketing Services: Farm versus Central Station.* North Carolina State College Agr. Inf. Ser. 74, 1960.

[356] ———. *Economies to Size in Hatching Chicks.* North Carolina State College Agr. Inf. Ser. 96, 1962.

[357] Hamann, J. A., and T. F. Todd. *Improved Designs for Commercial Egg Grading and Packing Plants.* USDA, AMS, Marketing Res. Rep. 422, 1961.

[358] Jackson, G., and O. D. Forker. *An Analysis of Factors Influencing Shell-Egg Distribution Costs.* Cornell University Agr. Exp. Sta. AE Res. 318, 1970.

[359] Jones, H. B. *Economies of Scale in Commercial Egg Packing Plants.* Georgia Agr. Exp. Sta. Bul. N.S. 120, 1964.

[360] ———. *Economies of Scale in Egg Packing Plants under Changing Cost and Technological Conditions.* Georgia Agr. Exp. Sta. Tech. Bul. N.S. 48, 1965.

[361] Judge, G. G., and R. L. Baker. "Time and Cost Functions for Egg Routes." *Poultry Sci.* 31:738-744, July 1952.

[362] Paulhus, N. G., and F. P. Delle Donne. *Candling, Sizing, Packing, and Materials — Handling Equipment and Methods Used in Egg Assembly Plants.* USDA, PMA, Marketing Res. Rep. 47, 1953.

[363] Pedersen, J. R. *Costs and Economies of Scale in Egg-Type Chick Hatcheries.* USDA, ERS, Marketing Res. Rep. 782, 1967.

[364] ———. *Economies of Scale in Turkey Hatcheries.* USDA, ERS, Marketing Res. Rep. 719, 1965.

[365] Peeler, R. J., Jr., and R. A. King. *In-Plant Costs of Grading and Packing Eggs.* North Carolina State College Agr. Econ. Inf. Ser. 106, 1963.

[366] Rollins, F. D., P. C. Clayton, and R. E. Cray. *Egg Marketing Costs Influenced by Size of Farm Shipments.* Ohio Agr. Exp. Sta. Circ. 83, 1960.

[367] Seaver, S. K. *The Effect of Variability in Supply of Eggs upon Wholesale Marketing Costs.* Connecticut Agr. Exp. Sta. Bul. 331, 1957.

[368] Vertrees, J. G., and H. E. Larzelere. *Factors Affecting Shell Egg Distribution Channel Costs.* Michigan State University Agr. Econ. Rep. 214, 1972.

[369] Williams, R. J., and J. S. Tobey. *Efficiency in Small and Medium-Sized Egg Handling Rooms.* Cornell University, Agr. Econ. Res. 166, 1962.

FRESH FRUIT AND VEGETABLE PACKING AND ASSEMBLY

[370] Andrews, B. G., and S. W. Burt. *Methods, Equipment, and Facilities for Receiving, Ripening, and Packing Bananas.* USDA, AMS, Marketing Res. Rep. 92, 1955.

[371] Bateman, L., and C. Price. *Packing Costs for Arkansas Pink Tomatoes — An Evaluation of Two Methods.* Arkansas Agr. Exp. Sta. Bul. 747, 1969.

[372] Bird, K. *Packing 10-Pound Sacks of Idaho Potatoes.* Idaho Agr. Exp. Sta. Bul. 265, 1956.

[373] Bohall, R. W., R. O. P. Farrish, and J. C. Podany. *Packing Mature Green Tomatoes: Costs, Efficiencies, and Economies of Scale in the Lower Rio Grande Valley of Texas.* USDA, Marketing Res. Rep. 679, 1964.

[374] Bowman, E. K., and E. Johnston. *Methods of Receiving Potatoes in Barrels at Maine Trackside Storages.* Maine Agr. Exp. Sta. Bul. 560, 1957.

[375] Bowman, E. K., A. H. Spurlock, S. Hedden, and W. Grierson. *Modernizing Handling Systems for Florida Citrus from Packing to Packing Line.* USDA, ARS, and Florida Agr. Exp. Sta., Marketing Res. Rep. 914, 1971.

[376] Bressler, R. G. *Efficiency in Fruit Marketing: Marketing Costs for Deciduous Fruits.* California Agr. Exp. Sta., Giannini Foundation Mimeo Rep. 127, 1952.

[377] Bressler, R. G., and B. C. French. *Efficiency in Fruit Marketing: Grading Costs for Apples and Pears.* California Agr. Exp. Sta., Giannini Foundation Mimeo Rep. 128, 1952.

[378] Brown, E. E., H. C. Spurlock, W. H. Thomas. *Reducing Injuries to Peaches through the Use of Field Box Pads.* South Carolina Agr. Exp. Sta., Dept. Agr. Econ., AE 175, 1959.

[379] Burt, S. W. *An Experimental Packing Line for McIntosh Apples.* USDA, AMS-330, 1959.

[380] ———. *Packing Apples in the Northeast.* USDA, AMS, Marketing Res. Rep. 543, 1962.

[381] Capel, G. L. *Comparative Costs of Alternative Methods for Performing Certain Handling Operations in Florida Citrus Packinghouses.* Florida Agr. Exp. Sta. Bul. 609, 1959.

[382] ———. *Costs for Handling Florida Oranges Shipped in Consumer Bags and in Bulk.* Florida Agr. Exp. Sta., Agr. Econ. Mimeo Rep. 58-12, 1958.

[383] ———. *The Use of Packing Labor in Florida Citrus Packinghouses.* Florida Agr. Exp. Sta., Agr. Econ. Mimeo Rep. 57-8, 1957.

[384] Capel, G. L., and H. J. Preston. *Cost of Prepackaging Potatoes in Maine, Michigan, and Pennsylvania.* USDA, FCA, Misc. Rep. 163, 1952.

[385] Carlsen, E. W., R. S. Duerden, D. L. Hunter, and Joseph F. Herrick, Jr. *Innovations in Apple Handling Methods and Equipment.* USDA, AMS, Marketing Res. Rep. 68, 1955.

[386] Carlsen, E. W., D. L. Hunter, R. S. Duerden, and J. F. Herrick, Jr. *Apple Handling Methods and Equipment in Pacific Northwest Packing and Storage Houses.* USDA, PMA, Marketing Res. Rep. 49, 1953.

[387] Carlsen, E. W., D. L. Hunter, R. S. Duerden, and G. F. Sainsbury. *Methods and Costs of Loading Apples in the Orchard in the Pacific Northwest.* USDA, ARS, Marketing Res. Rep. 55, 1954.

[388] Carlsen, E. W., and D. R. Stokes. *Prepackaging Apples at Point of Production.* USDA Agr. Inf. Bul. 29, 1951.

[389] Carman, H. F. *An Analysis of Apple-Packing Costs in Michigan.* USDA, ERS, Marketing Res. Rep. 786, 1967.

[390] Chambliss, R. Lee, Jr. *Labor Utilization in Apple Packing Sheds in Virginia.* Virginia Agr. Exp. Sta. Bul. 493, 1958.

[391] Chapman, W. Fred, J. F. Pittman, and A. B. Carroll. *Costs, Methods, and Facilities in Packing South Carolina Peaches, 1959.* USDA, AMS, Marketing Res. Rep. 425, 1959.

[392] Dickmann, F. H. J., and G. B. Davis. *Costs and Efficiencies in Handling, Storing, and Packing Onions.* Oregon State College Agr. Exp. Sta. Misc. Pap. 96, 1960.

[393] Enochian, R. V., F. J. Smith, and L. L. Sammet. *Cost and Efficiency in House Packing Western Head Lettuce.* California Agr. Exp. Sta., Giannini Foundation Mimeo Rep. 199, 1957.

[394] Evans, H. C., and R. S. Marsh. *Costs and Mechanical Injury in Handling and Packing Apples.* West Virginia Agr. Exp. Sta. Bul. 416, 1958.

[395] French, B. C. "Efficiency in Fruit Marketing: Costs of Lidding Packed Fruit Boxes Influenced by Type of Equipment. Size of Plant, Length of Season." *California Agr.* 7:10-12, January 1953.

[396] ———. *Packing Costs for California Apples and Pears.* California Agr. Exp. Sta., Giannini Foundation Mimeo Rep. 138, 1952.

[397] French, B. C., and R. G. Bressler. *Economy and Accuracy in Accounting to Growers for Fruit Received at the Packing House.* California Agr. Exp. Sta., Giannini Foundation Mimeo Rep. 149, 1953.

[398] French, B. C., and D. G. Gillette. *Cost of Assembling and Packing Apples As Related to Scale of Operation.* Michigan Agr. Exp. Sta. Tech. Bul. 272, 1959.

[399] French, B. C., and L. L. Sammet. *Wage Plans and Efficiency in Grape Packing.* California Agr. Exp. Sta., Giannini Foundation Mimeo Rep. 173, 1954.

[400] French, B. C., L. L. Sammet, R. G. Bressler. *Economies of Scale in Pear Packing.* California Agr. Exp. Sta., Giannini Foundation Mimeo Rep. 181, 1955.

[401] ———. "Economic Efficiency in Plant Operations with Special Reference to the Marketing of California Pears." *Hilgardia* 24:543-721, July 1956; also in California Agr. Exp. Sta., Giannini Foundation Monograph 5.

[402] Gaston, H. P., and J. H. Levin. *Equipment and Layout for Fruit Packing Houses.* Michigan Agr. Exp. Sta. Spec. Bul. 417, 1957.

[403] ———. "Grading Apples in the Orchard." Michigan Agr. Exp. Sta., *Quart. Bul.* 33:310-319, May 1951.

[404] ———. *On the Farm Refrigerated Storage.* Michigan Agr. Exp. Sta. Spec. Bul. 389, 1954.

[405] ———. "Time and Motion Studies of Apple Picking Made to Determine the Possibilities of Mechanizing Harvest Operations." Michigan Agr. Exp. Sta., *Quart. Bul.* 36:18-23, August 1953.

[406] Gillette, D. G., and B. C. French. "Costs of Packing Apples in Michigan." Michigan Agr. Exp. Sta., *Quart. Bul.* 40:286-299, November 1957.

[407] Ginn, J. L. *Prepackaging Firm-Ripe Peaches.* USDA, AMS, AMS-312, 1959.

[408] Godwin, M. R. *Consumer Packaging As a Method of Retailing Fruits and Vegetables Produced in the Northeast. Part II. Labor Requirements, Packaging Costs, and Reductions in Weight.* Cornell University Agr. Exp. Sta. AE 829, 1952.

[409] Greig, W. S., and A. D. O'Rourke. *Apple Packing Costs in Washington, 1971: An Economic-Engineering Analysis.* Washington State Agr. Exp. Sta. Bul. 755, 1972.

[410] Hale, P. W., and P. S. Chapogas. *Packing California Potatoes in Fiberboard Boxes.* USDA, AMS, Marketing Res. Rep. 214, 1958.

[411] Harris, R. G., and W. A. Lee. *Effects of Methods of Packaging Apples on Costs and Returns to Pennsylvania Growers, 1954.* Pennsylvania State University Agr. Exp. Sta. Prog. Rep. 141, 1955.

[412] Heffernan, R. E. *Apple Storage and Packing Facilities for Southern Illinois.* USDA, AMS, Marketing Res. Rep. 610, 1963.

[413] Herrick, J. F., Jr., D. L. Hunter, and R. A. Duerden. *The Comparative Efficiency of Current Methods and Types of Equipment Used for Receiving Field Boxes of Apples at Storage Houses in the Pacific Northwest.* USDA, PMA, January 1952.

[414] Herrick, J. F., Jr., and G. F. Sainsbury. *Apple Packing and Storage Houses Layout and Design.* USDA, AMS, Marketing Res. Rep. 602, 1964.

[415] Hunter, D. L., R. S. Duerden, F. Kafer, and J. F. Herrick, Jr. *Handling Empty Apple Boxes in Pacific Northwest Packing and Storage Houses.* USDA, AMS, Marketing Res. Rep. 71, 1954.

[416] Hunter, D. L., and F. Kafer. *Apple Sorting Methods and Equipment.* USDA, AMS, Marketing Res. Rep. 230, 1958.

[417] Lee, W. A., and W. M. Carroll. *Effects of Methods of Packaging Apples on Returns to Growers, Pennsylvania, 1953.* Pennsylvania State University Agr. Exp. Sta., 1953.

[418] Levin, J. H., and H. P. Gaston. "A Hand-Operated Mechanical Aid for Dumping Fruit." Michigan Agr. Exp. Sta., *Quart. Bul.* 33:193-198, February 1951.

[419] ———. *Fruit Handling with Fork Lift Trucks.* Michigan Agr. Exp. Sta. Spec. Bul. 379, 1952.

[420] ———. *Prepackaging Apples in Film Bags: Equipment, Layout Methods.* Michigan Agr. Exp. Sta. Spec. Bul. 396, 1955.

[421] Masters, B. M., J. C. Winter, and B. P. Rosanoff. *Potential Savings by Shipping Cauliflower in Double-Layer Packs.* USDA, AMS, Marketing Res. Rep. 78, 1955.

[422] Mathia, G. A. *Costs of Storing North Carolina Apples.* North Carolina State University Econ. Inf. Rep. 5, 1967.

[423] Mathia, G. A. *An Economic Analysis of Blueberry Packing Alternatives.* North Carolina State University Econ. Inf. Rep. 13, 1969.

[424] Mathia, G. A., and R. A. King. *Planning Data for the Sweet Potato Industry. Part 4, Costs and Returns from Curing, Storing, Grading, and Packing Sweet Potatoes.* North Carolina State College Agr. Econ. Inf. Ser. 108, 1963.

[425] Metz, J. F., Jr. *Grading and Packing Apples in Vermont.* Vermont Agr. Exp. Sta. Misc. Pub. 4, 1954.

[426] Meyer, C. H. *Comparative Costs of Handling Apples at Packing and Storage Plants.* USDA, AMS, Marketing Res. Rep. 215, 1958.

[427] ———. *Tomato Repacking Methods and Equipment.* USDA, AMS, Marketing Res. Rep. 597, 1963.

[428] Niebel, B. W., H. A. Knappenberge, R. S. Farwell, and W. A. Lee. *Improving Methods of Packing Apples in Consumer Packs.* Pennsylvania State University Agr. Exp. Sta. Bul. 639, 1958.

[429] Orr, P. *Powered Bulk Scooping in Potato Storage.* USDA, ARS, Marketing Res. Rep. 916, 1971.

[430] Pawski, L. *Handling and Shipping Potatoes in Bulk to Processing Plants.* USDA, AMS, Marketing Res. Rep. 625, 1963.

[431] Pearson, J. L., and J. R. Brooker, eds. *Planning Data for Marketing Selected Fruits and Vegetables in the South. Part 3, Fresh Vegetable Packing Handbook.* Southern Cooperative Ser. Bul. 152, 1970.

[432] Perkins, F. A. *The Cost of Packaging Maine McIntosh Apples in Consumer Units.* Maine Agr. Exp. Sta. Misc. Rep. 81, 1959.

[433] Perkins, B., and M. White. *Costs of Packing Fresh Peaches in Chilton County, Alabama.* Auburn University Agr. Exp. Sta. Bul. 358, 1965.

[434] Peters, C. W. *Costs of Marketing Carolina Peaches in 1954.* USDA, AMS, Marketing Res. Rep. 103, 1955.

[435] Pittman, J. F. *Worker Activity in Facing and Tubbing South Carolina Peaches.* South Carolina Agr. Exp. Sta. AE 180, 1959.

[436] Pittman, J. F., and B. J. Todd. *An Analysis of Costs in Early Potato Packing House Operations.* South Carolina Agr. Exp. Sta. Bul. 436, 1956.

[437] Podany, J. C. *Costs of Packing California Peaches in 1959.* USDA, AMS, Marketing Res. Rep. 443, 1960.

[438] ———. *Costs of Packing Michigan Peaches in 1957.* USDA, AMS, Marketing Res. Rep. 290, 1958.

[439] Podany, J. C., and D. E. Farris. *Costs of Packing Arkansas Peaches in 1958.* USDA, AMS, Marketing Res. Rep. 361, 1959.

[440] Powell, J. V. *Appalachian Apples — Packing Costs and Efficiency.* USDA, AMS, Marketing Res. Rep. 435, 1960.

[441] ———. *Costs of Marketing Appalachian Apples.* USDA, AMS, Marketing Res. Rep. 300, 1959.

[442] ———. *Costs of Packing Colorado Peaches in 1956.* USDA, AMS, Marketing Res. Rep. 179, 1957.

[443] Prosser, D. S., Jr., W. F. Grierson, E. Thor, W. F. Newhall, and J. K. Samuels. *Bulk Handling of Fresh Citrus Fruit.* Florida Agr. Exp. Sta. Tech. Bul. 564, 1955.

[444] Reed, R. H., F. G. Mitchell, J. P. Gentry, R. Guillon, M. H. Gerdts, B. C. Bilbo, and R. H. Dawson. *Technical and Economic Evaluation of New and Conventional Methods of Packing Fresh Peaches and Nectarines.* California Agr. Ext. Serv., Giannini Foundation Inf. Ser. 64-1, 1964.

[445] Sammet, L. L. *Costs and Efficiency in Packer Supply Operations for Fresh Table Grapes.* California Agr. Exp. Sta., Giannini Foundation Mimeo Rep. 187, 1956.

[446] ———. *Costs of Dumping Incoming Fruit As Related to Work Methods — Apple and Pear Packing Houses.* California Agr. Exp. Sta., Giannini Foundation Mimeo Rep. 153, 1953.

[447] ———. *Efficiency in Fruit Marketing — Orchard-to-Plant Transportation.* California Agr. Exp. Sta., Giannini Foundation Mimeo Rep. 131, 1952.

[448] ———. *In-Plant Transportation Costs As Related to Materials Handling Methods — Apple and Pear Packing.* California Agr. Exp. Sta., Giannini Foundation Mimeo Rep. 142, 1953.

[449] Sammet, L. L., and I. F. Davis. *Building and Equipment Cost, Apple and Pear Packing.* California Agr. Exp. Sta., Giannini Foundation Mimeo Rep. 141, 1952.

[450] Shaffer, P. F., and D. L. Anderson. *Some Comparative Methods of Packaging Potatoes and Onions at the Point of Distribution.* USDA, AMS-12, 1955.

[451] Sitton, G. R., and L. L. Sammet. *Economic Factors in Picking, Assembling, and Grading Sevillano Olives.* California Agr. Exp. Sta., Giannini Foundation Mimeo Rep. 155, 1953.

[452] Smith, F. J., L. L. Sammet, and R. V. Enochian. *Costs and Efficiency in Field Packing Western Head Lettuce.* California Agr. Exp. Sta., Giannini Foundation Mimeo Rep. 183, 1955.

[453] Smith, F. J. *Economic Analysis of Resource Combinations in Peach Harvesting and Packing.* North Carolina State University Agr. Econ. Inf. Ser. 124, 1965.

[454] Smith, R. J. *The Rapid Pack Method of Packing Fruit.* California Agr. Exp. Sta. Circ. 521, 1963.

[455] Smith, T. B., and J. W. Browning. *Fresh Fruit and Vegetable Prepackaging, Northeastern Region, Operating Season 1954-55.* USDA, AMS, Marketing Res. Rep. 154, 1957.

[456] Smith, T. B., and J. J. Valldejuli. *Fresh Produce Prepackaging Practices in the United States.* USDA, AMS, Marketing Res. Rep. 341, 1959.

[457] Stallings, D. G., and L. L. Sammet. *Plum Packing Costs and Efficiency: The Effects of Packing Methods and Type of Container.* California Agr. Exp. Sta., Giannini Foundation Mimeo Rep. 225, 1959.

[458] Stokes, D. R., and G. Barry. *Development of Carrot Prepackaging.* USDA, AMS, Marketing Res. Rep. 185, 1957.

[459] Stollsteimer, J. F. *Bulk Containers for Deciduous Fruits — Costs and Efficiency in Local Assembly Operations.* California Agr. Exp. Sta., Giannini Foundation Res. Rep. 237, 1960.

[460] Thor, E. *Cost Analysis of Bulk Handling Methods for Fresh Citrus.* Florida Agr. Exp. Sta., Agr. Econ. Mimeo Rep. 55-1, 1954.

[461] ———. *Economies of Scale in the Operation of Florida Citrus Packinghouses.* Florida Agr. Exp. Sta. Bul. 606, 1959.

[462] Thor, E., and L. D. Dohner. *Cost of Moving Citrus from Tree onto Highway Trucks As Related to Methods of Handling.* Florida Agr. Exp. Sta. Bul. 547, 1954.

[463] Thor, E., A. A. M. Goueli, and A. Hutchens. *Costs of Alternative Methods of*

Harvesting and Packing Lettuce. California Agr. Ext. Serv., Giannini Foundation Inf. Ser. 65-1, 1965.

[464] Toussaint, W. D., T. T. Hatton, and G. Abshier. *Hydrocooling Peaches in the North Carolina Sandhills, 1954.* North Carolina State College Agr. Exp. Sta., Agr. Econ. Inf. Ser. 39, 1955.

FRUIT AND VEGETABLE PROCESSING

[465] Davis, G. B., and H. M. Hutchings. *Costs and Efficiencies in Pea Freezing Operations. Part 2, Packaging and Freezing.* Oregon Agr. Exp. Sta. Mimeo Pap. 87, 1960.

[466] Dawson, R. H., and R. H. Reed. *Some Aspects of Labor Efficiency in Canning Asparagus Spears.* California Agr. Exp. Sta., Giannini Foundation Res. Rep. 281, 1965.

[467] Dennis, C. C. *An Analysis of Costs of Processing Strawberries for Freezing.* California Agr. Exp. Sta., Giannini Foundation Mimeo Rep. 210, 1958.

[468] Fairbanks, J. N., and L. Polopolus. *Economic Efficiency and Profitability of Okra-Tomato Canning Plants.* Louisiana State University, Dept. Agr. Econ., DAE Res. Rep. 339, 1965.

[469] Goble, W. E. *Costs of Processing Strawberries for Freezing in Tennessee.* Tennessee Agr. Exp. Sta. Bul. 378, 1964.

[470] Greig, S. W., and A. C. Manchester. *Cost of Peeling Potatoes by Lye and Abrasive Methods.* USDA, AMS, Marketing Res. Rep. 255, 1958.

[471] Hammond, L. H., and R. A. King. *Planning Data for the Sweet Potato Industry. Part 2, Costs and Returns for a Model Canning Plant.* North Carolina State College Agr. Econ. Inf. Ser. 93, 1962.

[472] Law, J. M., and B. E. Beeson. *Economic Efficiency and Profitability of Sweet Potato Flaking Plants.* Louisiana State University, Dept. Agr. Econ., DAE Res. Rep. 368, 1967.

[473] Mathia, G. A., J. L. Pearson, and O. Ela. *An Economic Analysis of Canning Leafy Greens, Lima Beans, and Southern Peas.* North Carolina State University Econ. Inf. Rep. 18, 1970.

[474] Pearson, J. L., and J. R. Brooks, eds. *Planning Data for Marketing Selected Fruits and Vegetables in the South. Part 2, Freezing Handbook.* Southern Cooperative Ser. Bul. 150, 1969.

[475] Pearson, J. L., and K. E. Ford, eds. *Planning Data for Marketing Selected Fruits and Vegetables in the South. Part 1, Canning Handbook.* Southern Cooperative Ser. Bul. 146, 1969.

[476] Pearson, J. L., G. A. Mathia, and O. Ela. *An Economic Analysis of Canning Okra, Dry Beans, and Squash in the South.* North Carolina State University Econ. Inf. Rep. 19, 1970.

[477] Rasmussen, C. L. *Economic Appraisal of Freezing Methods.* USDA, ARS 74-44, 1968.

[478] Reed, R. H. *Economic Efficiency in Assembly and Processing Lima Beans for Freezing.* California Agr. Exp. Sta., Giannini Foundation Mimeo Rep. 219, 1959.

[479] Reed, R. H., and L. L. Sammet. *Multiple Product Processing of California Frozen Vegetables.* California Agr. Exp. Sta., Giannini Foundation Res. Rep. 264, 1963.

[480] Scott, F. S., Jr. *An Economic Analysis of Passion Fruit Juice Processing.* Hawaii Agr. Exp. Sta. Agr. Econ. Bul. 18, 1959.

GRAIN ELEVATOR AND MILLING OPERATIONS

[481] Anderson, D. C., and D. L. Helgeson. *Economies of Size, Volume, and Diversification in Retail Grain and Farm Supply Businesses.* Nebraska Agr. Exp. Sta. Res. Bul. 261, 1974.

[482] Askew, W. R., C. J. Vosloh, and J. V. Brensike. *Case Study of Labor Costs and Efficiencies in Warehousing Formula Feeds.* USDA, AMS, Marketing Res. Rep. 205, 1957.

[483] Austin, P. E., and D. C. Nelson. *An Economic Analysis of the Costs of Manufacturing Commercial Feed in North Dakota.* North Dakota State University Agr. Exp. Sta. Agr. Econ. Rep. 47, 1966.

[484] Bouland, H. D. *Locating, Designing, and Building Country Grain Elevators.* USDA, ARS, Agr. Inf. Bul. 310, 1966.

[485] Brewster, J. M. *Comparative Economies of Different Types of Cottonseed Oil Mills and Their Effects on Oil Supplies, Prices, and Returns to Growers.* USDA, AMS, Marketing Res. Rep. 54, 1954.

[486] ———. "More Economical Cottonseed Oil Mills and Returns to Growers." *J. Farm Econ.* 36:429-465, August 1954.

[487] Brewster, J. M., and S. P. Clark. *Conversion of Small Hydraulic Cottonseed Oil Mills into Higher Oil-Yielding Mills.* USDA, AMS, Marketing Res. Rep. 187, 1957.

[488] Brewster, J. M., and J. A. Mitchell. *Size of Soybean Oil Mills and Returns to Growers.* USDA, AMS, Marketing Res. Rep. 121, 1956.

[489] Burbee, C. R., E. T. Bardwell, and A. A. Brown. *Marketing New England Poultry. Part 7, Economics of Broiler Feed Mixing and Distribution.* New Hampshire Agr. Exp. Sta. Bul. 484, 1965.

[490] Corley, E. M., and N. A. Briscoe. *Effects of Wheat Production Variations on Country Elevator Handling Costs in Northwestern Oklahoma.* Oklahoma State University Agr. Exp. Sta. P-516, 1965.

[491] French, C. E. *Labor Efficiency in Grinding and Mixing Feeds in Indiana Grain Elevators.* Purdue University Agr. Exp. Sta. Bul. 639, 1956.

[492] Gráves, A. H., and G. L. Kline. *Receiving Grain at Country Elevators — Hard Winter Wheat Area.* USDA, AMS, Marketing Res. Rep. 638, 1964.

[493] Graves, A. H., and D. W. Winter. *Unloading Box Cars of Grain at Terminal Elevators in the Hard Winter Wheat Area.* USDA, ARS, ARS-52-15, 1966.

[494] Hall, T. E. *New Country Elevators — Influence of Size and Volume on Operating Costs.* USDA, FCS, Circ. 10, 1955.

[495] Holder, S. H., Jr., W. R. Morrison, and H. D. Traylor. *Economic Models for Rice Mills in the South.* Southern Cooperative Ser. Bul. 187, 1974.

[496] Larson, A., and H. S. Whitney. *Relative Efficiencies of Single-Unit and Multiple-Unit Cooperative Elevator Organizations.* Oklahoma State University Agr. Exp. Sta. Bul. 5-426, 1954.

[497] Mitchell, J. A. *Supplement to Comparative Economies of Different Types of Cottonseed Oil Mills and Their Effects on Oil Supplies, Prices, and Returns to Growers.* USDA, AMS, supplement to Marketing Res. Rep. 54, 1959.

[498] Rowan, W. S., P. C. Bunce, A. R. Brown, and J. W. Simons. *Factors Affecting the Cost of Storing Grain in Georgia.* Georgia Agr. Exp. Sta. Bul. N.S. 27, 1956.

[499] St. George, G., and C. Rust. *Grain Trucking Costs for Montana.* Montana Agr. Exp. Sta. Bul. 638, 1970.

[500] Sorenson, V. L., and C. W. Hall. "Efficiency in Distribution of Mixed Feeds." Michigan State University Agr. Exp. Sta., *Quart. Bul.* 38:460-470, February 1956.

[501] Sorenson, V. L., and C. D. Keyes. *Cost Relationships in Grain Plants.* Michigan State University Agr. Exp. Sta. Tech. Bul. 292, 1962.

[502] Thurston, S. K., and R. J. Mutti. *Cost-Volume Relationships for New Country Elevators in Corn Belt.* USDA, FCS, Ser. Rep. 32, 1957.

[503] Thurston, S. K., and C. H. Myer. *Planning Large Country Elevator Facilities in the Eastern Corn Belt.* USDA, Farmer Cooperative Ser. Rep. 117, 1970.

[504] Trock, W. L. *Costs of Grain Elevator Operation in the Spring Wheat Area.* Montana Agr. Exp. Sta. Bul. 593, 1965.

[505] Van Ausdle, S. L., and D. L. Oldenstadt. *Costs and Efficiencies of Grain Elevators in the Pacific Northwest.* Washington State Agr. Exp. Sta. Bul. 713, 1969.

[506] Vosloh, Carl J., Jr. *Costs and Economies of Scale in Feed Manufacturing.* USDA, ERS, Marketing Res. Rep. 815, 1968.

[507] ———. *Ingredient Handling by Feed Manufacturers: Capital and Labor Requirements.* USDA, ERS, Marketing Res. Rep. 727, 1965.

[508] ———. *Labor and Capital for Mixing Formula Feeds.* USDA, ERS, Marketing Res. Rep. 564, 1962.

[509] ———. *Operating Costs in Packing Mixed Feeds with Emphasis on Labor and Capital.* USDA, ERS, Marketing Res. Rep. 658, 1964.

[510] ———. *Processing Feed Ingredients: Cost, Labor, and Capital Requirements.* USDA, ERS, Marketing Res. Rep. 731, 1965.

[511] Vosloh, C. J., Jr., W. R. Askew, and V. J. Brensike. *Custom Feed Milling in the Midwest.* USDA, AMS, Marketing Res. Rep. 273, 1958.

[512] Yager, F. P. *Country Elevators, Cost Volume Relations in the Spring Wheat Belt.* USDA, FCS, Ser. Rep. 63, 1963.

[513] Young, K. B. *An Analysis of the Cost of Assembling Grain by Farm Trucks in Manitoba.* University of Manitoba, Faculty of Agricultural and Home Economics, Res. Rep. 11, 1966.

MEAT PACKING AND ASSEMBLY

[514] Brasington, C. F. *Hotel and Restaurant Meat Purveyors — Improved Methods and Facilities for Supplying Frozen Portion-Controlled Meat.* USDA, ARS, Marketing Res. Rep. 904, 1971.

[515] Brasington, C. F., Jr., and D. R. Hammons. *Procedures for Handling By-Products Removed during Beef Boning.* USDA, ARS, ARS 52-29, 1968.

[516] Cassell, G. R., and D. A. West. *Assembly and Slaughtering Costs for Hogs in North Carolina.* North Carolina State University Econ. Res. Rep. 3, 1967.

[517] Daellenbach, L. A., and L. B. Fletcher. "Effects of Supply Variations on Costs and Profits of Slaughter Plants." *Am. J. Agr. Econ.* 53:600-607, November 1971.

[518] Franzmann, J. R., and B. T. Kuntz. *Economies of Size in Southwestern Beef Slaughter-Plants.* Oklahoma State Agr. Exp. Sta. Bul. B-648, 1966.

[519] Hammons, D. R. *Cattle Killing — Floor Systems and Layouts.* USDA, AMS, Marketing Res. Rep. 657, 1964.

[520] Hammons, D. R., and J. E. Miller. *Improving Methods and Facilities for Cattle Slaughtering Plants in the Southwest.* USDA, AMS, Marketing Res. Rep. 436, 1961.

[521] Leach, H. *Factors Affecting Costs for Alternative Meat Distribution Systems.* Missouri Agr. Exp. Sta. Bul. 866, 1968.

[522] Logan, S. H. "Economies of Scale in Cattle Slaughtering Plants." NCFM Tech. Study 1, Suppl. Study 2, 1966.

[523] ———. "Labor Costs of Slaughtering Hogs." NCFM Tech. Study 1, Suppl. Study 4, 1966.

[524] Logan, S. H., and G. A. King. *Economies of Scale in Beef Slaughter Plants.* California Agr. Exp. Sta., Giannini Foundation Res. Rep. 260, 1962.

[525] Marion, B. W., L. E. Ott, and F. E. Walker. *Meat Department Labor Requirements, a Tool for Improved Retail Management.* Ohio Agr. Exp. Sta. Res. Bul. 982, 1966.

[526] McIntosh, K. D., and C. E. Trotter. *Labor Utilization in Slaughtering Operations of Plants in Northeastern United States.* West Virginia Agr. Exp. Sta. Bul. 480, 1962.

[527] Schnake, L. D., J. R. Franzmann, and D. R. Hammons. *Economies of Size in Nonslaughtering Meat Processing Plants.* Oklahoma State Agr. Exp. Sta. Tech. Bul. T-125, 1968.

[528] Volz, M. D. *Systems and Equipment for Packaging and Price Marking Meat and Poultry in Retail Food Stores.* USDA, ERS, Marketing Res. Rep. 733, 1967.

[529] Volz, M. D., and J. A. Marsden. *Centralized Processing of Fresh Meat for Retail Stores.* USDA, AMS, Marketing Res. Rep. 628, 1963.

MILK COLLECTION AND DELIVERY

[530] Agnew, D. B. *How Bulk Assembly Changes — Milk Marketing Costs.* USDA, AMS, Marketing Res. Rep. 190, 1957.

[531] Babb, E. M., and W. T. Butz. *Improving Fluid Milk Distribution Practices through Economic-Engineering Techniques.* Pennsylvania State University Agr. Exp. Sta. Bul. 622, 1957.

[532] Baum, E. L., and D. E. Pauls. *A Comparative Analysis of Costs of Farm Collection of Milk by Can and Tank in western Washington, 1952.* Washington Agr. Exp. Sta. Tech. Bul. 10, 1953.

[533] Blakley, L. V., and J. Goodwin, W. B. Rogers, and K. B. Boggs. *Bulk Milk Assembly Costs in Oklahoma.* Oklahoma State University Agr. Exp. Sta. Bul. B-537, 1959.

[534] Boggs, K. B., F. A. Mangum, Jr., and L. V. Blakley. *Costs and Savings of Bulk Milk Tanks on Oklahoma Dairy Farms.* Oklahoma State University Agr. Exp. Sta. Bul. B-541, 1960.

[535] Boutwell, W. K., and R. L. Simmons. "Estimating Route Assembly Costs." *J. Farm Econ.* 46:841-848, November 1964.

[536] Carley, D. H. *Transporting Packaged Fluid Milk to Distant Markets: Costs and Systems in Georgia.* Georgia Agr. Exp. Sta. Tech. Bul. N.S. 30, 1963.

[537] Clarke, D. A., Jr. *Milk Delivery Costa and Volume Pricing Procedures in California.* California Agr. Exp. Sta. Bul. 757, 1956.

[538] ———. *Pricing Milk in Relation to Delivery Volume.* California Agr. Exp. Sta., Giannini Foundation, 1952.

[539] Cook, H. L., H. W. Halvorson, and W. R. Robinson. *Costs and Efficiency of Wholesale Milk Distribution in Milwaukee.* Wisconsin Agr. Exp. Sta. Res. Bul. 196, 1956.

[540] Courtney, R. H., and E. Brooks. *An Analysis of Wholesale Milk Delivery Costs and Volume-Pricing Procedures in California.* California Agr. Exp. Sta., Giannini Foundation Res. Rep. 317, 1972.

[541] Cowden, J. M. *Comparing Bulk and Can Milk Hauling Costs.* USDA, FCS, Circ. 14, 1956.

[542] Forker, O. D., and D. A. Clarke, Jr. *Changes in Milk Delivery Costs and Volume-Pricing Procedures in California.* California Agr. Exp. Sta., Giannini Foundation Mimeo Rep. 236, 1960.

[543] French, C. E., and J. R. Strain. *Market Planning for Farm Bulk Assembly of Milk.* Purdue University Agr. Exp. Sta. Res. Bul. 747, 1962.

[544] Goodwin, J. D., J. C. Purcell, and J. C. Elrod. *Analysis of Factors Affecting Time Requirements for Distributing Milk on Wholesale and Retail Routes in Georgia.* Georgia Agr. Exp. Sta. Res. Bul. 52, 1969.

[545] Groves, F. W., and H. L. Cook. *Hauling and Transportation Cost Functions for Wisconsin Milk.* Wisconsin College of Agriculture, Agr. Econ. 31, 1961.

[546] Ishee, S., and W. L. Barr. *Economics of Bulk Milk Handling.* Pennsylvania State University Agr. Exp. Sta. Bul. 631, 1958.

[547] ———. *Effects of Bulk Milk Assembly on Hauling Costs.* Pennsylvania State University Agr. Exp. Sta. Bul. 641, 1958.

[548] Jacobson, R. E., and G. F. Fairchild. *Hauling Costs and Rates in Bulk Milk Assembly.* Ohio Agr. Res. Dev. Center Res. Circ. 162, 1969.

[549] Kelley, P. L. *Cost Functions for Bulk Milk Assembly in the Wichita Market.* Kansas Agr. Exp. Sta. Tech. Bul. 96, 1958.

[550] Kerchner, O. *Costs of Transporting Bulk and Packaged Milk by Truck.* USDA, ERS, Marketing Res. Rep. 791, 1967.

[551] Moede, H. H. *Over-the-Road Costs of Hauling Bulk Milk.* USDA, ERS, Marketing Res. Rep. 919, 1971.

[552] Nolte, G. M., and E. F. Koller. *Economic Analyses of Farm-to-Plant Milk Assembly.* Minnesota Agr. Exp. Sta. Bul. 512, 1975.

[553] Shafer, C. E., and W. C. Pierce. *Bulk Assembly in the Outer Limits of the Philadelphia Milkshed.* Pennsylvania State University Agr. Exp. Sta. Bul. 726, 1965.

[554] Simmons, R. L. *Wholesale Milk Distribution Practices, Costs, and Pricing in North Carolina.* North Carolina State College Agr. Econ. Inf. Ser. 88, 1962.

POULTRY PROCESSING AND ASSEMBLY

[555] Abbott, J. C. *The Economic Implications of Recent Technical Developments in the Processing of Turkeys.* California Agr. Exp. Sta., Giannini Foundation Mimeo Rep. 172, 1954.

[556] ———. "Economic Results of Subscalding Techniques in the Marketing of Turkeys." *J. Farm Econ.* 38:62-67, February 1956.

[557] Baum, E. L., J. E. Faris, and H. C. Walkup. *Economies of Scale in the Operation of Fryer Processing Plants with Special Reference to Washington.* Washington (Pullman) Agr. Exp. Sta. Tech. Bul. 7, 1952.

[558] Burbee, C. R., and E. T. Bardwell. *Marketing New England Poultry. Part 6, Economies of Scale in Hatching and Cost of Distributing Broiler Chicks.* New Hampshire Agr. Exp. Sta. Bul. 483, 1964.

[559] Burbee, C. R., E. T. Bardwell, and W. F. Henry. *Marketing New England Poultry. Part 8, Effects of Firm Size and Production Density on Spatial Costs for an Integrated Broiler Marketing Firm.* New Hampshire Agr. Exp. Sta. Bul. 485, 1964.

[560] Childs, R. E., and P. D. Rodgers. *Methods and Equipment for Ice-Packing Poultry.* USDA, AMS, Marketing Res. Rep. 242, 1958.

[561] Donald, J. R., and C. E. Bishop. *Broiler Processing Costs.* North Carolina State College Agr. Econ. Inf. Ser. 59, 1957.

[562] Farrish, R. O. P., and S. K. Seaver. *Factors Affecting the Output, Size, Costs, and Location of Poultry Plants in Southern New England. Part 1, Cost, Efficiency, and Economies of Scale in Broiler Processing Plants.* Connecticut Agr. Exp. Sta. Bul. 342, 1959.

[563] Gerald, J. O., and H. S. Kahle. *Marketing Georgia Broilers through Commercial Processing Plants.* USDA, AMS, Marketing Res. Rep. 83, 1955.

[564] Harris, C. E., G. Amorelli, and C. M. Thrall. *Methods and Equipment for Processing Ducks.* USDA, ARS, 1971.

[565] Henry, W. F., and C. R. Burbee. *Marketing New England Poultry. Part 5, Effects of Firm Size and Production Density on Assembly Costs.* New Hampshire Agr. Exp. Sta. Bul. 482, 1964.

[566] Henry, W. R., J. S. Chappell, and J. A. Seagraves. *Broiler Production Density, Plant Size, Alternative Operating Plans, and Total Unit Cost.* North Carolina Agr. Exp. Sta. Tech. Bul. 144, 1960.

[567] Henry, W. R., and J. A. Seagraves. "Economic Aspects of Broiler Production Density." *J. Farm Econ.* 42:1-17, February 1960.

[568] Jewett, L. J. *Handling and Processing Broilers in Maine. Part 1, Costs and Efficiencies in Assembling Live Broilers for Processing.* Maine Agr. Exp. Sta. Bul. 592, 1960.

[569] Mountney, G. J., and F. A. Gardner. *A Survey of Labor Requirements in Six Texas Turkey Processing Plants.* Texas Agr. Exp. Sta. Misc. Pub. 113, 1954.

[570] Rogers, G. B., and E. T. Bardwell. *Marketing New England Poultry. Part 2, Economies of Scale in Chicken Processing.* New Hampshire Agr. Exp. Sta. Bul. 459, 1959.

[571] ———. *Marketing New England Poultry. Part 4, Structure and Performance of the Assembly System.* New Hampshire Agr. Exp. Sta. Bul. 482, 1964.

[572] ———. *Reducing Cost of Handling and Hauling Live Chickens from Farms to Processing Plants.* USDA Econ. Res. Ser. 81, 1962.

[573] Rogers, G. B., W. F. Henry, A. A. Brown, E. T. Bardwell, and D. L. Doess. *Economies of Scale and Current Costs in New York Dressing Broilers and Fowl.* New Hampshire Agr. Econ. Res. Mimeo 20, 1958.

[574] Rogers, G. B., and E. H. Rinear. *Costs and Economies of Scale in Turkey Processing Plants.* USDA, Marketing Res. Rep. 627, 1963.

[575] Rogers, G. B., and H. D. Smith. *Further Processing Industry and Impact of Economies of Scale in Poultry Plants.* Maryland Agr. Exp. Sta. Misc. Pub. 595, 1966.

[576] Stemberger, A. P., W. R. Henry, and J. S. Chappell. *Cutting Up Broilers in Processing Plants.* North Carolina State College Agr. Econ. Inf. Ser. 94, 1962.

WHOLESALE AND RETAIL FOOD STORE OPERATIONS

[577] Allegri, T. H., and J. F. Herrick. *Materials Handling in Public Refrigerated Warehouses.* USDA, ARS, Marketing Res. Rep. 145, 1957.

[578] Anderson, D. L. *Principles of Layout for Retail Produce Operations.* USDA, AMS, Marketing Res. Rep. 590, 1963.

[579] Anderson, D. L., and P. F. Shaffer. *Display Location and Customer Service in Retail Produce Departments.* USDA, AMS, Marketing Res. Rep. 501, 1961.

[580] ———. *Improved Handling of Frozen Foods in Retail Stores.* USDA, AMS, Marketing Res. Rep. 104, 1955.

[581] ———. *Improved Methods of Trimming Produce in Retail Food Stores.* USDA, AMS, Marketing Res. Rep. 192, 1957.

[582] Anderson, D. L., P. Shaffer, and M. Volz. *Improved Methods of Displaying and Handling Produce in Retail Food Stores.* USDA, AMS, Marketing Res. Rep. 551, 1962.

[583] Bartz, D. J., and J. C. Bound. *Improved Methods among Wholesale Food Dis-*

198 BEN C. FRENCH

tributors for Inventory Control, Sales Accounting, and Shipment of Merchandise. USDA, AMS, Marketing Res. Rep. 271, 1958.

[584] Bitting, H. W. *Factors Affecting Costs of Wholesale Distribution of Frozen Foods*. USDA, ERS, Marketing Res. Rep. 327, 1959.

[585] Bogardus, R. K. *Suggested Layouts for Warehouses for Service Wholesalers of Fruits and Vegetables*. USDA, AMS, AMS-228, 1958.

[586] ———. *A Warehouse Layout for a Fruit and Vegetable Service Wholesaler in a Terminal Market*. USDA, AMS, AMS-232, 1958.

[587] Bogardus, R. K., and S. W. Burt. *Loading Out Fruits and Vegetables in Wholesale Warehouses*. USDA, AMS, Marketing Res. Rep. 282, AMS, 1959.

[588] Bogardus, R. K., and R. T. Ferris. *Receiving Fruits and Vegetables in Wholesale Warehouses*. USDA, AMS, Marketing Res. Rep. 478, 1961.

[589] Bouma, J. C. *Methods of Increasing Productivity in Modern Grocery Warehouses*. USDA, AMS, Marketing Res. Rep. 94, 1955.

[590] Bouma, J. C., and M. Kriesberg. *Measures of Operating Efficiency in Wholesale Food Warehouses*. USDA, AMS, Marketing Res. Rep. 399, 1960.

[591] Bouma, J. C., and A. L. Lundquist. *Grocery Warehouse Layout and Equipment for Maximum Productivity*. USDA, AMS, Marketing Res. Rep. 348, 1959.

[592] ———. *Methods of Increasing Labor Productivity in Multistory and Small One-Floor Grocery Warehouses*. USDA, AMS, Marketing Res. Rep. 348, 1959.

[593] Brensike, J. V. *Formula Feed Warehousing Costs, a Study in Improving Efficiency in Marketing Farm Feeds*. USDA, AMS, Marketing Res. Rep. 268, 1958.

[594] Card, D. G., G. B. Byers, and W. C. Binkley. *Effect of Work Methods on Time and Ease of Loading Baskets of Tobacco in Sales Warehouses*. Kentucky Agr. Exp. Sta. Bul. 572, 1951.

[595] Crossed, C., and M. Kriesberg. *Evaluating Delivery Operations of Wholesale Food Distributors*. USDA, AMS, Marketing Res. Rep. 502, 1961.

[596] Guilfoy, R. F. J., and R. C. Mongelli. *A Method for Measuring Cost and Performance of Refrigeration Systems in Local Delivery Vehicles*. USDA, ARS, ARS 52-64, 1971.

[597] Harwell, E. M., and P. F. Shaffer. *Some Improved Methods of Handling Groceries in Self-Service Retail Food Stores*. USDA, PMA, Marketing Res. Rep. 7, 1952.

[598] Herrick, J. F., S. W. Burt, M. R. Kercho, and A. Zagarella. *An Analysis of Some Methods of Loading Out Delivery Trucks of Produce Wholesalers*. USDA, PMA, Marketing Res. Rep. 15, 1952.

[599] Holton, R. H. "On the Measurement of Excess Capacity in Retailing." *Rev. Econ. Stud.* 24:43-48, 1956-57.

[600] Kriesberg, M. *Methods of Handling and Delivering Orders Used by Some Leading Wholesale Grocers*. USDA, AMS, Marketing Res. Rep. 13, 1952.

[601] Lundquist, A., and J. C. Bouma. *Reducing Operating Costs in Affiliated Produce Warehouses*. USDA, ARS, Agr. Inf. Bul. 304, 1966.

[602] Marion, B. W., L. E. Ott, and F. E. Walker. *Meat Department Labor Requirements, a Tool for Improved Retail Management*. Ohio Agr. Res. Dev. Center, Res. Bul. 982, 1966.

[603] Mixon, J. A., and T. H. Allegri. *Some Improved Methods of Handling Frozen Food in Wholesale Plants*. USDA, AMS, Marketing Res. Rep. 107, 1955.

[604] Mixon, J. A., and J. S. Larson. *Planning a Wholesale Frozen Food Distribution Plant*. USDA, PMA, Marketing Res. Rep. 18, 1952.

[605] Shaffer, P., D. Anderson, P. Wischkaemper, and J. Karitas. *Packaging and Price Marking Produce in Retail Food Stores*. USDA, AMS, Marketing Res. Rep. 278, 1958.

[606] Snitzler, J. R. *Improving the Truck Delivery Operations of a Wholesale Grocer: A Case Study.* USDA, AMS, Marketing Res. Rep. 127, 1956.

[607] Stafford, T. H. *Methods and Costs of Distributing Beef to the Food Service Industry.* New York Agr. Exp. Sta. Food and Life Sciences Bul. 36, 1974.

[608] Wilmeth, J. B., and C. D. Bolt. *Handling Bales of Cotton in Public Warehouses.* USDA, AMS, Marketing Res. Rep. 250, 1958.

MISCELLANEOUS STUDIES

[609] Beal, G. M., and R. M. Jones. *The Market Structure and Use of Labor in Maryland Tobacco Auction Warehouses.* Maryland Agr. Exp. Sta. Misc. Pub. 492, 1963.

[610] Biederman, K., H. Mack, M. B. Neher, and O. Wilhelmy, Jr. *A Technical-Economic Evaluation of Four Hide-Curing Methods.* USDA Agr. Econ. Rep. 16, 1962.

[611] Binkley, W. C., G. B. Byers, and D. G. Card. *Easier and Time-Saving Work Methods for Receiving and Packing Burley Tobacco on Sales Baskets.* Kentucky Agr. Exp. Sta. Circ. 513, 1954.

[612] Bird, K. *Freeze-Drying of Foods: Cost Projections.* USDA, ERS, Marketing Res. Rep. 639, 1964.

[613] Brasington, C. F. *Livestock Auction Markets in the Appalachian Area — Methods and Facilities.* USDA, AMS, Marketing Res. Rep. 309, 1959.

[614] Brooks, R. C., and W. D. Toussaint. *Labor Requirements in the Market Preparation of Flue-Cured Tobacco.* North Carolina State College Agr. Econ. Inf. Ser. 98, 1963.

[615] Frazier, T. L., and J. T. Pudgett. *Factors Influencing the Efficiency of Livestock Auction Markets in Georgia.* Georgia Agr. Exp. Sta. Bul. N.S. 134, 1965.

[616] Gibb, R. D., and H. M. Riley. *An Analysis of Operating Costs at Michigan Livestock Auctions.* Michigan Agr. Exp. Sta. Tech. Bul. 283, 1961.

[617] Harp, H. H., and H. D. Smith. *Efficiency of Livestock Auction Markets in Maryland.* Maryland Agr. Exp. Sta. Bul. 457, 1956.

[618] Howell, L. D. *Costs of Manufacturing Carded Cotton Yarn and Means of Improvement.* USDA Tech. Bul. 1033, 1951.

[619] Jones, E. W., and R. A. King. *Economic Efficiency in Constructing and Operating Bulk Peanut Receiving Stations.* North Carolina State University Agr. Econ. Inf. Ser. 107, 1963.

[620] Kuehn, J. P. *Costs and Efficiencies of Model Livestock Auctions in West Virginia.* West Virginia Agr. Exp. Sta. Bul. 606, 1971.

[621] Moder, J. J., Jr., and N. M. Penny. *Industrial Engineering and Economic Studied of Peanut Marketing.* Georgia Agr. Exp. Sta. Bul. 286, 1954.

[622] Penny, N. M., and P. S. Akins. *A Comparative Study of Marketing Tobacco through Auction Warehouses.* Georgia Agr. Exp. Sta. Bul. N.S. 86, 1961.

[623] Thompson, J. C., P. V. Weaver, and M. E. Brunk. *Time and Skill Requirements for Handling Products at Fixed Work Places.* USDA, AMS, AMS-197, 1957.

[624] Thompson, J. W. *A Guide to Lower Costs and Greater Efficiency in Curing Cattle Hides.* USDA, ERS, Agr. Econ. Rep. 54, 1964.

[625] Turner, G. E., and C. F. Brasington. *Livestock Auction Markets in the Southeast, Methods and Facilities.* USDA, AMS, Marketing Res. Rep. 141, 1956.

Firm Optimizing Models

[626] Belden, S. A., and L. F. Schrader. *An Analysis of Coordination Decisions in a Turkey Production and Marketing System.* Cornell University, Dept. Agr. Econ., AE Res. 72-7, 1972.

[627] Cox, C. B., A. Glickstein, and J. H. Greene. "Application of Queuing Theory in Determining Livestock Unloading Facilities." *J. Farm Econ.* 40:104-116, February 1958.

[628] Frazier, T. L., R. E. Howell, and J. C. Fortson. *Optimizing Returns in a Swine Processing Plant.* Georgia Agr. Exp. Sta. Res. Bul. 3, 1967.

[629] French, C. E. "Activity Analysis: An Agricultural Marketing Tool." *J. Farm Econ.* 37:1236-1248, December 1955.

[630] ———. "The Managerial Factor and Research on Decision Making in Agricultural Marketing Firms." *J. Farm Econ.* 47:23-35, February 1965.

[631] French, C. E., M. M. Snodgrass, and J. E. Snyder. "Applications of Operations Research in Farm Operations and Agricultural Marketing." *Oper. Res.* 6:766-775, 1958.

[632] Kelley, P. L., T. W. Townsend, A. Feyerherm, and V. Hwang. *A Linear Programming Model of a Surplus Milk Plant.* Kansas State Agr. Exp. Sta. Tech. Bul. 123, 1962.

[633] Knop, D. R., and L. V. Blakley. *Optimum Organization and Operation of Oklahoma Country Grain Elevators with Sideline Activities.* Oklahoma State Agr. Exp. Sta. Bul. B-682, 1970.

[634] Kohls, R. L. "Considerations of Internal Firm Organization and Behavior Factors and Their Relation to Research on Market Structures." In *Market Structure Research*, P. Farris, ed. Ames: Iowa State University Press, 1964.

[635] Lee, R. E., and J. C. Snyder. *A Location-Logistics System for Feed Firm Management.* USDA, ERS, Marketing Res. Rep. 867, 1970.

[636] Lu, J. Y. "Optimum Super Market Check-Out Facilities: An Application of Queuing Theory." *J. Farm Econ.* 43:27-43, February 1961.

[637] Schruben, L. "Systems Approach to Marketing Efficiency Research." *Am. J. Agr. Econ.* 50:1454-1468, December 1968.

[638] Snyder, J. C., and C. E. French. *Disassembly-Assembly Models for Meat Packing Management.* Purdue University Agr. Exp. Sta. Res. Bul. 764, 1963.

[639] ———. "Selection of Product Line for Fluid Milk Plant by Activity Analysis." *J. Farm Econ.* 39:914-926, November 1957.

[640] ———. *Selection of Product Line for a Fluid Milk Plant by Activity Analysis.* Purdue University Agr. Exp. Sta. Res. Bul. 667, 1958.

[641] Snyder, J. C., L. L. Nelson, and T. L. Guthrie. *Profit Planning and Control, a Computer-Oriented System for Feed Industry Management.* American Feed Manufacturers Association, 1969.

[642] Sorenson, V. L. "Planning Efficient Operations for Cherry Processing Plants." *J. Farm Econ.* 40:406-416, May 1958.

[643] Streeter, C. L., and P. L. Kelly. *A Linear Programming Model of a Grain Elevator and Feed Firm.* Kansas State University Agr. Exp. Sta. Tech. Bul. 137, 1965.

[644] Vincent, W. H. *Methods and Models in Managerial Economics: A Bibliography.* Michigan State University Agr. Econ. Rep. 108, 1968.

Feasibility Studies

[645] Aspelin, A. *An Analysis of the Potential for Establishment of a Vegetable Canning Industry in Nebraska.* Nebraska Agr. Econ. Rep. 30, 1963.

[646] Baker, F. R., H. D. Traylor, and E. P. Roy. *Economic Feasibility of Soybean Oil Milling in South Central Louisiana.* Louisiana State University, Dept. Agr. Econ., DAE Res. Rep. 355, 1966.

[647] Brooker, J. R., and J. L. Pearson. *Commercial Freezing of Six Vegetable Crops*

in the South: Factors Affecting Economic Feasibility of Single-Product Operations. USDA, ERS, Marketing Res. Rep. 926, 1971.

[648] Brown, E. E., and W. A. Inglett. *The Economic Feasibility of Egg Breaking in Georgia.* Georgia Agr. Exp. Sta. Bul. N.S. 161, 1966.

[649] Cotton Economic Research Institute. *Feasibility Study of a Textile Mill in an Eight-County Area of West Texas.* Texas Res. Rep. 91, 1969.

[650] Cox, R., and F. R. Taylor. *Feasibility of Cooperatively Owned Slaughter Plants.* North Dakota State University Agr. Econ. Rep. 39, 1965.

[651] Dahle, R. D., E. W. Jones, and T. E. Nichols, Jr. "The Integration of Price and Cost Analysis in Developing Processor-Producer Feasibility Studies." *J. Farm Econ.* 46: 644-651, August 1964.

[652] Dalrymple, D. G. *Economic Studies Pertaining to Processing Plant Feasibility: A Partial Bibliography.* U.S. Fed. Ext. Ser. Mimeo D-61, revised October 1963.

[653] Daugherty, R. E. *Feasibility Study on Commercial Cattle Feedlot, Haskell County.* Oklahoma State University Agr. Ext. Ser., 1962.

[654] David, M. L., and G. M. Mennem. *Feasibility and Requirements, Commercial Cattle Backgrounding and Feeding, Lawrence and Randolph Counties, Arkansas.* A report to the Ozarks Regional Commission, 1971.

[655] Fox, R. L., and C. G. Randell. *Feasibility of Livestock-Meat Processing and Marketing Cooperatives in Vermont.* USDA, FCS, Econ. Dev. Administration, Department of Commerce, 1967.

[656] Fraase, R. G., and D. E. Anderson. *An Analysis of the Feasibility of Establishing Malt Plants in North Dakota.* North Dakota Agr. Exp. Sta. and USDC Econ. Dev. Admin. Bul. 407, 1970.

[657] Glover, R. S., and J. A. Raburn. *The Economies of Establishing a Cooperative Livestock Auction Faculty in Hall County.* Georgia Agr. Ext. Ser., Ext. Marketing Dept., 1968.

[658] Hammond, L. H. "Extension Approach and Role of Extension Marketing Workers in Plant Feasibility Studies." *Proceedings, Marketing Section, Association of Southern Agricultural Workers,* 1965.

[659] Hammond, L. H., and R. A. King. *The Feasibility of Expanding the Sweet Potato Canning Industry in the South.* USDA, ERS, Marketing Res. Rep. 603, 1963.

[660] Hammond, L. H., H. L. Liner, N. C. Miller, and H. M. Covington. *The Feasibility of Producing and Processing Certain Vegetables in Southeastern North Carolina.* North Carolina State University Econ. Res. Rep. 4, 1967.

[661] Holder, D., and K. Mathis. *Economic Feasibility Analysis Outlines for Livestock Marketing and Slaughter-Processing Firms.* Southern Extension Marketing Committee Pub. 71-1, 1971.

[662] Keppler, W. E., Jr., and W. T. Huxster, Jr. *Feasibility Guide for Charcoal Briquetting Plant.* North Carolina State College, School of Forestry, 1962.

[663] Kunze, J. H., E. E. Brown, and S. J. Brannen. *The Economic Feasibility of Secondary Processing of Light Fowl in Georgia.* Georgia Agr. Exp. Sta. Res. Bul. 29, 1968.

[664] Lackman, J., and C. R. Harston. *Economic Feasibility Study of a Proposed Livestock Auction Market at Kalispell, Montana.* Montana State College Agr. Econ. Coop. Ext. Ser., 1964.

[665] Manitoba Department of Industry and Commerce. *Feasibility of a Vegetable Freezing Plant in Manitoba.* Prepared by the Arthur D. Little Company, 1962.

[666] Mathia, G., J. L. Pearson, and O. Ela. *An Economic Analysis of Whole Tomato*

Canning Opportunities in the South. North Carolina State University Agr. Econ. Inf. Rep Rep. 17, 1970.

[667] McDermott, E. C., and J. R. Davidson. *The Feasibility of Cooperative Cattle Feeding and Slaughtering in Montana.* Montana Agr. Exp. Sta. Bul. 597, 1965.

[668] Mills, W. J. *Agricultural Processing Facilities in Southern Illinois — Factors Affecting Location and Expansion.* Southern Illinois University, School of Agriculture, Pub. 16, 1963.

[669] Moore, H. L. *Feasibility of Cattle Feedlot in Western Pennsylvania.* Pennsylvania State University, Dept. Agr. Econ., 1962.

[670] Polopolus, L., and C. Strebeck. *Feasibility of Additional Vegetable Processing Plants in South Central Louisiana.* Louisiana State University, Dept. Agr. Econ., DAE Res. Rep. 341, 1965.

[671] Reed, R. H. *A Synthesis of Operations, Costs, and Returns for Sweet Corn and Green Pea Canning Plants in Wisconsin and Minnesota.* Wisconsin Agr. Exp. Sta. Res. Rep. 26, 1967.

[672] Schaffner, L., F. R. Taylor, and L. Paulus. *Potentials for a Soybean Processing Plant for Southeastern North Dakota.* North Dakota Agr. Exp. Sta. Agr. Econ. Rep. 29, 1963.

[673] Schermerhorn, R. W. *Feasibility Analysis: A Must before Firm Reorganization.* Oklahoma State University, Dept. Agr. Econ., AE 7106, 1971.

[674] Schoeff, R. W., and R. J. Baker. *Determining Feed Plant Feasibility.* Kansas State University, Formula Feed Ext., 1961.

[675] Siebert, J. B. *An Analysis of the California Potato Industry's Market Alternatives.* California Agr. Ext. Serv., Giannini Foundation Inf. Ser. 67-2, 1967.

[676] Simmons, R. L. *The Economic Feasibility of Additional Milk Manufacturing Facilities in North Carolina.* North Carolina State College Agr. Econ. Inf. Ser. 99, 1963.

[677] Skadberg, J. M., R. J. Mikes, and A. P. Rahan. *The Feasibility of a Sheep and Lamb Slaughtering Facility in Southeastern Iowa.* Prepared for the Iowa Development Commission, Des Moines, 1970.

[678] Stollsteimer, J. F., A. J. Coutu, and R. D. Dahle. *The Economic Feasibility of Developing a Food Processing Industry in the North Eastern Region of North Carolina.* North Carolina State University Agr. Econ. Inf. Ser. 116, 1964.

[679] Tinley, J. M., and D. B. DeLoach. *An Economic Analysis of the Feasibility of Processing Potatoes in California.* California Agr. Exp. Sta., Giannini Foundation Res. Rep. 243, 1961.

[680] Western Extension Marketing Committee. *Economic Considerations in Determining Marketing Facility Feasibility.* Colorado State University Agr. Ext. Ser., Pub. 2, 1964.

[681] Williams, F. W. *Feasibility of Establishing a Vegetable Processing Plant in Jackson County, Florida.* USDA, ARA, Econ. Res. Ser., Case Book 2, 1963.

[682] Woodard, A. W. "Extension Programs to Aid Marketing Facility Location." In *Contemporary Agricultural Marketing,* Irving Dubov, ed. Knoxville: University of Tennessee Press, 1968.

Efficient Organization within Market Areas

[683] Alexander, W. H., and C. R. Ashley. *Optimum Number, Size, and Location of Milk Manufacturing Plants in Louisiana and Mississippi.* Louisiana State University, Dept. Agr. Econ., DAE Res. Rep. 418, 1970.

[684] Araji, A. A., and R. G. Walsh. "Effect of Assembly Costs on Optimum Grain Elevator Size and Location." *Canadian J. Agr. Econ.* 17:36-45, July 1969.

[685] Babb, E. M. *Effect of Assembly, Processing, and Distribution Cost on Marketing Fluid Milk.* Purdue University Agr. Exp. Sta. Res. Bul. 828, 1967.

[686] Baritelle, J. L., and D. W. Holland. "Optimum Plant Size and Location: A Case for Separable Programming." *Agr. Econ. Research* 27:73-84, July-October, 1975.

[687] Bobst, B. W., and M. V. Waananen. "Cost and Price Effects of Concentration Restrictions in the Plant Location Problem." *Am. J. Agr. Econ.* 50:676-686, August 1968.

[688] Brodie, R. J., and W. O. McCarthy. *Optimum Size, Number, and Location of Freezing Works in the South Island, New Zealand: A Spatial Analysis.* Lincoln College Marketing Res. Rep. 7, 1974.

[689] Candler, W., J. C. Snyder, and W. Faught. "Concave Programming Applied to Rice Mill Location." *Am. J. Agr. Econ.* 54:126-130, February 1972.

[690] Carley, D. H. *Factors Affecting the Location and Size of Fluid Milk Plants.* Georgia Agr. Exp. Sta. Bul. N.S. 155, 1966.

[691] Cassidy, P. A., W. O. McCarthy, and H. I. Toft. "An Application of Spatial Analysis to Beef Slaughter Plant Location and Size, Queensland." *Australian J. Agr. Econ.* 14:1-20, June 1970.

[692] Chern, W., and L. Polopolus. "Discontinuous Plant Cost Function and a Modification of the Stollsteimer Location Model." *Am. J. Agr. Econ.* 54:581-586, November 1970.

[693] Clay, K. O., and J. E. Martin. *Optimum Size, Number, and Location of Virginia Retail Farm Equipment Dealerships.* Virginia Polytechnic Institute Agr. Econ. Res. Rep. 6, 1971.

[694] Cobia, D. W., and E. M. Babb. "An Application of Equilibrium Size of Plant Analysis to Fluid Milk Processing and Distribution." *J. Farm Econ.* 109-116, February 1964.

[695] ———. *Determining the Optimum Size Fluid Milk Processing Plant and Sales Area.* Purdue University Agr. Exp. Sta. Res. Bul. 778, 1964.

[696] DeHaven, R. Kenneth. "Conjunctive Effects of Economies of Scale and Rate Structures in Establishing the Geographical Milk Supply Area of the Plant." *J. Econ. Theory* 3:199-206, June 1971.

[697] Haskell, J., and M. L. Manuel. *Efficient Distribution of Petroleum Products to Farms.* Kansas Agr. Exp. Sta. Circ. 397, 1971.

[698] Hicks, B. G., and M. B. Badenhop. *Optimum Number, Size, and Location of Livestock Auction Markets in Tennessee.* Tennessee Agr. Exp. Sta. Bul. 478, 1971.

[699] Hoch, I. "Transfer Cost Concavity in Stollsteimer Plant Location Model." *J. Farm Econ.* 47:470-472, May 1965.

[700] Holder, S. H. J., D. L. Shaw, and J. C. Snyder. *A Systems Model of the U.S. Rice Industry.* USDA, ERS, Tech. Bul. 1453, 1971.

[701] Holroyd, W. M., and B. V. Lessley. "Plant Location Models for a Honey Packer: Sensitivity of Findings to Some Alternative Specifications with Reference to the South." *South. J. Agr. Econ.* 5:217-221, July 1973.

[702] Hopkin, R. D., R. L. Christensen, E. T. Bardwell, and R. D. Andrews. *An Analysis of the Optimum Number, Size, and Location of Feed Mixing Plants in New England.* New Hampshire Agr. Exp. Sta. Res. Rep. 22, 1971.

[703] Hudson, J. F., and R. Jesse. *Number, Size, and Location of Processing Facil-*

ilities for More Efficient Marketing of Louisiana Cotton. Louisiana State University, Dept. Agr. Econ., DAE Res. Rep. 438, 1972.

[704] Hurt, V. G., and T. E. Tramel. "Alternative Formulations of the Transshipment Problem." *J. Farm Econ.* 47:763-773, August 1965.

[705] Jesse, E. V., W. G. Schultz, and J. L. Bomben. *Decentralized Processing Plant Design Costs and Economic Feasibility.* USDA, ERS, Agr. Econ. Rep. 313, 1975.

[706] King, G. A. *A Framework for Studies on Location of Agricultural Production and Processing.* University of California (Davis), Detp. Agr. Econ., 1970.

[707] King, G. A., and S. H. Logan. "Optimum Location, Number, and Size of Processing Plants with Raw Product and Final Product Shipments." *J. Farm Econ.* 46:94-108, February 1964.

[708] Kloth, D. W., and L. V. Blakley. "Optimum Dairy Plant Location with Economies of Size and Market Share Restrictions." *Am. J. Agr. Econ.* 53:561-566, August 1971.

[709] Ladd, G. W., and M. P. Halvorson. "Parametric Solutions to the Stollsteimer Model." *Am. J. Agr. Econ.* 52:578-580, November 1970.

[710] Leath, M. N., and J. E. Martin. "The Transshipment Problem with Inequality Restraints." *J. Farm Econ.* 48:894-908, November 1966.

[711] Logan, S. H., and G. A. King. "Size and Location Factors Affecting California's Beef Slaughtering Plants." *Hilgardia* 36:139-188, December 1964.

[712] Lytle, P. W., and L. D. Hill. "The Optimum Combination of Resources within and among Country Elevators." *Am. J. Agr. Econ.* 55:202-208, May 1973.

[713] Mathia, G. A. "Selection of the Optimum Number, Size, and Location of Processing Plants." *Proceedings, Marketing Section, Association of Southern Agricultural Workers,* 1963.

[714] Mathia, G. A.,a nd R. A. King. *Planning Data for the Sweet Potato Industry. Part 3, Selection of the Optimum Number, Size, and Location of Processing Plants in Eastern North Carolina.* North Carolina State College Agr. Econ. Inf. Ser. 97, 1962.

[715] Miller, E. A., and G. F. Henning. *Suggested Location of Ohio Livestock Markets to Reduce Total Marketing Costs.* Ohio Agr. Res. Dev. Center Res. Bul. 981, 1966.

[716] Miller, B. R., and R. A. King. "Location Models in the Context of a Regional Economic System." *Southern Econ. J.* 38:59-68, July 1971.

[717] ———. *Models for Measuring the Impact of Technological Change on Location of Marketing Facilities.* North Carolina State University Agr. Econ. Inf. Ser. 115, 1964.

[718] Olson, F. L. "Location Theory as Applied to Milk Processing Plants." *J. Farm Econ.* 41:1546-1556, December 1959.

[719] Peeler, R. J., Jr., and R. A. King. *Optimum Location of Egg Grading and Packing Plants in North Carolina.* North Carolina Agr. Econ. Inf. Ser 111, 1964.

[720] Pherson, V. W., and R. S. Firch. *A Procedure for Determining Optimum Warehouse Location.* Purdue University Agr. Exp. Sta. Res. Bul. 706, 1960.

[721] Polopolus, L. "An Analytical and Operational Framework for Solving Problems of Plant Location." In *Contemporary Agricultural Marketing,* Irving Dubov, ed. Knoxville: University of Tennessee Press, 1968.

[722] ———. "Optimum Plant Numbers and Locations for Multiple Product Processing." *J. Farm Econ.* 47:287-295, May 1965.

[723] Stollsteimer, J. F., R. H. Courtney, and L. L. Sammet. *Regional Efficiency in the Organization of Agricultural Processing Facilities: An Application to Pear Packing in*

the Lake County Pear District, California. California Agr. Exp. Sta., Giannini Foundation Monograph 35, 1975.

[724] Sanders, B., and L. B. Fletcher. *Least-Cost Egg Marketing Organization under Alternative Production Patterns.* Iowa Agr. Exp. Sta. Res. Bul. 547, 1966.

[725] Stollsteimer, J. F. "Fixed Production-Fixed Consumption Models with Processing Introduced." In *Interregional Competition Research Methods,* R. A. King, ed. North Carolina State University, Agricultural Policy Institute, 1963.

[726] ———. "A Working Model for Plant Numbers and Locations." *J. Farm Econ.* 45:631-645, August 1963.

[727] Takayama, T., and G. G. G. Judge. *Spatial and Temporal Price and Allocation Models.* Amsterdam: North Holland Publishing, 1971.

[728] Toft, H. I., P. A. Cassidy, and W. O. McCarthy. "Sensitivity Testing and the Plant Location Problem." *Am. J. Agr. Econ.* 52:403-410.

[729] Von Oppen, M., and L. Hill. *Grain Elevators in Illinois: Factors Affecting Their Number and Location.* Illinois Agr. Exp. Sta., Dept. Agr. Econ., AERR 108, 1970.

[730] Warrack, A. A., and L. B. Fletcher. *Location Efficiency of the Iowa Feed-Manufacturing Industry.* Iowa State University Agr. Exp. Sta. Res. Bul. 571, 1970.

[731] ———. "Plant Location Model Suboptimization for Large Problems." *Am. J. Agr. Econ.* 52:587-590, November 1970.

[732] Weinschenck, G., W. Henrichsmeyer, and F. Aldinger. "The Theory of Spatial Equilibrium and Optimal Location in Agriculture: A Survey." *Rev. Marketing Agr. Econ.* 37:3-69, March 1969.

[733] Williamson, J. C., Jr. "The Equilibrium Size of Marketing Plants." *J. Farm Econ.* 44:953-967, November 1962.

[734] Wilmot, C. A., and C. C. Cable, Jr. *Locational Models for Cotton Ginning and Warehousing Facilities.* USDA, ERS, Marketing Res. Rep. 969, 1972.

Central Market Studies

[735] Blackmore, W. E., and H. G. Clowes. *Detroit Wholesale Food-Distribution Facilities.* USDA, AMS, Market Res. Rep. 607, 1963.

[736] Boles, P. P., and W. E. Blackmore. *Food Distribution Facilities for Salt Lake City, Utah.* USDA, ARS, Marketing Res. Rep. 829, 1969.

[737] Clark, S. D., G. S. Abshier, and G. R. Cassell. *The Wholesale Produce Market at Winston-Salem, North Carolina.* USDA, PMA, 1951.

[738] Clark, S. D., and M. A. Faller. *A Plan for Development of a Wholesale Fruit and Vegetable Market at Baton Rouge, Louisiana.* USDA, AMS, AMS-20, 1955.

[739] Clowes, H. G. *New York City Wholesale Fresh Fruit and Vegetable Markets.* USDA, AMS, Marketing Res. Rep. 389, 1960.

[740] ———. *Wholesale Food Distribution Facilities of San Francisco.* USDA, AMS, Marketing Res. Rep. 226, 1958.

[741] Clowes, H. G., W. H. Elliott, and W. C. Crow. *Wholesale Food Market Facilities — Types of Ownership and Methods of Financing.* USDA, AMS, Marketing Res. Rep. 160, 1957.

[742] Clowes, H. G., and K. Utter. *The Wholesale Food Marketing Facilities at Grand Rapids, Michigan.* USDA, AMS, Marketing Res. Rep. 259, 1958.

[743] Crow, W. C. *Wholesale Markets for Fruits and Vegetables in 40 Cities.* USDA Circ. 463, 1938.

[744] Hanlon, P. J. *Food Distribution Facilities in Dayton, Ohio.* USDA, ARS, Marketing Res. Rep. 835, 1969.

206   BEN C. FRENCH

[745] Hefferman, R. E., and K. Utter. *The Benton Harbor, Michigan, Fruit Market: Present and Proposed Facilities.* USDA, AMS, Marketing Res. Rep. 390, 1960.

[746] Larson, J. S. *Wholesale Produce Markets — Management, Operating Expenses, and Income.* USDA, AMS, Marketing Res. Rep. 91, 1955.

[747] Manchester, A. C. *The Organization of the Wholesale Fruit and Vegetable Market in Boston.* USDA, ERS, Marketing Res. Rep. 515, 1962.

[748] Otten, C. J., S. D. Clark, A. B. Lowstuter, A. L. Owen, N. G. Paulhus, P. S. Richey, and J. I. Kross. *The Wholesale Produce Market at Milwaukee, Wisconsin.* USDA, PMS, 1950.

[749] Overheim, R. K., and P. J. Hanlon. *Food Distribution Facilities for Oakland, California.* USDA, ARS, Marketing Res. Rep. 874, 1970.

[750] Overheim, R. K., and J. T. Hayes. *Baton Rouge Wholesale Food-Distribution Facilities — Status Report.* USDA, AMS, AMS-536, 1964.

[751] Pittman, J. F., and F. W. Chapman, Jr. *The Organization of the Wholesale Fruit and Vegetable Markets in the South — Atlanta, Georgia.* South Carolina Agr. Exp. Sta. AE 249, 1964.

[752] ———. *The Organization of Wholesale Fruit and Vegetable Markets in the South — Raleigh and Winston Salem, North Carolina.* South Carolina Agr. Exp. Sta. AE 250, 1964.

[753] Pittman, J. F., and G. R. Von Tingeln. *The Organization of Wholesale Fruit and Vegetable Markets in the South — Columbia and Greenville, South Carolina.* South Carolina Agr. Exp. Sta. AE 251, 1964.

[754] Smalley, R. H., and T. J. Seabold. *Improved Urban Food Distribution Facilities for Denver, Colorado.* USDA, ARS, Marketing Res. Rep. 909, 1971.

[755] Stanford Research Institute. *Transportation and Handling Costs of Selected Fresh Fruits and Vegetables in the San Francisco Bay Terminal Market Area.* USDA, BAE, Marketing Res. Rep. 2, 1952.

[756] Taylor, E. G. *Boston Wholesale Food Distribution Facilities.* USDA, ARS, Marketing Res. Rep. 732, 1965.

[757] Taylor, E. G., and F. J. Miller. *A Study of Food Distribution Facilities for Cincinnati, Ohio.* USDA, AMS, Marketing Res. Rep. 825, 1968.

[758] Taylor, E. G., R. K. Overheim, and A. B. Lowstuter. *New Bedford Wholesale Food-Distribution Facilities.* USDA, AMS, Marketing Res. Rep. 613, 1963.

[759] Todd, F. R., Jr. *Pittsburgh Wholesale Food Distribution Facilities.* USDA, ARS, Marketing Res. Rep. 660, 1964.

[760] Traylor, H. D., and S. T. Warrington. *Wholesale Food Distribution Facilities in New Orleans, Louisiana.* Louisiana Agr. Exp. Sta. DAE Circ. 259, 1960.

[761] Turner, G. E., T. F. Webb, A. F. Schramm, J. G. McNeely, and J. Miller. *Fort Worth Stockyards, 1955: Proposed Facilities, Operations, Services.* USDA, AMS, Marketing Res. Rep. 260, 1958.

[762] Utter, K. L., E. G. Taylor, and A. B. Lowstuter. *Rhode Island Wholesale Food Distribution Facilities.* USDA, AMS, Marketing Res. Rep. 489, 1961.

[763] Utter, K. L., E. G. Taylor, A. B. Lowstuter, and P. J. Hanlon. *Wholesale Food Distribution Facilities for Knoxville, Tennessee.* USDA, AMS, Marketing Res. Rep. 404, 1960.

Part III. Policy for Commercial Agriculture, 1945-71

This review has been read by more than a dozen economists, most of whom were active in the field of farm policy during the period under discussion. Their critical comments were immensely helpful in improving the review. In some instances I felt justified in retaining interpretations objected to by one or two critics, and I assume responsibility for any questionable judgments, omissions, and outright errors that may remain. The review is limited almost entirely to literature addressed to a professional audience; to attempt to include popular and educational materials would have made the task unmanageable.

The review was authorized for publication January 18, 1973, as paper No. 4375 in the journal series of the Pennsylvania Agricultural Experiment Station.

G. E. B.

Policy for Commercial Agriculture, 1945-71

G. E. Brandow
Professor of Agricultural Economics
Pennsylvania State University

Farm Problems and Their Economic and Social Setting

Farm price and income policy is about an actual world, not an abstraction in which simple, homogeneous resources are frictionlessly allocated to production of want-satisfying goods, free of political influence or the clash of opposing value systems. Like most of the economy, the agricultural sector is constantly changing under the impact of new technology, shifting demands, and evolving institutions. It is in such a world that unrest about the state of affairs arises and creates policy issues. It is this world that economists studying farm policy try to understand and for which they analyze, and on occasion propose, policy alternatives. This review begins, therefore, by sketching the major economic developments in agriculture bearing upon price and income policy from World War II to 1971.

The Agricultural Experience

Total crop and livestock production has risen continually in this century with only small year-to-year variations in the aggregate except during the great droughts of the mid-1930s (figure 1). During the quarter century beginning with 1947 the rate of output expansion held remarkably close to 1.7 percent per year. Even so, the composition of total output changed significantly in this era; for example, production of poultry, beef cattle, and soybeans rose strongly, while production of cotton, tobacco, wheat, and milk increased slowly or declined.

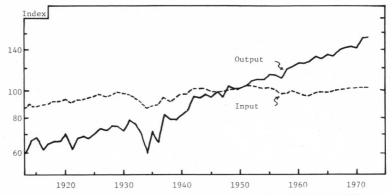

Figure 1. Total agricultural output and input, 1913-72 (1947-49=100).

Resources used in production changed dramatically. Tractors gradually began to push horses and mules aside at the end of World War I and had virtually completed the job by the late 1950s. Rapid increases in numbers, power, and versatility of farm machines followed World War II. The use of human labor, which declined slowly during the 1920s and 1930s, began to drop precipitously in the late 1940s. Farm employment was halved between 1950 and 1957 and was still falling in the early 1970s.

Large increases in the use of fertilizer and pesticides, together with the development of improved crop varieties, were instrumental in raising crop production per acre more than 50 percent in the quarter century beginning with 1947. The harvested acreage of crops, which was about the same in World War II as in World War I, declined slightly in the early 1950s and decreased again under acreage diversion programs begun in the late 1950s. The USDA index of total farm productivity (output-input ratio) rose persistently after World War II until about 1965, leveled off until 1970, and then rose again.

The number of farms varied within the narrow range of 6.5 to 6.8 million from 1920 to the late 1930s but had fallen to 6.0 million by the end of World War II. The number was 2.9 million in 1971. Farms became much larger in terms of acreage and still larger in terms of output. Except for irregular declines in persons and workers per farm, the size of the farm population and labor force followed the course of farm numbers after 1920.

Income in both the agricultural and nonagricultural sectors fluctuated widely in the 1920s and 1930s. Total agricultural income tended to decline slowly relative to total nonfarm income but averaged about one-tenth of the nonfarm amount during the two decades. Agricultural income rose somewhat more than nonagricultural income from 1939 to 1948 but took a much

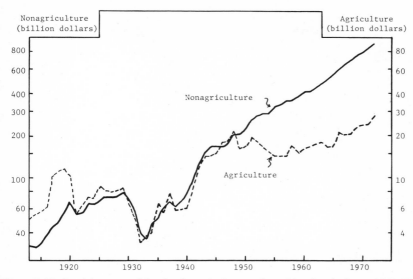

Figure 2. National income originating in agriculture and outside of agriculture, 1913-72.

different course after that, as figure 2 shows. Income originating in agriculture had fallen to 3 percent of nonagricultural income by 1971.

After World War II agricultural income was shared by a rapidly declining number of persons. Moreover, income of farm residents from off-farm sources rose from one-fourth of the total income at the end of World War II to more than one-half in 1971. A comparison of per-capita disposable personal incomes of farm and nonfarm residents shows a substantial decline in the relative position of farm people from 1948 to the mid-1950s, followed by a more than compensating gain from that point to the early 1970s. Farm residents had become so heterogeneous a group by the 1960s, however, that per-person and per-farm data tell us very little. Eighty-six percent of the income on farms with sales of less than $5,000 was from nonfarm sources in 1971 (table 1).

Farm prices collectively were highly unstable up to the mid-1950s, and prices of most individual farm commodities were even more unstable. The famous parity ratio compares the index of prices received by farmers with the index of prices paid by farmers, both indexes on a 1910-14 base. Farm prices were much below parity as thus defined during most of the 1930s, were at or above parity from 1942 to 1952, and fell below parity by increasing margins from the early 1950s to 1971.

Both farm land prices and net farm income nearly tripled in the fifteen years from 1939 to 1954. From 1954 to 1971, however, land values rose 134

Table 1. Income Comparisons on Farms of Different Size, 1944 and 1971

Class of Farm	Percentage of Cash Receipts	Percentage of All Farms	Net Income per Farm		
			Farm Sources	Nonfarm Sources	Total
			1944		
Medium and large commercial farms[a] . .	80	29	$5,467	NA	NA
Small commercial farms[b].	15	28	1,412	NA	NA
Other farms	5	43	384	NA	NA
All farms	100	100	$2,137	$688	$2,825
			1971		
Sales $20,000 or more.	79	21	$16,913	$4,898	$21,811
Sales $5,000 to $19,999.	16	27	4,723	4,442	9,165
Sales under $5,000	5	52	1,302	7,723	9,025
All farms	100	100	$ 5,581	$6,230	$11,811

[a]Minimum value of products $3,000 per farm unless value of land and buildings $20,000 or more.

[b]Minimum value of products $1,200 per farm unless value of land and buildings $8,000 to $19,999.

Notes: Farm prices increased 44 percent between 1944 and 1971; prices of items bought for farm family living increased 118 percent. Averages for small farms conceal poverty among families without substantial nonfarm income. Sources: 1944 data adapted from Brandow and Allison [29], together with census number of farms; 1971 data from USDA, ERS, *Farm Income Situation*, July 1972.

percent while net farm income increased only 30 percent. Farm proprietors' equity was high in relation to the value of farm assets — 91 percent — in 1950. Despite a fivefold rise in farm debts, it was still 81 percent in 1971.

Farm problems got on the nation's policy agenda because dissatisfied farmers put them there. Dissatisfaction became widespread during the price collapse of 1920-21 and was sufficiently strong throughout the 1920s to engender much legislative activity culminating in the Federal Farm Board of 1929. Extreme distress on farms in the early 1930s was part of the nation's economic and social condition to which the New Deal was a response. Extensive federal farm programs were firmly established by the end of the 1930s. Throughout the period under review political leaders had little reason to think that the federal government could withdraw from farm markets.

Before World War II many farmers were dissatisfied with incomes which they felt to be unfairly low. The immediate and often only reason perceived for poor incomes was unfavorable prices. After World War II memories of events following World War I led farmers to press strongly for price support.

Soon thereafter additional concerns received new emphasis. The steep decline in the numbers of farms and farmers was disquieting: it seemed wrong to fundamentalists, it meant a diminution of farmers' political power, it was an implied threat to the survival of many farmers who had not yet been forced out of agriculture, and it undermined rural communities in many of the farming areas of the nation.

Vertical integration by nonfarm business firms into farm production was dramatic in the poultry and egg industries in the 1950s and tended to spread into certain other branches of agriculture. Some new large-scale farms were formed, in a few cases by industrial firms strongly bent on conglomeration, and instances in which wealthy individuals invested in one way or another in farming seemed to increase. Farmers and many other citizens frequently viewed these developments as foreboding encroachments on family farming and often attributed them to unfair commercial or tax advantages. The charge of monopolizing practices by businesses with which farmers deal — a contention that is centuries, not decades, old — continued to be pressed by some farm groups.

Farmers' interest in self-directed collective action to improve prices and other terms of sales grew during the 1950s and 1960s. Farmers contrasted their own situation with that of labor unions and corporations in concentrated industries in demanding and getting higher wages and prices. Bargaining power became a central goal of a number of producer associations, including both general farm organizations and specialized commodity groups.

A dramatic turn of events in the summer of 1972, closely related to crop failures abroad and to inflation everywhere, caused farm prices and income to soar and fears about food shortages to replace preoccupation with surpluses. The year 1971, therefore, is an opportune point at which to end a review of farm policy literature.

The Macroeconomics of Agriculture

Understanding how the agricultural economy works is obviously important to policy analysis and prescription. Much of the effort to improve such understanding has been motivated by policy purposes. As agricultural economists observed the behavior of agriculture, there gradually emerged a dominant conception of the processes and structural attributes characterizing the sector and forming the milieu in which farm economic problems developed. The general model of agriculture was not agreed upon in full; disagreement remained concerning the relative importance of different components, the quantitative values of some key functional relationships, and the speed at which particular processes operated. Yet the general model became widely enough accepted to be the common framework within which discussions among agricultural economists about policy took place.

SCHULTZ'S 1945 ANALYSIS

Schultz's *Agriculture in an Unstable Economy* [174] is often remembered for relating farm economic fortunes to industrial instability and for a compensatory payments proposal, but most of the book was devoted to an analysis of the effects of persistent, long-term forces causing major changes in agricultural resource use, relative prices, and farm income. The ideas presented there are a convenient set around which to begin a description of the general model. Somewhat recast, the components of the Schultz model as of 1945 are as follows:

1. *Technology as an external, driving force.* Improved methods of farm production were being generated outside of agriculture — until 1945 mainly by publicly supported research institutions. The new technology caused the supply of farm products (in a schedule sense) to increase. The most dramatic current instance of this was the introduction of mechanical power on farms; as tractors replaced horses and mules, millions of acres were transferred from production of feed for draft animals to production of grain and forage for livestock for the market. Much farm machinery incorporated new technology that led to more capital and less labor in the optimal input mix.

2. *Land development.* Some new land was brought into agriculture not because farm price-cost relationships justified it but because development-minded communities had sufficient political power to induce the federal or state government to appropriate funds for irrigation, drainage, or clearing of land.

3. *Market and cost structure of agriculture.* Since agriculture was highly competitive (aside from the effects of government programs), "competition makes it necessary for farmers as producers to adopt the new technology or find themselves at a disadvantage relative to other farmers who do so." No producer restrained his output in order to influence prices. This was in contrast with oligopoly found "in the upper reaches of industry" where firms were in a position to decide whether or not to adopt technology and how much output to produce with it. Also, the importance of land and self-employed labor meant that farmers had high fixed costs that left them with no alternative but to keep their farms in full production.

4. *Slow expansion and low income elasticity of demand for farm products.* Population growth was expected to be slow. (Virtually all economists and demographers underestimated the rate of population increase that would prevail following World War II.) Since incomes in the United States were already

high, the income elasticity of demand for raw foods was low — on the order of .25. (Demand for services attached to foods after they left the farm was more income elastic.) Export demand was not expected to increase greatly, in part because other developed nations would also make technological advances in agriculture.

5. *Persistent maladjustment in farming.* Under the foregoing circumstances, the supply of agricultural products persistently advanced at a faster rate than the demand. The result was "chronic disequilibrium adverse to agriculture." Farming was constantly burdened with excess labor as outmigration lagged behind the reduction in the number of well-paying job opportunities. Farm prices were lower in relation to nonfarm prices than would have been the case if excess agricultural labor had not existed. The effects of the war, particularly shipment of food abroad, temporarily overrode this long-run tendency.

6. *Resource mobility: labor.* Average labor earnings in agriculture were persistently well below labor earnings in industry; the gap was not fully closed even at peaks of farm prosperity. Thus, outmigration from farming depended much more upon the availability of nonfarm jobs, as reflected in data on nonagricultural employment, than upon farm prices and income. Impediments to mobility (more often implied than explicitly developed) included lack of education and skills, poor health, lack of knowledge of nonfarm job opportunities, racial discrimination, employment barriers created by organized labor, and restrictive government regulations. High birthrates on farms added to the burden on labor mobility as a means of achieving equilibrium in agriculture.

7. *Resource mobility: land.* The land base was sometimes increased, as indicated under point 2, through political rather than economic decision making. Land was slow to be taken out of farming because it had little or no value in nonfarm uses. New technology often increased the productivity of land, even to the point of bringing poor land into cultivation; on the other hand, technology impaired the comparative advantage of land not suited to machinery or other innovations.

8. *Resource mobility: capital.* Advances in farm technology made capital, such as power machinery and equipment, highly productive and attracted capital into agriculture. (Schultz gave no analysis of the farmer decision process that led to an inflow of capital despite the decline of farm prices and labor earnings accompanying technological advance. His emphasis was on the labor resource; land and capital were discussed only incidentally.)

9. *Responsiveness of output to price.* There was a strong propensity for supply to increase despite low prices. The reasons lay in the exogenous nature of technology and new land development, together with the market structure

of agriculture and the fixity of land and labor costs. Agricultural expansion was "a one-way street"; it was "virtually impossible to bring about a contraction in total agricultural output during the course of a few years."

10. *Instability in agriculture.* Agriculture was highly sensitive to instability in the industrial economy in two principal ways: (a) demand and prices for farm products were affected by the level of nonfarm income, and (b) agricultural labor mobility, the amount of excess labor in agriculture, and farm labor earnings were influenced by employment in industry. In light of the experience of the previous two decades, instability in the nonfarm sector was heavily emphasized. On the supply side, inputs into agricultural production were highly stable from year to year, and total farm output ordinarily was nearly as stable. But for particular products and regions, output was much less stable. Weather, disease, and insects caused production and price variations that often meant special hardship for particular producers. The comparative stability of total output was attributable to the averaging out of results for many products over a large nation.

Schultz was pessimistic about the outlook for farm income: ". . . chronic agricultural surpluses in special commodities are likely to put in their appearance within two to five years after the war . . ."; prices received by farmers were expected to drop from 115 percent of parity to somewhere between 80 and 90 percent; and "there is a high probability . . . that the postwar period will find American agriculture substantially over-extended."

Most of the components of Schultz's model were, of course, already among the numerous reasons that had been put forth in explanation of earlier agricultural difficulties. For example, the January 1927 issue of the *Journal of Farm Economics* contained articles in which were described "portentous technological changes," the likelihood of "enhancing productivity at a rate faster than the growth of requirements for food and raw materials," prospects for changes in comparative advantage of farming regions, implications of the fixity of farm costs, and transfer of labor from rural to urban areas. "Stated as a paradox," wrote E. G. Nourse, "the outlook for agricultural production is so good that the outlook for agricultural prosperity is distinctly bad." But this view was by no means widely accepted even in the late 1920s, and the Great Depression of the 1930s, the devastating droughts in the same decade, and the effects of World War II overwhelmed the secular changes predicted by it. To select in 1945 the relevant variables for the future, to put them together in an appropriate way, and to make essentially accurate predictions of later developments was no small accomplishment.

OTHER CONTEMPORARY VIEWS

The winning papers on policy in a contest sponsored by the American Farm Economic Association (AFEA) were more explicit about policy proposals than about underlying circumstances creating policy problems [153, 159]. Apparently almost all of the authors would have accepted most of Schultz's points as containing at least a grain of truth, and all seemed to agree on the need for labor adjustment from agriculture to industry. But most authors seemingly would have put less emphasis on technology as a source of output expansion, on its intractability to the restraints of low prices and incomes, and thus on the severity of the chronic disequilibrium facing agriculture.

The USDA's *What Peace Can Mean to American Farmers* [217-220] was consistent with Schultz's book and with current thought among agricultural economists in emphasizing the importance of high-level employment in industry for maintaining demand for farm products and for giving alternative employment opportunities to excess farm labor. Discussions of problems of farm adjustment indicated implicit agreement with Schultz's points about farm size, changes in use of capital and labor, and shifts in comparative advantage of regions. Projections of output and prices for 1950 indicated that if, as strongly suggested, farm technology continued to advance, 23 million fewer acres would be needed for crops; a proposed program to upgrade diets of poor families would absorb the output of only about one-fourth of the prospective excess acreage. More clearly than stated in the text of the study, the data indicated looming agricultural surpluses that would be difficult to deal with.

A number of studies in the mid-1940s pointed to difficult adjustment problems facing cotton and wheat producing areas. It was expected that cotton would meet increasing competition from foreign growths and man-made fibers, and much of the cotton South was particularly burdened with excess labor, too-small farms, and eroded soils. The anticipated problem in wheat was inadequate demand to provide an outlet in the form of food for all the wheat likely to be produced.

Three questions frequently treated in the mid-1940s as basic, enduring problems were later to recede in importance. All had been prominent at least partly because of the special circumstances of the 1930s. One was soil conservation: Serious erosion in some areas was obvious; soil depletion had been forced on farmers by financial stringencies in the 1930s; memories of the dust bowl days were fresh. A second was farm credit: the difficulties faced by farmers in the 1930s had not been forgotten; needs for credit to finance reorganization and mechanization of farms in the future were impressive. The third was farm tenancy: renting by low-income operators had increased during the Great Depression; sharecropping was still important in the South. Better farm incomes in the 1950s and 1960s than in the depression years helped to ease all of these problems. Institutions created in the 1930s and modified later helped to overcome difficulties in soil conservation and farm credit. Some problems were partially eliminated if not solved by the onrush of events, as when many sharecroppers and small farmers with special credit needs disappeared from the scene. And, of course, some problems in these areas remain or have assumed new forms.

Events following World War II demonstrated that severe depression of the nonfarm economy was unlikely to be the source of agricultural difficulties that it had been in the 1930s. Events also demonstrated a pervasiveness and vigor of farm technological advance that had not been fully anticipated even by economists who had most emphasized the probable impact of new production methods. Accordingly, the general model was elaborated and modified in several respects described in the following sections.

AGGREGATE SUPPLY AND DEMAND

In a series of publications beginning in 1947 [50] and ending with his *Farm Prices, Myth and Reality* [51] in 1958, Cochrane emphasized the concept of the farm sector as an aggregate and presented a statistically supported analysis of a technologically based supply interacting with an inelastic demand to generate wide price gyrations. Cochrane argued that ". . . in the aggregate . . . there is a high degree of substitution between individual farm enterprises in most areas and at the extensive margin of all areas in response to commodity price changes . . . on the demand side, too, particularly in the case of foods, consumers are continuously substituting less expensive items for more expensive items." But intersectoral substitution was much less close: "To an important degree agriculture represents a water-tight compartment within which there is considerable fluidity, but the connective valve between the agricultural compartment and the rest of the economy works poorly and sometimes almost not at all."

Cochrane made no use of a long-run supply curve with all the complications of irreversibility, ratchet effects, and awkward shifts of position implied by the general model. Rather, he pictured a short-run aggregate supply curve as the relationship between planned total output and an index of "responsible prices" one production period (usually one year) earlier. This curve, he said, was perfectly inelastic or nearly so. When a shift of aggregate demand to the right caused high prices and optimistic expectations on the part of farmers, they had both the motivation and the financial resources to adopt new technology. As they did this, aggregate supply moved to the right, bringing down prices. When demand was static or declining, as in the 1930s, supply did not contract, but there accumulated a pool of unapplied technology to be put to use whenever demand expanded. Cochrane traced out in this way the course of farm prices from before World War I to the 1950s.

Though in retrospect Cochrane's analysis is seen to be generally consistent with ideas presented earlier by other economists, probably most specifically by Schultz, it is instructive to note that Cochrane's first articles did not present it in that context and that Schultz [176] so severely criticized the details and emphasis of Cochrane's analysis as to appear to reject it. This was not the first or the last time that economic ideas subsequently seen to be closely related were initially thought of as sharply different.

GENERATION AND ADOPTION OF TECHNOLOGY

Agricultural technology has been increasingly generated outside the farming sector as instances of innovations by farmers have dwindled in frequency. Hayami and Ruttan [105] recently drew upon the idea of induced innovation to argue that "... changes in input mixes represent a process of dynamic factor substitution accompanying changes in the production surface induced by the changes in relative factor prices." They contrasted factor supply conditions and types of agricultural innovations in the United States and Japan.

An alternative interpretation is that first-generation (basic) innovations like the internal combustion engine or fixation of atmospheric nitrogen often have little or no relation to a nation's farm economic situation. Once they are made, second-generation innovations adapting them to agriculture require only competent mechanical or biological engineering plus the prospect of economic feasibility. In this interpretation factor and product prices in agriculture importantly influence economic feasibility and thus the course of second-generation innovations; agricultural factor markets may or may not influence the pathbreaking, first-generation inventions. In this sense, farm mechanization was agriculturally induced only to the extent that the low cost of capital relative to labor encouraged exploitation of the basic invention. The low relative price of nitrogen fertilizer was largely traceable to a first-generation innovation and to later developments upon it, all external to American agriculture. Both mechanization and fertilizer profoundly affected the quantity and mix of inputs used in farming.

The detailed process by which technology was adopted on millions of farms was in the background of most agricultural economists' thinking in the 1940s and 1950s but was not often explicitly set forth. The incentive for an individual farmer selling under pure competition to adopt zero-cost or low-cost innovations (e.g., hybrid seed) was easy to see, even though such action by farmers collectively was likely to reduce incomes and to force additional withdrawals from agriculture. Farmers' financial position and access to credit were conceived as important limitations on the adoption of innovations requiring substantial investment (for example, expensive equipment). The importance of refined calculations of marginal costs and revenues in determining annual adjustments of output or in explaining the timing of adoption of new methods was questioned because the organization of resources on most farms was known to be far from the optimum defined by standard theory of the firm. A large lag in adopting such relatively simple technology as fertilization was easily demonstrated. Wilcox [235] showed the limitations of conventional analysis in predicting the effects of prices on farm output in the real economic world characterized by technical change and chronic disequilibrium.

Work by rural sociologists on diffusion of farm practices, pioneered by Ryan and Gross [168], described characteristics of early and late adopters. It supported the hypothesis that farmers who were sufficiently well financed and enterprising to stay several jumps ahead of the crowd often could manage to realize attractive rates of return on labor and investment, especially if prices were supported, even though returns in farming as a whole were substandard.

HETEROGENEITY WITHIN AGRICULTURE

Long before the 1950s large differences in rates of return to resources in different agricultural areas of the nation had been recognized. Explanations put forward had included differences in land quality, chronic difficulties afflicting crops dominating large areas (for example, cotton), the heritage of slavery, and area discrimination in transportation policy. Schultz [175] contended that area differences were in large part a function of the way the national economy develops. Economic development, he argued, takes place in a locational matrix and is industrial-urban centered. The economic organization works best close to industrial-urban centers and most poorly at long (economic and social) distances from them. The labor market is the chief culprit: economic and cultural distance impedes the labor mobility needed for income equalization. But also, he said, "the adjustments that are required in the allocation of capital will be achieved more satisfactorily in those parts of agriculture that are situated favorably to the centers of economic development than in those at the periphery."

Especially since an economic classification of farms was begun in the agricultural census of 1945, it has been well known that agriculture at any one time has contained many nominal units, that nonfarm income has exceeded the farm income of many "farm" families, and that most farms have been too small to achieve substantially full economies of size. Economists have recognized for decades that prices received for farm products can not solve the income problems of low-production farm families [155, 174, 220]. A closely related point, that prices and labor returns are not powerful allocators of resources in low-production agriculture, has been widely but less universally acknowledged.

ASSET FIXITY

The prevalence in family farming of inputs not recurrently purchased in markets has led to different views of the sense in which costs are fixed and the importance of fixed costs in explaining the behavior of output. In 1946 Brewster and Parsons [36] argued a position that had declining appeal in later years. On family farms, they said, the occupational unity of labor, technology management, and business management functions caused the first two functions to dominate the third. The farmer considered most costs fixed, gave little attention to marginal conditions for profit maximization, pressed output to the limit, and was not guided by price in making decisions about total output (and was only crudely guided by prices in adjusting enterprises within the farm). D. G. Johnson [125] went to the other extreme in considering labor, land, and other inputs as potentially variable costs to the farmer. He explained the behavior of farm input and output in terms of the characteristics of industry supply functions for inputs and the flexibility of certain input prices or opportunity costs.

G. L. Johnson [127, 128] reasoned that a production asset has two critical values. One is the acquisition price, which is applicable when utilization of more of the resource is being considered; another is the salvage value, which is applicable when less use is contemplated. When the marginal value product of the resource exceeds the acquisition price, the rational producer will acquire the resource and expand output. Only when the marginal value product falls below salvage value will the producer dispose of the resource and reduce output. When acquisition prices and salvage values are very different, assets will be fixed and cause no change in output despite rather wide variations in the price of output. Nonspecialized resources such as land and family labor are variable costs for particular enterprises and will be shifted from one to another in response to price. Important resources are fixed for the farm as a whole for long periods, however. G. L. Johnson's conclusions about the inelasticity of total supply in the short run, the greater responsiveness of longer-run supply to rising than to falling prices, and the concept of agriculture as an aggregate are consistent with characteristics earlier attributed to agriculture in the general model.

EFFECTS OF RISK AND UNCERTAINTY

Since the general model is intended to apply to the real world, risk and uncertainty permeate it. Especially when prices are not supported, farmers planting crops or breeding livestock are uncertain what prices will be when their products are marketed. Young men starting out in farming do not know what effects changing technology and market demands will have on the profitability of particular types of farming or of agriculture generally. Neither do producers know precisely how optimal size and organization of farms will change in the future.

Schultz and several of his associates held that uncertainty about selling prices when production decisions were made caused significant misallocation of resources. D. G. Johnson's analysis [123] pointed to undercommitment of capital, to the emergence of livestock cycles, and to similar imperfections. G. L. Johnson [128] has attacked the assumption of perfect knowledge incorporated in some models of the agricultural economy — certainly not an assumption of the general model described here — and has argued that farmers erroneously commit resources that, because of asset fixity, are not readily withdrawn though they cause excess capacity and its adverse consequences.

ECONOMISTS' VIEWS IN 1957

A study of policy for commercial agriculture by the Joint Economic Committee of Congress in 1957 produced a compendium of sixty-one articles, almost all by economists, on the existing farm situation, on underlying economic forces at work in agriculture, and on policy recommendations [132]. The concepts of the agricultural economy expressed or implied by most of the authors were generally consistent with the general model as developed to this point. That the committee chose to study policy for commercial agriculture — it had already made two studies of low-income farm families — demonstrated that heterogeneity within agriculture and its implications for policy were already well recognized.

The authors of the articles strongly emphasized the effects of technological advance and the myriad adjustments forced upon farming. Schultz added two points so far not mentioned in this review: (1) the tendency of wages in the economy, even in agriculture, to rise faster than prices of producers' goods, thus stimulating substitution of capital for labor, and (2) the rising quality of labor and managerial inputs and their effects on farm output. G. L. Johnson elaborated upon a point he and others had previously made, the increase in agricultural productivity resulting from greater specialization (1) on products by regions, (2) on products by individual farms, (3) on particular steps in production, such as hatching and growing birds in the broiler industry, and (4) on essential farm operations such as planting crops and feeding livestock while turning over to nonfarm firms such operation as liming fields and manufacturing feed.

CROPS-LIVESTOCK DISTINCTION

An idea implicit in econometric models of the feed-livestock literature of about 1960, alluded to in some policy analyses and most explicitly dealt with by Breimyer [34], was that crops occupy a different economic position than do livestock products within the agricultural sector. Livestock production, Breimyer argued, is a processing operation converting feed into secondary products. Feed crops are primary products of agriculture, as are other crops. (The difference is not clear-cut, for livestock grazing on nonarable land is primary production, and cropland can be pastured.) Production of meat animals and of poultry and eggs has been increasingly separated from feed production, making the distinction even sharper. Crop production, particularly because of its close association with land, has high fixed costs; feed is a highly important variable cost in livestock production. The major field crops are highly processed (including feed crops processed by livestock) before they reach the consumer; thus derived demands for feed crops at the farm level are particularly price inelastic.

Especially since much new technology has raised crop yields, some economists — not necessarily Breimyer — saw crop producers as being more vulnerable to the impact of technology than were livestock producers. Incomes were likely to be more severely depressed in crop production than in livestock production; and because of the low opportunity cost of most farmland, disequilibrium would persist longer in crops. Breimyer, with others, believed that the increasing use of inputs of nonfarm origin in both crop and livestock production increased the elasticity of farm supply, but he did not take into account greater specialization within agriculture and rising fixed costs associated with durable equipment.

GENERAL ECONOMIC CONDITIONS AND AGRICULTURE

The general model of agriculture continued to imply that a deep and prolonged economic depression would hurt agriculture through the product market, but expectations that such an event would occur faded if they did not entirely disappear. Several statistical studies confirmed the model's implication that slackness of industrial employment impeded the flow of labor from agriculture, with the likely consequence of prolonging farm-nonfarm disequilibrium.

Hathaway [99] argued in 1957 that farm output was more highly correlated with expansions and contractions of the business cycle than generally believed, but his data was largely for the years before World War II. Experience since the mid-1950s shows little, if any, relation between annual non-farm employment and farm output. Hathaway also argued, however, that the nonfarm economy affected agriculture through the prices of purchased inputs and that the effect was becoming more important as the use of such inputs increased. His expectation that mild business expansions would not have a positive contemporary effect on farm income (because of higher input prices) seems to have been confirmed.

MARKET STRUCTURES OF AGRICULTURE AND INDUSTRY

The significance attached to the purely competitive structure of agriculture as presented in Schultz's model of 1945 has continued to be accepted, with a modification here and an elaboration there, by most economists, though Schultz seems seldom to have mentioned it since then. But at no time has there been a consensus about the effect on agriculture of the varying degrees of oligopoly, oligopsony, and product differentiation often found on the other side of markets where farmers buy or sell.

Local markets for farm products or farm supplies are often highly concentrated, and instances unquestionably arise in the short run in which farmers receive less or pay more than if markets were purely competitive on both sides. The situation is a very old one and quite possibly has eased as local transportation has improved and as alternatives open to farmers have become more varied. It is not a reason why incomes of farmers collectively have been worse at any one time than they were one or five decades earlier. Concentration is high in a number of industries that process and distribute farm products or that manufacture farm supplies; accordingly, input prices and so-called marketing margins are more inflexible over time than they otherwise would be. But it is difficult to show that excess profits (above a competitive level) in such industries collectively are large in relation to prices received or paid by farmers or that the burden of any excess profits falls, in the long run, more on the farmers than on the general public.

Boulding [18] has argued that the mobility of farm resources largely vitiates any long-run effect of monopoly-like behavior in farm-related industries on earnings in agriculture. He has also contended that, the "relative stability of the [farmer] cooperative sector of the market . . . is evidence that the problem is no longer serious, and that there are no longer any areas of unusual profit for the cooperatives to undermine." He was unsure whether industrial oligopoly (he did not mention labor unions) impeded labor mobility from agriculture.

A contrasting view is illustrated in an article by Lanzilotti [140]. He concluded from observed concentration in processing and distribution industries and from actions by antitrust agencies that "farmers, as sellers, have found themselves at the mercy of oligopolies, collusion, and monopsony." He also contended that barriers to entry in industry were large and important in reducing labor mobility out of agriculture — again, no mention of the industrial labor market.

Several closely related ideas about the suitability of purely competitive structure for agriculture in a modern industrial world are most conveniently incorporated in the following section.

INDUSTRIALIZATION OF AGRICULTURE

The phrase "industrialization of agriculture" has been in the literature of agriculture at least since the 1920s. Then it usually meant a transformation of agriculture from a way of life to farming as a commercial business, a change that the general model of agriculture under discussion here assumes to be largely completed. Now the phrase often connotes, however vaguely, the presence of self-perpetuating technological and organizational forces sweeping through agriculture and industry alike and linking the two so intimately that the farming sector — itself becoming less identifiable — can be analyzed only in the context of the total industrial setting. The spirit and much of the content of "industrialization of agriculture" are contained in an article by Shaffer [181]. Galbraith [78] has displayed the role of management and planning in the larger framework of the total economy and has illuminated the organizational changes occurring in the economic environment of agriculture.

Two ideas are perhaps central to the implications of industrialization for agriculture. One is that production of technological change has become institutionalized as a means by which private economic units, mainly large corporations, achieve their varied (not merely profit) goals; together with such basic changes as increasing affluence of consumers, technology both outside and inside agriculture virtually requires redefinition of production processes, reorganization of firms, and reorganization of relations among firms. Heavy pressures are brought to bear on agriculture to rationalize supply and to operate in the fashion of an industry.

The second idea is the declining role of markets and prices as the means of coordinating economic activities, together with the growing role of administrative devices. Once, particular production processes, or at most closely related clusters of processes, were commonly associated with individual firms, and the activities of firms were coordinated by the price system. Increasingly, however, large blocks of activities, especially those in vertical sequence, are proving to be better coordinated administratively than through the market.

Either the activities are brought under the ownership of a single firm or firms use contracts or other arrangements to tie together their activities. The scope for planning, managing, and mutually supportive investing is greatly enlarged.

The literature of such fields as agricultural marketing and industrial organization develops these points much more fully. Vertical integration in the broiler industry and specification buying of farm products, together with the pressures exerted on the organization of farming, are familiar examples.

Ideas from industrial organization economics about oligopoly and administered prices (in the sense that firms have some control of prices) remain important. But probably more significant for the organization of agriculture and the discontent of farmers are "industrialization" forces at work and the ability of large firms to give effect to them, to capitalize upon them, and sometimes to absorb, subordinate, or outcompete the family farm. The suitability of price coordination of purely competitive firms independently specializing on particular production processes as a means of organizing agriculture is called seriously into question: the instability of purely competitive markets seems excessive for industrial-age farms with high investments; the consequences of full use of fixed resources to produce surpluses when yield-increasing technology becomes available seem unnecessarily disruptive; and administrative coordination apparently is more efficient than price coordination in a growing number of agricultural subsectors.

Breimyer [33] in particular has written on the forces reorganizing agriculture and on alternative ways of preserving what he calls the sociopolitical values of a system of independent farms. "Who will control agriculture?" became a challenge and a slogan among farmers and farm cooperatives; its economic implications are discussed in [238].

The hired farm labor force is also taking on an industrial character. Minimum wages and unionization increasingly mean that the farm wage is not a passive equater of supply and demand. Farming plays a reduced role as an absorber of unskilled labor because wages are less flexible as well as because farm employment is falling and a larger portion of remaining jobs require skills. Cost rigidities for producers collectively increase as wages become more uniform and inflexible under administrative determination.

THE GENERAL MODEL IN THE EARLY 1970S

Most of the modifications and elaborations of the general model of agriculture as Schultz described it in 1945 can be incorporated without basically revising it. Precisely how all the parts fit together is sometimes not entirely clear, though in principle they seem consistent. Individual agricultural economists differ in the emphasis given to different parts of the model, and they sometimes disagree rather widely on the quantitative value of key parameters.

Tweeten [202] has questioned the validity of asset fixity and other elements of the general model. Perhaps the principal exception to wide acceptance of some version of the general model concerns "industrialization of agriculture."

Even if industrialization operates as outlined, much of the general model remains releveant, for most of agriculture still consists of independent, purely competitive firms (aside from government programs). The implications for agricultural supply, resource adjustments between farming and other sectors, and farm income remain largely valid. But new relations must be brought into the model even for current use. Reasons outside of agriculture for vertically coordinating farm and nonfarm activities, together with the possibility that this can be done better by administrative arrangements than through the price system, need to be recognized. This point also has implications for size of farm and for availability of capital for farm production.

The most important implication of the industrialization thesis relates to the use of the general model for future situations. The ideal or target state implied by the early model was an agriculture in which firms achieved full economies of size but were still numerous enough to be purely competitive; resources were used in just such quantities and mixes that unrestrained output resulted in prices that returned to factors of production in agriculture rates of earnings just equal to rates elsewhere; and the price system and resource mobility held agriculture in the ideal state or exerted a pull toward it whenever the real world went off the track. It is now doubtful whether this ideal well suggests the future organization of agriculture or is a reliable guiding star for policy analysis. The needs of an industrializing agriculture for stability and for more effective coordination both internally and with outside firms seem likely to be met in part by organizational devices common to industry. But agriculture is still so far from industrylike organization, and it is so influenced by biological and weather uncertainties, that other means will be selectively needed for a long time. Government programs and cooperative action by farmers are means already in use and are potentially subject to large modification. Conflicts about the distribution of income generated in the system are likely to become sharper as administrative devices increasingly replace pure competition among producers and in labor markets. The resource allocation criteria implied by the early model will remain relevant, but the means of allocation seem likely to include large doses of private, cooperative, and government administration.

Empirical Knowledge about Key Economic Relations

Empirical work in price analysis, farm management, agricultural marketing, and related fields has been highly useful in supplying concrete information about key relationships in the general model of the agricultural sector.

The literature of those fields is discussed in other review articles. Only a few comments on particularly important points are included here.

Research in agricultural price analysis (for example, [23, 81]) has shown that demands for most of the leading farm products, especially at the farm level of marketing, are distinctly price inelastic. Despite some conclusions to the contrary (for example, [240]), long-run demands for most products do not seem notably less price inelastic than the demands usually inferred from year-to-year changes in prices and consumption. The principal exception is that persistently high prices may stimulate development of new substitute products; specific information on this point is poor, partly because new products often grow out of technological innovations not related to price. Demand for the aggregate output of agriculture is generally considered highly price inelastic despite the growing importance of exports, for which demands are more price elastic. Tweeten [200], however, argued on the basis of highly special assumptions and data that export demand is so price elastic as to make aggregate demand slightly elastic. Income elasticities of demand for most agricultural raw materials are low, and their weighted average probably is 0.2 or less.

Information about supply elasticities is less satisfactory than for demand, in part because technological advance and effects of government programs so often obscure pure output response to price. Houck and Ryan [117] found that more than 95 percent of the variation in corn acreage after World War II was associated with policy variables. The aggregate supply function for agriculture has been especially difficult to analyze. Griliches [86] and Tweeten and Quance [207] found very low short-run aggregate elasticities. Griliches did not suceed in showing a much higher long-run elasticity, but Tweeten and Quance, in an article evoking extensive critical discussion in subsequent issues of the *American Journal of Agricultural Economics*, found long-run elasticities of 1.5 for rising prices and 0.8 for falling prices. Whether the concept of a long-run agricultural supply function is operationally meaningful in a dynamic agriculture is doubtful. Cochrane's approach (discussed earlier) may be more useful, but how much shift of the short-run supply schedule to expect in different situations remains in doubt.

An alternative method is to use linear programming to estimate profit-maximizing adjustments of output in response to price changes for different type-of-farming areas of the United States and to combine the results into regional and national supply functions. The Economic Research Service of the USDA [182] has developed a model having this capability in order "to help answer policy questions asked by the Administration and Congress." The method seems highly useful for identifying the direction of output adjustments likely to result from hypothesized external impacts, including policy revisions, on agriculture. As the model builders recognized, however, the speed of adjustment is extremely difficult to predict.

Econometric analysis of the farm labor market (for example, [172]) has found that the short-run effects of farm wages and prices on farm employment are low, and that the effect of nonfarm employment opportunities is greater. Long-run adjustment of the labor force is best viewed as a process in which the following considerations apply: (1) income improvement is a highly important but not exclusive motivation of individuals: decisions; (2) age, family responsibilities, and ownership status greatly modify individuals' alternatives; (3) education and skills, both much influenced by society's investment in people, are critical for farm-reared individuals' opportunities to better their lot; (4) racial discrimination is an obstacle to successful mobility of members of minority groups; (5) institutions of the industrial labor market obstruct the process; (6) net mobility of labor from agriculture is the result of a large outflow partly offset by a substantial backflow; and (7) much of the transfer from the farm to nonfarm sector takes place when young people decide not to follow their parents in farming. Studies by Clawson [48], Hathaway and Perkins [103], and Hendrix [111] have effectively described elements of the total process. Adjustment of the farm labor force can be speeded up or slowed down, but large changes cannot be expected in a few years, and great changes require the turnover of generations.

Production Capacity, Current and Prospective

A continuing problem for framing future farm policy has been the need to know whether agricultural capacity generally would run ahead of or behind growth of the total market. If ahead, the nation would face, in Schultz's phraseology, a *farm* problem; if behind, a *food* problem.

As has already been indicated, Schultz in his *Agriculture in an Unstable Economy* and the USDA in its series *What Peace Can Mean to American Farmers* correctly anticipated overcapacity in agriculture in the post-World War II era. Schultz expected this to be a long-lasting situation. A USDA study [221] made in 1948 at the behest of the House Committee on Agriculture projected modest increases in crop yields to 1965 (which hindsight shows were grossly underestimated) and concluded that, if the rest of the economy was prosperous, production and markets would be in balance at about parity prices. The Korean War created concern about food supplies, and a joint USDA and land-grant college report [209] estimated that under favorable circumstances for producers farm output could be increased one-fifth in five years.

Black and Bonnen [12] concluded in 1956 that "rapid advances in technology . . . promise to continue with little slackening to 1965 unless prices are reduced to levels clearly below those now politically acceptable." A number of other economic studies of differing degrees of thoroughness in the 1950s indicated that no difficulty would be met in expanding farm output to keep pace with market growth, and some suggested that less cropland would be used if surpluses were not produced. Clark [47], viewing the American scene from Oxford, disagreed; he predicted in 1954 that by 1975 the United States would be importing half the farm products it consumed.

Several projections made in the 1960s showed that excess agricultural capacity was likely in the years ahead. A USDA study by Abel and Rojko [3] and others by Heady and associates at the Center for Agricultural and Economic Development at Iowa State University (for example, [108]) concluded that excess grain acreage continued to be likely in the United States. Tweeten and Quance [206], using a simulation model, concluded that excess capacity would persist in agriculture through the 1970s if the farm program of 1969 was continued.

In making projections of output capacity, agricultural economists generally drew upon their knowledge that recent trends were largely the result of technology-producing processes not likely to be ended soon or to cease to be productive. Nevertheless, simple extrapolation played a large role. The mistaken conclusion of the study made by the USDA [221] in 1948 resulted from departing from trend projections: "But yields cannot be expected to continue at this [recent years'] rate." In 1960 USDA economists worked closely with agricultural scientists in making rationalized yield estimates for 1975 [165]; actual yields of several important crops in 1971 already exceeded by 30 to 60 percent those estimated as "economic attainable" in 1975. Until 1972 extrapolation had a better record than more reasoned approaches; and no reasoned approach predicted the tight supply situation of 1972-73, for which a demand shift was largely responsible.

Excess capacity in agriculture usually has been taken to mean approximately the amount by which production would exceed market outlets at current prices if utilization subsidies, diversion to storage, and restrictions on output were discontinued. Tyner and Tweeten [208] estimated that excess capacity ranged from about 8 to 13 percent of potential output from 1955 to 1961. If certain disposals such as P. L. 480 were considered of some value, they said, the range might be lowered to 5 to 11 percent. This was consistent with estimates made on somewhat different bases by other writers (for example, [133]). Tweeten and Quance [206] put average excess capacity at the beginning of the 1970s at 6 percent.

Excess plant capacity in manufacturing as estimated by the Federal Reserve Board ranged from 8 to 25 percent over the period 1960-71. Though the concepts are not identical, plant capacity spontaneously withheld by manufacturing industries seems to have exceeded excess agricultural capacity dealt with in one way or another by farm programs.

Parity and Income Comparisons

Policy questions have required agricultural economists to attempt to measure personal incomes and returns to classes of resources in agriculture, to compare them with analogous incomes and returns outside of agriculture, to study the personal distribution of income, and to appraise legislatively defined standards for incomes and prices. For a few years following World War II much attention was given to parity prices and parity income as officially adopted objectives of farm programs.

The parity price formula was written into the Agricultural Adjustment Act of 1933. (For the history, basic indexes, and computation of parity, see [216].) In the main, the formula defined parity prices of farm products, both individually and collectively, as prices that had changed by the same percentage since 1910-14 as had an index of prices paid by farmers (the parity index). There had been, however, some changes in product base periods and in parity index components, usually to raise computed parity prices. The report of a committee appointed by the American Farm Economic Association to study redefinition of parity prices and incomes [155] summarized economists' views in 1947 and well reflected their traumas in dealing with the parity question.

Economists maintained that prices could not both allocate resources toward efficiency norms and raise farm income. The controversy over free markets versus government programs (described later in this review) spilled over into discussions of quantifying an equity norm for agriculture. Parity price relationships, depending as they did on a period already long past, were shown to be poor guides for future production and consumption. Full parity prices were accurately foreseen as leading to unmarketable surpluses; these, in turn, would require production controls and subsidies, to which many economists were opposed.

The AFEA committee recommended abandonment of parity prices for parity income, a concept already in the law but not used to that time (or later). If parity prices were to be retained, the committee proposed that the base be moved from 1910-14 to the latest peacetime period of high employment and that relationships among parity prices for individual commodities be made to reflect market price relationships in the most recent five or ten years. Congress adopted the second suggestion — a ten-year period was used — in 1950.

During the 1950s and 1960s farm policy literature increasingly contained the idea that a suitable policy goal was rates of return on labor and investment on efficient farms that were equal to rates earned on comparable resources outside of agriculture. Economies-of-size criteria were suggested, at least implicitly, as means of identifying efficient farms. No pretense was to be made that farm price programs could solve whatever income problems operators of seriously inadequate farms might have. Masucci [145] estimated the quantities of resources used on farms in two different size ranges in 1961, applied to resources rates of return deemed representative of rates earned in comparable circumstances outside of agriculture, computed the net income farmers would need to realize such nonfarm rates of return, and compared this parity returns income with income actually received. A later study by the USDA [156] provided similar computations for 1966 but introduced certain refinements, the most important of which was consideration of capital gains within and outside of agriculture.

Results showed that in 1961 the larger farms had average net incomes modestly below the parity returns standard and that in 1966, a particularly prosperous farm year, farms with sales of $20,000 or more had average net incomes somewhat above the standard. Net farm incomes on small farms were much below the standard, which was itself low because of the small resource base. (Nonfarm income was not included; many small farmers had substantial nonfarm income.) Farm prices would have had nearly to triple in 1966 to bring net income on farms with sales of less than $5,000 up to the parity returns standard. Taking capital gains into account did not drastically change results.

The two studies indirectly demonstrated the importance of more or less arbitrary judgments about valuation of farm assets and about comparable rates of earnings that must be made for a parity returns computation. Land poses an especially difficult problem. It is commonly inventoried at current value rather than at acquisition cost to farmers. If the value of land depends on income to be earned from farming it, how can one justify using the value of land to compute an independent standard for farm income? The wide range of choices to be made in calculations leaves much room for disagreement about whether or not any standard is fair.

Two studies [74, 156] of parity standards for different types of farming showed that one type may be much closer than another to attaining its standard in the same year, even if the commodities produced are much the same. Problems of translating a parity *returns* standard into a parity *price* standard for price support purposes are formidable.

The purchasing power of a dollar of net farm income may not be entirely comparable with that of a dollar of income received by nonfarmers because home-produced food consumed by farmers is valued at farm rather than retail prices, prices of goods and services are not necessarily the same in farm and urban areas, and for other reasons. Estimates made by Koffsky, Puterbaugh, and Hathaway (summarized by Hathaway [102]), indicate that the purchasing powers of farm and urban dollars tended to converge from 1941 to the late 1950s and that in 1959 the purchasing power of the farm dollar in consumption was about 6 percent greater than that of the urban dollar. More recently, the much reduced importance of home-produced food in farm consumption and the lower supply and sometimes inferior quality of social services in farm areas have led to the frequent conclusion that the purchasing power of income is about the same in farm and urban areas.

Age, sex, education, and similar characteristics of the farm labor force would result in a lower average rate of labor earnings in farming than in manufacturing even if labor of comparable earning power received the same reward in both sectors. D. G. Johnson [124] was the first to demonstrate this. A calculation taking into account three such factors was made for 1959 in connection with the resource-parity study by the Economic Research Service [156]. Various classes of farm labor were given the following ratings (ratios of labor earning power) in comparison with manufacturing workers: operators of large farms, 1.06; operators of small farms, 0.82; unpaid family workers, 0.73; and hired farm workers, 0.70.

Values, Beliefs, and Goals

The values and beliefs of farmers have much influenced American farm policy. Agricultural fundamentalism was strong throughout the history of the country, but it has declined in the decades following World War II. In its pure form, agricultural fundamentalism has strong religious, political, and economic components: as tillers of the soil who are close to nature, farmers are "the chosen people of God" (Jefferson) and provide the moral fiber of the nation; independent farmers are the bastion of democracy and the one true defense against tyranny; and as most wealth originates on the farm, the prosperity of farmers determines the prosperity of the nation. Papers by Fite [68] and Hadwiger[90] treated the subject at length and showed why in the 1950s and 1960s fundamentalism had little appeal to social scientists. Griswold [87] examined agricultural fundamentalism historically and in several countries; his findings amounted to a sympathetic deflation of its claims.

An analysis by Brewster [35] was particularly relevant to farm policy issues. He saw farmers in the era following World War II as torn by deeply held values and beliefs that had been well suited to agriculture as it had developed in the United States but were not consistent with rapid technological advance. The work ethic of this value-belief system gave the farmer a feeling of merit from his own industriousness; it offered justice in that men were believed to be duly rewarded for their efforts; and it promised that all might fulfill their ambitions. The democratic creed asserted the equal worth of all men and denied the right of any to have dictatorial power over others. The enterprise creed held that proprietors deserved full control of their businesses, free of government intervention. In an expanding America the family farm had been an efficient production unit, land had been plentiful, laissez-faire was an effective means of organizing agriculture, and both personal and national goals were well served by policy and conduct consistent with the dominant value-belief system.

But dramatic output-increasing technology in agriculture drove a wedge into the system. Technology's ability to increase production fitted well with the farmer's work ethic. When enlarged output pressed upon limited markets, however, the rewards were negative, not positive. "But, even though he may thus live under the very crack of doom, no article of faith is more deep seated than his unquestioning identification of technical advance with progress. Though it slay him, yet will he trust it." Should the farmer accept government programs to control output or support price? The enterprise creed said no.

Brewster's analysis captured much of the underlying explanation for farmers' political attitudes and their frustration with farm policy issues. It could have been expanded to other issues appearing to require a growing role for government. Disunity among farm groups grew after 1950 as the once dominant value-belief system broke down and farmers aligned themselves with different political-economic approaches to the farm problem.

Attitudes toward specific policy proposals may be determined by opinions of persons or organizations with whom the proposals originate, as Hathaway and Witt [104] found in a Michigan study at the time the Brannan Plan was an issue. The farmers who were interviewed were not well informed about direct payments but were not particularly hostile to the idea; they did, however, oppose by seven to one the Brannan Plan when it was identified by name (its principal novelty was direct payments).

Two collections of papers [41, 42] provide a sample of other views on policy and goals of agricultural economists. The topics on which goals have most frequently been formulated are (1) the responsibility of agriculture to produce an abundance of food and fiber for other sectors of society, (2) the income to which farmers are entitled in return, (3) farmers' preference for freedom of decision in operating their farms, (4) the desire for stability, (5) preservation of the family farm and the number of farmers, and (6) consistency of farm policy with other economic policy (for example, in international trade). Rarely have the statements of goals by economists included the situation of hired farm workers.

Economists have repeatedly said that farm policy goals conflict and that compromises must be made. The conflict arises not in the sense that high farm incomes, economic freedom, and other goals are mutually exclusive but in the sense that they cannot be achieved simultaneously under the circumstances often prevailing in agriculture. Hathaway [98] argued that most people do not have discrete priorities for individual goals (or values); rather substitution is rationally made at the margin — a little freedom may be given up for a little income — and maximization of satisfaction means getting on the highest iso-utility surface attainable under the constraints imposed by circumstances at the time. Cast in these terms, the obstacle to reaching consensus on policy goals is that different individuals have much different preference maps and have different degrees of knowledge (none perfect) about the possibilities available to them collectively.

The Politics of Farm Policy

The politics of farm policy is really too important to receive only the token treatment accorded it here. It is a difficult topic to discuss briefly, and much of what might be said belongs more to the field of political science than to agricultural economics. Extensive and fairly recent studies are provided by Talbot and Hadwiger [195] and Hardin [97], all political scientists who have given substantial attention to agricultural policy.

Much of what could be said about the politics of farm policy describes the workings of the American political system as it relates to a particular economic group. Farmers have their organizations and pressure groups (more divided than is usually the case), their strongholds in Congress, their contacts with administrative agencies, their political party affiliations, and their ways of influencing policy decisions. The great decline in the proportion of farmers in the total population and election reform giving the rural and city voter equal influence in electing legislators have much diminished farmers' political power. Significant power remains, nevertheless. Related groups such as the agricultural processing and supply industries exercise considerable influence on farm policy, but the general public is usually apathetic, poorly informed, and reacts to initiatives taken by interest groups instead of originating policy.

Is the USDA too politically vulnerable to permit it to do objective policy analysis of controversial issues involving deeply held values and beliefs of agricultural groups? The question was raised by the experience of the Bureau of Agricultural Economics from 1938 to its dissolution in 1953. Its economic investigations touched upon program objectives, commodity interests, and social conditions in ways that aroused the animosity of certain farm organizations, members of Congress, and rival parts of the bureaucracy. Hardin [96] examined a portion of this experience in a classic article. Later,

Cochrane [54] contended that evaluative policy research and policy education could best be done in the universities, in part because of its political vulnerability in a government agency.

Often the power structure centered around commercial agriculture has been lukewarm or even hostile to the development of policy to deal with rural poverty or with stimulation of nonfarm economic activities in rural areas. The research and education system of the land-grant colleges and the USDA has always received its principal political support from the agricultural power structure; but tensions grew within the system and between it and its political base as the dominance of commercial agriculture ebbed. In a slashing article Bonnen [15] attacked the failure of the agricultural establishment as he defined it to recognize the need for multiple goals and to adjust its policies to changing times. In a similar vein, Soth [192] called for acknowledgment that the day of agrarianism had ended.

Much farm legislation has been enacted in an ad hoc way with regard mainly for short-run results, with emphasis on particular commodities and corresponding neglect of aggregate problems, and with high vulnerability to doctoring in favor of special groups. One means proposed to bring greater rationality to the process has been an agricultural board having something of the quasi-independent status of the Federal Reserve Board. Tweeten endorsed the idea in his textbook [201, p. 355]; Hathaway opposed it in his [102, pp. 207-208].

Policy Issues and Proposals

Much of the economics literature on farm price and income policy deals with normative questions about what the nation's policy should be. This section contains a review of economists' proposals concerning farm policy and a very sketchy indication of the course that policy actually took. Analyses of the effects of particular types of programs will be examined in the next section.

Histories of Commercial Farm Policy

Though the substantive ideas in this section are presented chronologically, the section is not a history of farm policy. The most comprehensive history is Benedict's [9], which describes policy development over a broad front up to 1950. Another book by Benedict [8] deals with farm programs in a general way, and one by Benedict and Stine [10] concentrates on details of commodity programs; the coverage in both books terminates in the early 1950s. Short reviews of farm programs to the middle or late 1960s have been provided by Rasmussen and Baker [160] and Tweeten [201, pp. 300-321]. Hadwiger [91] made an intensive study of wheat programs to the late 1960s, and numerous articles give short sketches of particular programs. No comprehensive history taking up where Benedict's left off had been written as the 1970s began.

Evaluations and Proposals, 1945-50

THE GENERAL POSITION

As World War II drew to a close, both the central body of standard economic theory and the traditional economic policy of the nation emphasized free markets as the means of allocating resources and distributing income, and to this position most economists subscribed. Particularly among agricultural economists, however, experience with depression and droughts in the 1930s had created a common belief that a wholly free market policy would be defective in ways that required supplementary action by government. Departure from strictly laissez-faire views was also stimulated by observation of obstacles to resource mobility that helped to keep the agricultural sector chronically out of equilibrium both internally and with the rest of the economy.

The principal shortcomings of wholly free markets explicitly identified or implied in the writings of a number of agricultural economists were the following: (1) the industrial economy was subject to depressions that bore harshly upon farmers; (2) the need to adjust some portions of agriculture (for example, southern cotton and Great Plains wheat) and to correct the problem of inefficiently small farms was so formidable as to require government assistance; (3) price uncertainty inhibited optimal allocation of resources; (4) agriculture tended to be excessively unstable because of weather, production cycles, and other reasons not related to industrial instability; (5) even in a high-employment economy, but especially in depression, there were socially significant needs for food that were not adequately expressed through market demand; and (6) labor mobility out of agriculture was much impeded by lack of skills and job information and by frequent unemployment in industry. These views typically led to recommendations that reflected a strong loyalty to the free market yet proposed supplementary measures to improve its performance.

A poll of members of the American Farm Economic Association in 1945 [4] showed that 40 percent favored government price support or payments to prevent sudden changes in farm income but not gradual changes. Another 37 percent favored support of farm income in depression but no intervention at other times. About one-fifth (19 percent) favored wholly free markets, and very few members (4 percent) favored aggressive programs to achieve 90 percent of parity prices. The eighteen winning papers on policy in a contest sponsored by the association in 1945 [153, 159] all proposed at least some modification of free markets. The AFEA commitee on parity

[155] took a strong free market stand in 1947 but endorsed payments to farmers in depressions

Policy statements influenced by agricultural economists is the mid-1940s included a report [7] by the Committee on Agricultural Policy of the Association of Land-Grant Colleges and Universities in 1944. The report was strongly free-market oriented yet said that "the right mixture of freedom and control is needed." This report endorsed payments to farmers in times of severe depression, aid for production adjustments in problem areas of the country, and a long list of measures to improve social and living conditions for rural people. The USDA's *What Peace Can Mean to American Farmers* [220] was more specific and ambitious in suggesting ways to adjust agriculture in problem areas, and it admitted the feasibility of short-term price supports; but it argued for direct payments to farmers during depression and for food consumption subsidies as alternatives to supports. It, too, supported social services for farm people.

PAYMENTS DURING DEPRESSION

Proposals by D. G. Johnson, W. H. Nicholls, and others to make direct payments to farmers in time of depression appeared in [159]. Schultz [174] proposed compensatory payments to make up the difference between actual farm prices and perhaps 85 percent of predepression prices. Payments were expected to have little effect on resource allocation, would require no storage, and would not be conditional on farmers' compliance with any form of production control.

Norton and Working [154], as well as some of the winners in the AFEA policy contest, favored payments tied to farmers' incomes rather than to prices, mainly because compensatory price payments were considered capable of distorting the farm output mix. In the Norton and Working proposal, payments were to be a percentage of each farmer's sales less purchases of feed and livestock. The years in which payments were to be made and the amounts of the payments were to depend on the relationship of farm to nonfarm income rather than on industrial employment.

Several proponents of direct payments appealed to the ideas of Keynes' *General Theory*, published a decade earlier, to argue that payments to farmers would be countercyclical and thus stabilizing to the general economy. Later, the argument lost most of its force as fear of another major depression waned and as changes in net farm income were seen to have little positive correlation with minor business cycles.

AGRICULTURAL ADJUSTMENTS

The USDA's *What Peace Can Mean to American Farmers* [220] proposed a six-point program to convert certain southern and Great Plains areas to a more viable agriculture and to remedy the problem of inefficiently small farms. Competitive prices were to replace price supports in order to encourage resource shifts in the right directions; gradually declining payments were to be available to farmers for a limited time to cushion shifts from supported to competitive prices; supervised loans were to be made to some operators of small farms to build up their businesses; payments would also assist farmers to convert to other types of agriculture; assistance for soil and water conservation was to be provided; and retraining and job information were to be given to farm people wishing to leave agriculture. Most of the suggestions made by economists regarding agricultural adjustment following World War II were touched upon in one form or another in this publication.

J. D. Black was a leading advocate of extensive farm adjustment. He proposed [13] that payments due to farmers under an income support program be made in the form of assistance for carrying out farm and home plans that all farmers would be required to develop. The *Journal of Farm Economics* published numerous papers in the 1940s on research, extension, and policy aspects of agricultural adjustment.

UNCERTAINTY AND MISALLOCATION OF RESOURCES

T. W. Schultz, his close associates, and several other economists argued for "forward pricing" to reduce uncertainty and thereby to increase agricultural efficiency. This proposal, most fully developed by D. G. Johnson [123], called for government to announce expected equilibrium prices in advance of planting or breeding dates and to ensure that farmers received those prices, or a close approximation to them, at the time of marketing. Though the government might use a price support and storage program to make price guarantees for storable products effective, the preferred device was to make compensatory payments to farmers whenever market prices turned out to be significantly below the forward prices.

That fourteen of the eighteen winners in the AFEA's policy contest [153] favored some form of forward pricing was evidence of the proposals's attractiveness to agricultural economists in the mid-1940s. Advocacy of forward pricing ebbed as questions arose concerning (1) the government's ability to predict equilibrium prices, (2) the relative importance of the misallocation problems that forward pricing might remedy, and (3) the vulnerability of such a program to perversion to high-level price support. In 1957 D. G. Johnson [122] commented, "I am not now convinced that the American political system provides a setting that would permit forward prices to function in a manner that would reduce uncertainty without also being used as a means of raising the general level of farm prices." Announcement of support prices in advance of planting dates or marketing years became common practice under farm programs, but the prices were not expected equilibrium prices.

INSTABILITY FROM WEATHER, CYCLES

Forward prices were expected to stabilize farmers' realized prices (market prices plus payments) and output in addition to reducing uncertainty. Storage programs, usually accompanied by commodity loans, were favored by a majority of the AFEA policy contest winners [153] as a means of stabilizing supplies and prices. Proposals typically were aimed at stabilization rather than long-term price enhancement and were seldom tied to fixed percentages of parity. Farm and political leaders, however, frequently used "stabilization" to mean steady prices well above levels likely to prevail in free markets. As with forward pricing, perversion of stabilization programs to income support programs appeared to require only a short step.

FOOD CONSUMPTION SUBSIDIES

In the 1930s the presence of food surpluses on the one hand and obvious nutritional needs on the other had led to domestic food consumption programs, principally the food stamp plan, school lunches, and direct distribution to the poor. A majority of winners in the AFEA's policy contest [153] and the USDA's *What Peace Can Mean to American Farmers* [220] proposed consumption subsidies. The most popoular version of the food stamp plan provided for selling sufficient food purchase coupons for an adequate diet to poor families for a fixed percentage of their income [52, 170] ; the subsidy to the poorest families would be substantial, but the not-so-poor would find the program unattractive. J. D. Black and M. E. Kiefer [13] advocated a variety of nutritional programs ranging from improved diets for infants to in-plant feeding of industrial employees.

The potential for increasing demand for food through consumption subsidies was generally thought to be substantial. Meats, poultry, eggs, and dairy products then had comparatively high income elasticities of demand and were deemed to upgrade the nutritional quality of diets. Such products were high-resource-using foods and would increase utilization of agriculture's production capacity even if the consumption of calories did not rise. Factors leading later to declining per capita consumption of eggs, several dairy products, and fatty meats were not foreseen.

INCREASING LABOR MOBILITY

Better education for rural people was strongly emphasized in policy recommendations as a means of facilitating the shift from farm to nonfarm occupations as well as a valued end in itself. The land-grant policy report [7] candidly described the frequently squalid conditions and inadequate curricula of rural schools, the low-paid and poorly trained teachers, and the lack of financial support. Arguing that many rural areas were not able to afford good schools, the report recommended increased state aid and — when the idea was still anathema in many rural areas — federal aid for education. The USDA's *What Peace Can Mean to American Farmers* [220] took a similar position. Schultz [174] argued that education was an investment in people, increasing their productivity and mobility, and that the nation as a whole had an interest in and a responsibility for financing it. He particularly emphasized the need for preparing farm youth for nonfarm occupations.

Proposals for more directly facilitating labor mobility included a national job information service [159, 174]. Vocational training for displaced farm workers, location of new jobs for them, and payment of their transportation expenses also were recommended [159]. Later emphasis on rural development was foreshadowed by proposals by D. G. Johnson and W. H. Nicholls [159] for industrialization of depressed rural areas. Elimination of barriers to entry in nonfarm employment received some attention [159].

ADDITIONAL COMMENTS

Virtually all economists taking one or more of the positions discussed here rejected fixed percentages of parity prices as policy goals or guides. When some sort of price standard was needed, predepression prices, projected equilibrium prices, recent moving averages, a wide range of percentages of parity, or complete administrative discretion was suggested as a more flexible alternative. There was strong insistence on keeping prices near the path they would follow if high employment prevailed in industry and if weather and other short-term disturbances did not affect agriculture.

Individual economists emphasized particular combinations of the approaches considered in this section. W. O. Jones [134] identified a group of economists who tended to approach policy analysis in a particular way and who came to similar policy conclusions; this group, which he called the Schultzians, included T. W. Schultz, D. G. Johnson, W. H. Nicholls, O. H. Brownlee, and R. Schickele. A group in the USDA Bureau of Agricultural Economics largely responsible for the ideas in *What Peace Can Mean to American Farmers* [217-220] owed much to the leadership of H. R. Tolley and included, among others, B. W. Allin, W. W. Cochrane, J. G. Maddox, O. C. Stine, and O. V. Wells; J. D. Black in his pragmatic way worked closely with the Tolley group, S. E. Johnson, J. P. Cavin, and others in the USDA.

Widening Differences during the 1950s

DECLINING CONFIDENCE IN THE SUFFICIENCY OF PROPOSALS OF THE 1940s

Economists' proposals for aid to agriculture in depression, for ways of hastening agricultural adjustment, and for stabilizing farm income without raising it did not square well with the desires of the large body of farmers who wanted to stay in agriculture and to be prosperous there. The sharp decline of farm prices in the late 1940s increased farmers' concern about income support, a concern only temporarily abated by price inflation during the Korean War. The concern was fully reflected if not exaggerated by numerous farm leaders and political representatives from farm areas. The policy questions presented through the political process for resolution were not, in the main, those for which positive policy recommendations were being made by economists.

Three papers given at a symposium in 1952 expressed divergent opinions about how economists might deal with such a situation. Waugh [229] argued that public acceptability was a warranted requisite of policy proposals in a democratic society and that economists should not ignore equity issues involved in the farm policy controversy. Jesness [120] may be interpreted as arguing that participants in the policy debate did not fully understand — or were willing to ignore — the consequences of their proposals and that economists, with their greater insight, might well reject popular demands outright. Schultz [179] emphasized his own valuation of what was important: poverty was the significant equity question, and many farmers were not in poverty. Holding such divergent views and facing the fact that income support for farmers collectively was the main policy issue, economists took different positions on policy questions.

The decline in the importance of industrial depression as a source of farm difficulties and the impressive onrush of agricultural technology caused some reevaluation of farm policy positions common at the close of World War II. In a review of *Agriculture in an Unstable Economy* Davis [59] argued that Schultz had overstated both low earnings in agriculture and the severity of the pressures on farmers to be expected in the future, but, Davis commented ". . . it is gravely to be doubted whether the maximum progress along these lines [Schultz's proposals to increase labor mobility] can possibly solve the problems of underemployment and low earnings in agriculture, if these are of the magnitude that Schultz envisages." When events demonstrated that the burden placed on labor mobility by advancing farm technology had by no means been overstated, many agricultural economists (though not Schultz or Davis) gave greater attention to measures to support farm income.

Food consumption subsidies for the poor, relied upon by some economists in the 1940s as a means of disposing of surpluses, appeared less likely to be sufficient to absorb food surpluses as agriculture's production capacity grew [231]. Though interest among agricultural economists in food subsidies continued because of their potential significance to the poor, some consumption subsidy advocates turned to additional measures to support farm income.

THE FREE MARKET POSITION

Despite growing reservations, the mainstream of thought among agricultural economists in the early 1950s continued to oppose lasting farm income subsidies, support of prices above free market levels, production control, and export subsidies. General (that is, not agricultural) economists who occasionally interested themselves in farm policy were even more likely to be purists in their allegiance to strictly market solutions. It is barely a caricature of much respectable economic thought in the early 1950s to say that resource allocation was held to be the overwhelmingly important test of farm policy, that allocation problems were viewed within the framework of static models, that free market prices were considered to be virtually identical with good resource allocation, and that if any trade-offs with progressiveness or equity were recognized, the conflicts were to be resolved in favor of resource allocation.

In 1954 Galbraith [76] made the (for him) unlikely error of not going far enough in criticizing conventional thought but then may have overcorrected in a scathing commentary on agricultural economists' approach to policy issues [80]. *Turning the Searchlight on Farm Policy* [63], prepared by a committee of agricultural economists in 1952, became a symbol of conservative policy recommendations. It held that the outlook for American agriculture was "basically strong." Proposals "for a prosperous American agriculture that is sound in its basic fundamentals and consistent with the principles of maximum individual freedom" included direct payments to farmers in the event of severe depression, abandonment of price supports, no government storage except perhaps in depression and for military stockpiling, full development of educational and advisory services to help farmers make informed choices, and unspecified programs for noncommercial farmers.

High hopes were held by a few agricultural economists and numerous businessmen and politicians that promotion of farm products or development of new industrial uses would solve the excess capacity problem in agriculture within the framework of traditional free market operations. DeGraff [60] argued that a modest increase in consumption of livestock products would be adequate and could be achieved by promotion. McMillen [149] explained the "chemurgy" idea and urged that research on new industrial uses of farm products be increased. A common opinion among agricultural economists was that the science of chemistry was doing more to develop substitutes for farm products than to find new uses and that the high cost of basic compounds contained in farm products made this trend likely to continue.

DIRECT PAYMENTS FOR INCOME SUPPORT

Secretary of Agriculture C. F. Brannan [46] proposed in 1949 a new set of farm programs that gave direct payments a prominent role in supporting farm income year in and out. The plan (1) substituted a new parity formula for the old one, (2) set price targets generally higher than 90 percent of the old parity, (3) provided for price supports and output restrictions on leading storable crops, (4) called for direct payments on livestock products whenever their prices fell below target prices, (5) suggested that marketing quotas on livestock products might later prove desirable, and (6) limited the amount of payments a single producer might receive.

The proposed role for direct payments was a sharp departure from use only in depression or to effectuate forward pricing. Numerous economists who favored payments for the latter purposes opposed Brannan's proposed use of them. Several other economists willing to see payments used for continuing income support believed that the price targets were too high or that the plan would in practice restrict output and have little of the argued advantage of permitting a full flow of food to consumers at modest prices. Some economists supported the plan. The controversy well demonstrated that a tag such as "direct payments" is an insufficient basis upon which to identify and evaluate a program.

The Brannan plan failed to win congressional approval, but economists' proposals to support farm income with direct payments became more frequent. The Norton-Working type of proposal had preceded the Brannan plan.[1] Galbraith [77] argued in 1955 for direct payments with no price support or production control. Brandow [25] proposed that direct payments be made on a base amount of each farmer's output to support income but that marginal amounts of output be sold for market prices in order to promote resource allocation; he developed a more elaborate version of this proposal later [21]. Several proposals for direct payments included limitation on amounts going to individual producers.

PRICE SUPPORT AND SUPPLY CONTROL

As early as the Agricultural Adjustment Act of 1938 the idea of flexible price supports had been introduced into legislation. "Flexible" in this context meant that the support price for a crop was to be raised according to a prescribed formula when the supply was below normal and was to be reduced when the supply was above normal. Flexible supports had been written into the acts of 1948 and 1949 but had been superseded by other provisions of law [9, pp. 474-482]. Flexible supports became identified with groups favoring substantial reliance upon the market for resource allocation and income distribution, whereas the Brannan plan or supports at 90 percent of parity were favored by groups hoping to do more for farmers. From 1953 to 1960 flexible supports at low average levels were endorsed by Secretary of Agriculture Ezra Benson in his unflagging efforts to move toward a free market policy; basing price support on the average of recent market prices was also favored by Benson [11, pp. 184-201].

Prices of several leading crops and of dairy products were supported at higher than free market levels from the late 1940s to the 1970s except during the Korean War inflation. Stocks accumulated rapidly after 1952. Acreage restraints in use before 1956 either had little effect on output or merely shifted acreage from controlled to uncontrolled crops. The Agricultural Trade Development and Assistance Act of 1954 (P. L. 480) opened the way for large exports of agricultural products outside of commercial trade channels to poor countries under highly concessional terms.[2] Such exports may have kept the price support program from breaking down completely in the late 1950s, but they did not prevent stock accumulation.

Effective production control obviously was one approach to the farm policy dilemma. The Soil Bank program of 1956-58 experimented gingerly with payments to farmers to remove cropland entirely from production in order to avoid chasing surpluses from crop to crop. Bottum [16, 17] analyzed the cost and the expected results of different forms of land retirement in return for government payments and urged that policy move in that direction. Alternatives included (1) annual contracts for withdrawing from all production a portion of the crop acreage on participating farms, (2) annual contracts for diverting acreage from row crops to grass, and (3) long-term retirement of all cropland completely from production.

Cochrane [51] characterized the economic processes at work in farming as the agricultural treadmill — farmers adopted new technology in order to reduce unit production costs, but the resulting increase in total output forced prices and incomes down in highly competitive markets with inelastic demands; the farmers ran hard but went nowhere. He proposed comprehensive supply control to apply to substantially all of agriculture in order to attain fair prices (not necessarily parity prices) as defined by Congress [53]. Negotiable quotas on farmers' marketings were to be the principal administrative device. Much of the discussion among agricultural economists about the farm situation and supply control at the end of the 1950s centered on Cochrane's diagnosis and prescription.

MARKETING ORDERS

An important but rather detached component of policy from the mid-1930s onward consisted of marketing orders and agreements (the latter of only minor significance). Orders were authorized under federal and state legislation for certain commodities, mainly fruits, vegetables, and milk for fresh consumption. When approved by farmers, the orders applied to particular production areas or (for milk) to market areas rather than to the whole nation. In general, they were designed to increase producers' returns from sales by such means as grade and size regulation, smoothing the geographic and temporal flow of products to market, diversion of supplies to secondary uses, and (for milk eligible for fresh use) minimum producer prices. Usually their essential function, one that farmers' associations could seldom perform, was to apply measures of the type described to *all* handlers and producers in the relevant geographic area. The orders were (and are) government operated, but producers had substantial influence on them.

Marketing orders were the keystone for pricing milk eligible for fresh consumption from the mid-1930s onward. The work of dairy economists on the topic has been far too extensive to review here. Numerous economists regarded milk orders as important, even essential, for stability in milk markets. A smaller number favored their use to raise the average level of producers' returns. The proponents of orders for other commodities usually regarded orders as capable of increasing price stability and modestly raising producers' returns under some circumstances.

Marketing orders are closely related to the farmers' bargaining power issue because they provide areawide powers that producers' associations often cannot attain. Usually, economists have considered the marketing order approach as inadequate for dealing with such problems as excess national capacity for field crop production.

An Approximate Policy Equilibrium Emerging in the 1960s

THE EARLY 1960S

The high visibility of rising surplus stocks and government costs was forcing a change in farm policy as the 1960s began. Economists' work, of both positive and normative types, was perhaps more directly relevant to current policy decisions in the early and mid-1960s than in any other similar period.

A series of studies of the short-run effects of going entirely or nearly to a free market policy (to be discussed further in the next section of this review) showed that the immediate consequences for farmers would be severe. The Iowa State University Center for Agricultural and Economic Development, under the directorship of E. O. Heady, began publication of a series of studies of policy alternatives (for example, [43]); the series was still being continued in 1972 [108] . The Economic Research Service, a newly organized version of the old Bureau of Agricultural Economics, increased the USDA's output of policy analyses (several of these are cited in the next section). Economists outside these groups remained active in the ongoing policy debate. In 1967, the National Advisory Commission on Food and Fiber issued a report [151] containing majority and minority recommendations and a staff analysis of farm economic problems, together with several technical studies.

As before, policy recommendations pointed in widely different directions. Proposals for return to an essentially free market for farm products after a transitional period of five or more years were made by the Committee for Economic Development [55], by Houthakker [118], and by the minority group of the National Advisory Commission on Food and Fiber [151]. Declining direct payments not tied to farmers' current production (in order not to inhibit farm adjustments) were suggested to cushion the change from supported to free markets. Assistance for farm adjustments was advocated. The Committee for Economic Development especially emphasized measures to upgrade human skills and to increase labor mobility.

The administration elected in 1960 tried to swing farm policy toward comprehensive supply control of the Cochrane type, but Congress would not agree. The feed grain program initiated in 1961 relied upon annual retirement of a portion of the feed grain acreage on participating farms in return for a government payment (voluntary acreage control). A referendum among wheat growers in 1963 rejected compulsory acreage control and was followed by enactment of a voluntary acreage control program for wheat. The Food and Agriculture Act of 1965 combined the basic elements of the two programs with a similar one for cotton. Price supports on feed grains and cotton had been lowered sufficiently so that no export subsidy was required, and only a small export subsidy was needed on wheat. High payment rates on cotton and wheat supported growers' income despite lower prices. Production control under the modified programs of the 1960s reduced stocks generally to levels bearing some relation to stabilization requirements. Dairy supports continued. The 1965 act struck a balance of economic and political pressures bearing on farm policy, and policy became more settled than at any time since World War II.

FARMER BARGAINING POWER

An old but intensified issue, the bargaining power of farmers, received considerable attention from agricultural economists in the 1960s. Farmers had long sought to improve their incomes through cooperatives. The Sapiro movement of the 1920s [9, pp. 194-198] aimed at sufficient market control by large cooperatives to control marketing and prices. In the late 1950s and in the 1960s farmers were again strongly attracted by the idea of collective bargaining to increase their economic returns independently of government intervention. Roy [166] described the status of farm bargaining at the close of the 1960s.

Most agricultural economists' writing on collective bargaining for farmers has been descriptive or analytical rather than strongly advocative. The need for supply control and the apparent difficulty of voluntary farm organizations in exercising it frequently led to deflation of farmers' more glowing expectations. Examples may be found in [211]. Proposals for legislation conferring exclusive bargaining rights and authority to control supply upon farm organizations originated mainly with farm and political leaders. Economists taking a strong stand in favor of bargaining often were commodity specialists, especially in dairy marketing. An article by S. Johnson [131] provides an example, but frequently the work of this group was presented in reports or conference papers not part of the readily available literature. Fuller [71], among others, emphasized the importance of nonprice terms of sale, fringe benefits, and farmers' sense of self-reliance as potential benefits of collective bargaining.

SUBSIDING INTEREST IN FARM POLICY

The activity of agricultural economists in the area of farm policy declined in the late 1960s and the early 1970s. The set of programs largely incorporated in the Food and Agriculture Act of 1965 and continued without major change in 1970 was working well enough to reduce political pressure on farm policy. Growing concern about rural development, and in less degree rural poverty, attracted an enlarged proportion of research and educational resources. Environmental protection was a new field of substantial importance to agriculture and rural areas. The dramatic change from agricultural surpluses to shortages in 1972-73 drew attention once again to commercial farm policy, but the problems as then presented were much different from those of the preceding twenty-five years.

Farm Policy Analysis

This section is focused upon literature presenting analyses of the expected or observed effects of alternative farm policies. Particular types of programs are discussed one by one to show their effects on prices, production, product utilization, farm income, and related variables of interest to groups immediately involved in policy. Broader consequences such as those for economic efficiency and personal distribution of income are considered following the program-by-program review.

The Free Market

The first part of this paper, with its description of the economic model of agriculture and its brief comments on the quantitative values of key economic relations within the system, outlined in general terms how a free market for agriculture might have been expected to work during the period under review. Since government intervention was extensive, actual experience could not demonstrate the exact consequences of a free market policy. Neither was it possible to estimate the consequences with sufficient reliability to force consensus among economists whose judgments in the realms of both positive and normative economics otherwise would lead to disagreement on several issues.

One question on which methodology was sufficiently good to produce wide if not complete agreement was the short-term impact of abandoning programs in effect from the late 1950s to the early 1970s. Wilcox [236] estimated in 1958 that farm programs had accounted for one-fourth to one-half of net farm income. Beginning in 1960, several elaborate projections were made to show short-range results to be expected from a return to free markets. The usual assumption was that farmers would use available family labor, equipment, and land to the full, that variable inputs such as fertilizer would not be greatly reduced, that production methods would continue to be improved, and that market supplies of farm products would increase as production controls and diversions of products from commercial markets were dropped. Prices would fall to clear unsubsidized markets.

Five such studies [164, 187, 203, 224, 233] made in the early 1960s produced fairly consistent results when differences in assumptions about programs not eliminated were taken into account. The median projections of percentage changes from earlier levels are listed in the tabulation on the next page.

By implication, at least, the studies indicated that net incomes from field crop production would be hit harder than net incomes from livestock and poultry production. Later studies, including several projections made by E. O. Heady and associates at Iowa State University, were generally consistent with these results, although the reduction of price support levels and the rising use of direct payments of the 1960s altered the way in which termination of farm programs would affect net farm income.

Long-run consequences of a free market policy were not nearly so well agreed upon. Most economists making short-run projections thought that over a longer period production would be negatively affected by low prices

Prices:	*Percentage Change*
Corn	−25
Wheat	−50
Cotton	−27[a]
Hogs	−19
Beef cattle	−34
All farm products	−17[b]
Gross farm income	−7.5[a]
Production expenses	+ 5
Net income	−37

[a]Based on four studies reporting the figure.
[b]Change in farm prices of foods given in [224].

and incomes and that some recovery of prices and farm income would be expected. In a book reflecting much of the work on farm program alternatives at the Iowa State Center [108], Heady, Mayer, and Madsen made both short-run and long-run projections for a free market and compared them with the actual situation in 1967. Corn prices were expected to drop 33 percent in the short run but only 7 percent in the long run; the corresponding percentage changes for wheat prices were 39 and 12 and those for net farm income were 32 and 23. Loss of government payments was an important reason for the decline in net farm income.

Price Support

Separation of price support from several other programs is somewhat artificial, for price support usually must be accompanied by storage, production control, or disposal programs. Discussions of other programs and of combinations of programs follow this section on price support.

Price support at above the free market level increases gross and net farm income if the real support price can be maintained without production control. Support creates incentives for increased production and reduced utilization; information on supply and demand behavior, already reviewed, is highly relevant to the expected magnitude and timing of such response.

Added to the usual tendency of high prices to stimulate production sooner or later is the reduction of uncertainty resulting from support promised for the future. G. L. Johnson [126] concluded in 1952 that reduced uncertainty as a result of price support for burley tobacco led farmers to increase per-acre yields, though no way of distinguishing between the effects of increased certainty and of new technology was available. Gray, Sorenson, and Cochrane [84] found that (1) yields of potatoes increased in states not specializing in potato production under price support in the 1940s (though the trend of yields in specializing states was not altered), (2) price support encouraged specialization in potato production, and (3) price support eliminated a tendency toward cyclical potato production.

Farm policy literature, especially that published before 1960, abounds with conclusions, apparently taken to be self-evident, that price support leads to misallocation of resources and to reduction of welfare. Peterson's *The Great Farm Problem* [157] provides an extreme example. Such conclusions seem obvious to an economist who thinks in terms only of the perfect competition model, believes that free markets closely correspond to it, and accepts the resource endowments that underlie personal income distribution and market demands. But agriculture has been in chronic disequilibrium because of external forces acting upon it, modification of free market prices may have minor effects at most on basic long-run adjustments of resources, benefits of technology are often negative for producers, and opinions about the proper personal distribution of income are value judgments. Moreover, resource allocation and product utilization may be powerfully affected by production control or disposal programs associated with supports. Though price support raises extremely important questions about economic efficiency and equity, the questions are not answered simply by appeal to an unverified model; they must be answered by analysis of actual situations.

The most common device for supporting prices has been nonrecourse loans. Market prices can drop somewhat below loan levels, especially at harvest time, even when all producers are eligible for loans. Another support device, unlimited government purchases, has been effective for manufactured dairy products. Since outright waste is unacceptable, perishable products can feasibly be price supported only if they are first made storable by processing. The higher price of processed goods adds to the government's investment in price support stocks and often to its program losses.

Any loan program must establish an intricate system of loan values of different classes and qualities of product in different locations. Especially in cotton [67] the use of too narrow a range of premiums and discounts has at times caused government accumulation of less desirable qualities. Support of grain prices led to an enormous expansion of grain storage facilities in the 1950s. The government's participation in markets has affected the handling and processing industries, as well as the commodity exchanges, in numerous ways, many of them minor but nonetheless controversial; six discussions of the topic were published in the *Journal of Farm Economics* of December 1963.

Domestic Consumption Subsidies

The principal programs have been (a) direct distribution of food to needy families, (b) subsidies given to the poor in a form useful only for increased food expenditures (the food stamp plan), (c) the school lunch, special milk, and other programs for school children, and (d) assistance to institutions such as hospitals and to nutritionally vulnerable groups. The history of domestic consumption subsidies is given by Wetmore et al. [231] and Hoover and Maddox [115].

Southworth [193] summarized in 1945 most of the expected economic effects of food consumption subsidies. Direct cash grants to consumers are spent approximately as consumers would spend any income increment, with only a minor share going for food. Direct distribution of food largely replaces usual food expenditures by recipients and thus has much the same effect as cash grants (except that food consumption is concentrated on the types of food distributed). Effectively directed subsidies of the stamp plan type increase the food consumption and presumably the nutrition of the poor if supply is highly elastic; prices are then little affected. But if supply is highly inelastic, the subsidy to the poor tends principally to bid up prices as higher-income consumers, whose demands are inelastic, reduce their consumption only a little; then nutritional benefits to the poor are small but price benefits to producers large. When free choice is given to consumers to purchase the kinds of foods they want, demand for meats, certain fruits and vegetables, and other foods with relatively high income elasticities is increased; demand for bread, dry beans, and so on may be decreased.

If the objective of food consumption subsidies is to improve nutrition or to help farmers, programs that require the subsidy to be used only for food are preferred to cash grants or to programs having similar effects. But if recipients of subsidies are well qualified to judge what is best for their families, unrestricted cash grants should increase the welfare of the poor more than would any specialized subsidy of equivalent monetary value. Controversy exists about the accuracy of the assumption. Theory, once held unequivocally to support cash grants, gives indeterminate results when the desires of those who pay the subsidy are admitted into the consideration of welfare [57].

Near the close of the 1950s a comprehensive study at the University of Minnesota [2, 231] analyzed the potential effects of several approaches to demand expansion. The authors concluded, "There is little possibility that the surplus problem in agriculture can be fully alleviated by lifting the income restriction on food consumption for low-income families." [231]. They regarded the approach as a partial solution, one that might be justified entirely by the welfare of the poor.

Emphasis on the food stamp plan increased sharply at the close of the 1960s and raised a number of questions about operational details [115]. Some recent research suggests that the nutritional effects of the food stamp plan [142] and of a similar pilot program for infants and pregnant women [241] are minor; expenditure effects seem more like those of cash grants.

Should further research confirm these results for food stamps, the case for unrestricted assistance to low-income families as superior to assistance presumed to be directed to nutrition would be greatly strengthened.

Export Disposal

Export disposal of both the commercial and noncommercial types is mentioned only very briefly because a separate paper on international agricultural trade is included in this volume. The possibility of conflict between farm policy and international trade policy is evident. By the 1960s the nation's adverse balance of payments made the expansion of dollar-earning agricultural exports a matter of national, not merely sectoral, concern.

Farm price and income programs have existed in so many countries, and commercial world trade in agricultural products has been so obstructed by farm and general policy barriers, that classical "world markets" and "world prices" often have not even been approximated for many leading farm products. Retaliation by other countries is a possibility seriously to be considered whenever the United States untertakes export disposal programs. Devices such as the variable levy of the European Common Market can automatically offset the normal potential of lower prices to increase exports. A number of international commodity agreements have been developed in attempts to harmonize rivalries among export nations, but results commonly have been disappointing. The large comparative advantage of the United States in producing a number of farm products, particularly soybeans and feed grains, and the growing demand abroad for feedstuffs, again favoring soybeans and feed grains, have produced a rising trend in agricultural exports and have heightened the importance of commercial export policy for the future.

In contrast, disposal of farm products in noncommercial channels abroad, as under P. L. 480, was important through the mid-1960s but appeared in the early 1970s to have receded to a lower long-term level. The effects of the program on agricultural production in developing countries, on the countries' debt obligations for the future, and on other exporting countries have been complex. Though such effects cannot be reviewed here, the easy assumption that the program has been unqualifiedly beneficial to other countries is not warranted as a generalization.

Two-Price Plans

Two-price (or multiple-price) plans have usually been discussed in the farm policy literature as elements of export disposal programs, marketing orders for milk or for fruits and vegetables, or other price-raising devices. The theory of price discrimination applies to them, although agricultural programs have seldom carried the plans to the logical conclusions inferred from simplified assumptions by standard theory.

Multiple-price plans for agriculture were discussed in a USDA study [222] in 1954. Abel [1] used a price discrimination model in an analysis of export and import policies applying to agricultural products in the 1960s. In the 1930s Cassels [40] drew upon price discrimination theory in a realistic way in a study of fluid milk marketing, the field to which the theory has had by far its widest application in American agriculture. The literature on classified pricing of milk is too voluminous to permit more than a summary of certain conclusions here.

A classified price plan for milk eligible for fresh consumption in a particular area establishes a high price for milk sold for fluid use and essentially accepts whatever lower price is necessary to move production in excess of fluid use into manufacturing outlets [146]. Since demand for fluid use is distinctly inelastic and demand for *the particular area's* contribution to the nation's manufacturing milk supply is highly elastic, the gross income of the area's producers from production of a given volume of milk is increased by two-pricing. Prices are never set high enough in the fluid-use market to equalize marginal revenues there and in the manufacturing market, however, for practical reasons not entering into the usual price discrimination models.

Neither is output ordinarily restricted, though standard theory, assuming control of output, shows that producers' net income is maximized when the equal marginal revenues in the two markets also equal marginal costs. Producers are typically paid a blend price that is the weighted average of the high price for fluid use and the low price for manufacturing use. Output increments are thus seriously overvalued, thereby increasing farmers' incentives to produce surpluses. Failure to control output impairs the effectiveness of the program in achieving producers' objectives and may lead to social waste.

This result points up the difference between disposal control, which classified pricing for milk provides, and production control. Marketing order programs for fruits and vegetables ususally provide for some form of disposal control — sometimes of a two-price kind — but seldom for production control.

Classified pricing of milk has prompted much interest in two-price plans for other commodities. A major handicap has been the frequent lack of a secondary market readily separable from the primary market and capable of absorbing without large price declines substantial quantities diverted from the primary market. Area fluid milk markets are virtually unique in having the national market for manufacturing purposes as a large secondary outlet, and the capacity of that market to absorb excess milk has been increased by government price support for manufactured dairy products.

Supply Control

Cochrane presented a general case for supply control in [51], supplied program specifics in [53], and later commented on his experience in working for controls in government in [54]. Numerous discussions of the specifics of supply control, including [28], [169], and [167], have appeared in the literature. Representative writings that are moderately to sharply critical of supply control include [93, 102, 122, 184, 188].

It is obvious that if control is exclusively relied upon to increase producers' net income, producers' immediate gain will be the sum of change in total revenue and reduction in total costs. Since the latter is likely to be large only in a few cases (for example, broiler production), farm-level demand usually must be distinctly inelastic if potential income advantages to producers collectively are to be significant. Long-run results for producers depend upon long-run demand elasticity, changes in costs, and capitalization effects.

CONTROL OF PRODUCERS' SALES

Control might be placed on farmers' production, sales, or inputs. Control of sales often is more feasible than control of actual quantities produced and, in the case of storable products, permits growers to deal with the vagaries of nature by storage from year to year. Programs actually used in the United States provide only limited experience with direct control of sales.

In principle, limits on sales are preferable to limits on particular resources. Sales controls are direct and precise, but input controls are indirect and loose. Farmers' choice of inputs under sales controls probably would emphasize fixed resources such as land and family labor and deemphasize variable inputs such as fertilizer [102, p. 315]; the result should be more efficient use of resources and a greater net income for farmers from a given volume of production than if land controls were employed. Quantity sales quotas probably would encourage production of high-quality products. Evidence on farmers' use of variable inputs under acreage controls suggests that some of these presumed advantages might not be great in practice, but they would be in the right direction.

Virtually all proposals for outright sales controls call for assignment of quotas to individual producers in proportion to actual sales in a base period. Certificates issued to growers annually and required to be transferred to buyers as products are sold usually would be used to enforce the program against both buyers and sellers. Quotas would take on high values, as experience under some state marketing orders for milk indicates.

One of the oldest criticisms of supply control by economists is that quotas tend to freeze the pattern of production both among farms and among regions, thus preventing the shifts of production required for efficiency.

Cochrane [53] and most other economists have favored negotiability of quotas to avoid this. Farm leaders, especially leaders of organizations voicing concern about small farmers, usually have opposed negotiability, though injury to small farmers is not a necessary result.

A widely recognized limitation of sales controls is that they would be ineffective for commodities like feed grains that are or might readily be used on the same farm for feeding to livestock. Cochrane [53] proposed direct payments and perhaps acreage controls on feed grains if sales controls were applied to other products. Acreage controls have been the most common proposal as well as the means used in practice.

In light of farmers' inability to predetermine their production precisely, penalties for exceeding quotas on meat animals, milk, and poultry products (all perishable) probably should not prohibit sale of over-quota production but should only make it so unprofitable under normal circumstances that farmers would try to avoid it [28]. This is approximately what quota plans for fluid milk do when they assign Class I bases to producers and pay a sharply lower price for Class II milk [210]. The procedure would add administrative complications for most other perishable commodities.

For export products, some form of two-price plan would be attractive and perhaps essential under supply control. The administrative aspects would be awkward unless an export subsidy were paid for by the government. Several questions about resource allocation, income distribution, and capitalization of income benefits are deferred for consideration at the end of this section.

TAXING OUTPUT

Willingness to tax farmers' sales or production would open numerous possibilities for controlling supply and redistributing farm income. A tax might be most easily levied on processors (for example, the processing tax of the Agricultural Adjustment Act of 1933) and would ordinarily reduce farm prices. The proceeds could be used to reward farmers who complied with production or sales controls while the reduced prices would discourage farmers who did not comply. Or the proceeds could be used for payments redistributing income among farmers on some basis other than production.

A variant of the idea was discussed by Heady [107] in 1971. The government would receive a designated share of each farmer's production (say, 20 percent). The most favorable effect obtainable for farm income without production quotas would be achieved if the government simply removed its share from commercial markets (for instance, by giving the products to poor countries).

ACREAGE CONTROLS, GENERAL

Experience with supply control in the United States has been mainly with acreage restrictions. A long-recognized problem is the diversion of land removed from one crop to production of another crop. Several studies (for example, [31, 45, 100, 212]) show that such diversion takes place, with little loss of harvested acreage or even shift to hay or pasture, when acreage controls do not require land removed from a crop to be withheld from agricultural production. If the diversion takes the form of a shift from wheat and cotton to feed grains, as happened in the 1950s, livestock production is slightly encouraged despite feed grain price support [212]. Though output of controlled crops may be substantially reduced, total farm output may be little affected. Unless their products are price-supported, producers of crops to which acreage is diverted are made worse off.

Reduced acreage does not proportionately reduce output, of course, if yields increase. Effects of acreage control on yields frequently have not been distinguished from effects of the price supports that commonly accompany control. Probably this confusion, together with observation of upward trends in crop yields, accounted for a common belief at one time that per-acre yields increased so much under acreage restrictions that control was largely vitiated. But crop yields are now known to have increased greatly for technological reasons entirely apart from effects of controls or price supports. Comparisons of production practices and crop yields of participants in control programs with practices and yields of nonparticipants, together with questioning of farmers about why they adopted yield-increasing methods, showed that acreage controls as such has at most a small effect in inducing farmers to apply more fertilizer or otherwise to increase yields [6, 17, 30, 31, 101, 114, 147, 183, 225]. Comparison of yield increases over time showed that the rate was not greater than for nonquota crops after quotas went into effect [45].

Acreage controls have affected yields in ways other than influencing the levels of inputs. Under all types of land restrictions farmers are likely to leave in production of the controlled crop the most productive land on the farm. Thus, average yields increase when restrictions are imposed [45]. If rotation of idled acreage is possible, farmers can build up productivity by rotating or fallowing fields. Some programs appeal especially to farmers in areas having poorer land (or sometimes better land) than average. Programs aimed particularly at poor land automatically raise national average yields. In a study of land idled by acreage control programs in effect in 1966 Weisgerber [230] estimated that the combined effects of land selection within farms and the differential impact among areas caused land withdrawn from production to be, on the average, 80 to 90 percent as productive as the land in crops. Lower productivities of diverted land are not necessarily program defects, for they are usually consistent with efficient use of resources, and when programs are voluntary (paid for) the cost of attracting an acre into the program probably is lower when the farmer sacrifices less by enrolling the acre.

Acreage restrictions accompanied by price supports that did not adequately discriminate among qualities of the product have in several instances stimulated the use of varieties or cultural practices that increased yields at the expense of quality.

Whether inputs incorporating new technology would have been adopted less rapidly in a free market than under a joint program of acreage control, price support, and direct payments is a different question than the effects of acreage control alone. As indicated earlier, less technological advance and a somewhat lower level of inputs probably would have followed, with some lag, the abandonment of price and income programs.

Though rising technology and more use of fertilizer and other inputs per acre have not been much affected by acreage control alone, they have made land restriction more frustrating to farmers. When per-acre yields have risen faster than markets have expanded, as has happened at times for several crops, acreage allotments have had to be cut back. Minimum national allotments written into legislation have eventually become obstacles to effective control.

Except when whole farms are retired, acreage allotments ordinarily must be assigned to farms. Such allotments have been established, in practice, in proportion to acreages actually grown on individual farms in a base period. The use of soil conservation criteria has been proposed but given little attention. The acreage allotments or bases tend to freeze the historic pattern of production, as do sales quotas. Negotiability or administrative transfer of acreage bases is cumbersome because acreages should be translated into production equivalents if exchange of allotments between areas of different productivity is permitted.

WHOLE-FARM VERSUS PART-FARM RETIREMENT

The distinction here is between programs that retire all land on participating farms and those that retire only a minor fraction of the cropland on the farms. The principal part-farm programs — the acreage reserve of the Soil Bank program and the feed grain, wheat, and cotton retirement programs of the 1960s — retired land in proportion to past acreages of the controlled crops. In addition, upper limits were placed on the acreages of the controlled crops to be grown on participating farms. Under the Agricultural Act of 1970 the acreages to be retired were determined according to the earlier plan, but no upper limits were imposed on how much of the land permitted to be cropped could be devoted to the crops in question. In principle, the amount of land to be retired could be shifted from a specific-crop base to a total-crop base. Abandoning ties to specific crops in operating a part-farm retirement program increases the opportunity of farmers to adjust acreages of particular crops but decreases the precision of the government's supply management policies as they relate to individual commodities.

Closely associated with the whole-farm, part-farm distinction are the duration of land retirement contracts and the productivity of the land retired. Part-farm retirement is usually though not necessarily on an annual basis and is aimed at farms of all levels of productivity; whole-farm retirement makes sense only for periods of five, ten, or more years and usually is directed at poor land.

As Bottum [16] pointed out, voluntary (paid-for) supply control should be obtainable at lower cost to the government through whole-farm retirement than through programs idling some land on many farms. When some crop acres on an operating farm are withdrawn from production, the variable costs avoided by the farmer are small, with the result that the farmer will choose to idle the land only if he is paid a large share of the gross value of expected production on the withdrawn acres. When a whole farm is retired, however, a considerably larger proportion of total cost can be avoided, including family labor if it can be employed elsewhere or if the operator puts a high value on retirement from active work.

Research by Bottum et al. [17] indicated that under certain assumptions about other cost-influencing circumstances the government's cost of achieving a given amount of supply reduction through a voluntary whole-farm retirement program would be a little less than two-thirds the cost through voluntary part-farm retirement. A much more limited study [37] estimated the proportion at 84 percent. Brandow [27] calculated that the cost of obtaining a given reduction in output with the Conservation Reserve was roughly 50 to 60 percent of the cost incurred by part-farm retirement under the Acreage Reserve and early feed grain program. A similar estimate by Christiansen and Aines [45] based on a comparison of the Acreage and Conservation Reserves put the ration at 58 percent. The authors of a later Economic Research Service study [242] based on farmers' estimated costs and returns came to a different conclusion: achievement of a given amount of output restraint would be nearly as costly with a whole-farm retirement program, mildly restricted in the amount of land acceptable from any one county, as with a part-farm program. The preponderance of evidence is against this conclusion.

Several studies [17, 39, 45, 130, 147] show that whole-farm retirement, necessarily for an extended period of years, is attractive to elderly farmers, farmers with off-farm job opportunities, and other farmers who might especially want to do less farm work. Part-farm retirement apparently has few such effects except that farmers with off-farm work tend to participate more than others [30, 114, 183]. Whole-farm retirement is especially suited to marginal farmers as well as to marginal land.

Experience with the Conservation Reserve, recorded in references already cited, shows that whole-farm retirement on five-year to ten-year contracts speeds up the exit of land in areas going out of farming. But for the United States as a whole, most land is not shifted to trees, urban uses, or other purposes that prevent its return to agriculture, and much of it does return. To achieve permanent retirement some economists have proposed that contracts provide for easements against the use of the land for row crops or for any agricultural purpose after the contracts expire. Provisions for such easements would in most instances increase the government's cost of getting participation in a whole-farm retirement program. Easements have also been proposed as means, independently of any other device, by which to control agricultural use of land [85].

Some proposals [27, 213] for land retirement regard part-farm and whole-farm programs as complementary, as the Soil Bank program apparently did. In such proposals part-farm land retirement on an annual basis is considered an appropriate way of providing for and controlling the excess capacity needed for stability in the short run, whereas the function of whole-farm retirement is to hasten permanent withdrawal of submarginal land.

INTERFARM AND GEOGRAPHIC DISTRIBUTION OF RETIRED LAND

Theory and hypothetical calculations indicate that production can be reduced at lowest cost to government when voluntary programs are designed to retire land on which variable costs are highest in relation to value of output [186, 242]. High variable cost ratios generally are associated with low productivities of cropland. One means of giving priority to retirement of such cropland is to rate land for its productivity and to award contracts to farmers who submit the lowest bids relative to productivity ratings.[3] Giving priority to farmers who offered to retire cropland at the lowest rates per acre (without comparison with productivity) would be somewhat more expensive and would shift the location of the retired land [242].

Programs can be designed to be equally attractive to owners of good and poor land. This has been the general intent of annual, part-farm programs, whereas long-term, whole-farm programs have attracted the owners of poor land. The policy was one reason why the Conservation Reserve reduced farm output at lower cost than the feed grain program.

A major objection to programs designed to reduce output at lowest relative cost or lowest per-acre cost is that poor land tends to be geographically concentrated and that an unrestricted program would withdraw large proportions of cropland in the northern plains, in the southeast, and in some smaller areas. The local economies would thus be undermined. Political resistance to the consequences was the principal reason why whole-farm retirement was virtually discontinued after a partial trial through the Conservation Reserve.

Provisions to limit the amount of land retired in any county or other area subdivision to some percentage (for example, 20 or 40 percent) of the eligible land base would increase the government's cost of land retirement [17]. A series of studies at Iowa State University, based on a spatial programming model, have elaborated upon the location of land retired from agriculture and have compared costs under different policies; for examples, see [232] and [108].

COMPULSORY VERSUS VOLUNTARY LAND RESTRICTION

Mandatory restriction of land to be cropped has been strongly opposed by farmers on the grounds of compulsion and probably also because it is less profitable to farmers than alternative programs, including voluntary restriction. Under a voluntary program producers are offered sufficiently high payments for compliance to induce enough participation so that overproduction is avoided at the support price accompanying the program. Farmers' net incomes will be somewhat higher with a voluntary program than they would be if prices were supported at the same level without acreage restriction, for most farmers will not participate unless they gain more than from full production.

Compulsory acreage restriction accompanied by the requirement that land diverted from one crop may not be planted to another has been little used. Voluntary control has suffered from various "slippages" reducing its effectiveness [26, 141]. Apparently an important factor not explicitly recognized may be called the selectivity effect. Despite the stability of total crop acreage, many individual farmers in any one year make significant changes in their farming operations; moreover, land is going out of farming in some areas and coming into farming in a few others. When farmers are offered payments for retiring land and reducing output, the program is attractive to those who plan to cut down anyway and is rejected by those who think they have compelling reasons for expanding. The result is that the government pays for some reductions that would occur without a program and does not affect all expansions that would normally offset them. The selectivity effect apparently operates for both part-farm and whole-farm programs.

The actual reduction in total crop acreage typically has been less than the acreage enrolled in voluntary acreage retirement. A rule of thumb that worked fairly well in the 1950s and 1960s was that actual acreage was reduced 70 percent as much as program enrollment. This apparently is one reason why "on paper" calculations of expected costs (for example, [242]) are substantially lower than actual costs. The estimates for the Acreage Reserve and feed grain programs [27, 162, 186] generally agree that the cost of reducing the value of output by $1.00 with part-time retirement is nearly $1.00. Avoidance of storage and handling costs thus assumes importance as a reason why voluntary land retirement is cheaper to the government than price support without production control.

FROM ROW CROPS TO GRASS

Reduced intensity of land use and conservation have been emphasized in proposals to pay farmers for shifting from row crops to hay and pasture. Bottum et al. [17] estimated that a given reduction of crop output could be obtained a little more cheaply with a grass-use program than with complete retirement of crop land (voluntary part-farm retirement in both cases). As production of feeder cattle became an important bottleneck in agriculture in the late 1960s and early 1970s, shifting from row crops to grass became more attractive from a resource-use standpoint if not to established ranchers.

PIECEMEAL VERSUS COMPREHENSIVE SUPPLY CONTROL

Cochrane [53] argued for controls for all principal products of agriculture. Since demand is less elastic for an aggregate of competing products than for most individual products making up the aggregate, price and income effects of a given proportionate degree of supply restraint would be greater for comprehensive control than for control of one or a few products. Furthermore, producers of controlled commodities were expected to shift resources to uncontrolled commodities, with the result that all principal products would require control. Madsen and Heady [143] have defined supply control for agricultural bargaining power in a similarly comprehensive sense. The problem of getting sufficient consensus even to begin so all-encompassing a policy has led to other proposals emphasizing the desirability of control for some products but not others, with devices such as land retirement to impede shifts of resources from controlled to uncontrolled commodities.

Vertical relationships among farm products — for example, feed grains and eggs, or feeder cattle and fed cattle — complicate both the mechanics and the politics of comprehensive control. In light of farmers' attitudes, potential administrative problems, and consumers' probable objections, comprehensive supply control in Cochrane's sense ceased to appear to be a feasible policy alternative, a conclusion with which Cochrane apparently came to agree [54]. In another sense, however, comprehensive supply control became more important after 1960, for the acreage control programs intended to restrict production of particular crops without diversion of land to other crops were also significant as limitations on aggregate crop production. The "set-aside" provision of the Agricultural act of 1970 moved further in this direction.

CONTROL OF OTHER INPUTS

Little attention has been given to adminstrative control of inputs other than land as a means of controlling output. Shepherd et al. [186] reviewed the principal possibilities in 1963. None seemed promising, aside from voluntary withdrawal of labor. Perhaps the leading possibility here is that concern about the environment could be combined with efforts toward production control to limit use of agricultural chemicals.

Long-standing proposals to increase labor mobility by education, training, job information, financial aid, and the like have some relation to agricultural supply, of course, but they are not control programs in the sense used here. Virtually all economists proposing or analyzing supply control for agriculture have recognized that greater mobility of the labor force would ease the problems confronted by control programs and would be necessary if not sufficient for a wholly satisfactory farm income situation.

Direct Payments

As we saw earlier, the first proposals for direct payments usually intended payments to be strictly supplements to prices or incomes to compensate for their low level; payments were not thought of as inducements to comply with production controls. The first type of payment has sometimes been called a supplemental payment and the second a compliance payment to distinguish between the two purposes. As the 1970s began, only the wool program involved pure supplemental payments. Direct payments under crop programs were either wholly or partially compliance payments. A distinctive feature of an income payment plan proposed by Clawson [49] in the late 1960s was the extension of payments to rural nonfarm people made needy by the decline of agricultural population and employment.

Payments, even of the compliance type, have provided a degree of crop insurance as the programs have operated. Eligibility for crop payments has depended on acreage adjustments made by program participants; if yield per acre was low for reasons beyond the producer's control, the amount of payment was not altered.

BASE-LIMITED PAYMENTS

Unlimited supplemental payments can induce wasteful output expansion and create high costs for the government if supply is elastic. This has been one reason for the suggestion that payments be made only on a base amount — smaller than normal production — of each farmer's output. Market prices would then guide the farmer's marginal adjustments of production, the incentive to expand total output would be reduced (though farmers' financial ability to adopt capital-intensive technology would remain), and resource efficiency should be improved. If bases were changed each year to reflect the previous year's output, the marginal character of the plan would be lost. Freezing the bases, however, would introduce some of the inefficiency discussed in connection with supply control quotas. It would be possible at the cost of greater complexity to reduce this difficulty by relating payments to a total production base for each farm [21].

Whether because of economists' analysis or their own common sense, legislators set up the feed grain, wheat, and cotton programs as they operated in 1971 and 1972 so that producers could not enlarge the payments they received by expanding acreages beyond certain bases. Growers could, however, gradually increase their payments by raising per-acre yields.

ADJUSTING PAYMENTS TO AFFECT DISTRIBUTION OF FARM INCOME

Adjustment of direct payments of the supplemental type so that small growers received proportionately more than large growers was favored in some of the earlier direct payment proposals by economists [25, 155] and by such diverse sources as the Land-Grant College Committee on Postwar Agricultural Policy [7] and Secretary Brannan [46]. Economists' reasons included (1) the view that small farmers needed help more than large farmers and should have it, (2) large-scale farms were not generally more efficient than well organized family farms and should not be encouraged while this remained true, and (3) huge payments to a few very large farms would undermine public support for the program.

The opportunity to alter personal income distribution apparently was a leading reason for opposition by the American Farm Bureau Federation and some other groups to direct payments. The possibility that the small farms would be so heavily subsidized that inefficiency resulted was disturbing to some economists. Farmers' dependence upon highly visible appropriations for direct payments was held to be a restraint on their political freedom. Hamilton [94] gave a highly critical evaluation, mainly of supplemental payments, that summarized objections common during the 1950s.

The heavy reliance on compliance payments in conjunction with voluntary acreage control and price support in the 1960s and early 1970s complicated the issue. If payments are strictly for compliance, the principal income benefits of the joint program are realized through the market price and are not importantly modified by limiting payments to large growers. Limitations on pure compliance payments, moreover, may sharply reduce participation in production control by large growers, reduce the effectiveness of the supply management aspects of the joint program, and have the incongruous effect of idling proportionately large acreages on small farms while leaving large farms in full operation without much income sacrifice.

Some studies [171, 191, 234] implied that a limit of $10,000 on payments on each of the feed grain, wheat, and cotton programs would be feasible. They also pointed to a practical difficulty in limiting benefits to large farms: the owners of large farms might divide them up among family members, and lease arrangements could be made so that landowners received benefits through rent.

Farm Bargaining Power and Marketing Orders

Several article on economic, legal, and operational aspects of farm bargaining appear in [211] and in the December issues of the *Journal of Farm Economics* of 1963 and 1964. As Helmberger and Hoos [110] have remarked, standard price theory, not notably definitive for oligopoly and bilateral monopoly, usually assumes highly simplified situations and abstracts from significant elements of the total bargaining process. Helmberger and Hoos analyzed capture of excess profits of monopsonistic buyers in a setting in which producers' associations had no control of members' production. Most other writers and certainly farm bargainers have considered that higher prices to consumers, obtained through supply control, were also potential sources of benefits for producers. Moore [150] contended that profits in the food industry offer little general opportunity for large price gains by farmers through profit capture. As the tobacco industry has illustrated, high profits for processors and high prices for a farm product are not necessarily incompatible.

A point made by Ladd [138] and appearing in other terminology elsewhere distinguishes between (1) gains available to farmers by offering new service or product characteristics valued by buyers and (2) gains extracted from buyers by actual or threatened action that subjects them to losses. More efficient product assembly is an example of the first type; withholding products is an example of the second. The distinction is closely related to latent conflict between (1) the common desire of farmers to have cooperatives play a dominant role in vertical coordination wherever it develops and (2) the even more common desire to obtain higher farm prices by the exercise of economic power [26, 137]. If farmers attempt to coerce buyers in situations where substantial gains from vertical coordination are possible, the entry of buyers into farm production may be encouraged.

Economists have generally agreed that useful though not large benefits, mostly in nonprice terms of sale, are sometimes attainable by farm bargaining groups without control of market supply; but substantial price enhancement not offset by savings to buyers requires some form of supply control [26, 138, 166, 201]. Control of disposal of the product may be adequate in the short run; control of production is also necessary in the longer run. Madsen and Heady [143] analyzed bargaining power for farmers in much the same way they would analyze comprehensive supply control by the government.

Parallels as well as contrasts with collective bargaining by industrial labor have been noted [71, 166]. Several proposals for providing a broader legal base for farm bargaining are partially modeled on the Wagner Labor Act or minimum wage legislation [166, pp. 151-163]. The differing attitudes of farm groups toward such legislation, arising from their different interests and philosophies, is to some extent reflected in [198]. A proposed approach more closely resembling ordinary farm programs is the marketing board, an agency given government powers to enforce monopolylike policies for producers [239; 166, pp. 163-184].

A basic issue is the extent to which the government should create and hand over to farmers monopoly powers over production and prices. In arguing for supply control by the government Cochrane [53] contended that Congress would not and should not create unregulated monopoly for any industry. Farm groups, in contrast, often want private bargaining power partly because they resent the influence of government in ordinary farm programs. Several crucial questions involving conflict between antitrust laws and exemptions for farmers, begun under the Clayton and Capper-Volstead acts, are only partially resolved [61, 215].

Economic evaluations of the accomplishments of farm bargaining have been scarce and usually tentative. On the question of price Hoos [113] concluded in 1962 that "it is very rare that a lasting price-enhancement of as much as 10 percent emerges." The most impressive development since that time has been the formation of federated milk bargaining associations to negotiate for higher Class I prices than those provided in marketing orders and to control disposal of milk eligible for fluid use; Cook [56] concluded that direct and indirect price benefits for producers had been substantial. Appreciable savings in milk transport and handling have been made by some producers' associations formed primarily to bargain. Bits of evidence suggest that numerous gains improving the orderliness and equity of farmer-buyer relationships have been realized in several commodity fields.

The literature concerning marketing orders, especially for milk, is extensive. In 1957 a comprehensive survey of marketing agreements and orders was prepared by Hoos [112]. Farrell [64] made a detailed study of fruit and vegetable orders in 1966. Federal orders for milk through the late 1960s are described in [214].

Much of what has been said about the relation of means to ends in collective bargaining by farmers applies to marketing orders. Disposal control to effectuate two-price plans is common; production control is rare. In some instances the provisions of a marketing order and th* activities of a bargaining association reinforce each other, as in the marketing of cling peaches or (in numerous markets) milk eligible for fluid use. Marketing orders have clearly increased and have stabilized the price of milk used in fluid form. Several spatial equilibrium studies suggest that the location and volume of milk production have been modified. The effects of marketing orders on other commodities have been less clear-cut, and most price effects apparently have been greater in the short run than in the long run.

Storage and Market Stabilization

Support of market prices almost requires the government to operate a storage program because disposal outlets are not likely to absorb acquisitions as they are made. During most of the period under review the government financed large stocks of price support commodities either in the Commodity Credit Corporation's inventory or pledged as collateral for CCC loans. An important by-product of the joint support and storage program, intended primarily to support farm income, was the stabilization of market supplies and prices.

Price variability of crops was reduced, though livestock cycles were not elimated by more stable feed grain markets [32, 189]. Probably feed grain stabilization encouraged the growth of, and reduced risks on, specialized poultry, dairy, and meat animal farms not associated with grain production. When price support inventories were large, the trade usually carried only working stocks and ceded the longer-term storage function largely to government.

Sporadic attention was given to the question of how large storage stocks typically should be for stabilization purposes and how a stabilization program should be operated [70, 196, 222, 228]. Additional administrative studies were made by the USDA. It seemed generally agreed that no reserve policy could provide complete stabilization and that stocks adequate to guard against all but the most unusual circumstances would be substantially higher than private firms would normally carry in free markets.

The benefits that might justify a government stabilization program have not been agreed upon. Gustafson [89] concluded that if market demands are accepted as marginal social value functions, storage by private firms in a perfectly competitive market is optimal; the government, generally having no better information on future events than private traders have, cannot obtain better net social benefits. This result logically follows from the assumptions used in much conventional analysis.

Economists who have seen a role for government stabilization often have not been fully explicit about potential benefits admitted into their models, but the following considerations seem most important: (1) Specialized livestock (including poultry) operations have been built on a base of fairly stable feed grain supplies and prices; the social costs of instability in the livestock and processing sectors resulting from instability in feed grains are unlikely to be fully reflected in the decisions of private firms regarding feed grain storage. (2) Development of commercial export markets may be aided by dependability of United States supplies. (3) Food assistance to less developed countries in emergencies is desirable but will not be physically or politically possible unless ample stocks are available in the United States. (4) The dissatisfaction of consumers with unstable prices, the relation of food prices to industrial wage rates, and so on are not fully caught up in market demand functions. (5) Difficulties from national emergencies or exceptional crop failures will be alleviated by reserve stocks. Waugh [228] discussed a similar list of possible reasons for stabilization.

The rules or guidelines by which a true stabilization program would be operated constitute a complex question. D. G. Johnson [123], Gislason [82], Gustafson [88], and others studies the question in the context of the assumptions already described for Gustafson's work, with results as summarized by Gustafson [89]. Economists working outside this framework usually have tied their analyses to physical quantities rather than to prices. Substitution among crops should be considered (Waugh [228]). How much stabilization to attempt is a matter of judgment. Price stability should be considered if it will not follow automatically from stability of market supply, and price instead of (or together with) quantity guidelines might be used.

When some form of production control is in use, reserve stocks are a first line of defense against instability, and administratively determined changes in production are a second line of defense; both should be considered in a total stabilization program. Tweeten, Kalbfleisch, and Lu [204] have included reserve stocks, production control, and price and quantity criteria in a study of stabilization for wheat. A further complication is that price and income support probably will continue to be an objective of farm policy; if stabilization is also to be a recognized objective, procedures must be designed to accomplish both. The proper combination of price and quantity criteria becomes a sticky problem, and complete clarity about the relation of the two objectives is essential to avoid the familiar domination of stabilization by income enhancement. Finally, feasible price objectives of stabilization must be distinguished from effects of economywide price inflation.

Other Programs and Combinations of Programs

The complex sugar program has had an almost independent existence from other commercial farm policy. Its feasibility has rested largely on the fact that the United States is a large importer of sugar. Perhaps no other farm program entails so large a proportionate loss of efficiency or so obstructs economic opportunities of the less developed countries. Horton [116], among others, has reviewed past sugar policy and has proposed changes for the future.

Input subsidies have been little used in the United States. Irrigation water supplied at less than full cost, subsidies for liming, terracing, and so on under the former Agricultural Conservation Program, arrangements for grazing on public lands, and credit subsidies have been exceptions. A significant literature exists on these topics. Such subsidies have intensified the problem of excess capacity and may have modified interregional competition in agriculture, but they have not been highly important nationally.

Though such devices as consumption subsidies or supplemental direct payments can operate alone, most programs are effective only in combination with others. The feed grain policy of the late 1960s and early 1970s depended on part-farm land retirement to control output, compliance payments to induce farmers' participation, price support to improve and stabilize income, and storage to make price support effective. For wheat, payments supplemented income as well as inducing participation. For cotton, price support in 1971 and 1972 was so low that it played only an insurance and inventory financing role. In contrast, the old-style tobacco, rice, and peanut policies still operating in the early 1970s relied upon compulsory acreage restrictions without control of diverted land, high price supports, storage, and some form of export subsidy.

One defect of the organization in this part of the review is that comparative analyses of alternative programs for particular commodity producers are not sufficiently identified. Numerous such studies have been made. Among the more recent are analyses for cotton [194], rice [83], wheat [199], and grains, soybeans, and cotton [108].

Capitalization of Income Benefits

Running throughout the literature of farm policy is a point much emphasized by economists disposed to favor the free market and admitted, however reluctantly, by economists favoring farm programs of one kind or another: Income increments resulting from farm programs tend to be capitalized into land or other control instruments such as sales quotas, and eventually capitalization comes to mean higher costs for future farm operators.

Capitalization can be expected from any type of farm income program. It is most identifiable in a program like that for tobacco or peanuts wherein rights to produce for high prices are restricted to growers with allotments; farms with allotments sell for higher prices than do those without allotments [92, 109, 144, 180]. When allotments are transferable separately from land, they take on high values (for example, [62]), as do milk quotas under some state control plans. Unrestricted price support or supplemental payments for products in general would eventually raise land values, but it would not be possible to compare one farm with another to determine how much. Floyd [69] analyzed the effects of certain programs on returns to land and labor and pointed out that detaching sales quotas entirely from land would reduce land value while creating quota values.

Reinsel and Krenz [161] concluded that income benefits of farm programs are capitalized into land values at high discount rates or, alternatively, that if going rates of interest are used for discounting, a significant proportion of benefits go to resources other than land. Their findings suggested less capitalization than had usually been assumed. They calculated that only 8 percent of farm real estate values as of 1970 represented capitalized value of benefits from principal crop programs. Tweeten [201] estimated that up to one-third of land value gains from 1950 to 1963 were due to the farm programs.

The capitalization effect is considered by many economists to be a short-coming — by some a decisive one — of long-enduring income programs for agriculture. Most members of the generation entering farming after programs are initiated, it is argued, must buy their way in at higher land values than otherwise would be the case. Program benefits become imputed to land rather than labor. Wilcox [237] argued in rebuttal that ownership turnover is so slow that the effect is long delayed, and the Reinsel-Krenz findings tended to blunt the capitalization argument. Cochrane [53] agreed that the income benefits of comprehensive supply control would be capitalized in quota values but regarded that as a cost of achieving a stabilized market at fair prices.

Program Costs

Government outlays for farm programs are not unambiguously obtainable from the federal budget, and some judgment must be exercised concerning whether certain activities are chargeable to farm price and income support. One estimate [20] of annual outlay in the late 1960s was a little more than $5 billion. Most of the outlay transferred income from nonfarmers to farmers; one-fourth or less of the total outlay represented the absorption of resources for storage, administration, etc., useful for other purposes. Costs to consumers in the form of unduly high prices were considered low because the rates of return to resources on efficient farms would have been well below the rates in the economy at large if direct payments – the principal government outlay – had not substantially added to net farm income.

Efficiency

Farm programs create inefficiency if they cause resources to be used less effectively, under a given state of the arts, than they could be for satisfying citizens' wants. A much-used norm for appraising efficiency is the configuration of inputs and outputs expected under perfect competition, although, as noted earlier, acceptance of the personal distribution of resource endowments and income involves a value judgment. Economic evaluation of social costs associated with particular policies has frequently employed partial equilibrium analysis and the concepts of consumers' and producers' surplus. Harberger, a leading practitioner of such analysis, has made a strong plea for its acceptance in applied welfare economics [95]. Reservations on theoretical grounds often are based on a reluctance to aggregate personal utilities and on second-best considerations.

This reviewer is unwilling to aggregate personal utilities indiscriminately. He is particularly unwilling to accept the assumption that there exist empirical counterparts of either the perfect competition situation or the equivalent situation under the constraints of a program. As the general model of the agricultural sector discussed earlier indicates, agriculture has been and is in chronic disequilibrium. One of the best demonstrations of this has been provided by Kaldor and Saupe [135]. The neat alignment of resources, output, and prices specified by the perfect competition model is far from duplicated in free markets, and the equally neat alignment assumed under the constraints of a program is not experienced when programs are in effect. In particular, areas under empirically determined supply curves are unlikely to represent opportunity costs. The basic theory is invaluable in providing a conceptual orientation for the analysis of programs, but the assumptions implicit in the literal use of simple forms of it for policy conclusions are breathtakingly heroic.

Many, perhaps most, economists do not agree, so the findings of Harberger-style studies are of interest. Wallace [227] estimated social costs for Cochrane-type comprehensive supply control and for Brannan-type direct payments for all commodities. Because exact values of aggregate supply and demand elasticities were in doubt, Wallace used various combinations of elasticities. The highest ratio of social cost to value of output was less than 2 percent for the Cochrane program and less than 5 percent for the Brannan program. Johnson [129] concluded that the social cost of the tobacco program (characterized by high price support and compulsory acreage restriction without control of diverted acres) was relatively small if only the domestic market was considered and might be a net *benefit* for the nation (but not for other countries) if exploitation of the United States' presumed strong position in the export market was taken into account. Hushak [119] found that for the feed grain program during 1961-66 "in general, the net welfare costs were small and the income transfers were substantial." Dardis and Dennisson [58] compared the social costs of alternative ways of pro:iding protection for United States wool growers; differences between programs did not exceed 6 percent of the value of domestic consumption.

Thus conceptualized and measured, the loss of efficiency as a result of farm programs is small. A similar conclusion usually has resulted from the application of comparable methods to situations presumed to cause resource misallocation (for example, as under oligopolistic departures from competitive pricing) outside of agriculture [121]. At least for agriculture, however, a more fruitful approach appears to be to set forth hypotheses on how farm programs might impair or improve the efficiency expected to be achieved in the absence of intervention and then to attempt to measure the influence of each hypothesized effect. The approach, of course, could be easily adapted to comparing the effects of different programs. Although farm policy literature contains many intuitive or judgmental statements that fit into this framework, little searching, rigorous work has been done to support hard conclusions. The following paragraphs are a personal and often subjective summary of the implications of information so scattered in bits and pieces as to defy concise documentation.

Perhaps the principal way in which farm programs might affect efficiency is by retarding or speeding up the rate at which excess farm labor finds *productive* employment elsewhere in the economy. A large proportion of persons engaged in agriculture have been under strong economic pressure to go elsewhere, and, as the brief review of the labor adjustment process indicates, short-run mobility is not much affected by farm prices. Probably farm labor mobility has not been much different with farm programs than it would have been without them. Similar judgments have been made by many others; indeed, it is difficult to find statements by agricultural economists in the last ten years to the effect that programs have done much to hold labor in agriculture. the reimposition of cotton quotas in the 1950s forced some labor out of farming [212]. Fuller [72] emphasized the point that the departure of people from agriculture is not enough to assure an increase in welfare despite the statistical improvement in farm labor productivity and incomes; those who leave must be productively employed elsewhere.

Have programs tended to keep farms from becoming large enough to achieve the principal economies of size? In tobacco areas, yes [19] ; in areas of small cotton farms, probably; in most areas, apparently not. Acreage controls may have stimulated farm consolidation in some areas in order to get sufficient acreage of controlled crops. Though price supports are advocated by some groups to hold small farmers in agriculture and are said by some critics of supports to have done it, size and number of farms in the long run probably are determined largely by economies of size (broadly interpreted) and are little affected by the level of prices.

Have interfarm and interregional adjustments of output been impeded? Probably interfarm shifts have been substantially impaired for tobacco, and interregional shifts have been retarded or altered for cotton and milk, with significant efficiency losses. Though adjustments for other crops have also been affected, efficiency consequences seem slight.

Has the output mix been made less efficient? Significant damage may have been done to export markets and hence to production of cotton. High-cost sugar production in the United States is sheltered by sugar policy. Control programs of the late 1960s and early 1970s kept production of several crops about in line with utilization; other crops and livestock products were not controlled. Since demands for most controlled crops are distinctly inelastic, distortions of the output mix attributable to holding production in line with utilization at support prices cannot have a large value in relation to the value of total output. Expansion of cattle production in the Great Plains probably was retarded by grain programs.

Has the input mix been made less efficient? Probably substitution of variable inputs for fixed inputs, especially for land, in the production of a given volume of output has been too much encouraged. On the other hand, capital investment, which has not been generally excessive under government programs [135, 202], probably has been stimulated by higher and more stable farm incomes with programs in effect.

Have domestic consumption subsidies or export disposal in noncommercial markets created useless markets and wasted production costs? Values currently held by the majority of citizens justify most domestic consumption subsidies and, in less degree, emergency food relief abroad. If P. L. 480 has impeded agricultural development abroad, as some economists contend, the program's seeming contribution to welfare is diminished.

Has restriction of total farm output created social costs? The highly inelastic demand for aggregate output and the modest extent of output restriction suggest that the social costs incurred have been small in relation to the value of total output.

Progressiveness

The question is whether farm programs have influenced technological and managerial innovations that affect the productivity of agriculture. As Schultz [178] and others have pointed out, most total output gains and virtually all per-capita output gains, both in the economy at large and in agriculture, have come about through the application of knowledge to production processes. Tweeten and Plaxico [205] showed that gains in agricultural productivity between 1930 and 1960 save a large portion of the inputs that would otherwise have been needed to produce the farm output of 1960. The principal component of new knowledge in agriculture — technology — calls for constant reorganization of resources. A progressive agriculture is always out of equilibrium as defined by the static theory that underlies the concept of efficiency. Criteria for an optimal mix of progressiveness and efficiency are necessarily incapable of precise definition [22].

A general argument advanced by Cochrane [53] and others [28] is that production control has little effect in slowing down development of new technology (since it is largely external to farming) or in modifying farmers' incentives to adopt it. The general model discussed in the first section of this review strongly suggests that income support speeded up the adoption of technology by putting farmers in a better position to finance the investments that were often required. Reduced price risk probably also encouraged investment. It is also likely that to the extent innovations are induced, higher product prices resulting from farm programs speed up the development of new technology.

The gradual leveling off of the ratio of aggregate output to aggregate input in agriculture in the 1960s has not been thoroughly examined and has been taken by some economists [202] as an indication that the long increase in farm productivity has ended. It is possible that the leveling off was partly a statistical illusion arising from not properly taking into account the retirement of large acreages of cropland under the programs of the 1960s. In any event, the output-input ratio rose after 1970.

The brevity of this section reflects the fact that the economic organization and institutions of American society, together with a stage of development that science was in, had produced a high rate of progressiveness in American agriculture. Inadequate progressiveness was not the problem from 1920 to 1970, and agricultural economists devoted little attention to it in an analytical sense — they merely noted the presence of technolgy and the dramatic consequences of it. Progress and growth remain poorly understood in agriculture as elsewhere. Economists' much greater attention to efficiency in agriculture reflected in part a preoccupation with the static models of classical economics and in part a realization that many of the potential social benefits of technology are not won unless resources are reallocated in the direction of efficiency norms as development proceeds.

Income Distribution and Equity

Most equity considerations in farm policy are associated with the personal distribution of income and wealth and with the sharing of costs, but some — for example, the necessity for many people to change their occupation and residence — are not captured in dollar figures. As already emphasized, economists have long been well aware that the income benefits of simple price support, production control, and direct payment programs are shared among the members of the target farm groups approximately in proportion to the volume of sales. The distribution of sales or production is, of course, highly unequal. Robinson [163] concluded that possible disproportionate effects among farms of different size because of different net-gross income ratios were not important in practice.

Two extensive studies [14, 148] of the distribution of payments and price support loans did not much modify the general conclusion that benefits have been in proportion to farm size. All producers of a crop benefit from the level of price support maintained by a joint program of voluntary production control and nonrecourse loans. Which farmers decide to earn compliance payments or to use the loan is of secondary importance. Supplemental payments have been distributed about in proportion to production except for modifications at the extreme ends of the distribution, as under the 1971 cotton program.

The tendency for the benefits of price and income programs to be capitalized in land values implies that principal long-run benefits accrue to owners of farmland (and their heirs) at the time of its value appreciation. Part-owners and tenants, who are among the largest farm operators in some areas, probably have benefited proportionately less than landowners, some of whom have no other connection with farming. Gaffney [75] presented a catalog of objectives to programs tending to support or increase land values.

Emphasis of price and income programs on crops (on which the adverse effects of excess agricultural capacity have tended mainly to fall) suggests that crop producers have benefited most. Producers of meat animals and poultry products have had higher feed costs and product prices than otherwise would have been the case, along with somewhat lower aggregate output, greater stability, and small net benefits or costs. Dairy producers have been the exception in the livestock group — benefits to them have been significant. The geographic areas receiving principal benefits have been those where field crop acreage and milk production (especially for fresh consumption) are concentrated.

The effects of farm programs on income distribution within agriculture are considered good or bad depending on what goals are thought appropriate.

Heady [106], among others, has contended (1) that the leading purpose of farm programs is to compensate farmers for the adverse effects of technological change of great value to the general public and (2) that stabilization is needed for an inherently unstable agriculture. Benefits in proportion to size of farm operation are appropriate in this context. To economists who acknowledge only poverty problems, the personal distribution of the benefits of farm programs means that public funds are misdirected. Price and income programs clearly are grossly inefficient as solutions to poverty: Bonnen [14] estimated that the feed grain and wheat programs expended six or seven dollars for each dollar going to the smallest 40 percent of growers.

The distribution of income between farmers and nonfarmers also raises equity questions. Nonfarmers receive some benefits from farm programs (for example, assurance of adequate supply and stable prices in an event like the corn blight of 1970), but, in the main, income is transferred to farmers from nonfarmers through the tax and food bills. Farmers who sell more than two-thirds of all farm products (table 1) and who apparently receive a like share of program benefits have higher (net) incomes and substantially more wealth than does the average American family. Sharing of costs through the food bill is regressive compared with sharing through the tax bill [190, p. 47], though other considerations also influence the choice between market-finanaced and tax-financed programs. As for the within-agriculture case, conclusions about the appropriateness of income distribution depend in part upon emphasis given to the compensation principle or to alleviation of poverty as policy goals.

Much equity-oriented analysis has been focused upon returns to labor on the apparent assumption that persons receiving other factor returns, especially returns to land, are not generally among the needy. For farm families who own their farms, the distinction among factor returns is not important from an income standpoint in the short run. Except to the extent that income benefits are incompletely capitalized into land or quota values, it seems impossible for any conventional type of farm program to increase farm family labor returns in the long run if excess labor persists. Thus proposals to upgrade the skills of farm people and to increase labor mobility often have been motivated by a desire to improve personal distribution of income as well as by concern about resource allocation.

Concluding Topics
Farm Policy, Rural Poverty, and Development

As the first part of this review shows, agricultural economists in the late 1940s were well aware that many farmers had few resources, were poor, contributed little to total farm output, and could not be greatly helped by price support or similar programs for commercial farming. Serious examinations of policy for farm people, such as the land-grant college report on agricultural policy to follow World War II [7], the USDA's *What Peace Can Mean to American Farmers* [220], and a Senate study in 1948 of long-range policy [223], discussed the problems of low-income farmers. Included in these were such topics as education, vocational training, migration to sites of industrial employment, rural health and sanitation, nutrition, housing, electrification, recreation, Social Security for farmers, and migratory workers — indeed, virtually the whole gamut of topics to be discussed in the same connection twenty-five years later. Not until the mid-1960s, however, was the political climate right for much public attention to such matters.

Despite some concern with nonfarm economic problems of rural areas before the 1950s, agricultural economists once tended to regard the rural economy as directly or indirectly dependent on agriculture, with help here and there from forestry and mining. Not until well into the 1950s did a substantial expansion begin in resource economics and rural development in the sense of improving opportunities in, and performance of, the rural nonfarm sector. By the 1970s scarcely any economist identified rural economic problems as strictly agricultural.

The literature reflects some early ambivalence among agricultural economists about whether commercial farm policy, rural poverty, and rural development were distinct if overlapping topics. Though it was widely recognized that ameliorating the problems of commercial farmers would be of small help to the rural poor, it was less widely agreed that correcting the rural poverty problem would have little effect on commercial farmers. One view seemed to be that labor mobility was the solution to both problems; the two were on the same continuum although, of course, more education, vocational training, and so on were needed by the poor. Programs to accomplish these things for the poor, therefore, were the appropriate farm policy. The opposing view was that commercial farmers had important problems not capable of being dealt with adequately by labor mobility alone. It seems clear at present that the business characteristics of agriculture have opened up so wide a gap between commercial farming and rural poverty that policies for the two must be distinct; and, of course, many of the rural poor have no connection with farming.

Approaches and Methods

Most economists working in farm policy have been aware of the distinction between positive and normative analysis and, in principle, would have accepted the common view that the economist has no scientific basis for choosing among the value held by different persons regarding policy or among the persons holding the values. In practice, however, farm policy economists, like economists in other areas where values play a prominent role, have behaved in many individual ways and often have introduced value judgments as criteria for policy. Not much writing was done in the post-World War II period by farm policy economists on the methodological issues involved. Shepherd [185] argued in the 1950s that economists could affect values, but his difference with the conventional position seemed largely semantic. A more or less orthodox view of the role of values and of the scope of farm policy research was given in [24].

Values and economic assumptions often mingled in unclear ways when government programs were compared with free markets, especially before the mid-1950s. Cochrane [53] argued in 1959 that economists should not ignore the ancient question of fair prices. Allin [5], one of the dwindling school of institutional economists, called for consideration of ethics and freedom and for weaving other social sciences into the analysis of policy issues. Some agricultural economists (see, for example [22]) argued for looking at the economic world as a dynamic process and for reformulating criteria for policy accordingly. Kelso [136] expanded upon the old criticism of the concept of the economic man to challenge the analytical power of sophisticated economic and econometric models to provide true answers for real world problems, especially of prediction; policy prescription, he held, is art and goes beyond the limited valid information extractable from economic science. In all of these cases, of course, agricultural economists were dealing with questions about which much more has been written by general economists, other social scientists, and philosophers.

Techniques of analysis have been nearly as diverse as the multifarious problems investigated. Studies have ranged from integrative analyses as broad as Schultz's farm sector model in his *Agriculture in an Unstable Economy* to specific firsthand surveys of what farmers in particular areas did in response to acreage controls. Numerous studies have made use of programming models, estimation techniques for simultaneous equations, and similar analytical methods as they became part of the skills of agricultural economists. Farm policy questions have been studied in the context of game theory [66; 139; 90, pp. 364-374]. Control theory as an analytical framework has been discussed [38, 197]. A "state of the art" paper on policy simulation experiments is given in [152].

Comments on the Future

Understanding the macroeconomics of agriculture will continue to be fundamental to successful policy formulation. Nothing is so useful for farm policy analysis as accurate knowledge of how the agricultural economy works, fortified by reliable quantification of key relationships in the system. Awareness of values basic to what people want from the agricultural sector and of the political processes by which policy is made is also essential for successful work in political economy. Much of the research required is not called *policy* analysis, nor should it be; but policy analysis and prescription can make little progress without it.

The quick turnaround from farm surpluses to shortages in 1972-73 made dramatically evident the need to be able to anticipate the future supply-demand balance in agriculture. Policy should be capable of dealing with events as they unfold. This suggests the need for continuing examination of technological advance in agriculture, the availability and costs of inputs from nonfarm sources, production constraints required for environmental protection and food safety, changes in domestic demand, developments in foreign markets, and still other matters. Great uncertainty about whether agriculture will produce a little too much or a little too little may be inescapable, in which case policy should be designed to cope with either outcome.

If one had much confidence in the public's ability to discern its own interest in agricultural policy, one might predict that stabilization of agricultural markets would be given a higher priority than in the past. Whether agricultural capacity proves to be generally excessive, deficient, or about right in the future, much instability can be expected in free markets. The arguments for stabilization discussed in the preceding section are applicable, and the questions identified there deserve economists' attention.

Changes in farm structure — size of farm, ownership, vertical relationships with nonfarm firms, and so on — will continue to cause discontent among farmers and to raise issues about efficiency and the distribution of power in the economy. In-depth analyses are needed on those topics that the economist can get his teeth into: economies of size in the conventional sense; benefits of size in obtaining lower input prices, higher output prices, or other advantages in dealing with other firms; potential gains of several kinds from vertical integration; strategies available to conglomerate firms in obtaining markets, allocating costs, and payment of taxes; and the economic difficulties of family businesses in transferring ownership from generation to generation.

With the growth of food exports domestic agricultural policy and international trade policy will touch at more and more points. Supplies of and demands for food abroad and policies modifying trade will be essential considerations in the formulation of domestic policy. Food aid for poor countries will be almost a new problem if surpluses cease to exist.

Probably support of farm income, or at least provision for support should farm prices fall, will continue to be an important feature of farm policy. Questions on feasible policy alternatives and their economic consequences will remain relevant. The broader issues are well recognized among economists. A less appreciated need is for detailed knowledge of how programs actually work. There appear to have been provisions of law and administrative practices that conferred special advantages on some groups or incurred waste, neither justified by the avowed purposes of the programs. Such instances, if they exist in the future, should be widely recognized and discussed.

A particularly important aspect of policy analysis is the evaluation of the effects of programs on resource allocation or efficiency in the agricultural sector. As suggested earlier, the most fruitful appraisals are likely to come from addressing directly the real-world situations in which problems and programs are embedded, not from substituting unverified assumptions and static models for the dynamic world that actually exists. Though qualitative discussions along the lines proposed are plentiful, conclusions based on well-supported quantitative findings are scarce.

Questions bearing on personal income distribution are highly important but notably difficult to resolve. The difficulty is compounded by a common implication that commercial farm policy should deal primarily with poverty, something it does not and cannot do. Most of the economic policy problems with which the nation concerns itself are no more poverty-oriented than is farm policy. Industrial labor policy dealing with collective bargaining and unionization is not aimed at poor people; demands that the nation maintain a high level of output and employment come largely from business managers, stockholders, and workers not in poverty; inflation is denounced by almost everyone. The idea that economic policy must deal with poverty to be significant is an acceptable value judgment but obviously not one held by most citizens or economists.

That said, it can be agreed that the personal distribution of income and wealth is an important criterion for farm policy. The fact that the top farmers who market 80 percent of all farm products have higher average incomes and more wealth than the typical American family is relevant here. If generally understood, it probably would lead most citizens to conclude that support of farm income should receive a lower priority as a policy objective than in the past. The wide distribution of income among farmers, even within the strictly commercial sector, would suggest that programs should be designed, so far as they feasibly can be, to scale down benefits going to the wealthier producers. Accordingly, economists might well incorporate such equity considerations in their search for better farm policy.

Under the stresses of the 1930s and subsequent decades, farm policy became defined in practice as price and income policy. This emphasis should give way to a broader concept in which agriculture as an industry, forming part of a larger food and agricultural sector, is the contextual unit of analysis; and all aspects of the economic performance of the industry should be admitted to consideration. Farm policy specialists would be, first of all, knowledgeable about the macroeconomics of agriculture. Attention would be paid to the adequacy of agriculture's production capacity, changes in its product and factor markets, the structure of the industry, its sectoral relations to other industries, its stability, the generation and distribution of income in the industry, and the like. The position of hired farm labor, given too little attention in this review, would be included. Knowledge acquired across such an array of topics and integrated by the concept of industry is likely to be more applicable to policy issues in the future than is knowledge produced by exclusive attention to price and income questions.

The writer will indulge himself in two comments on methods and approaches. As has already been suggested, he has little confidence in the productivity of analyses anchored in the assumptions of perfect competition, focussed exclusively on resource allocation, and employing only logic, however elegant, to reach conclusions purporting to apply to policy issues. He would like to associate himself with the orientation toward the real world reflected in the presidential addresses of Leontief [141] and Galbraith [79] to the American Economic Association.

Economists would do well to go back to A. C. Pigou and forthrightly adopt his proposition that a narrowing of the personal distribution of income increases welfare if the national product is not reduced.[4] Post-Pigou welfare economics has been an intellectually fascinating exercise using constructs that relate to the economy as chess relates to war and guided by a criterion (Pareto's) that the public does not accept as a sufficient or necessary test of satisfactory policy. Pigou's defense of his position was impressive if not value-free; the ethic expressed in it, if not too finely drawn, is widely accepted by the American public today. Pigou's rule does not permit a resolution of all farm policy issues, but it does offer guidance in dealing with such questions as who should receive income support at a cost to the public.

In summary, work in farm policy can continue to be productive for qualified agricultural economists if it has four characteristics. It should be conceived in terms of agriculture as an industry, deal with a wide range of farm economic problems of significance to society, employ realistic if sometimes necessarily inelegant models, and be guided by Pigou's rather than Pareto's principle of the relation of personal income distribution to welfare.

Notes

1. In the early 1940s Schultz [177] had proposed payments to farmers to compensate for low income. The payments were not to be related to farm size or to production (to avoid making them regressive) but were instead to be available on equal terms to all families; they were to be made in kind (for instance, as food, medical services, education), and they were to be tied to the human agent rather than to property.

2. See "Postwar Policies Relating to Trade in Agricultural Products" by D. Gale Johnson in this volume.

3. An experimental program in 1958 asked farmers to submit bids for land retirement. Rough calculations of the values of production on land offered for retirement led to the disconcerting conclusion that the ratio of output to retirement payment was highest on the most productive land [17]. The sample was necessarily restricted to land offered for retirement.

4. This was subject to minor qualifications. Pigou also held that an increase in national product not accompanied by a decrease in the product accruing to the poor increased welfare.

References

[1] Abel, M. E. "Price Discrimination in the World Trade of Agricultural Commodities." *J. Farm Econ.* 48:194-208, May 1966.

[2] Abel, M. E., and W. W. Cochrane. *Policies for Expanding the Demand for Farm Products in the United States*, part 2. Minnesota Tech. Bul. 238, 1961.

[3] Abel, M. E., and A. S. Rojko. *World Food Situation, Prospects for World Grain Production, Consumption, and Trade*. USDA, For. Agr. Econ. Rep. 35, reprinted September 1967.

[4] "Agricultural Economists' Views on Farm Price Policy." *J. Farm Econ.* 28:604-609, May 1946.

[5] Allin, B. W. "Relevant Farm Economics." *J. Farm Econ.* 43:1007-1018, December 1961.

[6] App, J. L., and W. B. Sundquist. *The Feed Grain Program in Minnnesota*. Minnesota Agr. Exp. Sta. Bul. 464, 1963.

[7] Association of Land-Grant Colleges and Universities. *Postwar Agricultural Policy*. 1944.

[8] Benedict, M. R. *Can We Solve the Farm Problem?* New York: Twentieth Century Fund, 1955.

[9] ———. *Farm Policies of the United States, 1790-1950*. New York: Twentieth Century Fund, 1953.

[10] Benedict, M. R., and O. C. Stine. *The Agricultural Commodity Programs*. New York: Twentieth Century Fund, 1956.

[11] Benson, E. T. *Freedom to Farm*. Garden City: Doubleday, 1960.

[12] Black, J. D., and J. T. Bonnen. *A Balanced United States Agriculture in 1965*. National Planning Association, Spec. Rep. 42, 1956.

[13] Black, J. D. and M. E. Kiefer. *Future Food and Agriculture Policy*. New York: McGraw-Hill, 1948.

[14] Bonnen, J. T. "The Distribution of Benefits from Selected U. S. Farm Programs." In *Rural Poverty in the United States*. National Advisory Commission on Rural Poverty, 1968.

[15] ———. "Present and Prospective Policy Problems of U. S. Agriculture: As Viewed by an Economist." *J. Farm Econ.* 47:1116-1129, December 1965.

[16] Bottum, J. C. "The Soil Bank as a Solution to the Farm Price and Income Problem." In *Policy for Commercial Agriculture*. Joint Economic Committee, 85th Congress, 1st Session, 1957.

[17] Bottum, J. C., J. O. Dunbar, R. L. Kohls, D. L. Vogelsang, G. McMurtry, and S. E. Mogan. *Land Retirement and Farm Policy*. Purdue Agr. Exp. Sta. Res. Bul. 704, 1961.

[18] Boulding, K. E. "Does absence of Monopoly Power in Agriculture Influence the Stability and Level of Farm Income?" In *Policy for Commercial Agriculture*. Joint Economic Committee, 85th Congress, 1st Session, 1957.

[19] Bradford, G. L. Tobacco Programs and Program Choices." In *A Review of Agricultural Policy, 1970*. North Carolina State University Agr. Pol. Inst. Ser. 43, 1970.

[20] Brandow, G. E. "Cost of Farm Programs." In *Benefits and Burdens of Rural Development*. Iowa State University Center for Agricultural and Economic Development. Ames: Iowa State University Press, 1970.

[21] ———. "Direct Payments without Production Controls." In *Economic Policies for Agriculture in the 1960s*. Joint Economic Committee, 86th Congress, 2d Session, 1960.

[22] ———. "In Search of Principles of Farm Policy." *J. Farm Econ.* 44:1145-1155, December 1962.

[23] ———. *Interrelations among Demands for Farm Products and Implications for Control of Market Supply*. Pennsylvania Agr. Exp. Sta. Bul. 680, 1961.

[24] ———. "Methodological Problems in Agricultural Policy Research." *J. Farm Econ.* 37:1316-1324, December 1955.

[25] ———. "A Modified Compensatory Price Program for Agriculture." *J. Farm Econ.* 37:716-730, November 1955.

[26] ———. "The Place of Bargaining in American Agriculture." In *Cooperative Bargaining*. USDA FCS Serv. Rep. 113, 1970.

[27] ———. "Reshaping Farm Policy in 1961." *J. Farm Econ.* 43:1019-1031, December 1961.

[28] ———. "Supply Control: Ideas, Implications, and Measures." *J. Farm Econ.* 42:1167-1179, December 1960.

[29] Brandow, G. E., and H. E. Allison. "Per Capita Incomes on Commercial and Non-Commercial Farms." *J. Farm Econ.* 33:119-123, February 1951.

[30] Brandow, G. E., and J. P. Houck. *The Soil Bank in Southeastern Pennsylvania*. Pennsylvania State University, Dept. Agr. Econ. Rur. Soc., AERS 14, 1957.

[31] Brandow, G. E., and E. W. Learn. *Effects of 1954 Acreage Restrictions on Crop Production in Southeastern Pennsylvania*. Pennsylvania Agr. Exp. Sta. Prog. Rep. 128, 1954.

[32] Breimyer, H. F. "Emerging Phenomenon: A Cycle in Hogs." *J. Farm Econ.* 41:760-768, November 1959.

[33] ———. *Individual Freedom and the Economic Organization of Agriculture*. Urbana: University of Illinois Press, 1965.

[34] ———. "The Three Economies of Agriculture." *J. Farm Econ.* 44:679-699, August 1962.

[35] Brewster, J. M. "The Impact of Technical Advance and Migration on Agricultural Society and Policy." *J. Farm Econ.* 41:1169-1184, December 1959.

[36] Brewster, J. M., and H. L. Parsons. "Can Prices Allocate Resources in American Agriculture?" *J. Farm Econ.* 28:938-960, November 1946.

[37] Brown, W. G. and P. Weisgerber. "An Appraisal of the Soil Bank Program in the Wheat Summer Fallow Area of Oregon." *J. Farm Econ.* 40:142-148, February 1958.

[38] Burt, O. R. "Control Theory for Agricultural Policy: Methods and Problems in Operational Models." *Am. J. Agr. Econ.* 51:394-404, May 1969.

[39] Buse, R. C., and R. N. Brown. *The Conservation Reserve in Wisconsin, 1956-1959.* Wisconsin Agr. Exp. Sta. Res. Bul. 227, 1961.

[40] Cassels, J. M. *A Study of Fluid Milk Prices.* Cambridge: Harvard University Press, 1937.

[41] Center for Agricultural and Economic Adjustment, Iowa State University. *Goals and Values in Agricultural Policy.* Ames: Iowa State University Press, 1961.

[42] ———. *Farm Goals in Conflict.* Ames: Iowa State University Press, 1963.

[43] ———. *Farm Program Alternatives.* CAED Rep. 18, 1963.

[44] ———. *Farmers in the Market Place.* Ames: Iowa State University Press, 1964.

[45] Christensen, R. P., and R. O. Aines. *Economic Effects of Acreage Control Programs in the 1950s.* USDA, ERS, Agr. Econ. Rep. 18, 1962.

[46] Christenson, R. M. *The Brannan Plan.* Ann Arbor: University of Michigan Press, 1959.

[47] Clark, C. "Afterthoughts on Paley." *Rev. Econ. Stat.* 36:267-272, August 1954.

[48] Clawson, M. "Aging Farmers and Agricultural Policy." *J Farm Econ.* 45:13-30, February 1963.

[49] ———. *Policy Directions for U. S. Agriculture.* Baltimore: John Hopkins University Press, 1968.

[50] Cochrane. W. W. "Farm Price Gyrations — An Aggregative Hypothesis." *J. Farm Econ.* 29:383-408, May 1947.

[51] ———. *Farm Prices, Myth and Reality.* Minneapolis: University of Minnesota Press, 1958.

[52] ———. *High-Level Food Consumption in the United States.* USDA Misc. Pub. 581, 1945.

[53] ———. "Some Further Reflections on Supply Control." *J. Farm Econ.* 41:697-717, November 1959.

[54] ———. "Some Observations of an Ex Economic Advisor: Or What I Learned in Washington." *J. Farm Econ.* 47:447-461, May 1965.

[55] Committee for Economic Development. *An Adaptive Program for Agriculture.* New York, 1962.

[56] Cook. H. L. "The Standby Milk Pool — A New Strategic Bargaining Device." *Am. J. Agr. Econ.* 52:106-108, February 1970.

[57] Daly, G., and F. Giertz. "Welfare Economics and Welfare Reform." *Am. Econ. Rev.* 62:131-138, March 1972.

[58] Dardis, R., and J. Dennisson. "The Welfare Cost of Alternative Methods of Protecting Raw Wool in the United States." *Am. J. Agr. Econ.* 51:303-319, May 1969.

[59] Davis, J. S. "American Agriculture: Schultz's Analysis and Policy Proposals." *Rev. Econ. Stat.* 29:80-91, May 1947.

[60] DeGraff, H. "The Place of Food Promotion and Advertising in Expanding Demand for Farm Products." In *Policy for Commercial Agriculture.* Joint Economic Commitee, 85th Congress, 1st Session, 1957.

[61] Devlen, G. J. "Application of the Antitrust Laws to Agricultural Corporations." In *Dairy Marketing Facts.* Illinois Dept. Agr. Econ. AE-4294, 1972.

[62] Efstratoglou, S., and D. M. Hoover. *Variability in Rental Rates Paid in the Flue-Cured Tobacco Allotment Rental Markets in Selected North Carolina Counties.* North Carolina State University, Econ. Res. Rep. 12, 1970.

[63] Farm Foundation. *Turning the Searchlight on Farm Policy.* Chicago, 1952.

[64] Farrell, K. R. "Marketing Orders and Agreements in the United States Fruit and Vegetable Industries." In *Organization and Competition in the Fruit and Vegetable Industry.* National Commission on Food Marketing, Tech. Study 4, 1966.

[65] Farrington, C. C. "Impact of CCC Operation upon Marketing Agencies." *J. Farm Econ.* 32:943-953 (part 2), November 1950.

[66] Field, B. C. "Congressional Bargaining in Agriculture: Cotton." *Am. J. Agr. Econ.* 50:1-12, February 1968.

[67] Firch R. S. "Interregional Effects on CCC Pricing of Cotton." In *Cotton and Other Fiber Problems and Policies in the United States.* National Advisory Commission on Food and Fiber, Tech. Pap. 2, 1967.

[68] Fite, G. C. "The Historical Development of Agricultural Fundamentalism in the Nineteenth Century." *J. Farm Econ.* 44:1203-1211, December 1962.

[69] Floyd, J. E. "The Effects of Farm Price Supports on the Returns to Land and Labor in Agriculture." *J. Pol. Econ.* 73:148-158, April 1965.

[70] Fox, K., and O. V. Wells. *Reserve Levels for Storable Farm Products.* U. S. Senate Doc. 130, 1952.

[71] Fuller, V. "Bargaining in Agriculture and Industry: Comparisons and Contrasts." *J. Farm Econ.* 45:1283-1290, December 1963.

[72] ———. "Factors Influencing Farm Labor Mobility." In *Labor Mobility and Population in Agriculture.* Iowa State University Center for Agricultural and Economic Adjustment. Ames: Iowa State University Press, 1961.

[73] ———. "Political Pressures and Income Distribution in Agriculture." *J. Farm Econ.* 47:1245-1251, December 1965.

[74] Fuller, W., G. Purnell, L. Fiedler, M. Laursen, R. Beneke, and G. Shepherd. *An Alternative Parity Formula for Agriculture.* Iowa State University Agr. Exp. Sta. Res. Bul. 476, 1960.

[75] Gaffney, M. "The Benefits of Farm Programs: Incidence, Shifting, and Dissipation." *J. Farm Econ.* 47:1252-1263, December 1965.

[76] Galbraith, J. K. "Economic Preconceptions and Farm Policy." *Am. Econ. Rev.* 44:40-52, March 1954.

[77] ———. "Farm Policy: The Current Position." *J. Farm Econ.* 37:292-304, May 1955.

[78] ———. *The New Industrial State.* Boston: Houghton Mifflin, 1967.

[79] ———. "Power and the Useful Economist." *Am. Econ. Rev.* 63:1-11, March 1973.

[80] ———. "Review of Benedict's *Can We Solve the Farm Problem?*" *J. Farm Econ.* 38:878-882, August 1956.

[81] George, P. S., and G. A. King. *Consumer Demand for Food Commodities in the United States with Projections for 1980.* University of California, Giannini Foundation Monograph 26, 1971.

[82] Gislason, C. "Grain Storage Rules." *J. Farm Econ.* 42:576-595, August 1960.

[83] Grant. W. R. and D. S. Moore. *Alternative Government Rice Programs, an Economic Evaluation.* USDA, ERS, Agr. Econ. Rep. 187, 1970.

[84] Gray, R. W., V. L. Sorenson, and W. W. Cochrane. *An Economic Analysis of*

the Impact of Government Programs on the Potato Industry. Minnesota Agr. Exp. Sta. Tech. Bul. 211, 1954.

[85] Griffing M. E., and L. K. Fischer. "Government Purchase of Crop Limiting Easements as a Means of Reducing Production." *J. Farm Econ.* 47:60-73, February 1965.

[86] Griliches, Z. "Estimates of the Aggregate U. S. Farm Supply Function." *J. Farm Econ.* 42:282-293, May 1960.

[87] Griswold, A. W. *Farming and Democracy.* New York: Harcourt, Brace, 1948.

[88] Gustafson, R. L. *Carryover Levels for Grains.* USDA Tech. Bul. 1178, 1958.

[89] ———. "Implications of Recent Research on Optimal Storage Rules." *J. Farm Econ.* 40:290-300, May 1958.

[90] Hadwiger, D. F. "Farm Fundamentalism – Its Future." *J. Farm Econ.* 44:-1218-1230, December 1962.

[91] ——— *Federal Wheat Commodity Programs.* Ames: Iowa State University Press, 1970.

[92] Halsey, F. M., and W. L. Gibson. *Peanut Allotments – Comparison of Sale Value and Capitalized Net Income.* Virginia Agr. Exp. Sta. Bul. 574, 1966.

[93] Hamilton, W. E. "Comprehensive Supply Control: The Farm Bureau Viewpoint." *J. Farm Econ.* 42:1182-1189, December 1960.

[94] ———. "Direct Payments to Farmers Are Not The Answer." In *Policy for Commercial Agriculture.* Joint Economic Committee, 85th Congress, 1st Session, 1957.

[95] Harberger, A. C. "Three Basic Postulates for Applied Welfare Economics: An Interpretive Essay." *J. Econ. Lit.* 9:785-797, September 1971.

[96] Hardin, C. M. "The Bureau of Agricultural Economics under Fire: A Study in Valuation Conflicts." *J. Farm Econ.* 28:635-668, August 1946.

[97] ———. *Food and Fiber in the Nation's Politics.* National Advisory Commission on Food and Fiber, Tech. Pap. 3, 1967.

[98] Hathaway, D. E. "Agricultural Policy and Farmers' Freedom: A Suggested Framework." *J. Farm Econ.* 35:496-510, November 1953.

[99] ———. "Agriculture and the Business Cycle." In *Policy for Commercial Agriculture.* Joint Economic Committee, 85th Congress, 1st Session, 1957.

[100] ———. "The Effects of Agriculture Production Controls in 1954 on Four Michigan Farming Areas." Michigan Agr. Exp. Sta., *Quart. Bul.* 37:565-573, May 1955.

[101] ———. *The Effects of the Price Support Program on the Dry Bean Industry in Michigan.* Michigan Agr. Exp. Sta. Tech. Bul. 250, 1955.

[102] ———. *Government and Agriculture.* New York: Macmillan, 1963.

[103] Hathaway, D. E., and B. E. Perkins. "Occupational Mobility and Migration from Agriculture." In *Rural Poverty in the United States.* National Advisory Commission on Rural Poverty, 1968.

[104] Hathaway, D. E., and L. W. Witt. "Agricultural Policy: Whose Valuations?" *J. Farm Econ.* 34:299-309, August 1952.

[105] Hayami, Y., and V. W. Ruttan. "Factor Prices and Technical Change in Agricultural Development: The United States and Japan, 1880-1960." *J. Pol. Econ.* 78:1115-1141, September-October 1970.

[106] Heady E. O. *Agricultural Policy under Economic Development.* Ames: Iowa State University Press, 1962.

[107] ———. "Tax in Kind to Reduce Supply and Increase Income without Government Programs and Marketing Quotas." *Am. J. Agr. Econ.* 53:441-447, August 1971.

[108] Heady, E. O., L. V. Mayer, and H. C. Madsen. *Future Farm Programs*. Ames: Iowa State University Press, 1972.

[109] Hedrick, J. L., G. S. Tolley, and W. B. Back. *Effects of Flue-Cured Tobacco Programs on Returns to Land and Labor*. USDA ERS 379, 1968.

[110] Helmberger, P. G., and S. Hoos. "Economic Theory of Bargaining in Agriculture." *J. Farm Econ*. 45:1272-1280, December 1963.

[111] Hendrix W. E. "Income Improvement Prospects in Low-Income Areas." *J. Farm Econ*. 41:1065-1075, December 1959.

[112] Hoos, S. "The Contribution of Marketing Agreements and Orders to the Stability and Level of Farm Income." In *Policy for Commercial Agriculture*. Joint Economic Committee, 85th Congress, 1st Session, 1957.

[113] ———. "Economic Possibilities and Limitations of Cooperative Bargaining Associations." In *Cooperative Bargaining*. USDA FCS Serv. Rep. 113, 1970.

[114] Hoover, D. M., and R. O. Aines. *The 1962 Feed Grain Program in the Central Costal Plain of North Carolina*. North Carolina State University Agr. Econ. Inf. Serv. 118, 1963.

[115] Hoover, D. M., and J. G. Maddox. *Food for the Hungry: Direct Distribution and Food Stamp Programs for Low-Income Families*. National Planning Association, Planning Pamphlet 126, 1969.

[116] Horton, D. C. "Policy Directions for United States Sugar Programs." *Am. J. Agr. Econ*. 52:185-196, May 1970.

[117] Houck, J. P., and M. E. Ryan. "Supply Analysis for Corn in the United States: Impact of Changing Government Programs." *Am. J. Agr. Econ*. 54:184-191, May 1972.

[118] Houthakker, H. S. "Toward A Solution of the Farm Problem." *Rev. Econ. Stat*. 43:63-66, February 1961.

[119] Hushak, L. J. "A Welfare Analysis of the Voluntary Corn Diversion Program, 1961 to 1966." *Am. J. Agr. Econ*. 53:173-181, May 1971.

[120] Jesness, O. B. "What Sort of a Farm Price Policy Is Practical in the U.S.A.?" *J. Farm Econ*. 34:616-624, December 1952.

[121] Johnson, D. G. "Efficiency and Welfare Implications of United States Agricultural Policy." *J. Farm Econ*. 45:331-342, May 1963.

[122] ———. "Farm Prices, Resource Use, and Farm Income." In *Policy for Commercial Agriculture*. Joint Economic Committee, 85th Congress, 1st Session, 1957.

[123] ———. *Forward Prices for Agriculture*. Chicago: Univeristy of Chicago Press, 1947.

[124] ———. "Labor Mobility and Agricultural Adjustment." In *Agricultural Adjustment Problems in a Growing Economy*, E. O. Heady, H. G. Diesslin, H. R. Jensen, and G. L. Johnson, eds. Ames: Iowa State College Press, 1958.

[125] ———. "The Nature of the Supply Function for Agricultural Products." *Am. Econ. Rev*. 40:536-564, September 1950.

[126] Johnson, G. L. *Burley Tobacco Control Programs*. Kentucky Agr. Exp. Sta. Bul. 580, 1952.

[127] ——— "Supply Function—Some Facts and Notions." In *Agricultural Adjustment Problems in a Growing Economy*, E. O. Heady, H. G. Diesslin, H. R. Jensen, and G. L. Johnson. Ames: Iowa State College Press, 1958.

[128] Johnson, G. L., and C. L. Quance, eds. *The Overproduction Trap in U.S. Agriculture*. Baltimore: Johns Hopkins University Press, 1972.

[129] Johnson, P. R. "The Social Cost of the Tobacco Program." *J. Farm Econ*. 47: 242-255, May 1965.

[130] Johnson, R. D. *The Conservation Reserve in Nebraska*. Nebraska Agr. Exp. Sta. SB470, 1962.

[131] Johnson, S. "Collective Bargaining in Milk Marketing." *J. Farm Econ.* 49: 1376-1384, December 1967.

[132] Joint Economic Committee, 85th Congress, 1st Session. *Policy for Commercial Agriculture*. 1957.

[133] Jones, B. F., and D. E. Hathaway. "The Volume of Commodities Involved in Price Support Programs Related to the Indexes of Farm Output, 1948-1960." *J. Farm Econ.* 44:850-865, August 1962.

[134] Jones, W. O. "The New Agricultural Economics." *J. Farm Econ.* 34:441-450, November 1952.

[135] Kaldor, D. R., and W. E. Saupe. "Estimates and Projections of an Income-Efficient Commercial-Farm Industry in the North Central States." *J. Farm Econ.* 48:578-596, August 1966.

[136] Kelso, M. M. "A Critical Appraisal of Agricultural Economics in the Mid-Sixties." *J. Farm Econ.* 47:1-16, February 1965.

[137] Knutson, R. D. "Alternative Legislative Frameworks for Collective Bargaining in Agriculture." In *Agricultural Organization in the Modern Industrial Economy*. Department of Agricultural Economics, Ohio State University, 1968.

[138] Ladd, G. W. *Agricultural Bargaining Power*. Ames: Iowa State University Press, 1964.

[139] Langham, M. R. "Game Theory Applied to a Policy Problem of Rice Farmers." *J. Farm Econ.* 45:151-162, February 1963.

[140] Lanzilotti, R. F. "The Superior Market Power of Food Processing and Agricultural Supply Firms — Its Relation to the Farm Problem." *J. Farm Econ.* 42:1228-1246, December 1960.

[141] Leontief, W. "Theoretical Assumptions and Nonobserved Facts." *Am. Econ. Rev.* 61:1-7, March 1971.

[142] Madden, J. P., and M. D. Yoder. *Program Evaluation: Food Stamps and Commodity Distribution in Rural Areas of Central Pennsylvania*. Pennsylvania Agr. Exp. Sta. Bul. 780, 1972.

[143] Madsen, H. C., and E. O. Heady. *Bargaining Power Programs*. CARD Rep. 39, Iowa State University, 1971.

[144] Maier, F. H., J. L. Hedrick, and W. L. Gibson. *The Sale Value of Flue-Cured Tobacco Allotments*. Virginia Agr. Exp. Sta. Tech. Bul. 148, 1960.

[145] Masucci, R. H. "Income Parity Standards for Agriculture." *Agr. Econ. Res.* 14:121-133, October 1962.

[146] Mathis, A. G., and D. Fravel. *Government's Role in Pricing Fluid Milk in the United States*. USDA, ERS, Agr. Econ. Rep. 152, 1968.

[147] McArthur, W. C. *The Conservation Reserve Program in Georgia*. USDA ERS 31, 1961.

[148] McKee, V. C., and L. M. Day. "Measuring the Effects of U.S. Department of Agriculture Programs on Income Distribution." In *Rural Poverty in the United States*. National Advisory Commission on Rural Poverty, 1968.

[149] McMillen, W. "New Uses and New Crop." In *Policy for Commercial Agriculture*. Joint Economic Commitee, 85th Congress, 1st Session, 1957.

[150] Moore, J. R. "Bargaining Power Potential in Agriculture." *Am. J. Agr. Econ.* 50:1051-1053, November 1968.

[151] National Advisory Commission on Food and Fiber. *Food and Fiber for the Future*. 1967.

[152] Naylor, T. H. "Policy Simulation Experiments with Macroeconometric Models: The State of the Art." *Am. J. Agr. Econ.* 52:263-271, May 1970.

[153] Nicholls, W. H., and D. G. Johnson. "The Farm Price Policy Awards: A Topical Digest of the Winning Essays." *J. Farm Econ.* 28:267-283, February, 1946.

[154] Norton, L. J., and E. J. Working. "A Proposal for Supporting Farm Income." *Illinois Farm Econ.* 127:309-313, Department of Agricultural Economics, University of Illinois, 1945.

[155] "On the Redefinition of Parity Price and Parity Income." *J. Farm Econ.* 29: 1358-1374, November 1947.

[156] *Parity Returns Position of Farmers.* Report by USDA. 90th Congress, 1st Session, 1967.

[157] Peterson, W. H. *The Great Farm Problem.* Chicago: Regnery, 1959.

[158] Pigou, A. C. *The Economics of Welfare.* 4th ed. London: Macmillan, 1962.

[159] "A Price Policy for Agriculture, Consistent with Economic Progress, That Will Promote Adequate and More Stable Income from Farming." Award Winning Papers, *J. Farm Econ.* 27:737-902, November 1945.

[160] Rasmussen, W. D., and G. L. Baker. "A Short History of Price Support and Adjustment Legislation and Programs for Agriculture, 1933-65." *Agr. Econ. Res.* 18: 69-78, July 1966.

[161] Reinsel, R. D., and R. D. Krenz, *Capitalization of Farm Program Benefits into Land Values.* USDA ERS 506, 1972.

[162] Robinson, K. L. "Cost and Effectiveness of Recent Government Land Retirement Programs in the United States." *J. Farm Econ.* 48:22-30, February 1966.

[163] ————. "The Impact of Government Price and Income Programs on Income Distribution in Agriculture." *J. Farm Econ.* 47:1225-1234, December 1965.

[164] ————. "Possible Effects of Eliminating Direct Price Support and Acreage Control Programs." *Farm Economics* 218, Department of Agricultural Economics, Cornell University, 1960.

[165] Rogers, R. O., and G. T. Barton. *Our Farm Production Potential, 1975.* USDA Agr. Inf. Bul. 233, 1960.

[166] Roy, E. P. *Collective Bargaining in Agriculture.* Danville, Ill.: Interstate, 1970.

[167] Rudd, R. W. "Land Retirement Programs." In *Agricultural Policy: A Review of Programs and Needs.* National Advisory Commission on Food and Fiber, Tech. Pap. 5, 1967.

[168] Ryan, B., and N. C. Gross. "The Diffusion of Hybrid Seed Corn in Two Iowa Communities." *Rural Sociology* 8:15-24, March 1943.

[169] Schertz, L. P., and E. W. Lean. *Administrative Controls On Quantities Marketed in the Feed-Livestock Economy.* Minnesota Agr. Exp. Sta. Tech. Bul. 241, 1962.

[170] Schickele, R. "The National Food Allotment Program." *J. Farm Econ.* 28: 515-533, May 1946.

[171] Schnittker Study of Payment Limitations. *Congressional Record*, April 30, 1969, pp. 10867-10872.

[172] Schuh, G. E. "Interrelations between the Farm Labor Force and Changes in the Total Economy." In *Rural Poverty in the United States.* National Advisory Commission on Rural Poverty, 1968.

[173] Schultz, T. W. "Agricultural Policy for What?" *J. Farm Econ.* 41:189-193, May 1959.

[174] ————. *Agriculture in an Unstable Economy.* New York: McGraw-Hill, 1945.

[175] ————. *The Economic Organization of Agriculture.* New York: McGraw-Hill, 1953.

[176] ———. "Farm Price Gyrations by Cochrane." *J. Farm Econ.* 33:540-544 (part 1), November 1951.

[177] ———. *Redirecting Farm Policy.* New York: Macmillan, 1943.

[178] ———. "The United States Farm Problem in Relation to the Growth and Development of the United States Economy." In *Policy for Commercial Agriculture.* Joint Economic Committee, 85th Congress, 1st Session, 1957.

[179] ———. "What Sort of Price Policy Is Practical in the U.S.A.: Discussion." *J. Farm Econ.* 34:624-627, December 1952.

[180] Seagraves, J. A., and R. C. Manning. *Flue-Cured Tobacco Allotment Values and Uncertainty, 1934-1962.* North Carolina State University Econ. Res. Rep. 2, 1967.

[181] Shaffer, J. D. "The Scientific Industrialization of the U.S. Food and Fiber Sector, Background for Market Policy." In *Agricultural Organization in the Modern Industrial Economy.* Department of Agricultural Economics, Ohio State University, 1968.

[182] Sharples, J. A., and W. N. Schaller. "Predicting Short-run Aggregate Adjustment to Policy Alternatives." *Am. J. Agr. Econ.* 50:1523-1536, December 1968.

[183] Sharples, J. A., and J. R. Tompkin. *The Effect of the 1961 Feed Grain Program on West-Central Ohio Farms.* Ohio Agr. Exp. Sta. Res. Bul. 947, 1963.

[184] Shepherd, G. S. *Farm Policy: New Directions.* Ames: Iowa State University Press, 1964.

[185] ———. "What Can a Research Man Say about Values?" *J. Farm Econ.* 38:8-16, February 1956.

[186] Shepherd, G., R. Beneke, R. Heifner, and W. Uhrig. *Controlling Agricultural Production by Controlling Inputs.* Missouri Agr. Exp. Sta. Bul. 798, 1963.

[187] Shepherd, G., A. Paulsen, F. Kutish, D. Kaldor, R. Heifner, and G. Futrell. *Production and Income Estimates and Projections for the Feed-Livestock Economy under Specified Control and Market-Clearing Conditions.* Iowa Agr. Exp. Sta. Spec. Rep. 27, 1960.

[188] Simerl, L. H. "Adjusting Production through Administrative Controls." In *Policy for Commercial Agriculture.* Joint Economic Committee, 85th Congress, 1st Session, 1957.

[189] Simmons, W. M., and R. L. Rizek, "Performance of the Livestock-Feed Grain Sector." *J. Farm Econ.* 48:1455-1463, December 1966.

[190] Sisler, D. G. *Direct Payments as a Policy Tool in the Feed Grain Livestock Sector.* Cornell Agr. Exp. Sta. Bul. 1011, 1966.

[191] Slaughter, R. W. "Payment Limitation: Effect on Supply Adjustment and Income Distribution." *Am. J. Agr. Econ.* 51:1233-1236, December 1969.

[192] Soth, L. "The End of Agrarianism: Fission of the Political Economy of Agriculture." *Am. J. Agr. Econ.* 52:663-667, December 1970.

[193] Southworth, H. M. "The Economics of Public Measures to Subsidize Food Consumption." *J. Farm Econ.* 27:38-66, February 1945.

[194] Strickland, P. L., W. H. Brown, and W. C. McArthur. *Cotton Production and Farm Income Estimates under Selected Alternative Farm Programs.* USDA, ERS, Agr. Econ. Rep. 212, 1971.

[195] Talbot, R. B., and D. F. Hadwiger. *The Policy Process in American Agriculture.* San Francisco: Chandler, 1968.

[196] Thompson, L. S. "The Management of Reserve Stocks." *J. Farm Econ.* 34:713-718, December 1952.

[197] Tintner, G. "What Does Control Theory Have To Offer?" *Am. J. Agr. Econ.* 51:383-393, May 1969.

[198] Torgerson, R. E. *Producer Power at the Bargaining Table: A Case Study of the Legislative Life of S.109*. Columbia: University of Missouri Press, 1970.

[199] Tweeten, L. G. *Commodity Programs for Wheat*. Oklahoma Agr. Exp. Sta. Tech. Bul. T-118, 1965.

[200] ———. "The Demand for United States Farm Output." *Food Research Institute Studies* 12 (3):343-369, 1967.

[201] ———. *Foundations of Farm Policy*. Lincoln: University of Nebraska Press, 1970.

[202] ———. "Theories Explaining the Persistence of Low Resource Returns in a Growing Farm Economy." *Am. J. Agr. Econ.* 51:798-817, November 1969.

[203] Tweeten, L. G., E. O. Heady, and L. Mayer. *Farm Program Alternatives, Farm Incomes and Public Costs under Alternative Commodity Programs for Feed Grains and Wheat*. CAED Rep. 18, Iowa State University, 1963.

[204] Tweeten, L. G., D. Kalbfleisch, and Y. C. Lu. *An Economic Analysis of Carryover Policies for the United States Wheat Industry*. Oklahoma Agr. Exp. Sta. Tech. Bul. T-132, 1971.

[205] Tweeten, L. G., and J. S. Plaxico. "Long-Run Outlook for Agricultural Adjustments Based on National Growth." *J. Farm Econ.* 46:39-55, February 1964.

[206] Tweeten, L. G., and C. L. Quance. "Excess Capacity and Adjustment Potential in U.S. Agriculture." *Agr. Econ. Res.* 24:57-66, July 1972.

[207] ———. "Positivistic Measures of Aggregate Supply Elasticities: Some New Approaches." *Am. J. Agr. Econ.* 51:342-352, May 1969.

[208] Tyner, F. H., and L. G. Tweeten. "Excess Capacity in Agriculture." *Agr. Econ. Res.* 16:23-31, January 1964.

[209] USDA. *Agriculture's Capacity to Produce*. Agr. Inf. Bul 88, 1952.

[210] ———. *Base Plans in U.S. Milk Markets: Development, Status, and Potential*. ERS MRR-957, 1962.

[211] ———. *Cooperative Bargaining*. FCS Serv. Rep. 113, 1970.

[212] ———. *Effects of Acreage Allotment Programs, 1954 and 1955, a Summary Report*. ARS Prod. Res. Rep. 3, 1956.

[213] ———. *Farm Policy in the Years Ahead*. Report of National Agricultural Advisory Commission, 1964.

[214] ———. *The Federal Milk Marketing Order Program*. Marketing Bul. 27, 1968.

[215] ———. *Legal Phases of Farmer Cooperatives: Part III, Antitrust Laws*. FCS Inf. 70, 1970.

[216] ———. *Major Statistical Series of the U.S. Department of Agriculture: Vol. 1, Agricultural Prices and Parity*. Agr. Handbook 365, 1970.

[217] ———. *What Peace Can Mean to American Farmers: Post-War Agriculture and Employment*. Misc. Pub. 562, 1945.

[218] ———. *What Peace Can Mean to American Farmers: Maintenance of Full Employment*. Misc. Pub. 570, 1945.

[219] ———. *What Peace Can Mean to American Farmers: Expansion of Foreign Trade*. Misc. Pub. 582, 1945.

[220] ———. *What Peace Can Mean to American Farmers: Agricultural Policy*. Misc. Pub. 589, 1945.

[221] U.S. House of Representatives, Committee on Agriculture, 80th Congress, 2d Session. *Long-Range Agricultural Policy*. 1948.

[222] U.S. House of Representatives, Committee on Agriculture, 83d Congress 2d Session. *Long-Range Farm Program*. 1954.

[223] U.S. Senate, Committee on Agriculture and Forestry, 80th Congress, 2d Session. *Long-Range Agricultural Policy and Program*. Rep. 885, 1948.

[224] U.S. Senate, Committee on Agriculture and Forestry, 86th Congress, 2d Session. *Report . . . on Farm Price and Income Projections 1960-65*. U.S. Senate Doc. 77, 1960.

[225] Vermeer, J. *An Economic Appraisal of the 1961 Feed Grain Program*. USDA, ERS, Agr. Econ. Rep. 38, 1963.

[226] Vermeer, J., and R. W. Slaughter. *Analysis of a General Cropland Retirement Program*. USDA ERS 377, 1968.

[227] Wallace, T. D. "Measures of Social Costs of Agricultural Programs." *J. Farm Econ.* 44:581-597, May 1962.

[228] Waugh, F. V. "Reserve Stocks of Farm Products." In *Agricultural Policy: A Review of Programs and Needs*. National Advisory Commission on Food and Fiber, Tech. Pap. 5, 1967.

[229] ———. "What Sort of Price Policy Is Practical in the U.S.A.?" *J. Farm Econ.* 34:605-615, December 1952.

[230] Weisgerber, P. *Productivity of Diverted Cropland*. USDA ERS 398, 1969.

[231] Wetmore, J.M., M. E. Abel, E. W. Learn, and W. W. Cochrane. *Policies for Expanding the Demand for Farm Food Products in the United States*, part 1. Minnesota Agr. Exp. Sta. Tech. Bul. 231, 1959.

[232] Whittlesey, N. K. *Aggregate Economic Effects of Alternative Land Retirement Programs: A Linear Programming Analysis*. In cooperation with Iowa State University. USDA Tech. Bul. 1351, 1966.

[233] Wilcox, W. W. "Agriculture's Income and Adjustment Problem." In *Economic Policies for Agriculture in the 1960s*. Joint Economic Committee, 86th Congress, 2d Session, 1960.

[234] ———. *Economic Aspects of Farm Program Payment Limitations*. Library of Congress Legislative Reference Service, 1969.

[235] ———. "Effects of Farm Price Changes on Efficiency in Farming." *J. Farm Econ.* 33:55-65, February 1951.

[236] ———. "The Farm Policy Dilemma." *J. Farm Econ.* 40:563-571, August 1958.

[237] ———. "How Much of Farm Program Benefits Are Lost to Farm Operators via Capitalization into Land Values?" *J. Farm Econ.* 46:246-247, February 1964.

[238] *Who Will Control U.S. Agriculture?* North Central Reg. Ext. Pub. 32; Illinois Agr. Ext. Serv. Spec. Pub. 27, 1972.

[239] Wood, A. W. "The Marketing Board Approach to Collective Bargaining." *J. Farm Econ.* 49:1367-1375, December 1967.

[240] Working, E. J. *Demand for Meat*. Institute of Meat Packing, University of Chicago, 1954.

[241] Wunderle, R. E., and D. L. Call. *An Evaluation of the Pilot Food Certificate Program in Chicago, Illinois, and Bibb County, Georgia*. Cornell Graduate School of Nutrition, Contract Report, 1971.

[242] Zepp, G. A., and J. A. Sharples, *General Cropland Retirement: Analysis of Four Alternatives*. USDA ERS 462, 1971.

Part IV. Postwar Policies Relating to
Trade in Agricultural Products

The objectives of this review article are limited ones. The first objective is to show that there has been only a modest elimination of the conflicts between domestic agricultural policies and foreign trade policies in the world over the past quarter century. The second objective is to note and describe some of the policy analyses concerned with international trade in agricultural products and the conflicts between domestic and trade policies. The third objective is to present some important areas of research that have been neglected but that show promise of contributing to the possible resolution of the conflicts between domestic and trade policies and to the improved functioning of international markets.

It should be made clear that the literature review component of the article is selective. For instance, the review barely touches on the enormous analytical and policy literature on international trade and economic affairs. A significant part of this literature has been reviewed in recent years, especially in major articles in the *Journal of Economic Literature* [44, 45, 69]. Even within the rather confined scope of this article, the approach has been selective and illustrative rather than exhaustive. The potentially relevant bibliography is enormous. A bibliography prepared under the direction of Lawrence Witt almost a decade ago [13, part 3] and described as "an introduction to the literature on Food for Peace and on the use of surplus agricultural commodities in programs of assistance to developing countries" included 950 entries. Thus the failure to include an article, a monograph, or a book should not be interpreted as an indication that the particular contribution was unimportant or was flawed.

I am indebted to Barbara Blair and Deputy Director Carmen O. Nohre of the Foreign Demand and Competition Division, Economic Research Service, United States Department of Agriculture, for making available to me a listing of the references numbered [89] through [175].

D. G. J.

Postwar Policies Relating to Trade
in Agricultural Products

D. Gale Johnson
Professor of Economics
University of Chicago

Domestic and International Policy Conflicts

For at least four decades the United States has followed an ambivalent and inconsistent set of policies for trade in farm products. At no time were the conflicts between a liberal trade policy that would guide farm production in the directions implied by the principle of comparative advantage and the needs of domestic farm programs that required substantial interferences with international trade, for both imports and exports, resolved. Yet progress was made.

The United States was far from alone in the difficulties of resolving such conflicts. Numerous individual countries as well as such groups of countries as the European Economic Community have struggled with the seemingly inconsistent objectives of expanding international trade while vigorously protecting domestic agriculture. A significant part of the economic conflicts between Western Europe and the United States have arisen over the desire of the former to protect its agriculture from external competition and the efforts of the latter to expand exports in order to employ its farm resources fully.

Policy Conflicts at the End of World War II

Two somewhat lengthy quotations from the debate over the postwar farm and trade policy of the United States present in clear fashion the basic nature of the conflicts. Further, the quotations, the first from 1947 and the second from 1946, indicate how little the nature of the conflicts has changed in a quarter century. The first quotation can be said to represent the official position of the Department of Agriculture, since it is from the testimony of Carl Farrington before a joint congressional committee concerned with long-range agricultural policy [70, pp. 171-172]. The second is from a report entitled *Postwar Agricultural Policies* by the House Special Committee on Postwar Economic Policy and Planning, chaired by William M. Colmer [81, pp. 24, 33-34].

Foreign policy: We would be remiss if, in the formation of our domestic agricultural program, we did not give careful consideration to its relationship to international trade and the foreign policy of our government.

. . . in spite of adjustments in our pattern of production, we still need foreign markets for some commodities, such as cotton, wheat, tobacco, lard, rice, and certain fruits and vegetables. We know the great effort which our Government has devoted to breaking down barriers to trade throughout the world. We also know that price supports for farm commodities here in the United States also require a certain degree of protection through tariffs or other trade barriers. Without them foreign producers might flood our domestic market, with our Government buying the domestic production. In addition, it tends to become difficult to export farm products without an export subsidy. These trade barriers are in conflict, although not wholly irreconcilably, with our repeated declarations of a national policy which seeks international cooperation in reducing trade barriers. As long as this conflict exists, the best hope of reconciling it without increasing the burden on the United States taxpayer is in the possibility that international agreements can be negotiated for the individual commodities involved. Such agreements could recognize the special problems of such commodities and, in effect, lift them out of the general consideration of international trade practices for the duration of the agreements. In this way they could preserve the principle of international economic collaboration without sacrificing agriculture's interest.

. . . For the next few years, at least, we will need to continue having available section 32 funds to bridge the gap between domestic and world prices for some commodities which we export.

We recommend that section 32 of the Agricultural Adjustment Act be made applicable to all programs of the Department, particularly to programs of price support, inasmuch as imports could, as previously indicated, seriously interfere with the operation of any price-support program.

If a price is maintained at a level above that necessary to balance supply with demand, it tends to maintain production at levels in excess of market demand. Two alternative programs must then be considered; either production and marketing quotas must be established, or the surplus must be disposed of at lower prices by dumping abroad or by subsidized consumption at home. The committee believes that neither of these policies can be expected to yield the best results over the long run for the following reasons: (1) Production controls tend to maintain high-cost production and restrict expansion in low-cost areas as technological changes reduce costs. This is particularly true when acreage controls are made on an historical basis. At the same time prices to consumers are maintained at a high level, and the Nation as a whole is prevented from enjoying the benefits of lower costs resulting from improved techniques of production. (2) When production is not restricted, the Government is forced to buy up the surplus and take the loss involved through sale at a lower price.

. . . When prices are maintained on the domestic market and exports subsidized, other nations retaliate by applying similar export subsidies because the action of the Nation dumping its surpluses abroad tends to depress the world price. Any initial benefits are rapidly destroyed, world prices become less stable, and international friction is generated.

We suggest that the following principles be given serious consideration as embodying the objectives toward which we should work: (1) The support levels should be such that they would be below the levels that would balance the expected supply and demand of various products, and they should vary from year to year as supply and demand conditions change. (2) Except in the case of demoralized world market situations (against which the international cooperative arrangements discussed above might be invoked) support prices for export commodities should not exceed the prices expected to prevail on the world market over the production period.

The Department of Agriculture, while aware of the conflict between its programs and a liberal trade policy, was not prepared to equalize domestic and international prices but instead wanted to continue export subsidies and import quotas. It held out hope for the negotiation of international agreements that in effect would put farm products in a special category not bound by the principles of liberal trade. The Colmer Committee argued that in the long run prices could not be maintained at a level above that which would equate market demand with production and that efforts to do so would result in either the extensive use of export subsidies or production controls that would maintain high-cost production and high prices to consumers.

United States farm and trade policy has continued to be torn between the need to expand exports of some farm products — because otherwise the domestic adjustment problems could be met only by programs that were too costly to be politically viable — and the unwillingness to reduce significantly its barriers to the imports of several farm products that are produced at a comparative disadvantage. Although the support prices of major export products were aligned with international prices, export subsidies continued to be used extensively for wheat until September 1972. Export subsidies have been used to dispose of products of which we are not low-cost producers. In the absence of trade distorting measures would import rather than export, such as manufactured dairy products.

The conflict between domestic farm programs that result in market prices being maintained above world market levels and a liberal trade program has not yet been resolved for a rather simple reason — *it cannot be resolved.* However, during the 1960s support measures were adopted for cotton and the feed grains that resulted in a significant reduction in the interference with international trade while maintaining acceptable levels of returns to farmers.

United States Trade in Farm Products

As late as 1890 agricultural exports accounted for 75 percent of all United States exports. Over the next two decades the percentage declined to 50 percent; by the end of the 1920s only a third of total exports consisted of farm products. During the 1930s total exports and agricultural exports both declined, but farm exports declined the most [80, pp. 4-5]. The low point was reached in 1940 when agricultural exports fell to 9 percent of total exports, owing in large part to the outbreak of war in Europe. In the years following World War II agricultural exports increased in value and quantity and as a percentage of total exports. They declined again after 1951 and stagnated until 1957. Between 1957 and 1972 farm exports accounted for about a fifth of total exports [79].

Two measures of the importance of exports to agriculture are commonly used. One is the percentage of harvested acreage used for producing export products; the other is the percentage of cash farm receipts accounted for by the marketing of exports [79 (1952, 1972); 80, p. 10]. In 1910 approximately 12 percent of the cropland harvested was exported directly as a crop or indirectly as feed for livestock. During World War I and its aftermath about 16 percent of cropland output was exported, but the percentage declined gradually to a low of only 5 percent in 1935 and 1936. By the late 1940s the percentage had increased to nearly 15 percent. There were significant fluctuations in the percentage during the 1950s, ranging from less than 10 percent in 1953 to 19 percent in 1956. With some decline in cropland harvested and a significant increase in the use of land for exports, an all-time high (at least until 1972-73) was reached in 1963 when almost 26 percent of all crop-harvested area was used for export products. Approximately the same percentage was achieved in 1970 [51]. Thus measured by the cropland used for exports, the relative dependence of United States agriculture on exports is now substantially higher than it was before World War II.

Before World War II the value of farm exports was about 16 to 18 percent of the value of farm marketings; a peak of 28 percent was reached in 1918. The value of farm exports declined to less than 10 percent during the 1930s and increased to 12 percent in 1951; it declined to 9 percent in 1953 and slowly increased to 16 percent in 1957. Until 1972 exports fluctuated between 12 and 16 percent of cash receipts [79]. With the increased volume and price exports realized in 1973 and 1974, exports equaled or exceeded 20 percent of cash receipts [14].

Farm Programs and Trade Interferences

In retrospect it appears that there were three major periods of development of farm programs between 1933 and 1960. Each came into being at a time when the importance of exports to agriculture was low and/or declining.

The first period of development, when the basic framework of United States farm policy was determined, was 1933 through 1938; during this period exports accounted for a very small fraction of cash farm receipts and offered an outlet for relatively few cropland acres. It included three years in which the United States was a net importer of grains, an unprecedented occurrence.

Another major review of domestic farm programs occurred in 1947-49. In testimony to Congress in 1947, Assistant Secretary Charles F. Brannan presented projections of exports for 1950, but in terms of what was "assumed to be normal for future years . . ." [70]. For several important export products the projections were gloomy indeed. Wheat exports were projected at only 100 million bushels, only half above the low levels of 1937-41. Cotton exports of 3.5 million bales were projected, less than in 1937-41. Only tobacco exports were projected at levels that approximated prewar periods of reasonable world prosperity. Thus it is perhaps not surprising that at this time Congress gave little thought or emphasis to the conflict between domestic and trade programs.

Finally, after the change in national administration and the ending of price support commitments made in the Agricultural Act of 1949, an effort was made in 1953-54 to modify farm price support programs significantly. Little or nothing was accomplished with respect to domestic programs; the major piece of legislation affecting agriculture and trade was the Agricultural Trade Development and Assistance Act of 1954. This act was in response to three interrelated phenomena — very good crops in 1952 and 1953, a decline in exports of about a third from 1951 through 1953, and a substantial increase in stocks held by the Commodity Credit Corporation. By mid-1954 the value of CCC inventories was three and a half times the value two years earlier and loans outstanding were six times as large. The total of loans outstanding and commodities owned increased from $1.46 billion on June 30, 1952, to $6.0 billion two years later [79].

The 1950s fully confirmed the major points made by the Colmer Committee. The maintenance of price suports substantially above equilibrium levels required efforts to limit production and resulted in substantial stock accumulations and efforts to expand exports.

The first major response to the accumulation of grain stocks by the Commodity Credit Corporation was Public Law 480, the Agricultural Trade and Development and Assistance Act of 1954. Among the objectives of P.L. 480 were "to promote the economic stability of American agriculture and the national welfare, to make maximum efficient use of surplus agricultural commodities in furtherance of the foreign policy of the United States and to facilitate the expansion of foreign trade in agricultural commodities produced in the United States by providing a means whereby surplus agricultural commodities in excess of the usual marketings of such commodities may be sold through private trade channels and foreign currencies accepted in payment therefor." P.L. 480 has been revised several times, but it has served as the basis for our food aid programs and, until the mid-1970s, a primary method of disposing of agricultural products to the developing countries.

In the late 1950s and early 1960s agricultural exports began to increase, and price support policy was gradually changed for cotton, wheat, and the feed grains to improve the competitive position of the United States in world markets. Price supports were lowered to levels that were at or below export prices; this transition was completed by 1966. The market prices were generally aligned with export prices and the role of export subsidies was diminished, and the average return for the major crops was approximately maintained by direct payments to program participants.

The change in price support policy was not as effective as we might have hoped in eliciting responses from our trading partners. There were several reasons for this. First, the United States continued to use export subsidies until international market prices increased substantially in late 1972. Although it was true that the reliance on export subsidies declined, the United States never said that it would abandon the payment of export subsidies and still has not so declared. In fact, the cost of export subsidies was greater in 1970-71 than in 1966-67 or any subsequent period. Export subsidy costs were nearly as high in 1971-72 as in the previous year [14, April 1974, pp. 30-31]. Second, a convincing case was never made that the combination of price support and diversion payments and the diverted acreage had a significant effect on the level of production in the United States. Thus foreign farm groups and governments did not look simply at farm market prices but added in all of the payments and did not find the price disparities as large as we implied. Finally, it appeared that the United States was a liberal trader only for its export products and seemed to be about as protectionistic as anyone else when it came to dairy, peanuts, wool, sugar, and beef [86, 41].

During the period since World War II the United States has engaged in several negotiations to reduce the barriers to trade in all products, including agricultural products. The first effort culminated in the General Agreement on Tariffs and Trade (GATT), which was not only a negotiation about specific trade barriers but also an effort to devise a code of behavior for international trade. The General Agreement on Tariffs and Trade included exceptions to its general rule that the only legitimate trade barriers were import and export duties. These exceptions were made largely at the insistence of the United States [85] to permit the operation of domestic farm programs without significant interference from international trade. Quantitative restrictions were permitted when required for the enforcement of domestic production controls, marketing controls, or surplus disposal programs. Export subsidies were also permitted for essentially the same reasons. Neither quantitative restrictions nor export subsidies were to be used to change the pattern of trade, but the General Agreement on Tariffs and Trade has never developed adequate criteria for determining when such measures either restrict trade, as in the case of quantitative restrictions, or significantly expand exports, as in the case of export subsidies [78, *Papers*, vol. I, pp. 859-871].

Economists have discussed the numerous conflicts between domestic farm programs and a liberal trade policy. D. G. Johnson [35] outlined the major sources of conflict and indicated changes in domestic farm programs that could be made to remove most, if not all, of the conflict. Hardin [26] edited a special issue of *The Annals* which dealt largely with the interrelationships between agriculture and foreign policy. A volume edited by Tontz [71] included examples of economists' contributions to the discussion since World War II.

Most of the economists who wrote on the subject argued that the United States should remove the conflicts by significant modifications in its farm programs that would permit removing Section 22 import quotas and abolishing the use of export subsidies. The modifications included the reduction of price support levels and programs to encourage long-run resource adjustments through improved labor mobility and the achievement of income objectives by measures that would have minimum effect upon farm output [26, 35]. It should be noted that a case also has been made in favor of the United States farm and trade policies. As an example, Ioanes [71] argued that the United

States alone among major countries has tried to manage supplies, has had responsible stockpiling practices, and has thus added considerable stability to world supplies and prices of several important farm products.

Farm and Trade Policies of Other Countries

The inconsistency between domestic farm programs and a liberal trade policy is no monopoly of the United States. Two excellent reviews of the agricultural policies of the major industrial countries have been made by the Organization for Economic Cooperation and Development and its predecessor, the Organization for European Economic Cooperation [52, 53]. The Food and Agriculture Organization has presented data indicating that in the industrial countries self-sufficiency ratios for most farm products rose during the period 1955-57 to 1964-66 [77] and that if current policies continue until 1980 self-sufficiency ratios will continue to increase [74, *Papers*, vol. I, p. 70].

Perhaps the most striking event, and certainly the most publicized one, affecting international trade in farm products was the formation of the European Economic Community and the Common Agricultural Policy. Because the Common Agricultural Policy, which was designed to create a uniform agricultural policy within the Common Market and free movement of farm products among the members, was in an early stage of development, negotiations on farm products during the Kennedy Round were extremely difficult and largely fruitless [28, 78, *Papers*, vol. I, part 7].

Major components of the Common Agricultural Policy for a wide range of farm products — grains, flour, beef and veal, pork, poultry, eggs, and dairy products — are the variable levy and export restitutions [52]. The basic elements of the price policy consist of a target price (generally at both farm and market levels), an intervention price which is below the target price and is similar to the United States support prices, and a threshold price. The difference between the import price and the threshold price determines the variable levy — a measure designed to maintain the equivalence between the cost of imported and domestic products and the target price. Under this system a fall in world prices has no effect on the volume of imports. Export restitutions or export subsidies come into play when production exceeds consumption within the Common Market and exports are the alternative to increasing stocks.

The impact of the Common Agricultural Policy on Common Market imports and exports of farm products has been subject to substantial dispute. Studies in the United States Department of Agriculture indicate that there have been substantial restraints on imports as well as significant distortions of the pattern of trade [5]. Perhaps the most striking distortion has been the substitutions in livestock rations due to the varying barriers to imports. Soybean and oil-meal imports have increased rapidly as have the imports of certain starch products (manioc, for example) that enter duty free. The amount of grain included in mixed feeds has declined substantially since the policy was imposed [54].

Coppock [10, 11] contributed two excellent studies of farm and trade policy difficulties that confronted the Atlantic community in the early 1960s. These two books contain a great deal of relevant descriptive material on the structure of agriculture in Western Europe and North America. The statement of problems is still fresh and incisive.

Tracy [72] provides an informative description and analysis of farm and trade policy for the period since 1880. He indicates the circumstances that gradually resulted in a return to agricultural protectionism in the latter part of the nineteenth century and the early part of the twentieth century. For those who may think that the policy problems of agriculture today and our efforts to solve them represent something new, it is sobering to read the relevant parts of an article by Walford [83], especially tables IX and X, the latter dealing with restrictions on the export and import of grain.

Although it is quite appropriate to be critical of many of the agricultural and trade policies of the industrial countries, it must be noted that developing countries have also followed policies that have adverse effects upon their own agriculture. Schuh [59] has presented both an informative catalog of such policies as well as an analysis of a specific Brazilian example. In discussing general economic policies that affect agriculture he notes four such policies that have often been adverse to the interests of farm people and the expansion of agricultural production: (1) forced draft industrialization directed specifically to import substitution; (2) high protective tariffs or other import restrictions designed to reduce imports while failing to provide incentives to expand exports; (3) the overvaluation of exchange rates and the frequent establishment of multiple exchange rates; and (4) credit and fiscal policies to stimulate industries.

Taken together this mix of policies tends to penalize agricultural exports and to result in high prices for modern farm inputs and a loss of export markets for traditional agricultural products. Schuh estimated the effects of an overvalued exchange rate in Brazil upon the exports of corn for 1960-66. He estimated that potential exports of corn would have had an average value of about $103 million compared to actual exports of approximately $15 million [70].

Valdés [82] analyzed the effect of Chilean commercial and trade policies for the period from 1946 to 1965. He estimated that throughout most of this period there were significant negative rates of effective protection for wheat and beef, which were normally imported, and for barley, lamb and wool, which were normally exported. For all the commodities except barley the negative rate of effective protection ranged from -0.16 to -0.67. After 1951 barley generally, though not always, had either a slight positive or zero protection. The primary sources of the negative rates of protection were the overvaluation of the Chilean currency and the tariffs on farm production inputs.[1] Valdés concluded: "The results suggest that if during the 1950's Chile had opted for a commercial policy without negative protection for these farm activities, the trade balance deficit of agricultural goods would have been reduced to an insignificant level." For 1956-60 the trade balance deficit was approximately $50 million.

Measurement of Trade Policy Effects

Economists have argued repeatedly that the trade interferences accompanying domestic farm programs have a variety of adverse effects – on consumers, on the gains from specialization, on the export earnings of developing countries, and on taxpayers. Although much remains to be done in terms of providing verifiable estimates of these and related effects, considerable progress has been made since 1955. In this review four general areas will be considered: (1) the impact of P.L. 480 upon recipient countries; (2) the production and consumption effects of the enlargement of the Common Market; (3) the effects of farm and trade programs of the industrial countries on the export earnings of the less developed countries; and (4) the measurement of the benefits and costs of farm and trade policies.

P.L. 480 and the Recipient Countries

Schultz [62] presented estimates of the relationship between the money cost to the federal government of P.L. 480 food shipments, the marginal revenue that would have been earned from exporting the same quantity in commercial markets, the cost of P.L. 480 shipments to recipient countries, and the value to recipient countries. He estimated that the value of the shipments to the recipient countries was about 37 percent of the Commodity Credit Corporation costs. Based on the agreements that had been signed, he estimated the cost to the recipient countries at 10 to 15 percent of the CCC costs. He attempted to indicate the effect of P.L. 480 imports upon the farmers of the recipient countries. He felt that the price effect would be negative, though he noted that some of the price effect would be offset by the rise in real income in the recipient countries because of the resource transfer.

Sen [64] gave a rather more optimistic view in connection with the benefits that India had derived from P.L. 480 shipments. He argued that such food shipments had improved per-capita consumption, that other exporters had not been adversely affected, and that internal price supports had largely if not entirely, eliminated any adverse price effects for Indian farmers. He also argued that the availability of P.L. 480 grain had not slowed down emphasis upon agricultural development.

Witt and Eicher [87] summarized the results of several country studies of the impact of P.L. 480. They gave good marks to the program in providing food in emergencies caused by adverse weather. They concluded that the contribution of P.L. 480 to economic development depended very largely upon the internal policies of the recipient nations. Because of this they found that the case studies available to them did not permit an unequivocal conclusion concerning the adverse effects of shipments on local producers.

Mann [50], basing his work on an extension of an excellent theoretical article by Fisher [22], empirically estimated the impact of P.L. 480 imports on prices and domestic supply of cereals in India. Using a simultaneous equation model that included supply and demand equations for cereals, an income-generation equation, a commercial imports equation, and a stock equation, he found that the shipments lowered the price of cereals and reduced domestic production but that the reduction in domestic production was less than the shipments so that consumption was increased. Mann concluded that under the circumstances prevailing in India the net effect was a desirable one.

Srivastava [68], in a comment on Mann's article, argued that the existence of the fair price shops resulted in a sufficient increase in consumption and that there may have been no adverse effect on cereals prices received by farmers. He also implied that the elasticity of supply of cereals in India was zero. In response Mann [50] argued that there was an absence of evidence to indicate the price impact of the fair price shops.

Rogers, Srivastava, and Heady [56] presented empirical estimates of the effects of P.L. 480 grain imports by India, extending Mann's analysis by an equation that includes the demand for grains in the fair price shops. Their analysis indicates that the fair price shops did result in an increase in net demand for cereals and the effect of imports on domestic production was only a tenth as large as estimated by Mann.

Pinstrup-Andersen and Tweeten [55] estimated the effect of food aid shipments upon the commercial demand for wheat imports. The basic data used were from questionnaires from individuals resident in countries that had received food aid from the United States. Each respondent was asked to indicate how much commercial imports would increase for given reductions in P.L. 480 shipments of wheat. It was estimated that if there had been no food aid shipments of wheat during 1964-66 the world wheat price would have been increased by 28 percent *if* the wheat supplied as food aid had been with-held from the market. If the wheat supplied as aid had been exported commercially, the world price of wheat might have fallen by 21 to 41 percent.

The Enlargement of the Common Market

There has been an obvious interest in the consequences of the enlargement of the Common Market by those countries who feel their export trade will be adversely affected and by interests within the new members, especially in Great Britain, and several studies have been undertaken. Some have emphasized the effects on farmers and consumers in the new member countries [8, 41] ; others have concentrated on the effects on nonmembers [30, 51] .

It should be noted that these studies were preceded by a similar series of studies, sponsored by the United States Department of Agriculture, that analyzed long-term prospects for agricultural supply, demand, and trade for approximately thirty-five countries (see [89, 90] for a list of all studies that have been completed). Most of these studies assumed a continuation of existing policies and prices. But in two studies (for the United Kingdom and Denmark) the effects of joining the Common Market were included. There was keen interest in Great Britain in the effects of Common Market membership on farmers, taxpayers, and consumers [8, 42] .

Ferris and others [21] undertook a detailed study of the effect of enlarging the Common Market on United States agricultural trade. This study involved analyses of the supply and demand functions for all of the important farm commodities and projected the effects on imports and exports of the enlarged Common Market by 1980. Projections were also required of changes in production and consumption in the original six countries through 1980, and these were based on revisions of series of projections made earlier [67] . The enlargement was projected to reduce grain imports by more than 3 million tons; this reduction compares to total grain imports of the ten countries in 1968 of 10.9 million tons.[2] By 1980 it was projected that the enlarged Common Market would import only 1.8 million tons, but much of the reduction in imports reflected the reduction in imports by the original six countries −from exports of of 2.9 million tons in 1968 to projected exports of 1.8 million tons in 1980. Projections for milk, beef and veal, and poultry products indicated little change resulting from entry. It was projected that net exports of pork would increase somewhat.

One study [74] was based on the assumption that the Common Market would not be enlarged. A separate paper was prepared to consider the effects of the enlargement on production, demand, and trade in the member countries [76] . One conclusion was that the major impact on trade would be the result of consumption effects which were projected to be very substantial for feed grains and milk. The decline in demand for feed grains was projected at 3.6 million tons and for milk at 3.9 million tons; the production effect for feed grains was negligible but that for milk was about a quarter of the consumption effect.

Sugar is one of the most highly protected farm products of the industrial countries, and many developing countries have a significant comparative advantage in its production (Bates and Schmitz [3] ; D. G. Johnson [34]). Snape [65] undertook an empirical analysis of the effects of the protection of sugar by the industrial economies on the export earnings of the developing countries as of 1959. The effects were divided into consumption and production effects. The consumption effect, estimated by assuming that producer returns in the industrial countries would remain unchanged through the use of a deficiency payment, with consumers being permitted to purchase sugar at international prices, would have been sufficient to increase the sugar exports by more than $500 million for the world. An estimate of the production effect of protection in the industrial countries for seven countries (not including the Soviet Union) indicated that exports would have been increased by $675 million. The combined effects would have been nearly $1.2 billion.[3]

Although Snape committed one error — he ignored the returns in excess of the world market price obtained by sugar exporters with access to the markets of the United States, the United Kingdom, and France — his analysis was important and, unfortunately, neglected in policy decisions. A later article by Snape [66] included estimates of the excess resource costs, the loss of consumer surplus, and the income transfers in the major protected sugar market markets. Estimates were made for three different levels of world sugar market prices. As in similar analyses he found that the income transfers far exceeded the welfare losses. He also estimated the gains in exports for the major sugar producers that would result from free trade.

Bates [2] and Bates and Schmitz [3] used a spatial equilibrium model to analyze the effects of the United States sugar program on the sources and prices of sugar.[4] If the United States and the United Kingdom permitted free trade in sugar, United States imports in 1970 would have supplied about 85 percent of domestic consumption instead of less than 50 percent under the sugar program. The results of the model indicated that it made almost no difference to Cuba, to the United States, or to world production and price of sugar whether the United States continued its embargo on Cuban sugar.

D. G. Johnson [34] estimated that the income benefits to American producers of sugar resulting from the sugar program were, at most, $101 million annually. These benefits were derived from total costs to consumers and taxpayers of five to seven times that amount by 1972. He estimated that if the sugar program was abolished the long-run effect would be approximately to double United States sugar imports.

Industrial Country Policies and Agricultural Trade

In spite of the concern expressed in the less developed countries about the effect of the industrial countries' farm and trade policies upon the exports of the less developed countries and the continuing emphasis given to the subject by the Food and Agriculture Organization, only limited effort has been given to estimating the empirical magnitudes involved. Johnson [36] has estimated that the loss in the export earnings of the less developed countries may amount to $2 billion annually.

A major study was undertaken in the Department of Agriculture, and the summary results were published in *World Demand Prospects for Agricultural Exports of Less Developed Countries*. Several important publications presented the background information in greater detail [57]. Unfortunately, the changes in policies of the industrial countries that were projected from the underlying model of world production, consumption, and trade were quite modest. The major change that was considered was a more moderate pricing system for grains in the industrial importing countries. Even this rather modest change indicated a substantial increase in export earnings from grains for the less developed countries.

As part of its most recent projection exercise the Food and Agriculture Organization made estimates of the effect of the removal of protection in all countries on the exports and imports of developing countries in 1980 [75]. Compared with the level of projected exports and imports in 1980 if current policies of all countries were maintained until that date, the exports of developing countries to the rest of the world might increase by almost $6 billion and imports by $2 billion for an increase in net export earnings of approximately $4 billion. The projections were based on a world model of supply and demand and represented a major extension and improvement on previous work. Credit for the development of the basic model used in the projections is given to H. Alm, J. Duloy, and O. Gulbrandsen of the Institutionen för Ekonomi och Statistik at Uppsala, Sweden.

Benefits and Costs of Trade Policies

Given the very large financial costs imposed by the farm and trade policies of the industrial countries, it is surprising how few efforts have been made to estimate those costs. And even fewer attempts have been made to estimate aggregate benefits, their distribution, and the distribution of costs by income of group.

Most studies of the costs of trade restrictions emphasize the loss in national output through resource allocation effects. These losses are usually referred to as welfare losses and include the loss of consumer surplus and excess production costs. And generally such losses, as estimated, are very minor fractions of the value of national output. Thus, so it seems, trade restrictions do not matter very much. In what can be described as a tour de force Stephen Magee estimated the short-run and long-run welfare costs of United States restrictions on our exports to the rest of the world. He estimated that the combined effect of import and export restraints averages annually about $7.5 billion in the short run and $10.5 billion in the long run [49]. Approximately half of the total welfare losses in both the short run and long run were due to restrictions on United States agricultural exports.[5] But he equated the welfare cost with the actual increase in agricultural exports if there were free trade, and this is surely in error since additional resources would be required in agriculture to produce the added exports. But the important point, for present purposes, is that the welfare loss as estimated amounted to approximately 1 percent of the gross national product for the base year, 1971. This estimate is consistent with others made by Harry G. Johnson for Great Britain [39] and Arnold C. Harberger for Chile [25].

It is argued, and quite correctly, that such static estimates of welfare losses underestimate the total effects of trade restrictions [49, pp. 647-49]. Free trade could make additional gains through dynamic effects, economies of scale, reduction of monopoly, and the elimination of the waste of resources used in first seeking protection and then competing away most of the potential rents. But even if these desirable effects of free trade are substantial, the income transfers that result from trade interferences are many times as great as the welfare losses. It is rather surprising that most economists tend to emphasize the resource costs of protection but discuss the income transfers only in passing, if at all.

Estimates of costs to taxpayers and consumers of trade and farm policies have been made, based on the difference between domestic and import or export prices plus direct governmental costs. Schultze [63] and D. G. Johnson [36] made estimates for the United States that indicated costs on the order of $9 to $10 billion. Two similar estimates have been made for the Common Market, one by a group under the auspices of the Atlantic Institute [1] and the other by Kruer and Berntson of the Department of Agriculture [46]. The estimates ranged from $12 billion to $14 billion. The various estimates were for the late 1960s. Each of the estimates represents an overestimate of the actual costs borne by consumers, since if either the United States or the Common Market adopted free trade some international prices would increase and it is unlikely that any would decrease.

Josling [41] prepared a useful analytical framework for a more accurate indication of the various costs of farm and trade measures. He noted, correctly, that most efforts to measure costs are quite partial measures, sometimes emphasizing only balance of payment effects, and do not separate income transfers from real or welfare costs — the excess production costs and the loss of consumer surplus. As he indicated, based on reasonable estimates of parameters for Great Britain, most of the costs to consumers and taxpayers that result from farm and trade policies represent income transfers and not real costs or welfare losses.[6] D. G. Johnson [36, chapter 11] argued that the transfer costs are nonetheless important since some groups in the society are being taxed, either directly or through higher food prices, to give additional income to other groups and that the consequences of the transfers should be judged in terms of the social usefulness of the results.

Josling and others made estimates of the distribution of the costs and benefits of farm policy in Great Britain and compared these measures for four important policy options: no support, the United Kingdom deficiency payment scheme, a variable levy scheme that would give farmers the same return as the deficiency payment system and joining the European Economic Community and adopting the Common Agricultural Policy [42]. The results showed that with either the deficiency payment scheme or the variable levy scheme most income benefits went to the higest income quartile of farmers; the lowest income quartile of farmers received almost no gain from any of the three policies. An equally important result was the distribution of the costs of the various farm policies among households. Under the policy in 1969 the lowest income quartile of households paid a smaller fraction of the costs than their incomes (after transfers) represented of total household income, and the highest income quartile paid a substantially higher fraction of costs than their incomes represented of the total. The two middle quartiles paid the same fraction of costs as their incomes represented of the total. But the variable levy policy, either with United Kingdom or European Economic Community prices, resulted in a shift in the distribution of costs away from the highest income quartile to the other three quartiles, including the lowest income quartile [42].

The measurement of the degree of protection is closely related to the measurement of the costs of protection. An important development in this area has been the concept of effective protection. The traditional measure of protection has been that of nominal protection — a measure of the difference between internal and external (import or export) prices. However, the concept of nominal protection is not an accurate measure of the amount of protection provided a production activity because of the varying importance of purchased inputs used in the production process. The degree of effective protec-

tion is defined as the ratio of the difference between the value added at domestic prices and the value added at world prices to the value added at world
prices [24]. Very modest levels of nominal protection can result in effective
protection of 100 percent or more if a major input is imported free of duty
and the first processing, which results in little value added, is protected by a
duty as low as 10 percent on the products of that processing. The structure of
tariff rates in many industrial countries that provide for zero tariffs on raw
materials and seemingly low tariff rates on processed products effectively bar
developing countries from many processing activities.

Few estimates have been made of the rates of effective protection for farm
products. Wipf [86] has published estimates for United States agriculture for
1958, 1963, and 1968. He found rates of effective protection ranging from
negative for poultry and eggs to 144 percent for food grains and 662 percent
for sugar.

Dardis and Learn [12] estimated the degree of protection for major agricultural products for several countries in 1959-61. Their measure of the degree of protection was equivalent to the concept of nominal protection. The
study was designed to reflect the effect of nontariff as well as tariff barriers,
though direct income payments or input studies were ignored. The study, unfortunately, was flawed by numerous errors. For example, protection was
measured by the difference between the average producer price and the average export price for wheat in the United States. This calculation omitted the
domestic transport and marketing costs. As a result of this error the degree of
protection for United States wheat in 1959-61 was found to be only 2 percent, even though export subsidies of approximately 60 cents per bushel
($2.20 per quintal or 35 percent of the export price) were paid during the
three years. The degree of protection for wheat in Canada was indicated as a
negative 27 percent, apparently because of failure to include transportation
and marketing costs within Canada or neglect of all the delayed payments to
producers.

Dardis and Learn included discussion and estimates of the welfare cost of
protection. This part of their study deserves serious study. It is too bad that
the empirical results were marred by inaccuracies in the estimates of the degree of protection.

Josling and Earley [43] provided an informative discussion of various measures of protection and made estimates of each of the measures for five products (wheat, barley, maize, sugar, and milk) for Canada, the United States,
the United Kingdom, Germany, and France in 1968-70. An effort was made
to include the effects of all important subsidies and trade restrictions. The
measures of effective protection seem of little use since no independent estimate of value added was made for each commodity and country; instead, val-

ue added was assumed to be a fixed percentage of the value of output with the same percentage being applied across commodities within each country [43]. And, without explanation, the authors added: "Effective protection is not an adequate measure of resource allocation among countries for the same product." It is not clear whether the statement is meant as a generalization or is a reference solely to the calculations actually made.

The unique feature of Josling and Earley's paper is the estimation of the trade volume effects of the trade restrictions [43, pp. 55-60]. Space permits a summary of the results for wheat only. Free trade was estimated to result in a decrease of wheat exports of 0.6 million tons by Canada, 1.7 million tons by France, and 3.2 million tons by the United States. Import increases would have been 0.3 million tons for the United Kingdom and 1.72 million tons for Germany. These results, unfortunately, do not seem to take into account quality differences for wheat and thus the degree of protection provided in Germany and France is significantly underestimated.

New Directions for Research

There are many areas of research that impinge to some degree upon international trade in farm products. In fact, all research that deals with the production and consumption effects of domestic farm policies have an implication for trade. But there are four major areas of research that merit serious attention and have the potential for both a considerable impact upon policies and a contribution to our understanding of economic phenomena: (1) empirical estimates of the impact of trade restrictions upon production, consumption, and trade in farm products; (2) analysis of the adjustment problems of farm people that would result from substantial reductions in protection; (3) effects of trade restrictions upon price instability; and (4) appropriate methods of trading with centrally planned economies.

Estimates of Trade Restriction Effects

As we noted earlier, Dardis and Learn [12] and Josling and Earley [43] attempted to estimate the trade and price effects of the removal of trade barriers. These were important first steps, but much more work is required before our results can be said to be more than illustrative. In neither study was it possible to derive the best possible estimates of the relevant demand and supply functions.

A promising further effort was made in *A World Price Equilibrium Model* [75]. This was an enormously ambitious project in which supply and demand functions were estimated for all the major groups of farm products in the main agricultural areas of the world. The system was then solved for different assumptions concerning the degree of protection, including the case of free trade.

Though there has been a renewed interest in recent years in estimating supply and demand functions for farm products in the major areas of the world, much further work is required to provide a firmer basis for projections of the effects of trade restrictions and interferences upon production, consumption, trade, and the returns to resources.

Adjustment Problems of Farm People

The second area of research is one which we have largely ignored, even though we have the tools to permit us to inform farm people of the adjustments that would be required if there were a substantial reduction in the degree of protection for agriculture. Much of the resistance to freer or more liberal trade is the result of fear of the dislocation and possible loss of employment and income that might occur if barriers to trade were reduced or eliminated. Dairy and sugar farmers in the United States strongly resist any measure that would result in increased imports. Similarly farmers and farm organizations in Western Europe fear the impact of lowering grain prices.[7] Yet it is not self-evident that employment opportunities in agriculture in the Common Market would be reduced if grain prices were lowered. The present structure of protection provides high rates of protection for labor extensive products — the grains — and relatively little protection for the labor intensive products — livestock and milk — and at the same time prices. What is needed is research that will indicate the alternative resource use patterns that would emerge with freer trade and what implications these patterns would have for farm employment and income, especially the return to labor. Until such research is undertaken, it is highly probable that the efforts to reduce trade barriers will be strongly and probably successfully resisted.

A related area of research that needs emphasis is that of adjustment assistance. Although the majority of farm people might gain from freer trade, it is almost certain that some farm people would lose. We need to know how such groups can be identified and what kinds of assistance will best meet their needs and at the same time permit the resource adjustments to occur. All too often the impact of agricultural adjustment programs has been to maintain the status quo and not to respond to changing conditions. This may be one reason why emergency farm programs last several decades.

Trade Interferences and Price Instability

One of the important arguments for price policies such as the Common Agricultural Policy or the price support policies of the United States, Canada, and Australia is the desirability of achieving greater price stability than would prevail in the absence of these policies. What is ignored in this position is that the effect of such price support policies, including the associated interferences with trade, may greatly increase price instability in the international markets for the affected products. The price behavior of internationally traded farm products since late 1972 may have been due largely to trade interferences and not primarily to shortfalls in production or increased demand. I have argued that for the grains the production shortfalls that occurred in 1972 and 1974 were not large enough to explain the doubling and trebling of the prices of grains and soybeans, nor was the cyclical increase in demand that occurred in the major industrial countries from 1971 through 1973 sufficient, either alone or in combination with the production shortfalls, to explain more than a small fraction of the price increases [37, chapter 3]. Hathaway, on the other hand, has argued that increased demand plus the production shortfalls were largely responsible [27], and this seems to be the prevailing view.

I believe that the large price increases in the international markets occurred primarily because most consumers and producers were prevented from reacting to the price changes that resulted from governmental policies designed to stabilize domestic prices. Thus all of the adjustment to the production shortfalls and demand increases was imposed upon a rather limited segment of the world's market for feeds and grains.

The effect of trade interferences upon price instability could be determined if the research were undertaken. It may well be that the researcher would have available almost the equivalent of a laboratory experiment in the price increases from 1972 through 1974 and the price decreases in 1975 and later years. The behavior of sugar prices from early 1974 through early 1975 in the international markets and the relationships between the prices in the international markets and domestic price policies affecting both consumers and producers would be a highly suitable subject for investigation. In December 1974, when retail prices of sugar were 60 cents per pound or more in Canada and the United States, in several Western European nations retail prices were approximately 20 cents per pound, and in Brazil and Mexico retail prices were less than 10 cents per pound. In several major sugar producing and exporting countries producer prices had increased little if at all. It would appear that all of the demand and supply adjustments were forced upon a restricted part of the World market.[8]

Trade with the Centrally Planned Economies

If the Soviet Union has assumed a major role as an importer of grains and feedstuffs — and Schoonover [15] has made a convincing case for this possibility — it becomes necessary to consider the implications for world markets.

Mackie [48] estimated that 93 percent of the year-to-year changes in world imports of wheat from 1963 through 1974 occurred as a result of imports by the centrally planned economies of the Soviet Union, China, and Eastern Europe, and 80 percent of the fluctuation resulted from imports by the Soviet Union alone. Mackie also found that 92 percent of the year-to-year changes in world exports of wheat were absorbed by the United States and Canada, with the United States accounting for 83 percent of the total variation.

Grain production in the Soviet Union displays substantial year-to-year variability. In addition, the Soviet Union maintains a significant monopoly of information, with respect to the size of its expected production, the magnitude of its reserves, and its intentions. Are there measures that the major exporting countries could take that would make it easier to cope with imports by the Soviet Union and other centrally planned economies? Should the major exporters hold stocks to minimize the instability imposed upon their own economies and the economies of the other major importers? If such stocks were held, would it be possible to adopt trading arrangements that would permit recapturing the costs of holding the stocks from the centrally planned economies? If answers to these and similar questions cannot be found, there may be further fragmentation of the markets for grains and feed materials.

Notes

1. As Schuh [60] pointed out, developing countries are not alone in having overvalued rates. He showed that the dollar was significantly overvalued during the 1960s and that this affected agricultural policy (direct income transfers and export subsidies) and imposed significant and perhaps unnecessary adjustment problems upon American agriculture.

2. At the time the projections of the Common Market enlargement were made, it was assumed that Norway would become a member. This did not occur, but the projections were affected hardly at all since Norwegian farm prices were similar to the Common Market farm prices.

3. I have used the very helpful summary of Snape's results published by H. G. Johnson in his valuable study of United States economic policy toward the less developed countries [40, Appendix to chapter 3].

4. A good discussion of spatial equilibrium models may be found in Bawden [4]. A further application of spatial equilibrium models to the world wheat economy may be found in Schmitz and Bawden [58]. Both sources include useful bibliographies.

5. Unfortunately Magee's estimate of the effect of trade restrictions upon United States agricultural exports rested, at least in part, upon a possibly shaky estimate made by D. G. Johnson [33].

6. Josling compared the various elements of cost for different farm and trade policies — free trade, the actual policy of the United Kingdom in about 1970, the introduction of variable levies but with the current level of price supports and the entry of the United Kingdom into the Common Market — with the Common Market prices. Compared with free trade British entry into the Common Market was projected to transfer £ 560 million

to farmers. The welfare costs of entry would have been £ 34 million, of which the reduction in consumer surplus amounted to £ 13 million and excess production costs accounted for the remainder. Of the gross income transfers to farmers it was estimated that the cost of additional resources to produce the expanded output would have been £ 174 million, leaving an increase in net producer returns of £ 386 million [41].

7. For evidence on this point see D. G. Johnson and Schnittker [38, especially chapters 4, 8, and 9].

8. For a discussion of the limited nature of the international market for sugar, see Bates [2], Bates and Schmitz [3], Snape [65], and D. G. Johnson [34]. These studies were completed before the events described in the text occurred.

References

General References

[1] Atlantic Institute. *A Future for European Agriculture: A Report by a Panel of Experts.* Paris, 1970.

[2] Bates, T. H. "The Long-Run Efficiency of United States Sugar Policy." *J. Farm Econ.* 50:521-535, August 1968.

[3] Bates, T. H., and A. Schmitz. *A Spatial Equilibrium of the World Sugar Economy.* California Agr. Exp. Sta., Giannini Foundation Monograph 23, 1969.

[4] Bawden, D. L. "A Spatial Price Equilibrium Model of International Trade." *J. Farm Econ.* 48:862-874, November 1966.

[5] Berntson, B. L., O. H. Goolsby, and C. O. Nohre. *The European Community's Common Agricultural Policy: Implications for U.S. Trade.* USDA, ERS, For. Agr. Econ. Rep. 55, 1969.

[6] Blakeslee, L. L., E. O. Heady, and C. F. Framingham. *World Food Production, Demand and Trade.* Ames: Iowa State University Press, 1973.

[7] Britnell, G. E. "The Implications of United States Policy for the Canadian Wheat Economy." *Can. J. Econ. Pol. Sci.* 22:1-16, May 1955.

[8] Butterwick, M., and E. N. Rolfe. *Food, Farming, and the Common Market.* London: Oxford University Press, 1968.

[9] Cochrane, W. W. "Farm Technology, Foreign Surplus Disposal and Domestic Supply Control." *J. Farm Econ.* 41:885-899, December 1959.

[10] Coppock, J. O. *Atlantic Agricultural Unity: Is It Possible?* New York: McGraw-Hill, 1966.

[11] ———. *North Atlantic Policy: The Agricultural Gap.* New York: Twentieth Century Fund, 1963.

[12] Dardis, R., and E. W. Learn. *Measures of the Degree of Protection of Agriculture in Selected Countries.* USDA, Tech. Bul. 1384, 1967.

[13] Economic and Agricultural Development Institute, Michigan State University. *A Program of Research on Food for Peace.* 3 parts. Lawrence Witt, Project Director. 1966.

[14] Economic Research Service, United States Department of Agriculture. *FATUS, Foreign Agricultural Trade of the United States.* Monthly periodical.

[15] ———. *Prospects for Agricultural Trade with the USSR.* ERS-For. 356, 1974.

[16] Eicher, C., and L. W. Witt, eds. *Agriculture in Economic Development.* New York: McGraw-Hill, 1964.

[17] English, H. E., and K. A. J. Hay, eds. *Obstacles to Trade in the Pacific Area.*

Proceedings of the Fourth Pacific Trade and Development Conference, School of International Affairs, Carleton University, Ottawa, Canada, 1972.

[18] Ezekiel, M. "Impact and Implications of Foreign Surplus Disposal on Developed Economics and Foreign Competitors: The International Perspective." *J. Farm Econ.* 42:1063-77, December 1960.

[19] Farnsworth, H. C. "The Problem Multiplying Effects of Special Wheat Programs." *Am. Econ. Rev.* 51:353-70, May 1961.

[20] Fernon, B. *Issues in World Farm Trade.* Trade Policy Research Centre, London, 1970.

[21] Ferris, J., T. Josling, B. Davey, P. Weightman, D. Lucey, L. O'Callaghan, and V. Sorenson. *The Impact on U.S. Agricultural Trade of the Accession of the United Kingdom, Ireland, Denmark and Norway to the European Economic Community.* East Lansing: Michigan State University Press, 1971.

[22] Fisher, F. M. "A Theoretical Analysis of the Impact of Food Surplus Disposal on Agricultural Production in Recipient Countries." *J. Farm Econ.* 45:863-75, November 1963.

[23] Grubel, H. G., and H. G. Johnson, eds. *Effective Tariff Protection.* Geneva, General Agreement on Tariffs and Trade, 1971.

[24] ———. "Nominal Tariffs, Indirect Taxes, and Effective Rates of Protection." *Econ. J.* 77:761-68, December 1967.

[25] Harberger, A. C. "Using the Resources at Hand More Effectively." *Am. Econ. Rev., Papers and Proceedings*, 49:134-46, May 1959.

[26] Hardin, C. M., ed. "Agricultural Policy, Politics, and the Public Interest." *The Annals*, 331, September 1960.

[27] Hathaway, D. E. "Food Prices and Inflation." *Brookings Papers on Economic Activity* 1974:63-109.

[28] Hedges, I. R. "Kennedy Round Agricultural Negotiations and the World Grains Agreement." *J. Farm Econ.* 49:1332-41, December 1967.

[29] Hillman, J. S., and D. Loveday. "Surplus Disposal and Supply Control." *J. Farm Econ.* 46:593-602, August 1964.

[30] Honan, N. D. "Impact on Australia's Agricultural Trade of the United Kingdom's Accession to an Enlarged European Economic Community." *Quart. Rev. Agr. Econ.* 25:191-205, July 1972.

[31] Iowa State University Center for Agriculture and Economic Development. *Food: One Tool in International Economic Development.* Ames: Iowa State University Press, 1962.

[32] Johnson, D. G. "Agriculture and Foreign Economic Policy." *J. Farm Econ.* 46:915-29, December 1964.

[33] ———. "The Impact of Freer Trade on North American Agriculture." *Am. J. Agr. Econ.* 55:294-300, May 1973.

[34] ———. *The Sugar Program: Large Costs and Small Benefits.* Washington, D.C.: American Enterprise Institute, 1974.

[35] ———. *Trade and Agriculture: A Study of Inconsistent Policies.* New York: Wiley, 1950.

[36] ———. *World Agriculture in Disarray.* Fontana World Economic Issues. London: Fontana, 1973; New York: St. Martin's Press, 1973.

[37] ———. *World Food Problems and Prospects.* Washington, D.C.: American Enterprise Institute, 1975.

[38] Johnson, D. G., and J. Schnittker. *U.S. Agriculture in a World Context: Policies and Approaches for the Next Decade.* New York: Praeger, 1974.

[39] Johnson, H. G. "The Gains from Free Trade with Europe: An Estimate." *Manchester School* 26:247-255, September 1958.

[40] ———. *U.S. Economic Policy Towards the Less Developed Countries: A Survey of Major Issues.* Washington, D.C.: Brookings, 1967.

[41] Josling, T. E. *Agriculture and Britain's Trade Policy Dilemma.* Trade Policy Research Centre, London, 1970.

[42] Josling, T. E., B. Davey, A. McFarquhar, A. C. Hannah, and D. Hamway. *Burdens and Benefits of Farm-Support Policies.* Trade Policy Research Centre, London, 1972.

[43] Josling, T. E., T. Earley, and J. S. Hillman. *Agricultural Protection: Domestic Policy and International Trade.* Food and Agriculture Organization, C 73/LIM/9, Rome, 1973.

[44] Krauss, M. B. "Recent Developments in Customs Union Theory: An Interpretive Survey." *J. Econ. Lit.* 10:413-36, June 1972.

[45] Krueger, A. O. "Balance-of-Payments Theory." *J. Econ. Lit.* 8:1-26, March 1969.

[46] Kruer, G. R., and B. Berntson. "Cost of the Common Agricultural Policy to the European Community." *For. Agr. Trade of the United States,* October 1969, 6-12.

[47] Mackie, A. B. *Foreign Economic Growth and Market Potentials for U.S. Agricultural Products.* USDA, ERS, For. Agr. Econ. Rep. 24, 1965.

[48] ———. *International Dimension of Agricultural Prices.* USDA, ERS, FDCD Working Paper, 1974.

[49] Magee, S. P. "The Welfare Effects of Restrictions on U.S. Trade." *Brookings Papers on Economic Activity* 1972:645-701.

[50] Mann, J. S. "The Impact of Public Law 480 Imports on Prices and Domestic Supply of Cereals in India." *J. Farm Econ.* 49:131-146, February 1967. (Reply in *J. Farm Econ.* 50:145-147, February 1968.)

[51] Marsh, J. S. *British Entry to the European Community — Implications for British and North American Agriculture.* London: British-North American Committee, 1971.

[52] Organization for Economic Cooperation and Development. *Agricultural Policies in 1966: Europe, North America, Japan.* Agricultural Policy Reports. Paris, 1967.

[53] Organization for European Economic Cooperation. *Trends in Agricultural Policies since 1955.* Fifth Report on Agricultural Policies in Europe and North America, 1961.

[54] Pearson, W. E., and R. E. Friend. *The Netherlands' Mixed Feed Industry — Its Impact on Use of Grain for Feed.* USDA, ERS-For. 287, 1970.

[55] Pinstrup-Andersen, P., and L. G. Tweeten. "The Impact of Food Aid on Commercial Food Export." *Papers and Reports,* Fourteenth International Conference of Agricultural Economists, 1970.

[56] Rogers, K. D., U. K. Srivastava, and E. O. Heady. "Modified Price, Production, and Income Impact of Food Aid under Market Differentiated Distributions." *Am. J. Agr. Econ.* 54:201-208, May 1972.

[57] Rojko, A. S., and A. B. Mackie. *World Demand Prospects for Agricultural Exports of Less Developed Countries in 1980.* USDA, ERS, For. Agr. Econ. Rep. 60, 1970.

[58] Schmitz, A., and D. L. Bawden. *The World Wheat Economy: An Empirical Analysis.* California Agr. Exp. Sta., Giannini Foundation Monograph 32, 1973.

[59] Schuh, G. E. "Effects of Some General Economic Development Policies on Agricultural Development." *J. Farm Econ.* 50:1283-1293, December 1968.

[60] ———. "The Exchange Rate and U.S. Agriculture." *Am. J. Agr. Econ.* 56:1-13, February 1974.

[61] Schultz, T. W. *Economic Crisis in World Agriculture.* Ann Arbor: University of Michigan Press, 1965.

[62] ———. "Value of U.S. Farm Surpluses to Underdeveloped Countries." *J. Farm Econ.* 42:1019-1030, December 1960.

[63] Schultze, C. L. *The Distribution of Farm Subsidies: Who Gets the Benefits?* Washington, D.C.: Brookings, 1971.

[64] Sen, S. R. "Impact and Implications of Foreign Surplus Disposal on Underdeveloped Economies." *J. Farm Econ.* 42:1031-1042, December 1960.

[65] Snape, R. H. "Some Effects of Protection in the World Sugar Economy." *Economica* 30:63-73, February 1963.

[66] ———. "Sugar: Costs of Protection and Taxation." *Economica* 36:29-41, February 1969.

[67] Sorenson, V. L., and D. E. Hathaway. *The Grain-Livestock Economy and Trade Patterns of the European Economic Community, with Projections to 1970 and 1975.* East Lansing: Michigan State University, 1968.

[68] Srivastava, U. K. "The Impact of Public Law 480 Imports on Prices and Domestic Supply of Cereals in India: Comment." *Am. J. Agr. Econ.* 50:143-145, February 1968.

[69] Stern, R. M. "Tariffs and Other Measures of Trade Control: A Survey of Recent Developments." *J. Econ. Lit.* 11:857-888, September 1973.

[70] Subcommittee of the Committee on Agriculture and Forestry, United States Senate, and the Committee on Agriculture, United States House of Representatives. *Hearings, Long-Range Agricultural Policy.* October 6, 7, and 8, 1947. Washington, D.C.: Government Printing Office, 1947.

[71] Tontz, R. L., ed. *Foreign Agricultural Trade.* Ames: Iowa State University Press, 1966.

[72] Tracy, M. *Agriculture in Western Europe.* London: Jonathan Cape, 1964.

[73] Trant, G. I., D. L. MacFarlane, and L. A. Fischer. *Trade Liberalization and Canadian Agriculture.* Toronto: University of Toronto Press, 1968.

[74] United Nations, Food and Agriculture Organization. *Agricultural Commodity Projections, 1970-1980.* 2 vols. Rome, 1971.

[75] ———. *A World Price Equilibrium Model.* Committee on Commodity Problems, CCP 72/WP, 3, Rome, 1971.

[76] ———. *Implications of the Possible Enlargement of the EEC for Agricultural Commodity Projections, 1970-1980.* Committee on Commodity Problems, CCP 72/WP, 6, Rome, 1971.

[77] ———. *Provisional Indicative World Plan for Agricultural Development.* 2 vols. Rome, 1970.

[78] United States Commission on International Trade and Investment Policy. *United States International Economic Policy in an Interdependent World: Report and Papers.* 2 vols. Washington, 1971.

[79] United States Department of Agriculture. *Agricultural Statistics* (annual).

[80] ———. *United States Farm Products in Foreign Trade.* FAS Stat. Bul. 112, 1953.

[81] United States Special Committee on Postwar Economic Policy and Planning.

320   D. GALE JOHNSON

Postwar Agricultural Policies. Tenth Report, 79th Congress, 2d Session, House Report 2728. Washington, D.C.: Government Printing Office, 1946.

[82] Valdés, A. "Trade Policy and Its Effects on the External Agricultural Trade of Chile, 1945-1965." *Am. J. Agr. Econ.* 55:154-164, May 1973.

[83] Walford, C. "The Famines of the World: Past and Present." Part II, *J. Roy. Stat. Soc.* 42:79-265, 1879.

[84] Warley, T. K. *Agriculture: The Cost of Joining the Common Market.* London: Oxford University Press, 1967.

[85] Wilcox, C. *A Charter for World Trade.* New York: Macmillan, 1949.

[86] Wipf, L. J. "Tariffs, Nontariff Distortions, and Effective Protection of U.S. Agriculture." *Am. J. Agr. Econ.* 53:423-430, August 1971.

[87] Witt, L. W., and C. Eicher. *The Effects of U.S. Agricultural Surplus Disposal Programs on Recipient Countries.* East Lansing: Michigan State University, 1964.

[88] Zarembka, P. "Manufacturing and Agricultural Production Functions and International Trade: United States and Northern Europe." *J. Farm Econ.* 48:952-983, November 1966.

USDA Supply and Demand Studies for Foreign Nations and Related Summary Reports

All studies in this section were conducted by the United States Department of Agriculture or under its sponsorship.

[89] Abbas, S. A. *Supply and Demand of Selected Agricultural Products in Pakistan, 1961 to 1975.* Social Sciences Research Center, University of the Punjab, Lahore, Pakistan, 1967.

[90] Agricultural Economics Institute, The Hague. *Supply and Demand, Imports and Exports of Selected Agricultural Products in the Netherlands: Forecast for 1970 and 1975.* Rotterdam, Plantijn, 1967.

[91] Albornoz, M. E., et al. *Chile: Demand and Supply Projections for Agricultural Products, 1965-1980.* Economic Research Center, Catholic University of Chile. Published by Israel Program for Scientific Translations, 1969.

[92] Alminana, M. *Agricultural Supply and Demand Forecasts: Long-Term Forecasts of the Supply and Demand of Agricultural and Livestock Products in Venezuela.* Consejo de Bienestar Rural, Caracas, Venezuela, 1965.

[93] Andersen, P. S., et al. *Projections of Supply and Demand for Agricultural Products in Denmark (1970-1980).* Aarhus Universitets Okonomiske Institut, Aarhus, Denmark, 1969.

[94] Asfour, E. Y. *Saudi Arabia: Long-Term Projections of Supply and Demand for Agricultural Products.* American University, Beirut, Lebanon, 1965.

[95] Battelle Memorial Institute. *Projections of Supply and Demand for Selected Agricultural Products in Central America through 1980.* Published by Israel Program for Scientific Translations, 1969.

[96] Berg, E. R. *Nigeria, Senegal, and the Congo (Kinshasa) Projected Level of Demand, Supply, and Exports of Oilseed Products to 1975 with Implications for U.S. Exports to the European Economic Community.* Manning-Berg Research Associates Ltd., Edmonton, Canada, 1967.

[97] Bernitz, A. *Summary and Evaluation of Austria: Projected Level of Supply, Demand and Trade of Agricultural Products in 1965 and 1975.* USDA ERS-For. 56, 1963.

[98] Bockenhoff, E., et al. *Short-Term Forecasting of Livestock Numbers and Livestock Production in the Federal Republic of Germany, The Netherlands, and the United Kingdom.* Institut für Landwirtschaftliche Marktlehre der Universität Hohenheim, Stuttgart-Hohenheim, Germany, 1970.

[99] Centre de Recherches et de Documentation sur la Consummation. *Production and Uses of Selected Farm Products in France. Projections to 1970 and 1975.* Published by Israel Program for Scientific Translations, 1967.

[100] Chang, T. T. *Long-Term Projections of Supply, Demand, and Trade for Selected Agricultural Products in Taiwan.* Institute of Agricultural Economics, National Taiwan University, Taipei, Republic of China, 1970.

[101] Clark, C. *United Kingdom: Projected Level of Demand, Supply, and Imports of Farm Products in 1965 and 1975.* USDA ERS-For. 19. Oxford University. Published by Israel Program for Scientific Translations, 1962.

[102] Cohen, G. *Philippines: Long-Term Projections for Supply and Demand for Selected Agricultural Products.* USDA ERS-For. 34. Robot Statistics, Manila, Philippines, 1962.

[103] Crosson, P. R. *Economic Growth in Malaysia: Projections of Gross National Product and Production, Consumption, and Net Imports of Agricultural Commodities.* National Planning Association, Center for Development and Planning, Washington, D.C., 1966.

[104] De Ravizzini, E., et al. *Argentina: Projections of Supply and Demand for Selected Agricultural Products through 1980.* Instituto Nacional de Technologia Agropecuaria, Buenos Aires, Argentina, 1972.

[105] Elz, D. *Oilseed Product Needs of the European Economic Community, 1970: As Indicated by Livestock-Feed Vegetable-Oil Requirements.* Published by Israel Program for Scientific Translations, 1967.

[106] England, E., and A. Bernitz. *Summary and Evaluation of United Kingdom: Projected Level of Demand Supply, and Imports of Farm Products in 1965 and 1975.* USDA ERS-For. 50, 1963.

[107] Epp, D. J. *Changes in Regional Grain and Livestock Prices under the European Economic Community Policies.* Michigan State University, Institute of International Agriculture, Res. Rep. 4, 1968.

[108] Ferris, J., et al. *The Impact on U.S. Agricultural Trade after the Accession of the United Kingdom, Ireland, Denmark, and Norway to the European Economic Community.* Michigan State University, Institute of International Agriculture, Res. Rep. 11, 1971.

[109] Gayoso, A., and W. W. McPherson. *Effects of Changing Trade Systems in Latin America on U.S. Agricultural Exports.* Institute of Food and Agricultural Sciences, University of Florida, Gainesville, Florida, 1970.

[110] Getuilio Vargas Fund, Brazilian Institute of Economics. *Projections of Supply and Demand for Agricultural Products of Brazil through 1975.* Rio de Janeiro, Brazil. Published by Israel Program for Scientific Translations, 1967.

[111] Gill, A. H. *Hong Kong's Expanding Agricultural Imports: Projections to 1980.* USDA ERS-For. 296, 1970.

[112] Gruen, F. H., et al. *Long-Term Projections of Agricultural Supply and Demand —Australia, 1965 and 1980.* Monash University, Clayton, Victoria, Australia. Published by Israel Program for Scientific Translations, 1968.

[113] Huggins, H. D. *Jamaica, Trinidad and Tobago, Leeward Islands, Windward Is-*

322   D. GALE JOHNSON

*lands, Barbados, and British Guiana: Projected Levels of Demand, Supply, and Imports
of Agricultural Products to 1975.* USDA ERS-For. 94. Institute of Social and Economic
Research, University College of the West Indies, Jamaica. Published by Israel Program for
Scientific Translations, 1975.

[114] Jones, G. *United Kingdom: Projected Level of Demand, Supply, and Imports
of Agricultural Products, 1970, 1975 and 1980.* Institute for Agricultural Economics,
Oxford University. Published by Israel Program for Scientific Translations, 1969.

[115] Kampe, R. E. *South Africa's Agricultural Trade Projections to 1970 and 1972.*
USDA ERS-For. 236, 1968.

[116] Keefer, J. F. *Summary and Evaluation of the Philippines: Long-Term Projections of Supply and Demand for Selected Agricultural Products with Implications for
U.S. Exports.* USDA ERS-For. 58, 1963.

[117] Keefer, J. F., and A. H. Gill. *Taiwan's Agricultural Growth during the 1970's
— Supply, Demand and Trade Projections for Selected Agricultural Products.* USDA
ERS-For. 316, 1971.

[118] Le Baron, A., et al. *Long-Term Projections of Supply and Demand for Selected Agricultural Products in Iran.* Utah State University Agricultural Experiment Station, Logan, Utah, 1971.

[119] Lokanathan, P. S. *All India Consumer Expenditure Survey, Pattern of Expenditure. Vol. II.* National Council of Applied Economic Research, New Delhi, India, 1967.

[120] ———. *Long-Term Projections of Demand for and Supply of Selected Agricultural Products, 1960-61 to 1975-76.* National Council of Applied Economic Research,
New Delhi, India, 1962.

[121] Long, M. E. *Summary of Long-Term Projections of Agricultural Supply and
Demand, Australia, 1965 and 1980.* USDA ERS-For. 274, 1969.

[122] Mangum, F. A., Jr. *The Grain-Livestock Economy of Italy with Projections to
1970 and 1975.* Michigan State University, Institute of International Agriculture, Res.
Rep. 2, 1968.

[123] Moe, L. E. *Ghana: Supply and Demand Projections for Farm Products to 1975
with Implications for U.S. Exports.* USDA, ERS, For. Agr. Econ. Rep. 30, 1966.

[124] ———. *Israel: Supply and Demand Projections for Agricultural Commodities
to 1975.* USDA ERS-For. 137, 1965.

[125] ———. *Nigeria: Projected Level of Demand, Supply and Imports of Farm Products in 1965 and 1975, with Implications for U.S. Agriculture.* USDA ERS-For. 105,
1964.

[126] ———. *Saudi Arabia: Supply and Demand Projections for Farm Products to
1975 with Implications for U.S. Exports.* USDA ERS-For. 168, 1966.

[127] ———. *Turkey: Supply and Demand Projections for Farm Products to 1975
with Implications for U.S. Exports.* USDA ERS-For. 204, 1967.

[128] Mundlak, Y. *Long-Term Projections of Supply and Demand for Agricultural
Products in Israel. General View and Summary, Part I.* The Hebrew University, Jerusalem, Falk Project, 1964.

[129] National Council of Applied Economic Research. *Supply and Demand for Selected Agricultural Products in India — Revised Projections to 1980-81.* New Delhi, India, 1969.

[130] Nemschak, F. *Austria — Projected Level of Supply, Demand, and Trade of Agricultural Products in 1965 and 1975.* USDA ERS-For. 62. Austrian Institute, Vienna,
Austria. Published by Ahva Press, Jerusalem, 1964.

[131] Palmer, E. Z. *Agriculture in Turkey: Long-Term Projections of Supply and De-*

mand. School of Business Administration and Economics, Robert College, Istanbul, Turkey, 1967.

[132] Petit, M. J., and J. Viallon. *The Grain Livestock Economy of France with Projections to 1970 and 1975.* Michigan State University, Institute of International Agriculture, Res. Rep. 3, 1968.

[133] Pike, C. E. *Supply and Demand for Selected Agricultural Products in India, Projections to 1975-76.* USDA ERS-For. 100, 1965.

[134] Rossmiller, G. E. *The Grain-Livestock Economy of West Germany with Projections to 1970 and 1975.* Michigan State University, Institute of International Agriculture, Res. Rep. 1, 1968.

[135] Schmidt, H., and L. Grunewald. *Aggregation of Future Demand and Supply for Agricultural Products in the European Economic Community, 1970-1975.* Studien zur Agrarwirtschaft 5. Abteilung Landwirtschaft, IFO-Institut für Wirtschaftsforschung, Munich, Germany, 1969.

[136] Schmidt, H., and R. Ruf. *Summary of Long-Term Development of Demand and Supply for Agricultural Products in the Federal Republic of Germany.* USDA ERS-For. 228, 1968.

[137] Schmidt, H., et al. *Long-Term Development of Supply and Demand for Agricultural Products in the Federal Republic of Germany.* IFO-Institut für Wirtschaftsforschung, Munich, Germany, 1967.

[138] Secretaria de Agricultura y Ganaderia, Secretaria de Hacienda y Credito Publico and Banco de Mexico, S.A. *Projections of Supply and Demand for Agricultural Products in Mexico to 1965, 1970 and 1975.* Banco de Mexico, Ministry of Agriculture, 1966. Published by Israel Program for Scientific Translations.

[139] Shepherd, R. E. *Summary of the United Kingdom: Projected Level of Demand, Supply, Imports of Agricultural Product, 1970, 1975 and 1980.* USDA ERS-For. 248, 1969.

[140] Shinohara, T. *Japanese Import Requirements: Projections of Agricultural Supply and Demand for 1965, 1970, and 1975.* University of Tokyo, 1964.

[141] Sorenson, M. V., et al. *Projected Exports and Imports of Selected Agricultural Commodities of South Africa.* Cambridge, Mass.: Arthur D. Little, 1966.

[142] Sorenson, V., and D. E. Hathaway. *The Grain Livestock Economy and Trade Patterns of the European Economic Community with Projections to 1970 and 1975.* Michigan State University, Institute of International Agriculture, Res. Rep. 5, 1968.

[143] Stewart, I. G. *Nigeria: Determinants of Projected Level of Demand, Supply and Imports of Farm Products in 1965 and 1975.* USDA ERS-For. 32, 1962.

[144] Stewart, I. G., et al. *Ghana: Projected Level of Demand, Supply, and Imports of Agricultural Products in 1965, 1970, and 1975.* University of Edinburgh, Department of Political Economy, 1964.

[145] Tang, A. M. *Long-Term Economic and Agricultural Commodity Projections for Hong Kong, 1970, 1975, and 1980.* Chinese University, Economic Research Center. Published by Israel Program for Scientific Translations, 1969.

[146] Tsu, S., and E. Koenig. *Italian Agriculture: Projections of Supply and Demand in 1965, 1970, and 1975.* USDA ERS-For. 68, 1964.

[147] Urban, F. S. *Summary and Evaluation of Projections of Supply and Demand for Agricultural Products in Mexico to 1965, 1970, and 1975.* USDA ERS-For. 208, 1967.

[148] United States Department of Agriculture, Economic Research Service. *Summary and Evaluation of Jamaica, Trinidad and Tobago, Leeward Islands, Windward Is-*

324   D. GALE JOHNSON

lands, Barbados and British Guiana: Projected Levels of Demand, Supply and Imports of Agricultural Products to 1975. USDA ERS-For. 148, 1966.

[149] ———. Summary of Projections of Supply and Demand (1970-1980). USDA ERS-For. 303, 1970.

[150] ———. Summary of Supply and Demand, for Imports and Exports of Selected Agricultural Products in The Netherlands: Forecast for 1970 and 1975. USDA ERS-For. 245, 1969.

[151] Van de Hylke et al. Peru: Long-Term Projections of Demand for and Supply of Agricultural Commodities through 1980. Universidad Agraia, Programa de Investigaciones para el Desarrallo, La Molina, Lima, Peru. Published by Israel Program for Scientific Translations, 1969.

[152] Virenque, P. H., et al. Long-Term Development of Supply and Demand for Agricultural Products in Belgium, 1970-1975. Universitaire Faculteiten St.-Ignatus, SESO-Studiecentrum voor Economisch en Sociaal Onderzoek, Antwerp, Belgium, 1967.

Demand Studies for the Agency for International Development

[153] Barse, J. R. Japan's Food Demand and 1985 Grain Import Prospects. USDA, ERS, For. Agr. Econ. Rep. 53, 1969.

[154] Hutchison, J. E., et al. World Demand Prospects for Wheat in 1980 with Emphasis on Trade by Less Developed Countries. USDA, ERS, For. Agr. Econ. Rep. 62, 1970.

[155] Mackie, A. B., and J. E. Falck. World Demand Prospects in 1980 for Bananas with Emphasis on Trade by Less Developed Countries. USDA, ERS, For. Agr. Econ. Rep. 69, 1971.

[156] Magleby, R. S., and E. Missiaen. World Demand Prospects for Cotton in 1980 with Emphasis on Trade by the Less Developed Countries. USDA, ERS, For. Agr. Econ. Rep. 68, 1971.

[157] Moe, L. E., and M. M. Mohtadi. World Supply and Demand Prospects for Oilseeds and Oilseed Products in 1980. USDA, ERS, For. Agr. Econ. Rep. 71, 1971.

[158] Regier, D. W., and O. H. Goolsby. Growth in World Demand for Feed Grains Related to Meat and Livestock Products and Human Consumption of Grains, 1980. USDA, ERS, For. Agr. Econ. Rep. 63, 1970.

[159] Rojko, A., and A. Mackie. World Demand Prospects for Agricultural Exports of Less Developed Countries in 1980. USDA, ERS, For. Agr. Econ. Rep. 60, 1970.

[160] Rojko, A., et al. World Demand Prospects for Grain in 1980 with Emphasis on Trade by Less Developed Countries. USDA, ERS, For. Agr. Econ. Rep. 75, 1971.

[161] Timms, D. E. World Demand Prospects for Coffee in 1980 with Emphasis on Trade by Less Developed Countries. USDA, ERS, For. Agr. Econ. Rep. 86, 1973.

Selected USDA Foreign Agriculture Studies

All studies in this section were conducted by the United States Department of Agriculture or under its sponsorship.

[162] Aktan, R. Analysis and Assessment of the Economic Effects of PL 480 Title I Program, Turkey. University of Ankara, Turkey, 1965.

[163] Barlow, F. D., Jr., and S. J. Libbin. The Role of Agricultural Commodity Assistance in International Aid Programs. USDA ERS-For. 118, 1969.

[164] Cohen, M. H. The Agricultural Economy and Trade of Denmark. USDA ERS-For. 244, 1968.

[165] Coutsoumaris, G. *Analysis and Assessment of the Economic Effects of the U.S. PL 480 Program in Greece.* Special Studies Series I. Center of Planning and Economic Research, Athens, Greece, 1965.

[166] Friedmann, D. J., and H. C. Farnsworth. *The West German Grain Economy and the Common Market, 1925-1975.* Stanford University, Food Research Institute, 1966.

[167] Grunewald, L., et al. *Agricultural Marketing Systems in the United Kingdom, Ireland, Denmark, Norway and Sweden.* Vol. I, text; vol. II, tables. IFO-Institut für Wirtschaftsforschung, Munich, Germany, 1973.

[168] Grunewald, L., et al. *Agricultural Marketing Systems in the EEC-Member Countries.* Vol. I, text; vol. II, tables. IFO-Institut für Wirtschaftsforschung, Munich, Germany, 1971. Supplement to vol. II, *List of Tables.* USDA, ERS, 1972.

[169] Pritchard, N. T. *Food Marketing in Denmark: Developments, Prospects for 1980, Significance for U.S. Exports.* USDA, ERS, For. Agr. Econ. Rep. 72, 1971.

[170] Pritchard, N. T., and W. P. Huth. *Food Marketing in Benelux Countries: Developments, Prospects for 1980, Significance for U.S. Exports.* USDA, ERS, For. Agr. Econ. Rep. 72, 1971.

[171] Pritchard, N. T., et al. *Food Marketing in West Germany: Developments, Prospects for 1980, Significance for U.S. Exports.* USDA, ERS, For. Agr. Econ. Rep. 76, 1972.

[172] Regier, D. W. *Growth and Demand for Feed Grains in the EEC — Projections to 1970 and 1975 in Relation to Consumption of Meat and Livestock Products.* USDA ERS-For. 158, 1967.

[173] Smith, J. N. *Argentine Agriculture: Trends in Production and World Competition.* USDA ERS-For. 216, 1964.

[174] Steele, W. S. *France's Institutional Food Market — Developments And Prospects for U.S. Exports.* USDA, ERS, For. Agr. Econ. Rep. 87, 1973.

[175] Urban, F. S. *Agricultural Prospects in Central America.* USDA ERS-For. 270, 1969.

Part V. Agricultural Price
Analysis and Outlook

This paper reviews the literature of agricultural price analysis between 1946 and about the middle of 1973. Only brief reference is made to the literature published before World War II. We were offered the opportunity to update the review in January 1976 but did not have sufficient time to make an exhaustive review of additions to the literature since 1973.[1]

Agricultural price analysis is defined, for purposes of this review, as the study of agricultural product and input prices over time, space, form or quality, and market levels. In this context articles written in English, especially those appearing in United States publications, receive disproportionate attention. Even with these self-imposed restrictions, we found it impossible to summarize all of the literature, especially the numerous articles which report on empirical studies. Our major criteria in selecting literature for review are to indicate the major issues that have emerged in price analysis studies, to call attention to important empirical and theoretical results, and to illustrate the range of contributions made by agricultural economists in the subject of price analysis and outlook.

We are indebted to Ronald R. Piggott and W. Bruce Traill for their assistance in providing an annotated bibliography of publications related to price analysis. Our colleagues, Richard N. Boisvert and Timothy D. Mount, and the official reviewers, James P. Houck, Richard A. King, and Edward W. Tyrchniewicz, provided helpful suggestions. In addition, the assistance of Nancy L. Brown in typing and proofreading successive versions of the manuscript is gratefully acknowledged. Errors of omission, of course, are our responsibility.

W. G. T.
K. L. R.

Agricultural Price Analysis and Outlook

William G. Tomek
Professor of Agricultural Economics
Cornell University

Kenneth L. Robinson
Professor of Agricultural Economics
Cornell University

Recursive and Simultaneous Equations Systems

The theoretical basis for price studies is usually some variant of the competitive model of price determination; that is, price is assumed to be determined by the point of intersection of demand and supply functions. One theoretical view is that prices and quantities are determined simultaneously, and this model may be empirically relevant when sufficient time is allowed for interdependence to take place. An alternative view is that prices and quantities are determined sequentially, and this model may be empirically relevant when time lags between changes in variables are long or when the time unit over which variables are observed is short. An important issue in the price analysis literature of the 1940s and 1950s was the question of when and under what circumstances it is appropriate to use single-equation methods (based on the assumption of recursive relationships) to estimate supply and demand functions. Therefore, before turning to empirical studies of supply and demand, let us review the literature on recursive and simultaneous models as used in price analysis studies.

Before World War II price analysts commonly estimated demand and supply equations separately using least squares regression procedures. However, computation of multiple regression coefficients was tedious using desk calculators, and consequently emphasis was placed on simple linear regression or small multiple regression models. Warren and Pearson's work [350] is illustrative of the rather ingenious use of deflators and functional forms to construct simple regression models of supply-price relationships.[2] Prewar contributions in demand analysis culminated in Henry Schultz's *The Theory and Measurement of Demand* [292].

Although early empirical studies involved least squares estimates of single equations, E. J. Working's classic paper [370] did stress the implications of the simultaneous competitive model for the identification of supply and demand equations. Subsequently, Haavelmo [124] emphasized the inconsistency between using theoretical models which assume simultaneous determination of variables and using least squares estimation which assumes one-way causation from explanatory variables to a single dependent variable. This, of course, led to the development and use of simultaneous equations models and estimating procedures.[3]

The sequential nature of price determination in agriculture was also recognized in the prewar period and was incorporated in what has become known as the cobweb model. Bean [9] stressed the lagged relationship between price changes and the supply response of farm products. Thus, early studies supported the hypotheses that current production is a function of lagged prices and that current production is, in turn, an important determinant of current price. A statement of the cobweb theorem was provided by Ezekiel [77] in 1938.

The prewar literature provided a basis for the use of both simultaneous and recursive models in agricultural price analysis. In the postwar period Wold [366], among others, emphasized the importance of the recursive concept. If the values of the endogenous variables in a model are determined sequentially (in a recursive chain) and if certain assumptions about the disturbances of the equations are met, then the structural equations are identified and ordinary least squares applied singly to each equation provides consistent estimates of the parameters. These conclusions justify the use of single equations for some research problems.[4]

In the early 1950s Fox [87] stressed this point in slightly different language. If, for example, the quantity supplied and available for consumption in a particular time period is predetermined by prior events, then that quantity can be treated as an explanatory variable in a single price-dependent demand equation. Fox estimated, on the basis of 1922-41 data, that 95 percent of the production of pork in a calendar year was determined by events which had occurred in the previous year.

The cobweb model is perhaps the classic illustration of a recursive system. The simplest cobweb model assumes that (1) producers are price "takers" and supply response is based on price; (2) a clear time lag exists between a price change and a production change; (3) the total quantity planned to be produced is realized; (4) the quantity supplied in time t is sold in t, hence, determining price in t; and (5) the supply and demand functions are linear and do not shift.

Some of the assumptions of the elementary cobweb model, such as the static nature of the functions, are not particularly critical and can be modified in a more realistic model. Modifications to make cobweb models more realistic may include adding variables to each equation and adding equations to the model which capture the detail of the sector of the economy under study. Harlow's six-equation model [130] of the pork sector illustrates the manner in which the simple cobweb concept has been expanded in an attempt to specify a realistic model. The sequence of equations in this model explains (1) the number of sows farrowing, (2) the number of hogs slaughtered, (3) the pounds of pork produced, (4) the pounds of cold storage holdings of pork, (5) the retail price of pork, and (6) the farm price of hogs.

The cobweb model leads to a cycle in price and quantity with a period which is twice the length of the lag in the supply relation. Depending on the relative slope parameters of the supply and demand equations, the cycle may diverge, converge, or be continuous. As a result, two inconsistencies between the behavior of the model and reality have been noted. First, most cycles in agricultural prices and production neither converge nor explode. Second, some cycles are twice the length suggested by the model. For example, a market-weight hog can be produced in about twelve months from the time a breeding decision is made, suggesting a twenty-four-month period from peak to peak. However, the hog cycle has averaged four years from peak to peak [130].

Numerous explanations have been given for the continuity of agricultural price cycles in the context of the cobweb model [351]. Perhaps the least plausible is that the slopes of the functions are in fact equal and hence the special case of a continuous cycle is realized. A more plausible explanation for the observed inconsistencies is that actual production seldom equals planned production. Consequently, before a cycle can converge, a "random" shift in supply could start a new cycle. Shifts in the functions, however, have the potential to speed convergence to equilibrium as well as to prolong the cycle [3]. Thus, an argument based on the violation of assumption (3) is a two-edged sword. In any case a divergent cycle could not persist for long [285, p. 339], and by definition convergent cycles would inevitably die away so that only continuous cycles could be observed.

The assumption of straight line functions also may be violated. Continuous oscillation is possible with any pair of curved functions that go through points of a rectangle [351, p. 739]. Whether small deviations from the rectangle would converge back to the rectangle or not (stable or unstable oscillations) depends on the derivatives at the four corners. Nerlove [237] has developed the implications of a geometric form distributed lag supply equation for the possible alternative cycles.

Larson [199, 202] takes the view that the cobweb is not an appropriate model of price behavior. He proposes a "harmonic motion" model in which supply response is a *rate of change* in planned production through time (t):

$$\frac{dX_t}{dt} = kp_t,$$

where X is planned production. In this model, since the rate of change rather than the total level depends on price, the maximum in planned production is achieved only after a one-period lag following the price maximum. A second lag occurs between the maximum in planned production and actual production. Hence, this model produces a cycle twice the length of the one implied by the cobweb.

Assuming plans are realized, the level of production modifies price, and the cycle continues. However, a constant amplitude cycle would occur only with special slope conditions [199, p. 378]. In this respect, the harmonic motion model seems no more satisfactory than the cobweb model.

The harmonic motion model does recognize the "pipeline effects" (inertia) in the production process for livestock and livestock products, but it does not seem applicable to crops with periodic production. Also, the model assumes a fixed period in the cycle, but in fact producers have some discretion in modifying production plans. McClements [221] provides a critical examination of studies which have rejected the cobweb theorem in favor of a harmonic motion model.

Recursive models have been used to estimate structural coefficients, to forecast, and to explore the dynamic properties of certain commodity subsectors. Reutlinger [273], drawing on the work of Zusman [379], describes the analysis of time paths of endogenous variables in dynamic models. Research by Crom [58] and Walters [348] further illustrates applications involving description and projection and simulation of cycles for agricultural prices and output. Meadows [225] provides a summary of research as well as a simulation model of price behavior.

True cyclical behavior in prices and quantities is a self-generating process. High prices lead to larger quantities supplied which result in lower prices and so on. The recursive models discussed to this point attempt to capture this type of behavior. However, some agricultural economists believe that the so-called cycles in prices and quantities are not self-generated. The argument, as summarized by Breimyer [28] for the cattle cycle, is that random factors, such as weather, affect livestock production and prices through its effects on feed supplies.

Conditions sometimes exist under which a simultaneous specification may be preferred to the recursive alternative. First, in situations where the total quantity available for harvest is predetermined, the quantity actually harvested may still be simultaneously determined with current price and its relation to harvesting costs. For instance, Suits and Koizumi's model for onions [316] contains an equation in which unharvested production and current price are simultaneously determined.

Time lags exist in the production process for all farm products. However, a second condition exists when the lag is short relative to the time unit of observation. This situation obviously prevails for turkeys, broilers, and eggs; production of these commodities can be modified in response to price changes within a year. Hence, if interest centers on annual relationships, then a simultaneous equation model may be appropriate. Third, for some commodities, current supply need not equal current production. Quantities can be drawn from or placed in inventory. The supply in one country or region likewise may be influenced by imports and exports. Thus, current price and total supply may be simultaneously determined even when production is predetermined.

Another need for simultaneity arises from the fact that, although total production is predetermined, allocation among different uses is not. The current apple crop, for example, is fixed at a particular size by prior events, but the utilization of that crop as fresh fruit, canned applesauce, frozen slices, and juice depends in part on the relative prices of these uses. Hence, the quantities going into alternative uses and the corresponding prices are jointly determined.

Based on the foregoing distinctions, most simultaneous equations models in agricultural price analysis can be grouped into two categories. One type assumes demand and supply (or some important part of supply) are simultaneously determined; the second takes current supply as predetermined but treats the allocation of total supply to alternate uses as jointly determined with prices.

The earliest simultaneous price analysis models are of the first type. Girshick and Haavelmo [99] specified and estimated a five-equation model for all food in which price and quantity are jointly determined. Using 1922-41 observations, they estimated, by the limited information maximum likelihood method (LISE), the retail price elasticity of demand to be -0.25 and the comparable elasticity of supply to be 0.16, both seemingly reasonable numbers (see [19] for the sensitivity of these results to changes in model specification).

Tintner [328] estimated several two-equation (supply and demand) models for all meat. Nordin, Judge, and Wahby [246] specified a twelve-equation model involving a supply and a demand equation for six interrelated products. These early models sometimes provided illogical results in the sense that the estimated price elasticities of demand were much too elastic relative to what was known of the characteristics of the commodities. For example, in Tintner's overidentified demand equation for all meat, the estimated elasticity is -2.69. Such results may be attributed either to model misspecification or to multicollinearity.

Several studies made by USDA economists in the middle and late 1950s were based on simultaneous equations models [97, 226, 283]. Meinken's model [226] of the wheat sector is an example of the second general type of simultaneous equations model. Domestic production and carryin stocks of wheat for a given crop year are predetermined. This total supply is specified in Meinken's model as being allocated to four uses (domestic human food, domestic livestock feed, net exports, and end-of-year stocks).

In 1959 Cromarty [61] presented an econometric model of United States agriculture, which contains thirty-nine equations for eleven product categories. Since the model is constructed for the purpose of estimating aggregate behavior, index numbers of prices received and other variables are constructed from the disaggregated (product) estimates.

The specification and use of simultaneous equations models in the 1950s tended to have an experimental character; a contribution of this research was the experience gained in model building. Analysts hoped that the results would be better than those obtained from single equations, but the empirical results obtained from simultaneous equations models were often unreasonable or not useful. These experiences led to the recognition that the definition of a "correct" model (and the corresponding estimation method) depends, in part, on the problem under investigation. For example, a single price-dependent equation can provide useful predictions of the farm price of apples. But, to estimate the demand for apples for fresh use for a particular season of the year, a simultaneous equations model, such as the one specified by Pasour [252], seems preferable.

More recent simultaneous equations models have been designed to answer specific rather than general questions. Pasour's model was constructed to determine the optimal allocation of apples over the marketing year. Houck and Mann [159] used their model of the soybean industry to project the quantity and value of soybeans and soybean products into the 1970s "on the basis of alternative assumed combinations of prices and government operations in the market." Kip and King [188] estimated demand equations for selected deciduous fruits and projected the demands to 1980 in order to evaluate the potential effects of expanded supplies of these fruits in the San Joaquin Valley on prices and returns. A Washington State University project is developing a comprehensive model by product groups "to evaluate the effects of alternative government policies on the agricultural economy" [217, p. 1].

Simultaneous equations models have at the same time become more complex in the sense that they contain more equations and more variables (hence more information) than earlier models. The Houck-Mann soybean model [159] makes the commercial supply of beans predetermined, but the demand side contains thirteen equations — six identities and seven behavioral equations. The Langemeier-Thompson beef model [198] considers both the fed and nonfed subparts of the beef sector in twelve equations. The model contains margin, demand, and supply functions for both quality levels of beef.

If the objective of the research is to obtain the best possible estimates of certain structural coefficients and if the model involves simultaneity, then from the viewpoint of econometric theory a simultaneous equations estimation technique is preferred to ordinary least squares. One continuing problem in comparing estimates of structural coefficients from single and simultaneous equations models, however, is whether or not simultaneity is the dominant statistical problem and whether or not the alternative estimation procedures constitute the principal reason for contrasting empirical results.[5] The nature of the problem is illustrated by the alternative estimates of price elasticities of demand for beef (table 1).

Simultaneous equations models can have practical problems, other than multicollinearity, which perhaps have adversely influenced the quality of parameter estimates. Since estimation methods for simultaneous systems require a large number of observations relative to estimating single equations by least squares,[6] analysts have used long time series to estimate the models (for example, [61, 327, 347]). The use of a lengthy series can be treated as estimating the average structure, but such estimates may not be useful for current applications. Moreover, statistical analysis for a period containing structural change can give significant results by conventional tests (even though the coefficients are hybrid values not applicable to any period).

A second problem is that specifications usually limit the simultaneity to variables within the sector (for example, soybeans [159]) under study with other variables treated as predetermined. This treatment is often a necessary simplification to limit the scope of the model and to achieve identification. As a consequence, however, interrelationships among sectors are ignored or minimized, and some variables are treated as if they are predetermined when they are essentially endogenous.

Problems of contrasting estimation methods and time periods are, to some extent, illustrated in table 1. Three studies [27, 211, 352] of the demand for

Table 1. Selected Price Elasticities of Demand at Retail for Beef

Sources	Time Period	Estimation Method[a]	Elasticity
Nordin, Judge, and Wahby [246]	1921-41	ILS	-0.77
		OLS	-0.96
Fox [87].	1922-41	OLS	-0.94[c]
Wallace and Judge [347].	1925-55	LISE	-1.36
		TSLS	-0.77
		OLS	-0.76
Maki [214]	6/1947-12/56	OLS	-0.85[d]
Logan and Boles [211].	1/1948-12/59	OLS[b]	-0.65
Breimyer [27].	1948-60	OLS	-0.65[c]
Waugh [352]	1948-62	OLS	-0.69[c]
Tomek [329]	4/1949-3/56	OLS[b]	-1.00
	4/1956-3/64	OLS[b]	-0.90
Langemeier and Thompson [198]	1947-63	TSLS	-0.95

[a]ILS = indirect least squares; LISE = limited information maximum likelihood; TSLS = two-stage least squares; OLS = ordinary least squares.

[b]Elasticity derived from several OLS equations to take account of cross effects as described in [227]; this may be viewed as ILS estimates of system of demand equations, with supply predetermined.

[c]Elasticity computed as reciprocal of flexibility in price-dependent equation.

[d]Direct estimate from quantity-dependent equation.

beef, using a similar time period (within the period 1948-62) and single equation procedures, give similar estimates of the price elasticity. The Langemeier-Thompson [198] simultaneous equations estimates for a similar time period suggest a somewhat less inelastic demand. But, breaking the 1949-64 period into two parts and using least squares also gives estimates which are less inelastic than the single equation studies for the total period [329]. The unanswered question is how a simultaneous equations model would have performed for the shorter time periods.

Demand Analysis

The basic unit of demand theory is, of course, the individual consumer, but most empirical studies of demand consider market relationships. Research problems are usually concerned with aggregate behavior, such as predicting the national demand for beef, and data are more readily available for markets than for individuals. Analyses based on the behavior of individual consumers, however, have helped to provide useful simplifications and insights.

In this section demand studies are considered in two broad categories: those based on aggregate market behavior and those based on individual household or consumer behavior. We start with a review of conventional aggregate time-series studies and models of long-run demand. The second subsection covers miscellaneous topics related to parameters of demand models; these topics include structural change, the concept of total elasticity, and the relationship of flexibility coefficients to elasticities.

Two types of contributions related to individual consumers are reviewed in the third subsection. One type includes empirical studies using cross-section observations on individual households or consumers; the second type includes studies using restrictions on elasticities derived from basic demand theory as an aid in estimating empirical elasticities.

Analyses Based on Aggregate Time-Series Data

Certainly an important contribution of the post-World War II literature is the vast number of estimates of demand and price functions. This research provides estimates of structural coefficients and the basis for forecasts of levels of demand and prices. The studies cover numerous products at various market levels and degrees of aggregation. This literature also provides substantial insights into questions of model building. Foote [84], Rojko [284], and Waugh [352] summarize the state of the art as it existed in the late 1950s and early 1960s.

Work by Fox [87] and Stone and his colleagues [313] is representative of early postwar studies of demand. A "typical" equation fitted by Fox makes retail price a function of per-capita consumption (or production), per-capita quantity of a competing product, and per-capita disposable income. With respect to model specification, the selection of functional forms in demand analysis has been determined mainly on empirical grounds. Straight line and double logarithm forms are the most frequently used.

Disposable income is perhaps the most common shift variable used in demand analyses, with population reflected in per-capita variables. Income is usually treated as predetermined, though it is influenced both by prices and quantities sold. Analysts have argued that, for the most part, the error is not serious since the retail value of individual foods is small relative to total income in industrialized countries [84]. But this is not true in less developed countries. Moreover, even if the absolute size of the bias is small, the coefficient attached to the income variable also is likely to be small; hence, the relative bias can be quite large [189].

The measurement of the effects of substitutes is one of the more difficult problems in time-series analyses of demand. A potential lack of degrees of freedom and multicollinearity preclude using numerous variables for substitutes, and in any case their individual effects are often small and unmeasurable. Analysts (for example, [327]) have tried measuring the effects of all substitutes in one variable by using a sum, average, or index number to represent all substitutes.[7] Of course, if the commodity has just one or two close substitutes, then they may be represented in the model by separate variables. In recent years the theoretical restrictions on elasticities have been used to help estimate cross elasticities of demand (discussed in a subsequent section).

Another difficulty is the lack of a general, fundamental explanation for abrupt shifts in price-quantity relationships, which are sometimes observed with the passage of time. Such shifts are illustrated by Waugh [352, p. 41, figure 5.1] for beef, pork, lamb, and veal within the 1948-62 period. Changes in income and in population have been smooth, and hence cannot account for the abrupt shifts. Such changes might be explained by changes in the supply of close substitutes; but changes in substitutes do not appear to explain all of the abrupt changes in demand.

Goodwin, Andorn, and Martin [103] stress the idea of an irreversible demand relation for beef. Perhaps tastes and preferences change abruptly.[8] Larger production and lower prices, if they persist for some period of time, may induce a permanent increase in demand [330] ; consumers come to prefer the product when price is low and do not switch away (in the sense of movement along the old demand function) when prices subsequently rise. Conversely, small production and high prices may induce permanent shifts away from a commodity. Uvacek [341] makes an analogous argument in associating demand shifts for beef with changes in the beef cattle cycle. It is unclear at present whether or not similar arguments are applicable to the abrupt shifts in relationships for other commodities.

Many demand studies are based on annual observation, and the demands for individual farm products, based on such data, tend to be price inelastic at both farm and retail levels in the United States. An increasing number of demand analyses are conducted using daily, weekly, monthly and quarterly data. Such functions may be considered short-run or seasonal demand curves, and hence they might be thought to be more price inelastic than annual functions. Pasour and Schrimper [253] point out, however, that shorter period functions may involve the demand for storage (speculative demand) as well as the demand for current use. A price special on beefsteak could induce housewives to buy steak both for current use and for the freezer. At harvesttime, supplies move into storage as well as into current use. Thus, demand functions in the very short run can be highly price elastic relative to functions based on annual observations. Leuthold [209] obtained estimates which suggest a highly price elastic farm-level demand for hogs on a daily basis.

One method of estimating short-run elasticities is through the use of controlled experiments. This was done for fresh skim milk by changing prices in a particular location [13]. The point estimate of the elasticity based on the first two-day period following a price change was essentially zero. The elasticity tended to increase (in absolute value) and generally remained greater than 1.0 after the eighth two-day period. The elasticity was -0.86 for the first month and -1.29 for the second.

Among the studies based on monthly data are those conducted by Brown [35], Hayenga and Hacklander [139], and Farris and Darley [80]. Brown's paper summarizes a relatively comprehensive study for the United Kingdom based on the years 1953 to 1958. He also compares his results with those of Stone and his colleagues [313]. Quarterly data were used by Stanton [307], Logan and Boles [211], and Stent [308] to estimate demand relationships for meat. Logan and Boles, Stent, and Farris and Darley each accept the hypothesis of equal slope coefficients for each quarter (or month), but they found significant differences in the levels of the functions by seasons.[9]

Summaries of estimated demand elasticities for agricultural products are available in Buchholz, Judge, and West [37] and a committee report [360]. Manderscheid [216] has pointed out that estimated coefficients can reasonably be expected to differ from model to model and that correct comparisons among studies require that differences in models be taken into account. Less effort has been devoted, it seems fair to say, to summarizing ex post evaluations of forecasts for agricultural products (for an example for one commodity, see [142, pp. 73-89]). Beef, for example, is perhaps the most studied agricultural commodity, but the models available in 1973 did not appear to do a very good job of predicting beef prices.

There was some feeling in the early 1950s that traditional demand analyses based on annual observation were short-run in character. As a consequence, models to measure long-run demand were introduced. However, various definitions of long-run demand were in use (for a brief review, see [330, pp. 717-719]). A commonly accepted definition now is that the long run is the time required for a complete adjustment in quantity demanded to a one-time change in price, holding other variables constant. The idea of a delayed response of quantity to a price change is consistent with the concept of a distributed lag model.

Numerous potential reasons exist for delayed adjustments in quantities demanded [238, pp. 5-7], including imperfect knowledge, habit, technological factors, institutional factors, and uncertainty. Given these possible reasons for delayed adjustments, the long run might seem rather lengthy in terms of months. Tomek and Cochrane [330] argue, however, that the long run for individual foods need not be a long time period. Many foods are purchased frequently and food prices are well advertised; hence, knowledge of price changes should be relatively good. Technological and institutional factors seem to be relatively unimportant for foods. In a controlled experiment for skim milk (cited above), complete adjustment to a price change appears to have occurred within three weeks.

Elmer Working's study [369] of the demand for meat is perhaps the first empirical study of the long-run demand for a food product. Working took a rather ad hoc approach to model building, and he considered one year as the short run and periods longer than a year as the long run. Ladd and Tedford [196] show that the Working model is a special case of a linear form distributed lag model. Consider

$$Y_t = a + \beta_0 X_t + \sum_{i=1}^{n} \beta_i X_{t-i} + e_t,$$

where

$$\beta_i = \beta_1 + \lambda (i-1), i = 1, 2, \ldots, n. [10]$$

By substitution,

$$Y_t = a + \beta_0 X_t + \beta_1 \sum_{i=1}^{n} X_{t-i} + \lambda \sum_{i=1}^{n} (i-1) X_{t-i} + e_t.$$

The simple and weighted sums of X may be replaced by the corresponding simple and weighted averages with parameters β_1^* and λ^*, respectively, where

$$\beta_1^* = n\beta_1 \text{ and}$$

$$\lambda^* = \Sigma (i-1) \lambda.$$

The short-run coefficient is defined as β_0 and the long-run coefficient as the sum of all the β's.

As Ladd and Tedford point out, Working implicitly assumed $\lambda^* = 0$ by omitting the weighted average of X. Working selected n equal five and ten and found differences in the short-run and long-run price elasticities of demand for beef, pork, and all meat. Ladd and Tedford apply the more general model to the demand for meat using n equal three, five, and nine years. They found essentially no differences in short-run and long-run elasticities for any of the alternate values of n, and they concluded that the long run for meat does not exceed one year.

Waugh's model [352] of the long-run demand for cotton also uses simple averages of lagged prices, but by using three averages centered three, six and nine years previous to the current year, the lagged effect is specified as occurring in steps. Waugh estimated that the long-run price elasticity of demand for cotton is -1.84; a common estimate of the short-run elasticity is -0.3. Nerlove and Waugh's model [245] to measure the long-run effect of advertising on the demand for oranges is of the Working type with n equal 10. Other advertising studies have used geometric and polynomial form models.

Geometric form distributed lag models have been used quite frequently in studies of both demand and supply of farm products, their popularity stemming in part from papers by Nerlove [239, 241]. A partial adjustment model assuming static expectations, which is analogous to stock adjustment and flexible accelerator models, may be written

$$\overline{Q}_t = a + \beta P_t + e_t \text{ (long-run demand equation), and}$$

$$\gamma = \frac{Q_t - Q_{t-1}}{\overline{Q}_t - Q_{t-1}}, 0 < \gamma < 1.$$

This model (in a demand context) assumes (1) that the response in quantity demanded to a price change is delayed by factors such as imperfect knowledge and technological considerations but (2) that expectations are static so that changes in P_t are accepted as appropriate signals of price change and (3) that the adjustment process, given a price change holding other variables constant, is a specific proportional one as defined above, where γ is the coefficient of adjustment. $\overline{Q}_t$ is the unobservable long-run quantity demanded with complete adjustment, and P_t is the observed price. The two equations can be solved to obtain a relationship in observable variables. Namely,

$$Q_t = a\gamma + \beta\gamma P_t + (1-\gamma)Q_{t-1} + \gamma e_t.$$

The adaptive expectations model is an alternative approach that emphasizes expectations as the major factor in the lag process. Observed quantity is made a function of expected price, and in the adaptive expectations model, expected price is defined as the geometric average of current and past prices [239]. The model leads to an equation in observable variables which is analogous to the equation derived from the partial adjustment model; that is, the lagged dependent variable is one of the regressors.

Nerlove [239] argues for models of the partial adjustment or adaptive expectations type because they are derived from explicit hypotheses of consumer (or producer) behavior. The analyst may simply specify, however, that the form of the lag is geometric for whatever reason, and alternate geometric form models may lead to estimating equations with identical regressors (including the lagged dependent variable).

Tomek and Cochrane [330] use geometric and linear form models with quarterly observations to estimate long-run elasticities for beef, pork, and all red meat. The estimated lengths of the adjustment periods to price changes are three quarters, one quarter, and three to four quarters, respectively. The estimated long-run price elasticities are -1.0, -0.75, and -0.55 for beef, pork and all meat; this contrasts with estimates of -0.89, -0.73, and -0.44 using a conventional (non-lag) model with quarterly data.

The question of whether or not the adjustment parameter and length of lag might differ for quantity responses to changes in price and to changes in income was also considered [330]. It is quite easy to allow for different adjustment periods in a linear form model, but it is more difficult in a geometric form model. Martin [218], however, explicitly derives the model which permits different geometric form lags for two variables (price and income). Martin reports a lag of about four and a half years in quantity adjustments for pork to income changes and one year or less to price changes.

Griliches [117] provides a survey of literature for distributed lag models. Papers by Brandow [25], Ironmonger [167], Fuller and Martin [95], Ladd [195], and Mundlak [233] discuss specification problems related to applications in agricultural price analyses. The emphasis of these papers is on the sensitivity of estimates of parameters in geometric form models to specification error, autocorrelated disturbances, aggregation over commodities, and aggregation over time.

The omission of a relevant explanatory variable from an equation containing a lagged dependent variable can seriously bias the estimates of the remaining coefficients, such as the coefficient of adjustment [25]. In sum, there are many reasons why the estimates of parameters of geometric form models may be biased or misleading. Thus, while such models have been quite popular, particularly in estimating agricultural supply equations, the results from such studies, in the author's judgment, should be interpreted with caution.

Parameters of Demand Functions

The demand structures for farm products can change with the passage of time. Basic tastes and preferences change; a new government program is introduced; the income distribution of a population changes; or new substitutes become available. Experienced price analysts know that estimates of demand (or supply) functions frequently are sensitive to the time period selected for analysis, though few published comparisons are available (but see table 1). Moreover, if the time period selected for analysis included more than one structure, the resulting estimated coefficients represent an average which likely is not applicable to the problem under analysis but which may perform well in terms of conventional tests, such as the t-test or size of R^2 (see, for example, [332, p. 350ff.]). Thus, structural change presents a serious problem.

Basically, two approaches have been made to the problem: a search for and selection of a time period with a relatively homogeneous structure relevant to the research problem and the use of additional explanatory variables in the model [84, pp. 20-23; 284, pp. 43-44]. A trend variable may account for changes in tastes and preferences, at least when preferences have changed in a smooth, systematic way through time. Analysts have sometimes suggested using first differences of observations when a long time series is involved [26] ; the intercept parameter then becomes a measure of trend [84, p. 43]. Foytik [89] used a model which permits the slope parameters to change systematically with the passage of time.

Zero-one variables can also be used. A common example is the differentiation between wartime and peacetime. Zero-one variables are more flexible than a time trend in the sense that a trend constrains shifts in the function (which may be viewed as changes in the intercept parameter) to a fixed and equal amount each time period, and zero-one variables can account for abrupt or other uneven shifts with the passage of time. The analyst, however, must have sufficient knowledge to define the zero and one values properly for the appropriate time periods. The slope coefficient of a particular continuous variable can be permitted to change by using the concept of interaction between the zero-one and the continuous variable [11]. If a new substitute becomes available, a variable representing the substitute can be defined with values of zero in the earlier period (before introduction) and the observed values in the later period (after introduction). The effect of the substitute on the slope coefficients of other variables can be tested [84, p. 23]. Some novel methods of allowing for structural change in supply analysis are discussed later.

The selection of a structurally homogeneous time period has the advantage of permitting the use of a simpler model (fewer variables), which implies fewer opportunities for multicollinearity. But the number of observations may be severely limited,[11] and the methodology for selecting a suitable time period can present problems. Two recent theses [114, 299] have considered the time-period selection problem. It is rather common to delete wartime or other years involving effective price controls and/or rationing. In this situation the analyst is able to base the deletion of observations on a priori reasoning.

Given the sensitivity of some estimates to the deletion or addition of one or two observations, one might also argue that a random coefficients model is appropriate for certain price analysis problems. In this model the coefficients of the explanatory variables are specified as fluctuating randomly from one observation to the next (rather than being fixed numbers), and the mean and variance of the unknown random coefficients are estimated [325, pp. 622-627]. As of mid-1973 this model had not been used for agricultural price analysis problems.

Another important aspect of demand analysis is relationships among substitutes. The degree or closeness of substitution relationships depends on the physical or biological attributes of commodities and on relative prices. For instance, Armore [5] and Nyberg [247] point out that fats and oils (for example, coconut oil) often have certain special uses for which no good substitutes exist because of the physical properties of the oils; however, in other uses, food fats and oils can be viewed as essentially identical commodities. If the supply of an oil does not exceed the demand for it in the special use, then the price of this oil can be relatively high. As supplies increase, price declines, and at lower prices a high degree of substitutability becomes apparent.

The disaggregation of a commodity group, such as wheat or beef, into grades or classes represents a special case of closely substitutable products. Price elasticities of demand are much more elastic for the components than for the aggregate. Langemeier and Thompson [198] consider both the fed and nonfed components of the beef sector. Studies of demand by grade, variety, or quality groups have, however, been relatively limited in number (but see, for example, [166]).

If the price of a commodity remains at a relatively high level for a considerable period of time (say, because of a price support program), this may induce the development and use of new substitutes. Some analysts, for instance, believe that high prices of cotton stimulated the development of man-made fibers [352, p. 58]. It is difficult empirically to separate the long-run effects of a given price, which assumes other things constant (as defined above), from the price-induced changes in structure.

Close substitutes have large positive correlations among prices. Thus, while the price elasticity concept assumes "other things" constant, with the passage of time, other things cannot remain constant among close substitutes. If one price changes, the resulting chain of events results in new prices for all of the substitutes. The price elasticity measure alone is a poor predictor of the final net effect of a given price change on quantity. Buse [43] highlights this problem in his article on "total elasticities." He defines the elasticity of total demand response as "the percentage change in the quantity of a commodity demanded due to a one percent change in the price of the commodity, allowing all other variables in the market to vary as they must." This concept differs from the long-run price elasticity, which still assumes other things constant; total elasticity measures the price-quantity relationship after permitting other variables to respond as well to the initial price change.

Buse obtains the total elasticity measure by using an example for beef and pork. For pork, the following relationship is derived:

$$E_t = E_{ii} + E_{ij}S_{ji},$$

where

E_t = elasticity of total demand response for pork,

E_{ii} = price elasticity of demand for pork,

E_{ij} = cross elasticity of demand for pork with respect to price of beef, and

S_{ji} = effect of a one percent change in price of pork on the price of beef.

For substitutes, E_{ij} is positive, and its absolute value is less than E_{ii}; S_{ji} is positive and less than one [43, p. 889]. Thus, E_t is negative, and its absolute value is less than E_{ii}, which is the commonsense result.

Still another aspect of the literature on parameters is the relationship between elasticities and flexibilities. When price analysis models use price dependent demand equations, price flexibility, rather than elasticity, coefficients may be computed.[12] Houck [158] summarizes the general relationship between direct-price and cross-price flexibilities and direct-price and cross-price elasticities. In an earlier paper Meinken, Rojko, and King consider the special case for two substitutes, beef and pork, and provide details for computing elasticities from flexibilities, given the estimated price dependent equations [227, pp. 733-735].

The general relationship between flexibilities and elasticities is

$$FE = I, \text{ or } E = F^{-1},$$

where

F = n x n matrix of price flexibilities,

E = n x n matrix of price elasticities for the n commodities, and

I = n x n identity matrix.

Letting f_{ii} be the direct-price flexibility for the ith commodity and e_{ii} the corresponding elasticity, then from the logical signs of the parameters Houck [158, p. 792] states

$$| e_{ii} | \geq | 1/f_{ii} |.$$

Coleman and Miah [51], however, provide a detailed critique of the Meinken and Houck papers.

An implication of the above relationship is that the elements of F would be estimated from price dependent functions, and then $E = F^{-1}$. In contrast, Waugh [352, p. 29ff.] argues for obtaining the elements of E directly by estimating quantity dependent functions by least squares. This approach often may mean treating a current endogenous variable (price) as predetermined in a least squares regression, giving biased estimates of the parameters. If R^2 is near one, the bias is small [84, p. 68]. Waugh [354] also was a strong proponent of least squares estimation of single equations in forecasting problems, where the variable to be forecast determines the dependent variable.

Analyses Based on Individual Consumer Behavior

In aggregate time-series data estimates of parameters are based on the variation of variables with the passage of time, and the attendant problems of analysis are well known. A sample of interindividual observations (cross-section data) provides different and useful information to the analyst. Prices and consumer preferences can be taken as fixed at a point in time, and the effects of inter-individual differences in income (and other factors) on consumption can be estimated.

Prais and Houthakker [263] provide a comprehensive treatment of Engel functions. The preface to the second impression of their monograph (1971) includes citations of recent literature, which in general are not repeated here. Houthakker [164] also has summarized the results of household expenditure studies from a number of different countries. Three handbooks by Burk [39, 40, 41] include a survey of literature relating to the analysis of food-expenditure relationships in the United States. The latter two publications are devoted to sources of data and their interpretation; the first deals with social and economic factors affecting food consumption in the United States.

The responsiveness of food expenditures to a given change in income generally has been found to be greater than the responsiveness of quantity [104, p. 6]. George and King [96, p. 73] provide a useful summary of quantity and expenditure elasticities for forty-three food items, based on an analysis of the 1965 household consumption data for the United States (see also [278]).

Among the issues that arise in consumption function analysis is whether the analysis should be based on current incomes or total expenditures (or averages of incomes or expenditures). In some cases total expenditures are used as an estimate of income simply because income figures are not available. But, since total consumption expenditures may be viewed as simultaneously determined with expenditures for each product, least squares estimation is inappropriate with such data [317]. It is rather common in estimating Engel curves from cross-section observations to group the observations and to base the estimates on the averages of the groups. This greatly reduces the number of observations and need not cause problems in estimating the parameters of the equation, provided appropriate estimation procedures are used [263, pp. 59-62].

Evidence exists that within the observable range of household sizes, there are economies of scale; for a given level of income per person, per-capita expenditure on food decreases as the size of household increases [104, p. 5]. Household size is perhaps the most important explanatory variable other than income in Engel curve analyses of food consumption [189, pp. 56-57; 148, p. 827]. Other potential explanatory variables include the age distribution of members of the household, racial composition, rural-urban location, and the occupations of household members. Herrmann [148], using data from the 1955 United States household consumption survey, identified interactions between household size and income, between household size and urbanization, and among household size, urbanization, and income. Significant differences appear to exist between consumption functions for farm and urban consumers and between farm and rural nonfarm consumers. For example, Lee and Phillips [206] found that the income elasticity for all food consumption by farmers is less than the comparable elasticities for the other two groups (see also [278]).

The functional form of Engel curves has received considerable attention [104, 208, 263]. Factors to consider in selecting a functional form include (1) the simplicity and convenience of estimation, (2) the validity of the function over the plausible range of total expenditures (the elasticities implied should be logical), (3) the possibility of an initial income below which a commodity is not purchased, and (4) the possibility of a satiety level [208; 263, p. 82]. Prais and Houthakker, after considering alternatives, use a semilogarithmic form for food products; Goreux [104] uses mainly logarithmic, semilog, and log-inverse functions in his analysis.

Leser [208] also places considerable emphasis on functions meeting the "adding-up criterion." This is the constraint, when expenditure data are used, that the sum of the expenditures on all individual goods and services must equal the sum of total expenditures, the explanatory variable [263, p. 83].[13] Prais and Houthakker [263] argue, however, that the importance of the criterion can be overestimated and that "it may be unwise to restrain the formulation by imposing the same algebraic form on the curves for all items of expenditure." The algebraic form selected can influence the estimated income elasticity to an important degree. In the Prais-Houthakker study [263] the income (expenditure) elasticity for meat at the mean ranged from 0.44 for a hyperbola to 0.69 for the double-log form (see also [300, p. 114]).

Wold and Jureen [367] argue that income elasticities from cross-section studies are more nearly long-run coefficients than are those from time-series studies. Klein [189] believes that, in a carefully designed study, these differences can be overcome. Goreux [104] found the income elasticity for all food computed from time-series observations somewhat higher than that from cross-section data. This was attributed to the changing nature of food (the added services) through time. For individual products, income elasticities sometimes were smaller for time-series data, but this was not consistently true [104, p. 10].

Income elasticities for all food and for individual food products apparently have declined as incomes have increased. This assumption is, in fact, explicitly built into the algebraic form of most Engel curves, and massive amounts of empirical evidence confirm the idea of declining income elasticities for foods [104, 263, 268, 278, 309]. Harmston and Hino [131] also compare elasticities at alternative income levels but emphasize changes in elasticities for *given* income levels in two time periods.

Burk [38] points out that the small income elasticity for food and the high degree of urbanization in the United States weakens the usefulness of these variables for forecasting changes in demand. Burk argues for concentrating analyses on moderately high income families who may act as forerunners of changes in demand.

Food at retail can be split into a farm origin and a marketing service component. The service component has grown, but in the late 1950s and early 1960s economists disagreed about the magnitude of the income elasticity for marketing services for food. Anschel [4] summarizes the alternate results, which ranged from less than 0.5 to over 1.0. Anschel believes that the income elasticity for food marketing services is nearer 0.5 (see also [345]).

The development of consumer surveys on a regular basis, as in Great Britain, and the use of consumer panels also has permitted the use of individual household information to estimate price elasticities of demand (for example, [35, 267]). The Purcell and Raunikar study [267], based on an Atlanta consumer panel, indicates that the demand for food tends to become less elastic as the time interval over which prices change is lengthened, say from a weekly change to one that occurs over a year.

Most empirical studies of demand do not consider fully the interdependent nature of demand; few cross elasticities are estimated in a typical time-series analysis, and prices are treated as fixed in Engel functions. Yet, as previously observed, a change in the price of one commodity sets in motion events that influence the consumption and prices of other goods and services. A "complete" matrix of elasticities can be useful in answering price policy questions. There are at least two reasons, however, why such a large set of elasticities cannot be estimated directly from available data. One is the degrees of freedom problem. Given n commodities, there are n^2 direct-price and cross-price elasticities as well as n income elasticities. Second, the cross-price elasticities are often very small and, hence, unmeasurable by conventional econometric methods; but the aggregate cross effects for a group of products may not be negligible.

Certainly one of the important developments in agricultural demand analysis has been the use of restrictions on elasticities (derived from basic theory) as aids in obtaining estimates of elasticities. These restrictions, while derived from theory which applies to the individual consumer, are usually used in studies of market demand.[14] Thus, the results of applications of theoretical constraints must be treated either as applicable to a representative consumer

Table 2. Selected Relations from Demand Theory

Name of Relation	Statement
(1) Homogeneity condition (or row restraint)	$\sum\limits_{j=1}^{n} e_{ij} + e_{iy} = 0$
(2) Symmetry condition (or Slutsky condition)	$e_{ij} = \dfrac{w_j}{w_i} e_{ji} + w_j (e_{jy} - e_{iy})$
(3) Engel aggregation	$\sum\limits_{i=1}^{n} w_i e_{iy} = 1$
(4) Cournot aggregation (or column restraint)	$\sum\limits_{i=1}^{n} w_i e_{ij} = -w_j$ (for the jth column)
(5) Frisch equations	$e_{ij} = \dfrac{1}{\emptyset} e_{iy} e_{jy} w_j - e_{iy} w_j,\ i \neq j,$ and $e_{ii} = -e_{iy} w_i - \dfrac{1 - w_i e_{iy}}{\emptyset}$
(6) General expression for ordinal separability assumption	$\dfrac{\partial U_i / U_j}{\partial q_k} = 0$ for some $k \neq i, j.$

e_{ij} = price elasticity; $i = j$, direct; $i \neq j$ cross;
e_{iy}, e_{jy} = income elasticities for i and j;
w_i, w_j = expenditure weights;
$\emptyset$ = money flexibility coefficient (see [93]);
U_i, U_j = marginal utility of i and j, respectively;
q_k = quantity of k.
Adapted from George and King [96].

that meets the underlying assumptions or as approximations which still are useful for policy analyses and decisions [24, p. 14].

A classical approach to demand theory involves a consumer with a given income making choices from a commodity space of n items with given prices. The choice problem is stated as maximizing a utility function subject to the restriction that total expenditures equal income. Appropriate algebra gives n demand functions with each quantity a function of n prices and income. These functions satisfy a number of important relationships, which are briefly summarized in terms of elasticities in equations (1) - (4) in table 2. Bieri and de Janvry [14] and George and King [96] provide more complete summaries, including references to relevant theoretical literature.

Wetmore et al. [361, pp. 66-71] make use of equations (1) - (4) in their study of policies for expanding the demand for food. The homogenity, symmetry, and Engel conditions reduce the number of parameters to be estimated to $1/2(n^2 + n - 2)$, still a large number [96, p. 21]. Thus, Wetmore and colleagues also relied on reasonable assumptions (for example, the sum of cross elasticities is positive or zero) and judgment to complete a matrix of demand elasticities for foods.

Constraints such as the homogeneity condition also help analysts to appraise estimates obtained in applied research. For instance, if the income elasticity for food grains in India is estimated to be 0.5 and if the sum of the cross elasticities is zero or larger, then the direct-price elasticity is equal to or larger (in absolute value) than -0.5 [228, p. 973].

Separability concepts provide additional information for estimating a matrix of demand elasticities.[15] Frisch [93] proposed the assumption of "want independence" as a basis for computing all price elasticities.[16] This assumption permits Frisch to obtain equation (5) in table 2 for want-independent goods from the symmetry relation [96, pp. 22-23].

Brandow [24, p. 14] assumes food and nonfood are want independent and uses Frisch's conditions as a guide to obtaining cross-price elasticities between food and nonfood. George and King [96], expanding on Brandow, compute a complete set of elasticities for forty-nine foods as well as nonfood. They start by making estimates of direct-price and income elasticities for each commodity. The forty-nine foods are divided into fifteen separable groups, and "cross elasticities for commodities belonging to the same food group basically are obtained through direct estimation process" [96]. Extensive use is made of conditions (1) through (5) to complete the matrix of elasticities. In particular, the Frisch equations are used as guides to obtaining cross elasticities among groups [96, pp. 43-44].

In empirical analyses the grouping adopted necessarily has some degree of arbitrariness. George and King [96] describe briefly and use a grouping developed by de Janvry (see review in [14]). The groupings tend to be the "natural" ones such as meats (beef, pork) and fruits (apples, bananas).

Frisch assumes the marginal utilities of i and j are unaffected by the consumption of k (where k does not belong to the i, j group), but separability more generally requires only that the ratio of marginal utilities remain unchanged (that is, $U_i = U_j$) for a change in consumption of the kth commodity (equation (6), table 2).[17] Boutwell and Simmons [21] explore the implications of weak and strong (ordinal) separability for reducing the number of parameters to be estimated and apply a model to seven commodities (aggregates) divided into two groups. The restrictions derived from the separability assumptions are imposed on the demand functions. The final model is nonlinear in the parameters, requiring an iterative estimation procedure. Bieri and de Janvry [14] review alternative approaches to estimation which assume separability.

The implications of alternate models for the degrees-of-freedom problem can be illustrated by the Brandow study [24]. Brandow's elasticity matrix for 24 foods and one nonfood category contains 625 own and cross elasticities plus 25 income elasticities. These 650 coefficients can be reduced to 324 by the use of constraints (1) - (4). With two groups, as in Brandow, Boutwell and Simmons show that the assumption of weak separability requires the estimation of 301 parameters. Hallberg [126] asks whether or not saving 23 coefficients justifies the use of the more complex iterative estimation procedure implicit in the Boutwell-Simmons approach [21]. Hallberg also points out that for pragmatic reasons the functional form of the demand equation is restricted to the logarithmic type. In principle, however, the savings in degrees of freedom can be greater with a larger number of groups.

A recent study [14], using observations from Argentina to estimate demand elasticities, illustrates the simplifications made in a two-stage utility maximization-type model. Since, by assumption of the model, the total expenditures to be made for each commodity group is determined in the first step by the consumer, the group expenditure for individual demand functions is predetermined; that is, the consumer is assumed to determine the expenditures for the particular groups in the first step. Thus, the group expenditure is a predetermined variable for the demand function of an individual product within the group. Also, since the theory is related to individual consumers, prices are exogenous. If the assumptions are correct, least squares estimation is justified [14, pp. 20-22]. Of course, when aggregate market data are used, prices probably are endogenous.

The theoretical restrictions on elasticities derived from utility theory have counterparts for flexibility coefficients. Waugh [352] derives the conditions for an n equation model in which prices are on the left-hand side of the equal sign. Houck [155] provides a similar derivation, but starting with the traditional elasticity restrictions imposed on functions with *quantities* on the left.

Supply Analysis

The literature related to supply analysis for agricultural products can be conveniently divided into three main categories: (1) studies of the supply of individual commodities based on time-series data, (2) studies based on budgeting techniques or linear programming models using typical farms or regions as units of analysis, and (3) studies of aggregate supply including both the development of theoretical concepts and the estimation of the response of total farm output to changes in product and factor prices. Since studies of farm inputs have often been linked to analyses of product supplies, we review the literature on the supply and demand for inputs in a fourth subsection.

Fortunately, a number of excellent review articles covering both methods of supply analysis and empirical results are already available. Two of these [56, 244], which were written in the early 1960s, are still relevant and provide a useful summary of the contributions made by agricultural economists to the study of supply. More detailed descriptions of alternative techniques of supply analysis and summaries of empirical studies can be found in the book *Agricultural Supply Functions: Estimating Techniques and Interpretations* [140]. Some additional observations regarding supply analysis based on experience gained during the 1960s are contained in a series of papers presented at the December 1968 meetings of the American Agricultural Economics Association [175].[18]

Time-Series Analysis

Like many demand analyses, most studies of the supply response of individual commodities are based on time-series data using single-equation models and ordinary least squares estimation. Indeed, the similarity of the problems faced in time-series analysis of demand and of supply permit this subsection to be relatively short.

The most significant single contribution to time-series supply analysis in the postwar period undoubtedly has been the work of Nerlove. The concepts which he introduced in the late 1950s led to renewed interest in supply analysis [239, 240, 241, 243]. His distributed lag models (discussed earlier), in principle, make it possible to obtain separate estimates of short-run and long-run elasticities. These models, which have a rather elegant simplicity, frequently produce higher R^2 values than alternative models and in some cases appear to reduce or eliminate the problem of serial correlation in the residuals. In short, the marginal gains in terms of additional information (two elasticity estimates) and seemingly improved statistical properties are high in relation to the marginal costs. Under such circumstances, it is not surprising that this innovation was quickly adopted by agricultural economists.

The routine, and indeed almost universal, use of Nerlove-type models to obtain short-run and long-run estimates of supply has not escaped criticism, however. A number of agricultural economists have expressed reservations about the quality and interpretation of the estimated coefficients. Criticisms of the model run along the following lines. First, the equation contains the lagged dependent variable (usually acreage planted in supply equations for crops), and the coefficient of this lagged variable may very well embrace a collection of influences, including those associated with trends in the dependent variable such as technological change. This is simply a special case of the general problem of omitted variables which are correlated with included variables and hence bias the coefficients [25, 119]. In addition, multicollinearity may exist between the lagged dependent and other explanatory variables. For these reasons, great care must be exercised in interpreting the coefficients. As Griliches points out [116], such coefficients may measure more than an adjustment or expectation process.

A second major criticism is that the expectations model assumes price expectations are formed in a particular way (a geometrically diminishing lag). Clearly, farmers do not base their plans solely on past prices (for example, outlook statements may also play a role in their decisions); nor is it necessarily realistic to assume that weights are assigned to past prices in a geometric fashion. Equations with large R^2's and statistically significant coefficients may be obtained even though a geometric-form model is not applicable. Ultimately, additional experience with different lag forms (such as the Almon lag [45]) may place the geometric lag model in a clearer perspective.[19]

In order to have a reasonable number of degrees of freedom, supply analysts have been forced to select only a few of the many possible explanatory variables. Typically, analysts have used the product price (with varying lags and weights), lagged values of the dependent variable sometimes as an alternative or in addition to using a trend variable, either prices or an index of prices paid for inputs (such as fertilizer, machinery, or feed), and if appropriate some measure of the prices or returns from alternative crops or enterprises. In some cases, a variable reflecting off-farm job opportunities has been included. Reutlinger [274] suggests that supply may respond to the variance as well as the average level of price, though he concedes it is difficult to test this hypothesis empirically.

One of the more difficult problems in agricultural supply analysis is the specification and estimation of relationships for tree crops. French [91] made apple production a function of a simple average of price ratios lagged twelve years. French and Matthews' [92] supply model for perennial crops cites and builds on previous studies (see [12] for another approach).

The unexplained variance in supply equations is frequently large and usually greater than with demand equations. Moreover, coefficients, especially those attached to product and factor prices, tend to be unstable and are frequently small in relation to their standard errors [190, pp. 96-97]. Price elasticities, for example, vary depending on which years are used and whether or not trend or other variables are omitted or included. Elasticity estimates are also influenced by the functional form used. One automatically places certain restrictions of elasticity estimates if a straight line function is used [157]. In most equations shift variables account for a much higher proportion of the explained variance than the product price. Thus, own-price elasticity estimates obtained from time-series data are often weak.

The relatively large unexplained variance in supply equations can usually be attributed to one or more of three elements. First, random disturbances are associated with natural or biological phenomena such as variation in moisture availability or insect and disease damage. Second, abrupt or irregular changes in technology may occur which alter yields and the relative profitability of products. Finally, government programs have had a profound effect, especially in the United States, on the acreages planted to such crops as grains, cotton, and tobacco.

Agricultural economists have shown great ingenuity in devising variables to take account of these shifts in supply. For example, Stallings [306] constructed a weather index which could be incorporated in supply equations (for alternatives see [72, 249, 326]). Hathaway [135], G. Johnson [173], and Houck, Ryan, and Subotnik [160, 161] are among those who have incorporated variables to account for the effects of changes in government programs. Efforts to find a suitable proxy for technolgoy (other than trend) have been less successful. Halter [127] argues that the predictive power of supply equations will always be limited because the most critical factor in long-run supply is technology, and this is precisely the variable most difficult to incorporate into models and to forecast.[20]

Until the early 1960s supply analysis was limited mainly to the more developed countries, but work by Krishna (summarized in [192]), in which he successfully estimated supply equations for cotton, wheat, and other grain crops in the Punjab region of India, encouraged others to make similar studies. Krishna used the Nerlove model to estimate both short-run and long-run elasticities of supply based on annual data essentially for the period between the two world wars. The supply elasticities for cotton turned out to be somewhat larger than those estimated for the United States before the introduction of supply control programs. Somewhat smaller elasticity estimates were obtained for grain crops. Other published studies based on time-series analysis of supply in less developed countries include one on rubber in Malaya [363], wheat and rice in Pakistan [78], and rice and corn in Thailand [10]. The results of many of these studies have been conveniently summarized by Krishna [191]. These studies support the hypothesis that peasant farmers in poor countries respond positively to prices and particularly to changes in relative prices of cash crops. Supply elasticities generally are much smaller for subsistence (food) crops, especially if only a small proportion of the crop is sold, than for fibers or other cash crops.

For less developed countries, elasticities have been used, not only to test alternative hypotheses regarding farmers' production response to price but also to ascertain whether quantities sold are likely to diminish as prices rise. Several methods of estimating the response of marketings to changes in product prices (the elasticity of marketed surplus) have been devised. It is difficult to obtain reliable data on what happens to home consumption on subsistence farms when product prices (and hence real incomes) change. This problem has been circumvented by first estimating the response of total output to a change in price (own-price elasticity of supply) and then estimating the relationship between quantities marketed and produced (the elasticity of sales with respect to output) using either time-series or cross-section data. The price elasticity of marketed surplus is estimated by multiplying the elasticity of sales with respect to output by the price elasticity of supply. The empirical evidence suggests that elasticity of marketed surplus is positive even in subsistence agricultural economies [191, pp. 511-512].

Budgeting and Linear Programming Techniques in Supply Analysis

Time-series analysis is least useful for prediction when technology, government programs, or other supply shifters change abruptly or discontinuously. The limitations of time-series analysis led John D. Black to suggest building synthetic supply schedules from budget studies of "typical" farms. The logic of deriving supply schedules from firm data is appealing, but the practical problems of carrying out the analysis are enormous. Great care is needed in selecting farms for analysis, specifying input-output relationships on such farms, and deciding what alternatives to consider. Judgment obviously is involved at every step, and particularly in deciding what the farmer is most likely to do. Budgeting was the normal method of determining the most profitable level of output at alternative prices, but as Mighell and Allen [229] emphasized, "The step from the most profitable (output) to the most likely is a difficult one and cannot be entirely objective." Finally, there is the problem of how data from representative farms should be aggregated to reflect the response from a region. The results of one of the early studies which analyzes the effect of changes in milk prices on production of milk are reported by Mighell and Black [230].

The derivation of supply relationships from studies of individual farms probably would not have been pursued by very many economists if it had not been for the development and popularization of linear programming techniques in the 1950s. Unquestionably this innovation, along with the development of high-speed computers, was responsible for a renewed interest in the late 1950s and early 1960s in deriving supply schedules from farm data. Linear programming made it possible to test the effects of changes in prices, costs, and technology on the optimum output relatively inexpensively and rapidly. By using price-mapping techniques, boundary prices (those at which alternatives were equally profitable) could be readily identified (for an example of this type of analysis, see [224]).

But, as with budgeting studies, the practical problems of deriving useful estimates from programming representative farms proved to be very great. The difficulties involved in such studies are well summarized by Sharples [298]. Among the major problems encountered are the difficulty of allowing for changes in farm size and technology, induced changes in input or factor prices (externalities), deciding what assumptions regarding the behavior of decision makers should be built into the models (for example, whether simple profit maximization is an appropriate assumption), and the familiar problems of farm selection and aggregation. In addition, users of this technique found themselves overwhelmed in some cases by the multiplicity of results obtained. As more farms and alternatives were analyzed, straightforward conclusions were difficult to draw from the mass of computer outputs.

In an attempt to make the results of linear programming models more predictive (rather than normative), additional constraints designed to reflect behavioral or technological limitations to changing output from one year to the next were introduced. The research of R. H. Day [69, 70], building on the work of Henderson [146], unquestionably gave impetus to the use of "recursive programming." The technique involves only a simple modification of the traditional linear-programming model — namely, the introduction of "flexibility constraints" which impose upper and lower bounds to the expansion or contraction of each activity.

The flexibility constraints can be derived in a number of ways, but usually the coefficients are based on regression analysis of time-series data. The objective is to find the coefficient which expresses the relationship between, say, acreage in the current year and the preceding year — that is, $X_t = (1 \pm B) X_{t-1}$, where B is defined as the flexibility coefficient. Separate coefficients are customarily calculated for years of increasing and decreasing acreage. The model, in contrast to the traditional unrestrained linear programming solution, makes it possible to trace the path of adjustment in response to a change in the price of the product, a technological improvement, or an institutional modification such as a change in government programs. In the recursive model each successive solution is conditioned by the solution obtained for the preceding year.

The recursive programming model has been used mainly in attempts to explain or predict regional changes in the acreages planted to crops. The results obtained from recursive programming models and time-series analysis have been compared in several studies [289, 378]. These and other studies indicate that unrestrained linear programming models, and even recursive models, tend to overstate changes in acreage in relation to those that actually occur. In most cases regression equations based on time-series data have proved to be more accurate for forecasting than the results obtained from programming models; however, when large, discontinuous changes occur, such as with the introduction of new technology or modifications in government policies, programming results sometimes provide the basis for improved forecasts over those made using regression analysis. In general, supply elasticity estimates derived from programming models are too high for predictive purposes although such analyses are useful in calling attention to the probable direction of change in supply in response to a major change in structure.[21]

A review of supply analysis would not be complete without mentioning the efforts that have been made to derive supply elasticities directly from production or cost functions. In theory, of course, only the shape of the production function plus information about factor prices (or factor demand and supply equations) are needed to obtain an estimate of how output is likely to respond to changes in either product or factor prices (for a review of the formal theory of deriving supply relationships from production functions, see [140]).

In practice, differences in production functions between farms, attributable in part to differences in the quality of land resources available and in part to differences in capital constraints and managerial ability, have made it difficult to obtain usable results from production function analysis. Likewise, specifying useful cost functions, especially when alternative opportunities must be considered, is difficult. For the most part, supply analyses based on cost or production functions have been confined to single-product firms or data obtained from experimental plots (for example, see [141, pp. 143-153; 291]). However, Wipf and Bawden [365] attempted to derive supply elasticities from whole farm production functions separately for all crops and livestock products. The general conclusion emerging from these studies is that supply elasticity estimates derived from production functions are not reliable.

Powell and Gruen [261] demonstrate considerable ingenuity in attempting to derive estimates of cross elasticities of supply based on the principles of production economics. Their method involves the derivation of a constant elasticity of transformation production frontier from time-series data. The assumption of constant elasticity of transformation, they reason, is realistic if only modest changes in product/product price ratios from existing or average ratios are to be considered. Using the results obtained from the constant elasticity of transformation frontier, they calculated a complete matrix of supply elasticities, including all cross elasticities for six major agricultural commodities produced in Australia (wool, lamb, wheat, coarse grains, beef, and milk).

Greater use of producer panels to determine the response of farmers to changes in price or other factors affecting supply has been suggested on several occasions, notably by Nerlove and Bachman in 1960 [244] and more recently by Schaller [288]. Research by Conneman (see citations in [53]) illustrates the use of producer panel data in the economic analysis of milk production in the northeast. Conneman used Markov chains to analyze the implications of exits and entries of firms for milk supply,[22] but the translation of producer panel data into specific supply projections appears to be difficult. The same problems of sampling and aggregation apply to this technique as to linear programming analysis of supply.

Micro-Theory and Aggregate Supply

The concept of aggregate supply is especially important in agriculture, both for policy analysis and for forecasting. A knowledge of how total output is likely to change in response to an increase or decrease in the average level of farm product prices is necessary in order to predict the consequences of a change in price policy. Information concerning shifts in aggregate supply is essential in forecasting farm income since the average level of farm product prices is determined to a large degree by the shifts in aggregate supply over time relative to demand. As T. W. Schultz [293] emphasized, it is extremely difficult to match the growth of aggregate supply with demand. For this reason most countries are faced with one of two types of problems, either too much (a surplus problem and relatively low prices for farm products) if the growth of output exceeds that of demand or a food problem (deficits and high prices) if the reverse occurs.

Most of the concepts of aggregate supply now widely accepted by agricultural economists were developed in the 1950s and are embodied in papers by D. Gale Johnson [171], Willard W. Cochrane [47], T. W. Schultz [295], and Glenn Johnson [174]. These articles and especially the lengthy footnote to Glenn Johnson's paper, combined with the comments following it by Cochrane [49], provide a convenient summary of both the contributions and the controversies that have emerged regarding the concept of aggregate supply.

D. Gale Johnson's paper [171] emphasizes the critical role which factor supply elasticities play in explaining changes in factor/product price ratios (hence, factor use and output) when the average level of farm product prices declines. He argued, in conformity with the profit-maximizing principles of microeconomic theory, that a fall in product prices will be accompanied by a decline in the prices of at least some factors, particularly those with inelastic supply schedules. He found the empirical evidence consistent with his hypothesis, at least during the early 1930s. Since family labor, land, feed, and livestock had few alternative uses outside of agriculture during this period, the prices of these factors declined about as much as the prices of farm products. As a result, farmers found it economic to maintain the use of these factors at about the same level despite a substantial drop in farm product prices.

In contrast, the use of purchased inputs such as fertilizer, machinery, building materials, and hired labor declined because prices of these factors did not fall as much as average product prices.

Johnson cautioned against drawing general inferences about the elasticity of factor supplies, and hence the elasticity of total farm output, based on the experience of the depression years. Under conditions of more nearly full employment, the supply of labor undoubtedly would be more elastic, and hence the price elasticity of aggregate supply would be greater. Also, the analysis of the depression experience was based on the assumption of constant technology. A change in technology which shifted the production function upward could result in an increase in output despite a fall in average product prices.

Two contributions by Cochrane are especially noteworthy [47]. First, he drew a distinction between the static (ceteris paribus) supply function and a more general "response relation," which he conceded was a hybrid or mongrel relationship. The response relation perhaps is more useful for forecasting because it includes, among other things, the effect of technical change adopted in response to rising prices. Second, Cochrane was among the first to emphasize the importance of technical change in accounting for shifts in the aggregate supply function for farm products in the United States. As had other economists, he hypothesized that the aggregate supply response of producers to a fall in prices would be less than to a corresponding increase in prices. Cochrane's reasoning, however, was based more on the role of technology (as opposed to factor prices) and the differential rate at which technology was likely to be adopted in periods of rising prices in contrast to periods of declining prices. During periods of rising prices farmers have both the incentive and the necessary capital (out of retained earnings) to invest in output-increasing technology, but the process is not reversible. Once the new technology is adopted, it will not be abandoned. In periods of falling prices the output of the typical farm firm (and hence the total output) does not decline because of the lack of alternative uses for some factors of production, induced changes in the prices of factors with inelastic supply schedules, and a general commitment on the part of many of those in agriculture to continue farming despite low returns.

Technology, according to Cochrane [47], is the "dynamic force in agriculture, being involved in almost all production adjustments and explaining net increase in output on individual farms and in the aggregate." In Cochrane's view the modern farmer does not typically vary the proportions or quantities of existing factors over time; rather he changes to a new input mix based on a different technology. Since the rate of adoption of new technology is more likely to increase during periods of rising prices, the aggregate supply function is likely to shift to the right discontinuously, mainly during periods of prosperity for farmers, and to remain static and severely price inelastic during periods of depression.

Cochrane dismisses two other factors as being relatively unimportant, at least in the United States, in shifting the supply curve for farm products — namely the weather (which shifts the curve temporarily but not permanently) and the increased use of conventional inputs. His analysis seems to fit much of the twentieth-century experience in the United States, but not necessarily that prevailing in many less developed countries. In Brazil, for example, during the 1950s and 1960s, increases in total farm output were mainly a function of an increase in the land area and a corresponding increase in the amount of labor devoted to agriculture without any major changes in technology.

T. W. Schultz [295] also emphasizes the role of technology in shifting the aggregate supply function in the United States. Increases in conventional inputs, he points out, do not account for the sharp rise in aggregate output which has occurred in the United States. Hence, the increase must have been due to the addition of what he calls "unconventional inputs," mainly associated with improvements in the quality of the labor force and new technology. Since these appear to be the critical variables in increasing output, he stressed the importance of devoting more attention to methods of producing and distributing such inputs.

Glenn Johnson's contribution to the concept of aggregate supply has been to emphasize the role of fixed assets in limiting supply response to a change in product prices. An asset can be defined as fixed, according to Johnson [171], "so long as its marginal value productivity in its present use neither justifies acquisition of more of it or its disposition." The use of a factor is likely to remain constant over a wide range of product prices if the salvage value or opportunity cost of that factor outside of agriculture is much below the acquisition cost.

The Johnson model implies that the supply schedule for the fixed factor is a stepped function, highly elastic at the salvage value, and again at the price at which additional units can be purchased, but highly inelastic in between. The greater the length of the inelastic or vertical segment of the function, the less responsive factor use will be to changes in product prices (that is, the marginal value product or demand curve for the factor can move up or down over this range without affecting factor use). Johnson argues that the salvage value of such inputs as family labor, previously acquired machinery, and land is relatively low and likely to be less in most cases than their value in use; hence, such inputs remain employed even when a substantial decline occurs in farm product prices. While the conceptual model is useful in categorizing inputs, the conclusions drawn from the model are no different from those reached by other agricultural economists. Namely, the lack of profitable alternative uses for certain inputs such as family labor limits the response of supply to a fall in farm prices, at least in the short run, and especially in periods of general depression.

Empirical studies of aggregate supply are limited both by the lack of data in many countries and by the presence of strong trend factors in the dependent as well as the major explanatory variables. This makes it difficult to identify and separate the effects of shift variables such as technology from the effects of changes in relative prices. Despite the difficulties involved, agricultural economists have obtained what appear to be reasonable and useful estimates of the aggregate supply relationship for the United States. Among the empirical studies most frequently cited are those done by Cochrane [46, 48], Griliches [116, 118], Heady and Tweeten [141] and Tweeten and Quance [336]; for critiques of [336], see [42] and [368].

Cochrane's analysis is based on scatter diagrams with an index of per-capita food production for sale on the horizontal axis and an index of "responsible" prices on the vertical side. He determined by inspection approximately when the supply schedule had remained stable and when it had shifted. This analysis suggested that the schedule shifts to the right in a hopping or skipping fashion rather than smoothly and continuously. The two major shifts which appear to have occurred between 1910 and the early 1950s are attributed by Cochrane to the introduction of tractors in the early 1920s and the sharp rise in farm product prices during the war years of the early 1940s [48].

Griliches [116] was among the first to attempt to estimate the elasticity of aggregate supply based on an analysis of the response of factor use to a change in farm product prices. The elasticity of aggregate supply is simply a product of the weighted average of changes in factor use induced by a change in average farm prices. The weights are determined by the response of total output to a change in the quantities of each factor employed or simply by the elasticities of production. Algebraically, the relationship can be expressed as

$$E_{op} = \sum_{i=1}^{n} E_{oi} E_{ip}.$$

E_{op} is the elasticity of total output with respect to product prices; E_{oi} is the elasticity of production with respect to the ith factor; and E_{ip} is the elasticity of factor use with respect to product prices. Griliches used time-series data and a form of the Nerlove distributed lag model to estimate the response of several categories of inputs to a change in farm prices. He then multiplied the separate estimates of short-run and long-run elasticity of factor use by estimates of production elasticity based on factor share (the proportion of total value of output attributed to each category of inputs) to obtain aggregate short-run and long-run supply elasticities for United States agriculture.

Tweeten and Quance [336] used a similar procedure to estimate the aggregate elasticity of supply for the United States.[23] They also obtained direct estimates using time-series data. The most important variables in explaining changes in total output were the stock of productive farm assets (the value of real estate, machinery, livestock), lagged values of the ratio of prices received to prices paid by farmers, and a productivity index closely related to time or trend. The results, in general, confirm the hypotheses outlined earlier, namely that the elasticity of aggregate supply for the United States is positive but low, at least in the short run, and slightly greater during periods of rising prices than in periods of falling prices. Tweeten and Quance did not find any evidence of a significant change in elasticity in the postwar years as compared with the interwar period. This is contrary to the views of some economists who reasoned that aggregate supply should now be more elastic because of greater reliance on purchased inputs which are likely to have relatively elastic supply schedules.

Demand and Supply of Farm Inputs

Since changes in farm output depend on changes in the quantity and productivity of resources employed in farming, it is not surprising that the interest in product supply has led to the study of variables which are thought to explain the levels of resource use. The "farm problem" of surplus production and low prices generated substantial interest in the demand and supply of agricultural inputs in the 1950s and early 1960s (for example, [60, 115, 290]). T. W. Schultz [293], in particular, stressed the relationship of factor markets to the farm income problem. The zenith of such research in that period was Heady and Tweeten's *Resource Demand and Structure of the Agricultural Industry* [141]; this comprehensive book emphasizes estimates of demand relationships for numerous resources, including fertilizer, labor, machinery, plant and equipment, and certain operating inputs. In a limited amount of space it is impossible to examine all of the topics and issues related to the study of farm inputs. Our discussion focuses on traditional, as well as more recent, approaches to the estimation of structural relationships.[24]

Economic theory suggests that one could begin by estimating a production function and proceed to derive factor demand relationships. Heady and Tweeten [141, chapter 6] explored this approach, but in practice it is rarely used. Problems in deriving factor demand functions from production functions are similar to those discussed above in deriving product supply curves from production functions. Consequently, most estimates of input relationships have involved direct least squares regressions using time-series data. The models have often used a geometric-form distributed lag specification. The functional form of the demand equation is sometimes suggested by assuming a particular shape of the underlying production function [115]. Thus, the price of the input under analysis, prices of other inputs, and price of the relevant product (or products) are plausible explanatory variables in a demand equation for an input.

Renshaw [272] discusses the problems of specifying demand shifters and functional forms as well as the difficulties associated with geometric-form distributed lag models in the context of Griliches's study of the demand for fertilizer [115]. For instance, how does one take account of the effect of the adoption of hybrid corn on the demand for fertilizer? Notwithstanding Griliches's rather sharp reply [272], the difficulties of estimating and interpreting equations with a lagged dependent variable, particularly when this variable is trending, are now well documented.

Schuh's analysis [290] of the market for hired labor treats wages and employment as being simultaneously determined by the supply and demand for labor. The predetermined variables in the demand equation are an index of prices received by farmers, an index of technology, and the lagged dependent variable; the predetermined variables in the supply equation are the size of the civilian labor force, deflated nonfarm income, and the lagged dependent variable. This research was subsequently extended to a six-equation model involving the supply of and demand for hired labor, unpaid family labor, and operator labor [337].

Price (wage) elasticities of demand for hired labor were found to be inelastic in most studies, even in the long run. Recent work by Hammonds, Yadav, and Vathana [128] suggests, however, that the wage coefficient is becoming more elastic with the passage of time and perhaps is now about -2.0.

Two papers [147, 335] in 1966 were concerned with the puzzle of why farm real estate prices had risen in the face of low farm incomes. Herdt and and Cochrane [147], using a two-equation simultaneous model, conclude "that the expectation of rising income from technological advance in conjunction with supported farm prices . . . has been important in contributing to the rise in farm land prices." Tweeten and Martin [335], based on a recursive system of equations, reach a similar conclusion, though they use different terminology and attribute higher land prices "to pressures for farm enlargement and capitalized benefits from government programs."

Technological advance and changes in the quality of inputs create questions and problems beyond how a technological change may influence the demand for an input or how that change may be incorporated into the demand function. For example, the nature of the input itself can change. Studies of the demand for farm tractors have tried to take account of the important changes in the quality of tractors [271]. Fettig [81] discusses the problem of constructing an index of tractor prices which attempts to hold quality constant.

Since the demand for a durable input like tractors is a derived demand for a flow of services from the input, a problem exists in defining the price of the service. The price of a tractor represents the price of providing the stock of tractors from which services come. Another question in model specification for durable inputs is how to account for replacement investment. Rayner and Cowling [271] provide an excellent review of literature on the demand for farm tractors and the issues of model specification. Such variables as lagged farm income and the stock of tractors appear to be important explainers of gross investment in tractors in the United States, but "the parameter estimates are not well determined" [271].

Despite a considerable amount of research in the 1950s and early 1960s, agricultural input markets were considered a neglected area of research as late as 1962 [64]. In the past five to ten years there has been an increase in work in this subject area, but relative to product price analysis input prices still might be considered a neglected topic. A bibliography by Dahl, Anderson, and Peterson [64] provides a useful set of citations of research on purchased farm inputs, and a report edited by Nelson [236] gives additional references. Recent work covers such diverse inputs as feed, farm building, farm credit, and machinery.

Recent research continues to include conventional time-series analyses [143]. However, the newer work has also involved different data sources, such as farmer panels, and different research tools, such as probit and variance component models. Some recent developments in input research are summarized in [236].

An analysis by Daniel and Havlicek [67] illustrates the use of data from a farm panel to estimate fertilizer demand functions. Monthly observations were obtained from nine hundred Illinois farmers for the years 1961-65. The variables included in the models can be classified as economic factors, characteristics of the farm, characteristics of the farm operator, and trend, adjustment, and weather factors. Prices of fertilizers generally were statistically significant in the various equations, and the short-run demand for straight nitrogen was estimated to be price elastic while the short-run demands for phosphate and potash were inelastic.

Daniel and Havlicek [67] also compared their results with other studies, and the differences are disconcertingly large. While Heady and Tweeten found the demands for all of the various fertilizers to be quite price elastic (-1.24 to

-2.14) in aggregate analyses for the United States, Yeh and Heady reported inelastic demands (-0.40 to -0.45) for the same nutrients. These studies are, of course, based on quite different sets of data, but further research is required if the inconsistent results from aggregate time series, individual farmers, and production function studies are to be explained. In addition, it does not seem likely that the fertilizer models extant in 1973 could have accurately predicted the demand for fertilizer in 1974.

Analysis of Price Relationships

In theory, all prices are interrelated, though in practice some prices are essentially independent. An understanding of relationships among prices is important both for private and public policy decision making. Consequently, agricultural economists have explored a wide variety of price relationships. Those for substitutes were reviewed earlier. In this section we consider relationships under a competitive market structure at different stages of the marketing system, at different points in space, and at different points in time. In addition, the literature on price discrimination schemes in agriculture is briefly reviewed. We conclude this section with a short examination of the literature on farm-nonfarm price relationships.

Marketing Margins

Agricultural economists have devoted particular attention to the integrating role of price and especially to the relationship between prices at the farm level and those at the wholesale or retail levels. Among the questions they have sought to answer are whether or not changes in farm prices are promptly and fully reflected in retail prices, whether margins are too large, whether marketing margins remain constant per unit sold or vary with the volume sold, and whether and to what degree changes in margins influence farm and retail prices.[25]

Both theory and empirical observation suggest that changes in retail prices are likely to lag behind changes in farm prices and that retail prices tend to be somewhat more inflexible. Numerous hypotheses to explain the sticky response of retail prices in the face of increased or decreased farm supplies have been advanced. Inertia in the marketing system unquestionably accounts for some of the delay in transmitting price changes through the system. Breimyer [29] argues, in general terms, that stickiness in retail prices is due partly to the preference of marketing firms for price stability. Parish [251] attributes the same phenomenon to both cost and demand considerations.

Buse and Brandow [44] studied the relationship between marketing margins and quantities marketed for twenty commodities. In one type of equation [44, table 3] they found an inverse relation between the volume marketed and the farm-retail price spread. However, when quarterly observations were used for a few of the commodities, the results suggested the opposite conclusion. A problem may exist in the specification and identification of such equations; a price-quantity relation might be either a demand for or a supply of marketing services equation. In any case, the empirical evidence on the nature of price-volume relationships is inconclusive. Brandow, in his study of price interrelationships [24], ultimately decided to relate farm to retail prices by an equation which makes the total margin the sum of a fixed value plus a variable amount related to volume.

Among the most useful sources of information on the relationship between farm and retail prices are the publications on price spreads published by the USDA (for a recent summary, see [296]). Ogren [248, p. 1371ff.] summarizes some of the issues in interpretation and the problems of measurement. The National Commission on Food Marketing [235] considered whether or not farm-retail price spreads are too large. They concluded that few, if any, unnecessary physical functions exist in processing and distributing foods, but that some selling costs could be reduced without reducing the value of the final products to consumers.

Freeman [90] has investigated the impact of changes in marketing margins from 1947-49 to 1961-63 on the farm prices of selected commodity groups. His analysis indicates that the incidence of increased margins was on both farm and retail prices.

Spatial Relationships

Price relationships in physical space have been subjected to detailed analysis. A number of studies have been made of geographic differences in prices simply to determine whether or not serious imperfections exist in pricing systems. Such studies have recently included price behavior in less developed countries. (Studies of pricing institutions are reviewed in a later section.)

A knowledge of spatial price relationships is essential if the problem is to estimate the effect of a change in production or in demand in one region or the effect of a change in transfer costs on the competitive position of particular regions. Spatial price equilibrium models provide a framework for the analysis of changes in demand, supply, and transfer costs on the geographic structure of prices and on the volume and interregional movement of the commodity. This analytical technique also has been used to note the presence or absence of market imperfections since the model provides a set of theoretical prices which can be compared with actual prices. Spatial models provide a diagnostic tool, helping to define the existence of a problem rather than explain why it exists [186, p. 5]. These models also have been used to determine whether regional differences in support prices for grains are consistent with those expected under perfectly competitive conditions [205], and the regional impact of reducing grain production has been studied [57].

Fox and Taeuber [88] made one of the first applications of a spatial price equilibrium model to an agricultural commodity. Subsequently, Judge and Wallace [182] provided a succinct summary of a model and illustrated how internally consistent "shadow" prices can be obtained from the dual solution to the cost minimization transportation problem.

Agricultural economists have used various spatial price equilibrium models to estimate the geographic structure of prices for a number of commodities in the United States, including livestock [180, 183], grain [121, 205], apples [22], and milk [359]. In addition, models have been used to estimate the structure of prices of internationally traded commodities that might be expected to prevail among countries under competitive conditions (that is, in the absence of import restrictions or tariffs). Sugar [7] and oranges [380] are among the commodities that have been studied.

Leuthold and Bawden [210] prepared a bibliography of spatial studies in 1966. The spatial dimensions of market prices are explored in detail by Bressler and King [32]. Takayama and Judge [320] provide numerous spatial models in their comprehensive book; they start with the classical transportation model (supply and demand quantities given), move to models with regional supply and demand functions (quantities endogenous), and also extend the single commodity model to multicommodity formulations.

While spatial price equilibrium models provide a logical basis for estimating the geographic structure of prices, the squared correlation coefficients between actual prices and those computed from the models are usually less than 0.5 [346, p. 16]. The small correlations may be evidence of imperfections in the pricing system, but they also may be due to unrealistic models and inadequate data. The typical model assumes that all units of the commodity are homogeneous and originate or are consumed at a particular point in each region. Furthermore, decisions to move a unit of commodity are assumed to be based solely on an optimizing rule (for example, minimizing transfer costs). Thus, intraregional assembly and distribution costs as well as traditional relationships between buyers and sellers may be ignored. Ultimately, the adequacy of a spatial model must be judged relative to the problem under study [68].

Intertemporal Relationships

Studies analogous to those made for spatial price relationships have been made for seasonal and interseasonal price behavior (studies emphasizing imperfections in pricing systems and the intertemporal aspects of futures market prices are cited in a later section). Likewise, spatial price equilibrium models have been extended to include temporal price relationships. King and Henry [187] illustrate how time as well as space can be incorporated into the transportation model. Takayama and Judge [319] incorporate time as an element in a more complex quadratic programming model, which permits the use of regional and seasonal demand and supply functions. The recursive and simultaneous systems discussed earlier are of course models of intertemporal behavior. In this section, however, we limit the review to a brief discussion of the literature of intraseasonal and interseasonal storage rules.

Agricultural price analysis and agricultural price policy are closely associated in studies of storage rules, buffer-stock schemes, and other proposals which have such objectives as stabilizing prices or returns, increasing returns to producers, or increasing consumer welfare. The thrust of much of the analysis has been on the effects of proposed programs on price stability or on the revenue of producers. Eckstein and Syrquin [75] provide a useful summary of the relationship between the price elasticity of demand and returns from storage in the context of output instability.

A very large literature is available on price stabilization programs, buffer stocks, and related topics. Although this literature is not within the scope of our review, it is possible to observe that much of the literature is descriptive and assumes rather simple models of price behavior and that little of it involves empirical work (but see [355]).

Analyses of United States data by Gustafson [122, 123] and by Gislason [100] suggest that returns to producers based on optimal storage rules for year-to-year carryover of grains are very little larger than those obtained from competitive allocations of stocks. In a study of the Canadian Wheat Board Gislason [101] concludes that the board sustained substantial speculative losses in carrying inventories and hence "that the overall price to the Canadian farmers would have been greater if there had been no . . . interference with marketing Canadian wheat." Powell and Campbell [260], however, extend Gislason's paper by examining nonspeculative returns from buffer-stock schemes. Additional price analysis studies of real world data would be useful for appraising the effects of stabilization programs.

Price Discrimination

The principles of price discrimination have a long history of applications in agricultural economics (for example, [357]), and most of the contributions to the current literature involve applications of ideas developed in the 1930s. Forker and Anderson [86] provide a convenient bibliography.

A price discrimination model commonly considered in agricultural economics involves the allocation of a fixed quantity (a given crop) to alternative markets. The mathematical problem is to maximize revenue (net of allocation costs) subject to the restriction that the total quantity available is sold. With this equality constraint, Lagrangian (classical calculus) methods may be used to obtain the constrained optimum (see [352, pp. 87-91]).

One contribution in the postwar literature is the use of mathematical programming techniques to obtain solutions to the allocation problem. Models may be formulated so that the quantities sold to the alternate outlets are restricted to be equal to or less than the total supply available. With linear demand functions quadratic programming is used to compute the optimal allocations of quantities and the corresponding prices [197, 212]. Louwes, Boot, and Wage [212, p. 314] also illustrate how a policy constraint (to limit relative price changes to some "acceptable" level) can be incorporated into the optimization problem.

Numerous methods of separating markets have been explored in the literature. One approach is through alternate *forms* (say, fresh as opposed to processed forms) of a commodity. Milk [132, 197, 212] is an important example. Fresh fluid milk is treated as the primary market with the relatively price inelastic demand; processed dairy products are the secondary markets with the relatively less inelastic demands. The difference in form can be extended to include allocations based on quality or variety [356]. David Price [266] suggests that returns can sometimes be increased by discarding low-quality fruit even though the demand is price elastic.

Time is a second method of separating markets. Analysts, for instance, have explored the seasonal demands for apples to estimate the seasonal allocation of apples for fresh use to maximize returns to apple growers as a group [12, pp. 30-34]. *Space* is still another method of distinguishing between markets. Export demands are thought to be relatively more price elastic than domestic demand. Abel [1] argues, however, that as minimum-import-price schemes become more widespread it may become more profitable for exporters to charge higher prices in export markets than in their own domestic markets. For example, wheat exporters perhaps should sell wheat to developed countries (with trade barriers and relatively price inelastic demands) at relatively high prices and sell the remainder to less developed countries (with more elastic demands) at relatively low prices.

Lemons [152, 154] are illustrative of a commodity for which space, time and form all might be used in a price discrimination program. This would involve allocations between fresh use and processed products, allocations among seasons, and allocations between domestic and export markets.

The relatively long interest in the use of price discrimination models in agricultural economics has provided insights into the limitations of these models. The optimal allocations are necessarily based on *estimated* demand functions and allocation costs. Thus, the computed allocations and prices may be incorrect because the estimated information is wrong. (For alternate estimates of demand functions in [154], see [150, pp. 20-22].) Empirical models point to directions of change rather than to precise optimums.

Models often assume that markets are independent when in fact they are not. It may be necessary to take account of the substitutability among markets (for example, processed products are often, to some degree, substitutes for the fresh form). Roy J. Smith [302] outlines some limitations of discriminatory pricing with special reference to the experience with lemons. He argues, among other things, that since 1949 processed lemon products, such as frozen lemon concentrates and lemonades, have become more competitive with fresh products. Thus, elasticities based on earlier data (when the substitution relation was zero or small) do not reflect the current substitutability between fresh and processed lemons.

Closely related to the question of structural changes in demand (from new products) is the question of short-run versus long-run elasticities. A program which raises a price to a new level and holds price at that level should be appraised in terms of long-run coefficients.

Smith [302] also presents data which suggest a substantial supply response to the initial improved returns from the lemon program. With the increased production and the consequent increased diversions to the secondary processing market, average returns are reduced to producers. Thus, without supply control, Smith points out, in the longer run a two-price program does not necessarily increase returns to producers. Jamison [168] draws a similar conclusion in his study of cling peaches.

Farm-Nonfarm Price Relationships

Little of major significance has been added to the literature in recent years regarding the average relationship between prices received for farm commodities and prices paid by farmers for items used in production. This topic, of course, received extensive treatment in the United States during the 1920s and 1930s, and ultimately the parity concept was institutionalized in legislation. Current information on the relationship between prices received and paid is now available for at least nineteen countries. These figures are re-reported in the Food and Agriculture Organization's *Monthly Bulletin of Agricultural Economics and Statistics.*

The parity ratio and particularly the continued use of a 1910-14 base period have been widely criticized by agricultural economists in the United States (for example, [332, pp. 195-196; 344, pp. 369-371]). Nevertheless, some who use the figures seem unaware of the deficiencies and insist on using the parity ratio as a measure of the well-being of farmers and parity prices as indicators of the "fairness" of existing prices. A USDA publication [338] prepared mainly by R. J. Schrimper and B. R. Stauber, provides a concise summary of what parity does and does not measure. In response to a request from Congress the USDA prepared a lengthy report on parity in 1957, which contained a number of suggestions for modifications [259].

Farm prices continue to fluctuate with greater amplitude than the prices of most nonfarm goods and services. Thus, there is great instability in relative prices – the terms of trade of farm products. The factors which contribute to this instability are well summarized by T. W. Schultz [293], Cochrane [48], and Hanau [129]. Short-run fluctuations in farm prices are attributable mainly to fluctuations in supply, often arising from the biological nature of the production process, and to the relatively price inelastic aggregate demand and supply functions. Cochrane [48] and Tweeten [334] are among the authors providing empirical evidence on the inelasticity of aggregate demand. Longer-term trends in prices are often associated with shifts in demand relative to supply.

A number of contributions to the literature have considered relative prices in international trade, in particular the terms of trade of agricultural exporting countries. Prebisch [264] has hypothesized that a long-run tendency exists for the terms of trade to move against agricultural exporting nations. Studies of the relationship between the prices of agricultural commodities exported and manufactured products imported by less developed countries (alternatively, between agricultural imports and industrial exports of such developed countries as the United Kingdom), however, do not show any clearly established tendency for the terms of trade to move against primary products [222, 232, 258]. What the evidence does show is that the terms of trade are unstable and that conclusions drawn with respect to changes in the terms of trade are particularly sensitive to the beginning and ending years used to establish trends.

Analyses of the effects of inflation on agriculture, other than general descriptive studies, are limited. Brandow [23] has pointed out the differing impacts of demand-pull and cost-push inflation on agriculture. He also argues that resource misallocations in farming attributable to inflation are minor in comparison to the magnitude of resource adjustments attributable to technical change and to governmental farm programs. Hathaway [134] has summarized the general economic relationships between the nonfarm and farm sectors. Such interrelationships might be formalized in an econometric model, but most economywide models treat the agricultural sector as exogenous (for a succinct summary of large models, see [94]).

Topics in Quantitative Price Analysis

The literature reviewed to this point emphasizes models in which price and quantity variables are functions of certain explanatory variables. A considerable literature exists, however, on empirical descriptions of time-series variables. Emphasis is usually placed on decomposing such variables into systematic and random components. Another important area, not reviewed elsewhere, is the literature on handling qualitative variables in price analysis models. A qualitative variable, such as seasonality, could appear either in a behavioral equation like a demand function or in a descriptive time-series analysis. In this section we briefly review the literature on time-series models and on qualitative variables.

Models of Time-Series Behavior

An individual variable observed with the passage of time, such as price or production, is sometimes viewed as being composed of trend, seasonal, cyclical, and random (irregular) components. A very substantial amount of empirical price analyses has involved the description or decomposition of a time series into its components, in particular trend analysis. These applications are far too numerous to cite. We review selected developments.[26]

A random walk model is perhaps the simplest model of time-series behavior. This model states that price changes cannot be predicted from past price changes; they are equal to random disturbances.[27] Somewhat more complex models view time series as having moving average and/or autoregressive properties. Bieri and Schmitz [15] review various moving average and autoregressive models and then apply these models to predict wheat yields, daily hog prices, and daily hog supplies. The models and methods used, they argue, are more suitable for prediction than spectral analysis. Fuller [15], in discussing the Bieri-Schmitz paper, indicates that such models are not very new; recent developments emphasize ease of understanding models, estimation procedures, testing, and diagnostic procedures.

Common methods of measuring and removing seasonal and cyclical components, such as moving averages and indexes, are subject to criticism. Traditional seasonal adjustment methods may remove more from a times series than can properly be considered as seasonal [242], and they may introduce nonseasonal (nonrandom) elements into the series. In studying leads and lags between two series, emphasis is placed on subjective evaluation of what constitutes peaks and troughs of cycles and, hence, the length of a cycle. Thus, there has been some interest in using alternative procedures to measure components of time series.

Harmonic analysis, which makes the time series a function of sine and cosine variables, is especially relevant when the series contains a cycle with a known period, such as a twelve-month seasonal cycle. Doran and Quilkey [74] provide a useful review of the harmonic model, including relevant references and applications in agricultural economics.

Spectral analysis, an outgrowth of work in the 1940s, was applied to economic time series starting in the early 1960s [107]. It is a method with a rigorous mathematical foundation for decomposing time-series data into components. Spectral analysis decomposes a series X_t into a large number of independent components, each associated with a different frequency; the relative importance of any group of frequencies is measured by their contribution to the variance of X_t; the bands of frequencies which make relatively large contributions can be associated with particular periods (seasons, cycles).

Spectral methods may be used to determine the empirical characteristics of a time series (for example, the existence of a cycle), and they also may be useful in preliminary analyses of data to appraise leads and lags between variables, which in turn may suggest "causal" relationships. A large number of observations (say, larger than one hundred) is required to use spectral techniques. In addition, the spectral model is based on a stationary process (an assumption typically not met by economic time series), and hence some data transformation usually is required as a preliminary step to approximate this assumption [269, pp. 113-114].

Rausser and Cargill [269] have applied spectral analysis to monthly broiler price and supply variables. Traditional methods of time-series analysis imply a broiler cycle of about thirty months. Rausser and Cargill conclude that the spectral results do not support the hypothesis of well-defined cycles in the broiler industry. Weiss and Melnik [358], in a spectral study of monthly egg prices, find evidence for a thirty-two-month cycle, which they call "mild" but significant. Labys and Granger [193] apply spectral as well as other techniques to a variety of price series from commodity futures markets.

Doll and Chin [73] suggest a rather interesting application of principal components in price analysis. If a researcher wished to study the common and independent movements of a set of price series such as farm, wholesale, and retail beef prices, the principal components of the prices could be computed. If, for example, the first component is highly associated with all three series, then this component is related to those factors which "explain" the common movements of the prices, and if the second component (which by definition is orthogonal to the others) is closely associated with only one of the series, then this independent element of variation can be analyzed. Doll and Chin suggest using the principal components, rather than the prices, as dependent variables in regressions in order to analyze the common and independent elements of variation of the three time series.[28]

Analyses Involving Qualitative Variables

Price analysts have frequently made use of models to take account of qualitative explanatory variables; this is usually done by using zero-one variables in regression equations (fixed effects covariance models). Suits [315] provided one of the earlier discussions of dummy variables in the economics literature. A common use is to take account of seasonality in analyses of monthly or quarterly observations [211]; a second area of application involves using such variables to distinguish between regions or race in cross-section data [206].

The zero-one variable specification states that the intercept parameter changes as the alternate levels of the qualitative variable (say, season) change. The slope parameters are assumed not to change. This assumption is consistent with the typical specification of regression models, which assume that the parameters of explanatory variables are not systematically influenced by changes in the size of other explanatory variables. Interaction models are applicable for some research problems, however. Ben-David and Tomek [11] consider the possible interaction between a qualitative and a quantitative variable (hence, a slope change for the quantitative variable), and apply [12] such a model to a seasonal demand equation for apples.

In a study of supply the dependent variable could involve adopters and nonadopters of a new variety; in a study of demand the dependent variable could include buyers and nonbuyers. This dichotomy can be represented by a zero-one dependent variable.[29] While standard least squares procedures have often been used for such models, probit analysis (or a similar method) is usually preferable [325]. Kau and Hill [185] have applied a probit model to the problem of a purchase decision.

Somewhat related to the idea of a zero-one dependent variable is the idea of discriminating between groups. Blood and Baker [16] compare discriminate analysis and linear probability functions as techniques for delineating situations which favor wheat production versus range forage production in the northern Great Plains. This perhaps is one of the earliest applications of these tools in agricultural economics, though the tools certainly have had applications much earlier in other areas.

Time-series observations on a cross section of individual consumers, firms, or political units are becoming increasingly available. This suggests pooling time-series and cross-section observations for empirical analyses. The usual procedure has been to take the time and firm effects into account through a fixed effects covariance model. Recently, economists have turned to so-called variance components models, which have a much longer history in biometrics [297]. Models of this type have a composite error term, which includes random components specific to the cross-section effect, the time-series effect, and a component common to both. Girão, Tomek, and Mount [98] use such a model in estimating consumption and investment functions for a sample of farm households observed over seven years.

Supply-Demand and Price Outlook

Agricultural outlook work is, broadly speaking, of two types: short term, including time intervals up to one or two years, and long term. Both types of outlook involve empirical analyses combined with large elements of judgment. One of the potential applications of the models reviewed to this point is to aid in making forecasts. However, in 1970 Haidacher [125] examined the twenty-eight most recent issues of the *American Journal of Agricultural Economics* and found that only five of forty-one price analysis articles gave forecasting as the initial objective. Waugh [352] also argues that forecasting should be the primary objective of a much higher percent of price analysis studies.

Empirical techniques employed by those doing outlook work range from simple tabular analysis to the use of formal quantitative models. Most outlook work until recently has been based on fairly simple analytical procedures. Of the less formal procedures the balance-sheet approach is a way of summarizing large quantities of data to determine whether surpluses or deficits in supplies are likely to exist at some future date if current prices prevail [6]. This enables the forecaster to anticipate the direction of price changes. Graphic methods of analysis are used frequently in outlook work, and Waugh [353] provides a summary of these tools.

A simple but useful procedure in short-run outlook is to take advantage of known data on stocks, size of breeding herds, and biological time lags. For example, the number of beef calves available for placement in feedlots is limited by the size of the beef cow herd. Walters [348] uses this approach in forecasting the components of the beef cattle inventory.

Short-term outlook material prepared by USDA economists is published regularly in the well-known "situation reports." These provide useful summaries of current data and give general indications of prospective changes in prices in the next three to twelve months, but they seldom provide specific forecasts (with the exception of recent issues of *Livestock and Meat Situation*). Occasionally, a section or article is included which reports on specific econometric studies; an example may be found in a recent issue of *Fats and Oils Situation* [220].

Bargaining for prices by farmers and food processors often leads to the development of forecasting models. Work conducted at Michigan State University for apples and red tart cherries [275] and in California for cling peaches and other fruits [153] is illustrative of the response by agricultural economists in land-grant universities to the needs in this area.

Projections made by economists associated with private firms are generally prepared for internal use and consequently are less likely to be published. Outlook-related research of private firms, as well as other work, is considered in a recent series of articles [62].

Criticisms and suggested improvements in outlook are discussed in a series of papers presented in 1966 under the title "Is Agricultural Outlook Meeting Today's Needs?" [8]. Among the topics discussed are data problems, the analytical basis for outlook, the accuracy of forecasts, and the objectivity and independence of analysts. Less attention was devoted to whether outlook statements really influence decisions, and if so, whether there are feedback effects. Smyth [303] provides a theoretical model for considering the effect of public forecasts on price behavior, using a cobweb framework, and includes a brief review of the relevant literature. In theory, public forecasts should be price stabilizing.

Crom [58, 59, 318] stresses simulation as a tool to improve econometric models for making projections. Given the estimated model and the initial conditions, simulations are made both over and beyond the range of the original data. When substantial errors are observed between the simulated and observed data, the potential causes of the errors are analyzed. This analysis is used to make model revisions, to introduce operating rules, such as changing the value of a parameter under certain circumstances, and so forth. At each step the simulations are repeated to determine whether the changes create unexpected errors in an earlier period. This interplay between the model builder and the simulations continues until the historical data are reproduced with "acceptable accuracy" [58].

Agricultural economists have devoted thousands of man-hours during the past two decades to making long-term projections of demand and supply, both for individual products and for food in total. This is a response, at least in part, to a widespread demand on the part of national governments for information that can be used in formulating policies and development plans. For the most part, long-run projections are based on past trends. For demand, the analyst may consider trends in per-capita use (which of course reflect per-capita availabilities) and population; also, some attempt is usually made to estimate the effects of growth in real income on demand through the use of income elasticities. Goreux [105] describes techniques commonly used in making demand projections, summarizes the assumptions, and reviews the results of studies made in seven countries.

Projections of output are usually based on separate analyses of trends in yields and acreage (or animal units). The initial estimates may be modified on the basis of judgments of scientists regarding future developments in technology, hence changes in yields. Methods employed by USDA economists in making projections are reviewed by Daly [66] and Rogers and Barton [282].

Among the most frequently cited global projections are those published by the Food and Agriculture Organization [82, 83], the USDA [2, 36, 339], and the President's Science Advisory Committee [265]. In addition, a large number of projections of demand and supply, especially for export crops, have been made for particular regions (for example, [213]). Many countries have made similar studies (for a recent United States study see Culver and Chai [63]); some of the results have been published in English [120, 234, 343].

A detailed appraisal of the numerous long-range projections is beyond the scope of this paper, but some general observations are possible. Global forecasts of food shortages or surpluses tend to be conditioned by the situation at the time the forecasts are made. For instance, forecasts for the 1970-75 period made in the early 1960s emphasize the likelihood of surpluses, whereas forecasts made in the mid-1960s, when surpluses disappeared, tend to be much more pessimistic about the possibility of avoiding food shortages.

Another limitation of most projections is their inability to take account of the influence of weather variations. The weather is one of the most critical variables affecting supplies in a particular year and even over a period of years. In the case of tree crops, freeze damage may shift the whole pattern of production. Apple prices in the United States, for example, have not followed the cyclical pattern predicted by French [91], at least partly because a severe freeze killed or injured trees in a major producing area after the projections were made.

Forecasts of production have also been weak because of unanticipated technical improvements. This may also influence forecasts of changes in consumption since consumption is based on available supplies. For example, projections of United States beef consumption for 1975 made in the mid-1950s were much too low [66, p. 82]; similar errors were made in projecting United States corn yields [282, p. 9] and exports [66, p. 85].

Sanders and Hoyt [287], after reviewing four global studies of demand and supply projections for food, pointed out that the demand projections were of similar magnitudes (based on similar estimates of population, income, and income elasticities) but that the supply estimates were inconsistent. Yield projections tend to be much more variable than demand projections.

Most long-run projections do not include adjustments for the possible effects of changes in relative prices, but the study of Bonnen and Cromarty [18] is an exception. They used a two-step procedure in an attempt to incorporate price effects into the analysis. They first made tentative estimates separately for demand and supply relying on methods similar to those outlined above. They then resolved the separate projections by using available elasticity estimates.

Unfortunately, no attempt has been made to measure the benefits and costs associated with making long-term projections. We live in a society which needs and wants knowledge of the future, but in view of the inaccuracies of the longer-run projections the question of whether the returns have justified the costs can at least be raised. Short-run outlook statements obviously are useful to processors and other middlemen, but perhaps less so to farmers who generally have longer planning horizons. Hayami and Peterson [137] have attempted to measure the returns of reducing the sampling error of crop and livestock statistics. Benefits are potentially available from adjusting both inventories and production to new and better information. Hayami and Peterson [137, p. 129] conclude that "the investment in increasing accuracy for agricultural production statistics exceeds its cost by a wide margin." In general, additional work to improve short-run forecasts seems justified.

Price-Making Institutions

Price analysts, it seems fair to say, have emphasized the economic forces determining prices and have been less concerned with the influences of pricing institutions on price behavior. Nonetheless, the literature includes classification schemes for pricing methods and evaluations of pricing mechanisms, especially their influence on both the level and the stability of prices. Futures markets are sufficiently unique and have such a large body of literature that this component is reviewed in a separate subsection. Governmental policies and programs are, of course, important institutions, but they are the subject of separate articles by G. E. Brandow and by D. G. Johnson (parts III and IV in this volume).

Alternative Pricing Methods and Price Behavior

Several classification schemes for pricing arrangements in agriculture have been suggested [30, pp. 8-13; 279; 332, pp. 215-217]. Alternative mechanisms include price negotiations between individuals, group bargaining, organized marketplaces (including auctions), administered prices (including governmental regulation), and formula prices. Formulas may in turn be established by individual negotiation, group bargaining, or governmental action. The establishment of a price is sometimes viewed as having two components: the discovery of a base or reference price and the discovery of prices for specific lots of the product relative to the base. Studies have been conducted both with regard to the mechanisms for establishing base prices — say, for a particular grade of wheat in Chicago — and for specific prices — say, for those paid by elevator operators to farmers for particular loads of wheat.

Pricing institutions unquestionably do influence price behavior. Some provide greater stability than others. Criticisms of pricing mechanisms usually center on one or more of the following: price levels are biased; price fluctuations are too large; or prices fluctuate too frequently. Any of these may lead to the misallocation of resources.

One obvious problem of price analysis is to separate the influences of economic factors from the influences of the institutional factors. The latter effects are difficult to isolate since two different pricing mechanisms for a particular commodity cannot be observed under precisely the same economic conditions. Studies before and after an institutional change are subject to this limitation. Telser [323] did attempt to assess the effect of the United States support program for cotton on the variability of cotton prices. He did this by reconstructing the price behavior that would have existed in the 1933-53 period without price supports. He concluded that the support program reduced price instability for cotton, but he acknowledged that "the major difficulty [of the research] is that what actually happened is being compared to what did not in fact happen."

A second problem of research related to pricing institutions is the selection of criteria for evaluating alternative pricing methods. One common approach is to use the perfect competition model as a norm [17, 121, 133, 207] — that is, to observe how actual prices deviate from those expected to prevail under perfect competition. But, competitively determined prices still may not be very satisfactory from the standpoint of guiding resource use because of their instability, or they may yield incomes which for political or social reasons are deemed to be too low. Hence, the competitive norm is not the only criterion to be considered in attempting to evaluate the performance of a given pricing institution.

Among the studies made in the United States using the competitive model as a norm are those conducted by Hassler for manufactured dairy products [133] and for processed feeds. Studies of spatial and temporal price differences also have been made in which actual price differences between markets are compared with transfer costs and seasonal price changes are compared with storage costs. In a study of fresh winter lettuce prices, for example, weekly price changes at shipping points were found to be highly correlated with changes in prices at the twelve major wholesale markets[17].

Lele [207] and Jones[179] have used analogous procedures to analyze market and price performance for certain agricultural products in developing countries. It is commonly alleged that such markets have serious imperfections. Researchers found some evidence of price differences exceeding transfer costs between markets, but in reviewing the available evidence, it is perhaps fair to say that the claims of market imperfections are exaggerated [179, pp. 238-257; 207, pp. 214-220].

Studies of livestock auctions also have been made in an attempt to assess their performance or the possible biases they may impart to prices. Jack Johnson [172] concluded after studying southern United States livestock auctions that differences between prices at auctions and terminal markets were widest for the higher quality cattle. This was attributed to the small and erratic supply of such animals consigned for sale at auctions. Statistical analyses of price behavior at auctions [364] suggest that variables related to the pricing mechanism, such as size of market, as well as other variables, like weight, grade, and breed, significantly influence prices. Sosnick [305] suggests that on theoretical grounds prices might be expected to travel downward during the course of the auction since the most eager buyers might be expected to purchase first. But he found no empirical evidence to support this hypothesis. Among the possible explanations is that large quality differentials among lots can obscure any trends [305]. Indeed, auctions are a relatively time-consuming type of pricing system, and this pricing mechanism is likely to persist only for commodities with enough quality variation to justify pricing lots individually by inspection of the potential buyers.

Various studies provide empirical analyses of grower-processor contracts and of the effects of marketing orders on prices (for example, [194]). An analysis of contracts for sweet corn and peas suggests that the net price offered to farmers is about the same regardless of the particular contract signed [169]. This relative stability of net prices among contracts is considered to be evidence of a competitive raw product market for the commodities.

Farris [79] examined two aspects of price discovery for wheat in Indiana. He first considered the price paid for a standard grade of wheat, and he then looked at price differences associated with quality for specific loads of wheat. The objectives were to determine whether prices paid for wheat by local elevators were consistent with those prevailing on central markets and whether premiums or discounts for quality were appropriate.

With respect to the first objective, Farris found a range of prices which could not be explained solely by transfer costs. He concluded that these unexplained differences are probably related to local competitive conditions and to imperfect knowledge. With respect to quality differentials, Farris suggests two possible sources of error in pricing specific lots. First, the sample selected may not be representative of the entire lot, and second, the sample may be incorrectly graded. The first source of error could not be checked, but elevator grading was compared with laboratory grading. Apparently, errors in grading tended to favor farmers on the average, though wide differences existed for individual samples. Elevator grading also appeared to overvalue low-quality wheat and undervalue high-quality wheat. Farris concluded that more effort should be devoted to establishing appropriate price differentials.

A criterion related to the perfect competition norm is to ask how well a particular pricing system is performing particular functions. Some qualitative analyses have considered the implications of certain pricing methods for various roles of prices. For instance, a potential benefit of group bargaining for farm prices may be more stable prices, which may lead to better production and marketing decisions [30].

Another criterion for evaluating pricing institutions is alternative costs. These costs include the resources devoted to discovering prices, such as the time of the participants, as well as possible misallocation of resources associated with a pricing system. Available research seems to say little about relative costs of alternate pricing mechanisms (but see, for example, [177]).

From a commodity viewpoint the pricing of hogs has received considerable attention [138], perhaps because of a belief that prices paid farmers do not adequately reflect consumer demand for lean meat. Pricing systems for milk also have received special attention [34, 215]. An exceptional amount of effort has been devoted to egg pricing mainly because of the decline of trading on organized markets and because the performance of prices was thought to be unsatisfactory. The wholesale market has been studied by a number of analysts, and alternative pricing arrangements have been proposed. These and the possible consequences of using different pricing methods are reviewed by Rogers and Voss [280, 281].

A more fundamental question raised by agricultural economists is whether price is becoming less important as a coordinating mechanism for economic activities and whether existing prices are satisfactory for this purpose. A sequence of papers by Collins [52], Gray [112], and Hillman [151] highlight this issue. Collins argues that the shift from price to administrative coordination has occurred, in part, because the latter system leads to a more stable volume moving through the system and a more homogeneous quality. Gray agrees with Collins in one respect — namely, that administrative and engineering coordination have supplanted price at some intersections of economic activity. But Gray asks whether the importance of price is enhanced or diminished by this shift. He concludes that the change-inducing role of price is enhanced. The informal markets with a proliferation of prices "were not very good," and the development of precise specifications of product and delivery terms enhance the efficiency of price formation at the remaining price junctures.

Futures Markets

This review of commodity futures markets and prices stresses the literature on price behavior. Gray and Rutledge [113] provide a recent and comprehensive survey of the literature on futures markets.

Futures markets first developed for seasonally produced commodities with continuous inventories, such as the grains; thus, it is not surprising that much of the literature deals with price behavior on such markets. Observation of the constellation of futures and cash prices for a commodity indicates that price movements are correlated and that, as a delivery month approaches, the price difference between the futures contract and the cash commodity narrows. This price behavior is explained in an important paper by H. Working [377] as "the price of storage." This price for a particular commodity is defined as the difference between two other prices — namely, between a particular futures price (P_f) and a cash price (P_c). The price of storage is competitively determined by the demand for and the supply of storage, but the literature has tended to concentrate on the supply side.

Negative price differences (P_f-P_c) are associated with small inventories and positive price differences with large inventories. But the supply function, which presumably is related to the marginal cost of storage, tends to be flat over a fairly wide range of inventories. Brennan [31] sought to establish the nature of marginal costs which would lead to the functional form observed for the supply function. He attributes, following Working, negative price differences, in part, to the marginal convenience yield of inventories; some (small) inventories are needed for the sake of "convenience" even when the price of storage is negative.

Paul [255] points out that the flat segment in a storage supply function may merely reflect the fact that an individual commodity has good substitutes for the use of storage facilities. Consequently, he pools all of the commodities that compete for storage space and estimates an equation to explain the price of binspace. Price differences (essentially between futures and cash) are computed for all of the competing commodities, and the largest difference for a particular period for the various products is the basic component of the price of binspace.[30] The price of binspace is made a function of total stocks and of sales of grain (to reflect handling volume), both deflated by the total storage space available.

Working, who analyzed individual commodities, simply made the price of storage a function of the size of current inventory. Weymar [362] argues that the price should be a function of the expected behavior of inventories over the time interval covered by the price difference. Current inventory is probably a good proxy for expected inventory of a commodity harvested over a relatively short time period. It is perhaps a poorer proxy for a commodity with a long harvest period, such as cocoa.

Since the price of storage concept implies that the constellation of futures prices is linked through inventories, the price of a distant future in a new crop year should be correlated with the current spot price. This is in contrast to the view [342] that cash prices and futures prices are separately determined, the former by current conditions and the latter by expected conditions. Working [373, 374] was loath to treat prices of futures contracts as forecasts. Prices of cash grain, nearby futures, and remote futures are in his view jointly determined.

A futures price obviously cannot remain above the cash price by more than storage costs, but since no theoretical limit exists for the reverse relation, one can expect the variance of futures prices to be slightly smaller than the variance of cash prices when based on annual observations (for example, the year-to-year variability of the May price of the December corn futures versus the cash price in December). At the same time, the prices of futures contracts are closely tied to cash prices (for seasonally produced, continuous inventory products); hence, the two variances should be of roughly similar magnitudes [331].

With the development of new markets in the 1950s and 1960s, interest has turned to price relationships and behavior on such markets. The new markets include seasonally produced commodities with discontinuous inventories (potatoes), continuously produced commodities with inventories (pork bellies), and continuously produced commodities with no inventories in the ordinary sense of the term (fresh eggs).

Tomek and Gray [331] contrast potato futures prices with corn and soybean futures prices. Potatoes have a break in the inventory linkage between crop years. Thus, the daily prices of futures for different crop years are essentially uncorrelated. The springtime prices of new-crop potato futures are, in contrast to the grains, a function only of expected economic conditions, and in the spring, when little is known about the forthcoming crop, new-crop futures prices appear to be mainly an average of past prices. Consequently, the year-to-year variability of the November Maine potato futures price in April is much smaller than the variability of the November spot price.

Paul and Wesson [256] define the price of a relevant futures contract for fed cattle minus the value of feeder cattle and feed as a market-determined price of feedlot services.[31] Ehrich [76] extends this concept to explain the behavior of the price difference between fed cattle futures and spot feeder calves. He shows that price spreads are related in part to the cost of weight gain, particularly feed costs. The price spread can be negative.[32] The foregoing concept suggests a closer relation between fed cattle futures and spot feeder calf prices than between fed cattle futures prices.

Short-term commodity prices (say, day-to-day changes) seem to follow a random walk. Working's [376] theory of anticipatory prices was designed to explain the random walk nature of price changes. In a perfect market price responds immediately and correctly to new information, and since new information occurs randomly, prices change randomly (see also [286]).

While commodity prices appear to follow a random walk through time, empirical analyses suggest that such price series deviate somewhat from a formal random walk model. For instance, Claude Brinegar [33] observed negative autocorrelations (price reaction) over short periods of time (one or two weeks) and positive autocorrelations (price continuity) over longer periods (four to sixteen weeks) for grain futures prices (see also [165, 276, 301]). One hypothesis is simply that markets are imperfect and that time is required for new information to be incorporated into price changes (for additional hypotheses see [55, 165]). Larson [200] estimates that 81 percent of the appropriate change in price based on new information is incorporated into the price on the first day in the corn market. This is followed by an 8 percent price reaction (incorrect movement) in the next four days with the appropriate remaining 27 percent adjustment occurring over the next forty-five days.

Labys and Granger [193] also analyzed sequences of price changes using spectral analysis. They concluded that "most series obey a random walk or near random walk." Most evidence suggests, however, minor deviations from the random walk hypothesis; the serial correlation coefficients of daily price changes are small and of low order, but nevertheless are nonzero [113, p.97].

One of the long-standing controversies with respect to price behavior on futures markets has to do with the existence of a risk premium (for historical references see [113, pp. 63-71]). In essence, the risk premium theory implies that futures prices are biased estimates of the cash price in the delivery month. In an inventory-hedging market a downward bias is allegedly required to attract a sufficient supply of speculative services. Hedgers are typically short futures to cover inventory holdings, and consequently speculators typically hold long positions. Thus, according to the theory, prices must rise on the average for speculators to profit from the long positions. Presumably there would be an insufficient supply of speculators unless there is some return on the average from the speculative positions. Hedgers allegedly pay speculators to take the speculative risk of adverse price movements. Given this theory, a routine program of purchasing and then selling futures should provide profits.

A substantial amount of empirical research has been devoted to determining whether or not a risk premium exists. Several researchers find evidence of a small risk premium [54, 162]. The weight of evidence suggests, however, that there is no risk premium [111, 277, 321, 322]. Amateur speculators as a group are net losers in the zero-sum returns from futures trading [149, 310]. In addition, many speculators, particularly professionals, hold positions for very short periods of time, implying that they would not benefit from the trend in futures prices implicit in the risk premium hypothesis.

One of the difficulties in evaluating the risk premium theory, however, is the presence of trends in some price series. If futures prices do not fully anticipate long-term trends, holding long speculative positions in a period of rising prices is profitable and consistent with a risk premium hypothesis. Conversely, long positions are not profitable in periods of declining price levels. Thus, the selection of a time period for analysis can influence results. The existence of governmental support programs also has complicated the empirical analyses (see [113, pp. 72-75]). Moreover, Gray [109] argues that thinly traded futures markets have "characteristically biased prices" which do not represent transfers of risk premiums.

As the preceding discussion implies, the principal motivation of speculators has been the subject of some controversy. Return to speculators could be a payment for accepting risk (risk premium), a return to superior forecasting skill, or a return for providing market liquidity. Working [375] argues persuasively that profits earned by professional speculators are mainly returns for providing market liquidity; scalpers provide the service of temporally spreading the effects of large hedge transactions. While amateur speculators typically are losers, there is a (small) possibility of making a large gain. Thus, Telser [322] writes "to the amateurs speculation in commodities is comparable to the purchase of a lottery ticket . . . "

Research on price behavior also has developed in response to the alleged influence of futures trading on the behavior of cash prices. Trading in futures has been blamed both for low and high prices and for excessive price variability (for citations, see [113, pp. 85-91]). Although futures markets, like any financial institution, are occasionally subject to fraudulent price manipulations, this is not thought to be a serious source of biased prices. Most economists regard futures markets as *recording* the influences of factors affecting price and not as a factor which in itself influences price levels [113, p. 86].

A number of researchers, however, have sought to measure the effect of futures trading on the variability of cash prices. Among the procedures used is the one adopted by Powers [262]. A series of cash prices is divided into two parts: the systematic component and the irregular (random) components. Powers considers in particular whether trading in futures influences the size of the variance of the random component. Observations on weekly cash prices for pork bellies and beef cattle before and with futures trading are used to test the effect of futures trading on price variability. Tintner's "variate difference method" is used to eliminate the systematic component of the series [328].[33] Powers concludes that the variances are significantly smaller in the time period following the introduction of futures than in the preceding period. He attributes the result, at least in part, to the information role of futures markets.

Aaron Johnson [170] concludes essentially that futures trading did not influence price behavior in the cash onion market. Several previous studies suggested that trading in onion futures had reduced seasonal price variability, but Johnson detected little or no change in seasonal price behavior before, during, and after futures trading in onions. Johnson also concluded that, using the competitive model as a norm, price variation did not seem excessive during the period of futures trading. For certain commodities like potatoes and eggs, futures may provide more stable forward prices and the opportunity to hedge production decisions, thereby contributing to production and price stability [108, 201, 331].

T. W. Schultz [294], however, has maintained that resource misallocation is likely to be more serious for commodities with organized spot and futures markets than for commodities priced in other ways. In Schultz's view prices on organized markets fluctuate excessively (for whatever reason) and therefore do not provide reasonable guides for making production decisions (but see [371, p. 327]). Other economists [163, 223] have argued for the use of futures markets by government authorities as an integral part of price stabilization programs. Holbrook Working [371] concluded that the response of wheat inventories to wheat futures prices were "appropriate," which implies that futures markets, by guiding inventory adjustments, help to reduce price variability.

Implicit in the criticism of futures trading is the idea of excessive speculation. Speculation could be too large in at least two senses: trading by ill-informed persons causes prices to deviate from equilibrium levels, or the volume of trading by speculators exceeds the level required for adequate liquidity (even if equilibrium prices result). There is some evidence that speculation responds to hedging needs [375]. A more serious problem arises if the volume of speculation is inadequate to absorb hedging transactions without large price changes [110].

The literature contains alternative explanations of the motives (incentives) of hedgers. A few authors of research and extension publications have stated that hedging "eliminates" price risks, but this is more likely a poor choice of words rather than a literal theory of risk elimination through hedging. Most price analysts have observed the lack of perfect correlation between cash and futures prices (for example, [106]), and hence the reduction of price risk is often emphasized as a motive of hedging. Studies have considered basis risk (variation in the basis) relative to price level risk, and such research (particularly in inventory hedging contexts) usually concludes that hedging is useful in reducing risks of adverse price movements. Snape and Yamey [304] are among the stronger proponents of the risk reduction view of hedging.

In contrast, Working [372] stresses that the principal motive of hedging is profit based on changes in the basis (changes in the price of storage). He does not look upon hedging as a form of insurance but rather as "a form of arbitrage, undertaken most commonly in expectation of a favorable change in the relation between spot and futures prices" [371]. A positive basis can provide a return to holding inventory; a negative basis is a disincentive to carrying inventories. In an empirical analysis Heifner [144] concludes that "the information contained in cash-future spreads can be of value in forecasting storage earnings on hedged corn but is of little value in forecasting earnings for unhedged storage."

Agricultural economists have attempted to develop optimum hedging rules. An optimal level of hedging is defined in terms of maximizing returns for a given level of risk or in terms of minimizing risk for a given level of returns. Ward and Fletcher [349] extend L. L. Johnson's results [176] and develop a theoretical model of optimal firm decisions with respect to trading in cash and futures markets. Heifner [145] developed a model which enables the hedger to obtain an optimum combination of expected total profit and variance of total profit and applied it to hedging in cattle feeding. In general, both the theoretical and empirical analyses suggest that optimal decisions do not require a fully hedged position [145].

The concepts of price of storage, price of processing services, and price of feedlot services each imply a profit-increasing or risk-decreasing role of hedging on futures markets. The role of futures markets in forward pricing is closely related. This role is implicit in the forward sale of a commodity through futures, anticipatory hedging of ingredient requirements, and so forth. Alternate hedging uses of futures are summarized in numerous sources (for example, [332]).

Conclusions

One cannot help but be impressed by the large number of alternative models and techniques that have been developed and by the immense volume of empirical results accumulated over the past thirty years. Researchers now have available a much greater assortment of models and estimation techniques than they had before World War II. These developments probably have improved empirical results, but they also have compounded problems confronting price analysts and users of results. The analyst now has more decisions to make, and the user sometimes finds the results of separate studies inconsistent and confusing. Widely different elasticity estimates are frequently obtained, depending on the model and procedures used. This diversity can prove frustrating, but it also can be salutary if it leads to more critical and discriminating use of results. Clearly, good judgment remains a necessary ingredient in price analyses, both in developing models and in using results.

In agricultural price analysis, as in much of the economic literature, own-price elasticities probably have received more emphasis than is justified by their economic importance. The large changes in consumption, production, and prices have occurred as a result of shifts in demand and supply functions rather than as a result of movements along a static, ceteris paribus schedule. Preoccupation with price elasticities has in some cases led economists to ignore more critical variables. At least in our judgment there is a regrettable lack of empirical analyses of and comparisons among alternative forecasting models and techniques. Theil's imaginative suggestions for analyzing forecasts [324] perhaps have not received the attention they deserve from agricultural economists. While we unquestionably have better tools of analysis available today than a generation ago, it is less certain that forecasts have improved to a corresponding degree.

Forecasts are, of course, conditional on the values of the explanatory variables, and consequently the ability to forecast is constrained by unpredictable shifts in the supply and demand functions. Agricultural production is especially vulnerable to adverse weather, diseases, and pests; future changes in technology also remain something of an unknown quantity. On the demand side, political events such as the lessening of international tensions can open new markets, and modest changes in production in countries like India or the Soviet Union can have a profound effect on export demands and prices. But it is precisely events of this type which are difficult to anticipate. It is important to improve our ability to estimate changes in the explanatory variables, but to the extent these changes are random, a problem will remain.

Unfortunately, the magnitudes of structural parameters may not remain constant with the passage of time, and this also results in poor forecasts. A change in the structure of the demand for beef in the United States, for example, perhaps is responsible for the large underestimation of beef prices in the early 1970s using models based on pre-1969 data. We need a better understanding of structural change and of how to predict when these changes are likely to occur.

Price analysis probably has suffered somewhat from a lack of continuity in research efforts. Many studies are the product of "one-shot" research projects, often associated with a Ph.D. dissertation. This adds to the multiplicity of results but contributes little to our cumulative knowledge. While a diversity of research viewpoints is essential, it also seems important to have a few researchers doing in-depth studies over a period of years so that they may build explicitly on previous work and update their studies periodically. Analysts working for private companies probably do more of this than their colleagues in universities, but unfortunately their results are usually not published so that the profession as a whole can benefit. Why do equations with high R^2's and seemingly logical coefficients provide poor forecasts? What changes in the model improved the forecasts? These are among the questions we should attempt to answer.

The role of pricing institutions in influencing price behavior is receiving increased attention and probably deserves more. Traditional methods of pricing certain farm products such as fruits, vegetables, and eggs may be unsatisfactory in the light of changes in the location and concentration of production, the number of buyers, and processing technology. The need for research is apparent; however, attempts to evaluate pricing institutions often have proved frustrating. Existing institutions allegedly cause biased or highly variable prices, but these allegations are usually difficult to demonstrate. Moreover, our analytical tools do not seem adequate for the task of determining the economic consequences of adopting alternative pricing methods, and part of the dissatisfaction with existing pricing arrangements is related to conflicting views about the roles prices should perform.

Developments in research are generally influenced by contemporary problems. One of the principal aims of price studies is to provide a framework that policymakers can use to anticipate the consequences of alternative decisions. The demand for this type of analysis unquestionably will expand although the types of questions analysts will be asked to help answer probably will change. More specific, disaggregated models may be required to meet some of these demands. A review of recent literature leads one to be reasonably confident, however, that agricultural economists will demonstrate ingenuity both in adapting older methods of analysis to current problems and in developing new techniques to meet the changing needs of policymakers.

Notes

1. Among the contributions made in the intervening period are articles dealing with the role of risk in supply response models [184] and of marketable surplus functions based on individual farm observations [333]. Quantitative studies have continued to shift their emphasis toward prediction and simulation of policy alternatives (for ex-

ample, [219]). Concern about food prices and world food supplies generated by the events of the mid-1970s is reflected in recent publications [136, 340]. With market prices rising above support levels and greater price instability, commodity futures markets have drawn considerable research attention (for example, [257]), though price-making institutions in general continue to be neglected (but see [85]).

2. Many studies made important empirical contributions. Henry Moore [231] was among the early contributors. Stigler [311] has reviewed the very early (mainly pre-1915) history of cross-section and time-series analyses, and in 1929 Stine [312] reviewed the status of price analysis to that date.

3. Goldberger [102] argues that Sewall Wright is an important early pioneer in econometrics who had much to contribute to the identification and simultaneous equations problems but who has been neglected in the literature.

4. Much of the empirical price analysis is still based on estimating separate demand and supply equations; if such equations are part of a recursive model (perhaps with other equations not specified), then each equation is an identifiable structural equation which can be estimated by least squares.

5. Monte Carlo studies do demonstrate the general superiority of simultaneous equations estimators over ordinary least squares under most circumstances when the model involves true simultaneity [78, pp. 408-420]. But such comparisons hold everything else constant except the method of estimation. Unfortunately, similar comparisons cannot be made for real world results because the true model generating the observations is unknown.

6. Methods are available to reduce the data "requirements" of simultaneous estimators [178, pp. 393-395], but they have been applied infrequently in agricultural price analyses.

7. If, for example, a sum of the quantities of the substitutes for each time period were used, then the model specifies that a one-unit change in the quantity of any substitute has the same effect (regression coefficient) on demand, a tenuous assumption.

8. The measurement of changes in tastes and preferences is still another problem in demand analysis. This topic is considered in the next subsection.

9. Slope coefficients apparently do change seasonally for lamb [211]. Also, even when slope coefficients are equal but the level of the function differs seasonally, the season with the highest level has the most elastic (or least inelastic) demand for a *given* quantity marketed. In the Farris and Darley study broilers appear to have a more price inelastic demand in the summer although the level of the function is higher. This occurs, however, because the elasticities are computed at the mean level of marketings for each month, and marketings are larger in the summer; hence, the elasticity is measured in a more inelastic range of a constant slope demand function in the summer months.

10. Fisher developed the first linear form lag model in 1925 (see [238, p. 7ff.]). (Simpler lag models do not specify the separate effect for X_t.) The linear form model really is a special case of polynomial form models. In this form, the β_i are constrained to follow a polynomial of degree q (for an application in agricultural economics, see [45]).

11. It is obvious, of course, that many more degrees of freedom may be obtainable by "pooling" data and adding one or a few variables.

12. Foote [84, p. 81] states that the term "price flexibility" originated with Henry Moore. The direct-price flexibility is the percentage change in price associated with a 1 percent change in quantity, other variables constant.

13. A theorem states that "if the same form of Engel curve is fitted to all commod-

ities and the form is such as to allow the fulfillment of the adding-up criterion . . . , then the estimates of the curves obtained by the method of least squares will also satisfy the adding-up criterion" [263, p. 84]. The semilog function with individual expenditure as dependent is an example of a function which does not permit the fulfillment of the criterion [208].

14. George and King [96, pp. 3-5] review the basic axioms of consumer behavior that undergird the restrictions.

15. The general idea of separability is that consumers partition the list of n commodities into groups; it is assumed that consumers divide total expenditures into different groups and then further subdivide the amount allotted to a group among individual commodities belonging to that group. To use the two-stage allocation process, the utility function must satisfy certain properties [96, p. 24].

16. If commodities in two different groups are want-independent, then the marginal utility of a commodity in the first group is independent of the quantity consumed of a commodity in the second group.

17. For a more complete discussion of separability concepts, readers should refer to the sources noted in [96].

18. For those who read French, a useful annotated bibliography related to supply analysis was prepared in 1968 under the direction of Boussard [20].

19. A third problem area, not within the scope of this paper, is related to estimation. The model may eliminate autocorrelated residuals for the wrong reason, and least squares estimation is inappropriate if the disturbances are autocorrelated (see also citations in the section on demand analysis).

20. Stout and Ruttan [314] summarize the difficulties of using "output per unit of input" as a measure of technological change.

21. Learn and Cochrane [204] discuss regression analysis of supply functions undergoing structural change.

22. Coleman and Leech [50] evaluate Markov chains as a predictive device for producer numbers and output of milk in England (for other applications of Markov chains in agricultural economics, see [181]).

23. Rayner [270] used the same procedure to estimate the aggregate supply elasticity of aggregate output for the United Kingdom.

24. In considering factors that explain resource use, the question of whether or not farmers allocate resources efficiently, particularly in traditional agriculture, can be raised. Dillon and Anderson [71] provide a recent summary of the important issues, but we consider this topic to be outside the scope of this review. Also, as mentioned in the previous section, much of the growth in agricultural output has been attributed to technological change. Lave [203] has estimated the rate of technical change in United States agriculture, and considerable research effort has been devoted to such questions as returns to research in agriculture, the quality of labor inputs, and so on. We have taken this literature to be outside the scope of price analysis.

25. Dalrymple [65] summarizes one approach to the definition and measurement of margins. The nature of the margin has implications for the relationship between the price elasticity of demand at retail and at the farm for a given quantity marketed [65, pp. 8-9]. Houck [156] considers the relationship of the elasticities for joint products to the elasticity of the commodity from which the products are derived.

26. Granger and Hatanaka [107, pp. 4-9] provide a brief history of time-series analysis.

27. Prices may be predictable from, say, an econometric model which uses informa-

tion about variables influencing prices; a random walk simply says current prices are not predictable from past prices.

28. A much more common application of principal components analysis is to compute principal components for the explanatory variables of a model. Hopefully, the total variation of these variables can be captured in a smaller set of principal components. The principal components are then used as the regressors. There is an obvious saving in degrees of freedom, and since the components are orthogonal, there is no problem of multicollinearity.

29. Padberg [250] and others have used a model to analyze brand preferences for foods in which the dependent variable is a percentage (constrained to the range zero to one).

30. Paul makes a variety of adjustments in the basic component of price to obtain a measure of the concept of a price of binspace. The adjustments are made, in part, to avoid the problem of convenience yields from stocks and the possible negative prices of storage.

31. In an earlier paper Paul [254] considers the concept of a price of processing services. A price of processing services can be defined, for example, by the difference between futures for soybean oil and meal and cash soybeans.

32. Live cattle futures were new at the time of Ehrich's analysis. With a general upward trend in beef prices in recent years, futures have not always fully anticipated the trend. This factor appears to have contributed to the negative margins between fed beef futures and feeder calf prices.

33. The variate difference method assumes that the error term (component) is not autocorrelated, an assumption which may or may not be met for the price series considered. If the assumption is not met, the empirical results are questionable.

References

[1] Abel, M. E. "Price Discrimination in the World Trade of Agricultural Commodities." *J. Farm Econ.* 48:194-208, May 1966.

[2] Abel, M. E., and A. S. Rojko. *World Food Situation: Prospects for World Grain Production, Consumption and Trade.* USDA For. Agr. Econ. Rep. 35, 1967.

[3] Akerman, G. "The Cobweb Theorem: A Reconsideration." *Quart. J. Econ.* 71:151-160, February 1957.

[4] Anschel, K. R. "The Income Elasticity of Demand for Market Services in Cereal Products." *J. Farm Econ.* 45:304-308, May 1963.

[5] Armore, S. J. *The Demand and Price Structure for Food Fats and Oils.* USDA Tech. Bul. 1068, 1953.

[6] Ashby, A. W. "On Forecasting Commodity Prices by the Balance Sheet Approach." *J. Farm Econ.* 46:633-643, August 1964.

[7] Bates, T. H., and A. Schmitz. *A Spatial Equilibrium Analysis of the World Sugar Economy.* University of California, Giannini Foundation Monograph 23, 1969.

[8] Beal, G. M., session chairman. "Is Agricultural Outlook Meeting Today's Needs?" *J. Farm Econ.* 48:1154-1184, December 1966.

[9] Bean, L. H. "The Farmers' Response to Price." *J. Farm Econ.* 11:368-385, July 1929.

[10] Behrman, J. R. "Price Elasticity of the Marketed Surplus of a Subsistence Crop." *J. Farm Econ.* 48:875-893, November 1966.

[11] Ben-David, S., and W. G. Tomek. *Allowing for Slope and Intercept Changes in Regression Analysis.* Cornell University, Dept. Agr. Econ., AE Res. 179, 1965.

[12] ———. *Storing and Marketing New York State Apples, Based on Intraseasonal Demand Relationships.* Cornell Agr. Exp. Sta. Bul. 1007, 1965.

[13] Berry, C. H., G. K. Brinegar, and S. Johnson. "Short-Run Effects Following Controlled Price Changes: Skim Milk." *J. Farm Econ.* 40:892-902, November 1958.

[14] Bieri, J., and A. de Janvry. *Empirical Analysis of Demand under Consumer Budgeting.* University of California, Giannini Foundation Monograph 30, 1972.

[15] Bieri, J., and A. Schmitz. "Time Series Modeling of Economic Phenomena." Discussion by W. A. Fuller. *Am. J. Agr. Econ.* 52:805-813, December 1970.

[16] Blood, D. M., and C. B. Baker. "Some Problems of Linear Discrimination." *J. Farm Econ.* 40:674-683, August 1958.

[17] Bohall, R. W. *Pricing Performance in Marketing Fresh Winter Lettuce.* USDA Marketing Res. Rep. 956, 1972.

[18] Bonnen, J. T., and W. A. Cromarty. "The Structure of Agriculture." In *Agricultural Adjustment Problems in a Growing Economy,* E. O. Heady et al., eds. Ames: Iowa State University Press, 1958.

[19] Booth, E. J. R., and G. G. Judge. "The Impact of the Choice of Model on Measurements of Economic Behavior Relationships." *J. Farm Econ.* 38:570-583, May 1956.

[20] Boussard, J. *L'Offre de Produits Agricoles.* Economie et Sociologie Rurales, Institut National de la Recherche Agronomique, 1968.

[21] Boutwell, W. K., Jr., and R. L. Simmons. "Estimation of Demand for Food and Other Products Assuming Ordinally Separable Utility." *Am. J. Agr. Econ.* 50:366-378, May 1968.

[22] Brain, K., and R. L. Jack. *Interregional Competition in the Fresh Apple Industry.* West Virginia Agr. Exp. Sta. Bul. 612T, 1973.

[23] Brandow, G. E. "The Distribution among Agricultural Producers, Commodities, and Resources of Gains and Losses from Inflation in the Nation's Economy" (abstract). *Am J. Agr. Econ.* 53:913, December 1971.

[24] ———. *Interrelations among Demands for Farm Products and Implications for Control of Market Supply.* Pennsylvania Agr. Exp. Sta. Bul. 680, 1961.

[25] ———. "A Note on the Nerlove Estimate of Supply Elasticity" and reply by M. Nerlove. *J. Farm Econ.* 40:719-728, August 1958.

[26] ———. *A Statistical Analysis of Apple Supply and Demand.* Pennsylvania State University, A.E. and R.S. 2, 1956.

[27] Breimyer, H. F. *Demand and Prices for Meat: Factors Influencing Their Historical Development.* USDA Tech. Bul. 1253, 1961.

[28] ———. "Observations on the Cattle Cycle." *Agr. Econ. Res.* 7:1-11, January 1955.

[29] ———. "On Price Determination and Aggregate Price Theory." *J. Farm Econ.* 39:676-694, August 1957.

[30] ———, ed. *Bargaining in Agriculture, Potentials and Pitfalls in Collective Action.* University of Missouri, North Central Regional Extension Pub. 30, 1971.

[31] Brennan, M. J. "The Supply of Storage." *Am. Econ. Rev.* 48:50-72, March 1958.

[32] Bressler, R. G., Jr., and R. A. King. *Markets, Prices, and Interregional Trade.* New York: Wiley, 1970.

[33] Brinegar, C. S. "A Statistical Analysis of Speculative Price Behavior." *Food Res. Inst. Studies 9* (suppl.), 1970.

[34] Brinegar, G. K. "Economic Effects of Regulation and Price Fixing in the Milk Industry." *J. Farm Econ.* 39:1173-1185, December 1957.

[35] Brown, J. A. C. "Seasonality and Elasticity of the Demand for Food in Great Britain Since Derationing." *J. Agr. Econ.* 13:228-240, June 1959.

[36] Brown, L. R. *Man, Land and Food — Looking Ahead at World Food Needs.* USDA For. Agr. Econ. Rep. 11, 1963.

[37] Buchholz, H. E., G. G. Judge, and V. I. West. *A Summary of Selected Estimated Behavior Relationships for Agricultural Products.* University of Illinois, Dept. Agr. Econ., AERR-57, 1962.

[38] Burk, M. C. "Development of a New Approach to Forecasting Demand." *J. Farm Econ.* 46:618-632, August 1964.

[39] ———. *Influences of Economic and Social Factors on U.S. Food Consumption.* Minneapolis: Burgess, 1961.

[40] ———. *Measures and Procedures for Analysis for U.S. Food Consumption.* USDA Agr. Handbook 206, 1961.

[41] ———. *Trends and Patterns in U.S. Food Consumption.* USDA Agr. Handbook 214, 1961.

[42] Burt, O. R. "Positivistic Measures of Aggregate Supply Elasticities: Some New Approaches: Comment." *Am. J. Agr. Econ.* 53:674-675, November 1971; "Rejoinder" in *Am. J. Agr. Econ.* 54:528-529, August 1972.

[43] Buse, R. C. "Total Elasticities — A Predictive Device." *J. Farm Econ.* 40:881-891, November 1958.

[44] Buse, R. C., and G. E. Brandow. "The Relationship of Volume, Prices and Costs to Marketing Margins for Farm Foods." *J. Farm Econ.* 42:362-370, May 1960.

[45] Chen, D., R. Courtney, and A. Schmitz. "A Polynomial Lag Formulation of Milk Production Response." *Am. J. Agr. Econ.* 54:77-83, February 1972.

[46] Cochrane, W. W. *An Analysis of Farm Price Behavior.* Pennsylvania Agr. Exp. Sta. Prog. Rep. 50, 1951.

[47] ———. "Conceptualizing the Supply Relation in Agriculture." *J. Farm Econ.* 37:1161-1176, December 1955.

[48] ———. *Farm Prices: Myth and Reality.* Minneapolis: University of Minnesota Press, 1958.

[49] ———. "Some Additional Views on Demand and Supply." In *Agricultural Adjustment Problems in a Growing Economy*, E. O. Heady et al., eds. Ames: Iowa State University Press, 1958.

[50] Coleman, D., and D. Leech. "A Forecast of Milk Supply in England and Wales." *J. Agr. Econ.* 21:253-265, May 1970.

[51] Coleman, D., and H. Miah. "On Some Estimates of Price Flexibilities for Meat and Their Interpretation." *J. Agr. Econ.* 24:353-367, May 1973.

[52] Collins, N. R. "Changing Role of Price in Agricultural Marketing." *J. Farm Econ.* 41:528-534, August 1959.

[53] Conneman, G. J. "Farm Panels as a Source of Farm Management Data: The Cornell Producer Panel." *Am. J. Agr. Econ.* 51:1206-1210, December 1969.

[54] Cootner, P. H. "Returns to Speculators: Telser versus Keynes." *J. Pol. Econ.* 68:396-404, August 1960.

[55] ———. "Stock Prices: Random vs. Systematic Changes." *Ind. Manag. Rev.* 3:24-45, Spring 1962.

[56] Cowling, K., and T. W. Gardner. "Analytical Models for Estimating Supply

Relations in the Agricultural Sector: A Survey and Critique." *J. Agr. Econ.* 15:439-450, June 1963.

[57] Craddock, W. J. *Interregional Competition in Canadian Cereal Production.* Economic Council of Canada, Ottawa, 1970.

[58] Crom, R. *A Dynamic Price-Output Model of the Beef and Pork Sectors.* USDA Tech. Bul. 1426, 1970.

[59] ——. "Economic Projections Using a Behavioral Model." *Agr. Econ. Res.* 24:9-15, January 1972.

[60] Cromarty, W. A. *The Demand for Farm Machinery and Tractors.* Michigan Agr. Exp. Sta. Bul. 275, 1959.

[61] —— —. "An Econometric Model for United States Agriculture." *J. Am. Stat. Assoc.* 54:556-574, September 1959.

[62] ——, session chairman. "Agribusiness Research." *Am. J. Agr. Econ.* 54:779-800, December 1972.

[63] Culver, D. W., and J. C. Chai. "A View of Food and Agriculture in 1980." *Agr. Econ. Res.* 22:61-68, July 1970.

[64] Dahl, D. C., J. D. Anderson, and R. D. Peterson. *Purchased Farm Input Markets in the United States, 1950-71: A Bibliography of Economic Studies.* Minnesota Agr. Exp. Sta. Misc. Rep. 103, 1971.

[65] Dalrymple, D. G. *On the Nature of Marketing Margins.* Michigan State University, Dept. Agr. Econ., Agr. Econ. 824, 1961.

[66] Daly, R. F. "The Long-Run Demand for Farm Products." *Agr. Econ. Res.* 8:73-91, July 1956.

[67] Daniel, R., and J. Havlicek. "Farm/Ranch Firm Demand Relationships for Fertilizer Inputs." In *Farm/Ranch Input Research Yesterday, Today and Tomorrow,* P. E. Nelson, Jr., ed. Michigan Agr. Exp. Sta. Res. Rep. 208, 1973.

[68] Day, L. M. "A Critical Appraisal of Present Models." In *Interregional Competition Research Methods,* R. A. King, ed. North Carolina State University Agricultural Policy Institute, 1963.

[69] Day, R. H. "An Approach to Production Response." *Agr. Econ. Res.* 14:134-148, October 1962.

[70] ——. "Recursive Programming and Supply Prediction." In *Agricultural Supply Functions: Estimating Techniques and Interpretations,* E. O. Heady et al., eds. Ames: Iowa State University Press, 1961. (Reprinted in *Readings in Economics of Agriculture,* K. A. Fox and D. G. Johnson, eds. Homewood, Ill.: Irwin, 1969).

[71] Dillon, J. L., and J. R. Anderson. "Allocative Efficiency, Traditional Agriculture, and Risk." *Am. J. Agr. Econ.* 53:26-32, February 1971.

[72] Doll, J. P. "An Analytical Technique for Estimating Weather Indexes from Meteorological Measurements." *J. Farm Econ.* 49:79-88, February 1967.

[73] Doll, J. P., and S. B. Chin. "A Use for Principal Components in Price Analysis." *Am. J. Agr. Econ.* 52:591-593, November 1970.

[74] Doran, H. E., and J. J. Quilkey. "Harmonic Analysis of Seasonal Data: Some Important Properties." *Am. J. Agr. Econ.* 54:646-651, November 1972.

[75] Eckstein, S., and M. Syrquin. "A Note on Fluctuations in Supply and Farmers' Income." *Am. J. Agr. Econ.* 53:331-334, May 1971.

[76] Ehrich, R. L. "Cash-Futures Price Relationships for Live Beef Cattle." *Am. J. Agr. Econ.* 51:26-40, February 1969.

[77] Ezekiel, M. "The Cobweb Theorem." *Quart. J. Econ.* 52:255-280, February 1938.

[78] Falcon, W. P. "Farmer Response to Price in a Subsistence Economy: The Case of West Pakistan." *Am. Econ. Rev.* 54:580-591, May 1964.

[79] Farris, P. L. "The Pricing Structure for Wheat at the Country Elevator Level." *J. Farm Econ.* 40:607-624, August 1958.

[80] Farris, P. L., and R. D. Darley. "Monthly Price-Quantity Relations for Broilers at the Farm Level." *J. Farm Econ.* 46:849-856, November 1964.

[81] Fettig, L. P. "Adjusting Farm Tractor Prices for Quality Changes, 1950-62." *J. Farm Econ.* 45:599-611, August 1963.

[82] Food and Agriculture Organization. *Agricultural Commodities: Projections for 1970.* Supplement to FAO Commodity Review. Rome, 1962.

[83] ———. *Agricultural Commodities: Projections for 1975 and 1985.* 2 vols. Rome, 1967.

[84] Foote, R. J. *Analytical Tools for Studying Demand and Price Structures.* USDA Agr. Handbook 146, 1958.

[85] Forker, O. D. *Price Determination Processes: Issues and Evaluation.* USDA FCS Inf. 102, 1975.

[86] Forker, O. D., and B. A. Anderson. *An Annotated Bibliography on Price Discrimination.* Cornell University, Dept. Agr. Econ., AE Res. 241, 1968.

[87] Fox, K. A. *The Analysis of Demand for Farm Products.* USDA Tech. Bul. 1081, 1953.

[88] Fox, K. A., and R. C. Taeuber. "Spatial Equilibrium Models of the Livestock-Feed Economy." *Am. Econ. Rev.* 45:584-608, September 1955.

[89] Foytik, J. "Characteristics of Demand for California Plums." *Hilgardia* 20: 407-527, April 1951.

[90] Freeman, R. E. "Roles of Farm Productivity and Marketing Margins in Postwar Decline in Farm Prices." *J. Farm Econ.* 48:31-41, February 1966.

[91] French, B. C. *The Long-Term Price and Production Outlook for Apples in the United States and Michigan.* Michigan Agr. Exp. Sta. Tech. Bul. 255, 1956.

[92] French, B. C., and J. L. Matthews. "A Supply Response Model for Perennial Crops." *Am. J. Agr. Econ.* 53:478-490, August 1971.

[93] Frisch, R. "A Complete Scheme for Computing All Direct and Cross-Demand Elasticities in a Model with Many Sectors." *Econometrica* 27:177-196, April 1959.

[94] Fromm, G. "Implications to and from Economic Theory in Models of Complex Systems." *Am. J. Agr. Econ.* 55:259-271, May 1973.

[95] Fuller, W. A., and J. E. Martin. "The Effects of Autocorrelated Errors on the Statistical Estimation of Distributed Lag Models." *J. Farm Econ.* 43:71-82, February 1961.

[96] George, P. S., and G. A. King. *Consumer Demand for Food Commodities in the United States with Projections for 1980.* University of California, Giannini Foundation Monograph 26, 1971.

[97] Gerra, M. J. *The Demand, Supply, and Price Structure for Eggs.* USDA Tech. Bul. 1204, 1959.

[98] Girão, J. A., W. G. Tomek, and T. D. Mount. "Effect of Income Instability on Farmers' Consumption and Investment Behavior: An Econometric Analysis." Cornell Agr. Exp. Sta., *Search*, vol. 3, no. 1, 1973.

[99] Girshick, M. A., and T. Haavelmo. "Statistical Analysis of the Demand for Food: Examples of Simultaneous Estimation of Structural Equations." *Econometrica* 15:79-110, April 1947.

[100] Gislason, C. "Grain Storage Rules." *J. Farm Econ.* 42:576-595, August 1960. (See also Washington Agr. Exp. Sta. Tech. Bul. 37, 1961.)

[101] ———. "How Much Has the Canadian Wheat Board Cost the Canadian Farmers?" *J. Farm Econ.* 41:584-599, August 1959.

[102] Goldberger, A. S. "Structural Equation Methods in the Social Sciences." *Econometrica* 40:979-1001, November 1972.

[103] Goodwin, J. W., R. Andorn, and J. E. Martin. *The Irreversible Demand Function for Beef.* Oklahoma Agr. Exp. Sta. Tech. Bul. T-127, 1968.

[104] Goreux, L. M. "Income and Food Consumption." *Monthly Bul. Agr. Econ. Stat.* 9:1-13, October 1960.

[105] ———. "Long-Range Projections of Food Consumption." *Monthly Bul. Agr. Econ. Stat.* 6:1-18, June 1957.

[106] Graf, T. F. "Hedging — How Effective Is It?" *J. Farm Econ.* 35:398-413, August 1953.

[107] Granger, C. W. J., and M. Hatanaka. *Spectral Analysis of Economic Time Series.* Princeton: Princeton University Press, 1964.

[108] Gray, R. W. "The Attack upon Potato Futures Trading in the United States." *Food Res. Inst. Studies* 4(2):97-121, 1964.

[109] ———. "The Characteristic Bias in Some Thin Futures Markets." *Food Res. Inst. Studies* 1(3):296-312, 1960.

[110] ———. "Price Effects of a Lack of Speculation." *Food Res. Inst. Studies* 7 (suppl.):177-194, 1967.

[111] ———. "The Search for a Risk Premium." *J. Pol. Econ.* 69:250-260, June 1961.

[112] ———. "Some Thoughts on the Changing Role of Price." *J. Farm Econ.* 46:117-127, February 1964.

[113] Gray, R. W., and D. J. S. Rutledge. "The Economics of Commodity Futures Markets: A Survey." *Rev. Marketing Agr. Econ.* 39:57-108, December 1971.

[114] Griffiths, W. E. "Estimation of Regression Coefficients Which Change over Time." Unpublished Ph.D. dissertation, University of Illinois, 1971.

[115] Griliches, Z. "The Demand for Fertilizer: An Economic Interpretation of a Technical Change." *J. Farm Econ.* 40:591-606, August 1958.

[116] ———. "The Demand for Inputs in Agriculture and a Derived Supply Elasticity." *J. Farm Econ.* 41:309-322, May 1959.

[117] ———. "Distributed Lags: A Survey." *Econometrica* 35:16-49, January 1967.

[118] ———. "Estimates of the Aggregate U.S. Farm Supply Function." *J. Farm Econ.* 42:282-293, May 1960.

[119] ———. "Specification Bias in Estimates of Production Functions." *J. Farm Econ.* 39:8-20, January 1957.

[120] Gruen, F. H. *Long-Term Agricultural Supply and Demand Projections: Australia, 1965 to 1980.* Monash University, Clayton, Victoria, Australia, 1968.

[121] Guedry, L. J., and G. G. Judge. *The Spatial Structure of the Feed Grain Economy.* University of Illinois, Dept. Agr. Econ., AERR-78, 1965.

[122] Gustafson, R. L. *Carryover Levels for Grains.* USDA Tech. Bul. 1178, 1958.

[123] ———. "Implications of Recent Research on Optimal Storage Rules." *J. Farm Econ.* 40:290-300, May 1958.

[124] Haavelmo, T. "The Statistical Implications of a System of Simultaneous Equations." *Econometrica* 11:1-12, January 1943.

[125] Haidacher, R. C. "Some Suggestions for Developing New Models from Existing Models." *Am. J. Agr. Econ.* 52:814-819, December 1970.

[126] Hallberg, M. C. "Discussion: Estimation of Demand for Food and Other Products Assuming Ordinally Separable Utility." *Am. J. Agr. Econ.* 50:378-380, May 1968.

[127] Halter, A. N. "Evaluation of Time Series as Data for Estimating Supply Parameters: Discussion." In *Agricultural Supply Functions: Estimating Techniques and Interpretations*, E. O. Heady et al., eds. Ames: Iowa State University Press, 1961.

[128] Hammonds, T. M., R. Yadav, and C. Vathana. "The Elasticity of Demand for Hired Farm Labor." *Am. J. Agr. Econ.* 55:242-245, May 1973.

[129] Hanau, A. F. "The Disparate Stability of Farm and Nonfarm Prices." In *Proceedings of the Tenth International Conference of Agricultural Economists, 1958*. London: Oxford University Press, 1960.

[130] Harlow, A. A. *Factors Affecting the Price and Supply of Hogs*. USDA Tech. Bul. 1274, 1962.

[131] Harmston, F. K., and H. Hino. "An Intertemporal Analysis of the Nature of Demand for Food Products." *Am. J. Agr. Econ.* 52:381-386, August 1970.

[132] Harris, E. S. *Classified Pricing of Milk: Some Theoretical Aspects*. USDA Tech. Bul. 1184, 1958.

[133] Hassler, J. B. "Pricing Efficiency in the Manufactured Dairy Product Industry." *Hilgardia* 22:235-334, August 1953.

[134] Hathaway, D. E. "Agriculture and the Business Cycle." In *Policy for Commercial Agriculture, Its Relationship to Economic Growth and Stability*. Joint Economic Committee, 85th Congress, 1st Session, November 22, 1957.

[135] ———. *The Effects of the Price Support Program on the Dry Bean Industry in Michigan*. Michigan Agr. Exp. Sta. Tech. Bul. 250, 1955.

[136] ———. "Food Prices and Inflation." *Brookings Papers on Economic Activity* 1:63-109, January 1974.

[137] Hayami, Y., and W. Peterson. "Social Returns to Public Information Services: Statistical Reporting of U.S. Farm Commodities." *Am. Econ. Rev.* 62:119-130, March 1972.

[138] Hayenga, M. L. "Hog Pricing and Evaluation Methods — Their Accuracy and Equity." *Am. J. Agr. Econ.* 53:507-509, August 1971.

[139] Hayenga, M. L., and D. Hacklander. "Monthly Supply-Demand Relationships for Fed Cattle and Hogs." *Am. J. Agr. Econ.* 52:535-544, November 1970.

[140] Heady, E. O., C. B. Baker, H. G. Diesslin, E. Kehrberg, and S. Staniforth, eds. *Agricultural Supply Functions: Estimating Techniques and Interpretations*. Ames: Iowa State University Press, 1961.

[141] Heady, E. O., and L. G. Tweeten. *Resource Demand and Structure of the Agricultural Industry*. Ames: Iowa State University Press, 1963.

[142] Hee, O. *Demand and Price Analysis for Potatoes*. USDA Tech. Bul. 1380, 1967.

[143] ———. *A Statistical Analysis of U.S. Demand for Phosphate Rock, Potash, and Nitrogen*. Bureau of Mines Inf. Circ. 8418, 1969.

[144] Heifner, R. G. "The Gains from Basing Grain Storage Decisions on Cash-Future Spreads." *J. Farm Econ.* 48:1490-1495, December 1966.

[145] ———. "Optimal Hedging Levels and Hedging Effectiveness in Cattle Feeding." *Agr. Econ. Res.* 24:25-36, April 1972.

[146] Henderson, J. M. "The Utilization of Agricultural Land: A Theoretical and Empirical Inquiry." *Rev. Econ. Stat.* 41:242-259, August 1959.

[147] Herdt, R. W., and W. W. Cochrane. "Farm Land Prices and Farm Technological Advance." *J. Farm Econ.* 48:243-263, May 1966.

[148] Herrmann, R. O. "Interaction Effects and the Analysis of Household Food Expenditures." *J. Farm Econ.* 49:821-832, November 1967.

[149] Hieronymus, T. A. *Commodity Speculation as an Investment Medium.* New York Coffee and Sugar Exchange pamphlet, no date.

[150] Hildreth, C., and J. Y. Lu. *Demand Relations with Autocorrelated Disturbances.* Michigan Agr. Exp. Sta. Tech. Bul. 276, 1960.

[151] Hillman, J. S. "Collins' Changing Role of Price." and reply by Norman R. Collins. *J. Farm Econ.* 42:385-389, May 1960.

[152] Hoos, S., and G. M. Kuznets. *Impacts of Lemon Products Imports on Domestic Lemon Markets.* University of California, Giannini Foundation Res. Rep. 254, 1962.

[153] ———. *Pacific Coast Canned Fruits F.O.B. Price Relationships 1972-73.* California Agr. Exp. Sta., 1973.

[154] Hoos, S., and R. E. Seltzer. *Lemons and Lemon Products: Changing Economic Relationships, 1951-52.* California Agr. Exp. Sta. Bul. 729, 1952.

[155] Houck, J. P. "A Look at Flexibilities and Elasticities." *J. Farm Econ.* 48:225-232, May 1966.

[156] ———. "Price Elasticities and Joint Products." *J. Farm Econ.* 46:652-656, August 1964.

[157] ———. "Price Elasticity and Linear Supply Curves." *Am. Econ. Rev.* 57:905-908, September 1967.

[158] ———. "The Relationship of Direct Price Flexibilities to Direct Price Elasticities." *J. Farm Econ.* 47:789-792, August 1965.

[159] Houck, J. P., and J. S. Mann. *An Analysis of Domestic and Foreign Demand for U.S. Soybeans and Soybean Products.* Minnesota Agr. Exp. Sta. Tech. Bul. 256, 1968.

[160] Houck, J. P., M. E. Ryan, and A. Subotnik. *Soybeans and Their Products, Markets, Models, and Policy.* Minneapolis: University of Minnesota Press, 1972.

[161] Houck, J. P., and A. Subotnik. "The U.S. Supply of Soybeans: Regional Acreage Functions." *Agr. Econ. Res.* 21:99-108, October 1969.

[162] Houthakker, H. S. "Can Speculators Forecast Prices?" *Rev. Econ. Stat.* 39:143-151, May 1957.

[163] ———. *Economic Policy for the Farm Sector.* Washington, D.C.: American Enterprise Institute, 1967.

[164] ———. "An International Comparison of Household Expenditure Patterns, Commemorating the Centenary of Engel's Law." *Econometrica* 25:532-551, October 1957.

[165] ———. "Systematic and Random Elements in Short-Term Price Movements." *Am. Econ. Rev.* 51:164-172, May 1961.

[166] Hyslop, J. D. *Price-Quality Relationships in Spring Wheat.* Minnesota Agr. Exp. Sta. Tech. Bul. 267, 1970.

[167] Ironmonger, D. S. "A Note on the Estimation of Long-Run Elasticities." *J. Farm Econ.* 41:626-632, August 1959.

[168] Jamison, J. A. "Marketing Orders, Cartels, and Cling Peaches: A Long-Run View." *Food Res. Inst. Studies* 6(2):117-142, 1966.

[169] Jesse, E. V., and A. C. Johnson, Jr. "An Analysis of Vegetable Contracts." *Am. J. Agr. Econ.* 52:545-554, November 1970.

[170] Johnson, A. C., Jr. *Effects of Futures Trading on Price Performance in the Cash Onion Market, 1930-68.* USDA Tech. Bul. 1470, 1973.

[171] Johnson, D. G. "The Nature of the Supply Function for Agricultural Products." *Am. Econ. Rev.* 40:539-564, September 1950. Reprinted in *Readings in the Economics of Agriculture*, K. A. Fox and D. G. Johnson, eds. Homewood, Ill.: Irwin, 1969.

[172] Johnson, J. D. "Pricing of Cattle at Southern Auctions with Emphasis upon Factors Affecting Price and Farmer Price Uncertainty." *J. Farm Econ.* 39:1657-1664, December 1957.

[173] Johnson, G. L. *Burley Tobacco Control Programs.* Kentucky Agr. Exp. Sta. Bul. 580, 1952.

[174] ———. "Supply Functions — Some Facts and Notions." In *Agricultural Adjustments in a Growing Economy*, E. O. Heady et al., eds. Ames: Iowa State University Press, 1958.

[175] ———, session chairman. "The Supply Function in Agriculture Revisited." *Am. J. Agr. Econ.* 51:342-369, May 1969.

[176] Johnson, L. L. "The Theory of Hedging and Speculation in Commodity Futures." *Rev. Econ. Studies* 27:139-151, June 1960.

[177] Johnson, R. D. *An Economic Evaluation of Alternative Marketing Methods for Fed Cattle.* Nebraska Agr. Exp. Sta. Bul. 520, 1972.

[178] Johnston, J. *Econometric Methods.* 2d ed. New York: McGraw-Hill, 1972.

[179] Jones, W. O. *Marketing Staple Food Crops in Tropical Africa.* Ithaca: Cornell University Press, 1972.

[180] Judge, G. G., J. Havlicek, and R. L. Rizek. "An Interregional Model: Its Formulation and Application to the Livestock Industry." *Agr. Econ. Res.* 17:1-9, January 1965.

[181] Judge, G. G., and E. R. Swanson. "Markov Chains: Basic Concepts and Suggested Uses in Agricultural Economics." *Australian J. Agr. Econ.* 6:49-61, December 1962.

[182] Judge, G. G., and T. D. Wallace. "Estimation of Spatial Price Equilibrium Models." *J. Farm Econ.* 40:801-820, November 1958.

[183] ———. *Spatial Price Equilibrium Analyses of the Livestock Economy.* Oklahoma Agr. Exp. Sta. Tech. Bul. TB-78, 1959.

[184] Just, R. E. *Econometric Analysis of Production Decisions with Government Intervention: The Case of the California Field Crops.* University of California, Giannini Foundation Monograph 33, 1974.

[185] Kau, P., and L. Hill. "A Threshold Model of Purchasing Decisions." *J. Marketing Res.* 9:264-270, August 1972. (Also see *Am. J. Agr. Econ.* 55:19-27, February 1973).

[186] King, R. A., ed. *Interregional Competition Research Methods.* North Carolina State University, Agricultural Policy Institute, 1963.

[187] King, R. A., and W. R. Henry. "Transportation Models in Studies of Interregional Competition." *J. Farm Econ.* 41:997-1011, December 1959.

[188] Kip, E., and G. A. King. *The Demand for Selected Deciduous Tree Fruits with Implications for Alternative 1980 Production Levels.* University of California, Giannini Foundation Res. Rep. 309, 1970.

[189] Klein, L. R. *An Introduction to Econometrics.* Englewood Cliffs, N.J.: Prentice-Hall, 1962.

[190] Knight, D. A. "Evaluation of Time Series as Data for Estimating Supply Parameters." In *Agricultural Supply Functions: Estimating Techniques and Interpretations*, E. O. Heady et al., eds. Ames: Iowa State University Press, 1961.

[191] Krishna, R. "Agricultural Price Policy and Economic Development." In *Agricultural Development and Economic Growth*, H. Southworth and B. Johnston, eds. Ithaca: Cornell University Press, 1967.

[192] ———. "Farm Supply Response in India-Pakistan: A Case Study of the Punjab Region." *Econ J.* 73:477-487, September 1963. Reprinted in *Readings in the Economics of Agriculture*, K. A. Fox and D. G. Johnson, eds. Homewood, Ill.: Irwin, 1969.

[193] Labys, W. C., and C. W. J. Granger. *Speculation, Hedging and Commodity Price Forecasts*. Lexington, Mass.: Heath, 1970.

[194] Ladd, G. W. "Federal Milk Marketing Order Provisions: Effects on Producer Prices and Intermarket Price Relationships." *Am. J. Agr. Econ.* 51:625-641, August 1969.

[195] ———. "Temporal Aggregation in Distributed Lag Models." *J. Farm Econ.* 46:673-681, August 1964.

[196] Ladd, G. W., and J. R. Tedford. "A Generalization of the Working Method for Estimating Long-Run Elasticities." *J. Farm Econ.* 41:221-233, May 1959.

[197] Ladd, G. W., and G. E. Updegraff. *Allocation of Milk among Products to Maximize Gross Income of the Nation's Dairy Farmers under 1964 Demand Functions.* Iowa Agr. Exp. Sta. Res. Bul. 567, 1969.

[198] Langemeier, L., and R. G. Thompson. "Demand, Supply and Price Relationships for the Beef Sector, Post-World War II Period." *J. Farm Econ.* 49:169-183, February 1967.

[199] Larson, A. B. "The Hog Cycle as Harmonic Motion." *J. Farm Econ.* 46:375-386, May 1964.

[200] ———. "Measurement of a Random Process in Futures Prices." *Food Res. Inst. Studies* 1(3):313-324, 1960.

[201] ———. "Price Prediction on the Egg Futures Market." *Food Res. Inst. Studies* 7(suppl.):49-64, 1967.

[202] ———. "The Quiddity of the Cobweb Theorem." *Food Res. Inst. Studies* 7(2):165-175, 1967.

[203] Lave, L. B. "Empirical Estimates of Technological Change in United States Agriculture, 1850-1958." *J. Farm Econ.* 44:941-952, November 1962.

[204] Learn, E. W. , and W. W. Cochrane. "Regression Analysis of Supply Functions Undergoing Structural Change." In *Agricultural Supply Functions*, E. O. Heady et al., eds. Ames: Iowa State University Press, 1961.

[205] Leath, M. N., and L. V. Blakley. *An Interregional Analysis of the U.S. Grain-Marketing Industry, 1966/67*. USDA Tech. Bul. 1444, 1971.

[206] Lee, F., and K. E. Phillips. "Differences in Consumption Patterns of Farm and Nonfarm Households in the United States." *Am. J. Agr. Econ.* 53:573-582, November 1971.

[207] Lele, U. J. *Food Grain Marketing in India, Private Performance and Public Policy*. Ithaca: Cornell University Press, 1971.

[208] Leser, C. E. V. "Forms of Engel Functions." *Econometrica* 31:694-703, October 1963.

[209] Leuthold, R. M. "An Analysis of Daily Fluctuations in the Hog Economy." *Am. J. Agr. Econ.* 51:849-865, November 1969.

[210] Leuthold, R. M., and D. L. Bawden. *An Annotated Bibliography of Spatial Studies*. Wisconsin Agr. Exp. Sta. Res. Rep. 25, 1966.

[211] Logan, S. H., and J. N. Boles. "Quarterly Fluctuations in Retail Prices of Meat." *J. Farm Econ.* 44:1050-1060, November 1962.

402 WILLIAM G. TOMEK AND KENNETH L. ROBINSON

[212] Louwes, S. L., J. C. G. Boot, and S. Wage. "A Quadratic-Programming Approach to the Problem of the Optimal Use of Milk in the Netherlands." *J. Farm Econ.* 45:309-317, May 1963.

[213] Maizels, A. (assisted by L. F. Campbell-Boross and P. B. D. Rayment). *Exports and Economic Growth of Developing Countries.* Cambridge: At the University Press, 1968.

[214] Maki, W. R. "Economic Effects of Short-Run Changes in the Demand for Livestock and Meats." *J. Farm Econ.* 39:1670-1674, December 1957.

[215] Manchester, A. C. *Pricing Milk and Dairy Products: Principles, Practices and Problems.* USDA Agr. Econ. Rep. 207, 1971.

[216] Mänderscheid, L. V. "Some Observations On Interpreting Measured Demand Elasticities." *J. Farm Econ.* 46:128-136, February 1964.

[217] Marsh, J. M., and R. J. Folwell. *An Econometric Analysis of the U.S. Poultry Meats Sector.* Washington Agr. Exp. Sta. Tech. Bul. 67, 1971.

[218] Martin, J. E. "Isolation of Lagged Economic Responses." *J. Farm Econ.* 49:160-168, February 1967.

[219] Martin, L., and A. C. Zwart. "A Spatial and Temporal Model of the North American Pork Sector for the Evaluation of Policy Alternatives." *Am. J. Agr. Econ.* 57:55-66, February 1975.

[220] Matthews, J. L. "Conditional Market Forecasts and Implications for the U.S. Soybean Economy." In *Fats and Oils Situation.* USDA, FOS-268, 1973.

[221] McClements, L. D. "Note on Harmonic Motion and the Cobweb Theorem." *J. Agr. Econ.* 21:141-146, January 1970.

[222] McCrone, G. *The Economics of Subsidising Agriculture; a Study of British Policy.* London: Allen and Unwin, 1962.

[223] McKinnon, R. I. "Futures Markets, Buffer Stocks, and Income Stability for Primary Producers." *J. Pol. Econ.* 75:844-861, December 1967.

[224] McPherson, W. W., and J. E. Faris. "'Price Mapping' of Optimum Changes in Enterprises." *J. Farm Econ.* 40:821-834, November 1958.

[225] Meadows, D. L. *Dynamics of Commodity Production Cycles.* Cambridge, Mass: Wright-Allen, 1970.

[226] Meinken, K. W. *The Demand and Price Structure for Wheat.* USDA Tech. Bul. 1136, 1955.

[227] Meinken, K. W., A. S. Rojko, and G. A. King. "Measurement of Substitution in Demand from Time Series Data-A Synthesis of Three Approaches." *J. Farm Econ.* 38:711-735, August 1956.

[228] Mellor, J. W., and A. K. Dar. "Determinants and Development Implications of Foodgrains Prices in India, 1949-1964." *Am. J. Agr. Econ.* 50:962-974, November 1968.

[229] Mighell, R. L., and R. H. Allen. "Supply Schedules – 'Long-Time' and 'Short-Time.'" *J. Farm Econ.* 22:544-557, August 1940.

[230] Mighell, R. L., and J. D. Black. *Interregional Competition in Agriculture, with Special Reference to Dairy Farming in the Lake States and New England.* Cambridge: Harvard University Press, 1951.

[231] Moore, H. L. *Economic Cycles: Their Law and Cause.* New York: Macmillan, 1914.

[232] Morgan, T. "Trends in Terms of Trade and Their Repercussions on Primary Producers." In *International Trade Theory in a Developing World*, R. Harrod, ed. London: Macmillan, 1963.

[233] Mundlak, Y. "Aggregation over Time in Distributed Lag Models." *Inter. Econ. Rev.* 2:154-163, May 1961.

[234] ———. *Long-Term Projections of Supply and Demand for Agricultural Products in Israel*. Jerusalem: The Hebrew University, 1964.

[235] National Commission on Food Marketing. *Food from Farmer to Consumer.* Washington, D.C.: Government Printing Office, 1966.

[236] Nelson, P. E., Jr., ed. *Farm/Ranch Input Research Yesterday, Today and Tomorrow*. Michigan Agr. Exp. Sta. Res. Rep. 208, 1973.

[237] Nerlove, M. "Adaptive Expectations and Cobweb Phenomena." *Quart. J. Econ.* 72:227-240, May 1958.

[238] ———. *Distributed Lags and Demand Analysis for Agricultural and Other Commodities*. USDA Agr. Handbook 141, 1958.

[239] ———. "Distributed Lags and Estimation of Long-Run Supply and Demand Elasticities: Theoretical Considerations." *J. Farm Econ.* 40:301-311, May 1958.

[240] ———. *The Dynamics of Supply: Estimation of Farmers' Response to Price.* Baltimore: Johns Hopkins University Press, 1958.

[241] ———. "Estimates of the Elasticities of Supply of Selected Agricultural Commodities." *J. Farm Econ.* 38:496-509, May 1956. Reprinted in *Readings in the Economics of Agriculture*, K. A. Fox and D. G. Johnson, eds. Homewood, Ill.: Irwin, 1969.

[242] ———. "Spectral Analysis of Seasonal Adjustment Procedures." *Econometrica* 32:241-286, July 1964.

[243] Nerlove, M., and W. Addison. "Statistical Estimation of Long-Run Elasticities of Supply and Demand." *J. Farm Econ.* 40:861-880, November 1958.

[244] Nerlove, M., and K. L. Bachman. "The Analysis of Changes in Agricultural Supply: Problems and Approaches." *J. Farm Econ.* 42:531-554, August 1960.

[245] Nerlove, M., and F. V. Waugh. "Advertising without Supply Control: Some Implications of a Study of the Advertising of Oranges." *J. Farm Econ.* 43:813-837, November 1961.

[246] Nordin, J. A., G. G. Judge, and O. Wahby. *Application of Econometric Procedures to the Demands for Agricultural Products*. Iowa Agr. Exp. Sta. Res. Bul. 410, 1954.

[247] Nyberg, A. J. "The Demand for Lauric Oils in the United States." *Am. J. Agr. Econ.* 52:97-102, February 1970.

[248] Ogren, K. E. "Marketing Costs and Margins: New Perspectives in a Changing Economy." *J. Farm Econ.* 47:1366-1376, December 1965.

[249] Oury, B. "Allowing for Weather in Crop Production Model Building." *J. Farm Econ.* 47:270-283, May 1965.

[250] Padberg, D. I., F. E. Walker, and K. W. Kepner. "Measuring Consumer Brand Preference." *J. Farm Econ.* 49:723-733, August 1967.

[251] Parish, R. M. "Price 'Levelling' and 'Averaging.'" *The Farm Economist* 11 (5): 187-198, 1967.

[252] Pasour, E. C., Jr. "An Analysis of Intraseasonal Apple Price Movements." *Agr. Econ. Res.* 17:19-30, January 1965.

[253] Pasour, E. C., Jr., and R. A. Schrimper. "The Effect of Length of Run on Measured Demand Elasticities." *J. Farm Econ.* 47:774-788, August 1965.

[254] Paul, A. B. "Pricing below Cost in the Soybean Processing Industry." *J. Farm Econ.* 48:2-22 (part II), August 1966.

[255] ———. "The Pricing of Binspace — A Contribution to the Theory of Storage." *Am. J. Agr. Econ.* 52:1-12, February 1970.

[256] Paul, A. B., and W. T. Wesson. "Pricing Feedlot Services through Cattle Futures." *Agr. Econ. Res.* 19:33-45, April 1967.

[257] Peck, A. E. "Hedging and Income Stability: Concepts, Implications, and an Example." *Am. J. Agr. Econ.* 57:410-419, August 1975.

[258] Philpott, B. P. "Trends in Agriculture's Terms of Trade." *Proceedings of the New Zealand Institute of Agricultural Science.* New Plymouth: Avery Press, 1962.

[259] *Possible Methods of Improving the Parity Formula.* Report of the Secretary of Agriculture, Senate Document 18, 85th Congress, 1st Session, February 1957.

[260] Powell, A. A., and K. O. Campbell. "The Significance of Non-Speculative Returns in the Appraisal of Buffer-Stock Schemes." *J. Farm Econ.* 44:876-882, August 1962.

[261] Powell, A. A., and F. H. Gruen. "The Estimation of Production Frontiers: The Australian Livestock/Cereals Complex." *Australian J. Agr. Econ.* 11:63-81, June 1967.

[262] Powers, M. J. "Does Futures Trading Reduce Price Fluctuations in the Cash Markets?" *Am. Econ. Rev.* 60:460-464, June 1970.

[263] Prais, S. J., and H. S. Houthakker. *The Analysis of Family Budgets.* Dept. Applied Econ. Monograph 4. Cambridge: At the University Press, 1955; 2d ed., abridged, 1971.

[264] Prebisch, R. *Towards a New Trade Policy for Development.* Report prepared for the United Nations Conference on Trade and Development, New York, 1964.

[265] President's Science Advisory Committee. *The World Food Problem: A Report of the Panel on the World Food Supply.* 3 vols. Washington, D.C., 1967.

[266] Price, D. W. "Discarding Low-Quality Produce with an Elastic Demand." *J. Farm Econ.* 49:622-632, August 1967.

[267] Purcell, J. G., and R. Raunikar. "Price Elasticities from Panel Data: Meat, Poultry, and Fish." *Am. J. Agr. Econ.* 53:216-221, May 1971.

[268] ———. "Quantity-Income Elasticities for Foods by Level of Income." *J. Farm Econ.* 49:1410-1414, December 1967.

[269] Rausser, G. C., and T. F. Cargill. "The Existence of Broiler Cycles: An Application of Spectral Analysis." *Am. J. Agr. Econ.* 52:109-121, February 1970.

[270] Rayner, A. J. "The Demand for Inputs and the Aggregate Supply Function for Agriculture." *J. Agr. Econ.* 21:225-238, May 1970.

[271] Rayner, A. J., and K. Cowling. "Demand for Farm Tractors in the United States and the United Kingdom." *Am. J. Agr. Econ.* 50:896-912, November 1968.

[272] Renshaw, E. F. "Distributed Lags, Technological Change, and the Demand for Fertilizer" and reply by Z. Griliches. *J. Farm Econ.* 43:955-964, November 1961.

[273] Reutlinger, S. "Analysis of a Dynamic Model, with Particular Emphasis on Long-Run Projections." *J. Farm Econ.* 48:88-106, February 1966.

[274] ———. *Evaluation of Some Uncertainty Hypotheses for Predicting Supply.* North Carolina Agr. Exp. Sta. Tech. Bul. 160, 1964.

[275] Ricks, D. J., and D. Smith. *Economic Relationships in Tart Cherry Marketing, 1958-1970.* Michigan State University, Dept. Agr. Econ., Rep. 195, 1971.

[276] Rocca, L. H. "Time Series Analysis of Commodity Futures Prices." Unpublished Ph.D. dissertation, University of California, Berkeley, 1969.

[277] Rockwell, C. S. "Normal Backwardation, Forecasting, and the Returns to Commodity Futures Traders." *Food Res. Inst. Studies* 7(suppl.):107-130, 1967.

[278] Rockwell, G. R., Jr. *Income and Household Size: Their Effects on Food Consumption.* USDA Marketing Res. Rep. 340, 1959.

[279] Rogers, G. B. "Pricing Systems and Agricultural Marketing Research." *Agr. Econ. Res.* 22:1-11, January 1970.

[280] Rogers, G. B., and L. A. Voss. *Pricing Systems for Eggs.* USDA Marketing Res. Rep. 850, 1969.

[281] ――――, eds. *Readings on Egg Pricing.* College of Agriculture, University of Missouri, 1971.

[282] Roger, R. O., and G. T. Barton. *Our Farm Production Potential, 1975.* USDA Agr. Inf. Bul. 233, 1960.

[283] Rojko, A. S. *The Demand and Price Structure for Dairy Products.* USDA Tech. Bul. 1168, 1957.

[284] ――――. "Time Series Analysis in Measurement of Demand." *Agr. Econ. Res.* 13:37-54, April 1961.

[285] Samuelson, P. A. *Foundations of Economic Analysis.* New York: Atheneum, 1965. Originally published by Harvard University Press, 1947.

[286] ――――. "Proof That Properly Anticipated Prices Fluctuate Randomly." *Ind. Manag. Rev.* 6:41-49, Spring 1965.

[287] Sanders, J. H., and R. C. Hoyt. "The World Food Problem: Four Recent Empirical Studies." *Am. J. Agr. Econ.* 52:132-135, February 1970.

[288] Schaller, W. N. "Discussion: The Supply Function in Agriculture Revisited." *Am. J. Agr. Econ.* 51:367-369, May 1969.

[289] Schaller, W. N., and G. W. Dean. *Predicting Regional Crop Production: An Application of Recursive Programming.* USDA Tech. Bul. 1329, 1965.

[290] Schuh, G. E. "An Econometric Investigation of the Market for Hired Labor in Agriculture." *J. Farm Econ.* 44:307-321, May 1962.

[291] ――――. *The Supply of Milk in the Detroit Milkshed as Affected by Cost of Production.* Michigan Agr. Exp. Sta. Bul. 259, 1957.

[292] Schultz, H. *The Theory and Measurement of Demand.* Chicago: University of Chicago Press, 1938.

[293] Schultz, T. W. *The Economic Organization of Agriculture.* New York: Mc-Graw-Hill, 1953.

[294] ――――. *Production and Welfare of Agriculture.* New York: Macmillan, 1949.

[295] ――――. "Reflections on Agricultural Production, Output and Supply." *J. Farm Econ.* 38:748-762, August 1956. Reprinted in *Readings in the Economics of Agriculture,* K. A. Fox and D. G. Johnson, eds. Homewood, Ill.: Irwin, 1969.

[296] Scott, F. E., and H. T. Badger. *Farm-Retail Spreads for Food Products.* USDA Misc. Pub. 741 (rev.), 1972.

[297] Searle, S. R. "Topics in Variance Component Estimation." *Biometrics* 27:1-76, March 1971.

[298] Sharples, J. A. "The Representative Farm Approach to Estimation of Supply Response." *Am. J. Agr. Econ.* 51:353-361, May 1969.

[299] Silvestre, H. "Demand Analysis: An Attempt to Develop a Methodology for Detecting the Points in Time Where Structural Changes Took Place." Unpublished Ph.D. dissertation, Cornell University, 1969.

[300] Sinha, R. P. "An Analysis of Food Expenditure in India." *J. Farm Econ.* 48:113-123, February 1966.

[301] Smidt, S. "A Test of the Serial Independence of Price Changes in Soybean Futures." *Food Res. Inst. Studies* 5(2):117-136, 1965.

[302] Smith, R. J. "The Lemon Prorate in the Long Run." *J. Pol. Econ.* 69:573-586, December 1961.

[303] Smyth, D. J. "Effect of Public Price Forecasts on Market Price Variation: A Stochastic Cobweb Example." *Am. J. Agr. Econ.* 55:83-88, February 1973.

[304] Snape, R. H., and B. S. Yamey. "Test of the Effectiveness of Hedging." *J. Pol. Econ.* 73:540-544, October 1965.

[305] Sosnick, S. H. "Bidding Strategy at Ordinary Auctions." *J. Farm Econ.* 45: 163-182, February 1963.

[306] Stallings, J. L. "Weather Indexes." *J. Farm Econ.* 42:180-186, February 1960.

[307] Stanton, B. F. "Seasonal Demand for Beef, Pork, and Broilers." *Agr. Econ. Res.* 13:1-14, January 1961.

[308] Stent, W. R. "An Analysis of the Price of British Beef." *J. Agr. Econ.* 18:121-131, January 1967.

[309] Stevens, R. D. *Elasticity of Food Consumption Associated with Changes in Income in Developing Countries.* USDA For. Agr. Econ. Rep. 23, 1965.

[310] Stewart, B. *An Analysis of Speculative Trading in Grain Futures.* USDA Tech. Bul. 1001, 1949.

[311] Stigler, G. J. "The Early History of Empirical Studies of Consumer Behavior." *J. Pol. Econ.* 62:95-113, April 1954.

[312] Stine, O. C. "Progress in Price Analysis and an Appraisal of Success in Price Forecasting." *J. Farm Econ.* 11:128-140, January 1929.

[313] Stone, R., D. A. Rowe, W. J. Corlett, R. Hurstfield, and M. Potter. *The Measurement of Consumers' Expenditure and Behavior in the United Kingdom, 1920-38.* vol. 1. Cambridge: At the University Press, 1954.

[314] Stout, T. T., and V. W. Ruttan. "Regional Patterns of Technological Change in American Agriculture." *J. Farm Econ.* 40:196-207, May 1958.

[315] Suits, D. B. "Use of Dummy Variables in Regression Equations." *J. Am. Stat. Assoc.* 52:548-551, December 1957.

[316] Suits, D. B., and S. Koizumi. "The Dynamics of the Onion Market." *J. Farm Econ.* 38:475-484, May 1956.

[317] Summers, R. "A Note on Least Squares Bias in Household Expenditure Analysis." *Econometrica* 27:121-126, January 1959.

[318] Suttor, R. E., and R. J. Crom. "Computer Models and Simulation." *J. Farm Econ.* 46:1341-1350, December 1964.

[319] Takayama, T., and G. G. Judge. "An Intertemporal Price Equilibrium Model." *J. Farm Econ.* 46:477-484, May 1964.

[320] ———. *Spatial and Temporal Price and Allocation Models.* Amsterdam: North Holland Publishing, 1971.

[321] Telser, L. G. "Futures Trading and the Storage of Cotton and Wheat." *J. Pol. Econ.* 66:233-255, June 1958.

[322] ———. "The Supply of Speculative Services in Wheat, Corn and Soybeans." *Food Res. Inst. Studies* 7(suppl.):131-176, 1967.

[323] ———. "The Support Program and the Stability of Cotton Prices." *J. Farm Econ.* 39:398-408, May 1957.

[324] Theil H. *Economic Forecasts and Policy.* 2d rev. ed. Amsterdam: North Holland Publishing, 1965.

[325] ———. *Principles of Econometrics.* New York: Wiley, 1971.

[326] Thompson, L. M. *Weather and Technology in the Production of Corn and Soybeans.* Iowa State University, CAED Rep. 17, 1963.

[327] Thompson, R. G., J. M. Sprott, and R. W. Callen. "Demand, Supply, and Price

Relationships for the Broiler Sector, with Emphasis on the Jack-Knife Method." *Am. J. Agr. Econ.* 54:245-248, May 1972.

[328] Tintner, G. *Econometrics.* New York: Wiley, 1952.

[329] Tomek, W. G. "Changes in Price Elasticities of Demand for Beef, Pork, and Broilers." *J. Farm Econ.* 47:793-802, August 1965.

[330] Tomek, W. G., and W. W. Cochrane. "Long-Run Demand: A Concept and Elasticity Estimates for Meats." *J. Farm Econ.* 44:717-730, August 1962.

[331] Tomek, W. G., and R. W. Gray. "Temporal Relationships among Prices on Commodity Futures Markets: Their Allocative and Stabilizing Roles." *Am. J. Agr. Econ.* 52:372-380, August 1970.

[332] Tomek, W. G., and K. L. Robinson. *Agricultural Product Prices.* Ithaca: Cornell University Press, 1972.

[333] Toquero, Z., B. Duff, T. Anden-Lacsina, and Y. Hayami. "Marketable Surplus Functions for a Subsistence Crop: Rice in the Philippines." *Am. J. Agr. Econ.* 57:705-709, November 1975.

[334] Tweeten, L. G. "The Demand for United States Farm Output." *Food Res. Inst. Studies* 7(3):343-369, 1967.

[335] Tweeten, L. G., and J. E. Martin. "A Methodology for Predicting U.S. Farm Real Estate Price Variation." *J. Farm Econ.* 48:378-393, May 1966.

[336] Tweeten, L. G., and C. L. Quance. "Positivistic Measures of Aggregate Supply Elasticities: Some New Approaches." *Am. J. Agr. Econ.* 51:342-352, May 1969.

[337] Tyrchniewicz, E. W., and G. E. Schuh. "Econometric Analysis of the Agricultural Labor Market." *Am. J. Agr. Econ.* 51:770-787, November 1969.

[338] United States Department of Agriculture. *Major Statistical Series of the U.S. Department of Agriculture: Volume 1, Agricultural Prices and Parity.* USDA Agr. Handbook 365, 1970.

[339] ———. Economic Research Service. *The World Food Budget, 1970.* USDA For. Agr. Econ. Rep. 19, 1964.

[340] ———. *The World Food Situation and Prospects to 1985.* USDA For. Agr. Econ. Rep. 98, 1974.

[341] Uvacek, E., Jr. "A New Look at Demand Analysis for Beef." *J. Farm Econ.* 50:1501-1506, December 1968.

[342] Vaile, R. S. "Inverse Carrying Charges in Futures Markets." *J. Farm Econ.* 30:574-575, August 1948.

[343] Vargas Foundation. *Projections of Supply and Demand for Agricultural Products of Brazil through 1975.* Center for Agricultural Studies, Brazilian Institute of Economics, 1968.

[344] Waite, W. C., and H. C. Trelogan. *Agricultural Market Prices.* 2d ed. New York: Wiley, 1951.

[345] Waldorf, W. H. "The Demand for and Supply of Food Marketing Services: An Aggregate View." *J. Farm Econ.* 48:42-60, February 1966. (See also USDA Tech. Bul. 1317.)

[346] Wallace, T. D. "The General Problem of Spatial Equilibrium: A Methodological Issue." In *Interregional Competition Research Methods,* R. A. King, ed. North Carolina State University Agricultural Policy Institute, 1963.

[347] Wallace, T. D., and G. G. Judge. *Econometric Analysis of the Beef and Pork Sectors of the Economy.* Oklahoma Agr. Exp. Sta. Tech. Bul. T-75, 1958.

[348] Walters, F. "Predicting the Beef Cattle Inventory." *Agr. Econ. Res.* 17:10-18, January 1965.

[349] Ward, R. W., and L. B. Fletcher. "From Hedging to Pure Speculation: A Micro Model of Optimal Futures and Cash Market Positions." *Am. J. Agr. Econ.* 53:71-78, February 1971.

[350] Warren, G. F., and F. A. Pearson. *Interrelationships of Supply and Price.* Cornell University Agr. Exp. Sta. Bul. 466, 1928.

[351] Waugh, F. V. "Cobweb Models." *J. Farm Econ.* 46:732-750, November 1964.

[352] ———. *Demand and Price Analysis: Some Examples from Agriculture.* USDA Tech. Bul. 1316, 1964.

[353] ———. *Graphic Analysis: Applications in Agricultural Economics.* USDA Agr. Handbook 326, 1966.

[354] ———. "The Place of Least Squares in Econometrics." *Econometrica* 29:386-396, July 1961.

[355] ———. "Reserve Stocks of Farm Products." In *Agricultural Policy: A Review of Programs and Needs.* National Advisory Commission on Food and Fiber, Tech. Pap. 5, 1967.

[356] ———. "Withholding by Grade." *Am. J. Agr. Econ.* 53:500-501, August 1971.

[357] Waugh, F. V., E. L. Burtis, and A. F. Wolf. "The Controlled Distribution of a Crop among Independent Markets." *Quart. J. Econ.* 51:1-41, November 1936.

[358] Weiss, M., and A. Melnik. "Spectral Analysis as a Tool for Testing a Dynamic Cobweb Model." Econometrics Workshop Paper 6901, Michigan State University, 1969.

[359] West, D. A., and G. E. Brandow. "Space-Product Equilibrium in the Dairy Industry of the Northeastern and North Central Regions." *J. Farm Econ.* 46:719-731, November 1964.

[360] Western Extension Marketing Committee Task Force on Price and Demand Analysis. *A Handbook on the Elasticity of Demand for Agricultural Products in the United States.* Western Extension Marketing Committee Pub. 4, 1967.

[361] Wetmore, J. M., M. E. Abel, E. W. Learn, and W. W. Cochrane. *Policies for Expanding the Demand for Farm Food Products in the United States. Part I, History and Potentials.* Minnesota Agr. Exp. Sta. Tech. Bul. 231, 1959.

[362] Weymar, F. H. "The Supply of Storage Revisited." *Am. Econ. Rev.* 56:1226-1234, December 1966.

[363] Wharton, C. R., Jr. "Rubber Supply Conditions: Some Policy Implications." In *The Political Economy of Independent Malaya*, T. H. Silcock and E. K. Fish, eds. Canberra: Australian National University; Berkeley: University of California Press, 1963. (Also Agricultural Development Council Reprint 3, 1964.)

[364] Williamson, K. C., R. C. Carter, and J. A. Gaines. "Effects of Selected Variables on Prices of Calves in Virginia Feeder Calf Sales." *J. Farm Econ.* 43:697-706, August 1961.

[365] Wipf, L. J., and D. L. Bawden. "Reliability of Supply Equations Derived from Production Functions." *Am. J. Agr. Econ.* 51:170-178, February 1969.

[366] Wold, H. O. A., ed. *Econometric Model Building: Essays on the Causal Chain Approach.* Amsterdam: North Holland Publishing, 1964.

[367] Wold, H. O. A., and L. Jureen. *Demand Analysis; a Study in Econometrics.* New York: Wiley, 1953.

[368] Wolffram, R. "Positivistic Measures of Aggregate Supply Elasticities: Some New Approaches — Some Critical Notes." *Am. J. Agr. Econ.* 53:356-359, May 1971.

[369] Working, E. J. *Demand for Meat.* Chicago: University of Chicago Press, 1954.

[370] ———. "What Do Statistical 'Demand Curves' Show?" *Quart. J. Econ.* 41:212-235, February 1927.

[371] Working, H. "Futures Trading and Hedging." *Am. Econ. Rev.* 43:314-343, June 1953.

[372] ———. "Hedging Reconsidered." *J. Farm Econ.* 35:544-561, November 1953.

[373] ———. "Professor Vaile and the Theory of Inverse Carrying Charges." *J. Farm Econ.* 31:168-172, February 1949.

[374] ———. "Quotations on Commodity Futures as Price Forecasts." *Econometrica* 10:39-52, January 1942.

[375] ———. "Tests of a Theory Concerning Floor Trading on Commodity Exchanges." *Food Res. Inst. Studies* 7(suppl.):5-48, 1967.

[376] ———. "A Theory of Anticipatory Prices." *Am. Econ. Rev.* 48:188-199, May 1958.

[377] ———. "The Theory of Price of Storage." *Am. Econ. Rev.* 39:1254-1262, December 1949.

[378] Zepp, G. A., and R. H. McAlexander. "Predicting Aggregate Milk Production: An Empirical Study." *Am. J. Agr. Econ.* 51:642-649, August 1969.

[379] Zusman, P. "An Investigation of the Dynamic Stability and Stationary States of the United States Potato Market, 1930-1958." *Econometrica* 30:522-547, July 1962.

[380] Zusman, P., A. Melamed, and I. Katzir. *Possible Trade and Welfare Effects of EEC Tariff and "Reference Price" Policy on the European-Mediterranean Market for Winter Oranges.* University of California, Giannini Foundation Monograph 24, 1969.

Part VI. Agricultural Finance
and Capital Markets

This review covers the American literature of agricultural finance and capital markets since the end of World War II. It focuses on farm capital and financing needs, the financial structure of agriculture, rural financial intermediaries, and closely related topics. The first section of the review provides a perspective on the preceding research literature and an overview of postwar research trends and publications in the context of the historical events that helped to shape their content. A more detailed topical review constitutes the core of the paper. The concluding section presents a generalized evaluation and suggests some reorientations and challenges for future work.

Undoubtedly much deserving literature has been overlooked in this review. In fact, we had expected far fewer than the over two thousand professionally oriented publications which we compiled with the aid of Harriet Holderness and Marian Sayre, and even that list is probably incomplete. (A sequel to it, the *Agricultural Finance Bibliography*, is available from Emanuel Melichar, Federal Reserve Board, Washington, D.C. 20551.)

The review reflects the literature known to us as of April 1975. The data cited, however, have been updated to reflect revisions available as of July 1976.

Appreciation is expressed to our reviewers: Peter J. Barry, Fred L. Garlock, George D. Irwin, Lawrence A. Jones, Warren F. Lee, and John B. Penson, Jr. Their critical comments were most helpful. We, of course, are responsible for the final product, including errors of judgment, omission, or commission.

J. R. B.

E. M.

Agricultural Finance
and Capital Markets

John R. Brake
Professor of Agricultural Economics
Michigan State University
Emanuel Melichar
Senior Economist, Division of Research and Statistics
Board of Governors of the Federal Reserve System

In a field heavily influenced by historical events and public policies it seems a disservice to pick up the literature as of a certain date — say, January 1, 1946 — without briefly reviewing preceding work.

Agricultural finance specialists at that time — as demonstrated, for example, by Wall's contribution to *The Story of Agricultural Economics* [288] and by several textbooks published during the next few years — perceived their field as being concerned primarily with the role and performance of institutional and noninstitutional farm lenders and with other financial developments including capital investments and movements in land prices. For three decades professionals in agricultural finance had participated in recognizing the deficiencies of existing arrangements and in creating and molding major institutions: the federal land banks in 1916, the federal intermediate credit banks in 1923, the production credit associations in 1933, and the Farm Security Administration (later the Farmers Home Administration) in 1938. The description and analysis of the development, impact, and problems of farm lending institutions received primary attention in agricultural finance literature.

The major institutional alterations were, of course, prompted by equally turbulent events. Within their lifetimes, and in many cases during their careers, most agricultural finance analysts working in 1946 had witnessed (1) the speculative farmland boom of World War I, spurred by high farm product prices and incomes and accompanied by rapid and large increases in farm

413

mortgage debt; (2) the collapse of the farm boom in 1920 followed by thirteen consecutive years of declining farmland prices, severe debt repayment difficulties, and widespread rural bank failures; (3) the great national depression, involving massive farm foreclosures followed by greatly increased governmental involvement in agriculture, including the provision of credit; and (4) a recovery in farm income and land prices, soon transformed into another wartime boom.

From the beginning of professional work in finance, shortly after the turn of the century, the research emphasis was on credit. At the United States Department of Agriculture (USDA), early examples are a 1914 publication by Carver [76] on how to use farm credit and a 1916 study by Thompson [267] on factors affecting interest rates on short-term farm loans. The 1924 Yearbook of Agriculture, which presented a comprehensive description of the credit, insurance, and tax situation of farmers [221], indicates the primary interests of USDA finance personnel during the 1920s. In addition, the USDA Division of Land Economics annually published *The Farm Real Estate Situation*.

During the farm debt difficulties of the 1920s three men — Garlock, Murray, and Wall — launched professional careers that guided and shaped much agricultural finance research well into the period to be covered by this paper. By the late 1920s Murray and Garlock [208] had collaborated on a study of farm mortgage debt in Iowa. From his base at Iowa State University Murray continued to focus on farm appraisals and financing, while Garlock joined the USDA, where he and Wall each undertook several studies of rural banking difficulties [111, 113, 289].

In the 1930s Wall and Garlock became the nucleus of the agricultural finance staff in the USDA. Their ideas and efforts provided the foundation for data collection and ongoing analyses continued to this date. In 1938 they and others in the USDA initiated the *Agricultural Finance Review*, a periodical specializing in finance data and articles. Earlier, in 1931, both were involved in another landmark effort, coordinated by J. D. Black [37], to outline a far-reaching research program in agricultural credit, delineating the problem areas and specifying appropriate research approaches to each problem.

With the outbreak of World War II policy and research shifted rapidly toward coping with the probability of another boom-bust sequence. In 1941 Governor A. G. Black of the Farm Credit Administration was instrumental in organizing the National Agricultural Credit Committee, in which representatives of the major farm lenders could exchange information on farm lending experience and strive to present a united front against speculative excesses. Within the USDA agricultural finance workers collaborated on an urgent and major effort to measure and analyze the wartime changes in farm finances, in the process compiling the account of assets and debts that became known as the Balance Sheet of Agriculture. With some relief their report, *Impact of the War on the Financial Structure of Agriculture* [270], noted that farm debt had continued to decline rather than to rise as in World War I. But as the war ended and commodity price ceilings were removed, many analysts feared that a credit-financed boom might yet occur. Land prices were rising rapidly, and pent-up demand for farm machinery and buildings far exceeded available supplies.

In this setting agricultural finance work entered the period covered by this paper. The content of several agricultural finance textbooks that appeared at this time is indicative of the orientation and thinking of the principal workers in the field.

Murray's *Agricultural Finance* [207] appeared in 1941, followed by a second edition in 1947 and a third in 1953. After explaining the capital needs of farming, it emphasized the need to use credit soundly and wisely to avoid the possibility of repayment problems. A major portion of each edition was devoted to describing the alternative sources of credit, especially lending institutions.

A flurry of other textbooks that appeared during these years echoed this theme and emphasis with only minor variations. Norton's undergraduate text [219] featured rules for sound use of credit. Duggan, then governor of the Farm Credit Administration, collaborated with Battles on a text [93] that also emphasized lenders' procedures for effectively evaluating farm loan requests. (In reviewing this book, which he thought aimed at students of vocational agriculture, Butz [72] detected partiality toward the cooperative Farm Credit System.) Troelston's text [272], considered to be written from a borrower's point of view, presented more historical perspective and discussion of individual farm credit problems and principles but again emphasized sources of credit. In 1954 the American Institute of Banking [5] capped this prolific period of text production with an institutionally oriented volume for use in its educational programs for agricultural bankers. None of these efforts, however, enjoyed the success of Murray's work, which after its third edition in 1953 became the "standard" and virtually only college text employed in agricultural finance courses during the next twenty years.

Clearly, judging from these works and from Wall's detailed story of prewar agricultural finance research [288], the primary expertise of agricultural finance workers was regarded as knowledge of credit arrangements and sources, and their primary research roles dealt with the performance of the lenders and with the identification and management of credit problems.

Overview of the Postwar Literature

The first part of the postwar period was characterized by continuing concern about the possible aftermaths of the land and investment booms in progress and continuing examination of the performance and adequacy of farm lending institutions.

Lenders' apprehensions at the time are exemplified by Nowell's recitation [220] at the 1946 meeting of the American Farm Economic Association of the numerous factors responsible for what he feared to be the headlong rush of agriculture into financial disaster. That such fears were not confined to lenders was illustrated in 1945 by the North Central Regional Land Tenure Committee's bulletin, *Preventing Farm Land Price Inflation in the Midwest* [218]. As late as 1954, in introducing their comprehensive study of farm mortgage lending experience during the interwar period, Jones and Durand noted [170]: "In the past, such periods of high prices and incomes have been short-lived, and the ensuing periods of depression have been severe and characterized by widespread farm mortgage distress. Whether the rise associated with World War II will have a like sequel remains to be seen."

The evaluation of lending institutions continued with individual efforts such as Butz's study of production credit associations [73], organized projects such as the American Farm Economic Association committee report on Farm Credit System agencies in 1947 [30], and large-scale cooperative data collection efforts such as, in 1947, the Federal Reserve System's first national survey of farm loans and borrowers at commercial banks [39]. Subsequently, the development of detailed cross-section data using large samples of loans and borrowers at all major institutional farm lenders was undertaken in 1956 and again in 1966 as a coordinated effort of the USDA, the Farm Credit Administration, and the Federal Reserve System. Numerous publications resulted from each of these projects — at least forty, for example, were based on the 1956 surveys.

Monitoring of overall financial conditions and developments continued to be centered in the USDA, where it revolved around the annual *Balance Sheet of Agriculture*, surveys of farm real estate market developments, and additional surveys supporting a new annual publication, the *Agricultural Finance Outlook*. The Marshall Plan and Korean War years brought higher farm prices and, in contrast to World War II, sharp increases in outstanding debt. An equally rapid decline in farm output prices soon followed, accompanied by a drought in the Southwest, an upper turning point in the cattle cycle, and a national economic recession. Land prices and total farm debt fell in 1953; the next annual meeting of the American Farm Economic Association included a session on safe debt loads.

Disaster, however, did not follow as it had three decades earlier. Rather, there ensued a cost-price squeeze that could be attacked by increasing productivity and expanding the size of individual farms and enterprises. A resumed upward trend in land prices further rewarded those who employed credit boldly in such uses. Nelson's *Credit as a Tool for the Agricultural Producer* [212] exemplified the new order. This change in orientation was incorporated into the profession's standard text when Nelson joined Murray as coauthor of the 1960 edition [209]. The new text put more emphasis on differentiating among farm risks and on returns and repayment capacity as guides to credit use. Also, the perspective was broadened to include noncredit means of acquiring capital.

The farm credit problems that attracted research attention in the 1950s, as reflected in numerous publications and in sessions at meetings of the association, revolved around discrepancies between institutional lending practices and the financing terms sought by farmers desiring to enlarge their operations. Thus problems with land appraisal norms, the financing of beginning farmers, and the maturities on borrowing for intermediate-term investments were examined along with such approaches and solutions as land contracts, family partnerships and corporations, and budgeting methods.

When contrasted with prewar events, however, these represented relatively minor adjustments in financing arrangements. The institutional structure had essentially stabilized after the major innovations of the 1930s. Thus finance specialists were no longer in the front lines of formulating public farm policy. Their work involving the improvement of data collection and data quality, the suggestion and description of minor institutional adjustments, or, for example, the listing of factors influencing land prices suffered by comparison with the ongoing explosion of econometric supply-demand analyses and of linear programming applications to farm management. In some quarters professional regard for the theory, techniques, and research output of agricultural finance was at a low ebb in the late 1950s and early 1960s.

Several of the more ambitious basic research efforts of the 1950s were produced by USDA personnel on joint appointment with the National Bureau of Economic Research. In retrospect, these and other basic efforts at the time were severely limited by the unavailability of proper data, appropriate statistical techniques, and large-scale computational capability — all conditions later substantially alleviated through the passage of time, new data-collection efforts, and advances in the econometric and computer sciences.

For example, Tostlebe [268, 269] painstakingly constructed and examined the fund flows involved in capital formation and its financing. Although he succeeded in deriving useful insights, the same approach later produced much greater returns after being enhanced by the capability to estimate equations explaining each of the flows and then to make simulations and projections involving the entire system. Such empirical projects were also initially hampered because key capital, credit, and land price and transfer series were measured only on an annual basis, so that postwar observations available in the 1950s were too few to support meaningful empirical analysis, while use of data from the preceding three decades was suspect because of the particularly large structural changes that had obviously occurred in agriculture. In contrast, empirical work in many other fields could proceed using the more ample postwar observations on a quarterly, monthly, or even daily basis.

As another example, Horton [155] in 1957 published extensive analyses relating various farm characteristics to farm financial structure, using county-average data from the 1940 Census of Agriculture for a national sample of 108 counties. Its applicability to conditions in the late 1950s was immediately questioned [211]. More importantly, its approach and results were effectively rendered obsolete within a few years when the Bureau of the Census obtained similar but more detailed data for a national sample of over eleven thousand farms, and the quantum advances in computational capabilities permitted multivariate analyses employing all of these individual observations.

Thus in the 1960s agricultural finance staged its own revolution through newly found uses of theoretical concepts and quantitative analysis. Initiation of the transition was marked by a symposium on capital and credit needs in a changing agriculture (1959). The papers presented there by many leading agricultural economists, published in 1961 [28], helped to revive and refocus research attention on the structure and financing of agriculture.

At the macro level econometric work began to flourish. The parade of publications began in 1959, when both Griliches [117] and Cromarty [86] completed studies of the demand for farm machinery. In 1963 Heady and Tweeten [132] published extensive work on numerous types of capital investments as well as on land prices. By 1966 Herdt and Cochrane [136], Reynolds [242] and Tweeten and colleagues [274, 275] had all constructed detailed models of farmland prices. Additional work on these key elements of uses of funds continued to appear, both as specialized projects and as parts of broader farm sector studies and models. In contrast, econometric work on farm credit within a supply-demand framework has until recently languished after initial reports by Hesser and Schuh in the early 1960s [144, 145].

More recently, comprehensive models of capital and credit flows have been developed to explain past changes and to project future changes in total farm debt and to serve other related uses. After Brake in 1966 [62] reported projections for 1980 based on a largely judgmental flows model, subsequent work reflected progressively greater degrees of detail and sophistication. Melichar and Doll in 1969 [198] constructed several alternative projections

based mainly on the earlier work of others; then Melichar [192, 196] reported a comprehensive financial sector model which primarily estimated and
extrapolated past trends and relationships. In 1973 Lins and Penson each
completed large-scale sector models, with Lins [186] emphasizing disaggregation by sources of funds and Penson [225] by uses. The simultaneous equations model constructed by Penson and his colleagues — the Aggregative Income and Wealth Simulator — has been used in USDA studies of the impact
of alternative policies and was used to obtain the projections of capital formation, real estate transfers, and increase in outstanding debt published in the
Agricultural Finance Outlook for 1974 [278], the first such direct use of an
econometric model in any of the USDA's official outlook work.

In 1960 new possibilities for study of debt relationships among individual
farms were opened up when the Bureau of the Census, with assistance from
the USDA and the Federal Reserve System, conducted the first national sample survey of debts owed by individual farmers and farm landlords. These
data enabled Allen [2], Atkinson [10], Garlock [112], and others [90, 141,
194, 204] to explore various disaggregations of outstanding debt, to compare
indebted and debt-free farmers, and to relate debt to various characteristics
of the borrowers and their farms. Several of these studies employed econometric multivariate techniques. Similar census surveys were conducted in
1965 and 1970, with the sample size of the latter expanded to permit analyses
at the state level. A significant historical data base has been accumulated
through these efforts.

Evaluation of the performance of farm lending institutions continued during the 1960s, first in the form of several papers prepared in 1963 for the
Commission on Money and Credit [83, 84], then in numerous studies based
on the 1966 surveys of farm loans outstanding at all major lenders. Among
the latter were several multivariate analyses of factors affecting interest rates
charged on different types of farm loans [264, 265].

Institutions also undertook self-examination of their practices. Melichar
and Doll in 1969 [198] studied the farm lending problems of banks as part of
the Federal Reserve Board's reappraisal of its discount mechanism. The board
subsequently implemented a seasonal borrowing privilege particularly useful
to rural banks [199]. In 1968 and 1969 the cooperative Farm Credit System
undertook a broad reexamination of the credit needs of farmers and rural
residents [99, 100]. As a result, it changed several of its practices and in the
Farm Credit Act of 1971 obtained various new and broadened lending authorities, including the authority to make some types of rural nonfarm loans.
In the 1970s the Federal Reserve Board's special Committee on Rural Banking Problems sponsored work on various mechanisms that could be used by
rural banks to obtain nonlocal funds [42]. In all these and in other studies at-

tention began to turn to the process and efficiency of financial intermediation in agriculture and in rural areas in contrast to the previous narrower emphasis on lending agencies and farm financing.

Theoretical and analytical developments with equally signficant impact occurred at the micro level. Following Baker and Irwin's seminal work on lender restrictions as a factor in farming adjustments [18, 19, 161], many studies examined the means of acquiring control over capital resources, mainly in the context of growth models of the farm firm. Baker and his colleagues at the University of Illinois published a series of reports on the roles of liquidity and leverage in farm financial management and on the effects of external lender policies [12, 13, 23, 260, 286]. At Purdue University Patrick, Harshbarger, Boehlje, Eisgruber, and White constructed several simulation models permitting study of firm growth and estate transfers [44, 45, 128, 224]. Elsewhere, S. R. Johnson [169] and Martin and Plaxico [189] also developed multiperiod growth models. These new approaches, along with the new emphasis on financial intermediation and financial markets, were evident in the proceedings of a 1968 workshop at the University of Illinois that brought together many economists to discuss issues and problems in agricultural finance [152].

Revisions in textbooks provide further evidence of the changing orientation of agricultural finance. Nelson and Murray's fifth edition in 1967 [214] did not fully reflect the ongoing developments and consequently was sharply criticized on that account by John Lee [181]. Following the addition of Warren Lee as coauthor, the sixth edition in 1973 [213] took on a quite different emphasis with the inclusion of discussion of capital budgeting, cash-flow analysis, and financial markets and with less discussion of lending institutions.

In 1973 a new text by Hopkin, Barry, and Baker [153] also reflected the new approaches. Cash-flow budgeting was presented as the analytical tool for applying the concepts of liquidity and leverage to the problems of obtaining control over farm resources. Lending institutions were treated only briefly in the context of financial intermediation, with emphasis also given to leasing and nonfarm equity capital as alternatives in acquiring resource control. In neither of the 1973 texts does one find the cautious approach and warnings about debt that characterized texts only twenty years earlier.

A reorientation in agricultural finance research in the late 1960s was also evident in the Agricultural Finance Branch of the USDA Economic Research Service. New emphasis was put on the financial structure of the farming sector, flow-of-funds social accounts, and conceptualization of farm financial management. Examples of this new thrust were articles by Irwin, Lins, and Penson [163, 227] and Bostwick [46, 47]. In 1973, however, a reorganization of the Economic Research Service resulted in dissolution of the Agricultural Finance Branch. Researchers formerly in the branch were assigned to four different program areas, purportedly to consolidate similar areas of work. A useful review of the reorientation and subsequent reorganization, along with information on previous work and organization in the USDA, has recently been provided by Jones, Wiser, and Woods [172].

With the perspective provided by the foregoing overview, we now turn to a more detailed topical review of agricultural finance literature since 1945.

Capital Formation and Accumulation

Capital is not easily defined, in part because of continuing debate among economists. However, Solow [261] states that "the proper scope of capital theory is the elucidation of the causes and consequences of acts of saving and investment." As in most definitions of capital, the implication is that capital represents durable goods saved from consumption for the purpose of adding to future production. Belshaw [29] sees capital in a slightly different context, as the accumulated stock of real wealth, which covers land as well as produced goods. Saving and investment thus add to the stock of capital. Credit differs from capital in that it represents only one means of obtaining control over capital or assets.

At the micro level capital refers to the productive assets of a firm, including real estate, machinery, livestock, inventories, and cash balances. This concept is consistent with the general connotation of "capitalizing" a business, which refers to the acquisition of all its productive assets rather than just its plant and equipment. Over time, with capital becoming more important relative to labor inputs, increasing attention has been focused on the processes of capital formation and accumulation.

Theory

Economists in general have devoted considerable attention to the theory of capital formation and accumulation or growth. Agricultural finance workers have found this work generally applicable to their subject, if one may fairly judge from their limited attention to development of specialized formulations. However, Tuck [273] emphasized their need to employ theory applicable to individual proprietorships operating in a competitive environment. Thus, he contended, attempts to use generalized optimization models in studying the distribution of agricultural capital among individual farms must consider variation in management ability of farmers and must also recognize that price and production uncertainties tend to hamper ex ante optimization.

Some basic observations on aggregate farm capital formation have been summarized by G. L. Johnson [168]:

> Farm capital formation takes place rapidly when farmers are in a position to gain directly from reinvesting part of their income and when they have major responsibility for investment in direct farm production. . . . Rapid capital formation occurs when the public makes substantial investments in both the general and technical education of farmers, in improved technology for farming, and in its extension to farmers. . . . Formation of farm capital is accelerated when the transfer of capital from the farm to the nonfarm sector is left to voluntary processes, including transfers in the form of inherited monetary capital as well as training received by farm children who migrate to nonfarm occupations. On the other hand, programs designed to force income out of agriculture make private agricultural investment unattractive . . . Lagging farm capital formation can be stimulated with favorable price programs and credit assistance to individual farmers. . . . Both publicly and privately managed systems of direct agricultural production tend to be characterized by underinvestment in public facilities for agricultural research and extension and in general education, roads, and other public facilities.

There are, no doubt, other factors that could be listed. Certainly tax laws affecting capital gains, new investment, and depreciation are thought by policy makers to influence capital formation.

Researchers have also sought a conceptual framework for studies of financial management at the firm level. Bostwick [46] envisioned farmers as dealing with three sets of resources — productive, financial, and human — requiring the exercise of five managerial functions: investment, ownership, management, labor, and entrepreneurship. Later Bostwick [47] proposed, for analytical purposes, the partitioning of financial returns among the investment, ownership, and entrepreneurship functions.

Sources of Capital

Farm firms acquire capital in a variety of ways. Equity capital is obtained through gifts and inheritances, savings from farm and off-farm income, and investment from relatives or others through establishment of partnerships or corporations. Borrowing provides control over outside funds that are then used to purchase assets or inputs. Leasing and contract production constitute means of obtaining control over assets owned by others.

Arrangements through which outside capital could enter agriculture attracted considerable attention throughout the postwar period. In some types of farming substantial capital is provided by agribusiness firms seeking, through vertical coordination, to secure greater control over their production inputs or over the market for their output. Mighell and Jones [200] found large proportions of output being produced under integrated or contractual arrangements in the fluid milk, broiler, turkey, vegetable, seed corn, sugar, and citrus fruit industries. Financial arrangements associated with the rapid spread of vertical integration in the broiler industry during the 1950s were examined by a number of studies [123, 210].

Nonfarm venture capital was also attracted into certain farming enterprises that appeared to offer speculative or tax-shelter opportunities [127]. Scofield [249] studied agricultural ventures registered with the Securities and Exchange Commission during 1970-71. A majority were limited partnerships that intended to enter cattle feeding or to establish citrus groves, nut orchards, and vineyards. Most of the remaining registrations involved the direct sale of beef breeding herds. Only a few stock offerings were registered, and most of these had agribusiness as well as farming aspects.

Scofield [250] later estimated that as of 1973 large-scale cattle feedlots had raised between $200 and $300 million in equity capital from outside investors through the sale of limited partnership interests and other means. These funds provided from 15 to 20 percent of the total equity capital needed by the industry. A considerable portion of this capital was apparently lost during the financial reverses suffered by cattle feeders in 1974.

In 1967 the Secretary of Agriculture, in response to widespread concern about an apparent increase in corporate farming, directed the Economic Research Service to conduct a survey to determine the number, kinds, and general characteristics of corporations directly involved in farm production. In his analysis of these data Coffman [81] reported that the 13,300 corporations with farming operations accounted for 8 percent of annual sales of farm products. Four-fifths of the corporations, however, were controlled by individuals or families, and these accounted for 71 percent of the annual sales by corporations. Corporate farming was relatively most important in Hawaii, Florida, California, and the mountain states.

In 1969 the Census of Agriculture first provided for the identification of corporate farms. About 1,800 farms were found to be operated by corporations with more than ten stockholders. These nonfamily corporations operated 1.6 percent of all farmland and accounted for 2.8 percent of total production. Reimund [234], using 1969 data from the census and from Dun and Bradstreet, recently completed a report describing the activities of 410 large multiestablishment firms (including noncorporate firms) with farming operations. These firms accounted for 7 percent of total United States farm production, though their farming activities represented only 5 percent of their total annual sales.

Leasing of real estate and livestock owned by landlords is a common and traditional method of obtaining control over productive assets. The 1969 Census of Agriculture indicated that 13 percent of farm operators leased all of their land, and another 25 percent rented part of the land they operated. The decision to rent or to buy real estate is a major element in many "getting started," growth, and other studies that are reviewed later.

Leasing of farm machinery is a newer development. Irwin and Smith [165] found evidence that, as of 1970, such leasing was increasing rapidly but still involved only a minute proportion of the total machinery stock. Irwin and Penn [164] have reported that custom hiring, a more traditional practice, may enjoy new growth as a result of the rising capital flow required annually to maintain and add to the machinery stock, as well as because of the trend toward larger, more specialized machines. About 60 percent of commercial farmers reported expenditures for machine hire and custom work in 1969, with slightly over half of the custom work being performed by other farm operators.

As these studies of outside capital sources tend to indicate, the farming sector as a whole continues to acquire most of its capital through saving and borrowing. (In viewing the sector as a whole, most inheritances are merely intrasector transfers of title, and with the sector defined to include farm landlords, the same is true of shifts of ownership among operators and landlords.) A number of studies have therefore attempted to ascertain the relative importance of these two major sources. Because direct estimates of saving are not available, these studies have generally related borrowing to some measure of total capital flow.

Tostlebe [268] compared net borrowing (the change in outstanding debt) to the sum of the major elements of capital formation — purchases of machinery, buildings, and land improvements and the net increase in inventories of livestock and crops and in principal financial assets. He found that borrowing financed a relatively small proportion of capital formation during the first half of this century, except during World War I.

Tostlebe also estimated net capital formation by subtracting the depreciation of buildings and machinery from gross capital formation. Then, he noted, the difference between such net capital formation and net borrowing could be regarded as the net investment financed from farmers' net income. His estimates indicated that such net investment was negative during periods of agricultural depression before 1950.

A similar calculation has been published annually as the "farm business sector" of the national flow-of-funds accounts maintained by the Federal Reserve Board. Since the mid-1950s the annual net investment so calculated has consistently been negative, which has surprised some analysts who are unaware of the basis for these values. Melichar [195] pointed out that whereas the full amount of net borrowing entered into the calculation, at least one major capital flow financed in large part by such borrowing did not. Upon adding in estimates of the capital required to purchase real estate from persons leaving the farming sector, he found positive net investment throughout 1950-69. During the 1960s net investment so defined averaged 9 percent of net farm income and 5 percent of total net income (farm and off-farm) and financed about two-thirds of the total flow of capital for gross capital formation and the real estate purchases. Net borrowing financed the remaining one-third — a much higher proportion than in earlier decades.

With the recent downward revision in the USDA estimates of total farm debt, net borrowing during the 1960s is now shown to have averaged about one-fourth rather than one-third of total capital flow — still more than in previous periods.

The USDA has since 1973 employed a similar concept in its analyses of the agricultural finance situation and outlook [278, 279]. Between 1970 and 1973, as the total cash flow of capital doubled, net borrowing rose even more rapidly, reaching 40 percent of the total capital flow in 1973 and 37 percent in 1974. Since the late 1950s, therefore, borrowing has constituted a relatively more important source of capital than in most preceding years of this century; however, well over half of each year's capital flow continued to be financed from noncredit sources, mainly savings.

Demand for Capital by the Firm

The demand for capital is a derived demand based on the potential net returns from investment opportunities. Using this proposition as a point of departure, several researchers have estimated the capital needs of individual farm firms. For example, Wise, Plato, and Saunders [298] used linear programming to determine the minimum investment in operating and long-term capital required to achieve given levels of net farm income.

For estimating the returns to capital, some studies employed the Cobb-Douglas production function or other econometric approaches relating the demand for capital to its costs and returns. Yotopoulos [300] demonstrated that such analyses are improved if capital inputs are specified as service flows rather than as capital stocks. He also suggested a methodology for estimating service flow inputs from the more readily available data on capital stocks.

Burkett [70] explored the ability of farm operators to accumulate equity on various sizes of representative farms. On the larger farms more than one generation was typically required to accumulate, develop, and maintain the capital employed. Only on large farms did part-owners or tenants have sufficient farm earnings to make significant progress toward full ownership from this source alone.

Life Cycle of the Firm

Several studies have related the financial characteristics of farm firms to the life cycle of the firm or operator. Wirth [292] argued the need for more financial information specifically related to the establishment, expansion, and consolidation stages of the firm life cycle. Barry and Brake [24] suggested the life cycle as one important component of the conceptual framework for research on financial strategies of the firm.

The expansion stage of the firm life cycle has been found to be a particularly critical period, as farmers in this stage tend to have debt commitments that are high in relation to net incomes, cash flow, and assets [66]. Dorner and Sandretto [92] found that capital availability restricted firm growth during the early period of expansion, while later in the life cycle labor became the limiting resource and capital tended to be substituted for labor.

Some studies have concentrated on capital constraints facing beginning farmers. Kanel [173] estimated that farming opportunities could accommodate only one-third of maturing farm youth. Reiss [240] suggested that families beginning farming could minimize capital needs by shifting capital requirements to landlords through appropriate tenure arrangements, by substituting labor for capital, and by arranging for smaller annual cash payments when purchasing capital goods. In another study Shoemaker and Miller [257] attributed a successful start in farming to previous farm experience and training, substantial aid from relatives, and control of enough resources to employ the family labor force efficiently.

Rodewald, Larson, and Myrick [245], in their study of Montana dryland grain farms, described how the most common method of obtaining initial control over capital has changed since the years when land was obtained by homesteading. During the 1920s and 1930s land purchase was the most common method, but since 1940, and particularly after 1950, a large proportion of farmers were starting by renting all of their farmland. In Michigan Brake and Wirth [66] found that help from relatives had also become more important.

Problems of asset management also occur toward the end of the life cycle. A recent study by Lee and Brake [182] indicated that retiring farmers typically lost from 15 to 40 percent of the value of their farm assets in the course of liquidating them for retirement income. As noted later, Boehlje and Eisgruber [44] also found problems at this stage of the life cycle, and more analytical attention to it appears to be in order.

Management of Financial Resources

Various studies have examined the management of financial resources including liquidity management, effects of capital position and leverage on growth and adjustment, internal and external capital rationing, farm and family financial planning, firm-household relationships, and the effects of income, capital gains, and inheritance taxes on financial resources and income. In this literature considerations relating to capital and credit are often inexorably entwined, and the review has little choice but to reflect this condition.

Over the postwar period the nature of these studies underwent distinct changes as events altered attitudes and needs and as new analytical techniques became available. In the 1950s discussions were frequently phrased in the context of capital rationing, which was often considered synonymous with credit rationing. Attention focused on the attitudes, institutions, arrangements, and policies that affected the capital (credit) that farmers would employ and that lenders would make available.

The advent of multiperiod programming techniques provided a powerful tool for quantification and analysis of the relationships between these factors and the ultimate goal of progress in a farmer's income or net worth. Thus after 1960 more of these discussions appeared in the context of firm growth models. Emphasis shifted toward consideration of strategies for maximizing growth within the observed or hypothesized external and internal constraints, in contrast to the previous emphasis on ascertaining desirable changes in these constraints.

CAPITAL RATIONING

A study reported in 1949 illustrates attitudes commonly held directly after the war, which were significantly influenced by two prewar decades of difficulties in repaying farm debt. McNall and Mitchell [191], after surveying all 139 farms in one Wisconsin township in 1939 and again in 1946, asked, "What is the basis of farm financial progress?" The most influential factors explaining variation in progress among these farmers appeared to be size of farm and relative managerial ability. But, for this review, perhaps the most interesting aspect is the frame of mind from which the role of debt was examined: "Another of the factors which might conceivably influence the farmer's financial progress is the debt load he assumes when he buys his farm. There has been considerable speculation concerning the wisdom of the federal government policy during the past years of increasing farm ownership through 100 percent loans. Is that too heavy a load for a farmer to overcome?" The answer from the survey data was duly reported: "Such heavy loans of themselves need not represent insurmountable handicaps to owner-operators. . . . .

larger debts apparently do not slow up the process of asset accumulation to any extent when associated with large enough farms."

As noted earlier, these cautious attitudes born of prewar experience were widespread and were echoed in the agricultural finance textbooks of the time. Attention to the means of acquiring control over capital resources centered primarily on borrowing. Both lenders and borrowers were cautioned about the dangers of incurring debt in the face of uncertain prospects for farm income and land prices. Rules indicating the limits of "safe" debt loads were the order of the day. In other words, both external and internal capital rationing were advised to minimize the chances of debt repayment problems.

In contrast, some influential early postwar monographs on farm organization and policy took a rather different view of capital rationing. D. G. Johnson, in *Forward Prices for Agriculture* [167], asked why the bulk of American farms were relatively inefficient units of below-optimum size. His answer centered around external capital rationing — "the inability of the borrower to obtain all the capital funds desired at the going rates of interest." Given uncertainty about profit prospects, "lenders do not provide . . . loan funds in amounts which would equalize the rate of return and the interest rates. . . . In order to assure . . . the repayment of interest and principal . . . (1) the ratio of borrowed to owned capital is kept below some prescribed level . . . and (2) the rate of return on capital is kept at a high level." He therefore proposed policies designed to reduce uncertainty. When, as the postwar period progressed, actual governmental policies toward agriculture did have this effect, lender and borrower attitudes shifted toward increased use of capital as Johnson had anticipated.

Johnson also noted conditions which much later work would explore. The degree of external capital rationing, he observed, varied with the type and purpose of the credit request — cattle-feeding loans were favored over hog enterprises. The large down payments required on real estate loans were inducing beginning farmers to start with uneconomically small units or to lease their land. Loans to purchase farm machinery with a useful life of ten years had to be repaid within three years or less.

In *Production and Welfare of Agriculture* [247] Schultz took a similar tack: ". . . the customary practices of credit institutions are such that a farmer in the heart of the Corn Belt with less than $5,000 of assets is not permitted to establish a firm of optimum size except by renting. . . . It is necessary to go a step farther and examine why the practice of capital rationing has become established. . . . the tap root of this practice is grounded chiefly in economic uncertainty. . . . if it were only risk that was at stake in the gap which separates expectations and realizations . . . creditors and landlords would merely add the necessary risk premium and allow farmers to obtain all the resources which they would care to hire."

Rationing by borrowers, Schultz noted, varies directly with the ebb and flow of the general outlook; though creditors have developed a set of rules to safeguard their interests from unexpected changes, these exhibit an elasticity over time that stems directly out of the general state of confidence. Thus, "after a run of years when returns to agriculture were distinctly favorable, such as prevailed from 1900 to 1910, the effective margins required by creditors were lowered. Hence, also, the effects of capital rationing were less pronounced. In contrast, after the decade of more or less chronic depression experienced by much of the Corn Belt agriculture following 1920, creditors in a number of ways increased the effective margin even though the traditional ratios of debt to property values were not altered." Appraisals were stiffened, more operating capital was insisted upon, and shorter-term contracts were introduced. Meanwhile, interest rates declined even as uncertainty rose, which "further focuses attention upon the overall fact that the supply of resources which the farmer is permitted to hire in the capital market is rationed by factors other than price."

Earlier, in *Agriculture in an Unstable Economy* [246], Schultz had put his argument more bluntly: "The main deterrents [to enlargement of small family farms] are lack of knowledge about modern farm technology and its requirements, price uncertainty, and, most serious, the vise of capital rationing which squeezes the small farmer. Credit institutions, private and public, are geared too much to an outmoded farm technology and are not prepared to serve many farm families in enlarging their units, especially in the South where the need for this adjustment is greatest."

The needs perceived in these works ranked high among the concerns of the agricultural finance literature of the 1950s, particularly in view of the farm price, income, and organizational developments of the period. Public policy toward agriculture cushioned the adjustment to new output and input price levels after the Korean War but stopped short of preventing a cost-price squeeze. To maintain individual farm incomes in the face of that event, farmers sought greater efficiency through new technology and farm enlargement. In response to felt needs agricultural finance research and discussions centered on such topics as the increasing problems of getting started in farming or in transferring the farm estate, the use of credit in making farm adjustments, and the need for lenders to provide credit terms more appropriate for financing adjustments, enlargement, and greater machinery investment [7, 9, 59, 95, 124, 146, 183].

By 1960 more of the onus for capital rationing was being placed on farmers.

After surveying Indiana farmers, Hesser and Janssen [142] reported that three out of four farmers exhibited capital rationing in that they farmed units of below-optimum size but had the management ability to support expansion. Of these, only 13 percent were currently at debt limits imposed by external rationing. The others were practicing internal rationing. However, studies also continued to indicate deficiencies in credit availability to small operations [33, 183].

The positive impact of credit use on farm financial progress became well established. For instance, Hamlin, Wirth, and Nielson [121] described and analyzed the sources and use of credit by a panel of Michigan farmers during 1954-58. They concluded that the use of credit was strongly associated with financial progress. Credit was found most effective when used in increments that substantially increased the scale of farm operations. Brake [59] budgeted several farms in one area of Michigan to see how income could be increased by additional capital investment. Somewhat larger incomes could be obtained by operators with "a willingness and ability to use fairly large amounts of credit."

GROWTH MODELS

In the 1960s growth models became the primary vehicle for investigations of farm financial management. Such models ranged from algebraic formulations to applications involving linear programming and simulation techniques [45, 94, 162, 169, 184, 189]. These new analytical tools could be used to analyze the impacts of external and internal capital constraints on measures of financial progress or even to optimize an objective function reflecting financial progress. Also, the nature of the growth process and the effects of various financial strategies could be observed over time [94]. As Bailey [11] later noted: "Without growth, financial management of the farm is a one-time budgeting of debt and of income flows; with growth, debt becomes a powerful management strategy. Thus the concept of growth of the firm puts meaning into the term 'financial management.'"

Baker and Irwin pioneered research emphasizing liquidity and lender decisions. In 1959, at the symposium on capital and credit needs in a changing agriculture [19], they discussed the collection of data on production functions and lending limits of Illinois farms and a model for evaluating the impact of these variables on farm organization. Using this model, they later quantified some effects of differences in lender attitudes toward different loan purposes [161]. Thus the purchase of cattle, an enterprise favored by lenders, could displace the purchase of fertilizer in an optimal solution despite a higher marginal value product for fertilizer.

A series of studies at the University of Illinois, summarized by Baker [13], pursued this line of inquiry. Neuman (1962) found that an optimal farm plan called for a certain sequence of resource acquisitions during the production year, depending on lender reactions to the kinds and amounts of debt outstanding. Total credit obtained within a year could, for instance, be increased by purchasing cattle before, rather than after, purchasing machinery. Rogers (1963) reported that an optimum solution might include the use of merchant credit, in spite of its higher price, because more total credit could thereby be obtained. Vandeputte (1968) found that the level of annual repayment commitments on real estate debt influenced lenders' limits on non-real estate credit extensions, with consequent implications for the credit strategy that would optimize growth. According to Smith (1968), this reaction by non-real estate lenders to land contract debt tended to offset the growth rate advantage that land contract purchases would otherwise offer.

As these studies progressed, Baker [12, 13] evolved a conceptual framework for study of the behavior and growth of farm firms in an environment of external and internal constraints. A farmer's unused borrowing capacity ("credit" in Baker's terminology) represents a valuable liquidity resource. As debt is increased, "credit" is absorbed and liquidity is correspondingly reduced. Borrowing, therefore, entails a cost in reduced liquidity in addition to the direct interest charge. Internal capital rationing is thus a manifestation of the value placed on remaining liquidity. Pursuant to this concept, Barry and Baker [23] suggested a procedure for quantifying the liquidity value provided by unused credit ("credit reservation prices") and through case studies confirmed that it was inversely related to use of debt and to the rate of growth.

In the late 1960s another sequence of growth studies was carried out at Purdue University. Patrick and Eisgruber [224] developed a dynamic model to simulate the process of firm growth over a twenty-year period under various levels of managerial ability and capital market structures — the latter represented by variations in interest rates and in limits on loans of different maturities. For one thing, they found that the sooner a farmer was able to buy land, the greater was his net worth progress. Also, stringent limits on intermediate-term loans could be circumvented by refinancing long-term loans. But if low limits were imposed on both of these debt maturities, there was an impact on the management practices applied to crop rotations and the crop-livestock balance. (Baker and Hopkin [16] noted the macroeconomic implications of such effects for aggregate organizational structure and resource efficiency.) Harshbarger [128] extended this model by utilizing a random number generator to simulate weather variability while studying the impact of alternative land procurement policies and equity-ratio limits on borrowing.

In 1964 Baker and Holcomb [14] listed estate transfer and lender behavior as areas where modeling might yield attractive payoffs. Subsequently, Boehlje and Eisgruber [44] constructed a simulation model in which the impact of alternative estate transfer strategies could be studied. They found a need for joint consideration of growth and transfer strategies due to uncertainty concerning the timing of death. Thus estate transfer plans should be continually reviewed as various growth phases are entered or completed. They were further impressed with the need to coordinate the simultaneous process of exit and entry — exit of parents and entry of the operating heir. Their assessment: "Currently, little is known about the processes and the problems of either disinvesting from or getting established in farming, let alone how to coordinate these processes." Among the many variables involved and remaining to be considered in future work, they listed the retirement requirements of farmers, the equity capital outflow to nonfarm heirs, and changes in tax and transfer laws.

As research proceeded, additional considerations were suggested for inclusion in growth models. Brake [60] in 1968 pointed out that growth models then extant might be seriously incomplete because of their neglect of important cash withdrawals occurring through social security taxes, income taxes, and current family consumption. Vandeputte and Baker [287] subsequently discussed how income allocation to these uses might be specified in linear programming models. In another refinement Barry [22] evaluated the impact of asset indivisibility on firm growth. Other work examined problems of asset replacement in a decision-making context. Chisholm [78] and Perrin [231] offered criteria for determining optimum replacement patterns and demonstrated methodology useful in making such decisions. In an award-winning article Boussard [53] demonstrated that three major problems in using multiperiod linear programming models — the choice of objective function, excessive matrix size, and the introduction of uncertainty — are related and can therefore be managed through coordinated choices and procedures exemplified by the model he presented.

Several papers have reviewed and assessed developments in this research area in greater scope and detail than has been possible here. One contribution in this vein, by Baker, Scott, and Reiss [20], included considerable discussion of the implications for future research and applications. In addition, Bostwick [46] presented a nonmathematical outline of the theoretical framework, Irwin [159] provided a similar review of the principal growth models, and Harrison [126] compiled a bibliography of publications, ongoing work, and names of current researchers and teachers.

FARM AND FAMILY FINANCIAL PLANNING

Numerous extension publications have been devoted to farm and family financial planning, but not many research publications have addressed this subject. Attention has been given, however, to the use of cash-flow data and projections in financial planning and control, as in examining the need for and the ability to repay debt [26, 205, 293].

Because of the unique firm-household relationship in agriculture comprehensive financial planning requires information on factors such as family consumption functions, savings rates, income taxes, personal goals, and nonfarm investments. The importance of off-farm income as a source of capital, for instance, was demonstrated by Wirth and Nielson [295]. Research in these areas may employ data from the record-keeping projects conducted in several states, but typically such data are based on small samples that may preclude generalizations.

Several aspects of the role of federal income taxes in the firm-household relationship have been studied. In exploring income tax compliance by Wisconsin farmers Gardner [110] found that farm expenses were underreported in the aggregate, as were some kinds of farm income. Noncompliance generally occurred through omission or incomplete listing of both receipts and deductions.

Dean and Carter [88] illustrated how tax considerations, the form of business organization, and the optimum scale of the firm are interrelated. In the Imperial Valley of California individual proprietorships were the advantageous form of organization for farms up to five hundred acres whereas the corporate form provided tax advantages for larger farms. Their work also suggested that, given the current tax treatment of capital gains, a progressive tax rate structure stimulates investment in high-risk ventures.

Assets and Debts in the Farm Sector

There has been continual interest in the financial structure of the farm sector. Many studies have analyzed farmers' assets and debts. These include attempts to describe the credit situation in a locality, a larger area, an entire state, or the entire United States [10, 112, 156, 297].

Special surveys have provided extensive information on farmers' debts and assets. The 1960 Census Sample Survey of Agriculture obtained data on the debts of a large national sample of operators and landlords. Around December 1, 1960, debt was found on 62 percent of all farms [10, 40]. Lending institutions held two-thirds of the total debt reported by farm operators, individuals held one-fourth, and merchants and dealers held 8 percent. Borrowers typically operated larger farms, produced more, were younger, owned more farm real estate, and rented a higher proportion of the land they farmed than nonborrowers. Farmers with debt thus appeared to be more aggressive and more willing to take risks than debt-free farmers [112].

Similar sample surveys were made in 1965 and 1970 [282, 283]. Outstanding operator and/or landlord debt was found on 56 percent of all farms as of December 31, 1970. The proportion of indebted operators averaged 53 percent and ranged from 81 percent on farms with annual sales of $100,000 or more to 37 percent on farms with sales under $2,500. Among the indebted operators those with larger farms (measured by value of sales) exhibited higher average ratios of debt to real estate assets and to total (farm and off-farm) net income but lower ratios of debt to annual sales, expenses, and net farm income. Of the 1.9 million landlords 16 percent had outstanding debt, and among these the debt averaged 23 percent of the value of the farm real estate they rented out.

The 1970 survey embodied two new features that are permitting expanded analyses in work now planned or in progress (the data first became available late in 1973). Both operators and landlords reported the amount of credit obtained during 1970 in connection with each major type of capital purchase and operating expense, classified further by two maturity categories. Also, the sample size was substantially expanded to permit results to be tabulated and analyzed separately within most states [109]. In the previous surveys geographical disaggregation had been limited to three large regions — the North, the South, and the West.

The *Balance Sheet of the Farming Sector*, issued annually since 1945 by the USDA, is the standard source of aggregate information on farm assets and debt. After its introduction as an annual sequel to a study of the impact of World War II on farm finances [270], it rapidly became a popular and widely quoted USDA publication. The availability of Balance Sheet data for successive years has clearly facilitated the presentation of a comprehensive and organized discussion of aggregate changes in the value of farm assets and the amount of farm debt. As Burroughs noted in 1950 [71], the Balance Sheet represented "one of the first products of social accounting," covering agriculture for several years before similar data were compiled for most other sectors of the economy.

Over the years Balance Sheet data have sometimes been misinterpreted or misused. At first, Burroughs noted, social accounting was so new that only a few specialists were fully aware of the associated conceptual problems or the popular confusions that might result from applying the terminology of accounting for private enterprise to given sectors or to the whole of the national economy. He pointed out various conceptual limitations and valid and invalid uses. However, incautious or misinformed use continued, as noted more recently by Irwin [160]. For one thing, the Balance Sheet does not reflect the assets and debts of either farm operators or owners alone but rather assets and debts of farm operators, tenants, and landlords combined. Second, assets are valued at current prices, whereas data on assets of other economic sectors are generally available only as book values (cost less depreciation). Hence, Ir-

win noted, debt/asset ratios computed from the Balance Sheet are not directly comparable to those available for other sectors.

Subsequently the USDA also presented data on agricultural book values
[281]. However, analysts were not warned that agriculture/business comparisons based on book values may also be misleading for some purposes because many business assets (accounts receivable, inventories, goods in process
of production, and recently purchased plant and equipment) have book values
close to their market values whereas a large part of agricultural assets consists
of infrequently transferred real estate, for which the book value now averages
far below market value.

Trends in Capital and Resource Organization

Capital Formation and Land Prices

"Agriculture is a heavily capitalized industry. . . . The capital requirements
of agriculture have increased enormously since the middle of the last century.
. . . increasing land values, together with more intensive methods of farming
and the development of cooperative marketing, have made it necessary for
the farm to acquire larger working capital. . . . As the capital requirements of
farming have expanded, credit has become increasingly important in the
operation of the farm. . . . Now that the capital requirements of farming are
so great, farmers use credit facilities extensively . . ." [221]. These familiar
observations have been repeated, justifiably, many times during the past three
decades. The quotation, however, is from the 1924 Yearbook of Agriculture!
The trends described have indeed been long-term phenomena.

The general trends are familiar, but interruptions and significant variations
in their pace over time are less widely known and appreciated. Ironically,
when the quoted passage was written, agriculture had already entered a lengthy
period of depressed income, with severe consequences for land prices, capital
formation, and outstanding debt. After 1920 the national index of farmland
prices fell for thirteen consecutive years, dropping a total of 59 percent from
its postwar peak. Net capital formation for two decades was low and in many
years negative. Outstanding real estate debt peaked in 1923 and then declined
almost continuously to 1946; the total decrease amounted to 56 percent of
the volume outstanding in 1923.

During World War II farm income rose and the ongoing recovery in farmland prices accelerated to annual rates exceeding 10 percent (as noted, however, real estate debt continued to be reduced). With new machinery and
building materials largely unavailable, farmers added substantially to their
holdings of bank deposits and United States savings bonds. These helped to
finance a capital expenditures boom that got under way in 1946. Annual

gross spending trended upward through 1951, although net capital formation peaked earlier, in 1948. The boom was of very significant proportions. The stock of farm machinery measured in constant prices, for example, more than doubled between 1946 and 1951 and continued a slower rate of increase to 1956. Land prices, after softening in the late 1940s, rose by 27 percent during the first two years of the Korean War.

As Jones and Durand [170] noted, these events resembled four previous war-related capital spending and land price booms, each of which had been followed by agricultural depression. During the 1950s, however, farm income was supported by government programs while a more orderly adjustment in output capability took place. Crop acreage, for instance, was reduced by about 15 percent over the ten years following 1952. The machinery stock in real terms was reduced by 5 percent between 1956 and 1963. Except for a brief flurry in the mid-1960s net capital formation remained relatively low through 1972, which is consistent with Tostlebe's observations for previous periods in which net farm income was under pressure [268]. This time, however, the farm income squeeze was not severe enough to cause the widespread debt-repayment distress that had followed previous wartime booms.

In 1973 total net farm income nearly doubled that of 1972, again triggering the typical response — expansion of crop acreage and livestock production and increases in capital spending and land prices. Building and machinery purchases rose sharply, the latter being in effect limited by what manufacturers could produce. In the year ending March 1, 1974, the national index of farm real estate prices rose by 25 percent. On November 1, 1975, the index stood 81 percent higher than four years earlier — an average annual rise of 16 percent compared with an average annual gain of 6 percent over the ten years ending in November 1971. Net farm income in 1974 and 1975 receded from the 1973 peak but remained substantially above earlier levels; consequently, the sixth major boom in United States farm investment and land prices was still continuing in mid-1976.

The composition of physical capital underwent some significant changes during the postwar period. However, analysts unfamiliar with the USDA estimates of assets valued at their 1967 prices are often surprised when first shown the rather small shifts since the mid-1950s. The largest postwar changes were the increase in machinery and the decrease in liquid financial assets that occurred directly after the close of World War II. Machinery rose from 4.2 percent of total assets in 1945 to 10.3 percent in 1954. The ratio then fell off slightly before climbing again to 10.3 percent in 1967 and further to 11.2 percent by 1975. Holdings of currency, bank deposits, and United States savings bonds fell rapidly from 10.4 percent of assets in 1946 to 6.8 percent in 1952, and then continued a downward drift to 3.9 percent by 1975. Throughout the period the proportion represented by livestock fluctuated only between 6.4 and 8.1 percent — the latter also being the 1975 value. For the last twenty years the proportion in real estate has stayed at about two-thirds of the total.

Because prices of the various assets have moved very differently during the postwar period, the composition of assets valued at market exhibits somewhat different changes. Of greatest significance, the proportion represented by real estate has risen persistently from 56.8 percent in 1949 to 71.4 percent in 1975. The proportion in machinery rose from 4.6 percent in 1947 to 11.4 percent in 1954, but the latter percentage has not been exceeded. Liquid financial assets declined in importance rather steadily, from 13.1 percent in 1946 to 3.7 percent in 1975. The relative proportion represented by livestock fluctuated violently as a result of swings in livestock prices. The first peak of 11.7 percent in 1952 was followed by a drop to 6.2 percent by 1957. Another peak of 8.9 percent was reached in 1974, but a plunge in prices reduced the ratio to 4.7 percent only a year later.

Average assets per farm may also be computed from the Balance Sheet data; these are, of course, affected by changes in the number of farms. After increasing to an all-time high of 6.8 million farms in 1935, the number had already fallen to 5.9 million by 1946 and continued to decline each year to 2.8 million in 1975. Valued at market, total assets per farm rose from $17,500 in 1946 to $184,500 in 1975, real estate assets from $10,300 to $131,700, and machinery from $900 to $19,800.

Such comparisons, though commonly used to indicate the changes on typical farms, can be misleading because the farms that have been disappearing are, on average, much smaller than the remaining farms. Reinsel [237] pointed out the nature of this misconception in his estimates of the factors contributing to the change in average farm size from 1959 to 1964. The average size of farm increased from 302 acres to 351 acres over this five-year period. The forty-nine-acre average change came from four factors: (1) twenty-five acres from loss of farms through nonagricultural use or census redefinition; (2) eight acres from loss of farm numbers where land remained in agriculture; (3) thirteen acres from purchase or rental of additional farmland by operators of remaining farms; and (4) three acres from purchase or rental of land not previously in farming use by operators of remaining farms. Thus, those farms included in both the 1959 and 1964 censuses increased in size by only sixteen acres on average rather than by the forty-nine acres implied by the overall census averages.

Nevertheless, major structural changes occurred on individual farms. Capital was substituted for labor, new technology and larger-scale machinery were adopted, and increasing proportions of inputs were purchased rather than produced on the farm. Among the many studies of such resource adjustments and capital formation Dorner and Sandretto [92] examined those on a sample of Wisconsin dairy farms from 1950 to 1960. Labor input declined on these farms even though a greater volume of output was produced. Capital improvements made this possible, and 70 percent of them were financed from current income or accumulated savings. More of the farmers had supplemental nonfarm jobs in 1960. Operators who began as tenants or in family partnerships made more progress in enlarging their farms than did those who started as owners.

Farm Input Prices

After price ceilings were removed following World War II, farm input prices rose sharply, paused in 1949, and again rose rapidly in the first few months of the Korean War. By 1951 prices of production inputs averaged 55 percent above those of 1945, and prices of family living items had risen 47 percent. Except for 1949 these were also years of relatively high net farm income; furthermore, the rise in input prices was broadly based. Altogether, the emphasis was on expanding output rather than on adjusting to differentials or increases in input prices.

This experience was followed by a lengthy period, dating roughly from 1953 to 1967, characterized by stagnant total net farm income and "creeping" general price inflation. Prices of farm family living items, for instance, rose at an average annual rate of 1.3 percent. There was pressure, therefore, to improve individual farm incomes through resource efficiencies and adjustments.

The drive for higher income usually entailed farm or enterprise enlargement, and this in turn often required purchase of new or improved machinery. Also, farm wage rates were rising at an average annual rate of 3.7 percent, providing additional incentive for making labor-saving adjustments. Unfortunately, prices of farm machinery and motor vehicles advanced by 2.7 percent annually during this period, considerably faster than the rise of prices in general. This unfavorable relative price trend of an input basic to the adjustment process had major implications for capital decisions and financing needs.

On the other hand, some other major categories of farm inputs became relatively less expensive during this fourteen-year period. Prices of building materials and of motor supplies, including fuel, rose at annual rates near 1 percent. Prices of fertilizer and feed remained virtually unchanged. Thus a particularly dramatic rise in fertilizer use occurred, while the stability of feed prices removed one element of uncertainty from the highly cyclical livestock sector.

This experience was followed by a period, dating roughly from 1967 to

1972, characterized by accelerated rates of price rise but with little change in the differentials among the rates of increase for major input groups. Average annual increases rose to 7.3 percent for farm wage rates and 5.4 percent for farm machinery and motor vehicles. However, the price of motor supplies increased only 2.6 percent annually, and feed and fertilizer prices rose relatively little. Thus, insofar as price relationships were concerned, the appropriate resource adjustments continued to resemble those of the preceding period. The principal exception was that prices of building materials rose sharply. Pressure for expansion of individual farm incomes continued as prices of family living items rose at an average annual rate of 4.5 percent.

From 1972 to 1974 the pace of general price inflation rose sharply and, significantly, the previous input price relationships were violently altered. Over this two-year period the high rate of general price inflation was illustrated by the average annual rise of 14 percent in prices of family living items. In contrast to previous experience, wage rates and machinery prices rose less rapidly — wages by 10 percent annually and farm machinery and motor vehicles by 11 percent. But motor supplies, including fuel, rose at an annual rate of 19 percent, as did building materials. Finally, prices of feed and fertilizer — previously relatively stable — nearly doubled, exhibiting average annual increases of 33 percent and 38 percent, respectively.

Farm output prices initially led this period of rapid price inflation, and during this phase expansion of output took precedence over adjustment to changing input price relationships. But when livestock prices moved sharply downward after August 1973 while prices of feed continued upward, a brutal adjustment with severe financial implications rapidly ensued among livestock farmers. Cotton producers were next affected as cotton prices fell during 1974 while prices of fuel, fertilizer, and other inputs rose. By early 1975 farm income was being severely squeezed by a general decline in output prices; however, these prices soon staged significant recoveries and remained at generally profitable levels into 1976.

The financial implications of swings in farm input and output prices have seldom been more vividly demonstrated than by the experience of cattle feeders during 1973-74, and this should prove a fertile field for future studies. Over the entire postwar period feeder livestock prices were by far the most volatile and cyclical of major farm input prices. With feed prices relatively stable the swings of feeder livestock prices were magnifications of the fluctuations in slaughter livestock prices. Thus, as fat cattle prices rose strongly in the spring and summer of 1973, feeder cattle prices were bid up to extraordinary levels. In a final display of speculative euphoria, many feeders filled their lots in anticipation of still higher prices after the expiration of retail price controls in September, despite USDA analyses questioning such expectations.

The bubble burst as fat cattle prices began a prolonged decline, and these cattle feeders took large capital losses on the initial weight of the animals they had purchased earlier. To compound their dilemma, feed prices rose and they experienced operating losses as well. Scofield [250] estimated that cumulative losses of $1.7 billion were experienced by year-end 1974 in an industry that had started the year with an investment of $6.5 billion in livestock and feed. Some foreclosures and bankruptcies have occurred. Most outside investors have reportedly lost their investment and retired from the field. Many livestock producers are refinancing their short-term loans into long-term mortgage debt. The Congress in July 1974 passed the Emergency Livestock Credit Act of 1974, providing for loan guarantees by the Farmers Home Administration. Numerous popular descriptions of these events were published, but they are not as yet reflected in the analytical literature.

Earlier in the postwar period, when government programs attempted to maintain farm income, several studies examined their impact on returns to resource owners. For example, Seagraves [254] found that during the period 1953 to 1962 over 40 percent of the total revenue received from tobacco production was attributable to the tobacco allotment. Government programs that reduced the risk of farm ownership were found to increase the value of — and thereby reduce the rate of return on — the land resource.

Farm Consolidation

The trend toward increasing farm size and consolidation resulted in considerable research on financing implications. On the micro level one innovative approach was tried by Lindsey, who selected three representative low-income farm situations and then worked intensively with the operators and their credit institutions to develop viable commercial farms [183]. He concluded that with adequate credit and farm management assistance these families could receive personal income comparable to their potential earnings in nonfarm work. However, the families were faced with continual reorganization of their farms due to a persistent cost-price squeeze and new technological developments. He found that the amount of credit which existing agencies were prepared to extend to typical low-income families of North Carolina fell far short of that required to provide those families with adequate reorganizational capacity.

In a more recent study Benson and Brake [33] examined some of the problems dairy farmers faced in expanding their operations. The study concluded that debt maturities were often too short. Again, many lenders were not prepared to make sufficiently large loans to complete expansion plans. Real estate lending limits were unreasonably low. Still, the trend toward larger farms became well established in spite of such obstacles.

Other implications of this trend have been noted. Wirth and Rogers [296] concluded that significantly fewer, but larger, farms could meet United States food and fiber needs rather effectively. Brake [56], after calculating the equity that farmers might hope to accumulate over a working lifetime, hypothesized that the larger units among future farms would necessarily tend to involve partnership and corporate forms of organization. At the American Agricultural Economics Association meeting in 1970 Krause and Kyle [175] raised a number of questions concerning research needs and public policy in an agriculture increasingly dominated by large farms. And the association's Committee on Economic Statistics [3] concluded thus: "Technological change has led to a major reorganization of the production and marketing processes for food and fiber . . . processing and marketing functions formerly performed on farms [have] been spun off . . . inputs previously produced on farms . . . are now produced off farm. This has blurred the boundary and meaning of the *farm* sector and leaves behind some myths which we honor through continued statistical use." In short, recent literature has suggested that changes in the size and scope of farms have numerous implications that research in finance needs to recognize and examine.

Analysis of Land Prices

LAND PRICE TRENDS

Considerable research has been devoted to analysis of rising land values over the postwar period. Much of this research has been done by USDA personnel responsible for *Farm Real Estate Market Developments*, periodically published by the USDA. The real estate market group has continuously gathered and analyzed data on trends in farm real estate prices and related factors and is the source of the land price data used by most other workers.

At the close of World War II and again during the Marshall Plan and Korean War years, many agricultural economists feared the future consequences of ongoing land price increases. Typical was the alarm expressed by Nowell [220] that land prices were rising too fast relative to probable postwar income. Wall [290] and Larsen [180] also expressed concern over the ongoing increases but pointed out that prices were not yet very far out of line.

Land prices continued upward in the early 1950s but fell in 1953 as farm income declined. In 1954 they resumed an upward climb which has continued to date. Renshaw in 1957 [241] published regression results demonstrating that variations in prices of farmland between 1920 and 1953 could be explained largely by gross income, interest rates, and a time trend. He noted, however, that the rise in land prices between 1954 and 1956 was significantly above his projections and suggested that some structural changes had occurred in factors affecting prices.

Scofield in 1957 [251] reported that the resumed upward trend in 1954 was so unexpected, in view of the decline in net farm income, that USDA researchers had actually reviewed their survey procedures for possible bias. His explanation of the upward land price trend, which became the basic model for subsequent work, included the strong demand for land for nonagricultural uses, the technological changes resulting in strong demands for land to enlarge existing farms, the capitalization of farm program benefits into land prices, the ample supply of credit available to finance land purchases, and expectations of continued future appreciation of farmland. Later Scofield [248] reported that his estimates of imputed returns to land had continued to increase through the late 1950s and early 1960s.

Nevertheless, the divergence between farm income and farmland prices continued to be regarded as a paradox, which stimulated considerable research in the mid-1960s. Chryst [80] in 1965 hypothesized that the joint effect of technological advance and price and income supports decreases unit costs without comparable decreases in product prices, thereby raising the income that accrues to fixed factors. Herdt and Cochrane [136] also argued for the importance of the joint impact of technological change and price supports. Utilizing a simultaneous equations supply-demand model, they found a productivity index to be most important in explaining land prices.

Heady and Tweeten [132] found that farmland prices were related to size of farm (the primary influence), income, and the yield on common stocks. Their negative time-trend coefficient suggested that technological advance in and of itself decreased the value of farmland, thus supporting the hypothesis that price supports were a vital joint factor in its influence.

In 1966 Tweeten and his colleagues [274, 275] examined influences on farmland prices from 1950 to 1963. They concluded that 52 percent of the demand pressures were due to the combined factors of farm enlargement and government programs, 20 percent resulted from nonfarm demand, and 17 percent were related to expectations of further gains in real estate prices. The remainder was attributed to the reduction in the quantity of farmland. In 1969 Reynolds and Timmons [243] explained much of the variation in farmland prices between 1933 and 1965 with these variables: number of voluntary transfers, government payments for land diversion, conservation payments, expected capital gains, farm enlargement, the inverse of the rate of return on common stock, and expected net farm income.

Montgomery and Tarbet [203] presented data from the northwestern wheat-pea region supporting Scofield's hypothesis [248] that the effective demand for land came from successful farmers with above-average rates of return that allowed them to outbid the average operator. They also found that most of the successful buyers in their survey planned to operate their newly added acreage with their existing equipment — an interesting insight into the nature of the pressure for farm enlargement.

In some cases the effects of government programs were dominant. Hedrick [133] and Seagraves [254] found that peanut and tobacco allotments greatly increased the value of farmland. After a broader review of the capitalization of farm program benefits Reinsel and Krenz [239] estimated that in 1970 the capitalized value represented 8 percent of the market value of farm real estate nationally and as much as 33 percent in North Carolina and 19 percent in Kentucky and North Dakota.

The impact of federal income tax policies was also studied. Dean and Carter [88] observed that farmland in some areas could be priced above its agricultural value because investors in high tax brackets could afford to pay a higher price per acre. After budgeting financial flows and returns for cattle ranches, however, Martin and Gatz [190] concluded that ranches could not typically provide tax shelters large enough to affect greatly the general level of ranch prices. In contrast, they noted, typical investors in land development projects such as young citrus orchards would obtain tax savings, and this fact would tend to affect the general price level of such real estate.

Cross-sectional analyses have also been used in attempts to explain variation in land prices among states or within a given state. Using state data Reynolds and Timmons [243] found that positive effects on land values were exerted by expected net farm income, government payments for land diversion, conservation payments, expected capital gains, farm enlargement, nonfarm population density, technological advance, and the ratio of debt to equity. Negative effects were exerted by voluntary transfers of farmland, the capitalization rate, and the expected ratio of farm to nonfarm earnings.

Hammill [122] explained 90 percent of the variation in land prices among Minnesota counties by using the percentage of cropland, a crop productivity index, and the distance from urban centers as the main explanatory variables. Blase and Hesemann [38] found productivity to be most important in explaining variation in farmland prices within Missouri.

These studies and others have contributed much to the understanding of land price trends and variations. Recent work and events, however, continue to raise new issues.

In a time-series study Klinefelter [174] examined changes in the value of Illinois farmland from 1951 to 1970. Net returns, average farm size, number of transfers, and expected capital gains explained 97 percent of variation, with enlargement and expected capital gains exerting the more significant effects. This result suggests that expected capital gains are becoming a more important influence and illustrates the need for continual updating of such studies.

Reinsel [238] recently reported that the relationship between land values and rents (that is, the capitalization rate) had been relatively constant since 1940 in two relatively stable farming areas — Illinois and North Dakota — whereas it had increased markedly in two other states — Mississippi and New Jersey — in which dramatic structural changes in land use and tenure had occurred. These data imply a need for regional disaggregation in studies of the factors shaping land price trends.

Previously, Reinsel [236] had more generally questioned the ability of the national land price series to support the complex models that others had constructed, in view of its high correlation with fundamental economic factors. He dramatized his point by showing that the money supply and population — hypothesized as the basic forces behind general price inflation and the demand for farm products and land — explain 99 percent of the variation between 1947 and 1970 in the United States index of farm real estate prices.

Although some economists have speculated that liberalized credit arrangements tend to increase land prices, Engberg [96] in 1947 argued that the effect of the federal credit agencies had been to keep prices more nearly in line with long-run earning capacity of farms and to minimize the effects of short-term fluctuations in farm income. Perhaps Engberg's comments are outdated now that federal land banks may lend up to 85 percent of appraised market value. Secondly, the variable interest rate charged by the federal land banks lags when market rates of interest are rising, making their farm mortgage loans a relative bargain at such times. These new influences need to be studied. The impact of increased seller financing also warrants more attention.

As a result of the continued trend toward higher values per acre of farmland, Hill and Staniforth [148] suggested the need to experiment with adjustments in livestock-share leases to better reflect earnings and resources. They argued that 30-70 or 40-60 share leases might be more appropriate than the traditional 50-50 livestock-share lease.

Perhaps the only attention to supply of and demand for new land development was by Hoover [150]. He noted that policy errors could result from assuming, incorrectly, that the supply of farmland cannot be increased through development. With the level of demand for new land readily observed as the current market price for farmland, he suggested that a single-equation model could focus on the supply factors. Empirical work on these relationships would appear useful.

IMPLICATIONS FOR FINANCE

The persistent rise in farm real estate values had significant implications for virtually the entire spectrum of topics covered in this review — getting started in farming, financial progress of the farm firm, real wealth position of operators, aggregate capital and credit flows, and performance and adequacy of financing institutions, to name but a few.

At this point it is worth noting, however, that increases in farmland prices affect capital flows and the demand for credit mainly at the time land is transferred. The annual transfer rate of farm real estate, though basically determined by the productive life-span of farm operators, has fluctuated markedly with changes in agricultural income and credit conditions. In the year ending March 1, 1971, for instance, voluntary and estate sales of ten or more acres totaled 19.9 million acres valued at $5.1 billion, with credit financing of $3.2 billion. In contrast, three years later such transfers involved 41.8 million acres, a market value of $14.2 billion, and loans totaling $9.3 billion. Reynolds and Timmons [243] found that the annual number of farmland transfers during the period 1933-65 was affected by the debt-equity ratio, farm-to-nonfarm-earnings ratio, farm enlargement, expected capital gains, and technological advances.

The trend to higher land prices has been accompanied by a trend toward greater use of credit in land transfers. Annual surveys by the USDA, reported in *Farm Real Estate Market Developments,* show that the proportion of transfers on which debt was incurred rose from 43 percent in 1945 to 87 percent in 1975. Furthermore, among the credit-financed transfers the average ratio of the debt to the purchase price rose from 56 percent to 76 percent over the same time span. In fact, a Michigan study [85] found that over 40 percent of the farmers purchasing real estate had used 100 percent credit. Many had mortgaged part of their existing farms to avoid cash down payments.

Real Wealth Effects of Price Changes

With relative changes over time in farm production resource prices and other prices, writers began to ask how farmers were affected. Grove [119] pointed out that capital gains are important in assessing the welfare of farmers. He estimated nominal capital gains to be about 43 percent as large as average annual income during the period 1940-59.

Hoover [151] followed with a discussion of the importance, in many analytical uses, of adjusting the nominal capital gains for changes in the purchasing power of both investments in farm assets and holdings of financial assets and liabilities. His empirical analysis suggested that real capital gains on all farmer-owned assets were equal to about 2 percent of farmers' total income from all sources during the 1940s and to about 10 percent of such income in the 1950s. The relative importance of real gains was thus far below that of the nominal gains during this period of general price inflation.

Boyne [54] at about the same time undertook a detailed study of capital gains of farm operators between 1940 and 1959. He found that while farmers had experienced real capital losses on their financial assets and liabilities because of their net creditor position from 1943 to 1958, their per-capita losses were substantially less than those of nonfarmers, who as a group held a relatively larger net creditor position (the federal government held the net debtor position vis-à-vis these two private sectors). However, farmers gained substantially on their nonfinancial assets, resulting in total real capital gains over the period equal to 7.5 percent of operators' net farm income. The real wealth gain varied substantially within this time period — from a real loss equal to 7.0 percent of income in 1945-49 to a real gain equal to 27.3 percent of income in 1955-59 — and also by geographic region.

Huff and MacAulay [157] in a follow-up pointed out the importance of examining capital gains on a regional or individual component basis, not only to improve the results but to make the data more usable for policy purposes.

The estimates of real gains were updated through 1968 by Bhatia [34]. Between 1947 and 1968 total real capital gains in the farming sector were estimated at $99 billion, of which $88 billion came from farm real estate. Significantly, with financial liabilities becoming substantially greater than financial assets during the 1960s, net real capital gains of $4.5 billion were derived from this source, in contrast to the loss found by Boyne between 1940 and 1959. Also during the 1960s real estate began to yield more substantial and stable capital gains than it had from year to year in the preceding two decades. Consequently, real capital gains were obtained annually during the period 1961-68 in amounts that had previously been seen in only a few scattered years — 1950, 1956, and 1958.

No research publications have yet computed and analyzed the real capital gains of the early 1970s, a period in which the nominal gains considerably exceeded net farm income. The results should be interesting, if only for the sheer magnitude of the numbers involved. In 1973 — apparently the year of greatest gains — Balance Sheet asset increases less net capital formation indicate nominal capital gains on the order of $82.5 billion, or about $29,000 per farm! However, the price index for farm family living expenditures rose by 16.2 percent, resulting in a purchasing power loss of $58.5 billion on total investment in farm assets. The same price inflation, however, yielded $10.6 billion in real capital gains on the outstanding farm debt. Summing these results, total real capital gains were $34.6 billion, equal to 89 percent of total net farm income (including landlord rentals) of $38.8 billion. In contrast, nominal capital gains were 213 percent of such income. Then in 1974 nominal capital gains of $41.8 billion were not large enough to offset the purchasing power loss resulting from continued inflation, so that the sector experienced a real capital loss of $17.3 billion. These fascinating figures are the product of a period of rapid price inflation. The effects of such "paper" gains and losses on farmers' financial behavior — on money illusion, attitudes toward debt, and so forth — may be interesting and important.

In a slightly different context Carlin and Reinsel [74] combined income and wealth when analyzing family well-being in 1966. On this basis the distribution of farm families by well-being was substantially improved in comparison with that of all United States families, since farm families had about double the net worth of the national average. The authors pointed out, however, that older farm families with low incomes and substantial net worths face serious problems in transforming their wealth into cash flows.

Capital Flows and Their Financing

Studies of capital needs of farm units have for the most part dealt with the amount of assets required — the value of the machinery, real estate, and working capital. These are particularly useful in examining problems related to transfer, such as capital gains and inheritance taxes, and problems that beginning farmers have in acquiring control over a viable farming unit. However, in studying the growth of a farm firm and the acquisition and financing of capital investments one turns to cash-flow budgeting. Analogously, in studying aggregate investment and its financing, the flows of funds rather than the stocks of goods are the appropriate variables to measure and analyze.

Flow-of-Funds Accounts

In discussing the uses and limitations of the relatively new Balance Sheet of Agriculture, Burroughs [71] in 1950 wrote: "Thus a bridge is needed to articulate the BSA and the income statements for agriculture. This bridge is an accounting for money flows and other capital transactions. Some work has been done . . . but much pioneer work remains."

As in many investigations much of the initial work consisted of developing the concepts and constructing appropriate data series. Tostlebe [268] performed this monumental job for five-year intervals from 1900 to 1949, defining and measuring the categories of capital formation (uses of funds) and the sources supplying the funds to finance that total flow. Then, having measured the total uses of funds, the amount financed by increase in debt, and — as a residual — the amount financed internally, he was able to make interesting observations about the levels of, and trends and cycles in, such analytical ratios as the ratio of capital formation to farm income and the proportion of capital formation financed by debt. Diesslin's book review [89] highlighted the flow-of-funds segment of Tostlebe's work (which was somewhat buried in the last chapter) and its implications:

The source of gross funds for replacement and additions to physical capital and working cash is one of the interesting and important findings of the study. "Internal" financing, largely from gross farm income, was the major source and exceeded 70 per cent in every decade except one since 1900. More importantly, a trend toward more internal financing continues, totaling over 90 per cent for the 1940-49 decade. The great bulk of our teaching, research, and extension activities in the field of farm finance is directed to sources, procedures, and techniques of agricultural credit and lending institutions. Our activity has been concentrated on the external sources which provide only 10-20 per cent of the total funds for maintaining and increasing the capital plant in agriculture. The findings of this study are sufficiently significant that we could well afford to re-evaluate our emphasis in the farm capital picture. Certainly, greatly increased emphasis needs to be given to the internal financing of the agricultural plant.

Diesslin's last comment overstates the case, in that the large gross flows of credit extended and repaid during the year are not represented in the ratios that he quotes. On the other hand, as D. G. Johnson [166] noted later, some of the net increases in debt were employed to make purchases of real estate that are not included in capital formation and so, on the net basis shown, the indicated relative importance of debt might actually have been biased upward.

In 1961 Kuznets's tome, *Capital in the American Economy — Its Formation and Financing* [179], incorporated Tostlebe's series and updated them and the analytical comments through 1955. Goldsmith's 1965 volume in the National Bureau of Economic Research series, *The Flow of Capital Funds in the Postwar Economy* [115], updated the farm sector estimates through 1958.

In 1960 the Commission on Money and Credit, sponsored by the Committee for Economic Development to undertake a wide-ranging review of United States monetary policies and institutions, obtained a detailed study from D. G. Johnson on "Agricultural Credit, Capital and Credit Policy in the United States" [166]. Johnson found he could readily update Tostlebe's accounts from data published annually in *The Farm Income Situation* and *The Balance Sheet of Agriculture* and did so through 1958. He discovered that the downward trend in relative use of credit in financing capital formation had been broken during the 1950s and that by the period 1955-58 the sum of depreciation allowances and the increase in debt had in fact exceeded capital formation. In the first half century this situation had occurred only during farm depressions. Johnson, worried about the adequacy of his data, took a cautious approach toward this finding. However, Melichar [195] later noted, "it is now evident that Johnson's data for 1955-58 were reflecting an ongoing major change in farmers' financial behavior, toward a lower savings rate and more use of credit."

The USDA did not incorporate the new flow-of-funds accounts into its ongoing work. Had this approach been taken, perhaps the financial outlook work of the USDA would soon have been cast in this useful analytical framework. In that event a systematic effort to develop estimators for all flow-of-funds components might have been made by the mid-1960s, when substantial but uncoordinated econometric work on individual components was being undertaken elsewhere. The USDA eventually took both steps, which were first reflected in its outlook literature for 1974 [278].

The interest of the USDA was not kindled until Bobst [43] and Irwin, Lins, and Penson [163] proposed that a flow-of-funds social account for the farm sector could serve as a framework within which to examine financial aspects of policy questions. They noted that the Federal Reserve Board was already maintaining a highly aggregated account showing capital and net credit flows. If disaggregated by various classes of farms, for example, such an account could indicate the distributional impact of changes in credit policies or availability.

Penson, Lins, and Irwin initiated a USDA project to construct a flow-of-funds account and model. In 1971 [227] they noted that the definitions of several components of the Federal Reserve farm sector account differed from those of similar components of USDA asset and income accounts and that the Federal Reserve account also ignored internal noncash flows such as capital appreciation. They therefore proposed an alternative account that would include, for example, appreciation as both a source and use of funds and that would be consistent with the USDA Balance Sheet and farm income accounts. While in basic agreement with their goals, Brake and Barry [65] suggested that several additional flows should be entered, that flows should be entered on a gross basis, and that uses of funds should be limited to actual purchases. A reply [228] defended the inclusion of noncash items as consistent with social accounts for other sectors. In another reaction Melichar [195] also argued that real estate flows should be represented by actual purchases rather than by capital appreciation, and in addition he pointed out the close relationship of the new work to the previous analyses by Tostlebe and Johnson. The account eventually published by the USDA [278] reflected several elements of these discussions.

Flow-of-Funds Models

In 1966 Brake [62] used flow-of-funds concepts and the internal-external financing dichotomy as a means of obtaining a projection of increases in farm debt to 1980. In the real estate area Brake made a judgmental projection of funds to be required by farm transfers and then subtracted a judgmental projection of internal financing to estimate the required increase in mortgage debt. In the non-real estate area, he emphasized that the turnover (flow) of capital had to be considered in projecting future debt, but he did not specify the derivation of his estimate. His dramatic projection of an even $100 billion in outstanding debt in 1980 was widely publicized and served to alert lenders and others to the logical case for continued large increases in farm loan demands over a protracted period. As it turns out, the $100 billion debt level that startled many observers in 1966 (when farm debt totaled $39 billion) will be reached somewhat earlier, probably in 1977, largely because asset and input prices have recently risen faster than Brake assumed.

Melichar and Doll in 1969 [198] revived the Tostlebe flows account as the appropriate vehicle to employ in measuring past capital requirements and seeking insight into credit trends. They updated the capital formation series through 1968 and incorporated the new USDA series showing the annual value of farm real estate transfers. Debt was found to have provided 37 percent of total sources of funds between 1965 and 1968, compared with 13 percent in the early 1950s. The proportion of cash flow that farmers devoted to financing the capital flow had fallen during the 1950s and in the next decade fluctuated around its new lower level.

Melichar and Doll also exploited the flow-of-funds framework more fully as a vehicle for projecting increases in debt. Using three projections of 1980 capital stocks made, respectively, by Heady and Tweeten [132], Heady and Mayer [131], and Brake [62], they estimated the capital formation and value of farm transfers that were implied (making additional assumptions as necessary). They next projected the amount of internal financing by estimating future cash flow — the sum of net income and depreciation allowances — and then assuming that the proportion of this flow devoted to meeting capital needs would remain at recent levels. The projected increase in debt was thus obtained as the residual difference between these projections of capital flow and internal financing. The debt implied for 1980 by the three alternative models ranged from $91 billion to $137 billion.

In a continuation of this approach Melichar in 1973 [196] estimated structural or trend equations for each of the uses of funds, based mostly on the 1950-71 experience, and used the results to make long-term projections of capital flows and debt. The capital flow to be financed, which had averaged $7 billion in the 1950s, rose to around $11 billion in the late 1960s and was projected to rise further to $17 billion by 1980. Outstanding debt in 1980 was projected at $110 billion, assuming general price inflation of 2.5 percent annually during the 1970s. Melichar also demonstrated the use of the model to simulate the impact of different assumptions about variables such as price inflation.

In the early 1970s the USDA flow-of-funds project turned to the development of estimators for each of the components of a national flow-of-funds account, to be used to simulate hypothetical events or policy changes and to project capital and credit flows. Penson [226] and Lins [185] reported on segments of the work as it progressed, and in 1973 Lins [186] reported a simulation model in which the credit flows were highly disaggregated by lender groups. Also in 1973 Penson [225] completed the Aggregative Income and Wealth (AIW) Simulator, a model emphasizing the simultaneous determination of the year-end portfolio balance and corresponding flows for capital formation and other uses. With subsequent modifications, such as adoption of the real estate transfer approach urged by Melichar [195], the AIW Simulator was employed in making the USDA capital and credit outlook projections for 1974 and again for 1975 [278, 279]. The outlook statement also took on a flow-of-funds orientation useful in arriving at and conveying insights into farm financial developments and projections.

Much further work and many challenges remain in this area of macro-finance studies. The AIW Simulator could be enhanced by disaggregating the flow of loan funds by source. Linkage with a national econometric model is also being considered. To maintain the usefulness of the AIW Simulator over time, continual attention must be given to the validity of its estimators in the light of ongoing theoretical developments or structural changes. Importantly, the major estimators should also be reworked by analysts with varying viewpoints or approaches. The current situation is analogous to that existing when the first national econometric model was constructed. As in that field, the development of alternative equations and models will improve insights and projections and should stimulate lively discussions in the literature.

Demand for Non-Real Estate Assets

Studies investigating the aggregate demand for one or more farm assets began to appear in the late 1950s. In 1959 Cromarty [86] estimated demand for tractors, for trucks, and for all farm machinery. Machinery purchases during the period 1923-54 were found to have been influenced mainly by changes in machinery prices, farm output prices, total farm assets, and net farm income, all deflated by a general price index. In the separate tractor and truck equations, replacement-rate variables were also significant. Also in 1959 Griliches [117] employed a stock-adjustment model in studying the demand for tractors, which was found to be affected by the real price of tractors and the rate of interest. The short-run response elasticities were relatively low, but long-run elasticities were high. In 1966 Fox [107] used tractor horsepower as a more refined measure of purchases and found it to be related to the number of farms, the average age of existing tractors, and the ratio of tractor prices to farm output prices.

In 1968 Rayner and Cowling [233] reviewed the studies of United States demand and noted that the dominant variable was the ratio of tractor to crop prices, whereas the ratio of tractor prices to wage rates was relatively unimportant or did not have the hypothesized sign. In contrast, their work in the United Kingdom had indicated that the latter ratio was the dominant influence in that country and, further, that changes in farm size were not influential whereas they had been found to be significant in the United States.

Heady and Tweeten in 1963 [132] published a comprehensive set of demand functions. For machinery and tractors their results and elasticities paralleled those of Cromarty and Griliches. They also estimated the demand for all production assets, which was found to be related to net income, farm output, weather, and a time trend. Using these results and incorporating assumptions about future trends in the explanatory variables, farm sizes, numbers, assets, and total production were projected to 1980. The relative success of these projections to date is mixed. Some remain on target at this point while others, such as the machinery projection, are obviously far off the mark.

Demand for other farm assets was also studied. Penson [226] produced simultaneous-equations estimates of the demand for financial assets in a portfolio balance setting. Scott and Heady [252] found investment in buildings most strongly related to changes in physical output and also influenced by net income, interest rates, the equity ratio, and size of farms. In an interesting exchange with implications for all quantitative studies, Grove [118] questioned the ability of the USDA building investment series to support such investigations, as the series was not based on measures of current expenditures but rather was estimated annually using a hypothesized relationship to past net income. In response, Scott and Heady [253] pointed out the responsibility of the USDA to publish complete and updated information on its estimation procedures. Implicitly, this exchange also dramatized the need for independent annual measurement of the components of capital formation and debt to support further analytical studies.

Demand for Credit

One' significant point that emerged from the flow-of-funds and asset demand studies is that, perhaps contrary to popular impression, the rate of real capital formation in agriculture had been relatively low since the early 1950s. Over the postwar period growth in real estate stock had slowed to virtually zero, real cash balances were falling, and physical stocks of livestock and machinery, while highly cyclical, on balance showed only moderate growth. Thus the observed rapid growth in farm loan demands could not be ascribed to a high rate of physical expansion. Rather, as noted by Brimmer [68], the important factors were inflation in land and machinery prices plus the impact of farm reorganization and enlargement. In the latter process, existing farmers were raising funds to buy out nonfarm heirs and other farmers who were leaving the farm sector. More recently, in 1973, 1974, and 1975, demand for loans was also stimulated by unusually large increases in the prices of annual operating inputs.

Early supply-demand studies of farm mortgage loans were performed by Hesser and Schuh [144, 145]. Over the period 1921-59 both supply and demand were elastic with respect to mortgage interest rates. Demand also varied inversely with technological advance and the availability of internal funds and directly with changes in farm wage rates — the latter effect presumably reflecting the substitution of capital for labor.

Lins [185] extended such work by estimating separate supply-demand relationships for each of five major lender groups during 1947-69. The net change in real estate debt, especially from federal land banks and life insurance companies, was found to be more sensitive to changes in farm income than to changes in the value of capital assets. Debt changes were also related to changes in repayment ability, as measured by the ratio of money balances to production expenses.

Herr [140] formulated a model relating change in non-real estate debt to changes in farm cash expenditures and to the availability of internal funds, with the latter variable measured as the ratio of cash expenditures to cash receipts. Debt changes during the period 1949-65 were rather successfully explained by these factors, both by regions and in the United States as a whole. Lins [186] extended this work by separately examining debt changes at production credit associations and at commercial banks and by examining the influence of other factors, including the interest rates charged. However, the most significant factors — especially in the demand for bank loans — continued to be those proposed by Herr.

The flow-of-funds models discussed earlier [62, 196, 225] also incorporated procedures for estimating credit demand. These reflect two alternative approaches to projecting the relative contributions of credit and other sources to the total funds raised. Penson [225] employed estimators for credit demand, and thus internal financing constituted the residual supplier of funds. Melichar [196] projected internal financing, with the amount of credit derived residually. If the respective equations were "correctly" specified, the two approaches would yield the same result. However, so many diverse influences appear likely to be affecting the multiple sources of funds that future work may find a simultaneous subsystem desirable. In fact, the AIW Simulator already incorporates elements of a simultaneous system. To support such work, additional data series based on direct measurements of noncredit sources of funds are needed. This need was particularly demonstrated in Brake's fund-flows model of Canadian agriculture [61], which went further than any of the United States studies in attempting to measure and project various components of noncredit fund inflows. Improved data on credit from noninstitutional sources are also needed to support meaningful disaggregated analyses of total credit flows.

The flow-of-funds context is helping to focus attention on factors in credit demand and use which were not so easily visualized in the past. For example, Benjamin [31], after calculating that scheduled principal and interest payments on farm debt might approach $65 billion in 1974 and perhaps exceed $70 billion in 1975, noted that these debt service requirements seemed large relative to cash receipts from sales of farm products, which were under $100 billion in 1974. The apparent aggregate exposure to risk in the event of a significant decline in farm output prices may be a limiting factor in future credit demand or may even be indicative of future problems; however, adequate historical and other evaluations of these data have not been made. Working along similar lines, Robison, Barry, and Hopkin [244] found increasing ratios of debt repayments to gross farm income in Texas agriculture. In many years since 1962 repayments appeared to exceed gross income, necessarily implying significant loan carryovers and a build-up in outstanding debt.

A substantial amount of research has examined the credit demands of special groups such as low-equity farmers, young or beginning farmers, and rural nonfarm borrowers. For example, surveys made in 1956 indicated that borrowers from the Farmers Home Administration formed one such group, being generally younger and less wealthy than borrowers from commerical banks and production credit associations [36]. Hathaway [129] concluded that their Farmers Home Administration loans, with terms more favorable than those offered by other lenders, were responsive to their special credit needs. Herr [139] came to similar conclusions after studying data for 1966.

Throughout the postwar period there has been concern for the credit needs of young and beginning farmers. Some research indicated that lack of credit was not a major problem for this group [257], but more papers argued otherwise. Typically the latter felt that lenders' loan offerings had not kept pace with the rapidly increasing amounts of capital required to begin farming. In general, such research did not deal with the explicit question of whether more or less credit should be available to beginning farmers. Similarly, studies that examined rural nonfarm credit needs also generally focused on the adequacy and fairness of lenders' response to felt needs, rather than on the measurement and evaluation of the effective credit demands.

Credit Institutions and Policies

Sources and Operating Procedures

Many studies have described the institutions comprising the credit system in the United States. Typically these studies have been concerned with telling farmers about the organization, operating procedures, and lending criteria of financial institutions in their state. For example, in a bulletin addressed to farmers in Montana, Bostwick, Esmay, and Rodewald [48] discussed the nature of credit, the sources of credit, lender attitudes, and factors affecting the use of credit. Similar publications have been issued in many other states.

Some credit publications were more narrowly focused. For instance, Spitze and Bevins [262] described the agricultural representative program in commercial banks in Tennessee. The functions of agricultural representatives included public relations as well as farm lending, at a cost to individual banks ranging from $4,000 to $10,000 in 1957. Other studies examined specific farm lending institutions. For example, numerous studies have summarized lending procedures and loan volume of production credit associations, commercial banks, the Farmers Home Administration, and other lending agencies. Pursell [232], as one example, described the nature and extent of rural credit unions state by state and throughout the United States.

Some information is frequently updated as credit conditions change. For instance, researchers in the Federal Reserve System continually analyze the farm lending operations of commercial banks — particularly through quarterly surveys in the Chicago [103] and Minneapolis [104] Federal Reserve districts. Since 1962 the American Bankers Association has also conducted and published annual national surveys of various aspects of farm lending by banks [4].

Another large group of studies analyzed national surveys of the characteristics of borrowers and outstanding loans at the major farm lending institutions. Loans at commercial banks were surveyed in 1947 [39], 1956 [41], and 1966 [193]. In 1956 and 1966 coordinated surveys also covered loans outstanding at life insurance companies [77, 230], federal land banks [35, 229], and the Farmers Home Administration [36, 137, 139]. Production credit associations were surveyed in those years and also in 1962 and 1971 [101]. Recently, new analytical possibilities were opened when the federal land banks consolidated information on their loans at the Farmbank Research and Information Service in Omaha. Ongoing analytical programs have already been enhanced [201].

In one of the studies utilizing the survey data Herr [137] found that new farm-ownership borrowers at the Farmers Home Administration were more likely to have been tenants, to be younger, and to have smaller businesses and lower equities than farmers as a whole. Although most borrowers ranked below average in such important features as assets, cash farm sales, and equity ratios, they did not comprise the weakest strata of the farm population or those least likely to develop viable farms. Refinancing of existing debts or buying farms constituted the most important purposes of farm-ownership loans in the North and West. Loans in the South went mainly for farm enlargement, but refinancing was also important.

The first comprehensive information on the role of merchant and dealer credit in agriculture was obtained in the 1960 Sample Survey of Agriculture and analyzed by Morelle, Hesser, and Melichar [204]. Three characteristics exhibited the more significant relationships to farmers' use of merchant-dealer credit: type of farm, size of farm, and age of operator. Dairy farmers, young operators, and operators of medium-sized or larger farms were most likely to be users of merchant-dealer credit, but among indebted operators the cotton and tobacco farmers and the older farmers tended to employ higher proportions of such credit. Among the users, small farms and farms in the South were least likely to use credit from other sources as well.

There are similar studies available describing credit institutions and operations in many other areas of the world. For example, Tablante [266] described the rural agricultural credit system in the Philippines. Among the characteristics and problems he stressed were the importance of the noninstitutional credit market, high rates of interest, the use of loans for consumption purposes, and the lack of savings in rural areas. He concluded that more extensive use of supervised credit might be the answer to some of the credit problems in the rural Philippines. Oluwasanmi and Alao [222] described the rural agricultural credit system in Nigeria in much the same vein. After describing the agricultural credit institutions in the country, the authors stressed that nonrepayment of loans and misdirection of many loans to nonfarmers were major difficulties with Nigerian credit arrangements. Hendry [135] described credit and savings among a hundred households in a rural area in Vietnam. He found that informal sources of credit were very important and that much of the credit was used to cover farm operating expenses. He also reported that informal rotating credit associations were providing credit to households. Ardener [8] discussed how local rotating credit associations are important in mobilizing savings to provide credit to rural inhabitants in much of the world.

Many studies of credit institutions of various countries have been published, but perhaps the most extensive assembly of materials came from the Agency for International Development in its Spring Review of Small Farmer Credit

[284, 285], which resulted in twenty-one volumes describing and analyzing credit institutions and programs throughout the world. In addition, a recent Organisation for Economic Co-operation and Development report [223] provides such information for many member nations.

Interest Rates

Interest rates, credit terms, and factors affecting interest rates have been the subject of considerable study. Such studies fall into several categories. One type of publication typically presents interest rate concepts and formulas for calculating interest rates in different situations. Examples include Botts [52], Brake [63], and Gilson [114]. Numerous informational publications have also dealt with the calculation of interest rates including rates on installment loans. However, as Brake pointed out, typically the terminology in these publications has not been consistent with the terminology used in mathematics of finance, with some confusion resulting.

Another line of inquiry has dealt with factors affecting interest rates. Long [187] tested the hypothesis that high interest rates were evidence of monopoly forces at work. He concluded that, rather than evidence of monopoly influences, high interest rates can often be adequately explained by competitive factors such as scarce capital, high administrative costs, risk, production uncertainties, and seasonal credit demand.

Dahl [87] found the size of the loan to be the most important factor affecting interest rates paid by farmers on loans outstanding at fifteen Minnesota banks around 1960, as it had been in the Federal Reserve's national survey in 1956. But in examining rates on loans within each bank — an area which the Federal Reserve analyses had not explored — he also found evidence of rate discrimination among borrowers. He attributed this to a combination of factors, among them the tendency of bankers to lend to farmers they knew and the farmers' lack of information on alternative sources of credit. If, in addition, farmers do not discuss production loan terms with each other, he reasoned, bankers may be inclined to charge what the traffic will bear.

Bottomley [51] stated that the components of the rate of interest in underdeveloped rural areas are (1) the opportunity cost of the lender's loan funds, (2) the administration charge, (3) the premium for risk, and (4) any monopoly profit. The key to lowering rates charged by rural moneylenders, he therefore reasoned, is to build up the value of farmers' collateral. In general, the greater a farmer's collateral the greater his borrowing and the lower the risk to the lender. Thus both the unit administration cost on loans and the lender's premium for risk are reduced. The reduction in risk also gives farmers access to the low-interest urban money market, which tends to eliminate whatever monopoly profit the rural moneylenders had been able to obtain.

Following up on the policy implications of this reasoning, Bottomley [49] suggested that the opportunity cost of seasonal lending by village moneylenders could be reduced by providing short-term government securities in which they could profitably invest their funds during the off-season. In addition, this cost might be lowered by making the discounting facilities of the organized credit market more accessible through improvements in collateral instruments and associated institutional arrangements. He also argued [50] that a significant part of the interest rate is the charge for the risk of nonrepayment, which is best reduced by increasing the overall productivity of farmers. Though Bottomley's model and policy conclusions were presented in the context of underdeveloped nations, they appear more generally useful to those who seek to increase the amount and reduce the cost of loan funds in rural areas.

Adams [1] discussed the pricing of funds channeled into agricultural credit by aid agencies in Latin America. He argued that such credit had been priced too low, leading to misallocation of these funds, and that interest rates should therefore be raised to levels that reflect the opportunity costs of capital in rural areas. This step, he felt, would encourage the development of local financial markets, raise the yield on rural savings, and increase the proportion of agricultural loans made from such savings. Realistic prices on agricultural credit would also bring into sharper focus the major constraints slowing agricultural development, which he believed to be obscured by low-priced credit policies.

In a study of factors affecting farm loan interest rates in the United States during the period 1940-53, Jones and Garlock [171] found that the interest rate decreased as the size of loan increased and also as the term of loan increased. They concluded that the interest rates charged farmers paralleled the movement of interest rates in the nation's money markets.

More recently, Penson [225] found a statistically significant link between interest rates charged on new farm loans and interest yields on money-market securities. The specification of his model, which was patterned after the financial sector of the FRB-MIT national econometric model, permits analysis of the effects that changes in money market conditions have on the term structure of interest rates charged farm borrowers and subsequent demand for loan funds.

Relatively little research has focused on noninterest loan terms and conditions such as compensating balances, "points," and stock purchase requirements. A description of the extent of such practices and an analysis of their effects on credit costs would be useful.

Legal Aspects

Several studies examined legal aspects of credit institutions and policies. One important concern was farm-debtor relief policies. Munger and Feder [206] analyzed the impact of the Frazier-Lemke Act on farmers and lenders in the northern Great Plains. This act included farmer-debtor relief legislation (Section 75 of the federal bankruptcy laws), which was first proposed in 1933. They drew three main conclusions: (1) relatively few farmer-debtors availed themselves of the provisions of Section 75; (2) those who did were farmers who thought they had assets worth saving; (3) use of the act increased as general economic conditions began to improve in the late 1930s. Most farmers who petitioned under the act were in need of debt adjustment. In 82 percent of the cases debtors had an excess of liabilities over assets and could not meet their obligations. The direct use of Section 75 was not numerically significant, however. In only three states did the total number of petitions exceed one thousand between 1937 and 1949.

Even where Section 75 was used, there was little evidence that it reduced the chances of foreclosure. The original Section 75 provided only for voluntary conciliation. Hence, few settlements were reached. Many petitions were dismissed by unsympathetic district courts. Other debtors undoubtedly refrained from petitioning because they had scant hope of obtaining relief.

On the basis of his study Feder [102] offered several proposals to improve the effectiveness of relief programs: (1) a special credit fund for petitioners, which could be administered by an existing credit agency or preferably by an agency especially designed for that purpose; (2) redemption appraisals based on long-run farm earnings; (3) tenant-relief provisions that would freeze rental agreements; and (4) administration of the act by a federal conciliation office.

A great deal of attention was devoted to tenure and legal aspects of finance by members of the North Central Land Tenure Research Committee. For example, in 1950 they examined how land credit arrangements could be better adapted to variability in farm income [217]. After reviewing experiences in the 1930s with respect to credit problems, adjustments, and mortgage relief legislation, the committee suggested changes in contractual arrangements, new mortgage guarantees, and various adaptations of the credit structure to farming needs. It stated that, from the viewpoint of efficiency in production and general agricultural welfare, temporary delinquency in debt payments should not result in immediate foreclosure. Delinquency caused by forces clearly beyond the borrower's control should be handled differently from delinquency due to neglect or managerial incompetence of the borrower. Thus the committee believed that variable payment plans, deferments, extensions, and similar measures could have alleviated some of the problems in the 1930s with far less economic and social disruption than was experienced.

Primarily from interest generated by the North Central Land Economics Research Committee, a number of studies in the early to mid-1960s dealt with low-equity transfers of farmland — particularly transfer by installment contracts [95, 125, 147, 177, 188]. These publications stressed that both buyers and sellers must fully understand their legal rights and responsibilities under a land purchase contract and also urged both parties to obtain competent legal advice in drawing up contracts tailored to their individual needs. Land contracts often provided low down payments for buyers while sellers minimized capital gains taxes, and thus their use increased.

Knowledge and Attitudes of Farmers

Farmers were generally found to lack knowledge of credit sources and terms [7, 87, 105, 263]. Studies in the early 1960s revealed that farmers often could not indicate the names, locations, and types of existing credit sources. Nor could they describe the types of loans these sources made or the interest rates that would be charged. In general, the better-educated and larger-volume farmers had a better knowledge of credit institutions than the poorly-educated or small-volume farmers had.

In addition, some studies noted overly conservative attitudes toward credit use. Hesser and Janssen [143] found that Indiana farmers in 1958 hesitated to use credit in instances where it would have been profitable to do so. In fact, such internal credit rationing was more important than external credit rationing. Yet, as reported by Anderson and Coulter [7], a substantial number of North Dakota farmers at about the same time could not obtain sufficient credit for their farming operations. Nearly half indicated they would substantially adjust their farming operations if additional credit were made available to them.

Evaluation of Institutions and Policies

Farm surveys have often provided assessments of financing practices. According to Wittwer [299], farmers in the 1950s commonly complained that both real estate and intermediate-term loans were typically written with too short a maturity. Also, Wirth and Brake [294] determined that many capital investments were being financed with short-term loans.

Neuman's study of financing practices in southern agriculture [215] found a need for reorganization into larger farming units, with the adjustment potential dependent upon managerial ability and financial position. He concluded that financing practices and lender attitudes in many areas impeded the rate of transition. Specific practices of concern were (1) obsolete rules of thumb for determining loan limits, (2) unwillingness to finance enterprises new to the area, (3) capital loans with short maturities, and (4) piecemeal lending without attention to the total financial needs of the farm.

Another line of inquiry, already discussed in the section on firm growth models, was that taken by Baker and his colleagues at the University of Illinois. Credit terms and loan programs were evaluated not only from the standpoint of borrowers' demand but also in terms of lender preferences with regard to profit opportunities, risk, liquidity objectives, and other factors related to their economic environment. This approach provides considerable insight into the processes of financial intermediation.

Other studies have evaluated specific lending institutions or practices as opposed to financing practices of lenders in general. Many of these studies have focused on the Farmers Home Administration. Hendrix [134] noted that, in general, younger farm operators achieved greater increases in income and net worth than older operators while under the Farmers Home Administration program. The level of resources which borrowers commanded while in the program, rather than the amount they initially owned or used, was the crucial determinant of their income and financial progress. A sociological study by Hoffer, Boek, and Boek [149] revealed that families in the program had greater increases in level of living, organizational participation, and informal participation — but not in income — than similar families not in the program. Families who borrowed from the Farmers Home Administration did not lose status by doing so.

Typically, the studies concluded that the program was successful. In North Dakota Kristjanson and Brown [178] stated that the program reached thousands of qualified farm operators who were unable to obtain as much credit elsewhere, but the North Dakota borrowers were critical of some aspects of the program. Problems arose from (1) lack of understanding of the philosophy of the program, (2) the large case load of the supervisors, and (3) restrictions on the borrower's freedom to make capital purchases. The borrowers in Tennessee studied by Monhollon [202] had made significant progress in raising their income and level of living in the short run but less progress in the long-run resource adjustments required to turn their farms into viable units able to attract private sources of credit. And Herr [138] pointed out that it would take a very long time to eradicate farm poverty generally if special governmental credit programs of the size operated by the Farmers Home Administration in fiscal 1966 constituted the sole remedial measure.

Banfield [21] concluded that the tenant purchase program of the Farmers Home Administration was not suited to the postwar needs of the South. It was evident, he argued, that the eventual resolution of rural poverty and insecurity rested on adequate urban and industrial development. Thus the long-term farm credit program needed was not one that would create the maximum number of minimum-size farms, but rather one that would assist boldly and creatively in the reorganization of southern agriculture.

The supervised credit aspect of Farmers Home Administration lending has to be listed as one of the real contributions of the program. Various forms of supervised credit have been adopted by credit agencies in many underdeveloped countries. Colyer and Jimenez [82] reviewed the supervised credit programs of several public agencies in Colombia and concluded that they had induced changes in desirable directions.

Other studies have examined lenders' performance in servicing rural nonfarm credit needs, particularly in the area of housing. They generally indicated that the availability of housing credit in rural areas was not on a par with that in urban areas. For example, Hamlin [120] showed that in 1960 a smaller proportion of rural properties was mortgaged, the total first-mortgage debt was relatively smaller, and proportionately less financing was insured by the Federal Housing Administration or the Veterans Administration. Also, first-mortgage repayment terms were shorter, interest rates on conventional loans were higher, and debt-to-value ratios were much lower on both conventional and insured loans.

Similar findings came from a study by Hurst, Rose, and Yeager [158]. They concluded that government agencies and programs designed to aid the flow of mortgage funds into rural areas appeared to have had little effect in providing more mortgage funds at favorable terms to rural residents. Housing needs were not being met. The spread between appraised values and current prices of rural houses required down payments so large that rural people with limited equity could not utilize conventional loans. Relatively high down payment requirements prevented rural residents from obtaining home loans that could be economically justified by their repayment ability.

These findings were supported by Williams, Jones, and Miller [291], who concluded that rural areas had access to relatively few sources of home mortgage financing. Amounts and terms of housing credit were less favorable in rural areas than in larger towns and cities. Rural facilities for tapping the credit resources of larger institutions and metropolitan areas were found to be inadequate. Also, lending risks did not explain the inadequate credit and credit facilities in rural areas where, in general, loan repayment experience had been good.

Data used in these studies predated the enactment, beginning in 1961, of a series of laws and amendments authorizing the Farmers Home Administration to make and insure nonfarm residential mortgage loans in small towns and rural areas. The outstanding rural housing debt insured by the Farmers Home Administration rose rapidly to $9.9 billion on January 1, 1976, clearly indicating the large latent demand that had existed for such financing. The non-farm elements of Farmers Home Administration financing now comprise the greater share of its activity. In addition to the nonfarm housing, there is $2.1 billion outstanding in financing of community facilities and nonfarm commercial property. In contrast, the Farmers Home Administration held only $3.3 billion in outstanding farm mortgage debt and $1.9 billion in farm non-real estate debt.

The Farm Credit Act of 1971 also gave the federal land banks and production credit associations authority to make rural home and farm-related business loans. Outstanding loans under these programs had reached $551 million and $28 million, respectively, by January 1, 1976.

Clearly, new studies are needed to evaluate the impact of the Farmers Home Administration and other programs in relieving the rural housing credit deficiencies documented by earlier work. Also, studies of the credit situation facing rural business and industry are needed to permit evaluation of banking performance and of the need for the federally sponsored rural development credit banks that are frequently proposed; unfortunately, data deficiencies appear to present formidable obstacles to empirical work in this area.

Few studies have examined the efficiency of lender operations or lending decisions. Lenders themselves could well undertake or sponsor more such work. One line of inquiry that was pursued in a series of studies examined the ability of lenders to discriminate between loan applicants who were good versus poor credit risks. Brinegar and Fettig [69] found that the quality grade assigned to loan collateral by the federal land banks was not correlated with the final disposition of the loan. However, the ratio of the loan to the "normal agricultural value" of the property — the capitalized value of expected future net cash returns — was significantly correlated. Also, the credit rating placed on a loan by production credit associations, and in particular the change in that rating over the life of the loan, was closely related to the ultimate disposition of the loan.

Reinsel and Brake [235] estimated discriminant functions that indicated which borrower characteristics on loan applications were related to future repayment on schedule. Interestingly, the list of significant characteristics differed for Farmers Home Administration and production credit association borrowers. Evans [97] also found that certain borrower and financial characteristics in South Dakota were related to whether or not a borrower was in financial difficulty. In this case, however, a discriminant function using values for these variables as of the first loan application could not differentiate between the borrowers who were later financially successful or unsuccessful — the significant differences developed after the credit was extended.

Krause and Williams [176] examined whether behavioral personality variables were related to net worth progress — or the lack thereof — of South Dakota borrowers during the period 1960-64. Several significant variables were found, and the best relationships were obtained by employing personality variables for both husband and wife.

Capital Markets and Financial Intermediaries

Rural Credit Markets

Credit markets and institutions — historically among the first concerns of agricultural finance — continue to receive much research attention. Numerous publications present information on the farm lending activity of various institutions. Reports on outstanding farm loan volume by the major farm lenders are regularly assembled by the USDA, supplemented with estimates for nonreporting lenders, and published in *Agricultural Finance Statistics* [280] and other outlets. These data have been the major source of information on changes in the relative role of various lenders operating in the agricultural credit market.

The proportion of farm debt held by the banking system rose from 15 percent in 1940 to a peak of 29 percent in 1952, eased to 26 percent with the turn in the cattle cycle, and then held near this level through the next decade before rising to another peak at 31 percent in 1974 (all data cited in this section are as of January 1 and exclude Commodity Credit Corporation loans). Rapid growth in time and savings deposits of rural banks helped their lending resources to stay abreast of rapidly rising total farm loan demands, as did their willingness to move to higher loan/deposit ratios.

Conversely, the proportion of total debt held by the cooperative Farm Credit System declined from 31 percent in 1940 to 12 percent in 1952 before beginning a steady climb that reached 29 percent by 1975. Federal land bank loans (plus those of the Federal Farm Mortgage Corporation and joint-stock land banks) accounted for the pronounced swing, falling from 29 percent of total farm debt in 1940 to a low of 7 percent in 1952. Thereafter, the federal land banks increased their share of farm debt, reaching 16 percent in 1975. Production credit associations, on the other hand, exhibited relatively steady growth in their share, increasing it from less than 2 percent in 1940 to 12 percent in 1975. By employing national money markets as their primary source of funds, the cooperative agencies were generally able to obtain the volume of loanable funds desired even during years when restrictive monetary policy was holding down growth in lending resources of commercial banks and life insurance companies, their major farm lending competitors. In addition, surveys have indicated that the production credit associations have been attracting the larger, more successful farmers as loan customers [141].

Obviously, the proportion of farm debt held by some other sources has declined since the early 1950s. One of these was the life insurance companies, whose share hit a postwar high of 14 percent in 1957, decreased to 12 percent in the 1960s, and then fell rapidly to 8 percent by 1975. During the years of relative decline the farm mortgage departments of life insurance companies faced strong internal competition for funds from policy loans and from higher-yielding nonfarm investments — the latter especially during periods when usury laws placed effective below-market ceilings on their farm mortgage interest rates in some states or when widespread financial optimism resulted in euphoric projections of potential total yields from investments in common stocks or in bonds or commercial and multifamily residential mortgages with "equity kickers" attached.

Another declining source has been the mixed group generally labeled "individuals and others," composed of sellers of farms, landlords, merchants, dealers, machinery and farm supply corporations, and finance companies — that is, all lenders other than the major financial institutions that regularly report their farm loan volume. The share of total farm debt held by this group peaked at 44 percent in 1953 and has since dropped in almost every year, reaching 29 percent in 1975. Virtually all of the relative decline occurred in the non-real estate component of this debt, which decreased from 24 percent of the total farm debt in 1952 to 7 percent in 1975. The drop was especially rapid in the late 1960s, according to data from the Census Bureau sample surveys of agricultural finance in 1965 and 1970 [282, 283]. (After publication of the 1970 survey, the USDA series on outstanding farm debt was revised downward sharply, rendering obsolete portions of numerous earlier analyses and discussions.) In contrast, real estate debt held by "individuals and others" — mainly sellers of farms — has remained at about one-fifth of total farm debt for the past twenty-five years.

Contrary to reports appearing in some of the agricultural finance literature of recent years, the proportion of total farm debt accounted for by the Farmers Home Administration has remained at about 5 percent for the past twenty years, rather than falling sharply as these reports indicated. The mistaken impression occurred because the series published by the USDA did not include the insured loans which were made by the Farmers Home Administration and then sold to investors under repurchase agreements. The USDA series has now been redefined to credit the Farmers Home Administration with these loans.

Over the years, insights into factors reflected by these aggregate data have been provided by numerous surveys, on both large and small scales, covering specific aspects of rural credit markets. These have added to our knowledge; still, at any given point in time, it is plain that only a partial picture and understanding of rural credit markets were achieved.

Carson [75] described farmer use of merchant credit in Indiana after surveying both farmers and merchants. About two-fifths of production item purchases involved merchant credit, but most farmers could have obtained all of the credit they needed for such purchases from institutional lenders. In other words, the use of merchant credit did not result from unavailability of credit from other sources. Some farmers said they used merchant credit because it was free of cost; another group was not aware of its potentially high cost.

A study by Christiansen, Hartwig, and Staniforth [79] covering the 1950s found banks in Wisconsin decreasing their real estate financing in favor of financing farm machinery and livestock. Three situations were described. One set of banks was expanding its farm loan volume and specializing in such lending, a second group had little change in its farm loans, and a third set was reorienting toward more emphasis on nonagricultural lending.

A relatively detailed analysis of a rural credit market was undertaken by Nisbet [216]. He discovered two credit markets operating in Chile; one was serviced by banks and the other by informal sources. Wealthy farmers were more closely tied to bank credit, whereas poor farmers tended to be served by the informal market.

Rural Financial Intermediation

As Baker, Hopkin, and Brinegar [17] have pointed out, analyses of rural financial intermediation may examine the efficiency of an individual intermediary or may consider the efficiency of part or all of the financial intermediation system. Empirical models, they suggested, could be useful in pursuing either line of inquiry. So far, however, most attention has focused on the first approach.

Frey [108] conceptualized a multiperiod linear programming model which could be used to examine the asset and liability management options of a rural bank. The model included a feedback mechanism in which deposit growth was affected by the bank's local lending activity. Barry and Hopkin [25] further described how this approach allows the full range of returns, feedback, and constraints to be specified in a systematic manner. Without such a model analytical attempts might overlook some of these important relationships.

Fisher, Boehlje, and Roush [106] constructed a computerized rural bank management game. This gaming and simulation model uses credit and banking market equations estimated from data for rural Oklahoma counties in 1972. The game provides players with insight into the many ramifications of bank management decisions.

Rural financial intermediation systems as a whole, however, have yet to be modeled. But many aspects of these systems have been examined, especially by Federal Reserve economists. Swackhamer and Doll [264] studied how the flow and price of bank credit were affected by economic and institutional factors. Their data on interest rate differentials and trends suggested the presence of considerable restrictions on credit flows among regions and over time. In general, interest rates charged by banks on similar farm loans were significantly higher in the South and West than in the East and Midwest. Farm loan rates did not respond quickly to changes in the prime rate posted by large urban banks. Many small banks paid lower rates on savings deposits than larger banks which tended to pay the maximum allowed; yet both groups charged about the same average rate on farm loans.

Melichar [193] noted that the volume of farm loan participations — loans on which two or more banks collaborated — had increased sevenfold during the decade ending in 1966. Most of these arrangements arose because relatively small banks had received loan requests exceeding their legal limit on the amount of loans outstanding to any one borrower. While past growth in this area had been rapid, Melichar questioned whether urban banks would continue to increase such lending rapidly in their new environment characterized by reduced liquidity and more frequent periods of restrictive monetary policy. Subsequently, Benjamin [32] studied the correspondent banking arrangements of small banks in Illinois during 1968 and 1969 — the latter a year of tight monetary policy. He found that while correspondent credit from Chicago banks fell that year, substantially increased credit was provided by banks in smaller Illinois cities which served as the primary correspondents of many of the rural banks.

A number of studies pointed out that correspondent banking arrangements were relatively costly to rural banks and their communities because the outflow of funds through balances maintained in urban correspondent banks far exceeded the return flow of funds through participations in rural loans. Melichar and Doll [198] estimated that at heavily agricultural banks in 1966 the return flow through farm loan participations averaged only 22 percent of correspondent balances at member banks and 16 percent at nonmember banks. Shane [255], in one of a series of studies of rural-urban fund flows in the banking system, found a substantial net flow of funds from banks in rural Minnesota and North Dakota to banks in the Minneapolis-St. Paul area. Benjamin [32] noted that one factor responsible for these results might be lack of knowledge among rural bankers about the amount of correspondent balances required to reimburse urban banks adequately for noncredit correspondent banking services rendered. Using data supplied by urban banks, he calculated that a typical rural bank in Illinois could pay for noncredit correspondent services by maintaining balances equal to between 3 and 4 percent of its deposits. In contrast, such rural banks in 1969 on average maintained correspondent balances exceeding 6 percent of deposits. Others have suggested that rural areas would benefit if correspondent services were paid for by fees rather than through balances [42, 198].

Since 1970 production credit associations have been authorized to participate with commercial banks in making farm loans to customers of the banks. This arrangement obviously gives banks an alternative to seeking participations from correspondent banks. As yet, however, no research studies appear to have investigated the use and relative merits of this program.

Brake [58] studied the intermediary function that federal intermediate credit banks (FICBs) could provide for commercial banks. After surveying banks that were both current and potential users of this credit service, he concluded that with several changes in FICB policies this little-used mechanism could develop into a more important source of funds for rural banks. However, a survey of FICB officials raised doubts that such changes would be made, although a reexamination of the policies was under way at the time.

The discount mechanism of the Federal Reserve banks was also reexamined by Federal Reserve researchers during the 1960s [198]. As a result of this reappraisal a seasonal borrowing privilege for member banks was proposed and implemented in 1973. In a study of eligibility for and use of the privilege Melichar and Holderness [199] found it constituted a potentially significant source of funds for many rural banks. However, relatively few banks used it in 1973. The reappraisal in addition recommended a basic borrowing privilege that would also be useful to rural banks but which has not yet been implemented.

Baughman [27] described the basic economic function of financial intermediaries as linking suppliers and users of funds, with a variety of instruments and institutions linking the national financial market to local markets for farm securities. He argued that the rapid growth in investment and output per worker and the low rate of return on farm capital all suggested that capital and credit had been readily available in agriculture, implying that financial intermediaries had performed their roles reasonably well.

Sloan [259] agreed with this view but at the same time pointed out imperfections in financial markets — the relative inflexibility in the price of agricultural credit compared with the price of credit in other sectors of the economy and the significant geographical variation in interest rates on agricultural loans. He also noted legal restrictions that often interfere with the flow of capital, among them prohibition of certain forms of banking structure, usury laws, and ceilings on interest rates paid by banks and other thrift institutions.

In a later study for the Federal Reserve Board's Committee on Rural Banking Problems Sloan [258] urged that a new intermediary be interposed between small banks and the national money markets, since small banks are unable to raise funds in such markets directly. He proposed that the Federal Reserve System provide this function by establishing a pool of special time deposit certificates issued by small banks and then periodically auctioning participations in this pool to money-market investors, thereby effectively linking small banks to national money markets. The committee's report [42] advised the Federal Reserve System to consider establishing such a mechanism if other private or governmental initiatives were not undertaken to improve the ability of small and rural banks to raise money-market funds.

Rural financial disadvantages are not limited to credit markets. Brake [64] suggested that rural savers also operate in inadequate markets, in that their investment alternatives are limited and often provide only relatively low returns. He felt that investment information is less readily available, and its quality lower, in rural areas than in urban areas.

In another work on rural financial markets Hayenga and Brake [130] analyzed the effects of rural bank mergers on the banking services offered to citizens of rural communities. As a result of bank mergers customers had access to a wider variety of banking services, including new services not previously offered by independent banks. Markets for loans and savings became more closely tied to money-market conditions. Loan eligibility requirements were liberalized, making a wider range of people eligible for loans.

Other research concentrated more specifically on the relationship between banking structure and the ability of commercial banks to fulfill adequately their role as farm credit intermediaries. These studies have produced varied opinions and results. For example, Brake [55] concluded that without new institutions or changes in existing institutional arrangements rural banks would be unable to maintain their share of the farm credit business. Similarly, Hopkin and Frey [154] concluded that branch banking was needed to permit banks in Illinois to meet more readily the increased lines of credit demanded by Illinois farmers.

Melichar [197] found little support for these views in the aggregate relationships between state banking structures and the relative problems and importance of banks in farm lending during the 1960s. More banks in unit-banking states had encountered problems in financing farmers than had banks in branching states, but they had also made relatively more use of mechanisms designed to cope with such problems. Furthermore, farmers in unit-banking states in 1970 obtained a greater proportion of their credit from banks and also obtained more bank credit relative to farm income and assets. During the 1960s the relative importance of banks in farm lending increased slightly in the unit-banking states but fell in the states permitting branching. Interestingly, the relative total debt of farmers did not vary significantly among these groups of states, perhaps indicating that the farm loan demands had been similar and that nonbank lenders had offset variations in the farm lending activity of banks.

Several Federal Reserve studies [42] examined the relative proportion of farm loans in bank portfolios before and after banking structure changes, comparing banks involved in such changes with control groups of similar banks not involved. Taken together, their findings were inconclusive. In Ohio and Virginia no significant differences emerged, in Wisconsin banks that branched better sustained their relative farm lending emphasis, but in Florida banks acquired by holding companies rapidly reduced their farm lending. But such results do suggest the need for additional work to determine why the potential farm lending advantages of branch and group banking may not be realized in practice and what adjustments might be helpful.

These studies illustrate the growing volume of literature on financial markets, but it remains true that the literature has been disproportionately oriented to describing specific institutions — particularly lending institutions — rather than to improving the understanding of rural financial markets in a broader sense, including markets for savings and for debt and equity instruments. Among the work already mentioned, Baughman's analysis suggests the economic logic that could be employed in studies of financial markets. Sloan's discussion points out some suspected market imperfections which merit study. Certainly the time is ripe, as noted by Baker, Hopkin, and Brinegar, to undertake some modeling of financial markets. Such modeling will require both more empirical information than is currently available and a more macro-oriented and analytical approach to financial markets than that applied in most past studies.

Effects of National Monetary Policies

Only limited research has evaluated the impact of national monetary and credit policies on agriculture. Doll's empirical analysis of the 1950s [91] concluded that easing of monetary conditions — that is, increasing money supply — would not be beneficial to agriculture. He found the relationship between money supply and farm prices received to be inverse and statistically poor during the period 1947-57. Further, a comparison of farm costs and monetary conditions did not suggest that easy money policies would reduce farm costs.

Contrary to Doll's results, Gramm and Nash [116] found that agricultural incomes and investments had been responsive to changes in the money supply in the same manner as nonfarm incomes and investments. The elasticities of farm and nonfarm incomes in response to money supply changes were similar and statistically significant over the 1919-66 period. However, although farm investments were related to changes in the money supply, the elasticities of farm and nonfarm investments relative to changes in the money supply were dissimilar, perhaps because interest rates on farm loans were relatively inflexible. Given these results, the authors advised that farm policy "might be more effective if it were more closely coordinated with overall monetary and fiscal policy."

Sharpe [256] examined the impact of tight credit on farm mortgages during 1963-69, a period in which interest rates on farm mortgage loans rose from about 6 percent to almost 9 percent. Over this period federal land banks expanded their share of the market while commercial banks and life insurance companies accounted for reduced shares. In a tight-money year such as 1969 sellers of farms financed a greater proportion of farm real estate transfers. Evans and Warren [98] looked more generally at the impact of tight money in 1966 on both real estate and non-real estate credit experience. They concluded that while mortgage credit had been tight for both farmers and others, farmers had been served well with short-term and intermediate-term credit during a period when some other segments of the economy had experienced difficulties in securing such funds.

Trimble [271] examined the effect of the stringent monetary and credit policies of 1969 and 1970 on the cattle industry, testing the hypothesis that they had contributed to the higher farm-level beef prices of 1973 by causing increased herd culling or decreased investment in productive capacity. He found the effect to be relatively minor in that only 5 percent of the 1973 level of beef prices appeared to be attributable to 1969-70 credit conditions.

At its annual meeting in 1971, the American Agricultural Economics Association sponsored a session on the impact of inflation on agriculture. Brandow [67] pointed out that during the period 1953-70 demand-pull inflation had benefited farmers in some respects while cost-push inflation had been damaging to farmers. He felt that future inflation would more likely be cost-push in nature. Similarly, Tweeten and Quance [276, 277] concluded that the 1970 inflation rate in farm input prices — 4 percent annually — if continued would bring hard times to the farming industry. The more severe impact would arise from increases in the prices of inputs for which farmers have relatively inelastic demand, such as taxes, wages, and interest rates. In contrast, price inflation for cash operating inputs with an elastic demand, such as fertilizer, would not be so damaging.

In view of the rapid price inflation of 1973-75 and the apparently high probability of continued inflationary pressures, these results suggest a need for additional study of the impact of inflation and of anti-inflation policies on farming and on farm finance.

Suggestions for Future Research

The Question of Research Priorities

As one reviews the literature in agricultural finance, there is a temptation to evaluate the research in light of later developments. Often, however, important subsequent developments are not recognized in advance by researchers or are perceived by relatively few. Further, the literature contains a number of instances where problems and, indeed, proposed research directions were incorrectly perceived by the leaders of the time. Hence, the contribution subsequently deemed important came from the individual who went in a different direction and/or visualized a different priority.

Our reviewers urged us to indicate research priorities in agricultural finance on the basis of our review. We resisted these suggestions for several reasons. Most importantly, the review itself was a humbling experience as it revealed the wide range and the large number of publications in this field. It gave us little reason to believe that our priority set, necessarily influenced by our own special interests and experience, would be more useful than that of numerous other agricultural finance specialists. The review does, however, provide leads and ideas for researchers to consider while formulating their own priorities and interests. With the additional suggestions in this section, it supplements other extensive compilations of research needs [15, 37, 46, 57, 152]. But in this rapidly changing world research lists and priorities must shift as critical problems arise (or sometimes even disappear) almost overnight.

Less Duplication of Descriptive Research

The literature contains numerous publications on sources of farm credit, farmers' attitudes toward credit, calculation of interest rates, and farmers' debt levels. Although such information is necessary and useful for analytic and policy purposes, it is questionable whether each state needs to duplicate the efforts of others in these areas. Probably too little attention has been given to joint utilization of state or USDA publications.

At the beginning of a research project in agricultural finance a descriptive study is often necessary as a basis for further analysis in a second-stage project or for suggesting hypotheses to be tested in follow-up research. Too often, however, only the descriptive study is published. There is no analytical follow-up, and indeed, often the researcher then moves into a different interest area. A general criticism of past publications is relative overemphasis on "what is" or "what has been" at the expense of analysis of alternatives; that is, of "what might be."

Importance of Basic Data

If policy makers and researchers are to remain informed, there is an important need for continuing, accurate data on cash and capital flows, ownership of financial resources in farming, returns to those resources, and costs of resource services. The Balance Sheet and other USDA series represent a good foundation, but additional data are needed.

The Balance Sheet provides information on the capital stock and debt of agriculture, but there is no complete and comparable information on flows of cash or capital. For example, information is presently available on outstanding farm loans including both real estate and non-real estate. However, it is almost impossible to obtain full information on gross credit extended and repaid in any one year. Yet, such data are critical to the estimation of flows.

A similar need exists for information on the loss of capital from the agricultural sector in the course of intergenerational transfers. Two important aspects are involved: (1) the estimation of capital that leaves the sector through the sale of farms by retiring farmers or by nonfarmer heirs — capital that must be replenished by new entrants or through borrowing and saving; and (2) the impact of taxation and transfer laws on the individual farmer as well as on the sector. Each of these is important for different policy purposes.

In addition to a need for a breakdown of cash-flow detail by landlords, capital owners, and operators, improved information is desirable on the flows to resource services. It would be useful, for example, if the dollar value of leasing machinery and rental of real estate were available on a national and state basis. Such data would be revealing with respect to terms of trade on capital resources.

Other data that might well be updated from time to time are estimates of the real effects of price changes on the wealth of the farming sector. A number of such studies have been mentioned in this review. None of these studies, however, led to the establishment of a continuing series.

Consistency among data sources is also vitally needed. A single project may use data from the Census, the *Balance Sheet, Farm Income Statistics*, and lending institutions; yet, in many important respects these series are based on different definitions of farming. The various data sources providing financial information need to be consistent, one with the other, and they need to do a better job of presenting farm numbers and other assumptions going into their construction, calculation, and coverage.

Provision and analysis of the financial data discussed here have been traditional functions of the USDA. Some researchers are currently concerned that the recent reorganization of the USDA may adversely affect its ability to perform these functions. There seems some danger that the dissolution of the Agricultural Finance Branch and its focal responsibility for financial research may lead to fragmentation and loss of a unifying purpose rather than to improved data generation and analysis.

The observations of the American Agricultural Economics Association Committee on Economic Statistics [3] should be considered in formulating and revising agricultural finance data programs. The committee stressed the need for improved knowledge of capital investment structures, physical as well as human. Its comments relating to the need for better measurement of the increasingly diverse income and assets of farmers and the rural population should be heeded. As it noted, attention must be given to the fact that, for some problems and data, "farm" and "farm sector" are no longer meaningful concepts or feasible units of observation. And it is certainly true that information systems should provide data better suited for program evaluation, to permit analyses of the effectiveness of social programs and private institutions.

The rapidly changing nature of farm and rural society means that continued attention must be focused on updating and rethinking data needs, concepts, and future directions to enable our data systems to continue to support research that contributes effectively to problem solving and policy making.

Use of Theory and Modeling

Throughout the literature review there were numerous instances of the development of theoretical concepts or the adaptation of theories from related areas of work. Conceptualization, theory, and modeling are invaluable in establishing research directions and specifying data needs; they should receive continued attention in all areas of agricultural finance. Currently, theoretical and modeling efforts would seem to have particular potential in work on capital formation, decision theory under risk and uncertainty, sources and uses of funds, capital markets, and firm growth.

Evaluation of Potential Innovations

A number of innovations have been suggested in agricultural finance. Few of these have received serious research emphasis. Examples include variable (principal) repayment plans, permanent or semipermanent debt, new debt instruments, new financial institutions or changes in regulations governing financial institutions, provision of related financial services, and low-equity financing in combination with loan insurance. These types of questions are researchable. As one example, a simulator could be developed to examine effects of innovations such as variable payment loans in which the repayment of principal is related to farm profits, yields, or prices. Effects of permanent debt could similarly be described for both borrowers and lenders under a range of circumstances.

Given the increasing capital needs of farming throughout the period under consideration, there have been suggestions that lenders should provide lower-equity financing. Although low-equity financing has been evaluated in terms of its effect on growth, we have found no research evaluating low-equity financing from the viewpoint of the lender. Some analysts have suggested, often as part of proposals for low-equity financing, an insured farm loan program similar to the residential mortgage insurance programs of the Federal Housing Administration and the Farmers Home Administration. The experience of these institutions, in terms of its lessons for the feasibility, design, and administration of a similar farm agency, would seem to be worth exploring.

Another suggestion often heard is that credit institutions should provide additional related services. What is the potential for farm credit-related services such as record services, estate planning services, or management consulting services? Research should be able to shed light on the nature and extent of such needs.

Present farmland title registration and transfer procedures seem unduly cumbersome. How might such procedures be modernized and simplified? Could research suggest and evaluate procedures that would be useful in achieving this end?

Perhaps, given the increased variability in output prices and farm income, it is timely for thought and research to return to the area of overdue loans. In such an environment widespread financial setbacks could occur. There may be need for analyses of approaches to debt moratoria or changes in foreclosure proceedings. Past ideas such as the establishment of a debt-adjustment authority may also deserve to be reexplored.

Evaluation of Institutions and Arrangements

There has been a great deal of descriptive research on how various credit institutions operate, but much less evaluative and analytical research has been done on these institutions. An exception might be the Farmers Home Administration. Several studies have analyzed its operations and the extent to which they achieved stated purposes. Somewhat less research has been devoted to evaluation of the cooperative Farm Credit System agencies and the commercial banking system.

A number of institutional changes deserve research. Given what appears to be a continually rising need for capital and credit by American agriculture, can existing institutions meet future farm credit needs? What reorganization or changes might be useful? For example, should the relatively small rural banks be provided with new ways to obtain funds? By what means, such as pooling arrangements, might they increase their farm loans and at the same time keep their risks at acceptable levels? Would new financial institutions be useful — perhaps a counterpart of the Federal National Mortgage Association to insure farm loans? For many of these questions, modeling and simulation of intermediary institutions and systems serving the farming sector would be a useful approach.

Additional questions needing research are whether existing lending institutions could operate more efficiently and whether present credit arrangements are appropriate. Credit arrangements deserving of evaluation are one-stop credit, line-of-credit financing, and supervised credit. Some studies of these credit arrangements have been undertaken, but continuing analysis would be useful.

One recent institutional change that deserves evaluation is the federal land banks' new role in rural home financing. Have additional funds for rural home financing become available because of this program? Or do these funds substitute for funds from other agencies? Have rural home mortgage credit terms been liberalized because of the program? Has the implementation of this rural home financing option been detrimental to farm borrowers?

Credit institutions themselves have undertaken little research on innovations, policy changes, or their own operations. Probably the major exception is the Federal Reserve System, which employs a number of research economists who have examined policy questions and provided some meaningful information to decision makers. However, commercial banks as a group sponsor little research on farm credit. The Farm Credit System does some research, but this has, in general, focused on data gathering rather than analysis. Similarly, life insurance companies do little research in farm credit. All these institutions could well undertake or underwrite a larger share of the research responsibility.

Credit Policy Analysis

From time to time analysis is needed of the financial or economic effects of specific public policies. For example, it would be useful to know more about the effects of specific monetary policies and/or usury laws on farmers. During periods of tight money, do farmers cut back investment plans and thereby cause higher prices at some later time? Or are farmers relatively sheltered from the effects of monetary policy actions? What are the effects of state usury laws, rural bank mergers, and bank holding company acquisitions on the availability and cost of farm credit? What are the effects of various federal income and estate taxes on farmers? How would farmers be affected by being required to file income taxes on an accrual basis rather than on a cash basis? Such issues have received rather minimal research attention over the period since World War II; yet they are the questions facing policy makers and the public.

Perhaps researchers have treated credit policy issues to the greatest extent in speeches, interviews, legislative testimony, and popular periodicals. If so, there is need for a periodic or ongoing forum in which these thoughts are gathered and discussed. In this respect the Agency for International Development Spring Review of Small Farmer Credit can be cited as a noteworthy attempt to focus on some of the important issues in small farmer credit programs in developing countries [284, 285]. Similar treatment of domestic programs and policies would be useful.

Disinvestment from Farming

A neglected area of research has been disinvestment from farming. Perhaps this lack of interest came in part from the fact that many farmers continued to farm until they died. Yet now many farmers retire from farming. For those who do not, their widows may face retirement problems. They, too, need help in planning for retirement. What are the alternatives these retiring farm families face? How can they protect their capital from inflation and other drains to best meet their retirement goals? Where can they get qualified help in making the decisions that will affect their level of living for the remainder of their lives?

Rural Financial Markets

The rural financial market has been neglected until recently. This represents one place where a basic descriptive study is needed as a start. Questions to be answered are the extent to which rural borrowers and savers have access to credit and investment markets and whether such markets operate efficiently. While the credit market serving farmers appears to be relatively efficient, there is reason to believe that other rural borrowers face a more imperfect market. In both markets there is not enough continuing information on the volume and terms of real estate loans from individuals and non-real estate loans from merchants and dealers. It may be the case that more research has been done on the functioning of rural financial markets in developing countries than in the United States.

Too often the concern with rural capital markets is a concern only with their functioning from the standpoint of borrowers. One suspects that the market for savers functions less effectively than the market for borrowers. In many rural areas stock brokers have no offices within a reasonable driving distance; nor is it easy for rural savers to purchase debt instruments of governments or corporations. Probably many rural savers recognize only a savings account at the local commercial bank or the purchase of real estate as options for investing savings.

The linkage between rural and national capital and credit markets should also be explored. Capital should flow freely into and out of rural areas, depending on relative demand-supply relationships. What methods might be used to increase the efficiency of markets for debt instruments? Do the debt instruments themselves need to be changed? Are new markets necessary?

Another area for potential contribution concerns the effects of inflation on rural financial markets. Does capital flow less freely during a period of inflation? Do capital flows shift because of market imperfections? Or are such flows kept from shifting because of arbitrary restrictions? Is the rural borrower or saver at a disadvantage (or advantage) compared to his urban counterpart during inflation?

Analysis of Fund Flows

Recently attention has been given to the development of flow-of-funds accounts and models for the agricultural sector. However, considerable additional effort is needed. Understanding of the sources and uses of funds, whether in the context of the individual farm operator or the agricultural sector as a whole, is important to understanding what is happening financially in agriculture. From the standpoint of the farm operator this information is needed in planning the farm operation and in making plans for borrowing and repaying debt. Policy makers in government, in farm cooperatives, and in firms manufacturing or distributing farm inputs require similar information for the entire agricultural sector.

A cash or capital flows approach to agricultural finance research is one area in which considerable conceptualization and theory is needed. Theory and conceptualization should lead the way in specifying data needs and uses. For example, what data are useful in a decision-making context for the individual farm firm? How should debt service be related to cash flow? How do family living expenditures relate to the cash flow for the farm business unit? How does cash flow affect decisions on new equipment investments or upon timing of such investments?

What are the important relationships to be examined in a regional type-of-farming model or a national sector model? Can flows data be organized to tell us how farm balance sheets change from one year to the next, who finances the changes, what happens to the assets of farmers who leave farming, and how those who enter acquire capital?

Already a flows approach has shown much merit for projecting future capital and credit needs. The approach seems to offer potential for further research if data problems can be resolved and if data needs and uses are better conceptualized.

Problem-Oriented Research

Problem-oriented research necessarily depends on the times and hence the financing situation of farmers. Firm growth, for example, is an area that has received much attention, but more effort would reveal further insights. What are the choices and trade-offs among alternative sources of capital? What are optimal strategies for growth? To what extent do optimal strategies vary by type of farm, stage in life of the operator, or the economic setting of the country? How are risk and uncertainty considered in the context of firm growth? These and many other questions relating to growth need attention.

Some problem-oriented research also adds to our basic understanding of financing. For example, the major thrust of past work has emphasized external financing. Yet, the major financing of the farm business has been internal; that is, nondebt financing. The literature has surprisingly little to offer in the way of descriptions of internal financing or of theoretical and conceptual models dealing with internal financing decisions. Additional research may prove rewarding in terms of improved understanding of loan demands as well as of saving and investment decisions.

Additional theory and conceptualization are needed in management of financial resources. Replacement and investment decision models deserve further development. What factors should receive central focus in such models?

There is considerable room for development of management and decision-making strategies for risk and uncertainty situations. Insurance strategies need to be formulated and analyzed. Informal insurance, diversification-specialization questions, and other considerations involving risk and uncertainty merit similar study.

In the 1970s risk stemming from price changes has taken on new dimensions. The relative price stability of the 1960s has been replaced with both rapidly increasing input prices and highly volatile product prices. The financial manager must now give increased attention to the management of marketing and price risks arising from variations in national farm policy and international markets. Analysis of strategies for dealing with these risks appears very timely, as does the study of their implications for farm finance.

There is a continuing need for research to answer practical problems that farmers or farm families face. Often these problems are associated with stages in the operator's life cycle — for example, the problem of getting started in farming. The acquisition and control of capital by beginning farmers requires continuing study as farm income and credit conditions change. Expansion and disinvestment stages are additional problem points. With respect to each of these, continuing research should examine typical situations farmers face, their alternatives, and strategies to achieve family goals and objectives.

Research should continue to examine the effects of tenure and organizational forms on financial progress. Rental, leasing, owning, partnerships, and corporations all have their advantages and disadvantages, and as laws change and asset prices fluctuate new studies are needed to indicate the situations in which each is most useful. As farms increase in size and the partnership and corporate forms of organization are employed more often, the relationships between individual and firm life cycles may prove a rewarding research area. And if many farm firms achieve sufficient size to have their shares publicly traded, there will be new questions to examine.

Research emphasis on estate planning to achieve firm and family objectives should be continued. As tax laws change and as farmers' situations change, there is need to update analyses. Similarly, federal and state income tax changes should be analyzed for their impact on farmers' tax strategies.

Effects of Credit on Income Distribution

Credit policy over the years has implicitly assumed that credit represented a means of helping producers who could utilize additional resources to obtain those resource services. The tone of the early Farmers Home Administration programs and many of the credit programs in developing countries seemed to be built on this premise. In essence, credit programs provided a means of helping those without adequate resources to expand faster and become viable business firms.

Policy makers need analyses of the distribution of the income and other benefits of credit programs in order to help them choose among alternative programs. This would seem to be an area in which theory and conceptualization could point the way for research. For example, to what extent can alternative credit programs help disadvantaged individuals to better their situation? How would various restrictions or adjustments in credit policies affect the income distribution of the borrowers utilizing a given program or the distribution of the income or other benefits achieved under that program?

Concluding Comments

In concluding, two additional comments are offered. First, the total contributions in agricultural finance could have been greater had there been better coordination and communication among researchers. There is ample evidence both of needless duplication and of failure to build on previous research. Had there been more leadership exerted or more conscious efforts made to focus or coordinate research in agricultural finance, perhaps the results might have fitted better into a complete picture. A conference held at Allerton Park, Illinois, in 1968 represented such an attempt to promote discussion of problems and to focus research [152]. This was a useful undertaking. Future efforts of this type are to be encouraged.

Finally, in looking ahead to future social and economic needs, probably more emphasis should be put on rural financial research as opposed to farm financial research. This is not to argue that less emphasis should be put on farm finance but rather to suggest that rural nonfarm residents and businesses, as well as rural communities and governments, deserve more attention to their problems.

References

[1] Adams, D. W. "Agricultural Credit in Latin America: A Critical Review of External Funding Policy." *Am. J. Agr. Econ.* 53:163-172, May 1971.

[2] Allen, P. T. *Farm Real Estate Credit — An Analysis of Borrowers and Lenders.* USDA, ERS, Agr. Econ. Rep. 104, 1966.

[3] American Agricultural Economics Association, Committee on Economic Statistics. "Our Obsolete Data Systems: New Directions and Opportunities." *Am. J. Agr. Econ.* 54:867-875, December 1972.

[4] American Bankers Association. *Agricultural Banking Developments, 1974.* Washington, D.C., 1974.

[5] American Institute of Banking. *Agricultural Credit.* American Bankers Association, 1954.

[6] ———. *Agricultural Finance.* American Bankers Association, 1969.

[7] Anderson, D. E., and G. H. Coulter. *North Dakota Agricultural Credit Problems and Practices.* North Dakota Agr. Exp. Sta. Bul. 423, 1960.

[8] Ardener, S. "The Comparative Study of Rotating Credit Associations." *Journal of the Royal Anthropological Institute of Great Britain and Ireland* 94:201-229, July-December 1964.

[9] Arnold, L. L. *Problems of Capital Accumulation in Getting Started Farming.* Purdue University Agr. Exp. Sta. Bul. 638, 1957.

[10] Atkinson, J. H. "A New Look at the Farm Debt Picture." *Fed. Reserve Bul.* 48:1571-1588, December 1962.

[11] Bailey, W. R. "Necessary Conditions for Growth of the Farm Business Firm." *Agr. Econ. Res.* 19:1-6, January 1967.

[12] Baker, C. B. "Credit in the Production Organization of the Firm." *Am. J. Agr. Econ.* 50:507-520, August 1968.

[13] ———. "Financial Organization and Production Choices." *Am. J. Agr. Econ.* 50:1566-1577, December 1968.

[14] Baker, C. B., and J. M. Holcomb. "The Emerging Financial Problems in a Changing Agriculture." *J. Farm Econ.* 46:1200-1206, December 1964.

[15] ———, eds. *Research and Teaching Programs in Agricultural Finance.* Illinois Agr. Fin. Program Rep. 2, 1970.

[16] Baker, C. B., and J. A. Hopkin. "Concepts of Finance Capital for a Capital-Using Agriculture." *Am. J. Agr. Econ.* 51:1055-1064, December 1969.

[17] Baker, C. B., J. A. Hopkin, and G. K. Brinegar. "Research in Financial Intermediation with Respect to Agriculture." In *Research and Teaching Programs in Agricultural Finance*, C. B. Baker and J. M. Holcomb, eds. Illinois Agr. Fin. Program Rep. 2, 1970.

[18] Baker, C. B., and G. D. Irwin. *Effects of Borrowing from Commercial Lenders on Farm Organization.* Illinois Agr. Exp. Sta. Bul. 671, 1961.

[19] ———. "Estimating Productivity and Financing Limits for Resources." In *Capital and Credit Needs in a Changing Agriculture*, E. L. Baum, H. G. Diesslin, and E. O. Heady, eds. Ames: Iowa State University Press, 1961.

[20] Baker, C. B., J. T. Scott, and F. J. Reiss. "Research in Farm Finance." In *Research and Teaching Programs in Agricultural Finance*, C. B. Baker and J. M. Holcomb, eds. Illinois Agr. Fin. Program Rep. 2, 1970.

[21] Banfield, E. C. "Ten Years of the Farm Tenant Purchase Program." *J. Farm Econ.* 31:469-486, August 1949.

[22] Barry, P. J. "Asset Indivisibility and Investment Planning: An Application of Linear Programming." *Am. J. Agr. Econ.* 54:255-259, May 1972.

[23] Barry, P. J., and C. B. Baker. "Reservation Prices on Credit Use: A Measure of Response to Uncertainty." *Am. J. Agr. Econ.* 53:222-227, May 1971.

[24] Barry, P. J., and J. R. Brake. *Financial Strategies and Economic Decisions of the Firm*. Michigan State University Agr. Econ. Rep. 185, 1971.

[25] Barry, P. J., and J. A. Hopkin. "Financial Intermediation in Agriculture: A Suggested Analytical Model." *Southern J. Agr. Econ.* 4:179-183, July 1972.

[26] Barry, P. J., and T. P. Phillips. *Cash Flows and Short Term Financing of Selected Farm Types*. University of Guelph, School of Agricultural Economics and Extension Education, AE 71/10, 1971.

[27] Baughman, E. T. "The Economic Role of Financial Intermediaries — Challenges of a Changing Agriculture." In *A New Look at Agricultural Finance Research*, J. A. Hopkin, ed. Illinois Agr. Fin. Program Rep. 1, 1970.

[28] Baum, E. L., H. G. Diesslin, and E. O. Heady, eds. *Capital and Credit Needs in a Changing Agriculture*. Ames: Iowa State University Press, 1961.

[29] Belshaw, H. "Capital and Credit." In *Selected Readings in Agricultural Credit*, I. F. Davis, Jr., ed. International Conference on Agricultural and Cooperative Credit, University of California, 1952.

[30] Benedict, M. R., G. H. Aull, K. Brandt, G. W. Hedlund, and W. G. Murray. "The Federally Sponsored Credit Services to American Agriculture — Suggestions for Improvement and Coordination." *J. Farm Econ.* 29:1429-1502, November 1947.

[31] Benjamin, G. L. "Concern for Growing Farm Debt." Federal Reserve Bank of Chicago, *Business Conditions*, pp. 8-13, June 1974.

[32] ———. "Correspondent Banking in Illinois: Credit Flows and Pricing Practices." In *Improved Fund Availability at Rural Banks — Report and Study Papers of the Committee on Rural Banking Problems*. Board of Governors of the Federal Reserve System, 1975.

[33] Benson, R. A., and J. R. Brake. *Financing Expansion to Large-Scale Dairy Farming*. Michigan Agr. Exp. Sta. Res. Rep. 76, 1969.

[34] Bhatia, K. B. "On Estimating Capital Gains in U.S. Agriculture." *Am. J. Agr. Econ.* 53:502-506, August 1971.

[35] Bierman, R. W., and B. A. Case. *Farm-Mortgage Loans of the Federal Land Banks*. USDA ARS 43-86, 1958.

[36] ———. "The Farmers Home Administration and Its Borrowers." *Agr. Fin. Rev.* 21:40-67, July 1959.

[37] Black, J. D., ed. *Research in Agricultural Credit — Scope and Method*. Social Science Research Council, 1931.

[38] Blase, M. G., and C. Hesemann. "Farm Land Prices: Explainable or Illogical?" *Southern J. Agr. Econ.* 5:265-270, July 1973.

[39] Board of Governors of the Federal Reserve System. *Bank Loans to Farmers*. Washington, D.C., 1947.

[40] ———. *Farm Debt — Data from the 1960 Sample Survey of Agriculture*. Washington, D.C., 1964.

[41] ———. *Farm Loans at Commercial Banks*. Washington, D.C., 1957.

[42] ———. *Improved Fund Availability at Rural Banks — Report and Study Papers of the Committee on Rural Banking Problems*. Washington, D.C., 1975.

[43] Bobst, B. W. "An Input-Output Approach to the Study of the Flow of Funds to Agricultural Capital Markets." *Southern J. Agr. Econ.* 1:21-26, December 1969.

[44] Boehlje, M. D., and L. M. Eisgruber. "Strategies for the Creation and Transfer of the Farm Estate." *Am. J. Agr. Econ.* 54:461-472, August 1972.

[45] Boehlje, M. D., and T. K. White. *An Analysis of the Impact of Selected Factors on the Process of Farm Firm Growth*. Purdue University Agr. Exp. Sta. Res. Bul. 854, 1969.

[46] Bostwick, D. *Farm Financial Management Research — A Theoretical Analysis*. USDA ERS-389, 1968.

[47] ———. *Partitioning Financial Returns: An Application to the Growth of Farm Firms*. USDA ERS-390, 1969.

[48] Bostwick, D., J. Esmay, and G. Rodewald. *Agricultural Production Credit in Montana*. Montana Agr. Exp. Sta. Circ. 233, 1961.

[49] Bottomley, A. "The Determination of Pure Rates of Interest in Underdeveloped Rural Areas." *Rev. Econ. Stat.* 46:301-304, August 1964.

[50] ———. "The Premium for Risk as a Determinant of Interest Rates in Underdeveloped Rural Areas." *Quart. J. Econ.* 77:637-647, November 1963.

[51] ———. "The Structure of Interest Rates in Underdeveloped Rural Areas." *J. Farm Econ.* 46:313-322, May 1964.

[52] Botts, R. R. *Farmers' Handbook of Financial Calculations and Physical Measurements*. USDA Agr. Handbook 230, 1964.

[53] Boussard, J. "Time Horizon, Objective Function, and Uncertainty in a Multiperiod Model of Firm Growth." *Am. J. Agr. Econ.* 53:467-477, August 1971.

[54] Boyne, D. H. *Changes in the Real Wealth Position of Farm Operators, 1940-1960*. Michigan Agr. Exp. Sta. Tech. Bul. 294, 1964.

[55] Brake, J. R. "Can Rural Banks Meet Increased Farm Credit Demands?" *Banking* (Journal of the American Bankers Association) 60:80-83, April 1968.

[56] ———. "Capital and Credit." In *Size, Structure and Future of Farms*, A. G. Ball and E. O. Heady, eds. Ames: Iowa State University Press, 1972.

[57] ———. "Capitalizing Agriculture in Coming Years." In *Emerging and Projected Trends Likely to Influence the Structure of Midwest Agriculture, 1970-1985*, J. R. Brake, ed. Iowa Agr. Law Center, Monograph 11, 1970.

[58] ———. "Federal Intermediate Credit Bank Discount Services to Rural Banks: Experience and Prospects." In *Improved Fund Availability at Rural Banks — Report and Study Papers of the Committee on Rural Banking Problems*. Board of Governors of the Federal Reserve System, 1975.

[59] ———. *Financing Michigan Farms: The Thumb*. Michigan Agr. Exp. Sta. Res. Rep. 1, 1963.

[60] ———. "Firm Growth Models Often Neglect Important Cash Withdrawals." *Am. J. Agr. Econ.* 50:769-772, August 1968.

[61] ———. *Future Capital and Credit Needs of Canadian Agriculture*. University of Guelph, Dept. Agr. Econ., AE 70/3, 1970.

[62] ———. "Impact of Structural Changes on Capital and Credit Needs." *J. Farm Econ.* 48:1536-1545, December 1966.

[63] ———. *Interest Rate Terminology and Calculation*. Michigan State University Agr. Econ. Rep. 13, 1966.

[64] ———. "The Money Market – Is It Adequate for the Needs of Today's Agriculture?" *Am. J. Agr. Econ.* 52:695-696, December 1970.

[65] Brake, J. R., and P. J. Barry. "Flow-of-Funds Social Accounts for the Farm Sector: Comment." *Am. J. Agr. Econ.* 53:665-668, November 1971.

[66] Brake, J. R., and M. E. Wirth. *The Michigan Farm Credit Panel: A History of Capital Accumulation.* Michigan Agr. Exp. Sta. Res. Rep. 25, 1964.

[67] Brandow, G. E. "The Distribution among Agricultural Producers, Commodities, and Resources of Gains and Losses from Inflation in the Nation's Economy." *Am. J. Agr. Econ.* 53:913, December 1971.

[68] Brimmer, A. F. "Central Banking and the Availability of Agricultural Credit." *Am. J. Agr. Econ.* 50:357-365, May 1968.

[69] Brinegar, G. K., and L. P. Fettig. *Some Measures of the Quality of Agricultural Credit.* National Bureau of Economic Research, Tech. Pap. 19, 1968.

[70] Burkett, W. K. *Farm Size and the Capital Acquisition Problem on New Hampshire Dairy Farms.* New Hampshire Agr. Exp. Sta. Bul. 457, 1959.

[71] Burroughs, R. J. "Balance Sheet of Agriculture – Meaning, Conceptual Limitations, and Uses." *Agr. Econ. Res.* 2:86-95, July 1950.

[72] Butz, E. L. Review of *Financing the Farm Business,* I. W. Duggan and R. U. Battles. *Agr. Econ. Res.* 2:135-136, October 1950.

[73] ———. *The Production Credit System for Farmers.* Washington, D.C.: Brookings Institution, 1944.

[74] Carlin, T. A., and E. I. Reinsel. "Combining Income and Wealth: An Analysis of Farm Family 'Well-Being.'" *Am. J. Agr. Econ.* 55:38-44, February 1973.

[75] Carson, E. E. *Farmer Use of Merchant Credit in Indiana.* Purdue University Agr. Exp. Sta. EC-143, 1957.

[76] Carver, T. N. *How to Use Farm Credit.* USDA Farmers Bul. 593, 1914.

[77] Case, B. A. *Farm-Mortgage Loans Held by Life Insurance Companies.* USDA ARS 43-58, 1957.

[78] Chisholm, A. H. "Criteria for Determining the Optimum Replacement Pattern." *J. Farm Econ.* 48:107-112, February 1966.

[79] Christiansen, R. A., P. A. Hartwig, and S. D. Staniforth. *Bank Credit for Agriculture in Wisconsin.* Wisconsin Agr. Exp. Sta. Bul. 557, 1962.

[80] Chryst, W. E. "Land Values and Agricultural Income: A Paradox?" *J. Farm Econ.* 47:1265-1273, December 1965.

[81] Coffman, G. W. *Corporations with Farming Operations.* USDA Agr. Econ. Rep. 209, 1971.

[82] Colyer, D., and G. Jimenez. "Supervised Credit as a Tool in Agricultural Development." *Am. J. Agr. Econ.* 53:639-642, November 1971.

[83] Commission on Money and Credit. *Federal Credit Agencies.* Englewood Cliffs, N.J.: Prentice-Hall, 1963.

[84] ———. *Federal Credit Programs.* Englewood Cliffs, N.J.: Prentice-Hall, 1963.

[85] Cotner, M. L., M. E. Wirth, and J. R. Brake. "Credit Experience of Commercial Crop and Livestock Farmers in Purchasing Land in Michigan." Michigan Agr. Exp. Sta., *Quart. Bul.* 45:634-645, May 1963.

[86] Cromarty, W. A. "The Farm Demand for Tractors, Machinery, and Trucks." *J. Farm Econ.* 41:323-331, May 1959.

[87] Dahl, R. P. "Some Price Discrimination Aspects in Bank Farm Loan Interest Rates." *J. Farm Econ.* 44:126-140, February 1962.

[88] Dean, G. W., and H. O. Carter. "Some Effects of Income Taxes on Large-Scale Agriculture." *J. Farm Econ.* 44:754-768, August 1962.

[89] Diesslin, H. G. Review of *Capital in Agriculture: Its Formation and Financing since 1870*, A. S. Tostlebe. *J. Farm Econ.* 40:515-517, May 1958.

[90] Doll, R. J. "Farm Debt As Related to Value of Sales." *Fed. Reserve Bul.* 49: 140-148, February 1963.

[91] ———. "Some Implications of Monetary Policy on Agriculture." *J. Farm Econ.* 40:21-29, February 1958.

[92] Dorner, P., and C. Sandretto. *Resource Adjustments, Income Growth and Tenure — Their Interaction on Farms in Two Wisconsin Dairy Areas, 1950-1960.* Wisconsin Res. Bul. 242, 1963.

[93] Duggan, I. W., and R. U. Battles. *Financing the Farm Business.* New York: Wiley, 1950.

[94] Duvick, R. D. *Alternative Methods of Financing Growth on Michigan Dairy Farms.* Unpublished Ph.D. dissertation, Michigan State University, 1970.

[95] Elefson, R. V., and P. M. Raup. *Financing Farm Transfers with Land Contracts.* North Central Regional Pub. 122, Minnesota Agr. Exp. Sta. Bul. 454, 1961.

[96] Engberg, R. C. "Federal Credit Agencies As an Influence upon Land Values." *J. Farm Econ.* 29:150-162, February 1947.

[97] Evans, C. D. *An Analysis of Successful and Unsuccessful Farm Loans in South Dakota.* USDA, ERS, 1971.

[98] Evans, C. D., and F. G. Warren. "Farm Credit and Tight Money in 1966-67." *Agr. Fin. Rev.* 28:1-13, November 1967.

[99] Farm Credit Administration. *The Farm Credit System in the 70's.* Report of the Commission on Agricultural Credit. Washington, D.C., 1970.

[100] ———. *The Farm Credit System in the 70's — Appendix.* Report of the Commission on Agricultural Credit. Washington, D.C., 1970.

[101] ———. *PCA Borrowers 1971 — Their Characteristics, Their Loans.* Washington, D.C., 1972.

[102] Feder, E. "Farmer Debtor Relief: A Case Study." *J. Farm Econ.* 39:451-467, May 1957.

[103] Federal Reserve Bank of Chicago. *Agricultural Credit 1974/75.* 1975.

[104] Federal Reserve Bank of Minneapolis. *Agricultural Credit Conditions Survey.* January 1975.

[105] Fischer, L. K. *Farmers' Knowledge of and Attitudes toward Credit.* Nebraska Agr. Exp. Sta. SB 474, 1963.

[106] Fisher, G., M. Boehlje, and C. Roush. *A Management Game for Non-Metropolitan Commercial Banks.* Oklahoma Agr. Exp. Sta. Res. Rep. P-703, 1974.

[107] Fox, A. *Demand for Farm Tractors in the United States — A Regression Analysis.* USDA Agr. Econ. Rep. 103, 1966.

[108] Frey, T. L. *Optimum Asset and Liability Decisions for a Rural Bank: Application of Multi-Period Linear Programming.* Unpublished Ph.D. dissertation, University of Illinois, 1970.

[109] Frey, T. L., and D. A. Lins. "Use of Credit by Illinois Farmers." *Illinois Agr. Econ.* 14:39-45, July 1974.

[110] Gardner, W. D. "Farm Income Tax Compliance." *J. Farm Econ.* 42:686-692, August 1960.

[111] Garlock, F. L. *Effect of the Seasonality of Agriculture on Iowa Banking.* USDA, BAE, 1932.

486   JOHN R. BRAKE AND EMANUEL MELICHAR

[112] ———. *Farmers and Their Debts — The Role of Credit in the Farm Economy.* USDA Agr. Econ. Rep. 93, 1966.

[113] ———. *Loan Operations and Liquidity Requirements of an Iowa Bank.* USDA, BAE, 1933.

[114] Gilson, J. C. *The Cost of Credit.* University of Manitoba Agr. Econ. Bul. 3, 1961.

[115] Goldsmith, R. W. *The Flow of Capital Funds in the Postwar Economy.* National Bureau of Economic Research, 1965.

[116] Gramm, W. P., and R. T. Nash. "The Impact of Changes in the Stock of Money on Agricultural Income and Investment." *Journal of Money, Credit and Banking* 3: 712-720, August 1971.

[117] Griliches, Z. "The Demand for Inputs in Agriculture and a Derived Supply Elasticity." *J. Farm Econ.* 41:309-322, May 1959.

[118] Grove, E. W. "Econometricians and the Data Gap: Comment." *Am. J. Agr. Econ.* 51:184-188, February 1969.

[119] ———. "Farm Capital Gains — A Supplement to Farm Income?" *Agr. Econ. Res.* 12:37-42, April 1960.

[120] Hamlin, E. T. *Financing of Rural Nonfarm Housing in the United States.* USDA, ERS, 1970.

[121] Hamlin, E. T., M. E. Wirth, and J. Nielson. *Financing Agricultural Production on Michigan Farms.* Michigan Agr. Exp. Sta. Spec. Bul. 445, 1963.

[122] Hammill, A. E. "Variables Related to Farm Real Estate Values in Minnesota Counties." *Agr. Econ. Res.* 21:45-50, April 1969.

[123] Hansing, F. D. *Financing the Production of Broilers in Lower Delaware.* Delaware Agr. Exp. Sta. Bul. 322, 1957.

[124] Hansing, F. D., and W. L. Gibson, Jr. *Becoming a Farm Owner — Is It More Difficult Today?* Virginia Polytechnic Institute Agr. Exp. Sta. Bul. 473, 1955.

[125] Harris, M., and N. W. Hines. *Installment Land Contracts in Iowa.* Iowa Agr. Law Center Monograph 5, 1965.

[126] Harrison, V. L. *Financial Management Research in Farming in the United States.* USDA, ERS, Misc. Pub. 1222, 1971.

[127] Harrison, V. L., and W. F. Woods. *Farm and Nonfarm Investment in Commercial Beef Breeding Herds: Incentives and Consequences of the Tax Law.* USDA ERS-497, 1972.

[128] Harshbarger, C. E., Jr. *The Effects of Alternative Strategies Used in Decision Making on Firm Growth and Adjustment.* Unpublished Ph.D. dissertation, Purdue University, 1969.

[129] Hathaway, D. E. "The Federal Credit Programs for Individual Farm Development." In *Federal Credit Agencies.* Commission on Money and Credit. Englewood Cliffs, N.J.: Prentice-Hall, 1963.

[130] Hayenga, W. A., and J. R. Brake. *Some Effects of Rural Bank Mergers on Financial Services Available to Rural Michigan Residents.* Michigan Agr. Exp. Sta. Res. Rep. 243, 1974.

[131] Heady, E. O., and L. V. Mayer. *Food Needs and U.S. Agriculture in 1980.* National Advisory Commission on Food and Fiber, Tech. Pap. 1, 1967.

[132] Heady, E. O., and L. G. Tweeten. *Resource Demand and Structure of the Agricultural Industry.* Ames: Iowa State University Press, 1963.

[133] Hedrick, J. L. "The Effects of the Price-Support Program for Peanuts on the Sale Value of Farms." *J. Farm Econ.* 44:1749-1753, December 1962.

[134] Hendrix, W. E. *Approaches to Income Improvement in Agriculture — Experiences of Families Receiving Production Loans under the Farmers Home Administration.* USDA Prod. Res. Rep. 33, 1959.

[135] Hendry, J. B. "Credit and Savings in a Rural Community." Chapter 10, *The Small World of Khan Hau.* Chicago: Aldine, 1964.

[136] Herdt, R. W., and W. W. Cochrane, "Farm Land Prices and Farm Technological Advance." *J. Farm Econ.* 48:243-263, May 1966.

[137] Herr, W. M. *Characteristics of New Borrowers Obtaining Farm Ownership Loans from the Farmers Home Administration — Fiscal 1966.* USDA, ERS, Agr. Econ. Rep. 184, 1970.

[138] ————. "Credit and Farm Poverty." In *Rural Poverty in the United States.* Report of the National Advisory Commission on Rural Poverty, 1968.

[139] ————. "The Role of FHA's Farm Operating and Ownership Loan Programs As Indicated by Borrower Characteristics." *Agr. Fin. Rev.* 30:1-10, July 1969.

[140] ————. "Understanding Changes in Non-Real-Estate Farm Debt." *Agr. Fin. Rev.* 28:23-31, November 1967.

[141] Hesser, L. F. "Bank and PCA Lending to Farmers." *Fed. Reserve Bul.* 49: 1224-1234, September 1963.

[142] Hesser, L. F., and M. R. Janssen. *Capital Rationing among Farmers.* Purdue University Agr. Exp. Sta. Res. Bul. 703, 1960.

[143] ————. *Use of Credit by Farmers in Central Indiana.* Purdue University Agr. Exp. Sta. Res. Bul. 718, 1961.

[144] Hesser, L. F., and G. E. Schuh. "The Demand for Agricultural Mortgage Credit." *J. Farm Econ.* 44:1583-1588, December 1962.

[145] ————. "Factors Affecting the Supply of Farm Mortgage Credit." *J. Farm Econ.* 45:839-849, November 1963.

[146] Hill, E. B. *Impact of Taxes and Legal Costs on Farm Transfers and Estate Settlements.* Michigan Agr. Exp. Sta. Spec. Bul. 424, 1959.

[147] Hill, E. B., and J. W. Fitzgerald. *The Land Contract as a Farm Finance Plan.* Michigan Agr. Exp. Sta. Spec. Bul. 431, 1960.

[148] Hill, H. L., and S. D. Staniforth. "Adjusting Livestock-Share Leases to Meet Increased Capital Requirements." *J. Farm Econ.* 41:63-69, February 1959.

[149] Hoffer, C. R., J. K. Boek, and W. E. Boek. *Evaluation of Supervised Farm Loans in Hillsdale County, Michigan.* Michigan Agr. Exp. Sta. Tech. Bul. 257, 1956.

[150] Hoover, D. M. "An Economic Analysis of Farmland Development." *Agr. Econ. Res.* 22:37-44, April 1970.

[151] ————. "The Measurement and Importance of Real Capital Gains in United States Agriculture, 1940 through 1959." *J. Farm Econ.* 44:929-940, November 1962.

[152] Hopkin, J. A., ed. *A New Look at Agricultural Finance Research.* Illinois Agr. Fin. Program Rep. 1, 1970.

[153] Hopkin, J. A., P. J. Barry, and C. B. Baker. *Financial Management in Agriculture.* Danville, Ill.: Interstate, 1973.

[154] Hopkin, J. A., and T. L. Frey. *Problems Faced by Commercial Banks of Illinois in Meeting the Financing Requirements of a Dynamic Agriculture.* Illinois Agr. Exp. Sta. AERR 99, 1969.

[155] Horton, D. C. *Patterns of Farm Financial Structure.* National Bureau of Economic Research. Princeton: Princeton University Press, 1957.

[156] Hottel, J. B., D. S. Moore, and J. R. Martin. *The Financial Structure and Practices of Texas Rice Producers.* Texas Agr. Exp. Sta. Inf. Rep. 72-6, 1972.

[157] Huff, H. B., and T. G. MacAulay. "Summing Components of Real Capital Gains." *Am. J. Agr. Econ.* 55:69-72, February 1973.

[158] Hurst, J. R., B. B. Rose, and J. H. Yeager. *Financing Rural Homes.* Auburn University Agr. Exp. Sta. Bul. 333, 1961.

[159] Irwin, G. D. "A Comparative Review of Some Firm Growth Models." *Agr. Econ. Res.* 20:82-100, July 1968.

[160] ———. "Three Myths about the Balance Sheet: The Changing Financial Structure of Farming." *Am. J. Agr. Econ.* 50:1596-1599, December 1968.

[161] Irwin, G. D., and C. B. Baker. *Effects of Lender Decisions on Farm Financial Planning.* Illinois Agr. Exp. Sta. Bul. 688, 1962.

[162] Irwin, G. D., and L. M. Eisgruber. "Potential Methods and Methodologies Useful in Firm Growth and Financial Management Research." Paper presented at joint meeting of W-104 and GP-12 Regional Research Committees, Denver, 1970.

[163] Irwin, G. D., D. A. Lins, and J. B. Penson, Jr. "Flow-of-Funds: An Adjunct to Income and Balance Sheet Accounts in Understanding the Financial Structure of the Farming Sector." *Agr. Fin. Rev.* 31:11-26, June 1970.

[164] Irwin, G. D., and J. B. Penn. *Custom Farm Services in the United States: Status and Potential.* USDA ERS-583, 1975.

[165] Irwin, G. D., and L. N. Smith. "Machinery Leasing: Perspective and Prospects." *Agr. Fin. Rev.* 33:42-47, July 1972.

[166] Johnson, D. G. "Agricultural Credit, Capital and Credit Policy in the United States." In *Federal Credit Programs.* Commission on Money and Credit. Englewood Cliffs, N.J.: Prentice-Hall, 1963.

[167] ———. "Farm Size, Risk Aversion, and Capital Rationing." Chapter 5, *Forward Prices for Agriculture.* Chicago: University of Chicago Press, 1947.

[168] Johnson, G. L. "Agriculture: Capital." In *International Encyclopedia of the Social Sciences*, vol. 1, D. L. Sills, ed. New York: Macmillan and Free Press, 1968.

[169] Johnson, S. R. "A Multiperiod Stochastic Model of Firm Growth." In *Economics of Firm Growth.* South Dakota Agr. Exp. Sta. Bul. 541, 1967.

[170] Jones, L. A., and D. Durand. *Mortgage Lending Experience in Agriculture.* National Bureau of Economic Research. Princeton: Princeton University Press, 1954.

[171] Jones, L. A., and F. L. Garlock. *Factors Affecting Farm Loan Interest Rates.* USDA, ARS, Agr. Inf. Bul. 126, 1954.

[172] Jones, L. A., V. Wiser, and W. F. Woods. "History of Agricultural Finance Research in the Economic Research Service." *Agr. Fin. Rev.* 35:1-9, October 1974.

[173] Kanel, D. *Opportunities for Beginning Farmers, Why Are They Limited?* North Central Regional Pub. 102, Nebraska Agr. Exp. Sta. Bul. 452, 1960.

[174] Klinefelter, D. A. "Factors Affecting Farmland Values in Illinois." *Illinois Agr. Econ.* 13:27-33, January 1973.

[175] Krause, K. R., and L. R. Kyle. "Economic Factors Underlying the Incidence of Large Farming Units: The Current Situation and Probable Trends." *Am. J. Agr. Econ.* 52:748-761, December 1970.

[176] Krause, K. R., and P. L. Williams. "Personality Characteristics and Successful Use of Credit by Farm Families." *Am J. Agr. Econ.* 53:619-624, November 1971.

[177] Krausz, N. G. P. *Installment Land Contracts for Farmland.* Illinois Agr. Ext. Ser. Circ. 823, 1960; revised 1971.

[178] Kristjanson, B. H., and J. A. Brown. *The Farmers Home Administration Approach to Farm Credit Problems.* North Dakota Agr. Exp. Sta. Bul. 388, 1954.

[179] Kuznets, S., and E. Jenks. *Capital in the American Economy — Its Formation*

and *Financing.* National Bureau of Economic Research. Princeton: Princeton University Press, 1961.

[180] Larsen, H. C. "Relationship of Land Values to Warranted Values, 1910-48." *J. Farm Econ.* 30:579-588, August 1948.

[181] Lee, J. E., Jr. Review of *Agricultural Finance* (5th ed.), A. G. Nelson and W. G. Murray. *Agr. Econ. Res.* 20:142-143, October 1968.

[182] Lee, W. F., and J. R. Brake. *Conversion of Farm Assets for Retirement Purposes.* Michigan Agr. Exp. Sta. Res. Rep. 129, 1971.

[183] Lindsey, Q. W. *Transforming Low Income Farms into Profitable Commercial Farms.* North Carolina State College Agr. Econ. Inf. Ser. 76, 1960.

[184] Linke, C. M., and J. A. Hopkin. "Financial Aspects of Growth in Agricultural Firms." In *A New Look at Agricultural Finance Research*, J. A. Hopkin, ed. Illinois Agr. Fin. Program Rep. 1, 1970.

[185] Lins, D. A. "Determinants of Net Changes in Farm Real Estate Debt." *Agr. Econ. Res.* 24:1-8, January 1972.

[186] ———. *A Simulation Model of Farm Sector Social Accounts with Projections to 1980.* USDA, ERS, Tech. Bul. 1486, 1973.

[187] Long, M. "Interest Rates and the Structure of Agricultural Credit Markets." *Oxford Econ. Papers* (n.s.) 20:275-288, July 1968.

[188] Mann. F. L. *A Comparative Study of Laws Relating to Low-Equity Transfers of Farm Real Estate in the North Central Region.* North Central Regional Pub. 136, Missouri Agr. Exp. Sta. Res. Bul. 782, 1961.

[189] Martin, J. R., and J. S. Plaxico. *Polyperiod Analysis of Growth and Capital Accumulation of Farms in the Rolling Plains of Oklahoma and Texas.* USDA, ERS, Tech. Bul. 1381, 1967.

[190] Martin, W. E., and J. R. Gatz. "Effects of Federal Income Taxes on Cattle Ranch Prices." *Am. J. Agr. Econ.* 50:41-55, February 1968.

[191] McNall, P. E., and D. R. Mitchell. "What Is the Basis of Farm Financial Progress?" *J. Farm Econ.* 31:529-538, August 1949.

[192] Melichar, E. "Aggregate Farm Capital and Credit Flows since 1950, and Projections to 1980." *Agr. Fin. Rev.* 33:1-7, July 1972.

[193] ———. "Bank Financing of Agriculture." *Fed. Reserve Bul.* 53:927-953, June 1967.

[194] ———. "Factors Related to Farmers' Use of Credit: Least-Squares Analysis of Sample Survey Data." *J. Farm Econ.* 47:1468-1473, December 1965.

[195] ———. "The Farm Business Sector in the National Flow of Funds Accounts." In *1970 Proceedings of the Business and Economic Statistics Section.* American Statistical Association, 1971.

[196] ———. "Financing Agriculture: Demand for and Supply of Farm Capital and Credit." *Am. J. Agr. Econ.* 55:313-325, May 1973.

[197] ———. "Impact of Banking Structure on Farm Lending: An Examination of Aggregate Data for States." In *Improved Fund Availability at Rural Banks — Report and Study Papers of the Committee on Rural Banking Problems.* Board of Governors of the Federal Reserve System, 1975.

[198] Melichar, E., and R. J. Doll. *Capital and Credit Requirements of Agriculture, and Proposals to Increase Availability of Bank Credit.* Board of Governors of the Federal Reserve System, 1969. Also published in *Reappraisal of the Federal Reserve Discount Mechanism*, vol. 2, Board of Governors of the Federal Reserve System, 1971.

490 JOHN R. BRAKE AND EMANUEL MELICHAR

[199] Melichar, E., and H. Holderness. "Seasonal Borrowing at the Federal Reserve Discount Window." *Agr. Fin. Rev.* 35:42-51, October 1974.

[200] Mighell, R. L., and L. A. Jones. *Vertical Coordination in Agriculture.* USDA, ERS, Agr. Econ. Rep. 19, 1963.

[201] Mitchem, N. P. *Characteristics of Federal Land Bank Loans, 1973.* Farm Credit Administration Stat. Bul. 8, 1974.

[202] Monhollon, J. R. "The Farmers Home Administration and Rural Poverty in the South." *Southern Econ. J.* 32:204-215, October 1965.

[203] Montgomery, A. A., and J. R. Tarbet. "Land Returns and Farm Real Estate Values." *Agr. Econ Res.* 20:5-16, January 1968.

[204] Morelle, W., L. Hesser, and E. Melichar. *Merchant and Dealer Credit in Agriculture.* Board of Governors of the Federal Reserve System, 1966.

[205] Mueller, A. G. "Flow-of-Funds Analysis in Farm Financial Management." *J. Farm Econ.* 48:661-667, August 1966.

[206] Munger, J. A., and E. Feder. *The Frazier-Lemke Act: Its Impact on Farmers and Lenders in the Northern Great Plains.* USDA ARS 43-43, 1957.

[207] Murray, W. G. *Agricultural Finance.* Ames: Iowa State College Press, 1941 (2d ed., 1947; 3rd ed., 1953).

[208] Murray, W. G., and F. L. Garlock. *Farm Mortgage Debt in Iowa.* Iowa Agr. Exp. Sta. Current Econ. Ser. Rep. 6, 1927.

[209] Murray, W. G., and A. G. Nelson. *Agricultural Finance.* 4th ed. Ames: Iowa State University Press, 1960.

[210] Naden, K. D., and G. A Jackson, Jr. *Financing Western Broiler Production.* California Agr. Exp. Sta. Bul. 753, 1956.

[211] Nelson, A. G. Review of *Patterns of Farm Financial Structure,* D. C. Horton. *Agr. Econ. Res.* 9:114-115, July 1957.

[212] ———. *Credit As a Tool for the Agricultural Producer.* North Central Regional Ext. Pub. 4, Nebraska Ext. Ser. EC 57-804, 1957.

[213] Nelson, A. G., W. F. Lee, and W. G. Murray. *Agricultural Finance.* 6th ed. Ames: Iowa State University Press, 1973.

[214] Nelson, A. G., and W. G. Murray. *Agricultural Finance.* 5th ed. Ames: Iowa State University Press, 1967.

[215] Neuman, D. F. "Capital Requirements and Financing Practices for Restructuring Southern Agriculture." *J. Farm Econ.* 48:1550-1560, December 1966.

[216] Nisbet, C. T. "The Relationship between Institutional and Informal Credit Markets in Rural Chile." *Land Econ.* 45:162-173, May 1969.

[217] North Central Land Tenure Research Committee. *Improving Land Credit Arrangements in the Midwest.* North Central Regional Pub. 19, Purdue University Agr. Exp. Sta. Bul. 551, 1950.

[218] North Central Regional Land Tenure Committee. *Preventing Farm Land Inflation in the Midwest.* North Central Regional Pub. 4, Iowa Agr. Exp. Sta. Bul. P72, 1945.

[219] Norton, L. J. *Financing Agriculture.* Danville, Ill.: Interstate, 1940 (2d ed., 1948).

[220] Nowell, R. I. "The Farm Land Boom." *J. Farm Econ.* 29:130-149, February 1947.

[221] Olsen, N. A., C. O. Brannen, G. F. Cadisch, and R. W. Newton. "Farm Credit, Farm Insurance, and Farm Taxation." In *Agriculture Yearbook, 1924.* USDA, 1925.

[222] Oluwasanmi, H. A., and J. A. Alao. "The Role of Credit in the Transformation

of Traditional Agriculture: The Western Nigerian Experience." *Nigerian Journal of Economic and Social Studies* 7:31-50, March 1965.

[223] Organisation for Economic Co-operation and Development. *Capital and Finance in Agriculture,* vol. II. Paris, 1970.

[224] Patrick, G. F., and L. M. Eisgruber. "The Impact of Managerial Ability and Capital Structure on Growth of the Farm Firm." *Am. J. Agr. Econ.* 50:491-506, August 1968.

[225] Penson, J. B., Jr. *An Aggregative Income and Wealth Model for the U.S. Farm Sector: Its Description and Application to Policy Analysis.* Unpublished Ph.D. dissertation, University of Illinois, 1973.

[226] ———. "Demand for Financial Assets in the Farm Sector: A Portfolio Balance Approach." *Am. J. Agr. Econ.* 54:163-174, May 1972.

[227] Penson, J. B., Jr., D. A. Lins, and G. D. Irwin. "Flow-of-Funds Social Accounts for the Farm Sector." *Am. J. Agr. Econ.* 53:1-7, February 1971.

[228] ———. "Flow-of-Funds Social Accounts for the Farm Sector: Reply." *Am. J. Agr. Econ.* 53:668-670, November 1971.

[229] Penson, J. B., Jr., and F. G. Warren. *Federal Land Bank Farm-Mortgage Loans — A Statistical Study of Loans Outstanding, September 30, 1966.* USDA ERS-438, 1970.

[230] ———. *Life Insurance Company Farm-Mortgage Loans — A Statistical Study of Loans Outstanding, September 30, 1966.* USDA ERS-439, 1970.

[231] Perrin, R. K. "Asset Replacement Principles." *Am. J. Agr. Econ.* 54:60-67, February 1972.

[232] Pursell, A. H. *Rural Credit Unions in the United States.* USDA, FCS, General Rep. 49, 1958.

[233] Rayner, A. J., and K. Cowling. "Demand for Farm Tractors in the United States and the United Kingdom." *Am. J. Agr. Econ.* 50:896-912, November 1968.

[234] Reimund, D. A. *Farming and Agribusiness Activities of Large Multiunit Firms.* USDA ERS-591, 1975.

[235] Reinsel, E., and J. Brake. *Borrower Characteristics Related to Farm Loan Repayment.* Michigan Agr. Exp. Sta. Res. Rep. 59, 1966.

[236] Reinsel, R. D. *The Aggregate Real Estate Market: An Evaluation of Prevailing Hypotheses Explaining the Time Series Trend in the United States Average Farm Real Estate Values.* Unpublished Ph.D. dissertation, Michigan State University, 1973.

[237] ———. "Changes in Farm Size." *Farm Real Estate Market Developments.* USDA CD-69:33-39, June 1967.

[238] ———. "Land Rents, Values, and Earnings." Paper presented at the meeting of the American Agricultural Economics Association, Edmonton, Canada, 1973.

[239] Reinsel, R. D., and R. D. Krenz. *Capitalization of Farm Program Benefits into Land Values.* USDA ERS-506, 1972.

[240] Reiss, F. J. *Getting Started and Established in Farming with and without Family Help.* North Central Regional Ext. Pub. 8, Illinois Ext. Ser. Circ. 822, 1960.

[241] Renshaw, E. "Are Land Prices Too High: A Note on Behavior in the Land Market." *J. Farm Econ.* 39:505-510, May 1957.

[242] Reynolds, J. E. *An Econometric Investigation of Farmland Values in the United States.* Unpublished Ph.D. dissertation, Iowa State University, 1966.

[243] Reynolds, J. E., and J. F. Timmons. *Factors Affecting Farmland Values in the United States.* Iowa Agr. Exp. Sta. Res. Bul. 566, 1969.

[244] Robison, L. J., P. J. Barry, and J. A. Hopkin. "Cash Flows and Financing in Texas Agriculture." *Southern J. Agr. Econ.* 5:187-192, July 1973.

[245] Rodewald, G. E., Jr., D. K. Larson, and D. C. Myrick. *Dryland Grain Farms in Montana — How They Started, Growth, and Control of Resources.* Montana Agr. Exp. Sta. Bul. 579, 1963.

[246] Schultz, T. W. *Agriculture in an Unstable Economy.* New York: McGraw-Hill, 1945.

[247] ———. "Capital Rationing, Uncertainty, and Farm-Tenancy Reform." Chapter 12, *Production and Welfare of Agriculture.* New York: Macmillan, 1949.

[248] Scofield, W. H. "Land Returns and Farm Income." *Farm Real Estate Market Developments.* USDA CD-67:44-55, August 1965.

[249] ———. "Nonfarm Equity Capital in Agriculture." *Agr. Fin. Rev.* 33:36-41, July 1972.

[250] ———. "Operating Capital Requirements of the Cattle Feeding Industry." *Livestock and Meat Situation.* USDA LMS-200:28-30, November 1974.

[251] ———. "Prevailing Land Market Forces." *J. Farm Econ.* 39:1500-1510, December 1957.

[252] Scott, J. T., Jr., and E. O. Heady. *Aggregate Investment Demand for Farm Buildings: A National, Regional and State Time-Series Analysis.* Iowa Agr. Exp. Sta. Res. Bul. 545, 1966.

[253] ———. "Econometricians and the Data Gap: Reply." *Am. J. Agr. Econ.* 51: 188, February 1969.

[254] Seagraves, J. A. "Capitalized Values of Tobacco Allotments and the Rate of Return to Allotment Owners." *Am. J. Agr. Econ.* 51:320-334, May 1969.

[255] Shane, M. D. *The Flow of Funds through the Commercial Banking System, Minnesota-North Dakota.* Minnesota Agr. Exp. Sta. Bul. 506, 1972.

[256] Sharpe, D. B. "Farm Mortgages — The Impact of Tight Credit." Federal Reserve Bank of Chicago, *Business Conditions,* pp. 11-15, February 1970.

[257] Shoemaker, J. M., and F. Miller. *Financial Progress of Beginning Farmers in North Central Missouri, 1953-1959.* Missouri Agr. Exp. Sta. Res. Bul. 840, 1963.

[258] Sloan, R. L. "Marketing of Negotiable Instruments of Deposit Issued by Small Commercial Banks." In *Improved Fund Availability at Rural Banks — Report and Study Papers of the Committee on Rural Banking Problems.* Board of Governors of the Federal Reserve System, 1975.

[259] ———. "The Money Market — Is It Adequate for the Needs of Today's Agriculture?" *Am. J. Agr. Econ.* 52:695, December 1970.

[260] Smith, A. G., and C. B. Baker. "The Effect of Real Estate Debt Commitments on Non-Real Estate Credit and Liquidity of the Farm." *Illinois Agr. Econ.* 9:1-6, January 1969.

[261] Solow, R. M. *Capital Theory and the Rate of Return.* Chicago: Rand McNally, 1965.

[262] Spitze, R. G. F., and R. J. Bevins. *The Agricultural Representative Program in Commercial Banks of Tennessee.* Tennessee Agr. Exp. Sta. Bul. 289, 1958.

[263] Spitze, R. G. F., and J. T. Romans. *Knowledge of Credit by Tennessee Farmers and Its Effects upon Financial Practices.* Tennessee Agr. Exp. Sta. Bul. 339, 1962.

[264] Swackhamer, G. L., and R. J. Doll. *Financing Modern Agriculture: Banking's Problems and Challenges.* Federal Reserve Bank of Kansas City, 1969.

[265] Sweeney, R. E. *Bank Structure, Competition, and Interest Rates on Farm Loans.* Unpublished Ph.D. dissertation, Georgia State College, 1969.

[266] Tablante, N. B. "Implications of Credit Institutions and Policy for Savings and Capital Accumulation in Philippine Agriculture." *Philippine Econ. J.* 3:208-225, second semester, 1964.

[267] Thompson, C. W. *Factors Affecting Interest Rates and Other Charges on Short-Time Farm Loans.* USDA Bul. 409, 1916.

[268] Tostlebe, A. S. *Capital in Agriculture: Its Formation and Financing since 1870.* National Bureau of Economic Research. Princeton: Princeton University Press, 1957.

[269] ———. *The Growth of Physical Capital in Agriculture, 1870-1950.* National Bureau of Economic Research, Occas. Pap. 44, 1954.

[270] Tostlebe, A. S., D. C. Horton, R. J. Burroughs, H. C. Larsen, L. A. Jones, and A. R. Johnson. *Impact of the War on the Financial Structure of Agriculture.* USDA Misc. Pub. 567, 1945.

[271] Trimble, R. L. *An Economic Analysis of the Effect of Monetary Policy on the Beef Industry.* Unpublished Ph.D. dissertation, Michigan State University, 1973.

[272] Troelston, E. S. *The Principles of Farm Finance.* St. Louis: Educational Publishers, 1951.

[273] Tuck, R. H. "A Reconsideration of the Theory of Agricultural Credit." *J. Agr. Econ.* 11:20-40, June 1956.

[274] Tweeten, L. G., and J. E. Martin. "A Methodology for Predicting U.S. Farm Real Estate Price Variation." *J. Farm Econ.* 48:378-393, May 1966.

[275] Tweeten, L. G., and T. R. Nelson. *Sources and Repercussions of Changing U.S. Farm Real Estate Values.* Oklahoma Agr. Exp. Sta. Tech. Bul. T-120, 1966.

[276] Tweeten, L. G., and L. Quance. "The Impact of Input Price Inflation on the United States Farming Industry." *Canadian J. Agr. Econ.* 19:35-49, November 1971.

[277] ———. "The Impact on Net Farm Income of National Inflation." *Am. J. Agr. Econ.* 53:914, December 1971.

[278] United States Department of Agriculture. *Agricultural Finance Outlook.* ERS AFO-13, 1973.

[279] ———. *Agricultural Finance Outlook.* ERS AFO-15, 1974.

[280] ———. *Agricultural Finance Statistics.* ERS AFS-2, 1974.

[281] ———. *The Balance Sheet of the Farming Sector, 1969.* ERS, Agr. Inf. Bul. 340, 1970.

[282] United States Department of Commerce, Bureau of the Census. *1964 Census of Agriculture,* vol. 3, part 4, *Farm Debt,* 1968.

[283] ———. *1969 Census of Agriculture,* vol. 5, part 11, *Farm Finance.* 1974.

[284] United States Department of State, Agency for International Development. *Spring Review of Small Farmer Credit,* vol. 19, *Small Farmer Credit Analytical Papers,* 1973.

[285] ———. *Spring Review of Small Farmer Credit,* vol. 20, *Small Farmer Credit Summary Papers,* 1973.

[286] Vandeputte, J. M., and C. B. Baker. "Farm Mortgage Debt Management on Low Equity Dairy Farms." *Illinois Agr. Econ.* 7:17-23, January 1967.

[287] ———. "Specifying the Allocation of Income among Taxes, Consumption, and Savings in Linear Programming Models." *Am. J. Agr. Econ.* 52:521-527, November 1970.

[288] Wall, N. J. "Agricultural Credit." In *The Story of Agricultural Economics in the United States, 1840-1932,* H. C. Taylor and A. D. Taylor. Ames: Iowa State College Press, 1952.

494　JOHN R. BRAKE AND EMANUEL MELICHAR

[289] ———. *Agricultural Loans of Commercial Banks.* USDA Tech. Bul. 521, 1936.

[290] ———. "Review of Papers by R. I. Nowell and R. C. Engberg." *J. Farm Econ.* 29:163-166, February 1947.

[291] Williams, D., L. A. Jones, and F. Miller. *Financing Rural Homes in Missouri.* Missouri Agr. Exp. Sta. Res. Bul. 857, 1964.

[292] Wirth, M. E. "Lifetime Changes in Financial Problems of Farmers." *J. Farm Econ.* 46:1191-1197, December 1964.

[293] Wirth, M. E., and J. R. Brake. *The Michigan Farm Credit Panel: Cash Flows and Use of Credit, 1961.* Michigan Agr. Exp. Sta. Res. Rep. 8, 1964.

[294] ———. "The Michigan Farm Credit Panel: Loans to Farmers, 1961." Michigan Agr. Exp. Sta., *Quart. Bul.* 45:461-479, February 1963.

[295] Wirth, M. E., and J. Nielson. *Resource Ownership and Productivity on Michigan Farms.* Michigan Agr. Exp. Sta. Spec. Bul. 435, 1961.

[296] Wirth, M. E., and L. F. Rogers. "The Changing Nature and Environment of United States Farm Firms." In *A New Look at Agricultural Finance Research,* J. A. Hopkin, ed. Illinois Agr. Fin. Program Rep. 1, 1970.

[297] Wise, J. O. *An Analysis of Agricultural Credit in Laurens County, Georgia.* Georgia Agr. Exp. Sta. Bul. N.S. 148, 1965.

[298] Wise, J. O., G. E. Plato, and F. B. Saunders. *Minimum Capital Requirements for Specified Farm Incomes for Vegetable and General Type Farms in South Georgia.* Georgia Agr. Exp. Sta. Res. Bul. 73, 1970.

[299] Wittwer, E. E. *Financing Agriculture in Nevada.* Nevada Agr. Exp. Sta. Bul. 200, 1958.

[300] Yotopoulos, P. A. "From Stock to Flow Capital Inputs for Agricultural Production Functions: A Microanalytic Approach." *J. Farm Econ.* 49:476-491, May 1967.

Part VII. Technical Change in Agriculture

The main purpose of this paper is to present the major theoretical and empirical developments in the area of technical change in agriculture from World War II to the early 1970s. Although the paper is in large part a literature review, we attempt wherever possible to contribute at least in a small way to the overall state of the art.

As in any other emerging field the study of technical change in agriculture has generated its share of controversy and disagreement. Our aim is to search out the controversial issues and present as objectively as we can both sides of the major arguments along with the available empirical evidence bearing on the question. At the same time we try to point out areas of apparent agreement and areas where a consensus seems to have been reached, recognizing that some controversies are never settled but merely fade away because of lack of interest or because they are replaced by more urgent questions.

In order to keep the paper to a reasonable length, we have limited our coverage mainly to United States agriculture. We do not mention empirical studies of technical change in the nonagriculture sector unless we feel they contribute to our understanding of technical change in agriculture. Somewhat more attention is devoted to the theoretical developments of technical change presented in the general economics literature. (For a survey of the general economics literature on technical change, see Kennedy and Thirlwall [92] and Nadiri [114].)

We wish to thank Martin Abel, Hans Binswanger, Zvi Griliches, Lee Martin, Martin Pineiro, Vernon Ruttan, and Pan Yotopoulos for constructive comments and suggestions on an earlier draft on this paper. Although we have made a concerted effort to bring in all of what we considered to be the relevant literature in this area, no doubt there are some papers that we have inadvertently omitted. To the authors of these papers, our apologies.

W. P.

Y. H.

Technical Change in Agriculture

Willis Peterson
Professor of Agricultural and Applied Economics
University of Minnesota

Yujiro Hayami
Professor of Economics
Tokyo Metropolitan University

The Concept of Technical Change

It seems safe to say that during the post-World War II era technical change has been one of the most rapidly growing areas of study within agricultural economics. As an explanation for the growing interest in the topic, one can point to two major problem areas that have concerned agricultural economists since the end of World War II.

The first is the secular increase in the supply of agricultural products relative to demand in the developed countries, particularly the United States, leading to depressed farm prices and incomes and precipitating severe adjustment problems in the agricultural sector. As a consequence agricultural economists have sought to identify the sources of this output growth. Technical change is one such source, indeed a major source, which has become a subject of economic analysis.

A second problem area that seems to have contributed to the interest in technical change is the difficulty that the developing nations have experienced in increasing agricultural output. Many of these nations, particularly those with a rapid rate of population growth, have been faced with persistent food shortages and widespread malnutrition. It has become evident that development programs emphasizing the increased use of traditional inputs in agriculture have contributed only modestly to agricultural output gains.

Economists have increasingly turned to technical change as their major "engine of growth."

One should bear in mind that agriculture was the only sector of the United States economy for which the official statistical reporting agency collected and published input and output data and total productivity indexes [154]. Efforts to sort out and interpret these data, beginning with Griliches's seminal work, "Measuring Inputs in Agriculture: A Critical Survey" [50], no doubt contributed to the interest and research in the area of technical change.

The Definition of Technical Change

Technical change generally is defined in terms of either a productivity index or a production function. In the context of a productivity index, Ruttan's definition [122] of technical change as the production of a greater output with a given quantity of resources would seem to encompass most interpretations of the term. In other words, technical change results in an increase in output per unit of input. In a later article Ruttan [123] views technical change in a production function context and defines it as a change in the parameters of the production function or a creation of a new production function. In this case we can view technical progress as an upward shift in the production function.

Of course, these two ways of defining technical change are entirely consistent with each other. A productivity index implies the existence of a production function and vice versa. In fact, as Domar [35] points out, a Cobb-Douglas production function is simply a geometric index of inputs, each weighted by its elasticity of production. Conversely, the popular arithmetic productivity indexes such as the Laspeyres and Paasche type indexes imply an underlying linear arithmetic production function. Productivity indexes and production functions are discussed further in a later section of this paper.

It is important to recognize that in order to have changes in output per unit of input or to have shifts in a production function there must be changes in the quality of the inputs. The fact that we observe productivity changes means that some inputs have changed in quality and these quality changes are not reflected in the total input measure. (The problem of how to treat economies of scale is considered later in this section.) If a unit of input is defined in terms of its contribution to production, then total output must move in direct proportion to total input. It is just an accounting identity.

Schultz [141] argues that the ideal input-output formula is one in which the ratio stays close to one. But Heady [67] raises a relevant question: Of what value is it to keep the output/input ratio close to one? Surely, Heady argues, economists know about new inputs and technology and are aware that an increasing ratio is an indication that production is increasing faster than conventional inputs. Is it not better, then, to have this ratio increase over time?

Schultz's reply [137] to Heady provides the rationale for maintaining an accurate accounting of productivity growth. Here Schultz stresses that technical change is not "manna from heaven." In other words, resources must be devoted to improving the quality of inputs, and we ought to know the costs of producing new technology and the returns from it. Without knowing how much quality improvements in input contribute to output, we cannot answer this question. Moreover, Schultz cautions that allowing the production function to shift is an all too convenient way of disposing of the problem. Such a procedure in effect treats economic growth as exogenous to the system — something we have no control over, like the weather.

Indeed, one might argue, the mere fact that we use the term "technical change" is an indication that we do not know where at least a part of the output is coming from. As Abramovitz [1] so aptly stated, it is a "measure of our ignorance."

On the other hand, it is possible to measure only conventional inputs, avoiding input quality adjustments, obtain a measure of technical change (the residual), and then explain the residual by measuring the contribution of any new, nonconventional inputs or making quality adjustments in the conventional inputs. As Tolley [31] observes, there seem to be two approaches to the analysis of technical change — the "no-quality-change approach" and the "explain-everything approach." For example, Denison [31, 33] states that adjusting for input quality changes obscures the changes that productivity indexes are designed to measure. However, if input quality adjustments are made, Denison argues, the quality adjustment should reflect only the cost to society of bringing the higher quality input into use with the remainder being pure technical change. This might be called a "partial-quality-change approach."

The difference between the "explain-everything approach" and the "partial-quality-change approach" comes to a head in the Jorgenson-Griliches versus Denison debate of the late 1960s and early 1970s. By adjusting total output and input data for errors of aggregation, errors in investment goods prices, and errors of utilization of capital and labor, Jorgenson and Griliches [83] are able to reduce the unexplained portion of total real output growth from 1.60 to 0.10 percent per year in the United States economy. In response to Denison's criticism [32], mainly in regard to the capital utilization adjustment, Jorgenson and Griliches [84] revise the unexplained portion of output growth upward to 1.03 percent per year and admit that perhaps not all output can be accounted for by input quality adjustments. However, they still maintain that this should not prevent us from trying to minimize the unexplained portion of output growth.

Whether we prefer to account for output growth by input quality adjustments or to measure indexes of total factor productivity and to attribute the increase in output per unit input to an increase in knowledge, we still face the basic question asked by Schultz — namely, what is the return to investment aimed at increasing the quality of inputs or of producing new knowledge? If this return is relatively high, then such investment is a relatively cheap source of economic growth. (We consider attempts to measure the return to this investment later in the paper.)

The phenomena of input quality improvements or an increase in knowledge leading to an increase in output per unit of input are commonly referred to as either technical change or technological change. The two terms often are used interchangeably. Schmookler [131], however, preferred to use the term technological change to denote the act of producing new knowledge and to define technical change as the incorporation of this new knowledge in the production processes of firms. In other words, a change in the state of the art would be technological change, whereas a change in actual production techniques would be technical change. In this paper we are concerned with both phenomena, but for convenience we refer to them both as technical change.

Embodied versus Disembodied Technical Change

Embodied technical change, according to its most popular definition, refers to the introduction of new technology in the physical capital input. Solow [144, 146], in an attempt to measure how much investment is necessary to support alternative rates of growth, seems to have provided the major impetus for the embodiment hypothesis. He assumes that new technology could be introduced into the production process *only* through gross investment in plant and equipment. Admitting that such an assumption is not literally true, he nevertheless argues that embodied technical progress is by a substantial margin the more important kind. Salter [128] also emphasizes the importance of embodied technical change at about this time.

To test the hypothesis Solow estimates an aggregate production function for the United States in which he adjusts the stock of plant and equipment by a factor λ, defining 100λ as the percentage of improvement in capital goods from the previous year. Allowing λ to vary from 0 to 0.04 for equipment, Solow reports an improvement in the fit of the production function at the higher levels of λ. The results suggest that the unexplained residual can be accounted for by quality improvements in the capital input.

In spite of its intuitive appeal the embodiment hypothesis has precipitated a substantial amount of controversy and little empirical support. Utilizing Solow's technique of adjusting the capital input for quality change, Berglas [10] extends the capital adjustment factor (λ) upward from a 3 percent annual rate and finds that a 140 percent annual rate minimizes the sum of squares of the residuals. He concludes, therefore, that the embodiment hypothesis is implausible since a 140 percent annual rate of capital improvement is far removed from observed market behavior. In another attempt to test the embodiment hypothesis Griliches [51] uses the ratio of gross to net capital as a measure of the vintage of the capital stock in manufacturing and finds that the age of capital has little explanatory power in accounting for differences in output. For the embodiment hypothesis to be valid new capital should be more productive than old capital.

Denison [34] argues that the embodiment question is of little practical importance because it does not help to know the average fraction of technical progress embodied in capital goods because some innovation requires no investment in capital (unembodied), some requires a small amount of investment, and some requires much investment. Jorgenson [82], in an attempt to distinguish between embodied and disembodied technical change, argues that there is no way of distinguishing between the two if the assumption of a constant exponential rate of technical change is dropped. Solow [146] assumes that embodied technical change takes place at a constant exponential rate.

But why should we be concerned with the embodiment hypothesis? Isn't it little more than an academic question? Jorgenson [82] provides an answer to this question by pointing out that if Solow is right and embodied technical change is important, the rate of economic growth closely depends on the rate of investment. If it is not important, much can be done to stimulate growth without investment in capital goods.

A variant of the embodiment hypothesis seems to have emerged in agricultural economics even before the hypothesis became an issue in the general economics literature. Cochrane [22] in 1953 criticized Schultz [134] for placing too much emphasis on the weather and not enough on the unevenness of technical advance in explaining the uneven growth of the supply of agricultural products. Cochrane argued that technical change in agriculture involves the increased use of capital which in turn depends a great deal on favorable price relationships.

There is no reason, of course, why the embodiment hypothesis has to apply only to capital. Intriligator [77], for example, defines embodied technical progress as occurring because of quality improvements in both capital and labor. But pushed to its logical conclusion the embodiment hypothesis loses its empirical content. If we accept that technical change cannot be "manna from heaven," then all unexplained improvements are embodied in one or more of the factors of production, whether it be in capital, labor, or in any of the intermediate inputs such as fertilizer, new seed varieties, or herbicides.

Factor-Saving Bias

Technical change often is defined in terms of either Hicks or Harrod neutrality with respect to the direction of factor saving. According to the Hicks definition [75], technical change is neutral if the marginal rate of substitution between inputs is not affected. Nonneutral technical change in the Hicks context is generally described as either labor saving (capital using) or capital saving (labor using). Technical change is said to be labor saving (capital using) if the marginal product of capital rises relative to the marginal product of labor. (For a more thorough discussion of neutral and nonneutral technical change, see Brown [14].)

Harrod [58] defines technical progress as capital saving, neutral, or labor saving according to whether capital/output ratio decreases, remains unchanged, or increases with a constant rate of interest. Some controversy has arisen regarding the equivalence of the Hicks and Harrod definitions. Kennedy [89, 90] argues that the two are equivalent when technical change only takes place in the sector producing consumer goods. (See Amano [4] and Kennedy [89, 90] for a recent exchange over this question.)

We know that in the United States agriculture labor has been declining relative to other inputs. We can attribute at least a part of this change to an increase in the price of labor relative to other inputs. However, Stout and Ruttan [149] argue that technical change in United States agriculture has not been neutral because it seems unlikely that the rapid decline in farm employment from 1925 to 1955 can be accounted for entirely by the increase in the price of labor relative to other inputs.

In regard to the total United States economy David and Van de Klundert [29], using a CES function to measure labor and capital efficiency, cite evidence of a labor-saving bias in the technical change that has occurred between 1899 and 1960.[1] Utilizing a translog cost function which has the advantage of incorporating more than two inputs at a time, Binswanger [11] uncovers evidence of both factor-saving and factor-using biases in United States and Japanese agriculture since the turn of the century. In the United States there is evidence of a strong fertilizer-using and machinery-using bias during the period 1912-68. Technical change appears to be neutral with respect to labor until the 1930s and then exhibits a labor-saving bias, especially after World War II. Binswanger also reports that of the 60 percent decline in the labor share in United States agriculture between 1944 and 1968, the labor-saving bias accounts for about 35 percent and the direct price influence accounts for the remaining 25 percent. In Japanese agriculture efficiency gains take on a strong fertilizer-using bias even earlier than in United States agriculture, although after the 1920s fertilizer appears neutral with respect to technical change. Also in contrast to the positive machinery bias in the United States

Japanese agriculture exhibits an overall negative bias with respect to this input. Technical change is reported to be labor using until 1928 and then becomes labor saving, and land exhibits an overall negative bias over the period 1893-1962.

The David-Van de Klundert technique also was applied to Japanese agriculture by Sawada [129] and to New Zealand agriculture by R. W. M. Johnson [81]. Sawada reports that technical change in Japanese agriculture was biased toward the land-saving direction for the period before World War II, but the bias for the postwar period turned toward the labor-saving direction. The Johnson study indicates that the bias in technical progress in New Zealand agriculture was always toward labor saving during the period 1921-67.

Induced Innovation

Although it may be interesting to know whether technical change has progressed in either a capital-saving or a labor-saving fashion, an even more fundamental question is "Why?" The induced innovation hypothesis attempts to provide an explanation for the direction of technical progress. First proposed by Hicks [75] in 1932, the basic idea is that changes or differences in the level of relative factor prices influences the direction of innovative activity, hence the direction of technical progress. According to Hicks, "The changed relative prices will stimulate the search for new methods of production which will use more of the now cheaper factor and less of the expensive one" [75]. For example, if labor becomes high priced relative to capital, scientists and engineers will search for ways to save on the relatively high-priced labor and in so doing develop new forms of capital. The end result may be called biased technical progress in a labor-saving (capital-using) direction.

The contrasts in the direction of factor-saving bias in technical progress in agriculture between Japan and New Zealand as estimated by Sawada and Johnson seem to support the Hicks hypothesis. Technical progress was biased toward using labor in prewar Japanese agriculture, in which labor was more abundant (hence cheap) relative to land and capital, whereas it was biased toward saving labor in New Zealand agriculture, in which labor has traditionally been scarce (hence expensive) relative to land. As labor became increasingly more scarce in Japanese agriculture during the postwar period owing to rapid absorption of labor by expanding industry, the direction of technical progress began to bias toward labor saving. Those patterns are consistent with the Hicks theory of induced innovation. Comparisons of factor prices and factor proportions in the long-term agricultural development in the United States and Japan by Hayami and Ruttan [61, 63] also are consistent with the Hicks theory. In addition, Binswanger's study [11] comparing United States and Japanese agriculture provides empirical support of the Hicks hypothesis.

We should add, however, that the induced innovation hypothesis has not gained universal acceptance. For example, Salter [128] denies that relative factor prices influence the nature of invention: "When labour costs rise any advance that reduces total costs is welcome, and whether this is achieved by saving labour or capital is irrelevant. There is no reason to assume that attention should be concentrated on labour-saving techniques, unless, because of some inherent characteristic of technology, labour-saving knowledge is easier to acquire than capital-saving knowledge." On the other hand, Kennedy [91] maintains that if per-unit labor costs are high relative to per-unit capital costs, the entrepreneur will search for a labor-saving innovation because this will reduce his total cost in the greatest proportion. Thus Kennedy argues that it is only the level of relative factor prices and not changes in these prices that is essential for a theory of induced innovation.

Hayami and Ruttan [61] point out that part of Salter's disagreement with the induced innovation hypothesis stems at least in part from his broad definition of the production function, which he considers as embracing all possible designs conceivable by existing scientific knowledge. Hence, a change in relative factor prices would, according to Salter, amount to "factor substitution" rather than technical change.

Much of the early literature on the induced innovation hypothesis dealt with innovation in the context of the theory of the firm. Hayami and Ruttan maintain that no theory of induced innovation has been developed for the public sector. Since much of the new technology in agriculture is a product of public sector research, a rather large gap exists in our knowledge of how or whether relative factor prices in agriculture influence the direction of publicly sponsored research in agriculture. The authors attempt to fill this gap by extending the basic Hicksian theory of induced innovation to the public sector [61].

> Farmers are induced, by shifts in relative prices, to search for technical alternatives which save the increasingly scarce factors of production. They press the public research institutions to develop the new technology, and also demand that agricultural supply firms supply modern technical inputs which substitute for the more scarce factors. Perceptive scientists and science adminstrators respond by making available new technical possibilities and new inputs that enable farmers to profitably substitute the increasingly abundant factors for the increasingly scarce factors, thereby guiding the demand of farmers for unit cost reduction, in a socially optimum direction.

As the authors point out, the response of research scientists and administrators represents the critical link in the inducement mechanism.

Of course, a certain amount of public sector research is not directed at specific problems — that is, so-called basic research. For this type of research we would expect a weaker relationship between relative prices and research allocation than exists for the more applied type of research. Brozen [16] argues that nondirected research of universities and foundations accounts for many of the autonomous inventions that we observe. Also unexpected spin-offs coming from applied research on other problems or industries contribute to the error term.

Economies of Scale and Scale Bias

Economies of scale can be defined as a more efficient organization of traditional inputs stemming from an increase in the size of the firm or industry. And we have defined technical change as greater efficiency stemming from new inputs or quality improvements in traditional inputs. Although the two concepts at first glance may appear to be quite different, there is in fact considerable difficulty in separating the two, both conceptually and empirically, when technical progress is not neutral with respect to scale.

The problem occurs because new technology or new inputs may make it possible to realize scale economies that hitherto could not have been obtained. Poultry production provides a good example. Before the development of medicated feeds the difficulty of controlling disease generally made it uneconomical to keep a large number of birds in one location. By decentralizing production in smaller units a disease outbreak would affect a smaller number of birds and result in a smaller loss. A similar situation existed in hog production. More recently new technology in buildings, equipment, and machinery has probably contributed to the increase in the optimum size of farms. This hypothesis is supported by Ulveling and Fletcher's finding [157] of an increase in scale economies on Mexican farms using more capital-intensive technologies.

In economic terms we might say that technical progress is biased toward larger scale if the introduction of new technology or inputs increases the marginal productivities of traditional inputs at higher levels of output relative to their marginal productivities at lower levels. In such cases the effects of technical change and scale economies are inseparable.

Also, the distinction between scale bias and factor-saving bias is not clear-cut. For example, in the development of medicated poultry feeds, the technology biased toward larger scale probably increased the marginal productivity of capital relative to that of labor, thereby increasing the capital/labor at the same factor price ratio.

Supply Function Shifts and Technical Change

It is widely acknowledged that technical change by shifting the production function also shifts (increases) the supply function of the firm or industry.

Yet it should be kept in mind, at least in the case of agriculture, that supply function shifts are not limited to changes in agricultural technology alone. Reductions in input prices also shift the supply function of agricultural products to the right. These price reductions may stem from a number of sources including technical change, economies of scale, reductions in monopoly power, and an easing of import restrictions in the farm supply sector. It should be borne in mind that we are dealing here with price reductions of inputs of a given quality. An increase in the quality of an input more than an increase in its price also shifts the supply function to the right. We have labeled the latter phenomenon technical change.

Perhaps the most important example of this phenomenon in agriculture is the reduction in the real price of fertilizer (plant nutrients) over the past twenty years. In terms of a unit of plant food, quality has not increased but price per unit, particularly nitrogen, has declined substantially. As a source of this decline we can point to the adoption of new cost-reducing technology in the production of fertilizers, particularly the fixation of nitrogen, and in cheaper modes of transportation (Sahota [126, 127]).

Measurement of Technical Change

In keeping with the two ways of viewing technical change mentioned earlier, the magnitude of technical change can be measured either in terms of a change in the ratio of output to conventional inputs (usually an index when aggregation is necessary) or a shift in the production function consisting of conventional inputs. We first present a brief review of the various partial and total productivity indices that have been used to measure technical change in agriculture with their drawbacks and biases. Then we present alternative regression techniques for measuring technical change. In short, this section reviews what Tolley [31] refers to as the "no-quality-change approach."

Index Approach

Productivity is sometimes expressed in terms of output per unit of a particular input. Output per unit of a single input is a partial measure of productivity in the sense that it does not account for the effects of other factor inputs. However, a partial productivity measure can provide useful information on economic progress. For example, labor productivity is known to be a major determinant of farm income and wages and has often been used as a measure of economic progress. Land productivity is also a pertinent measure of agricultural productivity or, more broadly, agricultural development in most Asian countries where land is the limiting factor and farmers are primarily motivated to raise output per unit of cultivated land area.

These partial productivity indices are, in general, biased measures of technical progress because they include the effects of factor substitution together with the effects of advances in production techniques. In searching for the strategic factors in economic development economists have attempted to evaluate the influences of technical change and factor substitution independently. From their efforts total factor productivity measures have been developed. According to Ruttan [123], the total factor productivity approach was originally suggested by Copeland and Martin [23].

Total factor productivity is defined as the ratio of output to the aggregate of all factor inputs. Two major approaches have been developed to obtain a measure of total factor productivity. One uses a linear aggregation of various inputs with market factor prices as weights, and the other uses geometric aggregation with factor shares as weights.[2] Conceptually, the former assumes a linear form of aggregate production function and the latter a Cobb-Douglas form. However, a linear aggregation of inputs as utilized by the Laspeyres and Paasche indexes implies an elasticity of substitution between inputs of infinity. Aggregation in the Cobb-Douglas form implies an elasticity of substitution between inputs of one. In most situations we would expect the latter to fit reality more closely than the former.

Solow [145], one of the first to apply geometric aggregation to the construction of the productivity index, identified the index with technical change by explicitly introducing the concept of the aggregate production function. In order to permit identification of the index with technical change, the effects of factors other than technical change must be evaluated and allowed for. Such phenomena as scale economies and biased (nonneutral) technical progress have come to receive a good deal of attention as discussed in the previous section.

Both the linear and the geometric (linear in terms of growth rates) indices are inevitably subject to the well-known "index number problem." The index formulas commonly used are the Laspeyres formula, which uses the base-year weights, and the Paasche formula, which uses the end-year weights. As Ruttan [124] points out, the former tends to underestimate technical progress while the latter has the effect of biasing upward the measure of output per unit of input. The Divisia index, defined as the linear aggregate of growth rates using the base-year weights, is in effect a chain-linked index of Laspeyres indexes and may be recommended on the grounds that it is less vulnerable to systematic bias (see Jorgenson and Griliches [83]). However, on the bases of Jorgenson and Griliches's results, it appears that productivity growth as measured by the ordinary Laspeyres index is not appreciably different from what is obtained with the Divisia index. They report that during the period 1945-65 conventional inputs account for 52.4 percent of growth in total United States output using the Laspeyres index and 54.3 percent using the Divisia index.

With the use of either linear or geometric aggregation output over the aggregate of inputs can be identified as a shift in the aggregate production function under the following assumptions: (1) the economy is operating at the long-run equilibrium under perfect competition, and all factors are rewarded equal to their marginal value productivities, and (2) technical progress is a multiplicative factor of the aggregate production function (implying neutral technical progress). Mundlak and Razin [113] remind us that as a measure of technical change the productivity index is biased to the extent that these assumptions deviate from reality.

Regression Analysis with a Time Variable

For agricultural economists primarily interested in obtaining accurate estimates of production or supply parameters, technical change which shifts the production and the supply functions in a systematic fashion is a type of the disturbance that should be taken account of in the regressions.

A major statistical problem in the estimation of production and supply parameters in the presence of technical change is specification bias (Griliches [57]). Statistical estimates of regression parameters may be biased when such influential factors as technology are misspecified either by omitting these variables or by approximating them inadequately.

Another difficulty, which may be less serious, is the bias due to the application of single-equation least squares to the estimation of production functions on nonexperimental data. Originally, Marschak and Andrews [107] pointed out that input-output observations from cross-sectional or time-series samples are (we hope) generated as the result of producers' profit-maximizing behavior and, hence, factor inputs are not independent of the errors in the equation. This problem becomes more serious when differences in the levels of technology among sample observations are included in the error term.

These difficulties can be avoided if observations are such that they can be grouped into homogeneous subgroups. In this case unbiased estimates can be obtained for the respective groups, and the difference in the estimated parameters between the subgroups can be interpreted as an indicator of technical change. This method is admittedly ad hoc since homogeneous observations are not always available in sufficient number.

In time-series analysis it is common to represent technical progress by a smooth time trend. This convention fails when technical progress is in fact discrete or cannot be approximated by a statistically manageable function of time. Should technical progress represent a discrete shift of the production or supply function, covariance analysis or dummy variables may be utilized. Methods of measuring supply shifts from time-series data are presented by Cassels [17] and Cochrane [20, 21].

Covariance analysis is effective especially when data are cross-tabulated in two directions — for example, in terms of both region and time (Kaneda [85]). When at least two homogeneous observations exist in each cell of the two-way cross-tabulation, it is possible to obtain unbiased estimates of production parameters and, also, to estimate technical change or differences in technical efficiency. The usefulness of this technique in the measurement of technical change tends to be limited by the availability of adequate data, however.

Use of Partial Production Functions

Studies of partial production functions (for example, fertilizer response curves) by the use of experimental data constitute a well-established field of agricultural production economics (Heady and Dillon [71]). Partial production parameters from experimental data (which more closely satisfy the conditions for single-equation production function estimation) can provide a useful approximation of farm technology. Comparison of the partial production parameters estimated on experimental data over time could be a promising approach to the measurement of technical change. Surprisingly little has been done along this line, however. Usually interdisciplinary collaboration is required to compile an adequate time series of such parameter estimates for comparison.

The comprehensive study by Heady and Auer [70], in which they identify and measure the sources of yield changes in United States field crop production, represents an example of the use of partial production functions fitted to secondary data. In this study the authors measure the contribution of fertilizer, variety improvement, production location, and other crop yield variables to yield changes of field crops in the United States from 1939 to 1960. Herdt and Mellor [74] also demonstrate the usefulness of partial production functions in making interregional comparisons of production parameters in the United States and India.

Farrell's Index of Technical Efficiency

Farrell [41] attempts to measure the technical efficiencies of production units in terms of deviations from an isoquant representing the technological frontier. From a sample of observations on input per unit of output he constructs an isoquant by connecting the points which are not exceeded by the combinations of any other two points. Farrell's approach is useful in differentiating between technical efficiency (maximum output for a given combination of inputs) and price efficiency. As defined by Lau and Yotopoulos [97] economic efficiency includes both technical and price efficiency. The latter is defined as the ability of the firm to maximize profits by equating the value of the marginal product of each variable input with its price. Utilizing a profit function as first introduced by McFadden [110], Lau and Yotopoulos [97] test for differences in economic efficiency between large and small (less than ten-acre) farms in India and find that small farms attain a higher level of economic efficiency. In a subsequent study Yotopoulos and Lau [163] extend the technique to measure separately the differences in technical and price efficiency between groups of farms. Here they find that both large and small farms are equally price efficient but that small farms are more efficient in a technical sense, although the authors acknowledge that a possible explanation for their finding could be an inverse relationship between farm size and soil fertility. Applying the Lau-Yotopoulos model to a sample of Indian wheat farms, Sidhu [143] finds that large and small farms exhibit equal economic efficiency in both the technical sense and the price sense.

Sources of Productivity Growth

We have argued that the basic source of technical change is the improvement in the quality of inputs. In the previous section we reviewed various conventional techniques used to measure technical change. In this section we consider the attempts to identify the sources of technical change (productivity growth) in United States agriculture and to account for the measured productivity growth by the sources identified.

Quality Changes and Productivity Growth

Increase in skills of farm people. This topic falls within the broad area of the economics of human resources. Although it is a relatively new area of study for economists, the output of literature in this area in recent years has been prolific. Even an attempt to survey the literature on the economics of education, a subitem under human resources, would carry us far beyond the scope of this paper and its space limitations (Schultz [135, 136]). Our modest objective here is to offer a brief sketch of the work relating specifically to the effect the education and skills of farm people have on agricultural output.

The idea that education is an investment in human capital which contributes to the output and income of people, of course, is not new. Marshall [108] argued that "the most valuable of all capital is that invested in human beings." Early in the postwar period Schultz [140] argued that differences in per-capita income between communities is much more a function of acquired abilities than of innate abilities. Also it is reasonable to believe that differences in acquired abilities exist because of differences in both quantity and quality of education. The effect of differences in quality of schooling on earnings of rural farm people is clearly documented by Welch [159].

But, we might ask, why should more years of schooling or higher quality of schooling increase an individual's output? Nelson and Phelps [116] suggest that "education enhances one's ability to receive, decode and understand information, and that information processing and interpretation [are] important for performing or learning to perform many jobs." Along this line Welch [160] offers the hypothesis that the productive value of education has its roots in (1) the worker effect and (2) the allocative effect. The first increases the marginal product of labor given the level of other inputs. The second enhances the worker's ability to acquire and interpret information about costs and new inputs. Welch further argues that the allocative effect is the more important of the two for agriculture. This may explain why education does not appear to have a high payoff in a traditional agriculture setting characterized by long-run equilbria in the factor and product markets (Choudri [19]). Welch also points out that production function studies which in effect hold other inputs constant result in a downward bias to the returns to education.

If the allocative effect of education is important, then we should observe the early adopters of new technology to have a higher level of skills (schooling) than those who lag in the adoption process. This observation is borne out by Kislev and Shchori-Bachrach [94] in their study of winter vegetable production technology in Israel. In their study of the "innovation cycle" they find that an innovation is first adopted by the more highly skilled entrepreneurs and then diffuses down the skills scale. As additional evidence, Huffman [76] finds the level of education of farmers to be a significant variable explaining the adoption of nitrogen fertilizer in the United States corn belt. The diffusion of new technology is discussed further elsewhere in this review.

Increase in quality of nonhuman capital. Casual observation leads one to believe that the quality of machinery, equipment, and buildings has increased greatly in the United States over the past century. It is important to bear in mind here that a large share of capital improvement is produced by private sector research and development. As such, its supply price is more likely to reflect quality differences than would be the case if the research and development were carried out in the public sector and the knowledge were made freely available. Of course, to the extent that more productive capital requires more labor and materials to produce, its supply price also will exceed that of less productive capital. The demand for higher-quality capital also can be expected to exceed that of less productive capital, resulting in a higher overall market price provided that the supply curve of nonhuman capital is upward sloping (as we would expect it to be, at least in the short run).

However, in order to use value as a measure of capital quality, it is necessary to separate the price increases due to quality improvements from the effects of a general rise in the price level due to inflation. The work of Court

[24] and Griliches [49] on hedonic price indexes for automobiles documents the positive relationship between quality components such as automatic transmissions and automobile prices. Fettig [42], also using this technique, finds a similar relationship for farm tractors with respect to horsepower and type of engine (gasoline or diesel).

But Griliches [51] argues that the official USDA prices-paid index grossly overstates the "true" quality-adjusted prices of inputs purchased by farmers by not taking quality improvements into account. For example, the purchase of automatic transmissions or factory air conditioning with automobiles shows up as an increase in the price of automobiles, according to the USDA index. As a result the USDA prices-paid index overstates the true rise in prices and therefore results in a downward bias to the real (quality-adjusted and price-adjusted) stock of capital on farms. This is illustrated by a 56 percent rise in the price of automobiles between 1947 and 1958 according to the USDA prices-paid index but a 34 percent increase according to the consumer price index.

Increase in quality of other inputs. Among the other inputs (besides labor and nonhuman capital) that would appear to be sources of productivity growth in agriculture, we can point to commercial fertilizers with improved nutrient content, new and improved crop varieties, more efficient breeds of livestock and poultry, and new and improved agricultural chemicals, mainly herbicides and insecticides.

Increase in quality of output. In comparison to the attention given to input quality change, relatively little has been said about output quality. In part, the explanation may be found in the homogeneous nature of farm products. With the exception of the high-lysine variety of corn, a bushel of corn is a bushel of corn whether it be produced in 1910 or 1972. The same is true for wheat and many other field crops. However, in the case of fruits and vegetables and some livestock products, there is some indication that quality has improved. As examples, one can point to new and improved varieties of fruits and vegetables that are less subject to attack by insects and disease, and dairy products that are lower in bacteria count. On the other hand, some have argued that current varieties of fruits and vegetables are less flavorful than those in years past. The same argument is made for poultry meat. It is not clear which has changed — the product flavor or the consumers' appreciation of flavor given the increased and prolonged consumption of these items.

Of course, any quality improvements in farm products should be reflected in higher prices for these products over what they would otherwise be. However, in order to construct a price-weighted aggregate output index of the Laspeyres type it is necessary to use constant base-year prices. Although this procedure is necessary for the purpose of aggregation and to remove the effect of changes in the general price level, it tends to remove quality-induced price increases. To the extent that quality improvements are lost by this procedure, we underestimate the growth in aggregate farm output. Of course, converting improved quality into increased quantity of output has the effect of increasing the unexplained residual, which in turn throws an even greater burden on input quality adjustment in accounting for the unexplained residual.

Schultz [137] reminds us of several additional problems of measuring farm output. A major omission from our commonly used output measures is the "improvements in the farm plant resulting from the farmers' own labor or from other labor and materials on the farm." As Schultz argues, the formation of home-produced farm capital in the form of cleared land, drainage, fences, and buildings surely was substantial during earlier decades and is still much too important to leave out.

Secondly, no allowance is made for the increased leisure time of farmers, which is in effect a component of farm output. Nor do we take into account the reduction in the drudgery of farm work. Spending ten hours in the air-conditioned cab of a modern combine is a good deal less physically demanding than spending ten hours pitching bundles in ninety-degree heat. Also the mechanization of many farm chores such as feeding, barn cleaning, and milking undoubtedly has helped make farming a more desirable occupation than it was at the turn of the century or even ten to twenty years ago. Both the unmeasured creation of farm capital and the improved working conditions of farmers (including more leisure) give rise to an underestimate of agricultural output.

Schultz mentions the depletion of natural resources as a negative adjustment to output. Soil erosion and fertility depletion together with the depletion of forests no doubt have been important, especially up to the end of World War II. For example, Bray and Watkins [13] argue that corn hybrids deplete the soil more rapidly than the open-pollinated varieties. Thus the yield increase of hybrids probably overstates their economic gains. Since the beginning of the 1960s more attention has been given to the social costs, or externalities, of agricultural production, mainly fertilizer runoff, odors, and farm pesticide residue. Failure to take these negative aspects of output into account might be regarded as overestimating the "true" output, although it is perhaps more common to regard such externalities as resulting in an underestimate of the true cost of production.

Economies of scale. We are well aware of the substantial increase in the size of the average farm unit in the United States. As Stigler [147, 148] points out, this is an indication that large firms are more efficient than small ones and that economies of scale exist. We argued in a previous section that it is extremely difficult to separate pure scale economies (those resulting from more efficient combinations of traditional resources) from technical change. (See Griliches [57] for a discussion of specification bias and its effect on measured scale economies.)

Accounting for Productivity Growth

Now that we have identified what appear to be the major sources of the measured productivity growth, let us next review the attempts to account for the unexplained residual. Two general approaches have been used. One approach is to adjust inputs for quality, and the other is to measure the contribution of nonconventional inputs — research, education, and extension.

Adjustment for input quality. We have argued that changes in the quality of inputs represent the major sources of discrepancy between the growth in output and in inputs. If this be true, then adjusting inputs by an independent measure of quality should reduce the unexplained residual.

One procedure is to adjust inputs for quality changes before constructing a productivity index. An increase in the quality of an input is treated as equivalent to a larger quantity of that input. For example, labor should be measured in units of a given educational or skill level. An increase in skills then would be reflected as more units of labor of the previous skill level. In other words, a man-day of highly skilled labor is more labor than a man-day of unskilled labor. Similarly, a 100-horsepower tractor is more tractor than 1 50-horsepower tractor, 100 pounds of 12-12-12 fertilizer is more fertilizer than 100 pounds of 10-10-10 fertilizer, and so on.

The usual assumptions in the construction of total productivity indexes using quality-adjusted data are (1) linear homogeneous production functions and (2) competitive equilibrium in the factor markets (Jorgenson and Griliches [83]). Of course, input quality adjustments should be made on the basis of independent information rather than on the assignment of greater weight to higher-quality inputs by some arbitrary formula or rule. For labor, a convenient weight is years of schooling. One can "inflate" labor by either a simple index of education or by first adjusting the education index by an earnings index based on the earnings of people with various years of schooling (Griliches [51, 55, 56]). Griliches reports that for the United States rural farm population the index of education weighted by income is almost proportional to mean school years completed.

Capital poses a more difficult problem. Ideally we would like to measure its service flow, but in reality we usually are provided with information on its depreciated or market value. A good proxy for the service flow of capital would be the rental value of capital. The higher the quality of a capital item (the higher its productivity), the higher its rental value in a perfect rental market. Unfortunately, in agriculture the rental market for capital, particularly machines and buildings, is not well developed.

As mentioned earlier, the current market value of a capital item should reflect its quality or productivity. However, Griliches [51, 56] points out, the current market value of capital represents the market's estimation of the present value of all its present and future services. Hence, as a machine or building ages its market price declines, not necessarily because its current service flow declines but because it has fewer years of useful life remaining. Thus the current or market value would seem to underestimate its current annual service flow. An exception would be an increase in capital quality due to an increase in the durability or life of the machine. Here market value could increase without necessarily affecting the annual service flow.

Griliches [56] also points out that official USDA statistics on farm machinery reflect a depreciation pattern that reduces current value to about one-half of purchase price after the fourth year of use. But it is hard to imagine that the service flow of this equipment declines by a like amount. Thus the failure to take quality improvements into account in the prices-paid index, which understates the true stock of capital, and the practice of using the depreciated value of capital as a proxy for its annual service flow both result in an underestimate of the true service flow of farm capital. Hence Griliches argues that original purchase price or some constant fraction thereof provides a more accurate measure of the true service flow of equipment than the depreciated or current market value does. In effect, this procedure assumes that the annual service flow remains constant over the life of the machine. The fact that older machines tend to require more repairs in order to provide the same service flow as new equipment should be reflected by an increase in "other inputs" and labor.

Although the assumption of a constant service flow throughout the life of a machine probably is not too unrealistic in approximating the service flow of machines, Yotopoulos [162] argues that this is not likely to be the case for biological assets such as breeding stock, draft animals, and trees. For these assets the service flows are likely to increase during their early years, reach a peak, and then decline with age. To take account of this phenomenon Yotopoulos estimates the annual service flow of this type of asset by the expression $R_{it} = rV_t - (V_{it+1} - V_{it})$, where R_{it} is the service flow of asset i in year t, r is the rate of discount, and V_{it+1} and V_{it} are its values in years t + 1 and t, respectively. From the empirical results obtained it would appear that specification of production functions can be much improved by utilizing this simple technique. The technique would seem particularly useful for production function estimation in developing countries where biological assets make up a relatively large share of capital in agriculture.

From the standpoint of other inputs in agriculture, commercial fertilizer can be measured at a constant quality by measuring plant nutrients (N, P, and K weighted by their respective prices) as opposed to measuring units of total fertilizer materials including filler.

Nonconventional inputs as separate variables. Given that quality improvements of inputs are not free gifts of nature, there must be activities which produce these quality changes. In agriculture we can point to research, education, and extension as activities which produce or transmit knowledge that in turn produces quality improvements in agricultural inputs or gives rise to entirely new inputs.[3] If all quality improvements were the result of these activities, then we should be able to insert these variables directly into the production function instead of adjusting the traditional inputs for quality changes. On the other hand, G. L. Johnson [80] argues that management ability should not be included as a factor of production because it is already reflected in the quantities of other inputs used.

A major advantage of this approach is that it provides direct estimates of the marginal products of the activities engaged in improving inputs. As we have noted, these activities use up resources and therefore the really important question is whether or not it pays for society to invest in these input-improving activities.

Griliches appears to have been among the first to apply this approach by introducing the education of rural farm people as a separate variable in a cross-regional agricultural production function in the United States [48, 56], later including both education and public agricultural research and extension as separate variables [55]. Tang's study [150], which used time-series data for Japan, represents another pioneering effort in the use of this approach. Other authors using education, research, or extension as separate variables include Gisser [45], Kislev [93], Latimer and Paarlberg [96], Peterson [118], Evenson [37], Yotopoulos [161], Welch [160], and Fishelson [44] for the United States; Herdt [72] for India; Akino and Hayami [3] for Japan; and intercountry comparative studies by Hayami [60] and Hayami and Ruttan [62].

It is of course possible that these variables may not explain or take account of all the quality improvement in the traditional inputs. For example, an increase in the percentage of plant food in 100 pounds of commercial fertilizer is more likely to be the result of technical change and changing price relationships in the fertilizer industry than of public research and extension in agriculture. Also a substantial share (probably over one-half) of total agricultural research and extension is conducted in the private sector. Because of the lack of data on this research it may be necessary to adjust inputs affected by such research for quality change, even though public research is included in the production function. Private research and development would seem to bear heavily on the machinery, farm structures, and chemical inputs.

The inclusion of public agricultural research as a separate variable in an agricultural production function fitted to state-level cross-section data presents an estimation problem in that the results of the research carried out in a particular experiment station may be utilized in a larger area than just the state in question. This expected pervasiveness of research results prompted Latimer and Paarlberg [96] to argue that one should not be able to observe a relationship between agricultural research and farm output. However, it should be noted that the other authors mentioned above who utilized research as a separate variable obtained a statistically significant coefficient on this variable when including it in an aggregate agricultural production function fitted to cross-section data.

In this section we have attempted to review the methods of accounting for productivity growth in agriculture by various sources. Ideally, we would like to summarize these findings by stating what fraction of the unexplained residual is explained by each source. About the closest we can come to such a summary is that provided by Griliches for United States agriculture. On the basis of his studies [55, 56] he concludes that up to the early 1960s the residual can be attributed to three major sources, each contributing about one-third of the total: input quality change, economies of scale, and investment in research and extension. The last category can be looked upon as one of the ultimate sources of input quality change and possibly of scale economies. Hence, the three sources are not mutually exclusive.

The Production of New Technology

We can be quite certain that technical change in agriculture has not taken place by chance, nor has it been the result of "manna from heaven." The evidence strongly supports the hypothesis that technical change — that is, unexplained output — is the result of quality improvements in inputs which have not been fully reflected in the input measures and that these quality improvements are the result of knowledge-producing activities that require real resources. Our objective in this section is to survey the literature that has attempted to assess the costs and returns to knowledge-producing activities in agriculture and to analyze resource allocation in the production of knowledge.

Costs and Returns of Agricultural Research

In order to assess the economic returns to investment in agricultural research we must assume that research is a production activity. Inputs in this activity consist of labor (man-hours of scientists and supporting personnel), capital (laboratories, offices, computers, test plots), and other intermediate inputs (supplies, fuel, electricity), and output consists of new knowledge. The new knowledge itself becomes an intermediate input in the production of more productive, higher-quality inputs for agricultural production. The knowledge may be embodied in capital or in intermediate inputs such as pesticides, or it may be applied directly by farmers.

At the same time we should recognize that the research production function is likely to exhibit a sizable stochastic element. It is helpful to compare research with oil exploration. For every ten holes drilled, about eight are likely to be dry with only two yielding a portion of nature's bounty. In research, there are likely to be several projects that turn out to be "dry holes" yielding no new knowledge for every one that is able to add something to what we already know. Of course, the probability depends on the skill of the research worker just as it does for the oil explorer. It seems likely too that the probability of a significant contribution declines as one moves away from applied research to the more "basic" type of research. This does not mean that the expected return is lower for basic research than for applied research. But whatever the probability of success, it seems clear that little knowledge (output) will be gained unless resources (inputs) are allocated to its search.

VALUE OF INPUTS SAVED

We must credit Schultz [134] with the first attempt to quantify the benefits of agricultural research and extension. Using a total productivity index Schultz calculated the additional resources required to produce the 1950 level of output by 1910 techniques. The difference between this figure and the resources actually used to produce the 1950 output represents the value of inputs saved because of the increase in output per unit of input over the period. Schultz found that the savings in inputs for 1950 alone, $9.6 billion, was larger than all the expenditures of the federal and state governments on agricultural research and extension from 1910 to 1950.

We might expect some upward bias in the returns vis-à-vis the costs with this procedure. First, it is likely that the increase in the educational level of farm people had some effect in raising output per unit of input over this period. Second, as Schultz mentions, part of the improvement in production techniques should be attributed to private research and extension. Schultz points out, however, that some public expenditure allocated to activities is not specifically aimed at producing and distributing new production techniques. As a result, these activities would not be reflected in the productivity ratio, thereby introducing a downward bias to the return side. Also, it is not clear how activities which increase the quality of farm output are reflected in the productivity ratio.

Utilizing Schultz's technique and extending the data up to 1967, Peterson [119] finds that the *annual value* of inputs saved increases from about $10 billion in 1950 to nearly $26 billion in 1967 (constant 1957-59 prices). The more than doubling of annual resources saved in agriculture was the result of an increase in agricultural productivity (output per unit of input) and in the absolute value of agricultural output between 1950 and 1967. At the same time the annual cost of all research and extension (public and private) is estimated to have increased from $390 million in 1950 to $882 million in 1967. Thus the absolute difference between the annual value of inputs saved and the annual expenditure on research and extension appears to have increased substantially over time. Peterson also finds the *marginal* internal rate of return on agricultural research and extension in the early 1960s to be about double the long-run *average* rate, 42 percent versus 19 percent.

CONSUMER SURPLUS

In evaluating the returns to research with the inputs-saved technique we measure the reduction in resource cost of obtaining a given output by more efficient resources and techniques. In the consumer surplus approach we measure the extra value of output obtained from a given quantity of more efficient resources.

The consumer surplus approach was first used by Griliches [54] in his hybrid corn study. In this study Griliches obtains a measure of the area between the supply of corn using hybrid seed and the supply using open-pollinated seed bounded on the top (or the right) by the demand for corn. The increase in yields of hybrid corn (assumed to be 15 percent in this study) has the effect of shifting the supply of corn to the right of where it would be if open-pollinated varieties were used. (In the interest of obtaining a lower boundary to the estimated returns, or value of consumer surplus, Griliches measures the decrease in the supply of corn that would occur should hybrid seed disappear rather than the increase that occurs because of the availability of hybrid varieties.) Using a cash-flow technique with annual research costs as outflows and the annual value of consumer surplus as inflow, Griliches computes the widely quoted 743 percent rate of return to investment in hybrid corn research. We will discuss the meaning of this rate of return later in this section.

A major difficulty in such a study is to decide on and obtain the relevant research expenditure data. Griliches's expenditure data include both private and public research but only that research applying rather directly to hybrid corn. As such the data should not be interpreted as including all corn research during the period in question. Also, how much, if any, of the basic research on hybridization should have been included remains an open question. For example, Nelson [115] argues that George Harrison Shull, a geneticist, made the most significant breakthrough in hybrid corn development while working on genetic experiments with corn plants. Such research is not included in Griliches's measure.

Peterson's poultry study [118] applies in part the consumer surplus approach to a somewhat broader area. In this study a major problem was to obtain a measure of poultry productivity that reflected to a large extent the effect of new inputs stemming from poultry research. Improvements in feed efficiency and the decline in poultry output price relative to input prices are utilized as productivity measures to indicate the shift in the poultry supply function. The results turned up an average internal rate of return of about 20 percent on poultry research in the United States. Although at first glance this figure may appear modest in comparison with the 743 percent hybrid corn return, we will see shortly that the two figures are not comparable.

Schmitz and Seckler [130] utilize a similar technique to estimate the social returns to the development of the mechanical tomato harvester. In this case the authors use the reduction in harvesting costs to obtain a measure of the shift in the tomato supply function. Matching the social returns with the research costs, the authors obtain estimates of the rate of return in the range of 929 to 1282 percent. The procedure used to compute the rates of return is comparable to that used by Griliches in the hybrid corn study. However, because of the social costs involved (mainly displaced human tomato pickers), the authors question the desirability of the investment.

MARGINAL PRODUCT OF RESEARCH

As we have noted, Griliches, Peterson, Latimer and Paarlberg, and Evenson have included research as a separate variable in an agricultural production function using cross-section data. This approach has two major advantages: (1) it amounts to a rigorous test of the influence of agricultural research on agricultural output, and (2) the marginal product of research can be computed directly from the production function. Since decisions to invest or not to invest in agricultural research must be made continually, the relevant criterion is a marginal return rather than an average return.

In general, it appears that the marginal returns to investment in agricultural research are substantially larger than the overall average returns. Griliches [55] reports a $13 marginal product on public agricultural research and extension. Peterson [118] and Evenson [37] obtain estimates of a comparable degree of magnitude. We should caution, however, against interpreting these marginal products as marginal rates of return. To do so would require that the

Table 1. A Summary of Studies Estimating Average and Marginal Internal Rates
of Return to Agricultural Research and Extension in the United States

Author and Type of Study	Average Return (percentage)	Marginal Return (percentage)
1. Evenson, linear regression on residuals, time-series data [36]	--	48
2. Griliches, aggregate production function, cross-section data [55]	--	53
3. Griliches, hybrid corn study [54]	37	--
4. Peterson, poultry study [118]	18	50
5. Schultz, inputs-saved technique extended to 1967 [119, 134]	19	42

Source: Peterson [119].

returns be forthcoming in the same year the investment is made. Yet from our knowledge of the research process it seems unlikely that such would be the case. In fact, Evenson's work [36] reveals that the lag between the research input and the bulk of its output appears to be in the range of six to seven years. A marginal product can be converted to a marginal internal rate of return by finding that interest rate which makes the discounted present value of the marginal product of $1 of research forthcoming in year t + 6 equal to $1 in the year t (assuming a six-year lag). A marginal product of $6.50 (the Griliches figure reduced by one-half to take account of private research) converts to about a 53 percent internal rate of return with a six-year lag. Of course, a 53 percent rate of return still is extremely attractive by any standard.

RATES OF RETURN

We have seen that it is not correct to interpret a marginal product figure as a marginal rate of return if there is a substantial lag between research input and output. It is important also to distinguish between an internal rate of return and a so-called external rate. The latter figure is derived by first computing a benefit/cost ratio and then converting the numerator (the discounted stock of benefits) to an annual flow by multiplying it by the discount rate used. The external rate is equal to the annual flow of returns expressed as a percent of the accumulated costs (a stock). The 743 percent return obtained by Griliches in his hybrid corn study is such a figure.

The internal rate of return is defined as that rate of interest which makes the accumulated costs equal to the discounted benefits at any point. In other words, it is equal to the rate of interest that results in a benefit/cost ratio of one. The internal rate computed from the stream of costs and returns in the Griliches hybrid corn study is equal to 37 percent, which is quite different from 743 percent (see table 1). The large divergence between the external and internal rates is due to the long gestation period during which research was being done but no returns were forthcoming. The internal rate is quite sensitive to the length of the gestation period, especially if the rate of return is relatively high.

As a further precaution, one should distinguish between a long-run average rate of return on agricultural research and a marginal rate of return on additional investment. Although it may be interesting to know that the average return on all agricultural research has been high, a knowledge of the marginal return is necessary for making decisions on additional investment. The summary of rates of return presented in table 1 reveals that the marginal rate of return is substantially greater than the average rate.

The available evidence also suggests that the rates of return to investment in agricultural research in other countries are of a comparable order of magnitude. Ardito-Barletta's estimate [5] of the *average* internal rate of return to wheat research in Mexico (1943 to 1963) is about 75 percent. Ayer and Schuh [6] obtain a 90 percent average internal rate of return to cotton research in Brazil; Akino and Hayami [2] report an average internal rate in the range of 18 to 75 percent to rice-breeding research in Japan (1893 to 1950), and Evenson and Kislev [40] report substantial returns to investment in wheat and maize research based on cross-country observations.

The Allocation of Research

We know that the average or marginal rate of return to agricultural research in the aggregate is in part a function of the efficiency with which the research is allocated. For a given total expenditure the maximum return is obtained only if the marginal return is equalized among all possible research establishments and projects.

Although the allocation problem may be straightforward theoretically, empirically it is a great deal more complex. Until the late 1960s we had virtually no information on the actual allocation of agricultural research, let alone what the allocation should be. Peterson [117] employs a simple head count to determine the allocation of research, teaching, and extension activities by departments in United States colleges of agriculture from 1930 to 1967. Also in the 1960s a detailed and comprehensive inventory of agricultural research became available from the USDA [155].

Decisions bearing on the allocation of research funds both within and between experiment stations and other research agencies must, of course, be made regardless of the amount of information available. We might ask, however, what factors, if any, appear to influence these decisions. Federal funds are allocated by a formula which is based largely on a state's rural and farm population [153]. Regarding nonfederal (mainly state) funds, Schultz [132] argues and presents evidence to show that differences in total income between states is an important variable explaining differences in nonfederal and total funds available. Heady [68] also argues that appropriations to experiment stations are greatest in the large industrial states and tend to be smaller the larger the proportion of state income represented by agriculture. (For additional discussion on the funding of experiment station research, see Dalrymple [27, 28] and Latimer [95].)

The results of an econometric investigation by Peterson [117] support the Schultz and Heady hypothesis. Moreover, Peterson finds that within experiment stations departments such as agronomy and animal science bear a relatively close relationship to farm income while others such as horticulture and agricultural economics are more closely tied to nonfarm income.

The observed relationship between state income and the allocation of research funds, of course, says nothing about the efficiency of the allocation. It merely reports, "what is," not "what should be." The study entitled *A National Program of Research for Agriculture* [156], prepared jointly by the USDA and the Association of State Universities and Land-Grant Colleges, is an attempt to provide estimates of "socially desirable" levels of publicly funded research in 1972 and 1977 in each of ninety-one problem areas. Although eight criteria are used to weigh each problem area, the man-year recommendation contained in the report reflects in large part the subjective evaluation of the committee preparing the report. We still have no assurance that the proposed allocation would provide a higher overall rate of return than the actual allocation.

Griliches's hybrid corn study [54] reveals that the absolute size of the related output is an important factor influencing the rate of return to a given research expenditure. Comparing hybrid sorghum, also assumed to increase yields by 15 percent, with hybrid corn, Griliches obtains a rate of return to hybrid sorghum research of about one-half that to hybrid corn research even though the sorghum research expenditure is considerably less than the hybrid corn research figure. We might conclude, therefore, that given the probability of success, the expected return to research will be greater the larger the value of related output. Hence the observed practice of allocating the larger portion of the research budget to the most important output in each state might be defended as a fairly good rule.

An account of a number of decision-making experiments at the USDA and at the state levels are contained in the University of Minnesota symposium report, *Resource Allocation in Agricultural Research* (see Meyer [111], Puterbaugh [120], Mahlstede [101], and Fishel [43].) By and large, these efforts deal with the identification of goals along with the collection and summarization of information that may help research administrators to attain the goals.

Of course, the efficiency criterion is not the only consideration that bears upon the allocation of agricultural research. The distributional effects of agricultural research were brought to our attention long ago by Heady [65, 66, 69] and Schultz [138] and more recently by Schmitz and Seckler [130], Ayer and Schuh [6], and Akino and Hayami [2], and the environmentalists have reminded us of the possible social costs of our new technology on farms, mainly chemical inputs. The welfare aspects of agricultural research and technical change will be considered more thoroughly later in this paper.

The Diffusion of Technology [4]

It is evident that society cannot benefit from investment in research unless the results are made available and are adopted by producers. Here we review the literature on the process of interfarm and interregional diffusion within the United States and the process of international diffusion.

Interfarm and Interregional Diffusion

The process of diffusion of new technology among farms traditionally has been the domain of rural sociologists and geographers (see, for example, Beal and Bohlen [9]). The main focus of their studies has been on the impact of communication (or interaction) and sociocultural resistance to innovation on the pattern of diffusion over time and across space. There has been particular concern with understanding how the different sociocultural characteristics of adopters create a spectrum ranging from innovators to laggards and the resulting S-shaped diffusion curve. In general, these studies attempt to provide information on how such characteristics determine the means of communication that are most effective in accelerating the diffusion process.

In contrast, the main focus of economists in their approach to the diffusion of technology has been on how economic variables such as the profitability of innovation and the asset position of firms influence the rate of diffusion (for example, Mansfield [103, 104, 105, 106]). The study of hybrid corn diffusion by Griliches [50] and the subsequent exchange with sociologists bring out the contrast between the economic and sociological approaches as well as the role of economic and sociocultural factors in the diffusion process.

Griliches summarizes the diffusion path for each hybrid corn maturity area by fitting a logistic trend function to data on the percentage of corn area planted with hybrid seed. The logistic function is described by three parameters — an origin, a slope, and a ceiling. By observing differences in the slope (which measures the rate of acceptance) and the ceiling (which measures the level of acceptance at which use of hybrid seed tended to stabilize) of the S-shaped logistic curve, Griliches attempts to measure changes in the demand for hybrid seed. He finds that both the slope and the ceiling in the heart of the corn belt exceeded those of the marginal corn areas. A similar finding is reported by Martinez [109] regarding the adoption of hybrid corn in Argentina. He interpreted his results as indicating that differences among regions in the rate (slope) and the level (ceiling) of acceptance are both functions of the profitability of a shift from open-pollinated corn to hybrid corn. Maier's study [102] of the adoption of the mechanical cotton picker also reveals that the rate of acceptance of this machine was closely related to its profitability.

Griliches's study was criticized by a number of sociologists. Brander and Straus [12], citing as an example the case of hybrid sorghum adoption in Kansas, argued that familiarity (congruence) with a technique or an input is the critical factor explaining the rate of adoption. Havens and Rogers [59] argued that communication or interaction between people is the important factor. In reply Griliches [46, 53] argues that even if congruence and interaction are important, there is no reason to exclude profitability as a factor explaining the rate of adoption. Indeed, as Griliches points out, the "profitability" approach can be broadened by allowing for differences in information, risk preference, and so on, thus bringing it as close to the "sociological" approach as one would want to.

The work of Nelson and Phelps [116], Welch [160], Kislev and Shchori-Bachrach [94], and Huffman [76] mentioned earlier provides a basis for broadening the profitability approach to include the education or skill distribution of potential adopters.

Griliches also finds that differences in the origin (defined as the date an area began to plant 10 percent of its "ceiling" area in hybrid corn) can be explained largely by differences in the size and density of the hybrid seed market as measured by the size and density of corn production. As Hayami and Ruttan [61] note, this finding has an important implication for the induced innovation hypothesis in that it supports the idea that developers of hybrid seed, both private seed companies and public research institutions, are motivated by the potential returns from hybrid corn. In the case of private companies, the motivation is provided by the potential profits from the production and sale of hybrid seed. In the case of public research institutions, the desire to maximize social returns to the region and ensure its competitive position forms the basis for their actions. As Griliches [50] observes, "the contribution of the various experiment stations is strongly related to the importance of corn in the area. In the 'good' corn areas the stations did a lot of work on hybrids and in the marginal areas, less." This observation is consistent with the public sector induced innovation hypothesis advanced by Hayami and Ruttan.

This finding by Griliches also points out the critical role of adaptive research for the diffusion of agricultural technology among ecologically heterogeneous regions. Agricultural technology is typically location-specific or constrained by the local ecology. Techniques developed in a region often are not transferable to other regions without further adaptive research. Traditionally most of the diffusion models have been designed to describe or analyze diffusion among farms within a particular area over time. The attributes of technology and of potential adopters often are taken as given. Nevertheless, such models are not very helpful in explaining or predicting the diffusion of technology among heterogeneous regions, particularly among countries located in different climatic zones.

International Diffusion

The transfer of advanced technology existing in the developed countries to the less developed countries has been considered as the major means for promoting agricultural growth in the less developed countries. However, efforts to achieve rapid agricultural growth by the direct transfer of foreign technology have not been very successful. Modern agricultural technology has evolved largely in the developed countries of the temperate zone and is primarily adapted to their ecology and factor endowments. Inadequate recognition of the location-specific character of agricultural technology would seem to be a major reason for the lack of effectiveness of much of the efforts directed at international technology transfer. Also it seems that this perspective has resulted from the erroneous application of sociological interfarm diffusion models to the process of international technology transfer, in which local adaptation is essential.

We have argued that one of the merits of the Griliches model is that it incorporates the mechanism of local adaptation in the interregional diffusion of hybrid corn technology. This mechanism is based on the behavior of public research institutions and private agricultural supply firms. Modification of the model is needed, however, for the study of international technology transfer.

In the United States there exists a large stock of scientific and technical manpower, a well-structured federal and state experiment station network, and vigorous competition and entrepreneurship in the farm supply industry. When these conditions are not present, even if the potential profitability from the transfer of a particular technology is high, the required adaptive research may not be supplied. The problem of facilitating international technology transfer as an instrument of agricultural development is, therefore, how to institutionalize a system of adaptive research and development which is responsive to the opportunities of technology transfer that are profitable to society.

Based on the role of adaptive research in the process of diffusion, Hayami and Ruttan [61] distinguish three phases of international technology transfer: (1) material transfer, (2) design transfer, and (3) capacity transfer. The first phase is characterized by the simple transfer or import of new materials such as seeds, plants, animals, and techniques associated with these materials. Local adaptation is not conducted in an orderly and systematic fashion. The naturalization of plants and animals occurs primarily as a result of trial and error by farmers, usually involving a long gestation period.

In the second phase the transfer of technology is primarily through the transfer of certain designs (blueprints, formula books, and so on). During this period exotic plant materials and foreign equipment are imported for use in the development of new plant breeds and equipment designs, rather than for use in direct production. New plants and animals are subjected to orderly tests and are propagated through systematic multiplication.

In the third phase, the transfer of technology is made through the transfer of scientific knowledge and capacity which enable the production of locally adaptable technology, following the prototype technology which exists abroad. Increasingly, plant and animal varieties are bred locally to adapt them to local ecological conditions. The imported machinery designs are modified in order to meet climatic and social requirements and factor endowments of the economy. An important element in the process of capacity transfer is the migration of agricultural scientists, which is often of critical importance because scientific and technical manpower is in short supply in the less developed countries.

In support of their three-phase international technology transfer hypotheses Hayami and Ruttan point to the international diffusion of sugarcane varieties (Evenson, Houck, and Ruttan [39]) and to the transfer of tractors from the United States to the USSR (Dalrymple [25, 26]). Furthermore they argue that the dramatic appearance and diffusion of the higher-yielding varieties (HYV) of staple cereals in the tropics since the late 1960s (the widely heralded "Green Revolution") represents a case of capacity transfer: ". . . the development of the HYV's represents a process of agricultural technology transfer from the temperate zone to tropical and subtropical zones through the transfer of scientific knowledge and capacity. . . . These new HYV's adaptable to tropical ecologies were initially developed by international teams of scientists drawing on the principles that emerged in the process of developing HYV's that had been introduced earlier in Japan, the United States and other temperate zone developed countries" (Hayami and Ruttan [61]). In their view this process also represents an institutional innovation: the adaptive research that led to the development of higher-yielding varieties was primarily conducted at a new set of international agricultural research centers which typically were supported by large United States foundations. The centers are staffed by international teams of scientists of various agricultural science disciplines assisted by in-service trainees and coordinated by a common orientation to produce major breakthroughs in yield potentials of certain staple cereals. The establishment of these research and training centers can be considered as an institutional innovation facilitating the transfer of an "ecology-bound" location-specific agricultural technology from temperate zone developed countries to tropical zone developing countries (Hayami and Ruttan [61]). They conclude that the success of agricultural development via international technology transfer hinges on the ability to institutionalize the effective supply of adaptive research in the developing countries, given their limited endowment of research personnel. The importance of adaptive research in obtaining productivity gains in wheat, maize, rice, and cereal grains production is further documented by Evenson[38] and Evenson and Kislev [40].

Technical Change and Welfare

In recent years the long-accepted goal of promoting technical change in agriculture and thereby increasing its productive capacity has come under increasing scrutiny, at least in the United States. There can be little doubt that the mass exodus of people from farms and rural areas to cities is in large part the result of technical change in agriculture.

Moreover, it seems likely that this migration has contributed to the problems of congestion and pollution now troubling the nation, especially its cities. But it is equally certain that without a more productive agriculture the per-capita real output of goods and services would be considerably smaller than it is today. Nations that must devote a large share of their resources to the production of food generally are those with the lowest per-capita income. If a society must use the bulk of its resources to produce food, it cannot produce the other things that make for a high standard of living.[5] In this section we attempt to examine some of these issues, paying particular attention to the distinction between the output effects and the distributional effects of technical change.

Output Effects

Technical change is the name we have given to a phenomenon that provides an increase in output for a given level of conventional inputs. And we have already argued that the additional "unexplained" output is largely the result of unmeasured quality improvements in inputs or totally new inputs not accounted for on the input side. It is also evident that real resources are required to produce input quality improvements or new inputs. Thus we can treat the production of technical change as an investment which uses resources and yields a stream of returns over time in the form of increased output. In this sense the production of technical change is no different than any other investment. (Much of the discussion in an earlier section dealt with attempts to measure the returns to this investment.)

From all indications it appears that the rate of return on investment in agricultural research has been and is as high or higher than the rate of return on alternative investments. Thus we can infer that the total output of goods and services available to society is higher than if the resources devoted to agricultural research had been instead devoted to other investment alternatives. Since most societies prefer more to less, it is difficult to criticize the decision to allocate resources to agricultural research strictly on the basis of its output effect. Nor is it wrong on this basis to advocate continued investment in agricultural research in view of its relatively high marginal return.

Distribution Effects

With respect to the distribution effects of agricultural research we should consider its effects on both the personal and functional distribution of income in agriculture as well as in the total economy. It long has been argued that technical change resulting from agricultural research may result in greater inequality in the personal distribution of income among farmers and between farmers and nonfarmers (Heady [65, 66, 69]). Schultz [138] recognizing that farm progress leads to a relative decline in the price of farm products and a resulting decline to labor earnings in agriculture, argues that a high marginal return to agricultural research should be a signal to allocate more resources to research only if there is some way of "reckoning and reconciling" all gains and losses. Unfortunately a procedure for redistributing the specific gains and losses from technical change in agriculture has not been implemented.

It is clear that technical progress has benefited some farmers and harmed others. Those farmers whose labor is a complement to new and improved inputs, mainly the skilled farmers, no doubt have experienced an increase in their marginal products and consequently have enjoyed an increase in real income. On the other hand, farmers whose labor is a substitute for new inputs, mainly the unskilled farmers, have experienced a declining demand for their services and therefore have suffered a reduction in net income. Day's study [30] of sharecroppers in Mississippi provides an excellent account of the latter case. According to Day's estimates, the annual requirement for unskilled labor in the Mississippi delta declined from 170.2 million man-hours in 1940 to 13.7 million man-hours in 1957 while the annual requirement for skilled labor increased from 0.69 to 1.19 million man-hours during this period. Schmitz and Seckler [130] estimate that the mechanical tomato harvester will displace over 19 million man-hours per year after 1973 in the United States.

Unfortunately we have very little information on the effect of new technology on marginal productivity and the wages of labor retained in agriculture — that is, the labor to operate the cotton pickers, the tomato harvesters, and the like. Studies of the effect of research and development on the *total* agricultural labor market by Wallace and Hoover [158] and Bauer [8] reveal that, ceteris paribus, the demand for all farm labor is increased by agricultural research and development. When farm prices are allowed to adjust (decline) as a result of new technology, however, Bauer finds that a 10 percent increase in "technology" decreases the quantity of labor required in agriculture by 4.9 percent.

We should keep separate the income distribution effects of farm programs designed to increase all farm income from the distributional effects of technical change itself. We have strong evidence that past and current farm programs have benefited large, high-income farms to a much greater extent than their small, low-income counterparts (Schultz [139] and Schultze [142]). Surely the current personal distribution of income among farmers would be more equal if government payments to farmers would have been negatively correlated with farm income rather than positively correlated.

Kendrick [87] argues that technical change reduces income inequality because of the tendency for wage income to increase relative to property income, the latter being more important for higher-income people. And because low-income people tend to spend a larger fraction of their income on food than high-income people, it follows that lower food prices (relative to what they would otherwise be) resulting from agricultural research benefit low-income people to a proportionately greater extent than their higher-income counterparts. This fact is well documented by Tweeten [151]. Although the effect does not show up in the income distribution statistics, its net result is in essence similar to a shift to greater equality of income for a given price of food.

It also can be argued that income distribution will be affected by the kind of technology developed. For example, labor-saving technology can be expected to reduce the demand for labor and to displace more farm workers than neutral or labor-using technology. Also we might expect that mechanical innovations would more likely be labor saving than biological or chemical technology. Thus it appears that a greater allocation of agricultural research toward the biological and chemical spheres could have reduced the wholesale migration of farm people during the 1950s and 1960s.

Direct public control of agricultural research allocation is limited to the research conducted by agricultural experiment stations and the USDA (about one-half of the total agricultural research during the 1950s and 1960s). More-over, the major share of public agricultural research was already allocated to the biological area and, to a lesser extent, the chemical area, with the major share of mechanical research and development conducted in the private sec-tor. Thus it is not at all certain that even a complete abandonment of mechan-ical research in the public sector would have had much of an impact on the personal distribution of income in agriculture.

In regard to scale economies, we argued earlier that technical change prob-ably has been biased toward large-scale farms. But here again we might expect mechanical technology to have had the major impact. Although we know relatively little about the ultimate sources of scale economies, we should also consider the effect of increasing nonfarm per-capita incomes. As nonfarm earnings increase, farm size (in terms of output) tends to increase in order to provide farmers with somewhat comparable incomes. In economic terms we might say that as the opportunity cost of farm labor increases, unit labor costs increase on small farms relative to those on larger farms, hence scale economies appear and average farm size increases. Granted, agricultural research no doubt contributes to general economic growth and to rising per-capita nonfarm incomes, but this link between agricultural research and scale economies in agriculture is rather tenuous, to say the least.

The impact of technical change on the functional distribution of income between labor and capital (including land) in agriculture also is an important question. Herdt and Cochrane [73] argue that technical change benefits the landowner as opposed to the farm operator and manager. Their argument is that technical change shifts cost curves downward, resulting in pure profits. And as firms attempt to expand because of the new intersection between out-put price and marginal cost, the price of land is bid up. They estimate that a one-point rise in the total productivity index increases land price by an average of $1.59 per acre.

An important assumption in this analysis is that of a constant output price, for economic theory suggests that a reduction in marginal cost leads to a re-duction in output price and in the demand for inputs, ceteris paribus. Whether there is a net reduction in the demand for land in total depends on whether each particular parcel of land is a complement or a substitute to the new in-puts adopted by farmers. At any rate it is not clear whether the observed dis-tribution effects in the Herdt-Cochrane study are the result of technical change or of the particular characteristics of the farm income support pro-grams which have prevented output prices from declining, at least initially, in response to new technology.

Further in regard to the functional distribution of income between capital and labor in agriculture, Ruttan and Stout [125] report that labor's share of agricultural income declined between 1946 and 1957. This is in contrast to D. G. Johnson's previous finding that labor's share had increased slightly from 1910 to 1946 [79]. One might infer from the Ruttan-Stout results that technical change in agriculture has been of a labor-saving variety. Ruttan and Stout also report a convergence of relative factor shares between regions. They attribute this phenomenon in part to an increase in current expenses, particularly the cost of fertilizer which serves as a land substitute and thus reduces in importance the native land endowment of each region.

Externalities and Adjustment Costs

Generally we define an externality or social cost as a cost borne by society or individuals over and above the cost of resources directly utilized to carry on a production activity. In the case of agricultural research (public and private) the adjustment cost borne by farm people who have decided to leave agriculture because of declining farm prices and incomes brought on by technical change can be considered a social cost. These adjustment costs might be categorized as both pecuniary (reduction in income before and during the change in occupation plus moving costs) and nonpecuniary (the uncertainty and anxiety of leaving relatives, friends, and familiar surroundings).

The seriousness of these adjustment costs depends somewhat on the length of run considered. In the short run it cannot be denied that these costs are important for displaced farm people. (See Day [30] and Schmitz and Seckler [130].) In the long run, however, it is hard to deny that most displaced farmers have been able to increase their real incomes in nonagricultural jobs over what they could have earned in agriculture if technical change had not occurred.

Other social costs arising from technical change in agriculture might include the pollution caused by the increased use of farm chemicals, mainly pesticides and commercial fertilizer. However, the allegations of the environmentalists and the counterallegations of industry spokesmen provide little hard evidence to date on the magnitude of this problem. Also it seems necessary to consider the increased pollution that resulted from the acreage restriction characteristic of the farm income support programs. We would expect that the use of farm chemicals has been stimulated as farmers have searched for land substitutes because of acreage restrictions. To the extent that land is a complement to farm labor, one might argue as well that acreage restrictions have reduced the demand for farm labor and have hastened off-farm migration.

A somewhat different kind of social cost to technical change could occur if it brought about an agricultural industry made up of a few firms with extensive monopoly power. However, the spatial characteristics of agricultural production force us to dismiss this possibility at least in the foreseeable future.

Notes

1. The function they estimated was

$$V = [(E_l L)^{-e} + (E_k K)^{-e}] - \frac{1}{e}$$

where V is value added and E_l and E_k represent levels of efficiency of labor and capital, respectively.

2. It is common to call the ratio of output to the linear aggregate of inputs the index of total factor productivity and the ratio of output to the geometrical aggregate of inputs the index of technical change, though they are aimed at measuring the same thing. Empirical studies in United States agriculture using the arithmetic index have been carried out by Barton and Cooper [7], Kendrick [88], Loomis and Barton [100], Ruttan [121, 122], and Schultz [134, 138]. Studies using the geometric index have been conducted by Chandler [18] and Lave [98].

3. Strictly speaking, one can define an input of improved quality as a new input. For example, the farmer who learns that higher yields can be obtained by planting corn at an earlier date is in a sense a different person than before.

4. This section draws heavily on Hayami and Ruttan [61, pp. 169-190].

5. An exception to this rule occurs if a nation is able to export a large share of its agricultural output to other nations and buy other goods and services in return. Denmark and New Zealand, however, are about the only nations that have been able to do this on a relatively large scale. See Tweeten and Hines [152] for an attempt to measure the contribution of agricultural productivity and the resulting decline in the farm population to overall economic growth.

References

[1] Abramovitz, M. "Resource and Output Trends in the United States since 1870." *Am. Econ. Rev.* 46:5-23, May 1956.

[2] Akino, M., and Y. Hayami. "Efficiency and Equity in Public Research; Rice Breeding in Japan's Economic Development." SAP Rep. 5, Tokyo Metropolitan University, 1973.

[3] ———. "Sources of Agricultural Growth in Japan, 1880-1965." *Quart. J. Econ.* 88:454-479, August 1974.

[4] Amano, A. "Biased Technical Progress and a Neo-Classical Theory of Economic Growth." *Quart. J. Econ.* 78:129-138, February 1964.

[5] Ardito-Barletta, N. "Costs and Social Returns of Agricultural Research in Mexico." Unpublished Ph.D. dissertation, University of Chicago, 1970.

[6] Ayer, W. A., and G. E. Schuh. "Social Rates of Returns and Other Aspects of Agricultural Research: The Case of Cotton Research in Sao Paulo, Brazil." *Am. J. Agr. Econ.* 54:557-569, November 1972.

[7] Barton, G. T., and M. R. Cooper. "Relation of Agricultural Production to Inputs." *Rev. Econ. Stat.* 30:117-126, May 1948.

[8] Bauer, L. L. "The Effect of Technology on the Farm Labor Market." *Am. J. Agr. Econ.* 51:605-618, August 1969.

[9] Beal, G. M., and J. M. Bohlen. *The Diffusion Process.* Iowa State Agr. Exp. Sta. Spec. Rep. 18, 1957.

[10] Berglas, E. "Investment and Technological Change." *J. Pol. Econ.* 73:173-180, April 1965.

[11] Binswanger, H. P. "The Measurement of Biased Efficiency Gains in U.S. and Japanese Agriculture to Test the Induced Innovation Hypothesis." Unpublished Ph.D. dissertation, North Carolina State University, 1973.

[12] Brander, L., and M. Straus. "Congruence versus Profitability in the Diffusion of Hybrid Sorghums." *Rural Sociology* 24:381-383, December 1959.

[13] Bray, J. O., and P. Watkins. "Technical Change in Corn Production in the United States, 1870-1960." *J. Farm Econ.* 46:751-765, November 1964.

[14] Brown, M. *On the Theory and Measurement of Technical Change.* Cambridge: At the University Press, 1966.

[15] Brown, M., and J. Popkin. "A Measure of Technological Change and Returns to Scale." *Rev. Econ. Stat.* 44:402-412, November 1962.

[16] Brozen, Y. "Determinants of the Direction of Technological Change." *Am. Econ. Rev.* (supplement) 43:288-302, May 1953.

[17] Cassels, J. M. "The Nature of Statistical Cost Curves." *J. Farm Econ.* 15:378-383, April 1933.

[18] Chandler, C. "The Relative Contribution of Capital Intensity and Productivity to Changes in Output and Income." *J. Farm Econ.* 44:335-348, May 1962.

[19] Choudri, D. P. "Education and Agricultural Productivity in India." Unpublished Ph.D. dissertation, University of Delhi, 1968.

[20] Cochrane, W. W. "Conceptualizing the Supply Relation in Agriculture." *J. Farm Econ.* 37:1161-1176, December 1955.

[21] ———. "Farm Price Gyrations — An Aggregative Hypothesis." *J. Farm Econ.* 29:383-408, May 1947.

[22] ———. "Professor Schultz Discovers the Weather." *J. Farm Econ.* 35:281-283, May 1953.

[23] Copeland, M. A., and E. M. Martin. "The Correction of Wealth and Income Estimates for Price Changes." In *Studies in Income and Wealth.* National Bureau of Economic Research, vol. 2, 1938.

[24] Court, A. T. "Hedonic Price Indexes with Automotive Examples." In *The Dynamics of Automobile Demand.* General Motors Corporation, 1939.

[25] Dalrymple, D. "American Technology and Soviet Agricultural Development." *Agr. Hist.* 40:187-206, July 1966.

[26] ———. "The American Tractor Comes to Soviet Agriculture: The Transfer of a Technology." *Technology and Culture* 5:191-214, Spring 1964.

[27] ———. "Comments on Public Purpose in Agricultural Research and Education." *J. Farm Econ.* 44:444-453, May 1962.

[28] ———. "Public Investment in Agricultural Research and Education: Some Comments." *J. Farm Econ.* 47:1020-1022, November 1965.

[29] David, P. A., and T. Van de Klundert. "Biased Efficiency Growth and Capital Labor Substitution in the U.S., 1899-1960." *Am. Econ. Rev.* 55:357-394, June 1965.

[30] Day, R. H. "The Economics of Technological Change and the Demise of the Share Cropper." *Am. Econ. Rev.* 57:427-449, June 1967.

[31] Denison, E. F. "Measurement of Labor Input: Some Questions of Definition and the Adequacy of Data" and discussion by G. Tolley. In *Output, Input and Productivity Measurement.* National Bureau of Economic Research, vol. 25. Princeton: Princeton University Press, 1961.

[32] ———. "Some Major Issues in Productivity Analysis: An Examination of Estimates by Jorgenson and Griliches." *Survey of Current Business,* vol. 49, part II, pp. 1-27, May 1969. (Also included in *Survey of Current Business,* vol. 52, part II, pp. 37-63, May 1972.)

[33] ———. "Theoretical Aspects of Quality Change, Capital Consumption, and Net Capital Formation." In *Problems of Capital Formation.* National Bureau of Economic Research Conference on Income and Wealth, vol. 19, 1957.

[34] ———. "The Unimportance of the Embodiment Question." *Am. Econ. Rev.* 54:90-93, March 1964.

[35] Domar, E. "On the Measurement of Technological Change." *Econ. J.* 71:709-729, December 1961.

[36] Evenson, R. E. "The Contribution of Agricultural Research and Extension to Agricultural Production." Unpublished Ph.D. dissertation, University of Chicago, 1968.

[37] ———. "The Contribution of Agricultural Research to Production." *J. Farm Econ.* 49:1415-1425, December 1967.

[38] ———. "The 'Green Revolution' in Recent Development Experience." *Am. J. Agr. Econ.* 56:357-394, May 1974.

[39] Evenson, R. E., J. P. Houck, and V. W. Ruttan. "Technical Change and Agricultural Trade: Three Examples — Sugarcane, Bananas, and Rice." In *The Technology Factor in International Trade,* R. Vernon, ed. New York: Columbia University Press, 1970.

[40] Evenson, R. E., and Y. Kislev. "Research and Productivity in Wheat and Maize." *J. Pol. Econ.* 81:1309-1329, November/December 1973.

[41] Farrell, M. J. "The Measurement of Productive Efficiency" and discussion by M. G. Kendall. *J. Royal Stat. Soc.* 120:253-287 (series A, part 3), 1957.

[42] Fettig, L. P. "Adjusting Farm Tractor Prices for Quality Changes." *J. Farm Econ.* 45:599-611, August 1963.

[43] Fishel, W. L. "The Minnesota Agricultural Research Resource Allocation Information System and Experiment." In *Resource Allocation in Agricultural Research,* W. L. Fishel, ed. Minneapolis: University of Minnesota Press, 1971.

[44] Fishelson, G. "Return to Human and Research Capital and the Non-South Agricultural Sector of the United States, 1949-1964." *Am. J. Agr. Econ.* 53:129-131, February 1971.

[45] Gisser, M. "Schooling and the Agricultural Labor Force." Unpublished Ph.D. dissertation, University of Chicago, 1962.

[46] Griliches, Z. "Congruence *versus* Profitability: A False Dichotomy." *Rural Sociology* 25:354-356, September 1960.

[47] ———. "The Demand for Fertilizer: An Economic Interpretation of Technical Change." *J. Farm Econ.* 40:591-606, August 1958.

[48] ———. "Estimates of the Aggregate Agricultural Production Function from Cross-Section Data." *J. Farm Econ.* 45:419-428, May 1963.

[49] ———. "Hedonic Price Indexes for Automobiles: An Econometric Analysis of

Quality Change." In *Hearings on Government Price Statistics*. Joint Economic Committee, 87th Congress, 1st Session, 1961.

[50] ———. "Hybrid Corn: An Exploration in the Economics of Technological Change." *Econometrica* 25:501-522, October 1957.

[51] ———. "Measuring Inputs in Agriculture: A Critical Survey." *J. Farm Econ.* 42:1411-1433, December 1960.

[52] ———. "Production Functions in Manufacturing: Some Preliminary Results." In *The Theory and Empirical Analysis of Production*. National Bureau of Economic Research, vol. 31, 1967.

[53] ———. "Profitability versus Interaction: Another False Dichotomy." *Rural Sociology* 27:327-330, September 1962.

[54] ———. "Research Costs and Social Returns: Hybrid Corn and Related Innovations." *J. Pol. Econ.* 66:419-431, October 1958.

[55] ———. "Research Expenditures, Education, and the Aggregate Agricultural Production Function." *Am. Econ. Rev.* 54:961-974, December 1964.

[56] ———. "The Sources of Measured Productivity Growth: United States Agriculture, 1940-1960." *J. Pol. Econ.* 71:331-346, August 1963.

[57] ———. "Specification Bias in Estimates of Production Functions." *J. Farm Econ.* 39:8-20, February 1957.

[58] Harrod, R. *Towards a Dynamic Economics*. London: Macmillan, 1948.

[59] Havens, A. E., and E. M. Rogers. "Adoption of Hybrid Corn: Profitability and the Interaction Effect." *Rural Sociology* 26:409-414, December 1961.

[60] Hayami, Y. "Sources of Agricultural Productivity Gap among Selected Countries." *Am. J. Agr. Econ.* 51:564-575, August 1969.

[61] Hayami, Y., and V. W. Ruttan. *Agricultural Development: An International Perspective*. Baltimore: Johns Hopkins University Press, 1971.

[62] ———. "Agricultural Productivity Differences between Countries." *Am. Econ. Rev.* 60:895-911, December 1970.

[63] ———. "Factor Prices and Technical Change in Agricultural Development: The United States and Japan, 1880-1960." *J. Pol. Econ.* 78:1115-1141, September/October 1970.

[64] ———. "Professor Rosenberg and the Direction of Technical Change." *Economic Development and Cultural Change* 21:352-355, January 1973.

[65] Heady, E. O. "Economic and Welfare Aspects of Farm Technological Advance." *J. Farm Econ.* 31:293-316, May 1949.

[66] ———. *Economics of Agricultural Production and Resource Use*. Englewood Cliffs, N.J.: Prentice-Hall, 1952.

[67] ———. "Output in Relation to Input for the Agricultural Industry." *J. Farm Econ.* 40:393-405, May 1958.

[68] ———. "Public Purpose in Agricultural Research and Education." *J. Farm Econ.* 43:566-581, August 1961.

[69] ———. "Welfare Implications of Agricultural Research." In *Resource Allocation in Agricultural Research*, W. L. Fishel, ed. Minneapolis: University of Minnesota Press, 1971.

[70] Heady, E. O., and L. Auer. "Imputation of Production to Technologies." *J. Farm Econ.* 48:309-322, May 1966.

[71] Heady, E. O., and J. Dillon. *Agricultural Production Functions*. Ames: Iowa State University Press, 1963.

[72] Herdt, R. W. "Resources Productivity in Indian Agriculture." *Am. J. Agr. Econ.* 53:517-521, August 1971.

[73] Herdt, R. W., and W. W. Cochrane. "Farm Land Prices and Farm Technological Advance." *J. Farm Econ.* 48:243-263, May 1966.

[74] Herdt, R. W., and J. W. Mellor. "The Contrasting Response of Rice to Nitrogen: India and the United States." *J. Farm Econ.* 46:150-160, February 1964.

[75] Hicks, J. *The Theory of Wages.* London: Macmillan, 1932.

[76] Huffman, W. E. "Decision Making: The Role of Education." *Am. J. Agr. Econ.* 56:85-97, February 1974.

[77] Intriligator, M. D. "Embodied Technical Change and Productivity in the United States, 1924-1958." *Rev. Econ. Stat.* 47:61-70, February 1965.

[78] John, M. E. "The Impact of Technology on Rural Values." *J. Farm Econ.* 40: 1636-1645, December 1958.

[79] Johnson, D. G. "Allocation of Agricultural Income." *J. Farm Econ.* 30:724-745, November 1948.

[80] Johnson, G. L. "A Note on Non-Conventional Inputs and Conventional Production Functions." In *Agriculture in Economic Development,* C. K. Eicher and L. W. Witt, eds. New York: McGraw-Hill, 1964.

[81] Johnson, R. W. M. "Efficiency Growth in New Zealand Agriculture: A Review." *Economic Record* 48:76-91, March 1972.

[82] Jorgenson, D. W. "The Embodiment Hypothesis." *J. Pol. Econ.* 74:1-17, February 1966.

[83] Jorgenson, D. W., and Z. Griliches. "The Explanation of Productivity Change." *Rev. Econ. Studies* 34:249-283, July 1967.

[84] ———. "Issues in Growth Accounting: A Reply to Edward F. Denison." *Survey of Current Business,* vol. 52, part II, pp. 65-94, May 1972.

[85] Kaneda, H. "Regional Patterns of Technical Change in U.S. Agriculture, 1950-1963." *J. Farm Econ.* 49:99-212, February 1967.

[86] Kendall, M. G. "The Geographical Distribution of Crop Productivity." *J. Royal Stat. Soc.* 52:21-48, 1939.

[87] Kendrick, J. W. "The Gains and Losses from Technological Change." *J. Farm Econ.* 46:1065-1072, December 1964.

[88] ———. *Productivity Trends in the United States.* National Bureau of Economic Research. Princeton: Princeton University Press, 1961.

[89] Kennedy, C. "The Character of Improvements and of Technical Progress." *Econ. J.* 72:899-911, December 1962.

[90] ———. "Harrod on Neutrality." *Econ. J.* 72:249, March 1962.

[91] ———. "Induced Bias in Innovation and the Theory of Distribution." *Econ. J.* 74:541-547, September 1964.

[92] Kennedy, C., and A. P. Thirlwall. "Technical Progress: A Survey." *Econ. J.* 82:11-72, March 1972.

[93] Kislev, Y. "Estimating a Production Function from U.S. Census of Agriculture Data." Unpublished Ph.D. dissertation, University of Chicago, 1965.

[94] Kislev, Y., and N. Shchori-Bachrach. "The Process of an Innovation Cycle." *Am. J. Agr. Econ.* 55:28-37, February 1973.

[95] Latimer, R. G. "Some Economic Aspects of Agricultural Research and Education in the United States." Unpublished Ph.D. dissertation, Purdue University, 1964.

[96] Latimer, R. G., and D. Paarlberg. "Geographic Distribution of Research Costs and Benefits." *J. Farm Econ.* 47:234-241, May 1965.

[97] Lau, L. J., and P. A. Yotopoulos. "A Test for Relative Efficiency and Application to Indian Agriculture." *Am. Econ. Rev.* 61: 94-109, March 1971.

[98] Lave, L. B. "Technological Change in U.S. Agriculture: The Aggregation Problem." *J. Farm Econ.* 46:200-217, February 1964.

[99] Loomis, R. A. "Empirical Estimates of Technological Change in American Agriculture, 1850-1958." *J. Farm Econ.* 44:941-952, November 1962.

[100] Loomis, R. A., and G. T. Barton. *Productivity of Agriculture, United States, 1870-1958.* USDA Tech. Bul. 1238, 1961.

[101] Mahlstede, J. P. "Long-Range Planning at the Iowa Agricultural and Home Economics Experiment Station." In *Resource Allocation in Agricultural Research,* W. L. Fishel, ed. Minneapolis: University of Minnesota Press, 1971.

[102] Maier, F. "An Economic Analysis of the Adoption of the Mechanical Cotton Picker." Unpublished Ph.D. dissertation, University of Chicago, 1969.

[103] Mansfield, E. "Intrafirm Rates of Diffusion of an Innovation." *Rev. Econ. Stat.* 45:348-359, November 1963.

[104] ———. "Size of Firm, Market Structure, and Innovation." *J. Pol. Econ.* 71: 556-576, December 1963.

[105] ———. "The Speed of Response of Firms to New Techniques." *Quart. J. Econ.* 77:290-311, May 1963.

[106] ———. "Technical Change and the Rate of Imitation." *Econometrica* 29: 741-766, October 1961.

[107] Marschak, J., and W. H. Andrews. "Random Simultaneous Equations and the Theory of Production." *Econometrica* 12:143-205, July/October 1944.

[108] Marshall, A. *Principles of Economics.* 8th ed. London: Macmillan, 1936.

[109] Martinez, J. C. "Economics of Technological Change: The Case of Hybrid Corn in Argentina." Unpublished Ph.D. dissertation, Iowa State University, 1972.

[110] McFadden, D. L. "Cost, Revenue, and Profit Functions." In *The Econometric Approach to Production Theory,* D. L. McFadden, ed. Amsterdam: North Holland, 1972.

[111] Meyer, J. H. "The California Academic-Responsive Budget System." In *Resource Allocation in Agricultural Research,* W. L. Fishel, ed. Minneapolis: University of Minnesota Press, 1971.

[112] Mulleady, T. "Feasibility of Adopting Modern Technology in Corn Production in Argentina." Unpublished Ph.D. dissertation, Iowa State University, 1973.

[113] Mundlak, Y., and A. Razin. "Aggregation, Index Numbers and the Measurement of Technical Change." *Rev. Econ. Stat.* 51:166-175, May 1969.

[114] Nadiri, M. I. "Some Approaches to the Theory and Measurement of Total Factor Productivity: A Survey." *J. Econ. Lit.* 8:1137-1177, December 1970.

[115] Nelson, R. R. "The Simple Economics of Basic Scientific Research." *J. Pol. Econ.* 67:297-306, June 1959.

[116] Nelson, R. R., and E. S. Phelps. "Investment in Humans, Technological Diffusion, and Economic Growth." *Am. Econ. Rev.* 56:69-75, May 1966.

[117] Peterson, W. L. "The Allocation of Research, Teaching and Extension Personnel in U.S. Colleges of Agriculture." *Am. J. Agr. Econ.* 51:41-56, February 1969.

[118] ———. "Return to Poultry Research in the United States." *J. Farm Econ.* 49: 656-669, August 1967.

[119] ———. "The Returns to Investment in Agricultural Research in the United

States." In *Resource Allocation in Agricultural Research,* W. L. Fishel, ed. Minneapolis: University of Minnesota Press, 1971.

[120] Puterbaugh, H. L. "An Application of P.P.B. in the Agricultural Research Service." In *Resource Allocation in Agricultural Research,* W. L. Fishel, ed. Minneapolis: University of Minnesota Press, 1971.

[121] Ruttan, V. W. "Agricultural and Nonagricultural Growth in Output per Unit of Input." *J. Farm Econ.* 39:1566-1575, December 1957.

[122] ———. "The Contribution of Technological Progress to Farm Output: 1950-75." *Rev. Econ. Stat.* 38:61-69, February 1956.

[123] ———. "Research on the Economics of Technological Change in American Agriculture." *J. Farm Econ.* 42:735-754, November 1960.

[124] ———. *Technological Progress in the Meat Packing Industry.* USDA Marketing Res. Rep. 59, 1954.

[125] Ruttan, V. W., and T. Stout. "Regional Differences of Technical Change in American Agriculture." *J. Farm Econ.* 42:52-68, February 1960.

[126] Sahota, G. S. *Fertilizer and Economic Development.* New York: Praeger, 1967.

[127] ———. "The Sources of Measured Productivity Growth: United States Fertilizer Mineral Industries, 1936-1960." *Rev. Econ. Stat.* 48:193-204, May 1966.

[128] Salter, W. E. G. *Productivity and Technical Change.* Cambridge: At the University Press, 1960.

[129] Sawada, S. "Technological Change in Japanese Agriculture: A Long-Term Analysis." In *Agriculture and Economic Growth: Japan's Experience,* K. Ohkawa, B. F. Johnston, and H. Kaneda, eds. Tokyo: University of Tokyo Press, 1969.

[130] Schmitz, A., and D. Seckler. "Mechanized Agriculture and Social Welfare: The Case of the Tomato Harvester." *Am. J. Agr. Econ.* 52:569-577, November 1970.

[131] Schmookler, J. *Invention and Economic Growth.* Cambridge: Harvard University Press, 1966.

[132] Schultz, T. W. "Agriculture and the Appreciation of Knowledge." In *A Look to the Future.* W. K. Kellogg Foundation Conference Proceedings. Battle Creek, Michigan, 1956.

[133] ———. "The Declining Economic Importance of Agricultural Land." *Econ. J.* 61:725-740, December 1951.

[134] ———. *Economic Organization of Agriculture.* New York: McGraw-Hill, 1953.

[135] ———. *The Economic Value of Education.* New York: Columbia University Press, 1963.

[136] ———. *Investment in Human Capital.* New York: Free Press, 1971.

[137] ———. "Output-Input Relationships Revisited." *J. Farm Econ.* 40:924-932, November 1958.

[138] ———. "A Policy to Redistribute Losses from Farm Progress." *J. Farm Econ.* 43:554-565, August 1961.

[139] ———. "Public Approaches to Minimize Poverty." In *Poverty amid Affluence,* L. Fishman, ed. New Haven: Yale University Press, 1966.

[140] ———. "Reflections on Poverty within Agriculture." *J. Pol. Econ.* 58:1-15, February 1950.

[141] ———. "Reflections on Agricultural Production, Output and Supply." *J. Farm Econ.* 38:748-762, August 1956.

[142] Schultze, C. L. "The Distribution of Farm Subsidies: Who Gets the Benefits?" Brookings Institution Staff Paper. Washington, D.C., 1971.

[143] Sidhu, S. S. "Relative Efficiency in Wheat Production in the Indian Punjab." *Am. Econ. Rev.* 64:742-751, September 1974.

[144] Solow, R. M. "Investment and Technical Progress." In *Mathematical Methods in the Social Sciences,* K. Arrow, S. Karlin, and P. Suppes, eds. Stanford: Stanford University Press, 1959.

[145] ————. "Technical Change and the Aggregate Production Function." *Rev. Econ. Stat.* 39:312-320, August 1957.

[146] ————. "Technical Progress, Capital Formation and Economic Growth." *Am. Econ. Rev.* 52:76-86, May 1962.

[147] Stigler, G. "Economic Problems in Measuring Changes in Productivity." In *Output, Input and Productivity Measurement,* J. W. Kendrick, ed. Princeton: Princeton University Press, 1961.

[148] ————. *The Theory of Price.* New York: Macmillan, 1952.

[149] Stout, T., and V. W. Ruttan. "Regional Patterns of Technological Change in American Agriculture." *J. Farm Econ.* 40:196-207, May 1958.

[150] Tang, A. M. "Research and Education in Japanese Agriculture Development." *Econ. Studies Quart.* 13:27-41, 91-95, February/May 1963.

[151] Tweeten, L. G. "Distribution of Benefits and Costs of Agricultural Research and Education." *Oklahoma Current Farm Economics* 46:3-7, October 1973.

[152] Tweeten, L. G., and F. K. Hines. "Contributions of Agricultural Productivity to National Economic Growth." *Agricultural Science Review,* vol. 3, no. 2, Spring 1965.

[153] United States Department of Agriculture. *State Agricultural Experiment Stations: A History of Research Policy and Procedure.* Misc. Pub. 904, 1962.

[154] ————. *Changes in Farm Production and Efficiency.* Published annually.

[155] ————. *An Inventory of Agricultural Research.* Compiled by Science and Education Staff. Washington, D.C., 1970.

[156] United States Department of Agriculture and Association of State Universities and Land-Grant Colleges. *A National Program of Research for Agriculture.* 1966.

[157] Ulveling, E. F., and L. B. Fletcher. "A Cobb-Douglas Production Function with Variable Returns to Scale." *Am. J. Agr. Econ.* 52:322-326, May 1970.

[158] Wallace, T. D., and D. M. Hoover. "Income Effects of Innovation: The Case of Labor in Agriculture." *J. Farm Econ.* 48:325-338, May 1966.

[159] Welch, F. "The Determinants of the Return to Schooling in Rural Farm Areas, 1959." Unpublished Ph.D. dissertation, University of Chicago, 1966.

[160] ————. "Education in Production." *J. Pol. Econ.* 78:35-59, January/February 1970.

[161] Yotopoulos, P. A. "On Efficiency of Resource Utilization in Subsistence Agriculture." Food Research Institute Studies in Agricultural Economics, Trade, and Development, vol. 8, no. 2, 1968.

[162] ————. "From Stock to Flow Capital Inputs for Agricultural Production Functions: A Microanalytic Approach." *J. Farm Econ.* 49:476-491, May 1967.

[163] Yotopoulos, P. A., and L. J. Lau. "A Test for Relative Economic Efficiency: Some Further Results." *Am. Econ. Rev.* 63:214-223, March 1973.